Cultural Institutions of the Novel

Cultural Institutions of the Novel

Deidre Lynch and William B. Warner, Editors

Duke University Press Durham and London 1996

Printed in the United States of America on acid-free paper ∞
Typeset in Adobe Caslon by Tseng Information Systems, Inc.
Library of Congress Cataloging-in-Publication Data appear on
the last printed page of this book.

Contents

Deidre Lynch and William B. Warner

Introduction

The Transport of the Novel

❧ We were motivated in the initial stages of our work on this anthology by our common experience of a thoroughly institutional occasion: one of those occasions when the professional trumps the personal and individual agency gets folded into the way things have always been done. As teachers of eighteenth-century English literature, we are regularly compelled, by the design of the curriculum and by the customs of the discipline, to begin the course catalogued as "The Eighteenth-Century English Novel" with an explanation of why it is in this course and period, and not some other, that prose fiction makes its curricular and cultural debut. The usual business of historical lectures and close readings must be postponed at such moments to make room for accounts showing why *Oroonoko* or *Roxana* really are, despite their antiquity and unfamiliarity (their lack of chapter divisions, their plethora of capitalized nouns, their odd prefatory material), more like the "novels" by Dickens or Toni Morrison that our students encounter in the modern sectors of the curriculum than they are like the early narratives, by Chaucer, say, or Sidney or Bunyan, that they encounter elsewhere.

In short, these occasions oblige us to commit to a concept of genre: we must then reveal what makes the eighteenth-century narrative a novel. The results always dissatisfy. In delineating *what the novel is,* one invariably finds oneself resorting to outlines of what novels *are not* (e.g., they are not romances, and so, by implication, they are not "aristocratic" but bourgeois, and they are not French, or at least not yet, but English). And if one falls back on Ian Watt's list of the elements of formal realism (1957), at the point when one reaches the analogy between novelistic prose and empiricists' call for "the correspondence of words to things," students will, invariably, pull books like *Star Trek: Death Star* out of their backpacks and ask, "But isn't this a novel?"

Introducing the eighteenth-century "origins" of "the" novel, we validate the assumption that what novels are now was already immanent in what they were then. We ratify geopolitical boundaries (between, for example, England and France). We legislate for a canon of exemplary, "truly" novelistic texts and legislate against popular practices of reading and writing. These are problems endemic to efforts to ascribe a distinct, essential nature to the novel.

The shortcomings of this discourse of genre are, of course, hardly a secret. There is an everyday tension between the place of the novel in the classroom and novels' place in the corner store—where they appear not as instances of "the" genre but as "genre fiction," as romances, mysteries, westerns, and so forth. Nevertheless, in classrooms as well as in criticism, there is no end to definitions of the novel. With this anthology, we project a form of novel studies that would take as its object the semantic and social contests through which *the* novel keeps hold of its definite article and stakes a claim to cultural capital. By acknowledging novels' global circulation, we aim to redress the bias at work in restricting theoretical speculation about novels to fictions originating inside Europe or the United States.

This collection is shaped both to build on the novel studies of the 1980s and to take a logical next step. In British and American studies there has been a fruitful but inconclusive debate over the origins of the novel. Reworking the terrain of Watt's classic study *The Rise of the Novel,* participants in that debate have demonstrated how novels reshape the cultures in which they win currency and mediate conflicts within them.[1] At the same time, building on exemplary critical texts like Sandra Gilbert and Susan Gubar's *The Madwoman in the Attic* (1979), Edward Said's *Orientalism* (1978), and Henry Louis Gates's "The Blackness of Blackness" (1984; extended in *The Signifying Monkey* in 1988), new modes of historicist criticism and of cultural studies have analyzed broad cultural phenomena such as gender, sexuality, race, and class by analyzing how fictions exercise real power in the social order. Together, these strains of novel studies—that concerned with origins and that concerned with power—have redirected critical attention from refining the definition of the novel as a literary type to understanding how novels produce social divisions: from *what a novel is* to *what novels do.*

While endorsing this emphasis on novels' productive role in culture, we believe that there are two ways in which these studies fall short of what we are attempting. First, they fail to take into account how ideas about what counts as a novel themselves register and shape social struggles. The divisions that define genres—the divisions, for instance, between "realism" and "romance"—have frequently been articulated with the gender and class hierarchies that organize the social order. For this reason, efforts to define "the" novel—as either entertainment or literature, a conveyor of fantasy or reality—are implicated in the question of cultural power. Second, although these studies challenge the Jamesian project of locating the novel inside an aesthetic "House of Fiction," they have not fully acknowledged novels' mobility.[2] The global dissemination of novel reading and novel writing has, however, made "the" novel a discursive site where the relations among nations are brokered. By bringing the question of genre back into the foreground of novel studies, by attending to transnational institutions of the novel, this collection finds new ways to analyze the productive powers that novels exercise in culture.

In titling this collection *Cultural Institutions of the Novel,* we aim in part to exploit the customary sense of the word "institution," which gestures toward those establishments where ideas of "the" novel are endowed with a kind of solidity. Within such institutions as the university or the publishing house, "the" novel can seem perpetually *prior* to writers and readers, in a position to ghostwrite their practices. But, as Homer Brown notes in the prologue to this collection, since "institution" designates an action or happening as well as a place or a thing, the word can also designate the act of establishing that breaks with business as usual, providing a "novel" departure from institutional protocol. This second, active sense of "institution" interferes with the pledge of continuity and integrity inscribed in the term "the" novel. "Institution" in this sense evokes the contingency of what has happened. It encourages us to study the novel as that which was once "novel."

In order to clear the ground for a study of the cultural institutions of the novel, the authors of these essays investigate the implications of three principal ideas about novels: their status as print commodities, their mediation of national cultures, and their role in transnational exchange. While none of these ideas is new in itself, their alignment in these essays allows the collection as a whole to take a step forward in novel studies.

First, novels are the first literary genre to emerge into cultural centrality within the medium of print. Novels have accordingly a unique capacity for mobility. As commodities within the print market, novels have proven particularly adept at moving the desires of readers, often triggering identification with a central character and transporting readers into alternate identities. As commodities novels also have followed fashion and, by virtue of their adaptability and mobility, have circumvented the generic rules that authors and critics have laid down for the novel (Bakhtin 1981). Publishers and teachers, as well as critics and authors, have frequently resisted the commodity status of novels: by ascribing to fictions more elevated cultural functions—the moral improvement of readers, the representation of reality—they have tried to place the novel firmly inside the category of Literature. At the same time, novels' portability has allowed them to circulate among a diverse readership within the nation, to cross the frontiers of gender and class.

Second, their wide popularity has allowed novels to assume a crucial role in the constitution of the nation as an imagined community (Anderson 1983). To act in this way, novels exploit the claim to offer a detailed and inclusive representation of everyday life. From the great national literary histories of the nineteenth century, such as Taine's *The History of English Literature*, to the most recent multicultural syllabi, the novel has been privileged as a window opening onto the characters of nations and peoples. But the novel is more than a reflection of the social history happening outside its confines. Participating in the social practice of novel reading can give readers the sense of participating in a nation that they imagine to be the product of consensus. When novel reading traverses the social boundaries within the nation, novels' popularity can seem an index of the nation's essential coherence. This also means that efforts to define a select canon of paradigmatic instances of the national novel—and to define the terms of that consensus and the nature of that essence—are contentious. They render the novel the site where struggles over cultural identities are most acute.

Third, and finally, precisely because the novel is neither a Western invention nor a Western franchise, novels serve as a nexus of transnational exchange. Emphasizing the success novels have met with as components of a global import-export trade does *not* entail subscribing to the colonial sequel that has been appended to many European literary histories. If these literary histories often tell how the novel as a new type of narrative is invented in seventeenth-century Spain or France, or eighteenth-century Britain, their sequel recounts how the novel then disseminates its form and idea outward to the peripheries of the European empires, producing new inflections of the original paradigm. Such accounts of novelistic writing present the novel as a franchise, one whose export reaffirms the greatness and identity of its source. Certainly, it has sometimes appeared that the new nations emerging out of empires have been required to produce novels in order to certify their distinct and modern nationhood. "The" novel is the universally prescribed form for bearing witness to the locality of the group, and so every one "has to" have the local equivalent of the Great American Novel. Nonetheless, however this requirement is negotiated, novels' capacity for representing nations and peoples has enabled the novel to become a relay for transnational exchange, in a way that challenges the monopolies on representation sometimes claimed at the metropolitan center.

The interchanges among these three ideas about novels open up a global horizon for novel studies. Instead of an Enlightenment narrative of the novel's vertical "rise"—a narrative that is always normative as well as descriptive—this collection develops narratives of novels' horizontal displacements. By analyzing canon wars in Nigeria and New Zealand as well as the United States, Canada, and Japan, these essays bring into relief the function of novelistic canons in consolidating national identity. At the same time, by studying exchanges in the contact zones between nations, these essays modify our sense of what happens "within" national literatures: revising accounts of "the rise of the novel" means reworking the historical roles that have been imagined for an old canonical favorite like Jane Austen; and Austen's English novels will, when placed in this new context, seem less securely English. In short, by tracking the institutions of the novel within and between nations, and backward in time, this collection broadens our sense of what counts as the novel and of how novels do things in culture.

In "Why the Story of the Origin of the (English) Novel Is an American Romance," Homer Brown provides the prologue to this endeavor to relocate the novel. He reminds us of the disciplinary positions occupied by most of the writers and readers of the volume, and of academics' interest, in a double sense, in the narratives of origin that we transmit and by which we are empowered. Brown's engagement with the retroactive narratives that have made the 1740s look like the inaugural moment for "the" novel leads him to consider two moments of generic institution: the 1950s and the U.S. university's appropriation of the English novel as a component of American national identity; and the Scott phenomenon of the early nineteenth century, another deliberate reinvention of the novel, provoked in part by the Scottish invention of the discipline of English.

The double emphasis of Brown's meditation on institutions—on the novel's production *of* cultures and on the production of the novel in the spaces *between* cultures—is continued in part 1. There Michelle Burnham, Bridget Orr, Lisa Lowe, and Dane Johnson engage the questions of translation, assimilation, cultural belonging, and cultural authenticity that are brought to the fore when one situates novel reading and writing in "the contact zone." Burnham's account of the transatlantic circulation of "English" novels and "American" captivity narratives calls attention to the part that sentimentality plays in producing identities while brokering intercultural contacts. The pathos of the tales of transgressive mobility that Burnham engages, Mary Rowlandson's captivity narrative (originally published in 1682) and Richardson's *Pamela* (from 1740) among them, depends, paradoxically, both on readers' identification with the protagonist's displaced or liminal cultural location and on the obscuring of that movement through fantasies of integration and commonality.

Whereas Burnham's work in the eighteenth century treats an inaugural moment in the cooperative relations between novel, empire, and nation, the other three essays in part 1 engage a recent history of decolonization and diaspora as well as the increasing permeability of national boundaries in the face of economic globalization. Each of these essays asserts what Lowe calls "the paradoxical fluency of the colonized subject in the colonial language and culture." Lowe finds in contemporary Asian American novels a displacement of the forms of development and identification encoded within imperial institutions of the novel and Orientalist histories, forms invested with prescriptive force within the history of U.S. immigration, naturalization, and citizenship laws. Orr's essay first surveys a comparable field of cultural contestation—one created as the Maori, laying claim to "the" New Zealand novel, have become subjects rather than objects of representation—then provides a close analysis of how the operative premises of interpretation must change in this altered context. Her readings of two Maori novels break through the impasse created when critics polarize indigenous content and Western form and find themselves trapped between "the Scylla of ethnographic reductionism" and the "Charybdis of Eurocentric formalism." By contrast, in Johnson's examination of "the rise of Gabriel García Márquez and Toni Morrison" within the U.S. book market and classroom, the emphasis falls on failures of reading. The installation of the Latin American and African American authors' novels within a pantheon of Great Books may instance a new cosmopolitanism, but their "import" has yet to disrupt hegemonic systems of literary evaluation.

The remarks Johnson makes in passing on the resilience of the Great American Novel—an institution newly redeemed by its incorporation of "news from other worlds"—anticipate the questions about "(trans)-national canons" that are the focus of part 2. A canon is a receptacle for certain texts or aesthetic norms. It is also a site where the national heritage is displayed and produced, and a means of asserting the isomorphism of place and culture and nation. As such, canons are inevitably put under pressure by novels' movement across geographical divides and across the boundary lines that segregate the serious from the popular and underwrite ideas of the "real" novel.

The essays by Deidre Lynch and Katie Trumpener that open part 2 engage that mobility by displacing Jane Austen and Walter Scott from the positions of privilege they occupy in accounts of "the" novel's rise and illuminating the conflicted ways in which those figures have been scripted into national narratives that make both old and new states seem like home. Lynch examines the social contests mediated by the early-twentieth-century rearticulation of Jane Austen as an English national institution, a process that saw the Austen novel written into diverse discursive sites—from the English syllabus to the Regency romance, from detective fiction to the modernist program for a streamlined prose style. In her discussion of "Romantic fictions of empire and the narratives of Canadian literature," Trumpener first shows how Scott's novels offered colonizers and colonized a guide to subsuming national differences within the unifying frame of the British empire. She then identifies a countertradition to this imperial historiography of colonies' founding fictions, turning to the acerbic, "transcolonial" consciousness that John Galt and Thomas Chandler Haliburton elaborated in narrating the empire's flows of capital and peoples.

Like Trumpener, who traces how "a 'transcolonial' writing of empire is preserved and studied so partially that only 'national literatures' remain," James Fujii and Susan Andrade also confront the constitutive role of amnesia in national literary histories. Fujii considers how the canonization of Natsume Sōseki's *Kokoro* (first published in 1914) has enabled a definition of Japanese modernity that "writes out Asia," suppressing the colonial expansionism that is an integral element of Japan's emergence as a modern state. The failures of communication that structure Sōseki's narrative raise questions about the place that memory and narrative can claim in Japan, once the state's involuntary embrace of Western modernity signals the irrelevance of the past. It is nationalist literary histories' forgetting of women and of women's resistance to empire that prompts Andrade's essay. Against commemorations of Chinua Achebe as the "father" of the African novel, Andrade offers a genealogy of African literary "daughterhood," relating how Flora Nwapa and Buchi Emecheta renegotiate the territory of the Nigerian national novel and remembering the Igbo Women's War against colonial rule as an occasion for Achebe's own coming to writing.

Our final section, "The Romance of Consumption," puts the canonical into dialogue with the salable, while returning this book to the issue—first raised by Burnham's discussion of sentiment, fantasy, and transculturation—of how novels move and move their readers. Fiction is apprehended in part 3 as a social machinery that helps produce individuals as subjects of sexuality and aligns their desires with the norms of family and/or the demands of consumer capitalism. For many contributors to this section, attending in this manner to what novels do in culture involves engaging the romance, construed either as the novel's figure for its own origins or as the generic location in which narrative eludes the reality principle and responds to desire.

William Warner's account of the institution of formula fiction on the English print market of the 1720s reconsiders narratives labeled as "romances" and written out of histories of the novel's rise. Displacing the representational model in which female-authored fiction is interpreted as an expressive effort by and for "women," Warner emphasizes what the new "media culture" that Eliza Haywood helped to consolidate does: license the desires of a "general reader" and so offer "an infrastructure for the diverse ideologies and class positionalities contending in culture." In a parallel way, Dorothea von Mücke, reading William Godwin's *Caleb Williams* (from 1794), contests the presupposition that what makes the political novel political is its mimetic ambition to narrate "things as they are"—in this case, the persecutions inflicted on a servant narrator by his master. Instead, the political import of *Caleb* lies in how, by chronicling the paranoid interactions between servant and aristocrat, between the subject of the novel and the subject of the romance, Godwin models writing's pragmatic effects. Sexuality, the secret kernel of the subject's individuality, is here located in words not bodies, as the precipitate of the subject's encounter with the discourse of another. Jann Matlock's essay, "The Limits of Reformism: The Novel, Censorship, and the Politics of Adultery in Nineteenth-Century France," adumbrates other consequences of the power that novels wield in licensing desire. Auguste Luchet's 1842 publication of the scandalous *Le Nom de famille* occasioned a trial in which the state and the novel emerged as rivals in the effort to replot the reader's private life. Matlock shows how Luchet's polemics on behalf of a law guaranteeing the right to divorce allowed the novel to transgress its own fictive codes, and how new novels, no less than new law, could tantalize readers with "a second chance at sex."

Realism is again on trial, along with the system of literary value it organizes, in the critical discourse that Nancy Glazener analyzes in her account of Henry James and the romantic revival of late-nineteenth-century America. In addition to locating *The Turn of the Screw* as a canny response to this discourse's reconfiguration of reading, Glazener identifies the material effects of critics' promotion of adventure fiction and historical romance over realism. Explicitly, the project of reading like a boy or a primitive was advocated as a cure for "overcivilization"; tacitly, it operated to legitimize the commodification of novels. In her essay on Edna Ferber's 1926 novel *Show Boat* and its theatrical and cinematic adaptations, Lauren Berlant, like Glazener and Warner, asks us to consider the detours that attention to consumer fantasy might introduce into our narratives of the novel. In particular, she asks us to consider how the participation in the polis that national novels promise their readers is represented as access to consumer culture: thus Ferber's romance plot is the frame for a national history, one in which modes of entertainment are modernized as they are transported from the Mississippi to Hollywood, ex-slaves become consumers, and the memory of slave pain becomes the sentimental stuff of Americana.

The last word goes to Clifford Siskin, who argues that novels and the discourses that packaged them emerged in early-modern Britain to accommodate people to the nation, to the divisions organizing the disciplines, and, above all, to a new technological configuration of writing, print, and silent reading. Through "novelism," writing was naturalized. In the late twentieth century, Siskin avers, writing is again becoming strange, as a new media order takes shape. If, by virtue of its revivals (on stage, screen, video, c.d.), *Show Boat*'s story is also the never-ending story of the staying power of romance—and of the novel—within this new media order, Siskin's account of the "rise of novelism" invites us to write the sequel to the novel's success story. He provides the coda that historicizes and ironizes the project of this volume.

Notes

We would like to thank our readers at Duke University Press and our contributors for their patience and persistence over the course of this long and complex collaboration. Our gratitude also goes to Roy Roussel for an indispensable reading, Anne Graziano for research assistance, and Tom Keirstead and Lizzie MacArthur for their tolerance, humor, and eleventh-hour readings.

1. See, e.g., Davis 1985, Davidson 1986, McKeon 1987, Armstrong 1987, Bender 1987, and Hunter 1990. This debate has been conducted in rather different terms in French studies. See, e.g., DiPiero 1992.

2. For a notable exception, see Layoun 1990.

Homer Brown

Prologue Why the Story of the Origin of the (English) Novel Is an American Romance (If Not the Great American Novel)

Romance and real history have the same common origin. A moment's glance at the origin of society will satisfy the reader why this can hardly be otherwise. The father of an isolated family, destined one day to rise into a tribe, and in farther progress of time to expand into a nation, may, indeed, narrate to his descendants the circumstances which detached him from the society of his brethren, and drove him to form a solitary settlement in the wilderness, with no other deviation from truth, on the part of the narrator, than arises from the infidelity of memory, or the exaggerations of vanity.
—Sir Walter Scott, "An Essay on Romance"

We know the scene: there is a gathering, and someone is telling a story. We do not yet know whether these people gathered together form an assembly, if they are a horde or a tribe. But we call them brothers and sisters because they are gathered together and because they are listening to the same story. . . .

It is an ancient, immemorial scene, and it does not take place just once, but repeats itself indefinitely, with regularity, at every gathering of the hordes, who come to learn of their tribal origins, of their origins in brotherhoods, in peoples, or in cities. . . .

We know this scene well. More than one storyteller has told it to us, having gathered us together in learned fraternities intent on knowing what our origins were. Our societies, they have told us, derive from these assemblies themselves, and our beliefs, our knowledge, our discourses, and our poems derive from these narratives.
—Jean-Luc Nancy, "Myth Interrupted"

❧ Publication of arguments concerning a discrete eighteenth-century English origin for the novel might now seem to approach the dimensions of an American industry, the fulfillment of the American dream—that is, the basic American romance of second chances and new starts. After rejecting its Old World connections and traditions and declaring its own self-making, "the young genre" "rises" to its true, mature identity and home in an American institution—the university—where it settles down for what is predicted to be a long "recapitulation of the same" (McKeon 1987, 419). That it is a romance plot that relates the novel's fortunes is all the more ironic in that the old family from which the novel is said to have so stoutly denied its filiation is precisely romance itself. An early, curious version of this "American dream" is suggested in my first epigraph: Sir Walter Scott's story of the mythic origin of both the nation and the romance narrating that origin (and hence the origin, too, of the novel, which, according to Scott, is romance's "legitimate child" [Scott 1968]). I will return later, via Scott, to Jean-Luc Nancy's reflections on the Western obsession with mythic origins, in which theories of the "origin of the novel" must be implicated. It seems worth noting for the moment, however, that among the causes for deviations from the truth of such narratives are, according to Scott, the mystifications of "the king and the priest" (or one might add, professor), who "find their interest in casting a holy and sacred gloom and mystery over the early period in which their power arose" or the source of their empowerment (1972, 135). The most significant institutional features of such narratives are, that is, the principles that empower the executors, transmitters, and interpreters (kings and priests) of those narratives of mythic origin.

That the story of the institutional "rise" of the novel to a new legitimacy itself has a romance plot does not entirely subvert the fact that it also is part of an institutional history doubly "romantic." This story derives from one moment in the romance of English studies in the American university, a field reborn (and reformed) in the hegemonic rise of the New Criticism. That moment sees the publication by Ian Watt of *The Rise of the Novel* (1957), and sees the American novel's rechristening and reestablishment as romance when Richard Chase publishes *The American Novel and Its Tradition* (1957). It also bears witness, finally, to a revival of Romanticism. The Great American Novel in an Age of Criticism seems fated to have the plot of a quest for origins—which is both the Romantic myth and the plot of Romanticism itself.

In 1957, Ian Watt opened his magisterial inquiry into the novel's origins with a quintessential institutional gambit:

There are still no wholly satisfactory answers to many of the general questions which anyone interested in the early eighteenth-century novelists and their works is likely to ask: Is the novel a new literary form? And if we assume, as is commonly done, that it is, and that it was begun by Defoe, Richardson and Fielding, how does it differ from the prose fiction of the past, from that of Greece, for example, or that of the Middle Ages, or of seventeenth-century France? (9)

One could say of the object of this institutional gambit what Earl Wasserman said about the (as it turns out) not unrelated category, Romanticism:

We generally lop off a period of time, variously and arbitrarily determined, presuming it to be infused with some identifying quality whose name is "romanticism"; and then we set out, in fact, to constitute the *a priori* phantom by defining, with little resulting agreement, usually by naming the common features in manifestations of what we assume must be "romantic." The logic is that of the vicious circle: the definition assumes as existent and understood that which is to be defined and proved to exist. (Qtd. in Rieder 1994, 22)

Watt begins by assuming the existence of "early eighteenth-century novelists" and then goes on to "assume" as is "commonly done," that "the novel [is] a new literary form" and, finally, "that it was begun by Defoe, Richardson and Fielding." The "as is commonly done" that stands at the center of these assumptions points to the source of all of them in received opinion, and thus what needs most to be argued falls prey to "the logic . . . of the vicious circle." The fact that these assumptions are not explained is covered by a series of questions about the difference between this "*a priori* phantom," the novel, and previous prose fiction. It is not until almost a page later that we learn that the putatively originary "novelists," who mainly saw their work as "involving a break with the old-fashioned romances," "did not even canonise the changed nature of their fictions by a change in nomenclature—our usage of the term 'novel' was not fully established until the end of the eighteenth century" (Watt 1957, 10).

After his disclaimer, Wasserman goes on to distinguish his Romantic poets from the poets of sensibility and proceeds to a marvelously schematic account of the subject-object dynamics of four major "romantic" poets. John Rieder describes this apparently contradictory move as Wasserman's way of marking the difference between the term Romanticism's "conceptual validity and its institutional necessity" and of "defining the professional situation which allows—or forces—this designation to persist in spite of its intellectual and scholarly shortcomings" (1994, 23). By his resort to received doctrine, or what is commonly assumed, Watt is confirming anew what is already institutionalized. He is either confusing or leading his readers to confuse the history of the novel's institution with the institution's history of the novel. We call these works "novels" even though their authors did not so designate them, indeed could not have done so, because the novel, whenever it became "the" novel as instituted (the end of the eighteenth century? even later than that?), decided to claim *them* as its own.

Elsewhere I have argued for the uncertain, inchoate, and multiple institutions (in the active sense of that slippery word) that are associated with fictional narrative in the eighteenth and early nineteenth centuries and that problematize the "common" assumption about "the novel" that Watt's account transmits and by which it is empowered. These institutions are uncertain, because none of what are now considered "founding" novels were given that honorific generic name by Defoe, Richardson, or Fielding, who authored (and authorized) them by different names. The name "novel," in any case, had different semantic values then from those it took on during the nineteenth and twentieth centuries as what I am going to call an "institution." Inchoate and multiple, because whatever its influence on the way "the novel" came to be thought of in the next two centuries (and there were a lot of variations and differences in such thinking), no one work by Defoe, Richardson, or Fielding can be accepted as the "first," or originary, novel. No single one of them is sufficient to exemplify what later became "the" novel, given not only the radical differences of narrative form and thematic content among them but also their radically different "addresses" and the widely varying levels of social life they "represented" (in all senses of that term). Nor, despite Ian Watt's hope, are they in their differences from each other a "recapitulation" (1957, 301) of the variety of forms taken by the later novel, unless any difference is taken to symbolize difference as such. The fictions of Defoe, Richardson, and Fielding, it could be argued, only become "the novel" symbolically by means of retrospective histories that made them seem inaugural and exemplary at once.

Insistence that the novel fully realized its generic identity—that it was "institutionalized"—by 1750 is also based on a misconception of institution, not only implying an untenable confusion of intentionality with fully received acknowledgment but also tacitly evoking the ideological seventeenth- and eighteenth-century political presumption of strict genealogical determination. What an institution was in its beginnings it must always be. What an institution can become must be fully present in its origins (at least according to the way those "origins" are politically conceived retrospectively). Aside from the tautology of this claim in principle, in this particular case it sets a definite ideological limit on what kind of novel can claim entitlement, and for that matter on the definition of the very culture that produces and/or is produced by this increasingly effective narrative shaper of cultural and social desire.

Finally, to suggest that the novel fully achieves its identity by 1750 also presupposes that the identity of *the novel* is defined by its *contextualization* at this particular moment and precludes consideration of the massive change in meaning undergone not only by the term "novel" but also by the particular texts of Defoe, Richardson, and Fielding in the next two centuries, and especially the crucial next seventy years. We must always guard ourselves against the supposition that the meaning of any genre or institution, or even any text or utterance, is fully manifest, let alone contained, in any single historical moment or context. Ian Watt's conclusion to *Rise* demonstrates the reductive awkwardness of teleological solutions that respond, in part no doubt, to such a demand for closure. He adduces "the example of Sterne" to demonstrate that "the two major differences in narrative method between the novels of Richardson and Fielding are by no means manifestations of two opposite and irreconcilable kinds of novel, but merely rather clearly contrasted solutions of problems which pervade the whole tradition of the novel and whose apparent divergences can in fact be harmoniously reconciled" (Watt 1957, 296). Here Watt's "harmonious" solution to the differences between these "novels" brings him to the story of the novel promulgated by the New Criticism and F. R. Leavis's *The Great Tradition* (1954) and to the "first" (serious) novelist for both, Jane Austen, who is said to merge Fieldingesque and Richardsonian novelistic modes. Both stories—the resolution of difference as telos and that of the originator of the "great tradition" of the novel—are assembled in accordance with the allegory of natural growth and development: "Indeed, the *full maturity* of the genre itself, it can be argued, could only come when this reconciliation had been achieved, and it is probable that it is largely to her successful resolution of these problems that Jane Austen owes her eminence in the tradition of the English novel" (Watt 1957, 296; my emphasis). This narrative also more than implies the progressive improvement of the novel, as, a little later, Watt admits that "compared with Jane Austen, or with Balzac and Stendhal, Defoe, Richardson and Fielding all have fairly obvious technical weaknesses" (301). Historically, however, he grants them "two kinds of importance: the obvious importance that attaches to writers who" helped to create "the dominant literary form of the last two centuries" (a tautological argument); "and the equally great importance" that comes with their status as "essentially independent innovators," and the fact therefore that "their novels provide three rather sharply defined images of the form in general, and constitute a remarkably complete recapitulation of the essential diversities in its later tradition" (301).

This conclusion is oddly echoed in Michael McKeon's reworking of Watt, *The Origins of the English Novel, 1600–1740* (1987), when McKeon reverses the temporality of Watt's term—"recapitulate"—in his conclusion to make an even grander claim. For Watt, the trio Richardson-Fielding-Austen serves as a "recapitulation" of all the possibilities enjoyed by the novel to come in the next two hundred years. But if for Watt the whole complicated history of the development of the nineteenth-century and modern novels lies before it, he at least recognizes the difference between its future possibilities and its eighteenth-century past. For McKeon, one difference turns all other differences into versions of the same; the novel realizes its mature identity in the "institutionalization" of the conflict and a dialectical "*rapprochement*" between Richardson and Fielding. Well, almost. "If we distance ourselves from the details of this *rapprochement*," McKeon says, "we may catch a glimpse of where the novel goes after its origins." But, where it goes is not very far. After "the implications of the formal breakthrough of the 1740s are pursued with such feverish intensity over the next two decades," and after *Tristram Shandy* provides apparently the last novelty, what follows is that "the young genre settles down to a more deliberate and studied *recapitulation of the same ground*, this time for the next two centuries" (419; my emphasis). For both Watt and McKeon, there is a strange hiatus in the latter part of the eighteenth century, and, for McKeon, this hiatus seems to extend through the novel's whole future history. When McKeon's history closes, so does history as such. By the early nineteenth century, the novel is "history."

I would want to argue, contrary to this sense of the expression, that the novel really *is* history. I would also argue that the changes undergone by prose fiction during the "hiatus" heralded by Watt and McKeon essentially recontextualize the "novel" of midcentury and require for it a different reading, and that, furthermore, it is as necessary to "historicize" the discourse of the novel as it is the novel itself, given the implicitly transhistorical nature of the object as it is presented in most histories of its origin. This is so because historical accounts of the rise or origin of the novel, whatever their value as histories, have as part of their effect the establishment of protocols for reading novels, for determining what is important to read in them and *which* novels can be read "seriously" or even can be given the privilege of the curiously esteemed title "novel" instead of one of its déclassé and plebeian combination forms. Such lists of "real" novels have been notoriously variable from one point in time to another, probably because of the instability of "literary" involvement with the market, and because of ideological aspects of the popular and middle-brow culture to which novels have always ambiguously belonged.

Now that we have seen some of the problems that accrue, where accounts of the novel are concerned, to the traditional identification of institution solely with either origins or mature cultural formation, if not ossification, let me examine the word and concept "institution" and develop some of its implications regarding literature or the novel as institutions.

Literature, which only took its modern meaning in the late eighteenth century, has been called or thought of as an institution at least since Hippolyte Taine in the mid-nineteenth century. Before "literature," poetry was considered an institution by thinkers of the Scottish Enlightenment and at least as far back as Giambattista Vico's *New Science,* which first appeared in 1725. In the more or less modern meaning of the term "institution," both literature and the novel were referred to in the United States as "institutions" even during the New Criticism (e.g., Wellek and Warren 1956, 226; Levin 1963). These usages considered literature (or the novel) as a more or less organic, complete whole functioning in society but, like other institutions, autonomous (answerable only to itself) and affected by other social elements or forces only externally as an institution. This concept was part of a developing sociology of institutions which thought of society as the organization of such institutions.

According to Vico's modern English translators, Thomas Goddard

Bergin and Max Harold Fisch, it was something like this usage of the word *instituzione* in Italian political discourse during the early eighteenth century that made Vico eschew use of it, although he could be considered as a founder of modern social-cultural theory and its articulation of the cultural role of literature. As Bergin and Fisch point out, in Latin and the Romance languages, the cognates of "to institute" and "institution" "all imply deliberate contrivance, artifice, choice, will, intent"—all characteristics, interestingly enough, that we attribute to great "authors" in the modern institutions of literature. "One of the chief senses" of the term institution, Bergin and Fisch continue, referred to "formal education—planned systematic instruction—as distinguished from uncontrolled learning" (Vico 1970, li). Bergin and Fisch felt in 1970 that they were now able to translate various terms Vico used by forms of the word "institution," because this "rationalistic theory of the origin and nature of institutions" had begun to lose its status as "the accepted theory," at least partly because of Vico's work.

> The rationalistic theory assumed that the institutions of society were made by "men," in the sense of human beings who were already fully human, in whom the humanity of Vico's "age of men" was already fully developed. What Vico wanted to assert was that the first steps in the building of "the world of nations" were taken by creatures who were still (or who had degenerated into) beasts, and that humanity itself was created by the very same processes by which the institutions were created. Humanity is not a presupposition, but a consequence, an effect, a product of institution building. (Vico 1970, lii)

This point about the effects rather than the origins of institutions should serve as a caution for current convictions concerning the institution or origin of the novel, generated as they must be from within the culture that the novel has made possible. The danger of what might too simply be called "anachronism" (but could be understood in the Freudian term *nachtraglichkeit*) is also a danger of *institution*. Perhaps too familiar a word in common discourse, part of its function is to make the strange, unusual, singular, or the "novel" seem familiar, even common—legitimate and "authorized." There is another kind of ambiguity about "institution" that must also be noted—does it name a thing or an act, an act or an activity? Raymond Williams called it "a noun of action or process." Interestingly, the term always seems to require and elicit a narrative: thus Williams goes on to describe it as "a noun of action or process which became, at a certain stage, a general and abstract noun, describing something apparently objective and systematic; in fact, in the modern sense, an institution (1983a, 168).

Samuel Weber, in an essential study of institutions, sees the relationship between these two meanings in another way, insisting on construing institutionalization "differently from the way it has traditionally been treated in philosophy and, above all, in the social sciences. The dominant tendency . . . has been to reduce the concept to only one of its elements: the maintenance of the status quo, and thereby to eliminate its dynamic, transformative aspect." Citing René Lorau, Weber notes that the term " 'has been increasingly used to designate . . . the *instituted* (*institué*), the established order, the already existing norms, the state of fact thereby being confounded with the state of right (*l'état de droit*). By contrast, the *instituting* aspect (*l'instituant*) . . . has been increasingly obscured' " (Weber 1987, xv). Weber then goes on to describe his own use of the concept as "one in which *instituted* organization and *instituting* process are joined in the ambivalent relation of every determinate structure to that which it excludes, and yet which, qua excluded, allows that structure to *set itself apart*."[1]

Institution, then, designates at once an act, an action, a process, and the product of that action or process—at once, action and stasis, lingering effect, trace, or remainder as such. From the Latin *instituare,* to institute means literally to cause to stand or stand up, to move something to standing or at least the illusion of standing in one place—that is to say, something that *stays.* And that "something"—which almost always is or involves an assembling of collective acts or practices—is also of some social importance, which is acknowledged in that "standing" (both figurative and literal). There is a kind of reification at work in the term, an effect of the happening it names that makes the happening—institution—appear as something in itself. This effect explains why, when we think of institution, we almost always think of buildings—church, school, bank are all names of common institutions but also of the material buildings in which they are housed and with which they are often confused. The building sites and situates the institution. An "edifice" gives it not only an imposing presence but also a past and future, an appearance of duration and continuity. And while it shelters and arranges the practices and people that it houses, seemingly guaranteeing the internal unity of all it contains, the building also stands for and declares the institution's anteriority and alterity, its transcendance of any particular person or practice that it supports. Particular people or practices are made to seem accidental to the institution that names them and grants them distinction, while the notion of the material "house" is made to seem of the essence of institution. The history of the words "edifice" and "edification" captures this seeming reversal. They both come from the Latin *aedificare: aedes*—a temple or building—and *facere*—to make or build. Thus, to edify meant to build or establish before it meant to instruct or improve. All this suggests the operation of a powerful social imaginary that institution establishes and relies upon for its own authority—its seemingly material presence.

There is a paradoxical sense of the word institution that must needs be heard in all its contrariety in any use of the term. While it implies an origin, the establishment of something new for "the first time," institution, as an establishment, also implies social reception, acceptance, recognition, acknowledgment, legitimation. Does the Christian church as an institution begin as such when Jesus names (renames?) Peter? In a mystical sense, perhaps, but one that I doubt scholars of the novel would be willing to grant with respect to the naming of the novel as a genre. Or does the institution begin when the narrative of that naming is circulated and wins recognition? As Jacques Derrida (1989) points out, the paradox of any invention is that, on the one hand, it depends on absolute novelty, a break with the law and convention, and, on the other, it requires social recognition, by the law and institutional forms of legitimation—patents and so forth. Thus the institution of the novel takes place between a necessarily fictive (in a double sense) origin or first time and that time of legitimation and acknowledgment. Can there be generic status, and in this sense, *institution,* before general recognition?

> Power over another's mind, even to a simple degree, can be enormously dangerous. But that is education, and that is literature also.—Lewis Leary, "Literary Scholarship and the Teaching of English"

> Literature is that ensemble of objects and rules, techniques and works, whose function in the general economy of our society is precisely *to institutionalize subjectivity.* . . . if one wants to speak, even if only a word, about the Racinian *self*—one must expect to see . . . the most prudent critic reveal himself as an utterly subjective, utterly historical being.
> —Roland Barthes, "History or Literature"

When is that "moment" of institution for "the novel"? One important moment is in the second decade of the nineteenth century with the novels of Jane Austen (as Ian Watt acknowledges) and with the novels and criticism of Walter Scott (which Watt ignores), a moment significantly following three decades of great (and much maligned) novelistic and romance production. Another important institutional conjuncture is the controversial "aesthetic" elevation given the novel by Henry James and James's argument over the nature of the novel with H. G. Wells and others. This late-nineteenth-century conjuncture is, effectively, the moment when the novel "began" for the modernist New Criticism, and the enabling, foundational origin in what seems to me the most crucial institutional history of the novel. For it was this history that legitimated the New Critical appropriation of the novel for intensive close reading in university classes during the postwar expansion of American university enrollments (Graff 1987, 155). Already doctrine in courses on modernism, this notion of the novel's rise to aesthetic seriousness only with James and/or Flaubert was obviously a product of the criticism movement and not of academic scholarly research. But, in 1957, Watt deftly inserted his story of an earlier rise of the novel into this context, effectively combining historical with formalist considerations so as to recuperate the eighteenth-century novel as a *modern* form of literary art. Watt implied not only that the novels of Defoe, Richardson, and Fielding were modern but that they also played a major role in the invention of modernism as such.

That Watt's intervention came at a decisive moment for the institutionalization of the novel in American universities can be demonstrated by a glance at a few contemporary publications of novel theory. In addition to Watt's *Rise,* in 1957 there were Richard Chase's *The American Novel and Its Tradition,* Northrop Frye's *Anatomy of Criticism,* William K. Wimsatt Jr. and Cleanth Brooks's *Literary Criticism: A Short History,* and the English translation of Erich Auerbach's *Mimesis.* The English translation of José Ortega y Gasset's "First Meditation," from his *Meditations on Quixote,* was published in the *Hudson Review* as "The Nature of the Novel." One might see in this series an aspiration toward definitive works on the nature of fiction, its origin and rise, and its relation to nation and culture. These books also appeared at a turning point that could be described as the crisis of modernism in America, particularly in regard to the novel. The same year of the publication of *The Rise of the Novel,* which might more properly have been called *The Rise of*

Criticism of the Novel, there also appeared *The Living Novel: A Symposium,* edited by Granville Hicks. According to the dust jacket, Hicks, "alarmed at critical pronouncements that the novel is dead, . . . invited ten contemporary novelists to discuss the problems of their craft today," a group that included Saul Bellow, Paul Darcy Boles, Ralph Ellison, Wright Morris, and Flannery O'Connor. (Crisis and criticism seem to go hand in hand. This time was frequently described as "the" or "an" Age of Criticism.)

Whatever the problems of linear conceptions of history, this constellation of publishing events seems significant for understanding the institutional context of Watt's *The Rise of the Novel.* Luckily, for my purposes, this context is further illuminated by the more than coincidental publication in 1958 of a volume of essays by notable scholars and critics evaluating the current status of the academic disciplines of literary study in American colleges and universities: *Contemporary Literary Scholarship: A Critical Review,* edited by Lewis Leary for the Committee on Literary Scholarship and the Teaching of English of the National Council of Teachers of English. These scholars and critics are not simply surveying their disciplines according to the ordinary mandate of such periodic surveys. There is throughout the volume a sense that 1958 is a moment of decisive change for both the university and literature. The essays repeatedly celebrate the triumph of criticism in American English departments, criticism valued because it is "new" and defined as interpretation that is based on "analytical" close reading. But this triumph is also qualified by the sense that the era of a certain form of criticism—one that restricts the practice to close reading—had come to an end. William Van O'Connor, a prominent spokesman for the New Criticism, even adds as a postscript to his article, entitled "Modern Literary Criticism," the statement that "*Literary Criticism: A Short History* (1957) by William K. Wimsatt Jr. and Cleanth Brooks may prove to be a volume that ended an era of literary criticism" (Van O'Connor 1958, 233). What has changed the old criticism and consolidated the "triumph" of the new is the latter's accommodation to historical scholarship and the accommodation of both criticism and historical scholarship to the needs of classroom pedagogy. This accommodation defines "The Problem"—the title of the first section of *Contemporary Literary Scholarship*—and provides the theme of most of the volume's essays. It would seem to be called for by the very nature of departments whose courses and fields are structured according to historical periods and, to a lesser degree, genres, but this seems, for Lewis Leary's contributors, to be a fact that goes without saying. Instead, it is the felt deficiency of the strict New Critical approach that calls for correction. As Jacques Barzun points out in the first essay, "the interpretation which lighted up the refreshing new 'facts'" in the literary text ("facts" that had replaced the annotations of the old historical scholarship) was discovered itself to be "secretly loaded with history" and that "the pretense, moreover, of remaining 'inside the work' is an illusion." Barzun even goes on to wonder "whether the historical method is not, after all, the only one that the critic can use. It is, as we saw, the one that he has always used, even when he concealed it under new ideologies" (Barzun 1958, 7).

The relevance to Ian Watt's work of this combination of new historical scholarship and formalist interpretation should be obvious. Consider the novelty of Watt's work in the light of the values expressed in Bradford Booth's closing peroration for his essay, "The Novel":

> It has been for criticism an era of dramatic accomplishment. In its understanding of the intimate relationship between the novel and society; in its keen analyses of new psychological genres and of the intent and value of myth and symbol; in its lively awareness of technical problems, both new and old; and in its dedication to the scholarly principles and accuracy—in all these areas the study of the novel in the past quarter century has been pursued with skill, with devotion, and with high imagination. (Booth 1958, 287–88)

This statement encapsulates Watt's achievement and concerns not only in its references to thorough scholarship and to "the intimate relationship between the novel and society" but also in its allusion to the "psychologizing" of the eighteenth-century novel (I will comment shortly about what is coded in this term), its emphasis on the "technical problems" that fiction set out to solve, and even its mention of "myth." (It is easy to forget that part of Watt's first chapter on Defoe had been published in 1951 as an article entitled "*Robinson Crusoe* as a Myth.")

Booth's statement refers of course to critics of the *modern* novel, who in some sense must have been Watt's model. By "new psychological genres," Booth is referring to the twentieth-century novelist's "assumption of what Leon Edel calls the mind's-eye view" (Booth 1958, 264), an emphasis on the form of "consciousness" as such, which is more epistemological than psychological. Booth explains that "the Victorian novelists, not so unaware of the subjective life as is sometimes assumed, understood that it might be *reported,* but they did not perceive how it might be vividly and concretely *rendered*" (1958, 265). This last phrase suggests a Jamesian "origin" for this concern with the "technical" problems of the New Critical conception of the novel, and, indeed, Booth proceeds to comment on the fact that "since James, critics have been increasingly (and are now, indeed, almost exclusively) concerned with fiction as a technique, exploring the mechanics of a craft which has become subject to many of the organizational and philosophical principles which have historically governed older and more fully codified literary forms" (273). He then turns to a discussion of the two technical problems that have received the most "thoughtful consideration"—"point of view" and "the handling of time"—both of which are significant components of Watt's "formal realism" (Watt 1957, 32ff).

I will discuss here only the first of these. (The second—time—is defined and governed by the first.) Again, Henry James is the point of departure for this engagement with the novel, since, as Booth reports, James "solved the beguiling problem of finding a 'center' or 'focus' for his stories by framing the action not externally but within the consciousness of one of the characters" (1958, 274). Booth also quotes from "The Post of Observation in Fiction" by Allen Tate: "'The limited and thus credible authority for the action, which is gained by putting the knower of the action inside its frame, is perhaps the distinctive feature of the modern novel; and it is, in all the infinite shifts of focus of which it is capable, the special feature which more than any other has made it possible for the novelist to achieve an objective structure'" (275). Watt cites pretty much the same statement from Tate's "Techniques of Fiction," adding: "there is no doubt that the pursuit of verisimilitude led Defoe, Richardson and Fielding to initiate that power of 'putting man wholly into his physical setting' which constitutes for Allen Tate the distinctive capacity of the novel form" (1957, 27).[2] Though Watt's version of Tate allows a greater range of reference for the "formal realism" Watt espouses, his own epistemological focus places it within the New Critical problematic of point of view.

What is at stake for all these critics is the *consciousness* of experience or subjectivity; and the manner in which they conceived its "rendering" in the "form" of the novel seems to me highly significant. Once the subjectivity of fiction was considered in formal terms as "technique," "focus of narrative" (Brooks and Warren 1943), point of view, or narrative frame, the control of subjectivity was seen not only as the aesthetic essence of fiction but as what rendered fictional art "objective" (no doubt freeing the critic from accusations of impressionistic interpretations). Bradford Booth, for his part, turns in his survey to the two landmark works of the New Criticism on this topic (after, of course, Henry James and Percy Lubbock): Norman Friedman's schematic "Point of View in Fiction: The Development of a Critical Concept" (*PMLA* 1955), "an historical survey of critical thinking on the novelist's relationship to his material" (Booth 1958, 274), and Mark Schorer's much reprinted "Technique as Discovery" (*Hudson Review* [1948]). In this latter essay, as Booth says,

> Schorer examines "the uses of point of view not only as a mode of dramatic delimitation but, more particularly, of thematic definition." He contends that the devices of point of view offer a controlling medium by which the novelist may disengage his own prejudices from those of his characters and evaluate their predispositions dramatically. That such considerations are a commonplace of current criticism is the inference from the twenty-odd references which Friedman cites to this effect in the past fifteen years. (275)

It is by way of technique—control of subject form—that the subjectivity of language, of poetic art, and of interpretation as well, can be made *objective. Techne* then becomes the discovery or revealing of truth (*aletheia*), as Heidegger said it was for the Greeks.[3]

Not too much later, the revival of Romanticism studies, heralded in the 1958 Leary volume (by Richard Harter Fogle) and by at least three other volumes of critical essays published in 1957, would add other dimensions to the development of what is much more than a thematic. The "field" and canon of Romanticism had been more severely savaged than any other by modernism, as had its academic study by the New Criticism. In the late 1950s it was beginning to be clear that New Critical aesthetics owed a great deal to Romantic concerns and poetics. Soon, within the field of Romanticism as with novel criticism, concern with "psychology" would modulate into epistemological questions and into an engagement with subjectivity and consciousness along with narratives of "growth" and development. I necessarily foreshorten what is a complex "development" that is presently much contested (see, e.g., Siskin 1988; Favret and Watson 1994a). What interests me, however, is the curious intercourse apparent between novel criticism and romantic studies, a conjuncture with important pedagogical implications in 1958 and since. What takes place in the classroom in postwar America is (literally and on several other levels) the construction of subjectivity and the subject, at an institutional moment when more students than in any prior era, students of backgrounds that never before would have allowed them to dream about entering college, are studying what are considered to be significant literary works in terms of the naturalization of the construction of individual subjectivity. How to begin to evaluate the effects of such narratives of education as a narrative of education?

> Something is happening, I believe, and it may be of the utmost significance. —R. W. B. Lewis, "Contemporary American Literature"

That Watt's *Rise* is hardly mentioned in a volume of essays mostly written in 1957 (some even earlier) is not surprising, but the way Watt is mentioned casts some light on the state of the novel within the historical field of eighteenth-century English studies. James L. Clifford, who wrote an essay for the Leary volume entitled "The [i.e., English] Eighteenth Century," mentions Watt's *Rise* twice, first in a list of "discerning approaches" to Defoe (1958, 96), and later with the reservation that "although consideration of the rise of fiction properly belongs in another chapter, . . . for over-all commentary the most stimulating books are those by McKillop and Watt listed earlier in the section on Defoe" (101–2).[4] Although Clifford manages in his essay to include "some few remarks . . . about the major novelists, since they easily rank among the principal writers of the eighteenth century," the bias of the eighteenth-century specialist toward poetry over the novel, and the segregation of the more traditional early historical fields, is obvious, as is, elsewhere in the Leary volume, the marked expansion of criticism of the American and modern novel. As Bradford Booth says, "one of the results of James's critical awareness was the interest in fiction which it generated among persons trained in poetry and the drama" (1958, 259). One interesting thing about this statement is its twisted historical temporality. Booth refers to interest on the part of the New Critics, who tended to date the earliest moment the novel could be taken seriously as that of James and Flaubert, although they sometimes included Austen as a respectably conscious artist.

I want to pause for a moment here to pursue some of the institutional implications of this critical emphasis on the modern. Though this volume carefully marks the accepted disciplinary boundaries of the "fields" of the institution, as would seem to be the performative intent of such surveys, there is almost a sense of those fields being reinstituted in the light of modernist and American concerns. This reinstitution is most marked in the Leary volume's emphasis on recent criticism of British literature produced by American critics ("American" meaning U.S.). In the more traditional fields, the boundary marking in question is mostly defensive and supports more conventional canons in opposition to modernist revision. (Watt's *Rise* is certainly an example of this gesture.) But even here, "progress" is the key word, privileging innovative critical interpretation.

R. W. B. Lewis's essay, "Contemporary American Literature," in the Leary volume exemplifies and illuminates this phenomenon, which Lewis characterizes as "the persistent American nose for news":

> The formalised study of contemporary—that is, roughly twentieth-century—literature in America is itself a cultural phenomenon of the first order. . . . Indeed, a tense preoccupation with the present moment has long been a familiar American habit. . . . But it is hard to imagine in any other century what has taken place in this American century—the institutionalising of interest in the very recent and immediate. Courses have been introduced in colleges all across the continent, and they have proliferated to the degree that "contemporary literature" has become a formal and extremely popular field of academic study, . . . so that perhaps the first thing to notice about contemporary American culture is its fascination with its own form and pressure. (1958, 201)

Lewis relates this interest in the "latest" (which in fact defines the nature of all the surveys of scholarship in the Leary volume) not only to an American obsession but also to a persistent American question:

> As a corollary to the immersion in history, the study of contemporary literature is also a part of America's repeated effort to identify itself. We not only stand tiptoe to detect new trends; we are constantly taking stock. And we not only appraise our past, we are regularly changing our minds about its durable content. The rather tangled story I have to tell in this article is in fact the story of progressive determinations of the very substance of contemporary literature. (202)

What Lewis means to describe here is the establishment of the American literary canon (although he later calls canons "un-American"). But his statement in effect describes the project of the volume in which it appears, and also the renaissance of the institution of literary studies in the American university as such. If modernism characterizes the state of criticism (criticism as literature) throughout the academic fields surveyed in Leary's volume, and if it is precisely the genealogy of that modernism that is in question in terms of America's "repeated effort to identify itself," then what is taking place institutionally is the American critical appropriation of English literature as a component of its own national identity. However traditional the cultural genealogy at stake here might have been, and exacerbated as it might be by the massive new "melting pot" college population and, as Mary Favret and Nicola Watson have noted (1994a), by the antihistoricist pedagogy of the New Critics, what was happening was something new—English literature was being taken as America's own and read in a peculiarly American way in its own institution.

One could in fact apply R. W. B. Lewis's remark about Alfred Kazin's *On Native Grounds* to the Leary survey itself: "This is the stuff of a recognizably American point of view. . . . His thesis is that it is *that tradition* [which Kazin traces] which is authentically American. . . . Kazin's book thus belongs to the drama of American literature" (Lewis 1958, 204). Leslie Fiedler, in his essay on American literature for the Leary collection, writes: "For better or for worse, the criticism of American literature has been captured by the university departments; and conversely, those departments seem on the verge of being captured by the study of American literature" (1958, 159). We can see that final term as comprehending what is still called "English" literature. Recently Lawrence Lipking has remarked that

> Eighteenth-century English literature does not look quite the same when observed from England, the United States, France, India, or Australia. . . . One oceanic rift in particular underlies the field: the gulf between America and Great Britain. From an American perspective, eighteenth-century English literature is a foreign country. . . . Its politics, culture, ideas, and style require perpetual imaginative recreation. . . . If America and Britain are cultures divided by a common language, so the mirage of a common literature divides their scholars. . . . [T]he danger of American eighteenth-century studies, from a British point of view, lies in refining or vaporizing material practices into mere constructions of the mind. (1992, 20–22)

This question needs to be thought through in the light of Benedict Anderson's *Imagined Communities* (1983), and especially with reference to the historical context that Gauri Viswanathan describes in *Masks of Conquest: Literary Study and British Rule in India* (1989). Viswanathan cites the question posed by Richard Poirier's essay "What Is English Studies, and If You Know What That Is, What Is English Literature?" as "a useful one to bear in mind in connection with British Indian educational history, insofar as it draws attention to literary *education,* as opposed to *literature,* as a major institutional support system of colonial administration" (4). For Viswanathan, having distinguished between literary texts and the ideological instrument Literature, one can go on to comprehend how the "values assigned to literature—such as the proper development of character or the shaping of critical thought or the formation of aesthetic judgment—are only problematically located there and are more obviously serviceable to the dynamic of power relations between the educator and those who are to be educated" (4).

It is significant, if not surprising, that when Lewis Leary wants in 1958 to define the pedagogical role of the scholar-critic at the beginning of his survey, he does so in terms that ironically enough anticipate Viswanathan's. Jokingly, Leary even draws an outrageously unself-aware analogy via a 1950s nightmare catchword:

> The teacher of English is, or can be, perhaps even should be, a brain-washer, which is a coarser but more direct way of saying that he molds character. *Brainwashing* is a term of opprobrium used to describe what people we dislike do to people whom we think should view the world as we do. When Shakespeare or Milton, Albert Schweitzer or Billy Graham, tempts them to a view similar to ours, we call it something else. But the results, though not always the methods, are the same. Power over another's mind, even to a simple degree, can be enormously dangerous. But that is education, and that is literature also. (Leary 1958a, 18–19)

I want to pursue further this question of the "power" of the scholar-critic-teacher now, by considering the question of a metropolitan literature deemed useful for the administration of a colony. Robert Crawford's account (1992) of the lectures on rhetoric and belles lettres in mid-eighteenth-century Scotland and of the "Scottish invention" of English points to an even earlier origin of the teaching of English literature than that which occurred in India. For these lectures given by Adam Smith and Hugh Blair and others, a "canon" of English literature was effectively constituted, in order to provide a model of the best English writing for the aspiring Scottish professional who sought to rid himself of his "Scotticisms." Lists of "proscribed expressions," and, indeed, the popular lecture courses themselves, Crawford points out, indicate "the way in which discourse itself was politically important, a key to gaining power in Britain" (23). Moreover, "the fact that access to proper English Literature gave access to 'proper' language—and so to power—explains the popularity of the subject of Rhetoric and Belles Lettres in North America" (39). Crawford gives as examples Thomas Jefferson, who studied this subject with his Scottish tutor at William and Mary and later included it in his own plans for institutions of higher education, and the Scot John Witherspoon, who in 1768, when he became president of the College of New Jersey (Princeton), inaugurated the first formal rhetoric course in North America. (Witherspoon coined the word "Americanism" and published his own list of proscribed expressions.)

But if the learning of English letters provided only a modicum of power in the British empire for the Scot and even less for the East Indian —neither would ever be accepted as really "English"—the value of this discipline for the U.S. citizen after the Revolution was quite different. He gained by it immense symbolic capital in his own power structure. While the dominant position granted English literature in American education might now seem Toryishly reactionary or nostalgic, it might more accurately be thought of as American cultural imperialism since, as I suggested earlier in reading Fiedler's remark about the "capture" of English departments by American literature, what seems to be the unspoken trend is the "capture" of English literature by American criticism. One could as of 1958 supplement Poirier's title with "And If You Know What English Literature Is, What Is American Literature?"

This issue has a particular importance for the novel. Consider the opening of Leslie Fiedler's *Love and Death in the American Novel* (1960):

> Between the Novel and America there are peculiar and intimate connections. A new literary form and a new society, their beginnings coincide with the beginnings of the modern era and, indeed help to define it. We are living not only in the Age of America but also in the Age of the Novel, at a moment when the literature of a country without a first-rate verse epic or a memorable verse tragedy has become the model of half the world. . . . [L]iterature has become for most readers quite simply prose fiction; and our endemic fantasy of writing "the Great American Novel" is only a local instance of a more generalized obsession. The notion of greatness once associated with the heroic poem has been transferred

to the novel; and the shift is a part of that "Americanization" of culture which some European intellectuals continue ritually to deplore. (230)

Fiedler describes admirably America's "romance" with the novel and with modernism as it is described in Leary's collection, as well as the Americanization of other cultures, particularly for domestic consumption. "The Great American Novel" would no doubt be one constructing the myths of origin of both America and modernism, and thus its own form as well.

The hidden question here of the origin of the *American* novel emerges in an almost uncanny way in the last book of 1957 that I wish to discuss here. It is institutionally significant that the American novel, which has its beginnings during the later eighteenth and early nineteenth centuries, frequently played with the elements and the generic title of the romance. This identification of the difference of the American novel, by curious coincidence, is itself academically institutionalized in the American university at the same time that Watt marks the "realism of" the English novel. Like Watt's *Rise,* Richard Chase's *The American Novel and Its Tradition* launches an argument linking the origin of its subject with literary modernism; but by identifying the American novel as a kind of romance, Chase seeks to distinguish it from the great nineteenth-century *novel.* This opposition in coincidence suggests the same powerful institutional movement to define or redraw disciplinary territories that informs Lewis Leary's collection of essays. John McWilliams in an interesting recent essay on Chase's book suggests "strong institutional reasons" for its success and "persistence": "Chase's model of the romance gave Americanists a counter-theory of the American novel which justified the separate study of American fiction at a time of great expansion in higher education, including Ph.D. programs with increasing specializations in English or American literature" (McWilliams 1993, 73; see also Pease 1993a).

If we accept Chase's hypothesis about the Americanness of romance, a paradox arises. The American romance novel "rising" in the late eighteenth century suggests a response to English literary practices vastly different from those issued during the early to mid century as described by Watt (and more recently McKeon [1987]); but it also suggests that the changes the "novel" of Defoe, Richardson, and Fielding was subject to later in the eighteenth century were so enormous as to be almost unrecognizable by the same generic standards. Accepting both Watt's and Chase's theses would oblige literary history to engage a curious phenomenon in which America's "later" experience of the novel produces the novel's older, more primitive, and more aristocratic precursor, the romance. In this light, American academics' vociferous insistence on a discrete and complete mid-eighteenth-century origin of the English novel—and the category American academic should include Ian Watt—seems to exemplify how disciplinary and generic politics are imbricated with the politics of American identity and the politics of what America owes to its English "origins."

In this context, one figure that Richard Chase uses to distinguish American and English novels is notable. The English novel, he says, "has been a kind of imperial enterprise, an appropriation of reality with the high purpose of bringing order to disorder" (1957, 4). In contrast,

> the American novel has usually seemed content to explore, rather than to appropriate and civilize, the remarkable and in some ways unexampled territories of life in the New World and to reflect its anomalies and dilemmas. It has not wanted to build an imperium but merely to discover a new place and a new state of mind. Explorers see more deeply, darkly, privately and disinterestedly than imperialists, who must perforce be circumspect and prudential. (5)

Every bit as astounding as Lewis Leary's analogy between teaching and brainwashing, this statement combines the self-serving disingenuousness of Robinson Crusoe with that of Natty Bumpo. One could say of it what R. W. B. Lewis said of Kazin's *On Native Grounds:* this displacement of American imperialism is the "stuff of a recognizably American point of view" and "an example of its subject."

Chase engages a difference that is little difference at all, the explorer being merely the advance guard of the imperialist. However, the metaphoric field he sketches, with its engagement of frontiers, might offer us another possibility of understanding the complicated and constantly changing institution we call the novel. Perhaps the most confusing thing is to think of the novel as a genre. Genre (like institution) is a boundary concept: it deals with lines demarcating identities, excluding foreign elements, legitimating a difference. (Thus Watt's and McKeon's institutions of the novel seem set up to allow these critics to exclude from it, by a sort of generic cleansing, any contamination from "romance"—leading them to simplify Fielding and Richardson's attacks on romance, and leaving them ill equipped to account for how the term romance governs the multifarious production of prose fiction during the sixty-year "hiatus" that falls between Fielding and Richardson's production of novels and Jane Austen's.) By contrast, the notion of a frontier is that of a movable line of struggle and conquest. Perhaps that figure best describes the novel, which exists only by constantly incorporating new and alien territory. Perhaps the novel is more essentially imperialist than even Edward Said (1993) thinks it is.

Romance, by contrast, is too often conceived in outmoded ways. Modern, "social realist" critics have usually frozen romance as a generic category with the aristocratic, fantastic fictions of the Middle Ages or the courtly novel of the seventeenth century. (Frye's *Anatomy of Criticism* did much in 1957 to free the term romance from that definition, but few recent critics, other than Fredric Jameson, have paid it much attention.) The "revival of romance" in the second half of the eighteenth century in itself (as well as the more recent turn to romance) makes it foolhardy to assume that this generic term has any more stability than the term novel.

Moreover, "romance" also had a special importance for a Scottish sense—and so, by an extension we have already previewed, an American sense—of national identity. Scotland's position within a larger British Anglophone community was not entirely different from that of Anglo North Americans: it was neither exactly a colony nor exactly a separate nation, and it certainly had not come (nor for that matter had it been invited) to merge identities with England on an equal basis in their 1707 union. Mutual economic interests and problems connected the Scots with the American colonies. Romance tradition as it was reconstructed could seem to give both peoples priority over the English in terms of their relationship to the origin of "British" national identity. The romance read as a tale about the origin of the nation held also, as I have suggested, a special appeal for Americans, just as did the social and anthropological ideas about the origins of societies held by theorists in the Scottish Enlightenment, who, in turn, based many of those theories on what could be described as the American experience (see Crawford 1992). As, among other things, theorists of concepts of subjectivity, of personal identity, of national language and literature, and particularly of culture and its institutions, participants in the Scottish Enlightenment could be said to have had a major impact both on the novel and on a new understanding of the romance, one from which they in fact partially derived their theories. What is occluded by the institutional history that defines the novel by its eighteenth-century origin is this refiguring of the romance in the period of so-called pre-Romanticism and its role in the "institution" of the novel.

In this regard, it might be useful to look at the question of the novel from the vantage point of the early decades of the nineteenth century, only it is Walter Scott rather than Jane Austen who will give us that vantage point. As I noted earlier, Austen became the pivotal figure for modernists in the twentieth century. Watt chooses Austen for his pivotal figure and doesn't even mention Scott, because while he is implicitly writing against F. R. Leavis's downgrading of the eighteenth-century novelistic tradition, "New Critics" are the readers whose attention he solicits. I would argue that such neglect of Scott creates a confusion between the history of an institution and institutional history. The first is the history of the way an institution defines itself; the second is simply one of those fictions, the most recent history.

No historian of the institution of the novel could afford to ignore the Scott phenomenon occurring in the early nineteenth century. At any rate, although Austen had already begun to publish her novels with moderate success before the first appearance of the Waverley novels in 1814, Scott quickly dominated the field. (He also gave Austen's novels their first serious attention in print.) Among his contemporaries, Scott was thought to have either restored, or originally established, the novel as a major, serious, masculine English, and even European cultural institution. Scott's novels provided the model for the great nineteenth-century English novel and, for that matter, the European and American novel, or more precisely the novel of the Americas, as well.

In order to understand Scott's new novel-romance as displacing the earlier novel, and displacing its history into the history of romance, it is necessary to rehearse some contemporary notions about the status of narrative fiction and its past. By 1814, it is possible to say that Scott shared several assumptions about the novel with a number of other critics and historians: (1) that it had existed in one form or another at all times and all places; (2) that if there was a distinction to be made between the romance and the novel, it was not so much generic as "generational"—in Scott's words, "in its first appearance, the novel was the legitimate child of the romance"—that is to say, there was continuity in the difference;

(3) that the romance and the novel were also analogous in their social importance and power as both expressions and producers in the formation of individuals, cultures, and nations—if the chivalric romance served as the "epic" of ancient Britain, the modern romance or novel should perform the same function; and (4) that it was not performing this function because the novelistic resources it inherited from the eighteenth century were "exhausted" and the contemporary novel/romance had been largely appropriated by "female writers" writing for female readers (see Ferris 1991).

One version of this account of the novel may be derived from Scott's 1816 review of Jane Austen's *Emma.* Austen's novels, he says, "belong to a class of fictions which has arisen almost in our own times, and which draws the characters and incidents introduced more immediately from the current of ordinary life than was permitted by the former rules of the novel" (Scott 1968, 59). These rules he goes on to explain in the following way: "In its first appearance, the novel was the legitimate child of the romance; and though the manners and general turn of the composition were altered so as to suit modern times, the author remained fettered by many peculiarities derived from the original style of romantic fiction" (59). These fettering peculiarities were the requirement for improbable adventures and "violent changes of fortune" and exaggerated sentiments. The two examples Scott names of "earlier novels" that "differed from those now in fashion, and were more nearly assimilated to the old romances" are Fielding's *Tom Jones* and Tobias Smollet's *Peregrine Pickle* (62). He goes on to say that there was no doubt that, with their complications of plot and "ever new and wonderful incidents," these writers solicited "that obvious and strong sense of interest which arises from curiosity" and that "the idealized sentiments represented appealed to the better propensities of our Nature." Yet "strong and powerful as these sources of emotion and interest" might be, "they are, like all others, capable of *being exhausted by habit*" (62; my emphasis). Scott clearly implies that, for these reasons, and because of changes in social life, Fielding was now likely to be read as a romance, in the derogatory sense of the term.

In his later essay on Fielding for Ballantyne's Novelist's Library (later reprinted in *The Lives of the Novelists*), Scott reveals another agenda for his history of the novel. He implies that Fielding is "the first of British novelists" only by default, since his accomplishment is in fact more narrowly based than the term "British" suggests. It is true that Scott avers that when Fielding wrote *Joseph Andrews,* he "engaged in a mode of composition which he retrieved from the disgrace in which he found it, and rendered a classical department of British literature" (1906, 56). It is also true that Scott says that Fielding, in the prefatory chapters of *Tom Jones,* demonstrated that he "considered his works as an experiment in British literature" (67). Despite his fully detailed admiration for Fielding's artistry, however, Scott is more circumspect when it comes to naming what is actually produced. With *Tom Jones,* Scott says, "the first *English* novel was given to the public, which had not yet seen any works of fiction founded upon the plan of painting from nature" (63; my emphasis). At the close of the essay, Scott salutes Fielding as "father of the English Novel; and in his powers of strong and national humour, and forcible yet natural exhibition of character, unapproached as yet, even by his most successful followers" (70).

Indeed, Scott marks this more narrowly "national" emphasis from the very beginning of the essay, where he uses the terms "English" and "England" eight times in the first paragraph. He starts off with the claim that "of all the works of the imagination, to which *English genius* has given origin, the writings of Henry Fielding are, perhaps, most decidedly and exclusively her own" (Scott 1906, 46; my emphasis). Lest we fail to feel the force of the limitation, Scott "localizes" the difficulty even more pointedly in the second sentence. Fielding's writings, he says, "are not only altogether beyond the reach of translation, in the proper sense and spirit of the word, but we even question whether they can be fully understood, or relished to the highest extent, by such natives of Scotland and Ireland as are not habitually and intimately acquainted with the characters and manners of Old England" (46). One would think that the lack of such "reach" as might include Scotland and Ireland might diminish the imperial "British" achievement of Fielding's work. Scott's allusion to the problem of translation suggests a linguistic idiom perhaps difficult to capture in another European language. But this is not at all what he has in mind. The shocker comes with the mention of Scotland or Ireland, which implies that Fielding's idiom cannot travel across the ethnic boundaries within Anglophone culture. Finally, one realizes that what is involved in Scott's notion of "translation" is temporal or historical as well as cultural translatability. (Translation, in all these senses, might properly designate Scott's own project in his writings.)

The case made for Fielding's incarnation of the English genius that follows is itself comically redundant. His comic characters "are personages as peculiar to England as they are unknown to other countries"; but then, too, the (major) "actors . . . have the same cast of nationality, which adds not a little to the verisimilitude of the tale" (Scott 1906, 46). And then he goes on to make sure we understand their Englishness, paradoxically, as a limitation. "The persons in the story live in England, travel in England, quarrel and fight in England, and scarce an incident occurs, without its being marked by something which could not have happened in any other country" (46). Here then, Scott outlines his requirements for a truly "British" novel by suggesting what is *missing* from Fielding's "painting" of "national manners." For Scott, the role of the novel is that of the romance (and the epic before it): the foundation of a nation and a national identity that allows for Britain's "natural" heterogeneity.

In 1824, in his "An Essay on Romance," Scott provided a fable of the origins of romance that could serve as well for his history of the novel and of its relationship to romance. This form of narrative, he said, had developed in pace with society. In fact, he argued, "Romance and real history have the same common origin":

> A moment's glance at the origin of society will satisfy the reader why this can hardly be otherwise. The father of an isolated family, destined one day to rise into a tribe, and in farther progress of time to expand into a nation, may, indeed, narrate to his descendants the circumstances which detached him from the society of his brethren, and drove him to form a solitary settlement in the wilderness, with no other deviation from truth, on the part of the narrator, than arises from the infidelity of memory, or the exaggerations of vanity. (Scott 1972, 134–35)

According to Scott, these "deviations" from the truth in the story of the origin of the tribal patriarch (itself a story of an originary "deviation") are then multiplied by "the vanity of the tribe" and "the love of the marvellous, so natural to the human mind," as "the tale of the patriarch is related by his children, and again by his descendants of the third and fourth generation" (135). Finally, there are further turns of deviation, from "a third cause"—"the king and the priest find their interest in casting a holy and sacred gloom and mystery over the early period in which their power arose" (135). Hence, a great paradox. While the authority of a family, a tribe, a nation is authorized by a story of its original fathering, the power of its present authorities, including the control over the interpretation of the story itself, depends on the mystification of the processes transmitting both the narrative and the authority it makes possible—depends, in short, on the mystification of institution as such. Moreover, this mystification is also a main source of the "fictiveness" of the "tales of the patriarchs." I must pause for a moment over Scott's own mystification of origin, for if Scott's story of the origin of romance as the story of the origin of society is apparently always a story of the father-narrator's double deviation from the origin—from both his father and from the "truth" of that deviation—Scott's account is itself also deviant in a number of ways.

First, I want only to underline how Scott echoes without acknowledgment and how he changes the narrative that founds the authority of Judeo-Christian culture—the story of Yahweh's call to Abraham to leave his roots and set out for the wilderness to start a new nation, the story that begins the second major part of Genesis known as "the Story of the Patriarchs":

> Now the Lord said to Abram, "Go from your country and your kindred and your father's house to the land that I will show you. And I will make of you a great nation, and I will bless you, and make your name great, so that you will be a blessing. (Genesis 12:1–2)

Repeating with deviation, repeating deviation, Scott's story thus performs or reenacts exactly what it describes. Moreover, it also performs a double effacement of authority, since Scott leaves out both the attribution to the prior story and that story's attribution of the origin of the patriarch's break with his past to God's command. What is the meaning of this transformation? Is Scott's version merely a secularization of the sacred story? On the one hand, Abram leaves his father's house by divine command (becoming Abraham in the process), while, on the other, the departure of Scott's patriarch-to-be is unexplained. Might it stem from some unspecified "wandering inclination"? Does not the imperial narrative of the "explorer" Robinson Crusoe, among other eighteenth-century fictions, break apart between these choices?

Scott's story of the origin of romance as the story of the father itself serves as a "first" version of the "romance" of the novel. Scott sees romance's role as that of constructing culture; romance is a story of institution, the story as institution. For Scott, romance both chronicles and shapes the institution of modern culture—that is to say, romance is a story of institution that itself became institutional. In order to make this paradox clearer, I need to pursue the effects and implications of some of the deviations in Scott's account of the history of the romance and the birth of the novel.

One, in particular. Early on in the essay, Scott asserts that "the word Romance, in its original meaning, was far from corresponding with the definition now assigned. On the contrary, it signified merely one or other of the popular dialects of Europe, founded (as almost all these dialects were) upon the Roman tongue, that is, upon the Latin" (1972, 130–31). In other words before "Romance" named a mode of narrative, it named the language in which that narrative was sung or written. Even in this curiously indeterminate way it names not just a language of origin but a deviation or variation upon one—"one or other of the popular dialects of Europe," founded upon the classic language of the father, Latin. And so this story of a national father's break from his father and brethren to start a new family is also the story of the language in which it is told.

The "wild adventures" of Romance, the language, haunt—and perhaps shape—Scott's account of the rise and decline of romance, the narrative, and of the social order that was both mirrored and produced by it. I want to pause for a moment on this story of a language, which must have had a special, if overdetermined, meaning for Scott, his novels, and the context of their writing. Romance is not simply the name of a national language but precisely the precondition of several, each differing from the other as much as any one of them differs from their Latin original. Scott is charting here the beginning not only of the vernacular but also of "natural" or national languages, as a story of rebellion and exile. As Scott indicates, Romance is the general name for the various European languages that developed out of Latin. "The name of Romance was indiscriminately given to the Italian, to the Spanish, even (in one remarkable instance at least) to the English language"—this last example is most remarkable, in Scott's terms even laughable, because he will subsequently argue the poverty of English when it comes to romance. For even though the term has this general sense, "it was especially applied to the compound language of France; in which the Gothic dialect of the Franks, the Celtic of the ancient Gauls, and the classical Latin, formed the ingredients" (Scott 1972, 131). And this special language of Romance has a special kinship to the "British" (Celtic) sources of one of the two main branches of romance narratives. British, as opposed to English. In Scott's terms, the once and future nation.

The background and resources for this new view of both the romance and the novel came from more than a half-century of Romantic research and publication, fictional and historical. In fact, the second half of the eighteenth century was a time so known for its "Romantic" pursuits—that is, not only for its antiquarian ballad and romance research but also for its exploration of "Romantic" subjects such as sensibility, sentiment, Gothicism, and so on—that it has been called anachronistically "pre-Romantic." But is this term any more anachronistic than "eighteenth-century novel"? In fact, "Romantic," like its sometime associate "Gothic," is also itself a synonym for "anachronistic." "Romance," in various ways, is also a synonym for "history" but is especially so in its combination with "revival," as the name for the antiquarian enterprise of collecting and editing the old ballads and romances and researching the culture that produced them. That last phrase suggests just how much is at stake with the subject of romance. For this research opened onto a search for native, national origins and originary native poetic forms. If these forms were at first seen as parallel with early classical forms such as the Homeric epic, they were soon apprehended as more appropriate models for modern British (as sometimes opposed to English) literary forms. But what also emerged was a historicist notion of native, national culture.

Arthur Johnston, in *Enchanted Ground* (1964) thus says about Richard Hurd's *Letters on Chivalry and Romance* (1762) that "Hurd, for example, accepted that literature was the product of a particular type of society, and took its form from the predominant interests of that society. This long established view enabled critics to explain literature in terms of society, and to deduce a society from its surviving literature—whether the epics of Homer, the poems of Ossian, or the plays of Shakespeare. Holding to this doctrine, Hurd argued that the spirit of romance was born of the ages of chivalry, which were in turn the product of the feudal organization of society a particular attraction for many eighteenth-century writers" (52). Johnston's exposition of this research into what amounts to literature's relationship to historical culture and of the developing and consequential study of medieval romance by Thomas Percy, Thomas Warton, Joseph Ritson, George Ellis, and Sir Walter Scott demonstrates some of the struggle of emerging notions of "culture." The significance of the peculiarly nationalist aspects of this research for the Romantic novel and for, not the past, but the present of the British nation cannot be overestimated. Toward the end of his study, Johnston emphasizes that "those who theorized about the origin of romance were looking for the starting point of 'modern' literature. And it was not to Greece and Rome that the more rigorous theorists looked" (197). He then concludes his study with this statement, quoting Carlyle: "The Romance scholars from Percy to Scott left as their legacy the realization that the middle ages originated or perfected 'nearly all the inventions and social institutions whereby we yet live as civilized men'" (218).

The medieval romance offered possibilities for the revitalization of the modern poetic imagination because it was the originary native spring for poetry in *this place* (Britain); it was the natural (proper) expression of the culture and society rooted in this place at an originary and foundational moment in its historical past—in contrast with the neoclassical Greek and Roman past. ("Modern" literature is both what started and what should continue to start in this place.) Moreover, though romance had been (and continues to be) identified with the imagination in the sense of its fictional extravagances—its departures from historical truth—those extravagances are now seen to belong to the culture the romances portray and not merely to the genre, just as later elements of romance will be used to represent psychic interiority. Those "extravagances," belonging to the institutions of chivalry, the cultural/social system of the society represented/produced by the romance, can be understood as the foundation for modern British (and European) civilization, its institutions, and its "manners." (This is the sense of Johnston's quotation from Carlyle, a claim also made by Scott and others.)

In short, in the origins of romance we can find the origin of a specifically national literature and culture and the basis for a specifically national identity. Romance, then, becomes the name for the native imagination (always in both its good and bad senses)—the name for native fictions of origin and, by the same stroke, for history and the historical—the name for past and parent or for their traces in their felt absence. Yet it also, in complicated senses, becomes the name for difference and deviation—deviation from origins, from the parent, from history (and the truth) from and within culture and hence from proper identity or identification, deviation and difference from and within identity, and even difference and deviation from and within language. All this—these (re)emergent concerns, in nineteenth-century Britain and in the 1950s United States, about significant fictional narrative as an "expression" of a native culture, as a means of producing national identification as well as a sense of personal identity—could not *not* affect the way "the novel" of Defoe, Richardson, or Fielding was read and represented and instrumentalized. To insist that the novel had already fully matured into an institution is not only to confuse beginnings with establishment—the paradox of institution—but also to fall into the trap of institution and to think that either novels or the novel can be understood only in one context. Romanticism itself, Jean-Luc Nancy writes in terms applicable to Watt's and Chase's cultural moment and to Scott's:

could be defined as the invention of the scene of the founding myth, as the simultaneous awareness of the loss of the power of this myth, and as the desire or will to regain this living power of the origin and, at the same time, the origin of this power. . . . Concentrated within the idea of myth is perhaps the entire pretension on the part of the West to appropriate its own origin, or to take away its secret, so that it can at last identify itself, absolutely, around its own pronouncement and its own birth. The idea of myth alone perhaps presents the very Idea of the West, with its perpetual representation of the compulsion to return to its own sources in order to re-engender itself from them as the very destiny of humanity. (1991, 44–45)

Notes

Portions of this essay recapitulate arguments made in the introduction to my forthcoming book *Institutions of the English Novel* (Brown 1996), although the arguments are made in a different context there. I have also borrowed some sentences from that introduction.

1. In addition to Weber and Williams, see Bourdieu 1990, Douglas 1986, and Derrida 1989 and 1992.
2. Tate's "The Post of Observation in Fiction," appeared in a 1944 issue of the *Maryland Quarterly*. His "Techniques of Fiction" appeared in *Critiques and Essays on Modern Fiction, 1920–1951,* ed. John W. Aldridge (New York: Ronald Press, 1952), which was reprinted from a 1944 issue of the *Sewanee Review.*
3. It seems to me that this preoccupation should be thought through in relation to Heidegger's problematic of the *Ge-stell* ("enframing," as his American translators have it [Heidegger 1977, 19 n. 17]), his name for "the revealing that holds sway throughout modern technology" (14), which Heidegger describes as a "challenging claim [*Herausfordern*]" (14–15), a word that can also be translated as "interpellation." Heidegger's essay, full of difficulties and, no doubt, traps, should receive lengthy analysis. Of the many ironies with which such an analysis

might have to contend, I will note only that for my present context, this essay was first delivered as a lecture on 18 November 1955. Its relevance to the New Critical and later engagement with the question of the technology of subjectivity should be clear, however, on other grounds.

4. The chapter in which consideration of the rise of fiction belongs is, of course, Bradford Booth's. Booth's perfunctory paragraph on the eighteenth-century novel (much of it, significantly, on Jane Austen) doesn't mention Watt.

I

The Contact Zone

Michelle Burnham

1 Between England and America

Captivity, Sympathy, and the Sentimental Novel

❧ During her 1676 captivity by Algonquin Indians in the New England wilderness, Mary Rowlandson turns, in one of the numerous scriptural references that mark her 1682 narrative, to a particular psalm: "I fell a weeping which was the first time to my remembrance, that I wept before them . . . now may I say as, Psal. 137.1. *By the Rivers of Babylon, there we sate down: yea, we wept when we remembered Zion*" (Rowlandson 1913, 134). On the other side of the Atlantic and over half a century later, the captive heroine of Samuel Richardson's 1740 *Pamela* invokes the same tearful psalm:

> I remembering the 137th Psalm to be a little touching, turn'd to it, and took the Liberty to alter it to my case. . . .
>
> *When sad I sat in* B—n-hall,
> *All watched round about,*
> *And thought of ev'ry absent Friend,*
> *The Tears for Grief burst out.* (Richardson 1971, 127)

If these two captive women were moved to tears by their experiences, their accounts of captivity inspired a correspondent sympathy in their readers. Indeed, audiences were apparently captivated by these two books: both Rowlandson's narrative and Richardson's *Pamela* were transatlantic best-sellers, appealing to popular reading tastes in colonial New England as well as in England.[1] That popularity has been accounted for by the fact that these texts offered their audiences the highly desirable combination of a sensational and adventurous plot with moral and religious instruction—thereby inspiring not only tears but pious reform in their readers. The preface to Rowlandson's narrative, generally attributed to Increase Mather, uses the occasion of Rowlandson's recent captivity and of continuing Indian warfare to encourage religious conversion among readers. Mather insists that Rowlandson's particular account "makes deepest impression upon the affections" and that her example of piety "deserves both commendation and imitation" (Rowlandson 1913, 116, 115). When Mather instructs readers to "Peruse, Ponder, and from hence lay by something from the experience of another against thine own turn comes" (117), he anticipates that seventeenth-century Puritans, by imagining themselves in the captive's place, might strive to resemble the converted and reformed Rowlandson.

By the time Richardson made a similar argument for *Pamela,* however, novels were regularly being condemned as morally damaging, and for virtually the same reason that Mather had praised Rowlandson's earlier narrative: the capacity to inspire sympathetic identification in readers. Because moralists and educators assumed that sympathy led to imitation, they believed that readers would be encouraged to repeat the transgressive adventures of the novelistic heroes and heroines with whom they identified. Eighteenth-century novelists and romance writers therefore strategically attempted to position their work in order to evade condemnation within this model of reader identification. In 1705, for example, Delarivier Manley explained that the responses of "Fear and Pity" propel readers to imitate novelistic examples, since "we in some Manner put ourselves in the Room of those we see in Danger; . . . and the fear of falling into like Misfortunes, causes us to interest our selves more in their Adventures." She proceeded to argue that her *Secret History of Queen Zarah* would "instruct and inspire into Men the Love of Vertue, and Abhorrence of Vice, by the Examples propos'd to them" in the text (qtd. in Williams 1970, 35, 38). Not until Richardson, however, would this defense result in the profound combination of critical success and moral validation awarded to *Pamela.*

The eighteenth-century regulation of novel reading also operated within this paradigm of identification paired with imitation. Thus Maria and Richard Edgeworth, who in their 1801 *Practical Education* discouraged young women from reading novels, nevertheless deemed *Robinson Crusoe* suitable, because, they assumed, young women were simply incapable of imitating the appealing adventures and solitary travels of Defoe's hero (Armstrong 1987, 16–17). When Richardson successfully articulated his first sentimental novel as a deliberately ethical project, he did so not by disabling identification but by exploiting it. The instructive efficacy of *Pamela,* like that of Rowlandson's narrative, was theoretically inseparable from its ability to inspire affective sensation, for it was supposedly by sympathizing with these virtuous and pious heroines that readers were moved to imitate their exemplary behavior. It was precisely as a result of this sympathetic exchange between reader and text that Richardson could imagine English readers becoming a community of ethical individuals in response to the examples represented in his novel.

Eighteenth-century sentimental novels like Richardson's may operate within such a system of imaginative exchange, but they also develop within a context of other exchanges across cultural, national, and continental boundaries. The Atlantic Ocean is one such crossed and uncrossed border, an expanse that is implicitly invoked as a border whenever the labels "English" or "American" serve to define distinct and coherent literary traditions. Yet, as Ian K. Steele has pointed out, the Atlantic is as much a conduit facilitating connection as it is a barrier encouraging insulation. This relation was perhaps even more acknowledged in the eighteenth century when, Steele notes, "any informed adult living within the English Atlantic empire in 1739 knew that the Atlantic Ocean was traversed regularly, whether or not that person had crossed it. This same person also knew that the North American continent had never been crossed by anyone" (1986, 273). Popular texts such as colonial "American" captivity narratives and "English" sentimental novels also regularly crossed this border. The exchanges and transgressions both within and between these two genres are fundamental, I will argue, to the development and function of sentimental discourse during this period. The moving qualities of texts such as Rowlandson's and Richardson's depend not only on their stories of transgressive mobility but on the movement of the texts themselves across the border of the Atlantic, that watery margin which at once sealed and held open the ambivalent relation between the American colonies and the British empire. The acceptable popularity of these two accounts of female captivity is ultimately a measure of the degree to which they successfully obscured those transgressive elements.

Border Crossings

Like novelistic discourse, nationalist discourse relies on the profoundly affective experience of sympathy. From Ernest Renan's early claim that "nationality has a sentimental side to it" (1990, 18) to Homi Bhabha's recent assertion that the nation is a form of "cultural identification" (1990a, 292–93) with a deeply affective dimension, discussions of nationalism insist on the substitutive empathy of identification. When Benedict Anderson links the nation with the novel, he does so precisely through this feature of identification. Not only do these modern discourses both emerge simultaneously in the eighteenth century, but, he argues, both rely on a new conception of temporality, comparable to what Walter Benjamin calls "meanwhile," in which disparate and distant individuals are perceived to exist simultaneously. According to Anderson, it is in this open, transverse time associated with the novel—where separate characters live coincidental lives linked by a single narrative—that readers become able to imagine the community of the nation. New World Creoles came to conceive of themselves as contemporaneous national communities, as "Americans" or "Brazilians," for example, by reading about and imagining the existence of others who resembled themselves, a phenomenon facilitated by the development of print capitalism and the growth in literacy and in print languages. This sentimental experience of imagining others whose experiences are similar to, if not interchangeable with, one's own—experiences such as the journeys taken by Creole functionaries along particular routes or "the shared fatality of trans-Atlantic birth" (Anderson 1991, 57)—therefore becomes coincident with a feeling of stable national identity. Novel reading provided a way for these otherwise unrelated individuals to learn of their common experiences and thus "to visualize in a general way the existence of thousands and thousands *like themselves*" (Anderson 1991, 77; emphasis added). To this extent, for Anderson as well as for Richardson, the imagined community created through sympathetic identification is a community constructed and held together on the basis of resemblance or likeness.

The movement of printed texts across regional, social, and cultural boundaries is the indispensable condition for producing such an imagined community and the identification on which it is founded. This movement has its analogue in the process of sympathy, which requires a crossing of the boundary between reader and text. One might therefore expect to find the earliest formations of both the novel and the nation in a text notable for its own mobility as well as for its ability to move readers. Nancy Armstrong and Leonard Tennenhouse, in their analysis of the "origins" of the English novel and European nationalism, find precisely such a text in the colonial American genre of the captivity narrative. Mary White Rowlandson's 1682 narrative of her twelve-week captivity among the New England Indians chronicles her violent abduction in a 1676 Algonquin raid and her subsequent trials—both physical and spiritual—as she journeys with her captors through the wilderness. But it is the movement of the text itself, which traveled from the American colonies to England and found active readership on both continents, that is central to Armstrong and Tennenhouse's argument. By encouraging its readers to "care about" an unimportant Englishwoman and her sufferings, Rowlandson's captivity narrative constructs an imagined national community through the process of reader identification. Just as the abducted captive is "poignantly aware that survival depends on her ties to" her increasingly distant Anglo-American community, the narrative "asked its readers [in England] to imagine being English in America" (Armstrong and Tennenhouse 1992, 395, 394). Because the isolation of the Englishwoman in captivity among non-English people foregrounds her national difference, it enables readers to recognize their own position within a national community through identification with her.

The radical difference between the European captive and her Amerindian captors may have encouraged English readers to identify with Rowlandson, but that difference is presumably also what fascinated them so about her story. The circulation of Rowlandson's popular text across the boundary between colonial outpost and imperial center is therefore subtended by Rowlandson's own circulation across the even more profound cultural boundary between colonial Anglo-American society and tribal Algonquin Indian society. As Armstrong and Tennenhouse accurately note, the captive must sustain her ties to English culture in order eventually to reintegrate with the community she left behind. But securing that return also requires that Rowlandson develop relations within the Algonquin community she inhabits for nearly twelve weeks. The establishment of these latter ties complicates the model of reader identification on which Benedict Anderson's discussion of nationalism relies. Ultimately, Rowlandson's account calls into question the kind of imagined community produced by reader identification.

Throughout her captivity, Rowlandson continually asks her captors if and when she will be sold, and when asked by them "how much my husband would give to redeem me," she struggles to come up with a sum large enough not to "be slighted" by the Indian sagamores and small enough to "be procured" by her husband (1913, 151). Such dialogues reveal the captive's awareness that her return is contingent upon a mutually agreeable act of exchange between her Algonquin master and her Puritan husband. But if Rowlandson's return depends on both these parties, her survival depends almost entirely on her captors. She must learn to travel in Indian fashion through the wilderness, to recognize Algonquin words and customs, to barter for Indian food, and to tolerate it once it is given to her. Her narrative documents not only her early resistance to such alien customs, but her increasing familiarity with and practical acceptance of them.[2] To this extent, it is not Mary Rowlandson's Englishness at all that determines her survival during captivity but precisely the degree to which she abandons her Englishness in this process of acculturation.

In other words, as a captive Rowlandson occupies a position of cultural liminality rather than one of cultural integrity. That liminality requires that one ask what the readers of this captivity narrative identified with when they identified with Mary Rowlandson. While her narrative undoubtedly led readers in England to imagine "being English in America," it is equally likely that it led English readers on both sides of the Atlantic to imagine the possibility of not being English at all, to imagine a liminal if not an Indian cultural identity. Indeed, the captive's experience of transculturation—which is everywhere evident in her narrative—undoubtedly contributed to the book's unprecedented public appeal. This narrative implicitly critiques the assumption that readers can identify only with figures whose culture, race, or nationality resembles their own, for to identify with Rowlandson is necessarily to identify both with her English difference from the Indians and with her difference from English culture through her participation in Algonquin society, both with her insistent Englishness and with her departure from it.

When Rowlandson's narrative was originally advertised in the American edition of *The Pilgrim's Progress,* it was called a "pathetically written" story, a phrase that in the seventeenth century meant "movingly written" (Derounian 1988, 244). What is moving about this narrative, I suggest, is the fact that Rowlandson herself is always moving even while disclaiming that movement. Pathos inhabits the disjunction between the cultural identity that Rowlandson so insistently asserts and the textual evidence that contradicts that assertion. Franco Moretti has argued that "tears are always the product of *powerlessness*" and that "they presuppose a definitive estrangement of facts from values, and thus of any relationship between the idea of *teleology* and that of *causality*" (1988, 162). This very tension is apparent in the scene in which Mary Rowlandson herself is first moved to tears. When the captive arrives at an Indian village and finds herself the lone Christian among a "numerous crew of Pagans" who "asked one another questions, and laughed, and rejoyced over their Gains and Victories," she "fell a weeping which was the first time to my remembrance, that I wept before them" (Rowlandson 1913, 134). Rowlandson's Puritan reliance on typology and its promise that, like the captive Israelites, she too will be delivered from affliction clearly encounters a threat at this confrontation with the quantitative strength of the Indians. Rowlandson weeps at that moment when what should happen may not happen, when values and facts fail to coincide. Likewise, her readers are moved at those moments when what Rowlandson *claims* to be—a coherent English subject and a model Puritan goodwife—coincides least with what she *appears* to be—a mediating subject who participates in the tribal economy, is able to conform to Indian social practices, and has a command of at least the basics of Algonquin language. The captive professes an identity whose fixity is belied by the unstable and mobile process of identification that supports that identity.

Rowlandson's narrative points toward a model of identification that emphasizes disjunction and disavowal rather than resemblance and imitation. It challenges the notion that sympathetic identification constitutes an equivalent and seamless exchange in which individuals imaginatively substitute themselves for others "like themselves," a formulation that assumes rather than explains the sentimental affect that characterizes the narrative of novels and nations. Why should identification produce sympathetic tears even as it produces a coherent community? These tears which are so often a sign of sentimental identification—of the successful establishment of this relation of apparent equivalence—result, I suggest, not from the seamless substitution of self for other but from the necessary margin of inequivalence produced by such an exchange. In other words, what is sentimental about the imagined communities that novels create is the obscured fact that they are not based on likeness.

The psychoanalytic model of ambivalent identification that underlies Homi Bhabha's description of national narrative is able to account for this inequivalence that Anderson's discussion overlooks. For psychoanalytic theory, to align identification with imitation or resemblance is to miss what Bhabha calls its "dialogical or transferential" character, since any identification with a likeable image or feature is always "constituted through the *locus* of the Other" (1990a, 313), performed on behalf of a gaze from the perspective of which that image is seen as likable. Two seemingly incompatible but nevertheless interdependent relations constitute this process: an imaginary or specular identification with that which the subject is (or wants to be) like and a symbolic identification with that which the subject is not (and often does not want to be) like. The first is an identification with an appealing image, with the image of the suffering English captive piously reading a Bible and yearning for home. The second is an identification with the displaced location from which that image appears as appealing—with, in Rowlandson's narrative, the liminal position of cultural and national indeterminacy. Furthermore, readers are compelled to identify with the former only by identifying with the latter, since the image of Rowlandson's coherent Englishness takes on particular value only from the locus or perspective of her transgressive liminality. The circular movement between these two modes of identification generates a disjunctive gap between them, a gap that is concealed beneath the construction of fantasy.[3] For Anderson, the national identity of subjects arises from their identification with similarities, with others "like themselves." Here, identity is instead a retroactively determined effect of naming that works to erase any identification with difference.

This model of a doubled identification can account for the sentimentality of novels and nations in a way that identification understood as pure resemblance or imitation cannot. For the "moving" effect of novelistic and nationalist discourses results from the dialectical movement of identification across the gap or border between resemblance and its failure. The tears generated by sympathy function as a veil that masks the incommensurability between these two levels of identification, obscuring difference within the fantasy of sameness and commonality. This liminal gap of inequivalence marks for Bhabha the site of subjective agency, a site for the articulation of cultural difference and minority resistance. But that agency veiled by affective sensation can also constitute a violence aimed at difference, deployed in the service of preserving and reproducing a community based on resemblance. Such forms of active agency, I suggest, are disavowed by the passive sensation of "being moved." In this sense, sympathy is a movement that insistently denies its own activity, a border crossing that conceals its own transgressiveness.

As objects in motion across various borders, both Rowlandson and her text are in perpetual danger of going astray, a possibility that is suggested by Rowlandson's need to insist that she has returned physically and ideologically unviolated to her Anglo-American community.[4] Her narrative consistently disavows the transgression it documents. That disavowal is repeated by the model of identification that Armstrong and Tennenhouse borrow from Anderson, a model that allows the imaginary substitution of the English reader for the wholly English captive to constitute a balanced exchange that leaves no disabling remainder. The liminal space of acculturation within Rowlandson's narrative suggests that the operation of identification cannot be reduced simply to a function of mere resemblance or likeness but must account for the moments at which resemblance slips and equivalence fails. The narratives of female captivity published in the century following Rowlandson's reveal that it is precisely at such moments that identification acquires its affective property, its sentimentality. Although Rowlandson patiently awaits her deliverance from captivity, even choosing to "wait Gods time" (1913, 161) rather than accept one Indian's offer to help her escape, later captives often betrayed less faith in typology and divine providence. In the disjunctive moments when teleology's promise of what should happen failed to conform to causality's account of what was happening, those captives were sometimes prompted actively to escape from their captors. In order therefore to investigate the function of sentimentality within the discourses of the novel and the nation, it is necessary to pay attention to the strategies of later captivity narratives, to determine what happns when their captive heroines move across cultural frontiers, and to ask why readers are moved to tears by their stories.

Captivity and Escape

The popularity of Rowlandson's narrative, and its ideological usefulness in an era of persistent Indian warfare and waning Puritanism, prompted the publication of hundreds of editions and numerous collections of captivity narratives—both factual and fictional—throughout and beyond the following century. By the late eighteenth century, many of these texts—like the 1787 "Panther Captivity" and Ann Eliza Bleecker's 1793 *History of Maria Kittle*—are virtually indistinguishable from sentimental novels. Such developments clearly result in part from the incorporation of structural and stylistic elements from novels like Richardson's, which were among the most popular books read in the American colonies. But this consistent development cannot be explained solely by the later adoption of extrageneric elements, since the production of readerly sympathy serves a crucial function in the strategies of captivity narratives; indeed, some of the earliest narratives already rely on the sympathetic relation between reader and text that only later marks sentimental novels. My interest here, however, is not in positing a colonial influence on or origin to the sentimental novel but in putting these two overlapping genres into dialogue in order to determine the political implications of their production of sympathy around the scene of female captivity. As Armstrong and Tennenhouse suggest by linking Rowlandson's narrative directly with Richardson's *Pamela,* the captivity narrative and the sentimental novel were in cross-continental dialogue from the beginning. By reinitiating this exchange, I aim to expose the gap that these texts' sentimentality works to seal—the gap between an identification with the captive's virtuous and passive suffering and an identification with her transgressive and active agency. Although many eighteenth-century narratives of male captivity were often as sentimental as those of women,[5] I focus on the latter here because they more tellingly reveal the function and strategy of such affect. In these narratives, sentimentality works through reader identification to mask the agency of women held captive, an agency whose often startling violence encouraged colonial practices of genocide against Amerindians. At the same time, sentimentality works to performatively reproduce the Euro-American community, a process facilitated by the fact that so many captives were also mothers.

Captivity narratives nearly always begin with the moment of Indian attack, and the descriptions of these attacks incessantly focus the reader's attention on the abduction or death of infants. It has been estimated that at least one-fifth of the women taken captive from New England were either pregnant or had just given birth (Ulrich 1982, 205). While no evidence exists to suggest how many of those who published their stories were among that one-fifth, the number of narratives that begin with a woman being hauled into captivity from the delivery bed is staggering enough that any reader comes to expect this opening image. When the Indians carry away Elizabeth Hanson with her four children, the "youngest child but fourteen days old," Hanson claims that the Indians "immediately before my face knocked its brains out" (1981, 232). Mehetable Goodwin's Indian master "violently Snatcht the Babe out of its Mother's Arms, and before her Face knockt out its Brains" (Mather 1913, 210), while Hannah Dustan's captors literally pull her out of the bed in which she had only days earlier given birth, and "e'er they had gone many steps, they dash'd out the Brains of the Infant, against a Tree" (Mather 1913, 264). Clearly, this stylized scenario was both politically effective and potently affective, and later narratives capitalize on its sentimental potential. When the Indians arrive at the home of Frances Scott, Scott's young daughter "ran to her Parent, and, with the most plaintive Accents, cried, 'O Mamma! O Mamma! Save me!' The Mother, in the deepest Anguish of Spirit and with a Flood of Tears, intreated the Savages to spare her Child; but with a brutal Fierceness, they tomahawked and stabbed her in the Mother's Arms" (*Narrative of Mrs. Scott* 1978, 9). These narratives insistently subtract the captive mother's capacity to act in response to the violence against her family that she is forced to witness. Frances Scott's narrative even inserts details that further enhance the captive's passivity: the Indians instruct the mother to remain firmly in one place while her children are killed, and they subsequently throw the corpses onto the floor "near the mother" (9).

If the children of female captives happen to escape such early deaths, they are often immediately separated from their mothers. Mary Rowlandson claims that in the turmoil of the attack on her home, Indians were "ha[u]ling Mothers one way, and Children another" (1913, 143), and she expresses outrage over the fact "that I should have Children, and a Nation which I knew not ruled over them" (147). Jemima Howe, separated from her nursing infant, insists that "the Indians, I suppose on purpose to torment me, sent me away to another wigwam which stood at a little distance, though not so far from the one in which my distressed infant was confined but that I could plainly hear its incessant cries and heart-rending lamentations" (Drake 1990, 147).[6] Rachel Plummer's much later narrative recounts a similar incident in language that is even more explicitly sentimental. Plummer believes that the Indians deliberately "brought my little James Pratt so near me that I could hear him cry. He would call for mother, and often was his voice weakened by the blows they would give him. I could hear the blows. I could hear his cries; but oh, alas, could offer him no relief" (Drake 1990, 338). Repeatedly, the captive mother is portrayed as an unwilling spectator made to watch or overhear the violent murder or abuse of her child. Her sympathetic suffering is enhanced by her enforced lack of agency—a position that is shared by the captivated and sympathetic reader who, like the mother, can only passively endure this emotional scene.

The event of captivity is followed by an almost incessant mobility, as the captive must travel with the Indians into and through the wilderness. Within this entirely alien culture, Anglo-American assumptions, behavior, and morality invariably misfire and fail to elicit the responses they are accustomed to producing. While such failed gestures include pleading and fainting, the most common one is weeping. Cotton Mather writes that the worst hardship captives must endure is being made to watch "their Friends made a Sacrafice [*sic*] of Devils before their Eyes, but be afraid of dropping a Tear from those Eyes, lest it should, upon that provocation, be next their own Turn, to be so Barbarously Sacrificed" (1913, 208). Later he notes that "when the Children of the English Captives Cried at any Time . . . the manner of the Indians was, to dash their Brains against a Tree" (213). The captive's tears may lead to death, but as they do so they translate directly into tears of sympathy in the reader, as Mather's concluding words suggest: "*Nescio tu quibus es, Lector, Lecturus Ocessis; Hoc Scio quod Siccis scribere non potui*" [I know not, reader, whether you will be moved to tears by this narrative; I know I could not write it without weeping] (213).[7] As early, then, as 1699, tears in captivity narratives signal not only the sympathy of English captives for one another but, even more significantly, the reader's vicarious sympathy for the suffering captives—a response that explicitly distinguishes them from the unsympathetic Indians.

These strikingly recurrent narrative elements all insist on the captives' Christian and English difference from their captors, and they insistently encourage reader identification with that difference. Because the experience of captivity, however, entailed crossing the cultural frontier into Amerindian society, it often resulted for many of these captives in more startling forms of transgression. These transgressions amounted not to differences from the Indians but to differences from the English, since survival frequently necessitated abandoning Anglo-American cultural traditions, social and legal standards, and gendered codes of conduct. Captivity was, in this sense, a profoundly ambivalent experience—not only for the captives but for their readers. Often the same narratives that circulated horrifying accounts of victimization also circulated fascinating stories of escape from dominant social and moral norms. In fact, the act of escape from captivity was frequently the most ambivalent element in these narratives, since it was at once a heroic instance of female bravery and an often extraordinary act of female violence.

What is most remarkable about such stories is that they were so easily and readily legitimated by the very culture whose standards they blatantly transgressed. The white captive of the Indians most often returned to her community not as a criminal or as a threat to the social order but as a heroine and an exemplar of it. The strategies of sympathetic identification that we have seen at work in these narratives are, I suggest, central to this cultural legitimation. The increasingly sentimental discourse these narratives employ manipulates the transgression occasioned by captivity into a heroism that over the course of the eighteenth century would become more and more explicitly associated with nationalism. Narratives of female captivity fulfilled this nationalist function particularly effectively, largely because so many of the women taken captive were mothers whose bodies quite literally reproduced the nation and therefore had to be preserved. By encouraging readers to identify with the captive mother, these narratives attempt to veil her violent act of agency beneath the urgency of this reproductive necessity.

This strategy is evident in the famous captivity of Hannah Dustan, which Cotton Mather incorporated into no fewer than three of his publications between 1697 and 1702.[8] Mather clearly intended the narrative to serve as anti-Indian propaganda and at the same time to encourage Christian piety in his readership. Yet what is most remarkable about this brief account is its use of sympathetic identification with a captive's motherhood to sanction a lawless act of female violence. Mather's attempt to conceal the ambivalence of that identification by denying its transgressiveness provides a model for the operation of sentimentality in both novelistic and nationalist discourse. When Indians attack and enter Hannah Dustan's home in a 1697 raid, her husband is absent; she is taken from her lying-in bed, made to watch her newborn infant murdered before her eyes, separated from the rest of her family, and dragged through miles of wilderness by her Indian captors. Mather's narrative enhances the captive's fear of both ideological and physical violation by "those furious tawnies." Her Indian captors, converted to French Catholicism, will not allow her to say her "English" prayers, and they tell her that when they arrive at an Indian village she "must be Stript, and Scourg'd, and run the Gantlet through the whole Army of Indians" (Mather 1913, 265). The ritual of the gauntlet, in which an assembled file of Indian villagers beat the captives with sticks and rocks as they ran through them, frequently triggered fears of rape, since the captives were sometimes (or at least imagined that they would be) forced to disrobe and run naked.[9] It is apparently this frightening threat to her own body that leads Dustan to convince her midwife and a young boy captive with her to assist her in killing and "cutting off the Scalps of the Ten Wretches" while they sleep. The captive's deed dangerously resembles—in its method of attacking sleeping victims, the use of Indian tomahawks, and the practice of scalping—the same Indian threats it was an attempt to escape from. Mather easily justifies Dustan's murder of her Indian captors, however, by insisting that "being where she had not her own Life secured by any Law unto her, she thought she was not Forbidden by any Law to take away the Life of the Murderers, by whom her Child had been Butchered" (266). The captive's active violence is explicitly sanctioned by the violence she has passively witnessed and endured, and it is more specifically sanctioned by the conditions of motherhood and threatened female sexuality.

Mather's emphasis on these conditions attempts to subordinate the unavoidable possibility of the reader's identification with the act of female agency itself. From its beginning, the narrative places the reader into the position of the passive mother who must witness the destruction of her home and children. But this specular identification is supported by another identification, for it is precisely from the perspective of her transgressive act of violence that the image of Dustan as a passive victim acquires its forceful appeal. This necessarily doubled identification produces an inconsistency—and, in this case, a yawning gap—between the image of the innocent English mother and her incredible act of "Indianized" aggression. What is ultimately affective about this story is the imperfectly sealed margin between these two identifications, between a sympathetic grief for the mother's loss and a sympathetic approval of her aggressive compensation for that loss.[10] Affect fills the space of that disjunction, and in doing so it converts the subjective agency of the captive into (and conceals it within) the passive sensation of being moved.

Indian captivity stories like Dustan's often served to justify genocide, and Cotton Mather clearly appropriates her example in order to support and encourage anti-Indian sentiment and action. But Mather's careful explanation of Dustan's motivation and his strategic veiling of her own aggression suggest that her act may have represented as much of a threat as it did a response to one. Clearly, this Puritan goodwife's murder of ten Indians was unusual enough to require explanation. Laurel Thatcher Ulrich explains that although colonial American women were generally expected to respond to battle or captivity with submission and piety, actions like Dustan's might have been validated simply by the absence of her husband, for whom Dustan would have been acting as legitimate proxy (1982, 179). But even if such conditions sanctioned Dustan's refusal to submit to Indian captivity, the condition of coverture—which subjected seventeenth- and eighteenth-century New England women to legal, economic, and civic representation by their husbands—rendered wives captive in another sense, to a patriarchal authority that virtually required female obedience as a duty (Ulrich 1982, 6–7). In this context, Dustan's act of violence was not only unusual enough to require explanation but also radical enough to require containment by Mather's discourse. The necessity and the function of Mather's affective representation of her experience become evident in comparison with the best-known instance of female violence in New England before Dustan's legendary escape. Four years before he publicly celebrated Dustan for killing ten Catholicized Indians, Cotton Mather publicly condemned Elizabeth Emerson—Hannah Dustan's unmarried sister—for allegedly killing her newborn twins. Dustan received reward money in exchange for the Indian scalps, was invited to visit at the home of Judge Samuel Sewall, and became something of a celebrity. Emerson was tried, convicted of murder, and hanged. Mather's responses to these two events certainly mark the differences between Indians and English infants as victims of violence, but the relation between the two agents of violence suggests why Mather emphasized Dustan's reproductive motherhood and why that emphasis effectively obscured the very elements of female aggression that, in her sister's case, were considered most threatening and transgressive.

At the same time that he applauds Hannah Dustan's action, Mather demonizes her Amerindian victims. In this way, the narrative of her captivity, which circulated in an era of French and Indian warfare, works to construct an explicit border between the Protestant Anglo-American community and the outside threats to its coherence and identity, and it does so by constructing an impassible border of difference between the English captive and her Frenchified Indian captors. Like Rowlandson's narrative, Mather's account insistently denies that the captive herself transgresses that border. By forging an explicit identification with Dustan's motherhood, by asking in a sense that its readers imagine themselves as mothers, the text produces an imagined community and emphasizes the necessary reproduction of that community. Yet this identification, this crossing between reader and text, also involves a transgression that it denies. Only by acknowledging the ambivalence that surrounds her act of agency and readers' response to it can we account for how Dustan's narrative could produce an imagined English community in one century and an imagined American community in another.

By the nineteenth century, Hannah Dustan's story becomes an example of a specifically American national valor, and of a heroism that is encoded not by the doctrinal law of the state but by the sentimental law of motherhood. Robert B. Caverly, who published the *Heroism of Hannah Duston* in 1874, offers Dustan as an inspirational national heirloom to the living descendants of "old New-England mothers" (14) and cites her heroic escape as the originary moment of the colonies' eventual rise to independence. He includes in his book a genealogical list of her thirteen children, and compares her story to that of Hannah Bradly, who in 1736 shot one Indian and killed another by pouring a tub of boiling soap over his head when he entered her home. He notes that Bradly, like Hannah Dustan, "left numerous progeny" and that her "descendants are to be found in New England almost everywhere" (57). The inscription carved into the monument erected in her name virtually insists on her long-lasting reproductive value by describing her as one "of our ancient mothers" (379).

The collections of captivity narratives that began appearing in the late eighteenth century and continued to be published throughout the nineteenth, such as John Frost's *Heroic Women of the West,* often followed a principle of inclusion that privileged stories of maternal heroism such as Hannah Dustan's. While such narratives reproduce their readers as an imagined national community, however, they simultaneously produce an identification with the female transgression that a national rhetoric of maternal reproduction works to conceal. The affective appeal of these narratives can only be understood in terms of this dual identification. Sentimentality sutures the gap between these two levels of identification, as John Frost's introduction to his collection suggests: "The heroism of woman is the heroism of the heart. Her deeds of daring and endurance are prompted by affection. . . . Captured and dragged away from her home [she] endures fatigue, braves danger, bears contumely, and sometimes deals the death-blow to the sleeping captors, to save the lives of her children. Such is woman's heroism" (Frost 1976, iii–iv). These aggressive mothers are, in Frost's conventional formulation, less agents than victims who are passively moved to action by maternal feeling. The sympathetic tears that accompany the captive's reentrance into her community reaffirm the coherent identity of that community only by pretending to erase her incommensurable agency. As Franco Moretti has claimed, the blindness produced by tears "enables us *not to see.* It is a way of distracting us from the sight of what has upset us, or rather of making it disappear" (1988, 179). The operation of sympathy, like the experience of captivity, must be seen as transgressive in both senses of the word—as a crossing that is inevitably asymptotic and that within the remaining and irreducible space always retains the potential of going astray.

Sympathy and the Novel

The heteroglossia that, for Mikhail Bakhtin, characterizes novelistic discourse is not only an internal characteristic of the genre but an external condition for its production: novels appear out of the exchanges that take place across the zones of contact where cultures and nations chaotically cross.[11] Colonial American captivity narratives document the radical cultural contact that takes place at such a border, and their further passage across the border of the Atlantic puts the narratives themselves into dialogic contact with other texts. This ceaseless mobility suggests that novelistic discourse emerges not in fixed locations or static moments but within a constant movement *across* borders. If sympathy is a movement that obscures its own activity, then novels are transcultural and transnational products that sentimentally obscure those crossings. By reading Rowlandson with Richardson, Armstrong and Tennenhouse reenact a crucial trans-Atlantic exchange, one that significantly revises Eurocentric narratives of the novel. Sentimental novels like those of Richardson, however, insist on an equivalent notion of identification, one that Armstrong and Tennenhouse adopt when they argue that Richardson's *Pamela*—like its forbear the captivity narrative—creates a coherent national community. By reading Rowlandson through Richardson, by reading the captivity narrative as a sentimental novel, they overlook the transgressive level of identification that operates not only in captivity narratives but in sentimental novels. The possibility of transgressive identification becomes obscured beneath the fantasy of a coherent community of Englishness, much as the tears produced by captivity narratives veil the potential danger of an identification with the captive's agency. If, instead of reading captivity narratives as sentimental novels, we read sentimental novels as captivity narratives, the sympathetic identification on which their reproduction of an imagined community relies appears far more ambivalent than Richardson made it out to be.

Richardson's preface to *Pamela* insists that its readers, by being "*uncommonly* moved" by the incidents in the novel, will imitate its heroine's example of virtue and piety. The letters from readers that follow his preface confirm their sympathetic engagement with Pamela's suffering, but they also reveal an identification with the least virtuous aspects of her behavior. One anonymous letter claims that the novel's "Incidents are so natural and interesting that I have gone hand-in-hand, and sympathiz'd with the pretty Heroine in all her sufferings" (Richardson 1971, 6). But when this reader details those incidents which most engaged him, he claims to have identified not with Pamela's passive suffering but with her active attempts to escape from that suffering: "I have interested myself in all her Schemes of Escape; been alternately pleas'd and angry with her in her Restraint; *pleas'd* with the little Machinations and Contrivances she set on foot for her Release, and *angry* for suffering her Fears to defeat them" (6). In other words, what moves this reader are the moments of Pamela's own mobility, and specifically those moments when she uses deceptive "Schemes," "Machinations," and "Contrivances" to actively escape from her confinement and from her captor, Mr. B.

In fact, while Pamela Andrews may be a paragon of female virtue, modesty, and benevolence, her entrance into a condition of captivity leads her into a practice of deception that resembles her captor's behavior more than it adheres to her own principles of ethical conduct. She arranges a forbidden correspondence with Parson Williams, hides the pages of her journal, lies about her plans and motives, sneaks through the window while her guard, Mrs. Jewkes, sleeps, and attempts to escape over the garden wall. Like the heroines of captivity narratives who transgress their own moral standards by imitating their captors, Pamela learns this strategic trickery from Mr. B himself, who claims that "I believe I must assume to myself half the Merit of your Wit, too; for the innocent Exercises you have had for it from me, have certainly sharpen'd your Invention" (Richardson 1971, 202). Unlike the unquestionably immoral actions of her captors, however, the captive's deception is implicitly innocent, and it is innocent because it is legitimated by the condition of captivity itself. She momentarily subverts her own standards of conduct only in a grander effort to uphold those standards, and this logic of legitimation, which is also Cotton Mather's logic, obscures and dilutes her transgressive actions.

Pamela worries to her parents early in her captivity that she will become "an Intriguer by-and-by; but I hope an innocent one!" and prays for the success of "my dangerous, but innocent Devices" (Richardson 1971, 118, 149). When Mr. B later places her before a mirror, he exposes the gap between her evident innocence and honesty and the concealed "Tricks and Artifices, that lie lurking in her little, plotting, guileful Heart" (162). These latter qualities, which he discovers by reading her journal, are secrets that the mirror will not reflect. But it is precisely this gap between Pamela's virtue and her artifice, between the image the mirror reflects and the information her pages reveal, that finally transforms Mr. B when he reads the "very moving Tale" (208) that is her narrative of captivity. The inconsistency between these two modes of identification is evident in Mr. B's explanation of his reform to Pamela's father: "tho' she is full of her pretty Tricks and Artifices, to escape the Snares I had laid down for her, yet all is innocent, lovely, and uniformly beautiful" (255). The sentimental affect that Mr. B experiences while reading her journal works to suture the irreconcilable gap between two planes of identification; Pamela's active agency is disavowed by the reader's passive sensation of "being moved."[12] The prefatory letter from Aaron Hill, added to the second edition of the novel, offers Pamela's effect on her master as a model for the text's effect on its reader: "Not the charmer's own prattling Idea struck so close to the Heart of her Master, as the Incidents of the Story to the Thoughts of a Reader" (17).

Through this process of readerly sympathy, *Pamela* aims to reproduce a moral English community outside the text; it ideally transforms its readers into reformed Mr. Bs and virtuous Pamelas. This couple becomes, in effect, the textual parents of a nation distinguished by its "Example of Purity" from the vices of "a neighboring Nation; which now shall have an Opportunity to receive *English* Bullion in Exchange for its own Dross, which has so long passed current among us in Pieces abounding with all the Levities of its volatile Inhabitants" (Richardson 1971, 5). This letter to Richardson imagines that the novel itself circulates as though it were English currency, a piece of "our Sterling Substance" whose inherent morality prevents it from "*frenchify[ing]* our *English* Solidity into Froth and Whip-syllabub" (7). If the novel supposedly produces and preserves a particularly English integrity and value in its audience, the resolution of its plot performs the same function within the novel. Mr. B's authentic marriage to Pamela averts not only the immoral but the economically unproductive possibility that if she "should have a dear little one, it would be out of my own Power to legitimate it, if I should wish it to inherit my Estate; . . . as I am almost the last of my Family, and most of what I possess must descend to a strange Line, and disagreeable and unworthy Persons" (230). Indeed, following the conclusion of Pamela's journal, Richardson assures us that, like the heroic mothers of contemporary captivity narratives, "She made her beloved Spouse happy in a numerous and hopeful Progeny" (409). This assurance of reproduction with which the novel ends retroactively veils the agency that preserved the maternal body of the captive; the transgressive actions of the heroine are virtually washed away in the flood of tears produced by the sympathetic community within the novel and reproduced in the virtuous English community outside it. What the affect signaled by sentimental tears enables us not to see, in *Pamela* as well as in contemporary captivity narratives, is the efficacy of subjective agency.

That blindness has an efficacy of its own, particularly in the era of British warfare with the French and Indians during which *Pamela* was published. The novel's fantasy of a distinctively English community was no doubt particularly appealing to both continental and colonial English readers during this period, but it concealed an ambivalence capable of disrupting that community. When Esther Edwards Burr read Pamela's narrative of captivity in 1755, she was virtually immobilized at her home in New Jersey, afraid to travel to see her parents in Stockbridge or her friends in Boston because of the ongoing war. Burr records in her journal —written as a series of letters to her friend Sarah Prince—her response to *Pamela* along with her concern over "the state of our Nation and the French Nation, and how probable it was that the French might overcome in their desighns [*sic*] to this Country" (1984, 76).[13] Her responses to the novel and to the war, however, are equally ambivalent. Although she argues that Richardson "has degraded our sex most horribly, to go and represent such virtue as Pamela, falling in love with Mr. B. in the midst of such foul and abominable actions," she later claims that Pamela "was more than woman—An *Angel imbodied* [*sic*]" (99, 105). When she complains about "what a tender Mother undergoes for her children at such a day as this, to think of bring[ing] up Children to be *dashed against the stones by our barbarous enemies*—or which is worse, to be inslaved by them, and obliged to turn *Papist*" (142), her fears are torn between the local violence of the war and the national and religious implications of an English defeat. Her journal reveals the literal fear of captivity and the accompanying fear of mobility felt by New Englanders, and especially by New England mothers. At the news of increased fighting she claims that "no body stirs no more than if it was impossible" and singles out the "*Wo* [*sic*] to them that are *with Child,* and to them that give suck in these days!" (177). Upon finally attempting a delayed journey, Burr reasons that "if the Indians get me, they get me, that is all I can say" (223). Such conditions probably made reading *Pamela* and Indian captivity narratives particularly affective for New Englanders, and the sense of national community such texts created was no doubt consoling in an era when the borders of their community were challenged by both the French and the Indians.

Yet it is impossible to account for the political function of Richardson's novels and of sentimental captivity narratives within the later rhetoric of the American revolution against Britain without acknowledging their readers' more subversive identification with the captive heroine's transgressive actions. As Jay Fliegelman has argued, the later American reception of both *Pamela* and *Clarissa* tended to translate the heroine's "act of disobedience into a heroic rebellion" (1982, 130). The American Revolution appropriated these captive Englishwomen less as models of passive virtue than as victims whose suffering legitimated their active agency. Richardson's captive heroines, like Hannah Dustan, came to represent America itself as a "woman on the verge of bringing out a new and virtuous generation" (Fliegelman 1982, 122). The very texts, therefore, that enable the community of the nation to be imagined are also texts that enable the disruption and reconfiguration of that community to be imagined. This possibility is occluded by the reduction of identification to simple resemblance and by the assumption that nationalist and novelistic sentiment is a function of that resemblance. Sentiment appears rather at those moments when resemblance fails, and it appears as the blinding veil of tears that both masks and marks an unaccountable border of difference.

Nation and Identification

If sentimental novels offer the consoling illusion of a community based on resemblance, then it is no surprise that such novels enjoyed their greatest popularity in the eighteenth century during periods of crisis in national coherence. The publication of *Pamela* in England in 1740 ushered in the cult of sentimentality that remained popular until the 1780s, a period characterized by a series of military conflicts that challenged and established the borders of the British Atlantic empire. Significantly, after the American War of Independence, the popularity of these novels quickly declined in England in concert with the general cultural devaluation of sentiment. It was precisely at this time, however, that sentimental novels began to flourish in America, and to flourish as specifically American novels. William Hill Brown's epistolary novel *The Power of Sympathy,* published in 1789, was advertised as "the first American novel" and still remains the text most often nominated to that status. In a series of letters between Myra Harrington and Mrs. Holmes that discuss the function and course of female education, Mrs. Holmes warns her charge that "the books which I recommend to your perusal are not always applicable to the situation of an *American* lady" (Brown 1970, 77). She explicitly develops this critique of English literature and implicitly calls for an American national literature when she remarks that the ridicule of educated women "is evidently a *transatlantic* idea, and must have been imbibed from the source of some *English* novel or magazine" (80). Mrs. Holmes goes on to recommend American-authored books characterized by "sentiment, morality and benevolence" (81) but marked also by nationalist themes: Noah Webster's *Grammatical Institute,* Barlow's *Vision of Columbus,* and Dwight's *Conquest of Canaan.* If such texts are preferable, it is because "*English* books" are "filled with local descriptions, which a young woman here [in America] is frequently at a loss to understand" (77). The assumption undergirding Mrs. Holmes's claim is that the sympathetic identification that makes novels a form of moral education is hindered by the absence of a national identity shared by both reader and text.

Such assumptions, together with the persistent critique that American novels were poor imitations of British models, fostered a palpable anxiety in nineteenth-century America about producing and defining a distinct national literary tradition. The sentimental legacy of American exceptionalism continues to characterize the institution of American literary criticism. From F. O. Matthiesen's *American Renaissance* to David S. Reynolds's *Beneath the American Renaissance,* American literary criticism has repeatedly defined its object of study by distinguishing what is unique about literature that is produced in a place called America. The critical labels most often attached to American literature are also ones commonly affixed to the American nation: a commitment to democracy, the pursuit of freedom, the presence of the frontier.[14] While these definitions aim to construct a separate but equal literary tradition, they also confine American literature, American culture, and even American writers within a totalizing identity by asserting a kind of sympathetic resemblance between them.[15]

The undeniably affective appeal of exceptionalism suggests that its claim to distinctive and stable identity works only by obscuring mobility and difference. Indeed, the exceptionalist argument contains an ambivalence arising from the fact that it can only be from an external perspective—from the position of a European or British literary tradition, for example—that the uniqueness of American literature comes to seem so appealing. National literary traditions can be imagined as coherent, as structured on a principle of commonality, only by imagining the border between them to be fixed and uncrossed. By obscuring the movement and exchange of texts across borders like the Atlantic, exceptionalist discourse tends to reproduce those texts' sentimental fantasies of coherent national communities. These porous borders or frontiers are, however, precisely where Bakhtin locates the dialogism of novelistic discourse, and where Homi Bhabha focuses his study of the ambivalence of nationalist discourse. The narrative duplicity that characterizes the nation and the novel must also be recognized in the process of identification by which their discourses create imagined communities. The strategies of sympathetic identification within sentimental captivity narratives and novels elucidate the function of the "sentimental side" that Renan attributed to nationalism. If sentimental novels appear, not within a static topography but only in a context of exchange across cultural and national borders, then the process of identification on which that genre relies must accommodate the relation between individuals who lack, rather than share, commonality. The inevitable limitation of resemblance is concealed within the fantasy of a community based on resemblance—an imagined community that is sentimental precisely to the extent that it lacks resemblance. Perhaps what the novel and the nation most deeply share, then, are ambivalent relations between subjects who are, in fact, not alike. By repeating the strategies of discourses that insist on equivalence, exceptionalism reproduces the fantasy of resemblance and community and perpetuates its concealment of the sometimes violent agency that preserves the imagined body of the nation, that "mother country" which reproduces itself through the ambivalent strategies of sympathetic identification.

Notes

I would like to thank Ken Dauber, Deidre Lynch, Neil Schmitz, and Bill Warner for their helpful readings of earlier drafts of this essay.

1. Mott 1947 classifies both texts as best-sellers according to historically gauged sales figures. For the publication history of the four 1682 editions of Rowlandson's captivity narrative—three in New England and one in London—see Derounian 1988.
2. For a more detailed discussion of Rowlandson's process of acculturation, see Burnham 1993.
3. Jacques Lacan is describing the relation between these two modes of identification when he explains that symbolic identification "is not specular, immediate identification. It is its support. It supports the perspective chosen by the subject in the field of the Other, from which specular identification may be seen in a satisfactory light," and "from which the subject will see himself, as one says, *as others see him*" (1971, 268). My summary here relies on Lacan (1971, 244–58, 267–74) and on Žižek's lucid discussion of the Lacanian concept of identification (1989, 100–110). Žižek explains that "in symbolic identification, we identify ourselves with the other precisely at a point at which he is inimitable, at the point which eludes resemblance" (109); without this relation, identification itself dissolves. Furthermore, Žižek notes that identity, unlike the circular movement of identification, is constituted retroactively, through "the radical contingency of naming" (95). The name—a signifier such as "American"or "English," for example—works to transform differential relations into a homogeneous identity.
4. Teresa A. Toulouse has argued that Rowlandson's insistence on her "inviolate body" "points to her own need to be reintegrated into the community as the

same body (mentally and physically) that was wrenched from it—that went out into the wilderness but remained the same" (1992, 655–56).

5. The narratives of Peter Williamson (1757) and John Marrant (1785)—both reprinted in VanDerBeets 1973—offer examples of such sentimentality. Although captivity narratives were increasingly written *by* men during the eighteenth century, the narratives they wrote were most often *about* women.

6. The text here is from Drake's 1851 *Indian Captivities; or, Life in the Wigwam* (see Drake 1990), although Howe's narrative was first published as a pamphlet in 1793. She was taken captive in 1755/6, at the onset of the French and Indian War.

7. The translation is Lincoln's (1913, 213). Mather introduces these concluding lines with an anecdote about a "Petrified Man" whose body a traveler saw while visiting a ruined city in Italy. Mather virtually requires tears from his readers by claiming "That if thou canst Read these passages [about captivity] without Relenting Bowels, thou thyself art as really Petrified as the man at Villa Ludovisia" (1913, 213).

8. Dustan's narrative first appeared in *Humiliations Followed with Deliverances* (Boston, 1697) and was subsequently included in *Decennium Luctuosum* (Boston, 1699) and in *Magnalia Christi Americana* (London, 1702).

9. The gauntlet ritual, Axtell notes (1985), generally served the purposes of ritual adoption, since the captives who best survived this test were often chosen by tribal members to replace relatives who died in warfare.

10. Hawthorne's version of Dustan's story, published in his *Magazine of Useful and Entertaining Knowledge,* significantly eliminates all possibility of a sympathetic response to the captive by portraying her as a "raging tigress" and a "bloody old hag" who should either have drowned, sunk to her death in a swamp, or "starved to death in the forest, and nothing ever seen of her again, save her skeleton, with the ten scalps twisted round it for a girdle!" (Hawthorne 1941, 136, 137). By demonizing Dustan, Hawthorne eliminates the gap between an imaginary and a symbolic identification, effectively making any identification with her impossible. Sympathy in Hawthorne's story is reserved for her strikingly maternal husband, "that tender hearted, yet valiant man" condemned to live with "this awful woman" (137).

11. As Timothy Brennan points out, Bakhtin's notion of dialogism is not only textual but social (1990, 50). See Bakhtin's "Epic and Novel" in *The Dialogic Imagination* (Bakhtin 1981).

12. Like Hawthorne's version of Hannah Dustan's captivity narrative, Henry Fielding's *An Apology for the Life of Mrs. Shamela Andrews* makes sympathetic identification with the captive female impossible by eliminating the gap between her virtue and her agency.

13. Burr's father was Jonathan Edwards, her husband Aaron Burr was the president of what is now Princeton University, and her son the future vice president

of the United States. Her journal offers important insight into the conditions of women's intellectual and daily life in the colonial eighteenth century. I thank Susan Howe for bringing this book to my attention.

14. See, for example, Matthiesen 1941, Lawrence 1923, Poirier 1966, Henry Nash Smith 1950, and Reynolds 1989. This brief list merely hints at the persistence of exceptionalism and nationalism within American literary criticism.

15. William Spengemann exposes the concealed tautology on which such definitions inevitably rely when he suggests that any definition of American literature operates by first selecting a group of texts and authors that are implicitly considered to be American. It is only secondly, and on the basis of shared features or concerns (on the basis, precisely, of a shared identity based on resemblance), that these texts are explicitly labeled American (1989, 77–86). Because the second act of naming effectively obscures the first, the process of definition only appears to fill in the term "American" by, in effect, emptying it twice.

Bridget Orr

2 The Maori House of Fiction

I

In 1973, Witi Ihimaera published *Tangi,* the first novel by a Maori writer. In the twenty years since that first text emerged, many other novels by Maori, including Patricia Grace, Keri Hulme, Heretaunga Pat Baker, and Alan Duff have appeared, achieving recognition not only in Aotearoa/New Zealand but internationally. Although it is problematic for a variety of reasons to identify the texts produced by these authors as "Maori novels," the combined oeuvre provides a clear challenge to the dominant narrativization of New Zealand history and society.[1] Until recently, settler literature and historiography figured colonization as largely benign, celebrating the country's relatively harmonious "race relations," high rate of intermarriage, and lack of formal discrimination as an aspect of the national progressive liberalism that guided the creation of one of the earliest welfare states and first gave women the vote. The novelistic contestation of hegemonic colonial or settler myths by indigenous writers is a phenomenon observable in a wide band of postcolonial cultures: what is striking in the New Zealand context is the rapidity with which the texts that question the complacent assumptions of the settler majority have assumed a broad, cross-cultural authority. This authority is primarily legible in the public and mass media reception of the novels rather than in the literary-critical community. Keri Hulme's success in winning the Booker Prize for *the bone people* (1984) is widely known and helped make her novel a best-seller, while Alan Duff's *Once Were Warriors* not only was a popular success but has been made into a film that has broken local attendance records. But in a literary academy almost completely occupied by Pakeha—or Europeans—in which reading practices have until recently been governed by New Critical or slightly historicized

Leavisite principles, predominantly formal and ethical modes of analysis have proved largely ill equipped to address the broader cultural and political import of these texts. The result is an often vociferous public debate in the press over the novels and near silence by professional critics.[2]

This paucity of comment is not produced simply by the inadequacy of formalist modes of analysis in the face of the political charge of Patricia Grace's *Potiki* (1986) and Witi Ihimaera's *The Matriarch* (1986). Pakeha criticism often seems to sway between the poles of aggression and anxiety.[3] This unease is generally linked to a more pervasive sense of illegitimacy in the settler—or what Simon During (1985) has referred to as the "post-colonising"—community, one rendered peculiarly acute by engagement with texts that not only challenge cherished settler myths of racial harmony but assert the values of a "different," but local and authoritative, cosmology and epistemology. The problem for Pakeha critics is that monocultural commentary—which is all that most can provide—is likely to fall into the familiar traps of an appropriative interpretive "assimilation," the cultural equivalent of policies of racial "integration." This has tended to involve making aesthetic judgments in accordance with specifically and culturally inadequate European criteria or else anthropologizing Maori writing: treating it primarily as fictive ethnography.[4] The poststructuralist contribution to the debate has taken the form of suggesting that it is the obsession with the settler-other binarism that is itself the problem and that approaching texts by both Maori and Pakeha as postcolonial hybrids destabilizes the oppressively essentialized notions of identity that such binarisms sustain.[5] And the standard response to such celebrations of hybridity—usually made under the sign of "the political"—retains a certain cogency here; hybridity can all too easily end up looking like assimilation under another name. Cultural commentators such as Leonie Pihama (1994), in a position shared by a number of Maori critics, question the validity of the term "postcolonial" (and the unsettling of binary structures it implies) in the context of a settler society in which independence from the imperial power is nonetheless accompanied by the continuing, specifically colonial oppression of indigenous people.

These dilemmas are hardly specific to Aotearoa/New Zealand but inform the whole field of postcolonial studies and, to a lesser extent, colonial discourse analysis as well. Maori nationalists have invoked arguments over nativism from the discussions of Anglo- and Francophone African literature in order to contest novelistic practice and reception (Poananga 1986, 1987), and recent celebrations of cultural "cross-pollination" draw on postcolonial adaptations of poststructuralist positions (Hubbard and Craw 1990, 1992). But the kinds of analyses developed offshore always require a certain amount of adjustment to local conditions. In a recent essay pondering the epistemological and political implications of formalist and historicist approaches to African literature, Kwame Anthony Appiah's elegant deconstruction of the Eurocentric universalism lurking in the heart of nativism is followed by a suggestion that "we give up the search for Mr. Right; and speak, more modestly, of *productive modes of reading*" (1991, 158). Useful as his suggestion is, the example he offers, which contrasts appropriate ways of approaching African literature in American and African contexts, depends on the distance that informs the difference between the two locations. In a settler culture such as New Zealand/Aotearoa, there is difference but no distance. Separate realms exist, but there is always overlap; very few classrooms will contain a homogeneous set of interests. The tension this engenders in cultural analysis seems remarkably absent from another discussion of an arguably comparable problem, namely, Arnold Krupat's attempt to develop an "ethnocriticism" that allows for "progressive translation" between cultures (Krupat 1992). Krupat's primary concern is the relation between European Americans and Native American literature, and his cultural ideal is a radical cosmopolitanism that can produce a "polyvocal polity." Democratic as this Bakhtinian vision may be, it is articulated from a position of no doubt about the cultural—and sociopolitical—domination of Euro-Americans in the United States. It is in fact a classically pluralist model, one that seeks to make space for the cultural expression of an oppressed minority without seeing such expression as a political threat to the dominant order. That kind of certainty about the current and future primacy of their own authority is singularly lacking in recent Pakeha cultural production and commentary. During the 1980s, it was made clear to European scholars that historical and anthropological research on Maori topics was unacceptable without full agreement from the Maori concerned: one Pakeha historian was targeted by a firebomb planted by radicals. Newly conscious of the limitations of their perspective on New Zealand society, in a culture attempting to adjust political, judicial, and educational institutions to incorporate Maori customs and practice, settler academics and artists have tended to focus on specifically

Pakeha experience and to eschew attempts to represent the cross-cultural encounters of the past. The anxiety this reflects stands in contrast to the pervasive articulation, the continuing experience of oppression notwithstanding, of Maori (and Polynesian) confidence. As Irihapeti Ramsden has put it, "Our time of Maoritanga is exciting. We are recovering from colonisation" (1993a, 349). The sense on the part of Maori that they possess the cultural initiative is bound up with their increasing ability to reshape New Zealand society as a whole. That kind of specifically political power, with its clear and already effective challenge to the settler establishment, gives cultural debate a kind of urgency simply not imaginable in accounts such as Krupat's.

A certain defensiveness in Aotearoa/New Zealand's settler community is not unique. On the broadest front, it may be seen as symptomatic of the ongoing renegotiation of relations between the West and the rest produced by the dismantling of empires, the emergence of neocolonialism, and related intellectual developments, such as postmodernism and postcolonialism, which to some extent deprivilege European knowledge and cultural authority. More specifically, Alan Lawson (1993) has argued that while the continuing tendency to ground claims to authentic identity in terms of autochthony works to secure the legitimacy of both (imperial) metropolitans and indigenous peoples, it leaves the settler subject in a peculiarly problematic position. J. G. A. Pocock (1992) has come to a not dissimilar conclusion—by a radically different route—in a provocative essay suggesting that while both Maori and Pakeha intellectual traditions deplore vagrancy, it can be argued that both peoples, being explorers, navigators, and settlers, are what he terms *tangata waka,* or people of the canoe. This account questions the moral and political authority that attaches to aboriginality in both Maori and Pakeha traditions, and the concomitant cross-cultural assumption that the Maori have a special status as first inhabitants, arguing instead that it is the shared tradition of exploration and colonization that characterizes both kinds of New Zealanders. Pocock's view is a minority one, however, and the primacy of the position of Maori as *tangata whenua,* or people of the land, is becoming institutionalized in legal and bureaucratic discourse—without much visible settler dissent. Those without a comparable name—or, arguably, identity—are Pakeha, about whose status, as inhabitants of Aotearoa/New Zealand by virtue of the Treaty of Waitangi, argument continues.

The current renegotiation of power between Maori and Pakeha in the cultural sphere is an aspect of a multifaceted resurgence of the tangata whenua, or indigenous inhabitants, which has been called the "Maori Renaissance." From the early 1970s on, Maori have mounted a series of challenges to the dominant settler order through political action and the judicial system. The Treaty of Waitangi, signed by some two-thirds of Maori chiefs in 1840, and the primary instrument of legitimation for British colonization, has emerged as a crucial site of contestation—and possible settlement—between the two peoples. Through the seventies, many Maori nationalists decried the Treaty as a fraud: in the eighties, however, as revisionist historiography began to suggest its possible utility as a means of redressing grievances, the call came to "honour the treaty." A Tribunal has been established to hear the literally hundreds of claims relating to land, fisheries, and other resources, while the constitutional implications of the Treaty have shaped official policies of "biculturalism" that emphasize a notion of partnership between Maori and Pakeha.[6]

It is difficult to overstate the importance, politically and culturally, of the emergence of a Treaty discourse: as one Maori commentator put it recently, "the last twenty-five years of this century will probably be known as the Treaty years" (Jones 1994). And the kinds of debates over power, history, and identity that the revaluation of the founding contract—"New Zealand's birth certificate"—has produced (and of which it is symptomatic) are nowhere more apparent than in the domain of literature. The sites of greatest dispute are anthologies and novels, each of them generically burdened with a representative function in relation to a unified notion of national identity that seems increasingly anachronistic. Novelistic narration may have been vital in producing what Benedict Anderson (1983) calls the "imagined communities" of late-eighteenth-century European and twentieth-century Third World nations, uniting disparate groups of people through an appeal to a sense of shared history and interest, but recent novels from Aotearoa—a country uncertain even of its name—deconstruct rather than consolidate such a myth of nationhood.

Up to the 1970s, "New Zealand literature" was a substantially Pakeha project, in which Maori functioned as the objects rather than the subjects of representation. The initial period of colonization saw the emergence of a mythicization of Aotearoa/New Zealand as "Maoriland," with novelistic production that mimed the colonial genres of other settler cultures. Popular forms included romances set in a sentimentalized pre-European Maori context; stirring tales of settler hardship in the bush and in the Maori Wars of the 1860s; and comic sketches of rugged colonial characters and incompetent metropolitan "new chums." Toward the turn of the century, writers such as Katherine Mansfield and Jane Mander began ringing changes on these forms from a distinctly female perspective, while Roderick Finlayson inaugurated a tradition of "sympathetic" accounts of contemporary Maori life. Much of this literary production was intended for consumption abroad, whether in Australia or Britain, and much of the material was therefore concerned with exploiting New Zealand's exoticism rather than explaining the country to its new inhabitants. Much slower than neighboring Australia to develop any degree of anti-imperial feeling in the settler population, New Zealand witnessed the emergence of cultural nationalism among Pakeha only in the 1930s. The dominant writers of this movement, such as Frank Sargeson and Robin Hyde, did draw on overseas models such as Sherwood Anderson, but the regional realism they adopted provided much more satisfactory ways of representing local speech, manners, and ways of life than the sentimental or exoticizing modes used earlier. The search for an authentic literary discourse, ideally expressed in a Great New Zealand Novel, persisted through the fifties and sixties and established a preference for large-scale family dramas of provincial life and historical novels still noticeable in the novelistic practice of several leading Pakeha writers who came of age in the postwar period. The 1970s saw an end to this relatively homogeneous literary scene, not just because women and Maori writers rose to prominence, but also because realism began to lose its preeminence.[7]

The Pakeha domination of New Zealand literature existed alongside, but mostly in ignorance of, substantial and continuous Maori oral and written cultural production (McRae 1991; Ihimaera et al. 1993). After two decades of Anglophone publication by Maori writers in all the major genres, that domination is eroding, not least because the newly visible Maori writing has highlighted the thoroughgoing Eurocentrism of the legitimating institutions of literature. Witi Ihimaera commented in this regard in 1990 that "I look forward . . . for discussions of New Zealand literature to move from this European-biased and based analysis" (1). With rare exceptions, however, Pakeha critics prefer to remain silent about the significant area of Maori literary production, in a way that tacitly acknowledges their inability to make authoritative judgments in this domain. One can certainly argue that Pakeha critical silence is no bad thing—a series of controversies between the self-appointed standard-bearer of traditional European literary values, C. K. Stead, and other commentators who write with recognized authority about Maori culture has made it very clear that monophone Pakeha readers with limited knowledge of Maoritanga, or things Maori, however distinguished in their own context, lack the requisite knowledge to make informed judgments.[8] One interesting development in Maori studies has been the establishment of protocols to regulate relations between researcher(s) and subject(s), ensuring knowledge production is informed by two different epistemologies.

Novels occupy a somewhat different space and call for different strategies. The most cursory survey of recent work in the postcolonial field reinforces one's sense that the novel is still the genre in which struggles over cultural and political identities and authority are most acute.[9] As is obvious in the Aotearoa/New Zealand context, these kinds of textual conflicts are not simply a matter of a content unsettling to a settler or metropolitan reader; rather, they raise questions over the legitimacy of hitherto dominant reading practices and, by extension, the authority of the institutions that license and approve interpretive activity. In the face of these dilemmas, it is unsurprising that Bakhtin has emerged as the theorist of choice in so much postcolonial analysis. Bakhtin's emphasis on the novel as heteroglossial, a site in which the voices of many conflicting social groups interact, seems to provide a useful way of recognizing that these texts not only are internally divided but make a divisive address to a heterogeneous readership (Bakhtin 1981). Bakhtin's etiology of the novel, suggesting that the precedent epic was a specifically imperial narrative mode that displaced various types of tribal discourse, discourses that reemerge in the subversive form of the novel, reinforces the attractions of his account.

Developing this Bakhtinian emphasis on discursive difference and identity in the novel in relation to the categories of race and gender, Mae Gwendolyn Henderson suggests that the complex subjectivity of the black woman writer allows her to enter simultaneously into what she calls familial or testimonial and public or competitive discourses—both of which affirm and challenge the reader simultaneously. Thus she argues that black women writers enter into testimonial discourse with black men as blacks, with white women as women, and with black women as black women: conversely, they enter into a competitive discourse with black men as women, with white women as blacks, and with white men as black women. Novels such as Zora Neale Hurston's *Their Eyes Were Watching God* (1937) produce a plethora of reading positions that are themselves complex and internally divided (Henderson 1994).

The notion of polyvocality and multiple addressees that Henderson develops is highly suggestive. In one sense, the strongest reason I would adduce for critical engagement with the work of writers such as Patricia Grace and Witi Ihimaera from the Pakeha side is that their novels seem to solicit such a response; their texts are, precisely, polyvocal. That is not to say that Pakeha readers are of primary concern to either of these novelists—both have made it clear either explicitly or implicitly that their main addressees are Maori—but Pakeha do appear to be among the readers addressed, whether directly or obliquely.[10]

Mark Williams has already argued, in fact, in *Leaving the Highway: Six Contemporary New Zealand Novelists,* the only major monograph on the New Zealand novel published for some time, that Keri Hulme, author of the highly successful *the bone people,* has internalized and reproduces an essentially European projection of Maori culture as unified, harmonious, and organically rooted in Aotearoa, thus providing Pakeha as well as Maori with an idealized human origin for New Zealand society that can supplement, or substitute for, the messy, fragmented realities of history (Williams 1990, 110–38). Hulme's *the bone people* is an account of a triangulated relationship between Kerewin, a successful but doggedly solitary Maori woman artist cut off from her people, Simon, a young Pakeha boy orphaned in a shipwreck, and Joe, Simon's rescuer, adoptive father and abuser, and, like Kerewin, Maori. The novel can be read allegorically, as a figuration of the alienation of contemporary Maori and Pakeha from themselves and from each other, with violence as much as love informing the relationships. It concludes with a lengthy, almost phantasmagoric sequence in which ancient Maori magic is invoked to resolve the characters' problems. It is this sequence that critics such as Williams have generally found least satisfactory. Rather than simply dismissing the episode as overblown romanticism, however, one might read it as symptomatic of the difficulties Hulme faced in bringing an extraordinarily painful analysis of New Zealand domestic and racial conflicts to a hopeful conclusion. The shift to a fantastic register implicitly acknowledges the problematic nature of such optimism. Williams is not quite as dismissive of Witi Ihimaera's most ambitious novel, *The Matriarch,* but he is extremely critical. He suggests that Ihimaera's preference for the heroic and unified world of the epic renders his relation to the "ironic form" of the novel thoroughly ambivalent and results in a text marred by "overblown" prose, "structural incoherence," and "distortions of history" (Williams 1990, 87). However acute may be Williams's views on the settler guilt that helped make *the bone people* in particular so popular among Pakeha as well as Maori, his failure to pay systematic attention to the structure, language, or thematics of Hulme's and Ihimaera's novels seems to display the same cultural incompetence that Michael King (1993) has located in C. K. Stead's reading of Maori poetry. Williams's failure to offer a close reading of the texts in the terms they themselves propose—a procedure that stands in striking contrast with his careful exegeses of novels by major Pakeha writers such as Maurice Gee and Janet Frame—suggests that in addressing texts written by Maori, it is their apparent cultural effects Williams wishes to engage rather than the novels themselves. This would not be problematic per se if it weren't so obvious that the critical double standard at work here reinscribes Pakeha texts as embodiments of novelistic excellence, while Maori writing is treated, in the end, as the aesthetically unsuccessful epiphenomenon of cultural conflict.

The limits of Williams's Eurocentric formalism are legible not simply in this scholar's seeming inability to produce plausible readings of texts by Maori writers but also in his apparent incuriosity about the status of "the novel" in Maori terms. The categories of art and literature, national literature, and novels all have a specifically European provenance but have been transformed by their appropriation in various non-European contexts (some of which include traditions of lengthy prose narrative). These transformations cannot be understood simply, in formal or immanent terms, as changes of content, structure, imagery, characterization, and so on. The role of what in European terms is known as aesthetic discourse is also crucial in particular reconstructions of the cultural work that novels perform. While some non-Western cultures have long-established traditions of connoisseurship suggesting that cultural production operates within paradigms that seem relatively familiar, such is not always the case. If knowledge of what Terry Eagleton calls the "aesthetic ideology" that informs any literary text is necessary for the plausible interpretation of European writing (1978, 60–63), such knowledge will be no less, and arguably more, important in reading literature from non-Western cultures. Maori accounts of the function of cultural production suggest that novels might be understood as communal possessions—treasured objects, displays of skill, and sources of knowledge binding a people together—but also as challenges to non-Maori, occasions for debate, and even for revenge.

This, however, is the point at which the Scylla of ethnographic reductionism meets the Charybdis of Eurocentric formalism. A number of Maori artists have made forceful objections to having their work analyzed in terms that privilege "traditional" Maori culture, in that such analyses tend to reify and archaize their work, denying them modernity (Hubbard and Craw 1990, 1992). Others are equally emphatic about the necessity for critical familiarity with Maori culture.

Henderson's extrapolation of Bakhtinian dialogism seems to offer the most effective way of cutting this particular Gordion knot. Reading *The Matriarch* or *Potiki,* Pakeha readers will find themselves, to a greater or lesser extent, cultural outsiders in the world presented. But their position is not that of a distant spectator: for both these texts are intensively performative and undertake in turn to educate, to welcome, to argue with, and to accuse such readers. Performativity certainly figures in Ihimaera's accounts of his work: in one interview, this author suggested that theater was a form more suited than the novel to Maori culture given that culture's intensely communal nature (1985, 104–5). Writing more generally about the role of Maori artists, Hirini Moko Mead and Irihapeti Ramsden suggest that while objects or performances are produced by a particular creative individual or group, the origins of such work lie in the communal cultural work of the *iwi,* or tribe, and gain much of their meaning within that context (Mead 1993, 199–209; Ramsden 1993b, 320–22). This does not, however, limit the implied or possible audience of a given text; in one recent discussion, Ihimaera remarked in relation to *The Matriarch*'s use of European historical sources: "I visualised these as people with whom one could have a dialogue with [*sic*], a korero, on the nature of history and on their way of seeing it" (1990, 1).

Seeing *The Matriarch* as *korero,* or discussion, obviously emphasizes the work's performative and dialogic nature, and so does another of the terms Ihimaera has used to describe it. His early novels and stories Ihimaera has described as *waiata*—songs that are associated with love (*waiata aroha*) or mourning (*waiata tangi*) as well as greeting, farewells, and daily work. *The Matriarch,* however, he has said, can be understood as a *haka*—and a feminocentric haka at that (Ihimaera 1994). Among Pakeha, haka has usually been thought of as a war dance: in fact, it is performed without weapons, and although extremely various in its functions, it is not, strictly speaking, a war dance. Timoti Karetu's recent account (on which my remarks below are dependent) cites approvingly a definition of haka as an expression of "the . . . identity" of the Maori (Alan Armstrong qtd. in Karetu 1993, 25). Haka names all Maori dance but is currently associated with "that part of the Maori dance repertoire where the men are to the fore with the women lending support in the rear" (Karetu 1993, 24)—although the first *kapa haka* (haka troupe) is said to have been female (15). The number of people involved in a performance varies from a dozen or even fewer to over a hundred. Every part of the body is used: legs stamping and jumping, arms brandishing or shaking, eyes rolling, tongues thrusting in gestures and effects that are carefully calculated and expressive of eloquence and masculine power. There are some haka women who perform alone, but Karetu suggests that their traditional role was at the side of a troupe—armed—to protect the men. The spectacular visual effects—which early European observers compared to "the Saxon traditions of our ancestors, or any of the Gorgons whose looks were reputed to change into stones those on whom they cast a glance" (Joel Samuel Polack, qtd. in Karetu 1993, 28–29)—are accompanied by lyrics. Different forms of haka serve to welcome and entertain guests, to establish reputation, to express hatred, to prepare for conflict, to mourn the dead, and to comment on current problems—one recent prize-winning haka urged its audience to give up smoking and drinking. Haka texts are written by individuals but are usually associated with a particular tribe: in the case of *kaioraora,* however, a haka composed by women to express deadly hatred, the lyric is generally preserved by the tribe who are the butt of the composition, it being considered a great honor to have inspired such loathing (Karetu 1993, 47).

Haka were frequently remarked on by early European visitors to Aotearoa/New Zealand and have assumed a role in one of the most important areas of cultural overlap, namely, rugby. High schools often performed more or less bowdlerized versions of famous haka, and the national side, the All Blacks, always begins international test matches with a haka. Haka has more specifically political dimensions as well: during the protests against the South African rugby tour of New Zealand in 1981, I saw a Black Power group perform a haka to defy police outside the stadium where a test match was in progress. The performance of haka is now in fact carefully controlled: in the early eighties, a group called He Taua forcibly intervened, after years of fruitless requests, to prevent engineering students at the University of Auckland from including a desecration of haka in their graduation celebrations.

2

The reading that follows will attempt to suggest what might be at stake—for the Pakeha reader in particular—in thinking of haka as a governing metaphor for the cultural work performed by *The Matriarch.* The novel's eponymous heroine is Artemis Riripeti Mahana, head of a confederation of tribes from the east coast of Aotearoa. A figure of great beauty, power, and accomplishment, a priestess of the Ringatu faith (a Maori adaptation of Christianity), like other "women warriors," she has become famous for her efforts to recover land and sustain her people in the struggle against the disasters brought by the Pakeha. The novel's hero is Tama Mahana, who has been chosen by the Matriarch to take up her role but who can do so only after an exhaustive search into his family's and his people's history, while also ultimately confronting and defeating a rival for the position of leadership.

The novel's structure revolves around a central scene—in which the Matriarch fights to establish Tama as her heir at a particular *hui,* or meeting—a scene set up, revisited, and brought to a resolution only by threading it through a series of mythological, historical, and contemporary narratives that provide three different, albeit interrelated causalities for understanding the conflict. While the invocation and juxtaposition of mythological and realist modes of narration may remind readers of magic realist practice, *The Matriarch*'s schema is in fact determined by specifically Maori views of time and history. Thus the novel begins with a *whakapapa,* or genealogy, which provides the broadest possible frame—indeed, a cosmic one—for understanding the action that unfolds; then follow five "acts," the first, third, and last of which focus on Tama's upbringing, his developing relationship with the Matriarch, and his fight to maintain the right of succession; the second and fourth acts deal with

Te Kooti and Wi Pere, nineteenth-century religious-military and political leaders respectively. These leaders' struggle with the Pakeha informs that of the Matriarch and Tama and reframes the contemporary conflict yet again. The novel's spiraling structure thus embodies in narrative terms a chronology that positions its subjects, as Ranginui Walker has put it (1994), so that they back forward into the future, facing a past populated by a multitude of ancestral figures.

The novel's structure is describable in terms both of modernist narrative and Maori historiography, but the distinction itself emphasizes a polarity that the text renders questionable. As the division into "acts," one named " 'The Song of Te Kooti' " suggests, *The Matriarch*'s performance is as much informed by opera as by haka. The novel's invocation of a plethora of forms and practices both "Maori" (whakapapa, haka) and "Pakeha" (arias, parliamentary records) problematizes attempts to establish its "meaning" through reference to a single cultural origin. What remains irreducible is the text's mobilization of these heterogeneous representational strategies in the service of a particular politics; a project that, again, cannot be exhausted through either a Marxist or conservative formalist suspicion of the literature of commitment. Recognizing the novel as a haka—a form of address with which Pakeha readers are at least minimally familiar—renders transparent the Eurocentrism of the distinction between tendentious and "fine" (or avant-garde) writing while suggesting the inadequacy of critical judgments made in such terms of reference. Haka are often, though by no means invariably, "political" in theme and occasion, but they are performed with meticulous, often highly competitive concern for excellence in composition and effect. So while the Pakeha reader might wish to take issue with the text's account of the topics canvased—or even criticize the actual management of the narrative—complaints on the grounds that the novel is simply "too political" are to a large degree meaningless. What such criticism suggests, in fact, is a desire to displace the highly personalized but political confrontation established through the reading process by shifting into a familiar register of aesthetic assessment, rendering consideration of the substantive issues at stake moot.

The Matriarch establishes a range of reading positions, through discourse both familial and competitive, to invoke Henderson's terms. It is not always clear in the novel, however, who is performing for whom. Bakhtin's emphasis on the heteroglossial nature of novelistic discourse takes on a different valence in a context in which the textual metaphor of haka implies a communal cultural production—readers might at points perform with the text, as it were. Sometimes, as when the narrative invites the reader ceremoniously into Rongopai, the famous painted meeting house that provides the focus of life for a particular iwi, or people, the reader is treated as an honored guest but distinctly a stranger. At other points, when Tamatea's ancestors or immediate relations are addressed, the reader's position will depend on his or her own sense of recognition or relationship. This is not just a question of recognizing a particular rhetorical (and performative) practice transformed into novelistic discourse but an issue of identification and participation. While Maori readers generally are most likely to understand the symbolic implications of a particular rhetorical choice, their positions will vary in respect of their relationship to the characters represented. Given the historical nature of the novel, readers from different tribes would have quite different perspectives on both the "real" and the fictional characters, a common understanding of the terms of representation being invoked regardless.

My primary concern, however, is with another kind of reader. Certain sections of *The Matriarch* are explicitly and angrily directed at a Pakeha reader, conceived of adversarily. This is not, I would suggest, a generalized address to all whites but a haka directed at a specific group—the settler population of New Zealand. "The Song of Te Kooti," chapters 7 and 8 of *The Matriarch,* retells the story of the Matawhero Retaliation. The incident concerns the attack made by Te Kooti, the prophet and warrior chief of the Ringatu church and an ideological and military opponent of British power, on the small Poverty Bay settlement of Matawhero. Ihimaera has said that he was instructed by a *kaumatua,* or elder, to write about Te Kooti, who is a major figure in the pantheon of Maori resisters to colonial rule. During the mid-nineteenth-century British attempt to establish domination in Aotearoa, different Maori tribes adopted varying strategies to ensure survival or vanquish the invaders. These ranged from cooperation with the colonizing power to military and cultural resistance—the latter including the development of specifically Maori adaptations of Christianity. Te Kooti, who was missionary educated and began his military career fighting on the British side, is renowned for both his military prowess and his status as a prophet.

The particular incident concerning Te Kooti retold in *The Matri-*

arch occurred within Witi Ihimaera's tribal territory and is remembered locally (in popular memory)—and nationally (in scholarly accounts)—in different ways by two communities. For Pakeha, it is recalled in the familiar tropes of settler myth as a massacre of the innocents, women and children slaughtered in their beds, an act of excessive cruelty without strategic military value, comprehensible only as unrestrained savagery.[11] The novel provides another view, one that emphasizes both the role of *utu,* or revenge (a fundamental concept in Maori culture concerned with conflict and recompense), and holy mission in Te Kooti's decision to attack the home of his chief settler persecutor, Major Reginald Newton Biggs. Given that the Ringatu identified themselves as the last tribe of Israel, and the colonial government as Egypt, the blending of the desire for utu with an Old Testament understanding of divine justice as vengeance is shown to produce a powerful and legitimate motive for action against Biggs and his family and neighbors.

The narrative does not, however, effect its revision simply by focusing on a single Maori consciousness or providing "authoritative" contextual information. Rather, the chapter that precedes the account of the Biggs incident dramatizes the variety of perspectives on the event by providing a full narrative of Te Kooti's life from the lips of the hero's grandmother, the Matriarch herself; by quoting from a variety of contemporary Pakeha eyewitnesses; by rehearsing the extant historiographical positions; and by presenting snatches of action and dialogue from the day preceding the events. All these sections of the narrative are framed and given point by the chapter opening, which shows the Matriarch teaching Tama not just how to fight with traditional weapons—both the *taiaha,* or spear, and historical knowledge—but how to hate. This suggests that the narrative itself, driven on by a first-person narrator who rounds on certain Pakeha characters, is operating not just as reinterpretation but as reenactment: the text itself performs an act of vengeance on the Pakeha reader. The narrator's prose takes on the biblical cadences, the incantatory variations, and the repetitions of the Matriarch, creating an effect of increasingly focused purpose:

Some historians have puzzled over this and, ultimately, have decided that Te Kooti was too afraid to attack any of the well-garrisoned settlements. But the prophet could have taken Gisborne if he had wanted to. No, the reason for not razing Gisborne itself was that Te Kooti was not interested nor directed to do this. If there was to be an act of war, let it be a small act, and let it be directed against those who had in fact fired upon the prophet and thereby on Jehovah. Yes, let it be against Pharaoh, Major Biggs, the man who had exiled the prophet to Wharekauri and then, on Te Kooti's return, had pursued him through three battles to Puketapu Mountain. And let it be against Pharoah's cohorts, the militia who, with Major Biggs, were stationed at Matawhero. Let it be between the two armies of war. Major Biggs, Major Biggs, you walked three months in the valley of death. (Ihimaera 1986, 143)

The passage moves from the relatively detached initial reportage of the scholarly consensus to a directly partisan defense of Te Kooti's actions that quickly ratchets up the latter's *mana,* or prestige, by contemplating Gisborne not merely "taken" but "razed." The narrator's identification with Te Kooti motivates the sympathetic ventriloquism of the prophet's thoughts that culminates in the rhetorical address to Major Biggs, enemy it seems of Te Kooti and the narrator both. The tone here is not furious but menacing, creating its effect through the contemplation of possibilities dismissed before the turning to a considered aim. The repetition and modification of imperatives ("Yes, let it be . . . And let it be . . . Let it be . . .") in sentences of decreasing length that set the resonance of the Maori place names (Wharekauri, Puketapu, Matawhero) against the clumsy appellation "Major Biggs" marshall all the rhetorical power of Maori and biblical syntax and allusions to produce a sense of relentless purpose.

That narratorial relentlessness, and the vengeful purpose it sustains, drives the next two chapters, which focus on the Matawhero Retaliation in detail. It is a grim tale, not often told locally, but it is one, the narrator insists, that requires rehearsal:

Perhaps the reason for being tightlipped is that Poverty Bay citizens now pride themselves on their good record of race-relations, and rightly so. But they need to be told the truth. (159)

The text recounts the deadly episode by focusing on a dozen separate killings, of Maori and Pakeha both, providing rapid sketches of the victims' consciousness of events just prior to death. Each incident takes place along a deathly timeline with rapid shifts of scene that create a sense of mounting anticipatory horror: the narration seems as relentless and efficient as the executions. The attack begins on Tuesday, 10 November, at 12:01 A.M. with the deaths of Trooper Peppard, Lieutenant Dodd, and Richard Rathbone: next, at 2:20 A.M., is Robert Atkins, who is followed at 3:05 A.M. by Pera Kararehe.

Then, like shafts loosed from a bow, they descended upon the settlement.

3:45 A.M.

Lieutenant James Walsh, 33, his wife Emma, 26, and their infant daughter, Nora Ellen, were all asleep in the main bedroom of their cottage near the lower ford. The front door was open, and the raiders slipped in quietly. They were filled with passion, so much so that when Nora started to murmur in her sleep she was instantly decapitated.

. . .

3:55 A.M.

Piripi Taketake awoke quickly at the entry of raiders into the whare.

"Who goes there?" he demanded.

He heard the muffled sounds of his three children, Pera, Taraipene, and Te Paea. He roused his wife, Harata, and she began to call to the children. Even before Piripi could stop her, she was out of bed and on her way to them. But before she got to the door she was axed. (162–63)

It is not until the Matawhero killings cease that the narrator pauses to moralize. At this point the "they"—which refers specifically to the Pakeha of Poverty Bay—becomes "you," and the reader addressed in the account becomes Pakeha in general. Reflecting on the violence suffered by the white victims, the narrator asks:

All dead, and to what purpose? To serve the vanities of man or God? And who among you is ready to cast the first stone and say "Te Kooti is to blame?" . . . And do I hear you protest at the detailed descriptions of death? Again, your protests fall on deaf ears. (170)

The implied reader here is the shocked Pakeha, whose responses are anticipated and dismissed. A page later, that reader is named explicitly:

The curtain was coming down, but the show was not yet over. You, Pakeha, required a public sacrifice to be made, a symbolic killing, through which your feeling of horror about Te Kooti's retaliation at Matawhero could be transmuted into satisfaction. You didn't have Te Kooti himself, but, ah, you had caught one of his followers, hadn't you, at the fall of Ngatapa? (172)

This is an uncomfortable moment, I think, for the Pakeha addressee, imaginatively brutalized by the accounts of the Matawhero deaths but, equally, implicated in the injustice that gave rise to, and followed, the events. The resistant reader may dismiss the account of the Retaliation as "a distortion of history" or an inappropriate incursion of political polemic; but such responses seem transparently evasive in the context, just another symptom of the uneasy repression in the settler community described at the beginning of the chapter. The passage just quoted above aggressively fractures the identificatory contract that usually negotiates novelistic transactions: the Pakeha reader is not accorded the position of impartial witness or sympathetic observer, sharing in the narratorial perspective. Nor are the disconcerting effects he or she experiences the literary sleight of hand of a playful or amoral unreliable narrator. Rather, the textual sequence addressed to the Pakeha operates in accordance with another set of protocols; like haka, this rhetorical address to an adversary taunts, probes, and challenges.

> The killing of innocents, Pakeha. The blood is on your hands. Yes, Pakeha, you remember Matawhero. Let me remind you of the murder at Ngatapa. (172)

The onslaught is unrelenting, as the narrator, singing for, if not with, the prophetic and fierce Te Kooti, breathes with the force of Tumatauenga, God of Man and War.

My point here is emphatically not that the invocation of a single "traditional" Maori category can function as the hermeneutic key to a complex text like *The Matriarch;* it is rather that thinking about the text as a haka emphasizes the performative dimension of the novel and the particularly challenging relation it establishes with Pakeha readers.[12] Other novels by Maori, particularly Alan Duff's *Once Were Warriors,* might well also be seen as haka, but in the latter instance the addressee is certainly primarily other Maori, who, unlike the Pakeha invited to korero by Ihimaera, have not been slow to reply to its challenging account of contemporary Maori life.[13]

The extraliterary controversy over the historical, political, and cultural validity of Ihimaera's and Duff's texts bears witness to the extent to which their remarkably forceful reworkings of novelistic discourse have changed the nature of the cultural work done by this genre in Aotearoa. One extraordinary index of this is C. K. Stead's recent publication of a novel entitled *The Singing Whakapapa.* Stead's novel is a self-conscious vindication of the Pakeha presence in New Zealand, a playful variant of the historical detective story and family saga that contests representations of the early settlers as opportunistic land-grabbers. Given the role he has played in recent cultural debate, Stead's titular invocation of whakapapa, and his use of genealogy as a structural device, while presumably intended to reflect his own sense of having a hybrid cultural inheritance, cannot, as he is doubtless aware, avoid raising the question of cultural appropriation. Conscious of this, at least one, sympathetic, commentator has called Stead's gesture "mischievous" (Smithyman 1994, 6). It is possible, however, to refigure the writer—here, in an exemplary sense the Pakeha Novelist—less as the fully self-conscious agent of a recuperative settler discourse and more as a defensive participant in cultural practices he does not fully understand but, equally, cannot ignore. It is difficult not to see *The Singing Whakapapa* as Stead's haka as well as his whakapapa.

Novelistic practice as haka is forceful, often combative. Patricia Grace's *Potiki* offers another central metaphor for narrativization, one that also significantly refigures novelistic relations. Grace's novel tells the story of a small *hapu,* or subtribe, whose community is threatened by the attempts of developers to build a holiday resort on their land, thus disrupting their whole way of life. The conflict is framed by the life histories of all the Tamihana family—eschewing a single protagonist, the text nonetheless assigns great importance to the eponymous Potiki, who is a Maui and Christ figure both. The prologue to this novel focuses on the man who carved the *wharenui,* or meetinghouse, which serves as the center of the Tamihanas' lives. We are told that the role of the carver is to provide "a house for the people" (Grace 1986, 8), where the carving of ancestral figures tells the story not only of the iwi but also of human and divine origins:

> The people were anxious to have all aspects of their lives and ancestry represented in their new house. They wished to include all the famous ancestors to which they were linked, and also to include the ancestors which linked all people to the earth and the heavens from ancient to future times, and which told people of their relationships to light and growth, and to each other. (10)

Later, discussing the role of the wharenui in the context of the Tamihanas' dissatisfaction with the dominant modes of schooling, knowledge, art, and media offered, Roimata, one of the main narrators, remarks:

> We could not afford books, so we made our own. In this way we were able to find ourselves in books. It is rare for us to find ourselves in books, but in our own books we were able to find and define our lives.

> But our main book was the wharenui which is itself a story, a history, a gallery, a study, a design structure and a taonga. And we are part of that book along with family, past and family yet to come. (104)

While most emphasis is placed on the role of carving in the wharenui's symbolic embodiment of the people's history and values, *tukutuku,* or paneling, and weaving also play a part:[14]

> I would sit comfortably in my chair close to the tukutuku frames, often with my sister Tangimoana on the opposite side, and taking the strips of pingao or kiekie, crosswork the half-round sticks to the backboard. As the strands worked to and fro, so did our stories, what we had in our hearts and minds. We sang to and fro, latticing down and along the strips of black, red, white and gold, which had become the strands of life and self. (144)

The linkage between carving, tukutuku, and storytelling, between books and the wharenui, encourages us to understand the novel as analogous to these other arts. As is the case with *The Matriarch, Potiki* recapitulates the origin stories of Maori cosmology, and the characterization, structure, and language are all shaped not only by recent historical events but by creation myths and genealogy. Like the wharenui, *Potiki* is not simply a "story" but also a "history, . . . a study, . . . and a taonga."

How does the figuring of the novel as wharenui position us as readers? As with *The Matriarch,* one recognizes an immediate complication in the novel's address. For *tauiwi,* or strangers, the novel provides an educational introduction to crucial aspects of Maori life, past and present. Sometimes implicitly (as in Roimata's meditation on the way in which the original sibling hostilities of the gods still inform human conduct) and sometimes explicitly—as in the explanations of the role of the wharenui cited above—the novel welcomes and informs cultural outsiders as *manuhiri,* or guests, directly communicating central aspects of its characters' lives.

The novel's considered deliberation in regard to the portrayal of cultural outsiders is evident in the delicacy with which the Maori-Pakeha divide itself is figured. The narrative mostly eschews both terms, and in so doing reinforces the sense of the fictional space as simultaneously Maori and general: for this is a "Maori" world in the original sense of the term as ordinary or usual. (Although the word "Maori" now refers to the indigenous people of Aotearoa as a whole, that is a postcontact usage. Before contact with the West created a settler-indigenous binarism, people defined themselves primarily in terms of a tribal affiliation, not in a manner that collectivized them "racially.") Threats to this world are presented as motivated by greed masquerading as an ideology of progress, and are resisted not only by the Tamihanas and other iwi, but also by "those not of our race."

However, while the novel is interpretable by tauiwi, its status for those who recognize their own selves, lives, and stories within it—those who are quite clearly its principal audience—is different. Here too, the address is complex. If the wharenui is traditionally the embodiment of the history and future of a particular people, sited on ancestral land, novels seem to stand in some contrast, given that they are individually produced commodities, free-floating movable property. But while *Potiki* can be consumed as an exotic pleasure, a whole range of other reading positions remain. The novel might be seen as the meetinghouse of an urban *marae,* or tribal center, offering a welcome to those who have left, or have lost touch with, their iwi and *turangawaewae*—the latter being the place where you stand and are at home. The text thus provides resources to those Maori at the hard end of the colonial process: urbanized, proletarianized, or with an eviscerated relation to traditional cultural practices. Further, while *Potiki* can be read as hospitable, extending an invitation to strangers, including those "not of our race," who feel welcomed as manuhiri, it is also important to register the effect of the novel's vision of future cataclysmic social conflict. Roimata's meditations on the reenactment of the struggles of the gods in her children's play suggest that such conflict is an inescapable part of the human condition, but it seems equally clear that the coming conflagration will be between the tangata whenua and the shadowy forces of "progress"—the Pakeha. As is the case in visiting a wharenui, the warmth of the welcome and the beauty of its decoration do not disguise the formidable power of the figures who line the walls of the house.

Thinking of novels as haka or wharenui may seem to run the risk of archaizing anthropologization—but only if one thinks of such cultural forms as themselves moribund, an impossibility now for Pakeha as much as for Maori. Thinking of novels as haka or wharenui does problematize interpretation—for Pakeha if not for Maori—but an incitement to discourse and interlocution remains implicit in the positioning such metaphors suggest. Maori protocol enjoins the visitor to respect the *kawa,* or custom, of one's hosts. If Pakeha critics want to step into the Maori house of fiction, we will have to learn to respond to the resulting challenges to our identity, our history, and our reading practices in dialogic terms, as participants in korero. This is a prospect for Pakeha as exhilarating as it is . . . unsettling.

Notes

I would like to express my gratitude to Witi Ihimaera for his patience and generosity in discussing his work.

1. See Mereta Mita (1984) for an argument that only novels written in the Maori language can be defined as "Maori literature."
2. One notable exception to this is Peter Beatson, whose *The Healing Tongue* (1989) was one of only two entries in the New Zealand National Library's subject catalogue under "Maori Literature in English."
3. For a useful discussion of this issue, see Lamb 1986.
4. C. K. Stead is the critic most unabashed about invoking European criteria to assess Maori writing, as in his discussion of the inclusion of translations of Maori poetry in an anthology of New Zealand verse (Stead 1985). One of the most careful commentators on Witi Ihimaera's work has been Trevor James—based in Australia—who has provided a series of close readings of Ihimaera's novels that explore traditional categories such as theme, imagery, structure, characterization, and temporality through reference to Maori cosmology and social, political, and cultural practice (James 1988). While James's work is most helpful to those unfamiliar with Maori culture, it does have the effect of translating the novels into comprehensible European terms, a process Eric Cheyfitz (1991) regards as useful only to Westerners. The only monograph on a Maori writer to appear to date has been written, interestingly, by a Nigerian (Ojinmah 1993).
5. Christine Prentice (1991, 1993) is the strongest advocate of this view.
6. For background on the Treaty of Waitanga, see Kawharu 1989.
7. For the best recent overview, see Sturm 1991.
8. Probably the best known of these disputes occurred in the pages of *Metro* magazine. A (Pakeha) historian who has written extensively on Maori, Michael King, accused Stead of advocating "the ethnic cleansing of New Zealand literature"—a phrase that was withdrawn after a threat of legal action (King 1993). King focused on Stead's attack on the inclusion of translations of Maori oral poetry in *The Penguin Book of New Zealand Verse* (1985). Another controversy erupted over Stead's editorship of a Faber anthology of short stories from the Pacific when five prominent Maori and Polynesian writers withdrew from the

project on the grounds that Stead lacked the *mana,* or prestige, to edit a representative collection of this kind.

9. See for example Bhabha 1990b.

10. In a review article about *The Matriarch,* Ihimaera is quoted as saying that "if I am writing for Pakeha as well as Maori then I am acknowledging that our history is a shared one" (Young 1986).

11. For another, useful discussion of novelistic treatments of this episode by both Maori and Pakeha writers, see Dowling 1989.

12. It is worth noting that—as Henderson's schema might suggest—*The Matriarch* did divide readers along gender lines. Ihimaera is emphatic that it is a "woman's haka," but objections were made to the matriarch's characterization by Maori women critics such as Atareta Poananga (1986, 1987).

13. See for example Ranginui Walker's comments in *Metro* (1994, 134–35).

14. Tukutuku is an elaborate form of paneling. See Miniata 1967.

Lisa Lowe

3 Decolonization, Displacement, Disidentification

Asian American "Novels" and the Question of History

To articulate the past historically does not mean to recognize it "the way it really was" (Ranke). It means to seize hold of a memory as it flashes up at a moment of danger. —Walter Benjamin, "Theses on the Philosophy of History"

Frantz Fanon directs our attention, in *Black Skin, White Masks* (1967), to the importance of language as the medium through which a colonizing culture forms the colonized subject: "To speak means to be in a position to use a certain syntax, to grasp the morphology of this or that language, but it means above all to assume a culture, to support the weight of a civilization" (17–18). In alluding to the paradoxical fluency of the colonized subject in the colonial language and culture, Fanon astutely names the twofold character of colonial formation. The imposition of the colonial language and its cultural institutions, such as the novel, demands the subject's internalization of the "superiority" of the colonizer and the "inferiority" of the colonized, even as it attempts to evacuate the subject of "native" language, traditions, and practices. Yet the colonized subject produced within such an encounter does not merely bear the marks of the coercive encounter between the dominant language and culture, constructed as whole, autonomous and disinterested, and the specificities of the colonized group's existence. Such encounters produce contradictory subjects, in whom the demands for fluency in imperial languages and empire's cultural institutions simultaneously provide the grounds for antagonism to those demands.

In this essay I will be extending Fanon's analysis of the role of colonial narratives to modes of cultural imperialism that cross national boundaries, are in excess of a single nation-state formation, and are complicated by displacement and immigration. I will be considering literary countertexts as sites in which such imperialist modes are thematized, disorganized, and ultimately, critically resituated in relation to alternative cultural forms. Through discussions of "novels" written by "Asian Americans" in English, this essay considers the novel as a cultural institution that regulates formation of citizenship and the nation, that genders the domains of "public" and "private" activities, that prescribes the spatialization of race relations, and, most of all, that determines possible contours and terrains for the narration of "history." In other words, the cultural institution of the novel legitimates particular forms and subjects of history; it subjugates or erases others. In this regard, I observe the institutional and formal continuities between the novel and historical narrative.

With the emergence of print culture as an institution of modernity in the "West," the Anglo-European and U.S. American novel has held a position of primary importance in the interpellation of readers as subjects for the nation, in the gendering of these subjects, and in the racializing of spheres of activity and work. Franco Moretti (1987) has analyzed the *bildungsroman* as the primary form for narrating the development of the individual from youthful innocence to civilized maturity, the telos of which is the reconciliation of the individual with the bourgeois social order. For Benedict Anderson (1983), the novel as a form of print culture constitutes a privileged site for the unification of the citizen to the "imagined community" of the nation. Likewise, David Lloyd (1987) has argued that the national literary canon functions to unify aesthetic culture as a domain in which material differences are resolved and reconciled; the *bildungsroman* has a special status among the works selected for a canon, for it elicits the reader's identification with the *bildung* narrative of ethical formation, itself a narrative of the individual's relinquishing of particularity and difference through identification with an idealized "national" form of subjectivity.[1]

We can view Austen's *Pride and Prejudice* (1813), for example, as an important artifact and producer of nineteenth-century English discourses on middle-class morality and propriety, of women's domestic role within the ideology of separate "public" and "private" spheres, and of the reconciliation of bourgeois individualism and the social order through the marriage contract. Yet as a result of the institutionalization of the novel in England as well as in the British empire's systems of colonial education, the powerfully determining divisions and narrative resolutions of Austen's novel extend well beyond her nineteenth-century English public to the globalized readers and recipients of popular culture in the late twentieth century. In reckoning with that legacy, we might think of the ways in which the orthodoxy of domestic womanhood emerges as a ruling category and terrain of contestation in postcolonial Anglophone novels. Buchi Emecheta's novel *The Joys of Motherhood* (1979), for example, portrays a Nigerian woman in the 1930s and '40s poignantly caught between "traditional" Ibo definitions of motherhood within the extended family and the "modern" capitalist gender relations prescribing female domesticity within the nuclear family imposed by the colonial British state. The description of colonial education in Jamaica in Michelle Cliff's *Abeng* (1984) also offers an apt allegory for the widespread communication of English "civility."[2] Just as the Jamaican schoolgirls of *Abeng* are required to recite William Wordworth's poem "Daffodils," so they are disciplined to conform to received notions of proper middle-class English "femininity." "No doubt the same manuals were shipped to villages in Nigeria, schools in Hong Kong . . . Probably there were a million children who could recite 'Daffodils,' and a million who had never actually seen the flower, only the drawing, and so did not know why the poet had been stunned" (85). Though the resolutions narrated in Austen's *bildungsroman* were by no means uniform and complete in her own time—there were certainly growing contradictions between the notion of separate spheres and nineteenth-century social practices, between her narrative of class reconciliation through sentimental marriage and the turmoil of the period that E. P. Thompson described in the *Making of the English Working Class*—I would argue that in the institutionalization of the English novel in the British colonies, there was an even greater contradiction between the values and norms of the colonizing culture and the bifurcated, unequal colonial society that the colonial education functioned to sustain and reproduce.[3] And the cultural and political identifications of the United States with Britain ensured that the bourgeois English formation detailed in Austen's novels has been disseminated with a scope almost equivalent to that of television reception. Just as the English novel was a central cultural institution in British colonial education and contributed to the formation of subjects in the British colonies of India, Nigeria, and Jamaica, so, too, did the American novel from *The Scarlet Letter* to *The Sound and the Fury* exercise its formidable authority on the literary and cultural traditions of African Americans, Chicanos/Latinos, and Asian Americans in the United States. I do not intend to imply an always oppositional relationship between an imperial metropolitan culture and its subordinated others, nor am I claiming that the Anglophone writing by colonized or minoritized groups in every case transgresses the imperatives of the English or American novel. Rather, let us emphasize that owing to complex, uneven material histories of colonization and the oppression of racialized groups within the United States, the sites of minority or colonized literary production are at different distances from the canonical nationalist project of reconciling constituencies to idealized forms of community and subjectivity. As I have argued elsewhere, the structural location of U.S. minority literature may produce effects of dissonance, fragmentation, and irresolution even, and especially, when that literature appears to be performing a canonical function.[4] Even those novels which can be said to conform more closely to the formal criteria of the *bildungsroman* express a remarkable contradiction between the demand for a univocal developmental narrative and the historical specificities of racialization, ghettoization, violence, and labor exploitation. The kind and degree of contradiction between those historical specificities and the national narrative served by the cultural institution of the novel generates formal deviations whose significances are misread if simply assimilated as modernist or postmodernist aesthetic modes. The effects of these works are more radically grasped in terms of their constant interrogation of the discrepancies between canonical historical narratives and what Walter Benjamin would term the material "catastrophes" those histories obscure.

In the discussions that follow, I examine three contemporary Asian American texts that interrupt the traditional functions of the novel as a medium for narrating the development of the individual and its reconciliation to the social order, as a site of interpellation for the citizen-subject of the nation, and as a work that enacts the separation of autonomous aesthetic culture from material stratification and gender and racialized differences. These texts challenge the concepts of identity and identification produced within a universalized narrative of development. They skew the relationship of the citizen-subject to the nation by interrogating the constructions of both "Asian" and "American." The discussion of these Asian American texts begins with the observation of the rhetorical and institutional congruence between U.S. historical narratives about Asia and Asian Americans on the one hand and the institution of the Anglophone novel on the other. The Orientalist histories take up the realist aesthetic that governs representation in the novel, and they borrow the formal devices of the novel as a means of situating Asia and narrating the incorporation of Asian immigrants into the U.S. American nation. In contrast, the "novels" by Asian immigrant and Asian American women explore other modes of telling, revealing, and spatializing history. In meditating on the notion of blood as ground and figure of representation in Theresa Hak Kyung Cha's *Dictée* (1982), on *tsismis* (gossip) as an antifiguration of narrative in Jessica Hagedorn's *Dogeaters* (1990), and on the excavation of urban space in Fae Myenne Ng's *Bone* (1993) as a disruption of temporalization as the novel's privileged mode, I trace how these Asian American novels displace the representational regimes of the institutionalized novel by writing out of the limits and breakdowns of those regimes.

I

> The concept of the historical progress of mankind cannot be sundered from the concept of its progression through a homogeneous, empty time. A critique of the concept of such a progression must be the basis of any criticism of the concept of progress itself.
> —Walter Benjamin, "Theses on the Philosophy of History"

Throughout the twentieth century U.S. Orientalism has been determined by several differentiated but interconnected apparatuses of rule. Orientalism was deployed to justify the use of brutal military force in the colonization of the Philippines, the war against Japan in 1941–45, culminating in the nuclear bombing of Hiroshima and Nagasaki, the war in and partition of Korea (1950–53), and the war in Vietnam (1954–75). Orientalism also bears a crucial relationship to the history of Asian immigration, exclusion, and naturalization. Immigration Exclusion Acts in 1882, 1917, and 1924 barred entry to the United States to Chinese, Japanese, and Koreans, and, though the Magnuson Act of 1943 repealed Chinese exclusions, the exclusion of other Asians continued. While the McCarran-Walters Act of 1952 established quotas of one hundred for each country within the Asia-Pacific triangle, it also specifically screened for "subversives" and allowed deportation of immigrants with Communist affiliations (Takaki 1989). Immigration and naturalization laws have thus been not only means of policing the terms of the "citizen" and the nation-state but part of an Orientalist discourse that defines Asians as "foreign" in times when the United States has constructed itself as ideologically at war with Asia (Gotanda 1995).

The crisis of U.S. national identity during the period of war in Asia, coupled with the imperatives of racializing and proletarianizing the Asian populations immigrating to the United States from a variety of national origins, has necessitated a complex and variegated discourse for managing "oriental otherness." A racialized and gendered anti-Asian discourse produces and manages a "double front" of Asian threat and encroachment: on the one hand, as external rivals in overseas imperial war and global economy, and on the other, as a needed labor force for the domestic economy. The "blood-will-tell" anti-Japanese racial discourse during World War II, propaganda about the traitorous Asian as subhuman, and the extensive conflation of Asian women with accessible "foreign" territories to be conquered and subdued are all parts of a mid-century U.S. Orientalism tailored to homogenize and subordinate both internal and external Asian populations (Dower 1989). World War II inaugurated an acute figuration of the Asian as racial enemy; and, throughout the postwar period until 1970, war films and popular novels as well as "official" historical narratives deployed this discourse for the purpose of unifying national identity, justifying the cold war, and assisting the expansion of the domestic American market (Browne 1992).

In the post-cold-war period, though the traditional anti-Asian figurations persist, the emergence in Asia of formidable capitalist rivals has also given rise to a discourse of economic penetration and trade with those overseas nations that the United States had previously caricatured as enemies. In the meantime the abolition of national origin quotas in 1965, allowing for 170,000 immigrants annually from the Eastern Hemisphere, has enormously changed the profile of "Asian Americans," rendering the majority of the constituency Asian-born rather than multiple-generation: the new immigrants from South Vietnam, South Korea, Cambodia, Laos, the Philippines, India, and Pakistan have diversified the already existing Asian American group of Chinese, Japanese, and Filipino descent. "Multiculturalism," leveling the important differences and contradictions within and among racial and ethnic minority groups, has since emerged as a discourse that seeks to integrate Asian immigrant workers into the domestic capitalist economy. And, finally, as U.S. capitalism shifts production to the Third World, making use, in low-cost export assembly and manufacturing zones, of Southeast Asian and Latin American female labor in particular, the proletarianization of nonwhite women has led to a breakdown and a reformulation of the categories and the relations of national, racial, and gender difference that were characteristic of the earlier, more nationalist-inspired Orientalism.

This contemporary shift toward the transnationalization of capital is not exclusively manifested in the "denationalization" of corporate power; more important, it is also expressed in the reorganization of oppositional movements and constituencies against capital that articulate themselves in terms and relations other than the "national," notably movements of U.S. women of color and Third World women (Sandoval 1991; Mohanty 1991a).[5] Thus an important dimension of my discussion is to urge consideration of Asian immigrants, with specific attention to Asian immigrant women, as a group emerging out of colonialism and neoimperialism in Asia as well as immigrant displacement to the United States. Asian immigrants are determined at once by the histories of Western expansionism in Asia *and* by the racialization of working populations of color in the United States.[6] Especially in light of post-1965 Asian immigrations to the United States, "Asian American" subjectivity is a complex site of different displacements, among which figures prominently the displacement from a decolonizing or neocolonized Asian society to a United States with whose sense of national identity the immigrants are often in contradiction. Once Asians have arrived in the United States, the demand that they insert themselves into liberal capitalist discourses of development, assimilation, and citizenship provides the grounds for antagonism to such demands. The imperatives that the subject identify —as national, classed, and gendered subject—arise within the materially differentiated conditions of racialized workers of color that simultaneously produce *disidentifications* out of which critical subjectivities may emerge. Disidentification expresses a space in which alienations, in both the cultural and economic senses, can be rearticulated in politically oppositional forms. But disidentification does not entail the formation of even oppositional identities against the call to identification with the national state. On the contrary, it allows for the exploration of alternative political and cultural subjectivities that emerge within the continuing effects of displacement. The discussions that follow explore three recent Asian American "novels" that produce alternative "histories" out of the conditions of decolonization, displacement, and disidentification.

Western theorists of modernity and postmodernity, as well as postcolonial intellectuals, Subaltern Studies historians, and feminist critics of colonialism, have articulated critiques of the realist aesthetic as a regime for the production of history. In studies of the rhetoric and tropology of nineteenth-century historical narratives, Hayden White (1973) and Dominick LaCapra (1985) target verisimilitude, development, and teleology as fundamental to European history's truth effects; for Jean-François Lyotard, famously, the postmodern moment is one witnessing the breakdown of such master narratives of dominant culture and aesthetics (1984). That Western historiography itself establishes the congruence of historical narratives with a realist representational project suggests that this aesthetic constitutes not only the historiographical means through which empires narrated their own progress, not only the aesthetic imperial subjects used to represent colonies as peripheral objects, but also the aesthetic they imposed upon their colonies and within which they demanded those colonies narrate themselves. Accordingly, critiques of Orientalism have linked the aesthetic interrogation of the project of representation to the historiographical critique of narrative as an apparatus of European colonial rule (Said 1978). Postcolonial theorists have written about the way in which colonial powers imposed modes of historical representation on the colonized (Prakash 1990; Chakrabarty 1992) and have analyzed the violence done to, but failed containment of, the colonized within the modes of literary representation (Niranjana 1992b; Lloyd 1993). Radical historians of India and the Philippines have argued that both official colonialist histories and the elite nationalist histories they have implicated and engendered have favored the narrative structure of progressive development of a unified subject and people, a structure that has subjugated the fragmented, decentralized activities of mass uprisings, peasant revolts, and laborer rebellions (Guha 1988; Pandey 1988a, 1988b; Ileto 1988). Feminist theorists have further challenged Orientalist historiography by interrogating narrative histories as technologies of patriarchal rule (Sangari and Vaid 1990; Mohanty 1991a): their insistence that all aspects of colonial society are gendered has provided a basis for moving the critique of Orientalism beyond a privileging or universalizing of the colonized subject—male or female—as a means of decentering Orientalist history.

In this sense, the authority of Orientalist narrative falters on a number of frontiers; yet quite evidently, the documentations of its failure take place differently, depending on the locations and contexts of their production.[7] While U.S. Orientalism makes use of the representational and narrative regimes of an earlier Orientalism that expressed the European empires' desire to institutionalize colonialism elsewhere, it has also been transformed by a different state formation, and by the global and national contexts of U.S. expansion in Asia. Keeping this in mind, it is useful to consider how U.S. historical accounts of Asia take up the formal features of the aesthetic governing the novel.

In Eric Goldman's *The Crucial Decade—And After: America, 1945–1960,* the commencement of the Korean War lies in a conversation between Truman and the State Department. Goldman writes:

> The American government had long known that Korea was a trouble spot.... In the spring of 1950, the American Central Intelligence Agency was reporting that the North Koreans were continuing to build up their military machine with Soviet assistance and might launch a full-scale offensive. (1960, 148)

> Harry Truman had heard enough. He told Acheson that he would order his plane, the *Independence,* readied immediately and asked the Secretary of State to get together with the military chiefs and prepare recommendations.... Bess Truman waved good-by to her husband with a look very much like the one she had on that eerie evening when Vice-President Truman suddenly became President Truman. Margaret stood a bit apart from the airport crowd, staring at the plane with her hands clasped under her chin as if in silent prayer. (152)

> The very nature of the Presidential decisions disarmed critics of the Truman-Acheson foreign policy.... They put their faith, above all, in General Douglas MacArthur. It was at the General's recommendation—and this fact was generally known—that full intervention had been decided upon, and Douglas MacArthur was in command in Korea. (172)

> For one moment, suspended weirdly in the bitter debates,... the reckless plunge of the North Korean Communists and the bold response of Harry Truman had united America. (173)

In Goldman's narrative, history is developmental. A succession of events leads up to a crisis, and then the crisis is resolved. History is made by elite heroes (the president and secretary of state), whose foes are U.S. public opinion and intragovernmental relations, and the drama is played out before Bess and Margaret, a loyal feminine spectatorship. The narrative structure implies that Korean leaders and mass groups are merely a passive, perhaps colorful backdrop for the drama of the central noble protagonist, President Truman. The dynamics of Korean nationalism in its relationship to the Japanese occupation, the generational and political schisms within Korean nationalism that were expressed in the division of North and South Korea, as well as the larger scope of U.S. involvement in Asia before 1950—all are erased or obscured by the central drama of the U.S. government's decision to send General MacArthur into South Korea.

The account of Korea offered by James Thomson, Peter Stanley, and John Curtis Perry's *Sentimental Imperialists: The American Experience in East Asia* (1981) also elucidates features of U.S. Orientalist narrative:

> Korea's tragedy has been that the nation is alone, precariously situated between the major cultures of China and Japan, with no neighbors comparably small or weak. . . .
>
> With one language, one ethnic group, and one society, Korea is one of the world's oldest and most homogeneous nation-states, stubbornly retaining its distinct cultural identity despite periodic invasions and recurring waves of foreign influence. Perhaps this cultural tenacity is in part due to the challenge posed by the outside world. (236)

"Korea" is here posited as a fixed, static victim, without differentiation from itself. Unlike the West, which possesses self-consciousness and can know itself through the universal reason of its own histories, "Korea" is fundamentally unphilosophical and atavistic. Thomson, Stanley, and Perry narrate the history of Korea as tragic; their narrative exemplifies the paternalism that figures the West as the father and Asian nations as backward children in need of emancipation. It positions Korea with reference to a West-Other axis, obscuring the relations between Korea and other Asian peoples and suppressing any recognition of Korea as internally complex: as a country of differently classed and propertied populations, men and women, many religions, official and unofficial nationalisms.

The larger project of *Sentimental Imperialists* reiterates the narrative form and function of the *bildungsroman;* it documents the history of imperialist war in Asia as a story of the progress of the United States from youthful "innocence and grandiosity" through the "dashing of hopes" to the maturity of a nation seasoned by the trials of war in Asia. It narrates the national reconciliation of a United States made wiser by the errors of having entered into difficult and not always victorious wars, "educated" by the lessons of anti-Communism and imperialism. Fundamentally, it exemplifies a narrative of nationalist unification, celebrating the triumph of liberal tolerance and a magnanimous state that protects and incorporates immigrants.

We have observed that this link between historical narratives of the United States as a nation and novelistic narratives of the individual is mediated by adherence to a realist aesthetic, a fetishized concept of development, and the narration of a single unified subject. Having mentioned already the Euro-American poststructuralist or "postmodern" critique of the congruence of historical narrative and the novel (White, La Capra, and Lyotard), we must differentiate such "Western" challenges to representation from the "decolonizing" writing that emerges from Third World, diaspora, and racialized U.S. American sites. In *The Wretched of the Earth* (1968), Frantz Fanon defines decolonization as a process of thorough social transformation that disorganizes the stratified social hierarchy beyond the nationalist party's capture of the state from the colonizer. Decolonization, in Fanon's sense, does not prematurely signify the end of colonialism but refers rather to the multifaceted project of resistance struggles that can go on for decades in the midst of simultaneous neocolonial exploitation. Associating bourgeois nationalism and the colonial state's structures of domination, Fanon designates decolonization as a third alternative to colonialism and nationalism, an ongoing project exhausted neither by the political narrative of constitutional representation promoted by the state nor by the notion of a nationalist aesthetic that posits national culture and the representative work as sites of resolution. Decolonization can be defined as necessarily antagonistic to existing institutions of representation, aesthetic and literary, as well as constitutional or political. We can therefore read Asian American writing as emerging out of decolonization in this sense. Euro-American postmodernism dissolves the notion of a homogeneous "West" as it has been constructed within Enlightenment literary and philosophical categories; like poststructuralism, it contests the "modern" within European terms, and reveals the difference internal to the making of the "West."[8] In contradistinction, "decolonizing" writing, which may include features associated with postmodernism (such as nonlinear, antirepresentational aesthetics), emerges not from a terrain of philosophical or poetic otherness within the West but out of the contradictions of what Bipan Chandra (1980) has called the "colonial mode of production."[9] Whereas the relations of production of nineteenth-century industrial capitalism were characterized by the management of the urban workers by the urban bourgeoisie, colonialism was built on the split between colonial metropolis and agrarian colony, organizing the agrarian society into a social formation in which a foreign class functioned as the capitalist class. In order to maximize the extraction of surplus, the necessary reproduction of the relations of production in a colonial mode of production was not limited to the reproduction of class relations but emphasized the reproduction of hierarchical relations of region, culture, language, and, most particularly, race as well. "Decolonization," then, is the social formation that encompasses a multileveled and multicentered assault on those specific forms of colonial rule; that project of decolonization is carried forth in the "postcolonial" site as well as by immigrant and diasporic populations.

In other words, if we understand "decolonization" as an ongoing disruption of the colonial mode of production, then Asian American writing participates in that disruption from a location already marked by the uneven and unsynthetic encounters of colonial, neocolonial, and mass and elite indigenous cultures that characterize decolonization. These material pressures produce texts that resist the formal abstraction of aestheticization that is a legacy of European modernism and a continuing feature of European postmodernism. In this sense, the writing of the "decolonizing novel" takes place necessarily by way of a detour into the excavation of "history," as we will see in Theresa Hak Kyung Cha's *Dictée.*

2

> . . . the angel of history. His face is turned toward the past. Where we perceive a chain of events, he sees one single catastrophe which keeps piling wreckage upon wreckage and hurls it in front of his feet.
> —Walter Benjamin, "Theses on the Philosophy of History"

In Theresa Hak Kyung Cha's 1982 Korean American text, there is no full narrative account of the Japanese occupation of Korea from 1910 to 1945, no linear history of the brutal suppressions of a resistant Korean nationalist movement that originated in the Tonghak Rebellion of 1884–95 and flowered in the March First movement of 1919.[10] There are no emancipationist narratives of the Korean War of 1950 and the partition of Korea in 1953, or of the exodus of Koreans and their dislocations in the United States, on the one hand, and no explicit narrative history of the U.S. neocolonial role in the military dictatorship and the development of state capitalism in South Korea, on the other. Rather, *Dictée* juxtaposes a series of episodes, scenes, and evocative fragments, including an account of a period of Korean nationalism during the Japanese colonial occupation, a description of the adult narrator's displaced situation as a Korean American immigrant, and a memory of the narrator's return to a military-ruled South Korea after the Korean War.[11]

Making use of fractured memory, poems, and dreamlike impressions, *Dictée* resists the core values of aesthetic realism. Rather than constructing a narrative of unities and symmetries, with consistencies of character and plot, it emphasizes fragmented recitation and nonidentity. Repetition is taken to its parodic extreme and disengaged as the privileged mode of mimesis and realism. *Dictée*'s unfaithful relationship to realism resonates with critiques both of the traditional novel and of official historical accounts.

Images of blood—spilling from the open wound, staining the pavement as a crowd is assaulted by troops, seeping from students caught and beaten—punctuate the episodes in *Dictée.* Descriptions of blood hemorrhaging, emptying, and flowing, erupt in a text that refuses continuous narration of the wars, insurgencies, containments, and violences that are central to both U.S. neocolonial and South Korean nationalist accounts of the Korean people during this century. Allusions to splitting, breaking, and dividing—of tongue, body, family, and nation—pervade *Dictée.* One scene in particular, depicting the splitting and severing of the represented body in relation to representation and narrative technique, alludes to the military suppression of the 19 April people's revolt of 1960, and, in this scene, blood becomes the ground of representation as well as the figure of erasure.

I feel the tightening of the crowd body to body. . . . The air is made visible with smoke it grows spreads without control we are hidden inside the whiteness the greyness reduced to parts, reduced to separation. Inside an arm lifts above the head in deliberate gesture and disappears into the thick white from which slowly the legs of another bent at the knee hit the ground the entire body on its left side. *The stinging, it slices the air it enters* thus I lose direction the sky is a haze running the streets emptied I fell no one saw me I walk. Anywhere. In tears the air stagnant continues to sting I am crying the sky remnant the gas smoke absorbed the sky I am crying. The streets covered with chipped bricks and debris. Because. I see the frequent pairs of shoes thrown sometimes a single pair among the rocks they had carried. Because. I cry wail torn shirt lying I step among them. No trace of them. *Except for the blood. Because. Step among them the blood that will not erase with the rain on the pavement that was walked upon like the stones where they fell had fallen. Because. Remain dark the stain not wash away. Because. I follow the crying crowd their voices among them their singing their voices unceasing the empty street.* (Cha 1982, 81–82; my emphases)

This passage dramatically disrupts not only syntax but also the grammars of predication and causality fundamental to the novel and history: both presuppose closure (telos) and character (subject of development). Just as the passage portrays bodies that are wounded and separated, so too is syntax interrupted and truncated. There is a conspicuous absence of purposive narrative context, and no explanation for either the disrupted syntax or the fragmented bodies; there is only blood, as if blood, which issues from the breaking of both syntax and limbs, were the only language that emerges out of the violence of grammar. Blood is not merely the representation of violence but the trace whose stain, whose flow, whose indelibility is the measure of what cannot be represented, is the index of the violence of historical representation itself. A subversion of predication occurs in the repeated separations of subjects from modifiers, and the repeated dislocations of subject and predicate, as in "The stinging, it slices the air it enters," in which it is an unnamed firing that is the subject of "slices" and "enters" and that presumably results in "the stinging." Predication and causality are disrupted as well by the temporal inversion through which the stinging precedes the slicing and entering.

"Because," the conjunction conventionally used to express cause or reason, has a peculiar status in this passage. "Because" usually precedes a logical sequence or inference, indicating an unequivocal causal relationship, but here, the four repetitions of the conjunction defy this grammar and are followed by blood staining the pavement. In this sense, not only does the inverted grammar (splitting—"because"—blood) register the failure of temporal narrative, but the repetitions of "because" followed by blood ("that will not erase with rain") assault causality as a trope of official history. They interrogate predication as one among several discursive orthodoxies for producing historical truth, and ultimately target the violent regimes of official representation and narrative themselves: both the U.S. narrative of Korean emancipation from Japanese colonialism by U.S. intervention on the one hand and an official South Korean narrative about the rise of Korean nationalism and its role in the modernization of society and the capitalist economy on the other (Choi 1993).

We have in this passage from *Dictée* a conception of history that treats the "historical" not as a continuous narrative of progress, maturity, and increasing rationality, not as a story of great moments and individuals, but as a surplus of materiality that exceeds textualization, that renders inoperable the vocabularies and grammars of nineteenth-century post-Enlightenment narrative with its belief in the individual, reason, and the linear evolution of civilization. The materiality of history is, in this passage, what will not be ordered, what does not coagulate and cohere. This materiality does not become accessible with a mere change of perspective, or even a shift to another narrative; it is not exclusively a question of creating more "accurate" narratives. Rather, "history" becomes "visible" not in its narrative representation but in its defiance of the dominant regimes of representability. Like the blood that is itself not a "fixed" material but materiality's belated sign, it spreads, skews, seeps, and will not cohere into the developmental progress that narrative history and the novel demand.

Dictée's treatment of the relationship of a mobile, nonunivocal narrating subject to official events suggests that narrative accounts giving priority to elite groups against a backdrop of the institutions of government, political assembly, the military are partial and obfuscating. It dramatizes the fact that the investigation of nonelite, popular activity requires not only a deviation from the well-documented, official account but also a transformation of historical understanding and a revaluation of what is considered to be significant. Such an investigation demands that we become literate in what may appear, through the lens of traditional representation, to be only confused, random, or violent incidents. Rather than provoking cynicism about the possibility of writing history, the challenge to representation signals the need for alternative projects of many kinds and suggests that the writing of *different* histories—of nonelites, of insurgencies, of women, from the "bottom up"—inevitably runs up against representation and linear narrative as problematic categories. In this respect, texts like *Dictée* provide an opportunity to reflect on the possibility of alternative modes for historical retrieval and recollection, at the very level of the form in which they are written and conceived.[12]

3

> The tradition of the oppressed teaches us that the "state of emergency" in which we live is not the exception but the rule.
> —Walter Benjamin, "Theses on the Philosophy of History"

Jessica Hagedorn's 1990 *Dogeaters* is a Filipina American text that also radically alters the form and function of the novel and of historical narrative through explorations of alternative means for representing the history of "the popular." Like *Dictée,* it poses institutions of "official" historical representation against a notion of history as fragments and against the telling of history as a process of partial, imperfect recollection. *Dogeaters* thematizes the displacement of an Asian immigrant/Asian American narrator who "remembers" the Marcos era. It foregrounds the connections and discontinuities between her diasporic location and the Filipino nationalism that emerges as a consequence of and a challenge to Spanish colonialism (sixteenth century–1896), U.S. colonialism (1902–World War II), and neocolonial martial law (1954–1972). The Filipina American character Rio's national identifications with the United States and with the Philippines are each thematized, and yet disrupted, by her temporal and geographical dislocation.[13] Rio's "recollections," from her standpoint as an immigrant to the United States, both mediate and defamiliarize the "homeland"; at the same time, the "Asian American" writing of a culturally heterogeneous and class-stratified Manila of her past grounds Rio in a multivalent collective memory that diverges repeatedly from the voice of the subject interpellated within a single national discourse. The collage structure of the text also interrupts the development of a national subject: *Dogeaters* places together discontinuous, simultaneous first- and third-person narratives about characters as different as a general, a senator's daughter, movie actors, a mixed race "callboy," *bakla* transvestite hairdressers, and a department store salesgirl. An episodic multiperspectivism replaces character development; melodrama and pastiche parody realism. The integrity of "official" historical representations—such as an 1898 address by President William McKinley justifying his decision to invade the Philippines, news articles from the Associated Press, or an 1846 history of the Philippines by Jean Mallat—is subverted by the fragmented citation of these documents, and by the "popular" genres of text to which the cited documents are juxtaposed: transcripts from a radio melodrama entitled *Love Letters*, scenes from Douglas Sirk's "All That Heaven Allows" and other Hollywood films, quotations from advertising, or bits of talk show or tabloid gossip.

In discussing *Dogeaters*, I wish to focus on the role of gossip as a popular discourse that interrupts and displaces official representational regimes. Extravagant and unregulated, gossip functions as an "unofficial" discursive structure—or perhaps we might better characterize it as an antistructure or a destructuring discourse—running distinctly counter to the logic of verisimilitude and the organized subordination of written narrative. Though gossip is unofficial, I do not mean to imply that it occupies a terrain that is separate or discrete from official narratives; rather, gossip is peculiarly parasitic, pillaging from the official, imitating without discrimination, exaggerating, relaying. In this sense, gossip requires that we abandon binary notions of legitimate and illegitimate, discourse and counterdiscourse, or "public" and "private," for it traverses these classifications so as to render such divisions untenable. Rather than mere "postmodern" experimentation, *Dogeaters* disorganizes official history through its multiple performances of gossip, moving from particular citations and instantiations of gossip—*tsismis* (Tagalog for "gossip"), hearsay, anecdote, slander—to gossip's informal sites and institutions—the beauty parlor, the television talk show, the tabloid "Celebrity Pinoy"—to staging gossip as a trope of popular insurgency itself. By "gossip," I do not mean to refer to gossip practices that function as commentaries upon, and primarily "domestic" excursions from, bourgeois propriety, of the sort we find in Austen's *Emma* or George Eliot's *Middlemarch*. Rather I wish to associate "gossip" in *Dogeaters* with the concept of "rumor," as elaborated by Subaltern Studies historians and others, in order to locate it as a public form of popular discourse in colonized societies in which relations of rule force popular modes of social organization (from subcultures to acts of insurgency) into unsanctioned sites and discourses. Historian Vicente Rafael, for example, has elaborated the importance of rumor in the Japanese-occupied Philippines as a popular strategy for "fashioning alternative bases for recounting, and accounting for, [the colonized's] sense of deprivation" (1991, 67). Rafael argues that unlike practices that seek to stabilize social institutions, rumor does not result in "the conservation of the social formation" but rather produces "evanescent communities" (75).[14]

In this regard, we might fruitfully extend Rafael's notion of rumor through the terms offered by historian Reynaldo Ileto in his "Outlines of a Nonlinear Emplotment of Philippine History" (1988). Ileto discusses the relationship between elite linear, developmental history and the popular knowledges, practices, and sites that are subjugated by official accounts. He argues that

> in examining historiography, criminality, epidemics, and popular movements, one has only begun to reflect upon those crucial moments when the state, or the historian, or whoever occupies the site of the dominant centres, performs a cutting operation: remembering/furthering that which it deems meaningful for its concept of development, and forgetting/suppressing the dissonant, disorderly, irrational, archaic, and subversive. (154)

One focus of Ileto's critique is the internalization of European colonialist ideology evidenced in the developmental histories produced by the nineteenth-century Philippine nationalist elites who led the challenge to Spanish rule. He characterizes Teodoro Agoncillo's history of the Philippines as paradigmatic of this nationalist tradition, showing how it relies on the following categories in sequence: a golden age (pre-Hispanic society), the fall (conquest by Spain in the sixteenth century), the dark age (the seventeenth and eighteenth centuries), economic and social development (the nineteenth century), the rise of nationalist consciousness (the post-1872 Katipunan revolt), the birth of the nation (1898), and either suppressed nationalism or democratic tutelage (post-1901, U.S. colonialism). After arguing that nineteenth-century discourses of modernization privileged a small elite and subjugated the knowledges of "others," a second focus of Ileto's work is the assembling of a "counter-history" of the Philippines that gives priority to "irrational," disorderly, "popular" phenomena. A "history" that attends to the popular and regional activities of bandits provides an account of mobile, dispersed insurgency, and of the official modes of regulation erected to police and suppress that insurgency.

"Gossip" in Hagedorn's text responds to Ileto's call for more articulations of a "nonlinear emplotment of Philippine history." By featuring gossip as an element of, and as an organizing principle for, social relations, *Dogeaters* offers scenes, dialogues, and episodes that are not regulated by plot, character, progress, or resolution. Both the gossip it features and the format of the novel itself move by way of a horizontal, or metonymic, contagion rather than through the vertical, or metaphorical, processes of referentiality and signification. Spontaneous, decentered, and multivocal, gossip is antithetical to developmental narrative. It seizes details and hyperbolizes their importance; it defies the notion of information as property. Gossip exemplifies both antinarrative and antirepresentational strategies that dehierarchize linear historical accounts, be they Orientalist and nationalist, with a popular, multiple record of very different kinds of activities and modes of social organization.

Gossip in *Dogeaters* is recognized as having a superior authority and giving greater pleasure than other discourses: "Pucha signals me with her eyebrows, then whispers she'll call me first thing in the morning. We'll go over the night's *tsismis,* the juicy gossip that is the center of our lives. If the laundress Catalina is really the General's mother, then who is Apolinaria Cuevas? Who is the red-haired foreigner's wife *Tito* Severo is fucking?" (66). Yet precisely owing to its popular status, members of the ruling oligarchy are also keenly aware of gossip and rely on it for the information on which they will base their economic and military decisions: "*Tsismis* ebbs and flows. According to a bemused Severo Alacran, richest of all the richest men and therefore privy to most of the General's secrets, the best *tsismis* is always inspired by some fundamental truth" (101). For those pragmatically in need of instruments with which to stay in power, gossip is acknowledged to be a more valuable discourse than a discourse of "truth." Yet defying possession by a single owner, and moving easily across the class boundaries that express the concept of property, gossip is always in circulation, without assignable source and without trajectory or closure. Mobile and promiscuous, it collects significance as it travels from site to site; orality and speed make it "common" and yet difficult to detect or trace.

Gossip often plagiarizes, and in doing so satirizes, official civil institutions: government, marriage, family, the law. Adultery, bastardy, homosexuality, criminality, intoxication, profanity—each corresponds to the tropological structure of gossip, which cites the official and yet is in excess of it; these affinities underline the location of gossip as the terrain of such activities. As it is parasitic upon the details of "private" life, it derides the separation of "public" and "private" spheres, transgressing these separations symbolic of bourgeois order. Since gossip is unwritten, it does not respond to demands for linguistic purity; it deviates from the laws of national languages, as well as from the linguistic separations of "high" proper language and "low" colloquialisms. In *Dogeaters,* gossip combines colloquial English with Tagalog and Spanish slang. This hybrid text circulates in and around Manila, a city that is itself the expression of a Philippines colonized and occupied at different times by Spanish, Japanese, and U.S. powers.

> After dinner we drag ourselves to the adjoining living room for coffee, cigars, and Spanish brandy. "We're out of French cognac, I'm afraid," my mother apologizes. "Excellent, excellent. The French are overrated! Spanish brandy is actually the best in the world," Uncle Augustin says . . . "Johnny Walker Black, on the rocks for me," my cousin Mikey says . . .
>
> "That Johnny Walker is *sprikitik,* boss!" Mikey cracks up . . .
>
> My mother turns to my father. "I don't get it, Freddie. What's the difference between *putok* and *sprikitik?* Don't they both mean fake?"
>
> My father thinks for a moment. "You might say Congressman Abad *sprikitiks* when he plays golf, but General Ledesma rewards his army with cases of *putok* liquor."
>
> *Tita* Florence fans herself with a woven *pye-pye.* "*Dios mio,* Freddie. What are you making *bola-bola* about? . . ."
>
> "The General is from a good family," *Tito* Augustin says to my mother. "Do you remember the Ledesmas from Tarlac?" My mother shakes her head. *Tita* Florence puts down her fan to correct her husband. "Wrong, Augustin, as usual. Nicasio is the outside son of Don Amado Avila and the laundress Catalina. I know because my mother is from the same town as the Avilas— "
>
> My mother's eyes widen. "You mean he's actually Senator Avila's half-brother?"
>
> "And the president's former chauffeur," *Tita* Florence nods triumphantly. (63–64)

The Saturday night talk of the Gonzaga clan exemplifies the many dimensions of gossip. This evening, the talk turns around the distinction between authenticity and inauthenticity—of ancestry, of nationality, of liquor, of sexual fidelity, of the military government—in the liminal space that is indeed the "proper" site of gossip. Yet as Rio's father Freddie differentiates between the uses of the informal Tagalog terms *sprikitik* and *putok,* the distinction between different orders of inauthenticity becomes crucial: on the one hand, acceptable acts of apparition or seeming and, on the other, the unacceptable counterfeit or the "bogus." While *sprikitik* is associated with magic or spiritualism, *putok* connotes illegitimacy and scandal; Freddie's comparison ("Congressman Abad *sprikitiks* when he plays golf, but General Ledesma rewards his army with cases of *putok* liquor") establishes *putok* as a lower order of deception than the "abracadabra" magic of *sprikitik.* Thus the gossip moves from one connotation of *putok* to the next: not only does General Ledesma give *putok* liquor labeled "Dewar's Scotch" or "Johnny Walker" to his soldiers (which "is so terrible, their guts rot and burn"), but the Gonzagas speak of the General as if he himself is a *putok,* an "outside son," a "former chauffeur" "outside" the network of ruling families. Initially, the meditation on two orders of inauthenticity opens up an implicit subtext of the conversation—government power and rule; when the ruling military dictatorship is backed by the U.S. government, the former colonizer of the Philippines from 1902 to World War II, who *sprikitiks* and who is the *putok?* Who has the semblance of the usurper and who the semblance of the usurped? Gossip, as the instrument of the masses, becomes the terrain for the critique of degrees of deception, and for the organization of actions against the apparatuses of rule.

In another turn, the discussion of inauthenticity in relation to birth moves from the particularity of the General's illegitimate birth to the allegorical level of the heterogeneous cultures, languages, and races *in excess of* the legitimate nation provided for by the "birth" of the Philippines in 1898. In a country with 7,100 known islands in which eighty dialects and languages are spoken, and a cultural and racial hybridity that has mixed Spanish, Malayan, Chinese, Arab, Hindu, North American, and others with "native" groups over the course of four centuries, the distinction between the "authentic" and the "inauthentic" (hybridized by the history of colonial and commercial encounters) may be less salient than the turn around different kinds of "seeming," the cultural, racial, and linguistic admixtures that are the contemporary expression of the Philippines. Like the composite, multileveled languages of the conversation, the drinks mentioned in this scene are themselves marked by the history of hybridizing colonial encounters.[15] The reverence for Spanish brandy, the taste for imported Johnny Walker Black, as well as the

TruCola and coffee Hagedorn's characters are drinking—each alludes to different parts of the history of the Philippines: three centuries of Spanish rule, U.S. colonialism and the subsequent penetration of the Philippines by U.S. commodity capitalism, and the emergence of Philippine industries emulating U.S. products.

Daisy Avila, the "demure and solitary" daughter of the high-profile oppositional leader Senator Avila, begins as a dutiful daughter sequestered in the "private" family home and emerges into the alternative "public" sphere as a leader of armed insurgent guerrillas. Her first step toward this transformation takes place just before her twentieth birthday when she is crowned beauty queen of the Philippines. When Daisy denounces the beauty pageant as a farce on Cora Comacho's talk show "Girl Talk," she "becomes a sensation, almost as popular as her father. The rock band Juan Tamad records a song dedicated to her, 'Femme Fatale.' Banned on the radio, the song surfaces on a bootleg label, Generik; it is an instant underground hit. Condemned as NPA [New People's Army] sympathizers, band members are rounded up by plainclothesmen from the President's Special Squadron Urban Warfare Unit" (109). Gossip produces figures around which other social discourses are organized. Daisy is just such a figure, and in this instance, the scandal of Daisy becomes a hub around which discourses of gender and sexuality, as well as discourses of counterinsurgency, revolve.

The representation of Daisy occurs always through forms of gossip—the tabloids report her marriage and divorce to Malcolm Webb, *tsismis* circulates about her pregnancy: "Daisy Avila is pregnant with Tito Alvarez' baby, Daisy Avila is secretly married to the President's only son, Daisy Avila is a junkie" (107). Headlines scream "Fickle Daisy in Hiding!" (111). This construction of "Daisy" reveals the decisively reactionary dimension of gossip, historically a key purveyor of the control and regulation of women's bodies, sexualities, and agency. As *woman*, Daisy is figured as carrier of community, and the gossip about her is concerned with the containment of her sexuality, and with her transgressive movement across "private" and "public" domains as she changes from pious daughter to revolutionary.[16] In this sense, while I focus on gossip in *Dogeaters* as an antirepresentational and antinarrative form, I would not suggest that it is anything like a counterethical system; we cannot understand gossip as intrinsically progressive or subversive. Nonetheless, Daisy's transgression of gendered roles and spheres is instantly linked with acts of political insurrection: indeed we might understand the eventual armed insurrection in which she participates as a mobilization that is not a univocal, linear development of politicization, that takes place according to gossip's model of spontaneous displacement and contagion. Revolutionary activity in *Dogeaters* is not teleologically narrated; it does not privilege heroes, martyrs, or the development of the revolutionary subject. The association in *Dogeaters* of insurrection with gossip may refer implicitly to a history of guerilla strategies that were not centrally organized, and to different modes of political practice that have been obscured by the stage of oppositional party nationalisms.[17]

4

> History is the subject of a structure whose site is not homogeneous, empty time, but time filled by the presence of the now.
> —Walter Benjamin, "Theses on the Philosophy of History"

In Fae Myenne Ng's novel *Bone* (1993), Mah, a sewing lady in San Francisco Chinatown, who, like the other women, brings home her sewing to finish in the evenings, urges her daughters, Leila, Ona, and Nina, to help with darts, seams, and zippers. The narrator, Leila, writes:

> It was an easy pattern: four darts, four straight seams, and a simple zipper. Six dollars per dozen. Mah could finish a dozen in a little over an hour (Miss Tsai took at least two). A pattern like this came around once a season, and every shop in Chinatown was rushing its orders. On Stockton Street, ladies stopped their rivals from other shops and compared wages. Every lady smiled, every lady nodded: This pattern was easier than eating rice. All the ladies were working overtime at the shop. Mah even had Tommie deliver bundles to our apartment, and I helped to sew them on our Singer. (177)

That the women of *Bone* provide the labor for a consumer market in which they scarcely participate, sewing clothing their meager wages will not allow them to buy, demonstrates how the geographical, cultural, and linguistic boundedness of their Chinatown community is a product of the spatially uneven development of a capitalist economy that supplies the dominant center by managing and extracting from the peripheries. The policy of paying the worker by piece exploits the women in ways that extend beyond the extraction of surplus value from hourly low-waged factory labor. The incentive to complete as many pieces as possible ensures that the sewing women will work overtime without compensation and will make the home an additional site of labor. Thus the lives of the members of the Leong family are imprinted by Mah's work as a sewing woman: from the central motif of the sewing machine in all of their lives to the vulnerability of the immigrant home to capitalist penetration to the tense contrast between Leon's difficulty staying steadily employed and Mah's "over-employment."

Leon and Mah, their marriage and their employment histories, express how discriminatory immigration and naturalization policies transformed Chinatown from the bachelor society of the 1940s to a family society. These laws also changed the garment industry, whose sweatshops made use of Chinese male labor during the industry's growth from the 1920s to the '40s and then turned increasingly to female labor (Loo 1991) after the Magnuson Act of 1943 repealed Chinese exclusions, after the McCarren-Walters Act of 1952 permitted wives and children to enter as nonquota immigrants, and after the Immigration Act of 1965 abolished Asian national origin quotas.[18] Most of all, the family relations in *Bone* express the constraints put on individuals when the "private" space of the home is a "workplace" that prioritizes the relations of production over Chinese family relations. With the erosion of the "private" sphere, the boundaried space of Chinatown becomes the "frontier" upon which antagonism to racialized exploitation of Chinese workers by the dominant society is articulated. From the breakdowns in communication between the parents to the various "flights" of the three daughters (emotional, mortal, and physical)—the affective, cultural ties of the Leong family members bear the weight of immigrant laws, geographical segregation, and the imposed relations of production.

Having meditated on "blood" and "gossip" as disruptions of official regimes of representation and narrative, I turn to Ng's *Bone* in order to explore another mode through which Asian American writing addresses the problem of history. *Bone* confronts the narratives that have so often suppressed events and peoples that do not conform to the logic of development, and the equally vexing problem of how alternative records might adequately attend to those suppressed materials. Just as Ileto proposes a "nonlinear emplotment of history" that *maps* rather than narrates spaces of insurrection and suppression, Ng's *Bone*, in my view, explores *space* as a category in which to read about the emergence of, and the obstacles to, Asian American social life over the past century. Meditations on the produced locality of community, records of the affective dimensions of the "everyday," excavations that trace the regulation and transformation of the physical and psychological spaces of otherness give priority to space over the temporality that is stressed by the traditional novel and official history. History in *Bone* is the history of place, an archaeology of the richly sedimented, dialectical space of urban Chinatown community. The buildings and streets, the relations between spaces, the relations between human individuals to work, to leisure, to life and death are all material testimonies not only to the means through which U.S. society has organized Chinatown space to enhance production and reproduce the necessary relations of production but also, and equally, to the means through which Chinatown society has reconfigured spatial discipline and rearticulated the ethnic ghetto as a resistant, recalcitrant "historical" space. *Bone* exemplifies what Edward Soja (1989) has termed a "critical human geography," one that excavates the uneven geography of locality within the pressures of universal temporalized history.

San Francisco Chinatown, the site explored in *Bone,* emerged in the late nineteenth century in response to intense periods of anti-Chinese violence between 1870 and 1890 and the government's authorization of residential segregation in 1878. The old core area is the most densely populated: stores, restaurants, and family-association houses that apparently have withstood the penetration of urban, industrial culture from the outside are concentrated on Grant Avenue and off Portsmouth Square. Since 1947, and the lifting of the restrictive covenant, Chinatown has grown beyond its old borders and through the valley that lies between Nob and Russian Hills west to Van Ness Street and eastward to the financial district; outlying satellites of Chinatown dot San Francisco and can be identified by the presence of Chinese businesses and grocery stores (Nee and Nee 1972). Chinatown is a "social space" that is produced and reproduced over time in connection with the forces of production. Yet a social space cannot be adequately accounted for by simply describing its objects or its chronological history. As Henri Lefebvre (1991) reminds us, the mediations of groups and social factors within knowledge, ideology, or the domain of representations must all be taken into consideration. Social space contains a great diversity of objects, and these objects are not merely things but also relations. Labor transforms these objects and their spatial relations; indeed, social space infiltrates, even collides with, the concept of production, becoming a central dimension of the latter's content. Lefebvre writes: "No space disappears in the course of growth and development; the *worldwide does not abolish the local*" (86). In other words, "Chinatown" is produced by the interrelation of spaces—from worldwide networks of capital, labor, and commodities to national, regional, and local markets. Its space emerges as an expression of this heterogeneity and dialectic, with all of its objects eloquently testifying to that spatial interrelation, and ultimately calling into question the hierarchy of these networks of interrelated markets.

In a posthumously published essay, "Of Other Spaces," Michel Foucault (1986) discusses "heterotopia," those spaces of alterity which call into question the hierarchical organization of all other social space. Foucault defines heterotopia as sites of crisis and deviation (prisons, sanitariums, or cemeteries) or sites juxtaposing several incompatible spaces or temporalities (the festival, museum, or colony). Heterotopia function in a critical relation to the binarized space that remains: they expose the untenability of the hierarchized divisions of space into domains of public and private, leisure and work, or legitimacy and illegitimacy. Chinatown can be considered such a space: a sedimented community space that condenses at once barbershops, boardinghouses, and gambling halls (traces of late-nineteenth-century bachelor societies) with schools, churches, or family service businesses (signs of the transition to family society and the influx of women after World War II) and with the restaurants, stores, and factories in which newer Chinese immigrants work. Chinatowns are at once the deviant space ghettoized by the dominant configurations of social space and the resistant localities that betray the internalization of "others" within the national space. The heterotopia of Chinatown challenges what Akhil Gupta and James Fergusen (1992) have called "the isomorphism" of space/place/culture/nation. It marks the disunity and discontinuity of the racialized urban space with the national space. It is a space not spoken by or in the language of the nation.

The elaboration of space particular to *Bone* is permitted by the reverse chronology of the narrative. If an overemphasis on temporality actively submerges and peripheralizes the "geographical" as a category of social life, then *Bone*'s narrative reversal works to criticize the overdevelopment of temporal contextualization as a source of meaning. The narrative moves backward in time, in a reverse approach to the suicide of the middle sister, Ona. One effect of the reverse narration is that *causality* as a means of investigation is disorganized. While Ona's death appears initially as the originating loss that would seem either to motivate the reverse chronology or to resolve a progressive one, when the event of the suicide is at last reached, it dissolves, apprehensible not as an origin but as a symptom of the Leong family's collective condition. The opening chapter represents the ongoing schism between Leon and Mah as if it were the effect of Ona's death, but as the chapters move backward, we learn that the painful divide between the parents precedes the death, resulting from a steady stream of losses: Mah's loss of her first husband, Lyman Fu; Leon's absences when he worked as a seaman; Leon's loss of his "original" history and antecedents upon immigration; his successive job losses; his loss of Mah to her affair with Tommie Hom; and finally, the loss of paternal authority that obliges his daughters to chaperone and care for him.

The novel investigates Chinatown space as a repository of layers of historical time, layers of functions, purposes, and spheres of activity. The Hoy Sun Ning Yung Benevolent Association, for example, is a building that condenses many different activities into a space that is undifferentiated, in which leisure and work, family and business coexist. If the rationality of production seeks to organize space in accordance with a sequence of actions that accomplish a certain "objective"—the production of an object, in this case, a garment—then the spatial arrangement characteristic of the building skews this rationality. Leila narrates her visit to the Benevolent Association:

> Friday after school, I walked down to the five-story building at 41 Waverly Place. The narrow staircase squeaked. I stepped aside on the first landing to let some Italian guys carrying white carnation wreaths pass. On the second floor, the rumble of machines and the odor of hot steamed linen made my nostrils feel prickly; these sensations brought back memories of working in Tommie Hom's sweatshop, helping Mah turn linen pockets. Ironing the interfacing for the culottes. The time I sewed my finger. The awful exactness of the puncture point where the needle broke nail and skin. An exacting pain.
>
> A racket of mah-jongg sounds, plastic tiles slapping and trilling laughter of winners filled the third floor. The fourth smelled of sweat. Sharp intakes of breath, sudden slaps, guys grunting. Master Choy, White Crane Gung-Fu Club.
>
> The office of the Hoy Sun Ning Yung Benevolent Association was like many other Chinatown family-association offices: family and business mixed up. To

the right, a long counter; to the left, the reception area, made up of two hand-me-down sofas, old arm touching old arm. (75)

Though the prioritizing of the relations of production organizes the "private" space of the Leong home as a workspace, the collective space of the Benevolent Association is not organized with production as its sole end; work is not the privileged referent of its arrangement of space. The Benevolent Association is a space of multiple functions in which activities are simultaneous, not hierarchized or temporalized. Its condensed simultaneity of activities ultimately comments on that other organization of social space which relegates Chinatown to the periphery serving the dominant center. Where the Benevolent Association tiers one floor of activity on top of another, other buildings alternate and double activities into a single space. Leila learns that the funeral house where Grandpa Leong was prepared for burial was also a makeshift storefront with "nailed-together benches" and "stacks of boxes"; the funeral parlor doubled as a warehouse for Shing Kee's Grocery. Then the space went on to house other things: "Everybody's Bookstore, Master Kung's Northern-style Martial Arts Club, and the Chinese Educational Services" (83).

The hybrid space that doubles as family association and business, exercise space and work space, space of life and space of death finds an analogue in the suitcase of papers that Leila's stepfather, Leon, keeps. In the informal "archive" of Leon's papers, we are offered an ethnological, bibliographical, and demographic space containing records of the everyday life that Leon has lived, of the work he has done, of what he has dreamed and remembered:

> I lifted the suitcase up on to the kitchen table and opened it. The past came up: a moldy, water-damaged paper smell and a parchment texture. . . .
>
> . . . this paper son saved every single scrap of paper. I remember his telling me about a tradition of honoring paper, how the oldtimers believed all writing was sacred. . . .
>
> I made paper files, trying to organize the mess. Leon the family man. Airmail letters from China, aerograms from Mah to Leon at different ports, a newsprint picture of Ona graduating from the Chinese Center's nursery school, of Nina in her "boy" haircut and an awful one of me and Mason.
>
> Leon the working man: in front of the laundry presser, the extractor; sharpening knives in the kitchen; making beds in the captain's room. Leon with the chief steward. Leon with girls in front of foreign monuments.

A scarf with a colored map of Italy. Spanish pesetas in an envelope. Old Chinese money. Dinner menus from the American President Lines. The Far East itinerary for Matson Lines. A well-used bilingual cookbook . . . Had Leon been a houseboy?

Selections from newspapers. From *The Chinese Times:* a picture of Confucius, a Japanese soldier with his bayonet aimed at a Chinese woman, ration lines in Canton, gold lines in Shanghai. From *Life* magazine: Hitler, Charlie Chaplin, the atom bomb. (57–59)

The suitcase of papers is a material archaeology of Leon's life, just as Chinatown is a sedimented site of collective memory for the Chinese in America. Sedimented space is an emblem for history as excavation rather than projection, simultaneity rather than sequential time, and collective geography rather than individual biography. The suitcase of papers is also the record of the conversion of "blood" to "paper" that is required when Leon renounces his Chinese past in order to assume the legal identity of citizen. Leon Leong is a "paper son" who, like thousands of other Chinese, claimed a paper identity in order to pass through the Angel Island immigrant detention center. According to U.S. law, the children of Americans were automatically citizens, even if they were born in a foreign country. After the 1906 San Francisco earthquake and fires destroyed municipal records, many young men purchased the birth certificates of American citizens of Chinese ancestry born in China and then claimed they were citizens in order to enter the United States (Lai, Lim, and Yung 1980). Leon had exchanged five thousand dollars and the promise to send Grandpa Leong's bones back to China for a "paper son" identity. After Grandpa Leong dies, and his bones remain in the United States, Leon attributes the misfortune of Ona's death and all the losses to this unpaid debt. Contemplating the contents of the suitcase—Leon's affadavit of citizenship, remnants of travel and migration (maps, currency, cookbooks) and of work lives (pay stubs, diaries), along with receipts, photographs, letters, and newspaper clippings—Leila remarks: "I thought, Leon was right to save everything. For a paper son, paper is blood" (61). The paper in the suitcase is the residue, the trace of the "conversion" of Chinese into "Americans." The conversion can never be completed, and like the "blood" in *Dictée,* it retains "the physical substance of blood as measure, that rests as record, as document" (Cha 1982, 32), becoming an integral part of the contemporary present. The paper archive, like Grandpa Leong's bones, is figured as the material trace of early Chinese immigrant life: a trace that paradoxically testifies to a loss of history yet simultaneously marks the production of "community" that commences with the investment, through memory and narrative, in that loss.[19]

The Chinatown represented in *Bone* is a recalcitrant space that cannot be wholly or univocally translated. Its heterogeneity is not assimilable to the capitalist logic that would organize the ethnic ghetto for production; its contemporaneity does not yield to the gaze that seeks to exoticize it as antiquated artifact. The tourist, the voyeur, the immigration service may enter, but they are all deceived.

> From the low seats of the Camaro, I looked out. . . .
>
> . . . I thought, So this is what Chinatown looks like from inside those dark Greyhound buses; this slow view, these strange color combinations, these narrow streets, this is what tourists come to see. I felt a small lightening up inside, because I knew, no matter what people saw, no matter how close they looked, our inside story is something entirely different. (Ng 1993, 145)

In discussing blood as ground and figure of representation in *Dictée,* gossip as an antifiguration of narrative in *Dogeaters,* and Chinatown urban space as a disruption of overdeveloped temporalization in *Bone,* I have suggested that these Asian American novels displace the orthodoxies of both historical and novelistic representation and excavate the material histories that have been subjugated or erased by these aesthetics. Engagement with the "past"—as catastrophe, as memory, as space—forms the core of all three projects. The three novelists do not through their respective engagements seek to find and represent an essential authenticity, to articulate the past "the way it really was." Rather, like Walter Benjamin's historical materialist, they "seek to brush history against the grain" (1969, 257). If historical narrative is, as Benjamin suggests, a narrative that has "empathy with the victor," the material memory of the unvictorious is not simply repressed by that narrative; it returns dialectically, to pressure and restructure precisely the regimes of uniformity that seek to contain it as representation. In this sense, *Dictée, Dogeaters,* and *Bone* each suggest that the project of writing as a subject who remembers is not merely a matter of finding better modes of representing or renarrating the "histories" of colonialism, modernization, underdevelopment, and immigrant displacement from a posterior point; it is not exclusively a matter of projecting and narrating a new subject of history. Rather, such writing reconstructs a relationship to the past that embodies a contradiction between representation and the violences that are part of representational institutions themselves.

Notes

Many ideas in this essay were born in the fertile space of teaching graduate students: I wish to thank George Lipsitz for the seminar we taught together in the fall of 1993, and to appreciate the outstanding graduate students with whom we have the opportunity to work. Portions of this essay were presented at Cornell University, Clark University, U.C. Berkeley, U.C. Riverside, U.C.L.A., the University of Iowa, the University of Southern California, and the Association of Asian American Studies. I would like to express my gratitude to generous interlocutors and discussants at these sites, particularly Satya Mohanty, Gary Okihiro, Oscar Campomanes, Parminder Bhachu, King-kok Cheung, Geeta Patel, and Vincent Cheng. My special thanks to Deidre Lynch for her most remarkable gifts as an editor.

1. See the following studies for further explorations of the interpellating function of the novel in the production and management of the individual, the family, the nation, and the empire: Armstrong 1987; Reid 1993; Bhabha 1990b; Sharpe 1993; and Said 1993.
2. Colonial education in *Abeng* is discussed further by Niranjana 1992a.
3. On the teaching of "English literature" as an apparatus of the British colonial project in India, see Viswanathan 1989; Loomba 1992.
4. See Lowe 1995.
5. Aihwa Ong (1991) has argued that contrary to the literature on Fordism that predicted the increasing adoption of mass-assembly production, since the early 1970s, subcontracting firms and sweatshops have come to typify industrialization in Asia and Central America. As corporations attempt to remain competitive in a global arena, new patterns of "flexible accumulation" have emerged, relying especially on the use of Asian female labor.
6. By "racialization," I am referring to the theorization of the construction of race in the United States in Omi and Winant 1986.
7. Elsewhere, I have argued that Orientalism, neither monolithic nor stable, is a heterogeneous discourse whose diverse articulations have been engendered differently by material circumstances that were located within national contexts and specific historical crises, and that we might better understand both the "West" and the "Orient" as contested categories by giving attention to the heterogeneity,

hybridity, and multiplicity of Orientalist objects, whose contradictions and lack of fixity mark precisely the moments of instability in the Orientalist discourse founded on such a binary. See Lowe 1991a, 1991b.

8. I have learned from Winifred Woodhull's critique of French poststructuralism in terms of its reiteration within some Francophone postcolonial writing. See Woodhull 1993.

9. Other discussions have differentiated "postcolonial" or "third world" texts and contexts from "postmodernism": see Sangari 1990; San Juan 1991; Chow 1992.

10. For accounts of Japanese colonialism and Korean nationalist opposition, see, for example, Robinson 1982–83; Cumings 1984.

11. For a fuller discussion of *Dictée,* see Kim and Alarcón 1994.

12. While I want to underscore the potential access to historical understanding that texts like *Dictée, Dogeaters,* and *Bone* provide, I do not mean to privilege the Asian American "literature" over Asian American "history." The discussion of historical narratives would need to take place elsewhere, but it might be said here that just as Asian American literature emerges out of the contradiction between, for example, racialization and U.S. narratives of citizenship, so too do Asian American histories. This contradiction expresses itself in the historiographical work by John Kuo Wei Tchen, John Cheng, or K. Scott Wong, for example, on Chinatowns, immigrant labor history, and community life, which provides alternatives to univocal, totalizing historical modes.

13. On Filipino American identity, see Bonus 1994. Bonus's work explores the important part played by Filipino immigrant nostalgia and longing for the "homeland" in the construction of ethnic and national group identity.

14. In their analyses of peasant revolts in India, subaltern historians emphasize the phenomenon of "rumor" as a means of communication that proved powerful in peasant mobilization precisely because it was popular, unstable, and unmediated by dominant codes. See Guha and Spivak 1988; Rafael 1991.

15. By "hybridity," I do not mean simply cultural or linguistic mixing or "ambivalence" but rather a material form that expresses the sedimented traces of a complex history of violence, invasion, exploitation, deracination, and imposed rule by different colonial and neocolonial powers. On Philippine hybridity, see Joaquin 1988.

16. On the function of the figure of woman in official and unofficial discursive systems, see Spivak 1988b.

17. On decentered insurgent movements in the Philippines, see Guerrero 1979.

18. In thinking about how immigration and naturalization laws have affected Asian American women's labor, I have benefited from reading Neil Gotanda (1995).

19. In relation to German history and the Holocaust, Eric Santner (1990) as-

sociates mourning with the historical "task of integrating damage, loss, disorientation, decenteredness into a transformed structure of identity, whether it be that of an individual, a culture, or an individual as a member of a cultural group" (xiii). Though the ostensive narrative drive of *Bone* appears to be the mourning of Ona, it seems important to recast that representation of individual or familial mourning as an echo of the "community" mourning of the loss of Chinese American history, of which Grandpa Leong's bones are the emblem.

Dane Johnson

4 The Rise of Gabriel García Márquez and Toni Morrison

❧ When the Swedish Academy awarded the Nobel Prize in Literature to Gabriel García Márquez and Toni Morrison, in 1982 and 1993 respectively, they lauded an "overwhelming narrative talent" (Michener 1982, 81) and spoke of a "richly composed world of the imagination" ("Magic, Matter, and Money" 1982), "visionary force and poetic import" (Blades 1993, 1), and "epic power" (Skube 1993). These seemingly interchangeable terms of literary celebration—terms to be expected for recipients of the world's most prestigious literary award—suggest a universal and timeless appeal for both authors. Now, a new novel by Gabriel García Márquez or Toni Morrison is a gala publishing event complete with full-page advertisements in the key industry organs and a front-page review in the *New York Times Book Review*. Morrison and García Márquez are not only authors of literary fiction but well-known cultural icons. This was not, to put it mildly, always the case. Prior to 1970, Morrison was told that there was no audience for *that* type of novel. Morrison herself has spoken of being inspired to write by "huge silences in literature . . . about black girls, black women" (Blades 1993, 25). Similarly, translations from the other America were considered a certain loss, a sort of publisher's "Good Neighbor Policy." Latin America was perceived to have no true literary tradition, just a long string of derivative novels about land and dictators.

The rise of García Márquez's and Morrison's prestige and sales goes beyond the recognition of great writing. Their enthusiastic incorporation into an American novelistic tradition is symptomatic of changes in the ways in which Latin American and African American fiction is read by the mainstream U.S. literary community. This essay studies how these authors who wrote out of previously low-status literary traditions came to represent (that is, depict *and* speak for) their race, nation, or region for a larger public. Here and throughout this essay, I play off the dual sense of representation as "speaking for" in the political sense and "re-presentation" in the artistic sense. Internationally successful novelists from "other" places are valued in part for their natives' depiction of strange lands. They are then called upon or given the opportunity to speak for African Americans or Latin Americans in international forums.[1] García Márquez and Morrison participate in and complicate the battle of cultural representation and the creation of literary value[2] by inscribing debates on misreading and cultural appropriation in their novels. In a double movement, the inclusion of these two authors diversifies what is meant by the term "American literature," while it reinforces Western aesthetic criteria of art.

The first "rise of the novel" I study focuses on Latin American narrative of the 1960s. I examine how García Márquez's *One Hundred Years of Solitude* became *the* Latin American novel in the United States, showing how the most celebrated Latin American novel fits stereotypical images of exotic lands south of the Rio Grande. In the 1970s, African American women writers became another international "discovery" in the history of the novel. Reviewers often employed similar metaphors in describing Morrison's work and that of García Márquez, suggesting that Morrison, too, is weaving stories of "strange, pristine, fecund, doomed land[s]" (Mead 1970, 35). Whereas before, African Americans and Latin Americans were objects of the stories told by social science, history, and government centered in the metropolis, the arrival of the Latin American and African American novel in Europe and North America suggests that the space of the other is now being mined for stories.

An examination of the fate of *One Hundred Years of Solitude* in the U.S. market, when compared with the trajectory of Morrison's reception, also suggests a functional parallel between a translated, foreign novel and an indigenous minority text. In both cases, most nonprofessional readers accept the history they encounter in fiction as truth. In the United States, the majority of these readers (and the reviewers and editors who serve them) are European Americans relatively unfamiliar either with African American or Latin American culture. Given the unconscious tendency to deny in others the capacity for semiotic mediation that we acknowledge in ourselves, popular minority and foreign texts are likely to be read as guidebooks to the culture.

Morrison and García Márquez have positioned themselves as mediators between the place from which they come and the culture they perceive to be controlled by the large metropolises. On the basis of these writers' explicit self-positioning and on textual analysis of *Song of Solomon* and *One Hundred Years of Solitude,* I develop the notion of a "noncosmopolitan aesthetic." These authors revere and respond to the metropolitan literary tradition while fearing, resisting, and critiquing metropolitan mores, politics, economics. Made to pass as "classic," their texts appear to be valuable in different, sometimes contradictory ways for a variety of readers. Casting their oppositional texts in forms familiar to the Western tradition, García Márquez and Morrison, and the tradition within which they have been appropriated, leave intact a system of literary evaluation and a concept of cultural difference that still exclude cultural forms that do not adhere to Western ideas of high art. Although sensitive to systems of exclusion, aspects of both writers' texts make them easily exportable into a world literary marketplace that desires classic stories from exotic places.[3]

How *One Hundred Years of Solitude* Became Latin America

I start from the assumption that literary value is not the exclusive property of the text but "the product of the dynamics of a system" (Smith 1988, 15). Different moments of reception can be studied by asking, "What is this text valued *for?*" Pierre Bourdieu's work on culture as a relational sytem of evaluation further undercuts both essentialized statements of value and the move to isolate readings of texts from their production. Since the literary field "is a field like all the others"—"it involves power—the power to publish or to refuse publication, for instance; it involves capital—the capital of the established author which can be partly transferred into the account of a young and still unknown author by a highly positive review or a preface" (Bourdieu 1990, 141)—its games can be studied. The author is clearly a participant in this game, but not only as producer of the literary text. Thus my analysis of the rise of Morrison and García Márquez weaves together multiple discursive strands—reviews, advertisements, nonprofessional readers, academic criticism, author's speeches and interviews, the novels themselves—to more fully understand the dynamic process of the creation of literary value.

Richard Ohmann's "The Shaping of a Canon: U.S. Fiction, 1960–

1975" is one of the few efforts to describe the process of canonization in the United States after World War II. Ohmann identifies a gatekeeping process whereby "a small group of book buyers formed a screen through which novels passed on their way to commercial success; a handful of agents and editors picked the novels that would compete for the notice of those buyers; and a tight network of advertisers and reviewers, organized around the *New York Times Book Review*, selected from these a few to be recognized as compelling, important, 'talked-about'" (1983, 203–4). Such recognition made it more likely for a novel to attract attention among academic critics, thereby begetting placement in college curricula, "where the very context . . . gave it de facto recognition as literature" (205–6). Thus, a small segment of the professional-managerial class based in Manhattan has an inordinate—albeit mostly hidden—effect on the canonization of contemporary fiction. I follow Ohmann, then, in paying particular attention to categories according to which members of the New York literary community judge García Márquez and Morrison. Both authors clearly have been able to appeal to this group, although their success in doing so challenges Ohmann's conclusion that in the final instance class is the major component of canonization.

What sense of Latin America did Gabriel García Márquez capture in *One Hundred Years of Solitude* that North American readers of literary fiction were so eager to hear, so quick to pass on to their friends, so willing to move into that mythological space of great books—books that everyone has heard of, books that pop up as cultural references and generate the names of future bookstores and cafés? To address this question, I turn to the trajectory of Gabriel García Márquez's reception in the United States through an examination of the contemporary reviews of *One Hundred Years of Solitude*.

When published in English in 1970, *One Hundred Years of Solitude* was almost unanimously reviewed as a masterpiece and implicitly marked as a tale to sate our desire for stories from exotic southern lands. Although widely and almost wildly acclaimed, García Márquez's extensive impact outside of the community of literary professionals would have to await the eventual success of the Avon paperback edition of the novel (1971) and the further push that the 1982 conferral of the Nobel would supply to his career.

Although the Knopfs had prompted occasional interest in Latin American literature from the 1940s on (and there had always been at least a trickle of translations), the late 1960s was a period when Latin America began to receive wider notice within the New York literary community.[4] In a review essay from 1969, Rodman Selden wrote of the belated discovery of "literary gold in South America" (1969). The use of the term "belated" suggests that, like African American literature, Latin American literature is constantly being *re*discovered and only rarely becoming a permanent presence in the United States. *One Hundred Years of Solitude* is the one and only recent text that has moved from "discovery" to apparently permanent cultural referent, making literature in Spanish, in the world's most boiled-down canon, run straight from *Don Quixote* to this novel, the two works separated by a vast, uncharted wasteland.

Prepublication reviews of *One Hundred Years of Solitude,* a key marker of industry interest in the product, were extremely laudatory. The normally restrained *Publishers Weekly* declared: "This extraordinary Latin American novel, rich, fanciful and extravagant, stands by itself, unlike anything else in a long, long time" (Review of *One Hundred Years of Solitude* 1970, 58). The review also noted the selection of the novel as a Book-of-the-Month-Club alternate choice, another significant sign to booksellers that this was a book to promote since, as Janice Radway has shown (1989), the Book-of-the-Month-Club editors pride themselves on being able to find literary fiction that will appeal to the "middlebrow" tastes of their club members.

Success in the places that matter continued with a very positive notice in the *New York Times Book Review,* followed by the novel's selection as one of the editors' twelve best books of the year. "Part chronicle, part myth, at once surreal and realistic, it tells the story of the rise and fall of one archetypical family and one town which represents an entire continent," the *Times* editors wrote ("Editors' Choice" 1970, 2). While not an inaccurate description of the novel, significant slippage occurs with the phrase "represents an entire continent." In an influential forum like the *New York Times Book Review,* where depictions of Latin America are few, this epic representation of the continent (which is, to be sure, a selective representation) crowds out alternative representations within the world of the Latin American novel while becoming almost the sole representative of that world in the United States. The novel—rather than being seen, for example, as providing ground for symbolic confrontation—becomes, with surprising ease, a stand-in not only for all Latin American literature but also for Latin American reality.[5]

I call this tendency to let *One Hundred Years of Solitude* represent all of Latin America the perfect creole fantasy: the unstated—and perhaps unconscious—assumption is that "we" can represent all of Latin America because only we know and understand all parts of Latin America. I use the term "creole" as a translation for the Spanish *criollo,* which means, in the first instance, a person born in Spanish America but of Spanish descent—that is, neither mestizo, mulatto, nor indigenous. In the twentieth century, *criollo* is more generally used to designate educated middle- and upper-class males, who happen to be, for the most part, those of lighter skin (although there is regional variation in the deployment of this term). Thus, "creole" is a shifting cultural category, not a strictly racial one. It is under these terms that I label García Márquez a creole writer.

Taking a wider look at creole writing, Mary Louise Pratt (1993) notes that the foundational texts of the Latin American independence period contain a common trope: "a panorama of the vast and empty American wilderness, the future national territory onto which the writer goes on to inscribe the march of human history" (95). This description fits *One Hundred Years of Solitude.* But not just anyone is likely to co-opt such a trope: "The potential master is the creole speaking subject, the new American citizen who is the seer in these panoramas and who himself remains unseen" (95). García Márquez both takes on this trope and is called upon to play this role.

Thus the "local," the "minor," the part that does not purport to represent the whole is then overlooked or erased or considered less important, being less grand. This is not a move endemic to U.S. criticism of the novel. However, in the context of a system of translating and publicity that already places foreign novels at a considerable disadvantage in the marketplace, this sort of filtering almost ensures that an "epic" male voice will be the voice of the Americas.

The reception that authorized García Márquez in this manner meant that a book full of (and playing with) exotic stereotypes about the *tristes tropiques* was quite often taken not only as an arresting representation of Latin America but as reality. Robert Mead's article in the *Saturday Review* was careful and elegant; Mead soon moved, however, as many other reviewers did, into equating Macondo with Latin America:

> Macondo may be regarded as a microcosm of the development of much of the Latin American continent: a strange, pristine, fecund, doomed land where,

in the beginning, magic, "impossible" things are made to happen by innocent, natural, iron-willed men. . . . Although it is first and always a story, the novel also has value as a social and historical document. (1970, 35)

García Márquez's prose may encourage this reading. However, when Latin America is allowed to be subsumed as "a strange, pristine, fecund, doomed land" of "magic" and "innocent, natural, iron-willed men," then we are clearly in the land of overdetermined "othering." In an incisive analysis of García Márquez in the United States, Johnny Payne (1993) focuses on the sense among U.S. writers that *One Hundred Years of Solitude* (and its magically real brethren) might rescue fiction north of the border—where "an infusion of the tropic staved off the entropic" (15). Payne's work also describes some of the dangers and limits of what he calls "the New Word myth," pointing to the reduced possibilities for Latin American fiction to represent more than a monologic exotic other.

By consolidating García Márquez's position as *the* Latin American novelist, Alistair Reid's long piece in the *New Yorker* upon the release of *Autumn of the Patriarch* in 1976 was a pivotal article for the Colombian novelist within the New York literary community. Reid lauded the manly virtues of the Latin American novelists, who were willing to go after that most fearsome quarry: the Great American Novel.[6] Embracing the exotic and encouraging the colonialist attitude of constructing Latin America as a place without history (literary or otherwise), Reid wondered: "Is there something about the Latin-American experience, apart from its labyrinthine variety and the fact that it is *largely unwritten as yet,* that makes it exceptionally fertile ground for inventive fiction?" (1976, 181; emphasis added).[7] Reid took as his guide in these matters the Cuban creole writer Alejo Carpentier and his theory of "the marvelous in the real." While *lo real maravilloso* is a complex concept, it is in part predicated upon considering the norm to be elsewhere. For Carpentier, one might say that the "real" real is in Europe, the "marvelous" New World retaining the Edenic, magical qualities believed to be there by the first European conquerors. Following Carpentier, Reid concluded: "For Latin Americans, theory is the enemy, human eccentricity the norm" (181). Not surprisingly, *One Hundred Years of Solitude* is held up as evidence (183). This in itself would not be so limiting except for the tendency, exhibited in Reid's article as in so many others, to read *One Hundred Years of Solitude* as representing the Latin American essence. As Reid summarized, "these attitudes implicit in the book exude from the history and being not just of Aracataca-Macondo and Colombia but of the Latin-American continent. Yet the manner in which this fate is accepted and come to terms with is what gives Latin Americans their distinguishing humanity" (198). Analyzing metropolitan discourses on the Third World, Jean Franco (1988) describes the point at which heterogeneity is valued by the routinized metropolis: "At this moment, the Third World becomes the place of the unconscious, the right source of fantasy and legend recycled by the intellegentsia" (505). *One Hundred Years of Solitude* has become that place.

Through a segue that is only apparently paradoxical, the generalized particularity attributed to this novel allows reviewers to insert *One Hundred Years of Solitude* easily into a web of universalist "world literature." The tension that John Leonard's review in the daily *New York Times* underscored by, on the one hand, interpreting Macondo as "Latin America in microcosm" and, on the other hand, inserting the novel into the matrix of world literature reflects the move whereby *One Hundred Years of Solitude* became a text that captures all of Latin America and—simultaneously—speaks to all people (Leonard 1970). This ambidexterity sometimes leads to the novel being read in ways that would be anathema to the author's own sense of mission. García Márquez's smooth assimilation into a narrative of classic literature is a gesture of inclusion that ends up excluding the diversity of Latin America. The focus on connecting García Márquez's or any other work to canonical texts or authors (e.g., the Bible, Dostoyevsky, Faulkner) ensures that texts replete with Western literary allusions—like *One Hundred Years of Solitude*—will be more likely to be embraced in the metropolis.[8] At the same time, a discussion of this text in terms of Western literature minimalizes the possibility of its representing and retaining a Latin American difference (as opposed to a Latin American essence or some idea of no difference at all in the final instance—the eternal verities and all that).

Taken as a whole, García Márquez's rise complicates Ohmann's model of canon formation, described earlier. If class is the major component of canonization, as Ohmann suggests, then how does an anti-U.S.-multinational-capital narrative from a supporter of Cuba (one among the many narrative and thematic strands in the novel) become so successful during the cold war? One might ask this question more generally of the novel's nonprofessional readers: do they just gloss over the political content of the book and, instead, revel in the exoticism of it all? Or are the satisfied readers also opposed to the Vietnam War, with García Márquez providing them a critique of the United States as a colonial nation while still allowing them to believe in the salutary effects of a trip to the tropics for a dose of universal humanism? As the reviews suggest, *One Hundred Years of Solitude*'s enormous success is at least partly related to its compatibility with North American stereotypes about Latin America. Paradoxically, many of the stereotypes readable within the text—the volcanic sexuality of the Latin Americans, for example, whose bodies forever seem to be holding sway over their minds—were previously used to exclude Latin America from the world literary marketplace.

One Hundred Years of Solitude is also a central text for North American critics who have quite diverse cultural-political ideals. Earl Fitz and José David Saldívar, for example, integrate it quite variously into their respective conceptions of "the New World" and "Our America." Fitz finds García Márquez most attractive where he can be discussed as representing universal human values, whereas Saldívar focuses on his representation of economic dependency, seeing García Márquez as providing the critique that we in the United States lack. While both critics are interested in the motif of solitude in the novel, they provide divergent interpretations of its significance: for Fitz, solitude in García Márquez symbolizes "people everywhere" who "have only a limited time on earth" (1991, 202); Saldívar, by contrast, observes that solitude in *One Hundred Years of Solitude* "is metaphorically allied with the Marxian idea of alienation and to a biblical alienation from meaning" (1991, 38), both tied to a legacy of colonialism. The fact that *One Hundred Years of Solitude* appeals to critics who have little intellectual common ground is a powerful indicator of García Márquez's mastery of multiple discourses, as well as a hint to how a novel informed by anti-imperialist politics can still be accepted by Ohmann's professional-managerial class. Neither interpreter can let the local be local, can, as Jean-François Lyotard puts it in *The Differend* (1988), allow for difference to remain unresolved.

Based on García Márquez's cultural work as a novelist and intellectual, Saldívar reconstructs "an image and function of the writer that many Anglocentric writers and intellectuals have lost—the writer who combines the traditional intellectual's commitment to language and image with the organic intellectual's commitment to politics and revolution" (1991, xiii). This combination also coincides with Morrison's vision of the artist. Still, in order for a novel to pass into widespread acceptance in the metropolis, politics must drop out or at least be pushed to the side. The political edge can, however, continue to buttress the author's support among some readers.

In short, the success of Gabriel García Márquez in the United States is a victory, but with limits. The southern void has been filled, the Latin American plain has been peopled with memorable characters. Reverence for *One Hundred Years of Solitude* repudiates the prior belief that no art comes from the so-called Third World. Nevertheless, the ways in which this novel is read and used show that the stereotypes according to which Latin American literature has been excluded before remain largely intact. Furthermore, the celebration of this particular novel makes it easy to believe in the myth of a unified Latin America and its single, authorized voice. While the region's diversity is more patent but perhaps less savory in genres like *testimonio* or in Afro-Hispanic and mestizo novels that do not posit a unified Latin American subject (e.g., José María Arguedas's *Deep Rivers*), none has captured the North American fancy like García Márquez's "South American Genesis" (Kiely 1970).[9]

The Rise of Toni Morrison: "The Last Classic American Writer"

In advertisements for *Jazz* from the spring of 1992, Toni Morrison peered down at the readers of the *New York Times* as an African American female sage. The quotations accompanying the photo trumpeted her importance: "She is the best writer in America. Jazz, for sure; but also Mozart" (John Leonard, qtd. in Advertisement for *Jazz* 1992). "She herself may be the last classic American writer, squarely in the tradition of Poe, Melville, Twain and Faulkner" (David Gates, qtd. in Advertisement for *Jazz* 1992). As exemplified in this advertising pastiche, Morrison had been transformed from a well-known, well-respected writer into a cultural icon of African American and American writing.

What is perhaps too easily forgotten is that a scant twenty years ago or so, Morrison's success would have been an outlandish impossibility. Contemporary African American women's writing was barely visible, past writing by black females had been almost wholly erased, and when either women or blacks as a subject position were recognized, it seemed as if "all the women were white, and all the blacks were men" (to paraphrase the title of Gloria Hull, Patricia Bell Scott, and Barbara Smith's groundbreaking anthology [1988]). In *Discourse and the Other: The Production of the Afro-American Text*, W. Lawrence Hogue (1986) concludes: "There is an unstated consensus in the American literary establishment that if a novel is great, it cannot be black. For it to be black, it has to be limited because within the dominant American ideological apparatus, the Afro-American is defined as the Other, as different, as inferior" (170). Toni Morrison's career, especially after *Beloved* (1987), disrupts this opposition, for she has attained the highest recognition possible from the literary establishment for a living writer—as well as considerable commercial success—while writing resolutely African American texts—novels, as she puts it, "about those Black people the way I knew those people to be" (qtd. in Giddings 1977).

Many of the tensions inherent in the gradual approval of Morrison's writing—which went from "good black writing" to "classic American writing"—have been analyzed in the past, yet they persist today in structuring critical response to Morrison's work. In "Criteria of Negro Art" (originally published in 1926), W.E.B. Du Bois succinctly put forth three recurring issues for the African American literary community as it comes into contact with the European American literary community. The first is the general problem of black representation in the wider culture, at the level both of what images African American authors ought to be producing and of which representations will likely be distributed. The status of black consciousness vis-à-vis white-dominated culture is another issue. Marginality—"double-consciousness" in Du Bois's memorable phrasing—can be seen as a problem or as a source of power (as Du Bois puts it, "We who are dark can see America in a way that white Americans can not" [1971, 87]). Du Bois suggests that the misappropriation and misreading of African American culture are a general problem, even when it comes to goodwilled European Americans.

In publishing circles, the late 1960s was the period of the black male writer, especially in nonfiction, with Eldridge Cleaver's inflammatory *Soul on Ice* gaining considerable notice.[10] This wave of interest in African Americans and other ethnic minorities contributed to Morrison's initial recognition, although many African American female writers were already separating themselves from the male-dominated Black Arts movement by 1970. Separation seemed necessary for writers who had been systematically erased from a tradition in which they had fully participated.[11] In fact, Toni Morrison and other contemporary black female writers seem to attract an audience more integrated by race and gender than the black male writer's market. The reviews show Morrison becoming increasingly relevant to an ever-widening audience book after book, suggesting that Morrison is writing more universally. A close reading of the reviews, however, demonstrates that the paradigms of the reviewers have shifted. In other words, Morrison's success is not merely a case of increased enthusiasm; rather, the terms of enthusiasm for Morrison's writing have changed over time.[12]

Morrison had not set out to be a writer, but while teaching at Howard University in the early 1960s, she became involved in a group in which everyone shared their writing. Obligated to produce something, Morrison brought a story of a young black girl who wished to have the "bluest eyes." A few years later, this became Morrison's first novel, *The Bluest Eye,* published in 1970. Morrison's powerful tale of Pecola Breedlove growing up in a land where the "soil is bad for certain kinds of flowers" (1972, 160) focused attention on, to quote Morrison, "the true devastation of racism on the most vulnerable, the most helpless unit in the society—a black female and a child" (qtd. in Dreifus 1994, 74). Although by no means a major publishing event, *The Bluest Eye* did garner significantly more attention than the average first novel by an unknown author, partly because of its "hot" subject and partly because of Morrison's status as someone who worked within the publishing business.[13]

The ambivalent effects and dubious distinction of being read for "blackness"—the prevailing paradigm of the time—are clear in the trade journal reviews. Summing up the novel's prospects, *Library Journal* reviewer Patricia H. Marvin (1970), for example, praised Morrison as "a new and considerable talent," but at the same time she preselected and narrowed the novel's audience: "Of particular interest to young adults and social caseworkers" (3806). The tendency was to see African American fiction as not exactly art but rather as the direct "testimony" of the black experience. Thus an African American novel could, at best, be sociologically interesting and perhaps useful for educational purposes.

In a development quite rare for a first-time novelist, *The Bluest Eye* was also reviewed in *Newsweek,* the *New Yorker,* and the daily *New York Times.* The *Newsweek* review lends credence to the notion that some of Morrison's success in the white-dominated literary community arose out of her distance from the cultural and political black nationalism of the time. Raymond A. Sokolov (1970) began his review by commenting on the "forensic" tone of much black writing, a tone that "has been used to persuade or frighten whites into action and to cajole or exhort other blacks into solidarity and revolution." Morrison's tone, by contrast, he sees as "a more private tone, the tone, as it were, of black conversation. All of which is not meant to imply that Mrs. Morrison has no political consciousness, far from it, but only that she has found a way to express that consciousness in a novel instead of a harangue" (95A).

The treatment of Morrison's second novel, *Sula* (1973), in the *New York Times Book Review* is indicative at once of Morrison's success and of the conditions placed on that success by the still prevailing paradigm in the European American literary community. Sara Blackburn's review (1973) began with both lavish praise and a surprising attack on the attention given to *The Bluest Eye,* implying that the glowing reception accorded that novel was merely affirmative action. Blackburn was working within a mindset in which black equals regional equals not quite Art: "Toni Morrison is far too talented to remain only a marvelous recorder of the black side of provincial American life. If she is to maintain the large and serious audience she deserves, she is going to have to address a riskier contemporary reality . . ." (3). What actually changes, however, in Morrison's rise is *not* her subject matter but rather the idea that writing centered on African American life might be limiting.

In 1977, Morrison's editor at Knopf, Robert Gottlieb, felt certain that *Song of Solomon* would be a breakthrough novel with universal appeal. In his editorial fact sheet, Gottlieb stressed Morrison's prior praise and his belief that her latest would receive rave reviews. Morrison and Gottlieb had managed to generate a buzz throughout Knopf. African American support for Morrison came early and has been important for her rise. And her publisher solicited such support. With *Song of Solomon,* for example, in addition to sending galleys to all the most important mainstream reviews, Knopf also targeted outlets with direct contacts in the black community, asking that they bring this novel to the attention of their readers. In the interlocked literary community of New York, internal excitement of this magnitude tends to stir up external excitement too.[14]

Gottlieb's rosy predictions were seconded when the Book-of-the-Month Club announced that *Song of Solomon* would be a "September Dual Selection" and awarded the book a fifty-thousand-dollar advance. The Book-of-the-Month-Club selection suggests Morrison's ability to appeal to an audience beyond both the New York literary community and the African American community. Janice Radway's study of the Book-of-the-Month Club's selection process suggests criteria Morrison had met in order to be valued beyond the African American community and literary professionals:

> On the one hand, the editors seem to share the assumption of high culture aesthetic that fiction should be technically complex and self-consciously *about* significant issues. On the other, they demand that such fiction be pleasurable to read, a stipulation that differs little from that made regularly by readers of best-sellers and genre fiction who desire always to be entertained. (Radway 1989, 271)

It seems that for most Book-of-the-Month-Club editors, "the crucial molar unity seems to be the coherent, unified personality. They approach the books they read as stories about people" (272). Radway concludes from her research that "what matters in commercial fiction is not primarily the congruence between fiction and the real but rather the capacity to catch the reader up in a story that seems to propel itself forward with force" (276). There is little doubt that *Song of Solomon* has more of that kind of narrative propulsion than Morrison's previous work.

Still, it takes a certain kind of selling to convince a largely white audience that stories of Morrison's people are both important and pleasurable. The description of *Song of Solomon* in the *Book-of-the-Month-Club News,* something between a review and an advertisement, showed how one might sell an African American novel to an audience largely ignorant of African American culture and the African American literary tradition. After calling it "the best novel of the black experience in America since *The Invisible Man* [*sic*]," the reviewer, Mordecai Richler continued, barely able to contain his enthusiasm:

> A writer who does more than bring us news of another world, . . . Toni Morrison alters our perception of the black experience. . . . Ostensibly *Song of Solomon* is about grindingly poor blacks trapped in the slums of Detroit, and other seemingly ignorant blacks . . . vegetating in the backwoods of Virginia, and yet . . . one emerges from the other end of this book envying the characters for their way of seeing. (Richler 1977, 2)

Here, as we saw in reviewing the reception of *One Hundred Years of Solitude,* the "other" is there to be mined for experience. Richler was a careful reader of the novel, but his report showed how a "magical book of mysteries" could still contribute to stereotypical images of blacks as "grindingly poor" or "ignorant."

As Gottlieb predicted, most reviews of *Song of Solomon* were raves. Furthermore, the book garnered even more reviews than Morrison's previous novels, the quantity of reviews being both indicative of and constitutive of success. Nevertheless, despite the marketing push for *Song of Solomon,* despite the accolades, the paradigm in which Morrison remains an African American writer and not just an "American" had not yet been undone. In the *New York Times Book Review,* Reynolds Price (1977) began full of praise, pointing to the unresolved ending and wider canvas of *Song of Solomon* as signs "of the book's larger truthfulness." Addressing the novel's "problems," Price cited the "weakening omission of active white characters" (48). The stress on "wider" as better and blackness as narrow illustrates again the double bind of the African American author: writing of blacks is not the norm, so that representation is either valuable as a view into "another world" or limited by not taking on supposedly more universal topics.

It is not until *Beloved* (1987) that a novel centered on black women is read as "universal"—as both "black" and "great." Besides affirming Morrison's high status, the reviews showed that her "little postage stamp of soil"—the inner life and history of a group usually represented as having none (that is, slaves and, in this case, a former slave who sacrifices her child rather than have her returned to slavery)—was now considered relevant as more than just news from the other side. Michiko Kakutani (1987) of the daily *New York Times* placed *Beloved* in the highest category of art, comparing it to opera or Greek drama while insisting that "the novel also remains precisely grounded in an American reality—the reality of black history as experienced in the wake of the Civil War" (C24). Wilfrid Sheed's review/advertisement for *Beloved* in the fall 1987 *Book-of-the-Month-Club News* suggested how affirming Morrison's universal appeal opens a number of different ways that the novel could be valued: "on one level *Beloved* might simply be read as a hair-raising parable of mothers and daughters everywhere; on another it could almost be a genuine folk tale of the period, discovered in some old trunk—the writing is timeless, and the characters epic; on any level at all it is also a unique piece of living social history" (Sheed qtd. in Samuels 1990, 9). Sheed invoked all the high rhetoric used to distinguish masterpieces from mere contemporary fiction: "parable," "genuine," "timeless," "epic." At the same time, as Elizabeth Long's analysis of book clubs suggests, if a writer is already a "name," already considered a "classic," readers are more willing to translate the works into parable (Long 1986). I would suggest that *The Bluest Eye* is just as much a parable—a parable, for example, of the anxieties everyone feels about whether or not they are accepted for who they are. But because *Beloved* was published at a point in Morrison's career when she was already considered a major writer (and also at a time when African American culture was not considered a completely alien world), that novel was more likely than *The Bluest Eye* to be described in terms of the timeless, of Literature, of Art. And, paradoxically in this context, the specific representation of blackness is now even part of the novel's greatness.

With the publication of her most recent novel, *Jazz* (1992), the long-term acceptance of Morrison as one of the best contemporary novelists clearly affects the categories used for reviewing her work. Wendy Steiner's formulation in the 1992 review of Morrison's *Playing in the Dark* (on the front page of the *New York Times Book Review*) suggested a crucial change in the meaning of African American writing for American literature: "Toni Morrison is both a great novelist and the closest thing the country has to a national writer. The fact that she speaks as a woman and a black only enhances her ability to speak as an American, for the path to a common voice nowadays runs through the partisan" (Steiner 1992, 1). The idea that Morrison can be most fully "American" as both African American and female clearly breaks from the suggestion in the 1970s that she write more "universally" by including European Americans. Steiner allows Morrison to be at the center without having to assimilate, although she still implies that women and blacks are marginal—"partisan"—allowing white males to remain the unstated norm.

The rise of Toni Morrison shows that categories are always complex and contested, and open to mutation. Writers and their fiction are not just "African American" or "American," "male" or "female," "protest" or "art," "local" or "metropolitan," "national" or "universal." To study the reception of Morrison's writing over the arch of her increasingly public circulation is to watch these categories and critical terms come into considerable confusion and crisis.

The trajectory of Morrison's reception within the literary community suggests a shifting paradigm according to which it is no longer impossible for a novelist to be both "great" and "black." Morrison has had similar success with the majority of readers who are not literary professionals, but the ways in which they read and value her are distinct. To understand a different context within which novels from previously excluded traditions are read into the Western tradition, I will briefly discuss the way Morrison's *Song of Solomon* was read in a "Great Works" class in which I did ethnographic work on how students respond to sections led by teachers with starkly divergent positions on what "great works" should signify.[15]

Clearly, how students define a "great work" affects their reading of *Song of Solomon*. Analysis of student answers to the question "What is a Great Work and why?" shows that notions of greatness have changed much less than the canon itself in the recent process of canon transformation. The inclusion of formerly excluded texts or traditions works perfectly in the sense that these texts are accepted and read as great works (with the attendant seriousness and investment). The restructuring of the canon is less successful in leading students to question the notion of "greatness," even when the question is put directly to them. The implied definition of a classic for many of the students is a book for which the process of being marketed and sold is no longer visible; it is this invisibility that this essay is attempting to unveil. In short, eighteen-year-olds have little difficulty integrating disparate texts into traditional ideas of "greatness." Although the students' reasons for approval vary in startling ways, there was uniform appreciation—even love—for *Song of Solomon*. The book appealed to both those who read literary fiction on their own and those who read very rarely. By and large, these readers took pains to distinguish *Song of Solomon* from the merely "popular," which for most students meant "mere entertainment." Morrison's ability to grab the nonreaders' interest is part of her diverse appeal.

In discussions that took place in "Great Works," *Song of Solomon* had two principal and contradictory uses, both somewhat incompatible with Morrison's own sense of her project. On the one hand, the book was used as "real" information about a history and culture with which most Stanford students were unfamiliar. On the other hand, "lessons" were extracted from the novel—and whether the characters are black or white seemed unimportant. In one exchange that suggests a possible split in ways to value this text, two African American female students chastised the character Macon Dead (the stern father of the protagonist Milkman) by relating the novel's discussion of family and especially generational conflict to their own lives and their sense of African American culture. These students saw Morrison raising questions specific to the black community—here, the question of whether parents who are becoming affluent should give their children an easier life than they had growing up. European American and Asian American students, on the other hand, saw universal value in these questions.

Although Morrison has been smoothly accepted by students into the narrative of great works at Stanford, canon change is still controversial. What attention to these nonprofessional readers suggests is that Morrison's success might in some ways reinforce exclusionary borders. Paraphrasing a Du Bois question, we still need to ask if Morrison's inclusion in the canon in some ways reduces the urgency of attending to questions of difference in American culture. Can success lead to readings that silence, perhaps in new ways? Yet the presence of a "relentlessly black book" or the sense that Morrison may be "the last classic American writer" changes the ease with which people of color can be excluded from America's grand narrative or myths of origin. Using Morrison's metaphor for her grandmother's perspective on race relations to summarize the shift, one might conclude that "like the slow walk of certain species of trees from the flatlands up into the mountains, she would see the sign of irrevocable and permanent change" (Morrison 1976, 105).

One Hundred Years of Solitude, Song of Solomon, and the Noncosmopolitan Aesthetic

What is the writer's role in the creation of literary value? How do Morrison and García Márquez conceptualize their role as Artist and negotiate with notions of tradition? What are their strategies for coping with the burdens of representation, that is, the tension between the universal and the particular, between the desire for recognition and the fear of being mis-taken? Despite their differences in cultural background, Morrison and García Márquez are quite similar in their approaches to writing: their goals and their vision of writing's possibilities are congruent with a humanist, Romantic version of the literary and the literary artist. Nevertheless, both self-consciously position themselves in dialogue with a perceived metropolitan tradition, reconstructing the notion of a noncosmopolitan positioning for their texts.

My reading of the appropriation of Morrison and García Márquez parallels that of Timothy Brennan (1989) in his discussion of Salman Rushdie and other "Third World Cosmopolitans." Like Brennan, I see the celebration of these novelists as allowing for a sense of change that ensures some kinds of continuity. Their acceptance and even adoration in the mainstream (and I include myself there) contributes to a new mythology of "world" inclusion. As Brennan puts it, "Alien to the public that read them because they were black, spoke with accents or were not citizens, they were also like that public in tastes, training, repertoire of anecdotes, current habitation" (ix). At the same time, by describing their positioning as "noncosmopolitan," I wish to highlight ways in which their own writing contests such appropriation, while also suggesting that these writers may never be considered wholly metropolitan or, as Homi Bhabha so adroitly raps, "almost but not quite; almost, but not white" (1984, 126, 130).

Morrison sees no contradiction in writing "black" and writing "universal": "if you hone in on what you write, it will *be* universal" (Bakerman 1978, 59). At the level of mainstream critical reception, however, she is less optimistic, because "critics generally don't associate black people with ideas" (Tate 1983, 121). Yet Morrison still insists on a fundamental humanism across cultural boundaries, for "the subjects that are important in the world are the same ones that have always been important" (121).

Morrison has labeled her goal as a writer—her solution to the dilemmas of African American representation—"village" or "peasant" literature. The objectives for her novels are clear: "They should clarify the roles that have become obscured; they ought to identify those things in the past that are useful and those things that are not; and they ought to give nourishment" (LeClair 1981, 26). The old village literature, however, is no longer serviceable because the village has disintegrated. Morrison's solution is to cast old ideas in modern form, for "the books that mean something—treat old ideas, old situations" (26).

Preservation of the village is often expressed and experienced in terms of separation from the culture, with Morrison, as a "noncosmopolitan" writer, mediating between her "tribe" and the city. With evident nostalgia, she posits, "There must have been a time when an artist could be genuinely representative *of* the tribe and *in* it" (1984, 339). Knowing this moment to be past, Morrison writes with a sense of loss, representing processes of cultural transformation and all the while maintaining that a novel can confront important ideas and still be "a beautiful thing" (Washington 1987, 137). Part of the noncosmopolitan aesthetic, then, is to question the rigid boundary between artistic and political writing. Self-conscious about striving for multiple goals, Morrison attempts to reach multiple audiences. Commenting on the opening to *Sula*, for example, Morrison acknowledges she was "writing about, for and out of black culture while accommodating and responding to mainstream 'white' culture" (Morrison 1989, 26).

García Márquez also shows himself to be responding to cosmopolitan culture while representing his own. He often plays with metropolitan ignorance of Latin America, noting in accepting the 1972 *Books Abroad*/Neustadt International Prize for Literature, that he hails "from a remote and mysterious country" (qtd. in Ivask 1975, 440). In his Nobel Prize acceptance speech in 1982, García Márquez made the question of Latin American representation even more complex. He noted that recently "Europeans of good will—and sometimes those of bad, as well—have been struck, with ever greater force, by the unearthly tidings of Latin America, that boundless realm of haunted men and historic women, whose unending obstinacy blurs into legend" (1988, 231). "Unearthly," "boundless," "haunted"—these are the words of legend, but do they represent the European vision of the "New World," García Márquez's version, or Latin American reality itself?

Like Morrison, García Márquez laments his separation from his people, his Colombia, talking about homesickness and "losing contact with . . . [his] myths" (Harss and Dohmann 1967, 318). This sense of possible loss leads him to write and to preserve. Nevertheless, only separation could lead him to see Latin American reality as "fantastic," "unbelievable," "incredible" (García Márquez 1985, 13–15), for it takes the normative reference point of an Other to see and represent one's "own" reality as exceeding the norm. The job of the Latin American artist is not to invent but to make this reality credible—for the incredulous European or North American. This multiple perspective on Latin American reality is built into the very structure of *One Hundred Years of Solitude.*

While often discussed in unified, purified ways—as African American Literature or Latin American Literature—the novels of Morrison and García Márquez are clearly arts of the contact zone, to use Mary Louise Pratt's phrase (Pratt 1992, 6–7). Savvy border negotiators who know the metropolis but retain their critical difference and distance, these authors trade on both their urbane understanding of the metropolis as well as their authenticity as exotic others. There seems to be no other option for breaking into the cosmopolitan discourse. The concept of "border aesthetics" is integral to my comparative of analysis of these novels. Instead of allowing *Song of Solomon* and *One Hundred Years of Solitude* to singularly represent a particular race or region, I see the two novels as reflecting forms, possibilities, and conditions for representational exchange. My collocation of Morrison and García Márquez, and of these two texts in particular, highlights the complex relationships and blurring of boundaries among race, region, and nation.[16]

At the base of the semiotic confrontation between North and South in *Song of Solomon* and *One Hundred Years of Solitude* is a sense that the authors and protagonists are compelled to represent not only themselves but also the "tribe" from which they come to some other group that does not understand them. As a result, identity is formed through attempts to explain not only oneself but also one's culture to another. During this symbolic confrontation stereotypes are deployed, turned upside down, and twisted. In Morrison's *Song of Solomon* most of the questioning of broad paradigms of North and South comes out in explorations of the North-South dynamic within the African American communities Morrison describes. García Márquez, by contrast, plays with many of the North-South stereotypes by turning the center-periphery models inside out, with Macondo becoming the center of the universe around which the rest of the world—even Sir Francis Drake—revolves. The "North" comes in many guises, from the bullying U.S. banana company to the snotty highlanders, one of whom, Fernanda del Carpio, manages to infiltrate—but is not integrated into—the Buendía clan.

Although the ultimate goal in the exchange of stories is to replace stereotypes with a more nuanced cross-cultural understanding, in situations of unequal power the humorous deployment of stereotypes is used to undermine the force of cosmopolitan othering. In *One Hundred Years of Solitude,* for example, the characters Fernanda and Petra are set up as a duel between North and South, and the South wins. Fernanda's cosmopolitan culture is useless in the new Latin America of Macondo, the noncosmopolitan world (in pointed contrast to the natural education of Remedios the Beauty and in a manner reminiscent of the role played by First Corinthians in *Song of Solomon*):

At the end of eight years, after having learned to write Latin poetry, play the clavichord, talk about falconry with gentlemen and apologetics with archbishops, discuss affairs of state with foreign rulers and affairs of God with the Pope, she returned to her parents' home to weave funeral wreaths. She found it despoiled. . . . she had never heard mention of the wars that were bleeding the country. (García Márquez 1971, 195–96)

Here, knowledge of "the best that has been thought and said"—the vaunted arts and letters of the West—means distance from reality, living in a dream world, a Northern irrationality. Petra, by contrast, is the best of the Americas, "a clean young mulatto woman" with "a generous heart and a magnificent vocation for love" (180).

Song of Solomon engages the North-South dynamic by exploring how this paradigm has seeped into and divided African American culture. First, Morrison reinscribes Northern and Southern boundaries by contrasting the urban milieu of the first half of the book with the rural communities of the second and by representing the North-South split within the fictional northern city. Then she overturns this duality by having Milkman revalue the "southern" (the repository of his African heritage) and by exposing the arbitrariness of North-South boundaries. Here is what Guitar Bains (Milkman's Southern-born best friend who has a killing rationality) has to say about those boundaries: " 'Goddam, Milk, I do believe my whole life's geography.' . . . 'for example, I live in the North now. So the first question come to mind is North of What? Why, north of the South. So North exists because South does. But does that mean North is different from South? No way! South is just south of North' " (Morrison 1978, 115).

The North-South confrontations enacted in these texts illustrate unequal economic and political exchange as well as the differential exchange of stories. Within the play of stereotypes is a resistance to those who might misread stories from Southern lands. While the complicating of stereotypes does not in itself ensure a large readership, it does suggest that Morrison and García Márquez apprehended the diverse audience to which their novels would appeal. One can imagine a reader who enjoys these tales for their depiction of an exotic alternative land—but, almost as easily, one can also see how these texts would help a cosmopolitan reader interrogate his or her desire for and creation of such exotic others.

The blurring of history, story, and genealogy is another form of resistance to the official story embedded in each of these narratives. Colonized groups often find that getting their story straight and protecting their heritage against attempts to erase it takes the form of genealogy or family history, which then stands in opposition to the official story. *Song of Solomon* makes gestures toward a patriarchal family history, following the various Macon Deads, but it is through the intervention of Pilate (Milkman's aunt and spiritual mother) and through Milkman's eventual discovery of his grandmother that he, the last Dead, is able to resolve the tension of competing heritages. In *One Hundred Years of Solitude,* the passing down of Macondo's history, in writing, is a male activity—and a self-destructive one. Úrsula's longevity (she serves as mother to them all), however, allows her to influence that written history by way of oral corrections, though she begins to place things in circles toward the end of her long life.

While not cyclical to the same extent, *Song of Solomon* initially depicts a world in which the past is a present burden. When Milkman first hears of his mother's strange ways, it is from his father's perspective.

> What was he supposed to do with this new information his father had dumped on him? Was it an effort to cop a plea? How was he supposed to feel about the two of them now? Was it *true,* first of all? Did his mother . . . He didn't want to know any of it. There was nothing he could do about it. The doctor was dead. You can't do the past over. (76)

Immediately after this reflection, Milkman walks into the city, becoming "the solitary man" who knows his mother's alleged "crime" (77) of unspeakable affection for her father. Milkman finds himself walking alone on one side of the street, the whole black world, seemingly, going the other way: "He wondered if there was anyone in the world who liked him. Liked him for himself alone" (79). And his quest becomes a quest for unified subjectivity, to be himself but as part of the African American community.

It is through a reflection on names that Milkman first changes his quest from the pursuit of gold to the pursuit of a self that is of and in the tribe. For Morrison, knowing one's name and knowing the hidden history inscribed in names are essential to recovering the story of African Americans. Milkman's father, Macon Dead, tries to erase what he sees to be the problematic history of black naming. On the door to his real estate office, for example, he has painted simply, "office," but one can still discern the words "Sonny's Shop" underneath, Macon Dead thus failing to cover over that history of a more personalized business. Mr. Dead wishes for an ancestor "who had a name that was real": "a name given to him at birth with love and seriousness. A name that was not a joke nor a disguise, nor a brand name" (17). Macon Dead's parents, however, had received—and agreed to keep—a name from the thoughtless North: "Dead" having come from a mistake on the part of a drunken Yankee clerk. Morrison hints at some lack in the patrilineal heritage, "a literal slip of the pen handed to his father on a piece of paper and which he handed on to his only son, and his son likewise handed on to his" (18).

Having unlocked himself through unlocking his family's past, Milkman naturally begins to question the lost heritage of others in the official, dead history:

> He read the road signs with interest now, wondering what lay beneath the names. The Algonquins had named the territory he lived in Great Water, *michi gami.* How many dead lives and fading memories were buried in and beneath the names of the places in this country. Under the recorded names were other names, just as "Macon Dead," recorded for all time in some dusty file, hid from view the real names of people, places, and things, names that had meaning. (333)

Naming may be controlled by the powerful, but the power of understanding and embracing one's name is available to those who can look behind the visible signs. The noncosmopolitans turn out to be the most careful readers, and the insertion of African American stories behind the recorded ones is essential for revitalizing all American culture.

In *One Hundred Years of Solitude* the clash between the official story and what is known to be true by a select few is even more explicitly laid out. Bear in mind that the turning point in the history of Macondo is the transformation of the town that occurred as a result of the incursion of the North American banana company and of their ruinous departure amid a massacre—the latter action having been completely erased from the history books. This episode and its aftermath represent a more direct form of questioning the value of literacy—the written, official history—for if the official words can eliminate horrendous actions, then words alone have very little positive value but much potential power. When the banana company's workers consider going on strike, words drive them out of existence after company lawyers do their work: "by a decision of the court it was established and set down in solemn decrees that the workers did not exist" (García Márquez 1971, 280). The real elimination of the workers and their families comes in the form of a massacre that only José Arcadio Segundo survives. Not even his twin brother will believe his story: "The official version, repeated a thousand times and mangled out all over the country by every means of communication the government found at hand, was finally accepted: there were no dead, the satisfied workers had gone back to their families, and the banana company was suspending all activity until the rains stopped" (287). Unable to make himself heard, José Arcadio Segundo dedicates himself to the perusal of the manuscripts of Melquíades, turning to reading prophecy when talk was found to be without value.

Taken as a whole, the noncosmopolitan aesthetic offers possibilities for accepting cultural difference without homogenization, while the appropriative mechanisms for international fiction move in the opposite direction, dissolving the other into something almost like us. Morrison and García Márquez are in many ways "conservators of culture" that is never exactly theirs.[17] Standing between the metropolis and their tribe, they preserve a vision of past fullness for the group they represent. And the "pastness" of their stories—their representations of, among other things, metropolitan atrocities—make them safer in the present for the politically conservative metropolitan. Thus the Nobel Prize for Morrison and García Márquez is not surprising, not a clear break from the past. Instead, the Nobel is business as usual, even if the usual business has become more transnational and more multiethnic. I believe it is fruitful to consider cultural systems as canon-making machines, for a canon, in a general sense, is about narrowing choices and establishing relationships between consumers and producers (whether spiritual or financial). Further inquiry into the construction of traditions will ultimately lead, I hope, to seeing reading and writing as valuable in a multiplicity of ways beyond a narrowly conceived tradition of formal expertise. Recognition of the profound transformation visited upon authors like Morrison and García Márquez by a reception that reads "universally" should encourage readers of all kinds to reread specificity back into novelists who have long been considered part of the Great Tradition. At the same time, a new attention to the mechanisms through which we find and read tales from strange lands as allegories of "otherness" ought to move us to acknowledge the complex history and diversity of these "new found lands."

Notes

1. For further explication of this duality, see Spivak 1988a, especially 275–76.
2. The term "value" suggests the complex intertwining between the economic and the aesthetic, the commercial and the ethical.
3. William Faulkner is an obvious influence on and analogue of these two writers and their cultural value. While both Morrison and García Márquez openly acknowledge Faulkner's position as a lodestar for their own writing, I see the multiple and intertwining connections as more than just influence. Faulkner's road to the Nobel, for example, parallels in some ways the cultural shifts necessary for acceptance of Latin American and African American writing, Faulkner being the rescued genius from a languid land that time and art forgot. Ironically, the success of Morrison and García Márquez has contributed to a resituation of Faulkner allowing him to be read now as simultaneously "classic" and "postcolonial," as Southern, black, Caribbean, and even as "our most Latin American writer" (Chevigny 1993, 355; see also Spillers 1991). I analyze these complex relations in my forthcoming book *Which Difference Makes a Difference: William Faulkner, Gabriel García Márquez, Toni Morrison, and the Creation of Literary Value.*
4. Important background for the rise of the Latin American novel in the United States is the story of the disparate forces that came together in Barcelona around 1960 and enabled access to and interest in Latin American novelists for an international audience. My research in Barcelona and Madrid has convinced me that literary scholars underestimate the importance of extraliterary forces (e.g., export subsidies, the personal biases of powerful editors, Franco's censorship) in shaping what has come to be accepted as the natural recognition of great writing. In this case, many factors combined to create a "Boom" (the label given to the sudden international prominence of Latin American novelists in the 1960s) that could only have been male and that had to consist of high Western art. Authors already known internationally were then passed on to New York publishers.
5. That García Márquez's novel was reviewed in both *Time* and *Newsweek* is significant, since these two most prominent U.S. newsweeklies present only a very low percentage of the novels they receive. The publication of this novel was not just literature but news, and in the *Time* review, that news stands as the story of Latin America itself (a varied group of nations usually gracing the pages of the weeklies only when there is an uprising or an earthquake) ("Orchids and Bloodlines" 1970; see also Wolff 1970).
6. See Nina Baym's "Melodramas of Beset Manhood" (1981) for a discussion of how paradigms of literary art fulfillable only by white male protagonists (and likely to be written by male authors) are translated into "universal" or "American." Reid performs a similar action for recent Latin American fiction by unifying and universalizing what is actually a small selection of Latin American au-

thors. The interlocking friendships of the "Boom" writers are well documented, and it is clear that their sense of being a *Latin American* generation was important to their creative process, but this was no open club (see, for example, the memoirs of José Donoso [1977] and Carlos Barral [1978 and 1988]; Ángel Rama's "El Boom en perspectiva" [1982] is still the best single source for a discussion of the complexity of the Latin American "Boom" as a material and artistic phenomenon).

7. Homi Bhabha suggests that this is a typical colonizing move: "The colonial space is the *terra incognita* or the *terra nulla,* the empty or wasted land whose history has to be begun, whose archives must be filled out; whose future progress must be secured in modernity" (1991, 205).

8. In the case of *One Hundred Years of Solitude,* "replete with Western literary allusions" may be an understatement. One critical study spends some 250 pages attempting an exhaustive survey of the novel's "three thousand years of literature" (García 1977).

9. George Yúdice (1991) sees Latin American testimonial writing as challenging the traditional role of the intellectual or artist as spokesperson for the "voiceless" (19). Earlier Latin American literary institutions permitted only certain classes of individuals to establish standards of taste within the public sphere: "This explains why contestatory writers like Neruda or Gabriel García Márquez, trained within the institution, have not had trouble performing in the literary sphere" (20). Despite the publicity surrounding Rigoberta Menchú (and acknowledging the recent additions of the magic-realist "sisters" Isabel Allende and Laura Esquivel and the continuing presence of his "Boom" brethren) García Márquez retains a hegemonic position as the voice of Latin America for most North American readers of literary fiction.

10. A 1969 *Newsweek* article on "the black novelists" revealed publishers' attitudes toward this "new" phenomenon. The journalist acknowledged that there was a clear history of prejudice toward black fiction, but the national absorption in the growing black-white crisis had spurred publishing houses to add black writers to their lists. As an editor at William Morrow told the reporter, "People are after a black experience; they want to be black" (Gross 1969).

11. Prior to the 1970s, scholars within the African American literary community contributed to the exclusion of female authors. Mary Helen Washington (1990) notes that African American literary histories "set forth a model of literary paternity in which each male author vies with his predecessor for greater authenticity, greater control over *his* voice." Thus "women's writing is considered singular and anomalous, not universal and representative, and for some mysterious reason, writing about black women is not considered as racially significant as writing about black men" (33). Early reviews of Morrison's work reflected this older paradigm.

12. As with García Márquez, Morrison's rise in the public eye complicates Ohmann's model of canon formation (1983). I follow Ohmann's lead again in focusing on Morrison's status in New York, but his class analysis fails to account for the two most important "insurgencies" in the New York literary world in the past two decades—blacks and women and, in this case, African American women.

13. Prior to publishing her first novel, Morrison was one of the first black female editors at a New York trade publisher. She continued in her position as a senior editor at Random House until 1984, working with Angela Davis, Gayl Jones, and Toni Cade Bambara, among others.

14. This paragraph is based on research in the Random House Records at Columbia University Library. See especially Box 1522.

15. All student and instructor comments come from my ethnographic study of the "Great Works" class at Stanford University in 1992, where I was a participant-observer in two sections of the "great works" track of the required first-year humanities course.

16. In describing aspects of *Song of Solomon* that she sees as characteristic of African American writing, Morrison ends up providing a schema for the kind of literary-historical border hopping that I advocate, for her analysis easily applies to *One Hundred Years of Solitude.* Morrison discusses, for example, the way she blends "the acceptance of the supernatural and a profound rootedness in the real world at the same time with neither taking precedence over the other." She also mentions the "oral quality" of the writing and "the presence of an ancestor" (1984, 342–43).

17. I borrow this term from Theodore Mason's article on *Song of Solomon,* "The Novelist as Conservator." While I share Mason's view that many critics miss Morrison's "traditional view of the relation between literature and culture" (Mason 1988, 564), my reading follows different, albeit not contradictory, lines of inquiry.

II

(Trans)National Canons

Deidre Lynch

5 At Home with Jane Austen

The Eighteenth century was an age such as our imagination can barely comprehend; weltering as we do in a slough of habitual ugliness, ranging from the dreary horrors of Victorian sham gothic to the more lively hideousness of modern jerry-building, with advertisements defacing any space that might be left unoffendingly blank, and the tourist scattering his trail of chocolate paper, cigarette ends and film cartons, we catch sight every now and again of a house front, plain and graceful, with a fanlight like the half of a spider's web and a slip of iron balcony.
—Elizabeth Jenkins, *Jane Austen: A Biography*

❧ In the opening sentence of her life of Jane Austen (originally published in 1938), Elizabeth Jenkins swivels between celebrating the miraculous survival of a Georgian house and railing against the untidiness of those who might visit it. Doing so, she enacts an irony that will be central to my discussion of the ideological work of Janeisms in interwar England, ideological work performed by a concept of the "classical novel," on the one hand, and by widely circulated narratives about English homes and a home-loving author, on the other. Jenkins helped preserve the Hampshire cottage in which Austen wrote her novels and in May 1940 helped found the Jane Austen Society—while a more celebrated mission of national salvation unfolded at Dunkirk. By such means Jenkins perforce participated in recasting Austen's fictions so that they would suit new functions within the literary system and, more urgently, so that they would suit definitions of nationality that were themselves being transformed. The creation of the Austen Society, the proliferation of Shakespeare festivals, and the curricular rise of "English" were so many early-twentieth-century testimonies to the notion that select literary works constituted a preserve for real Englishness. Such Englishness metamorphosed in turn between 1918 and 1945. The idiom of that identity politics moved away from the outsized epic rhetoric suited to imperial missions toward an emphasis on the "inward-looking, domestic, and private" and toward the proposition that the real locus of national history was the middle-class woman's life in a house (Light 1991, 211).

The scorn that Elizabeth Jenkins directs toward just those sightseers for whose sake Chawton Cottage was preserved can stand for the moment as a paradigmatic instance of the tensions that accompanied the process of repackaging Englishness as an article of domestic consumption. Those tensions arise, in more general terms, whenever a token of aesthetic value—a talisman of a "touch of class"—is released from its point of origin in the social formation and redeployed as a *national* heritage, whenever it is made subject to capitalism's constant recycling of commodities and displayed across the modern formats and reprographic techniques that compose a culture of mass leisure. For the rhetoric that Jenkins draws on to decry loutish town-dwellers on tour emerged in tandem with yet another new, widely circulated story about Englishness. This story nominated rural England—more specifically the landscape of the "Home Counties" (to the exclusion of the Midlands and North England)—as the site of that all but lost traditional national essence. The interwar period witnessed a series of conflicts issuing directly from the nationalization that made rural beauty spots into a notional permanent residence for England's urban majority. The rights of way claimed by tourists who used modern technologies (Shell guides and Southern Railway package tours) to escape to a "green nook" (a site that invoked, so the pioneering Professor of English Literature Arthur Quiller-Couch claimed, every "Englishman's" nostalgia) were soon pitted against the property and privacy rights claimed by farmers and by the hunting, shooting, and fishing gentries. What was rehearsed through these clashes over who did and did not have a legitimate relation to "the country" was, of course, the history of the same enclosure acts that had, back in Austen's era, produced this ostensibly timeless, sacred landscape of hedgerows, checkerboard fields, and Hampshire cottages in the first place.[1]

The teaching of English literature (perhaps the teaching of the English novel most of all) has long been grounded in comparable conflicts, between the project of preserving the aura that accrues to objects of minority ownership and tastes and the project of nationalizing a public consciousness—of turning citizen-subjects away from rival forms of allegiance (those of class, for a start) and convincing them that England is where they are most themselves and most at home. Thus while it lobbies for literary pedagogy the English Association's 1918 report on the curriculum of the national education system advocates what is in effect a doubled definition of "English in England." Wherever "English" is manifested as "art," it transcends narrow class interests; when manifested as "education," "its function [is] to refuse and actively combat the influence of majority cultures rather than be democratically responsible to them" (Doyle 1989, 43). Most studies of this tension in English studies' mission of national cultivation have focused on the plural mobilizations of "Shakespeare" and on the neo-Elizabethanism that the English cultivate on public occasions of state (see, e.g., Holderness 1988). The timing of Jenkins's preservation of Chawton Cottage suggests, however, that Austen as much as the Bard was in 1940 deemed vital to the warfare being waged on what was called, after all, "the home front." Where analysis of "the Shakespeare Myth" delivers one sort of perspective on Englishness, tracing the competing, legitimizing and delegitimizing modes in which Austen's domestic fiction was reproduced illuminates rather different fractures in the nation's consensual notions about the unity of the national literature and national character. The history of Jane Austen's reinscriptions discloses conflicting perspectives on women readers' and writers' place in the nation and state. And because the Austen novel came to function in the interwar era within new intertextual systems—systems that, as we shall see, brought it into relation with mass-marketed historical romances and whodunits as well as with highbrow redefinitions of "women's fiction"—the history of its reinscriptions also illuminates that double play which has "the feminine" serve in the English context both as a sign for high culture and as a byword for such mass-culture menaces as the leveling-down process, Americanization, and escapist pleasure seeking.

The Austen novel's high-cultural, classical credentials first become an article of faith for reading audiences of the 1920s and '30s. A. C. Bradley and Virginia Woolf, as well as Elizabeth Jenkins, cast Austen as the Shakespeare of the female sphere. Associations of *Emma* with *Electra* and references likening Austen's wit to "sunlight [playing] upon some flawless antique marble" suggest that for this era Austen also became in effect a novelist-denizen of Athens, and so more classical still (Woolf 1937, 42; Priestley 1931, 137). "A 'classic' text . . . has the complex presence of a Scripture (which blocks, reifies its iteration and appropriation by other systems of writing)," John Frow writes: "the social function of the classical text is in the first place to *be* a classical text, to signify its own value as cultural capital" (1986, 228, 230). If we wish, as Frow advocates, to withdraw the classical text from that hermetic context—and if as feminist critics, we want to take seriously the anomaly presented by a woman writer who is as "at home" in the canon as Jane Austen is—we need both to acknowledge and to query the ideal of durability that is invested in hypercanonical novels like *Emma* or *Pride and Prejudice.* Austen still operates as a sign for the charms of permanent residence. At least since her novels' 1909 republication in the *English Idylls* series, readers have been invited to enter into an elegiac relation to the world they enclose. (D. A. Miller gives somewhat facetious expression to this homesickness in "The Late Jane Austen": "For many years after I first left home, whenever I got sufficiently sick . . . to need to 'take to bed,' I would take Jane Austen there with me" [1990, 55].) Over the last decade feminist and materialist critics' studies of Austen within her historical context have challenged the authorial image that informs these desires for settlement and settled meanings, enclosure and closure. Austen no longer invariably appears as a feminine counterpart of the solitary Romantic genius, someone set apart from her era's well-established network of women novelists, self-possessed and unflappable in a cottage of her own. Nonetheless, such criticism has generally sidestepped how those same desires are writ large in the institution of literary studies.

Notwithstanding its current determination to admit historical vicissitude inside Chawton Cottage, literary studies still operates according to the unwittingly elegiac assumption that "forms of writing are . . . active within history once and once only" (Bennett 1990, 112) and that the Austen novel, like any text, bears into the future an enduring significance that it derives from a past moment of origin. My presupposition in this essay is, by contrast, that the meanings and uses of the Austen novel, or any text, are not fixed or unitary but should be understood as a function of multiple and overlapping historicities. Conforming to that presupposition involves questioning the conventional determination to segregate Austen's century from ours, or to segregate "Austen herself"—the meanings *in* the novels—from the institutional and public contexts of her reception—matter deemed to be "outside literature." Accordingly, I offer the following partial history of how Austen's name and text were mobilized in one terrain of cultural contention, English society between 1918 and 1945, as an illustration of what it might mean to acknowledge the interdependence between the intratextual and the extratextual. This essay means to account, that is, not for the Austen novel's pastness but rather for its productive interaction with distinct historical systems, their practices of reading, and their intertextual and institutional coordinates. Once we unsettle Austen's texts from their place in tradition and in the literary histories that regulate and contain "the" novel, the history of these most literary of novels can be reseen—as one in which "Austen" still represents a cultural site supportive of new inventions.

Repeatedly rescripted as source material for competing, sometimes contradictory definitions of England as home, the Austen text also served in interwar England to articulate and rearticulate the shifting boundaries between elite and mass culture, between "the realist novel" and "romance fiction," and, by extension, to articulate and rearticulate the nation with the desires and needs of some classes of readers, to the exclusion of others. Just that serviceability may lie behind the assertion John Bailey made in introducing his new "Georgian" edition of Austen—"We cannot do without the classical novel" (1931, 53). The English state's new definition of classic literature as a national asset meant that, throughout Bailey's era, wider, more mixed readerships were ushered into the enchanted, hedgerowed landscapes of "Austen-Land" (Hill 1902, 1). Yet this discourse of legitimation also depended on retaining the Austen novel's cachet as the exclusive property of the country-house set. As commentators idealized agrarian England under the Regency into an era of gracious living, the Austen novel provided a means of preserving old-fashioned images of class differentiation. At the same time, however, other uses of Austen indicate how her novel was equally available through the 1920s and '30s as an unmistakably modern source of entertainment and inducement to further consumption. Thus the name of "Jane" operated in the interwar literary system to countersign the identification of Regency and Romance that Georgette Heyer inaugurated in her series of best-sellers (published almost annually from 1923 to 1972) set in turn-of-the-nineteenth-century pleasure spots like Bath and Brighton.[2] And allusions to Austen's novels gave a high-cultural sanction to the breezy backgrounding of history and attention to the quotidian that distinguished interwar detective fiction as well as the Regency Romance; simultaneously, Austen's reputation for a genteel immunity to sentimentality alibied the lady crime-writer who catered to a mass market from the charge of also catering to lowbrow tastes for romantic passion.

To apprehend these conflicting agenda in the ways "Jane" was set up to confer and acquire significance will mean tracking the histories of gender inscribed in the relations English readers have had to literary tradition, house, and homeland, tracking the histories of class inscribed in those relations, and also, crucially, remarking how these histories diverge. For the tension between those two ways of telling is something we have always to reckon with, inside feminist literary classrooms, when we resort to Austen to teach "the" novel. Within the wider terrain of culture that literary studies brackets, a terrain that mediates our access to the literature that is our professional base, Austen's classical novel has been effective precisely (but not exclusively) *as* a classic, in representing and maintaining hierarchies. To ignore that overdetermined effectivity while we produce scrupulously contextualized readings of "Austen herself" is to ignore the power that we, too, wield as teachers and critics: the power to legitimize and to delegitimize literariness. To ignore Austen, conversely, is to give a hostage up to a singular, capitalized notion of Literature, and to ignore the ways in which the latter is always a contested object. In these ways, Austen's classical novel, as well as its author's status as the icon of an irredeemably genteel femininity, at once compels and puts to the proof our efforts to locate a common ground for feminist literary history and cultural studies. The history of the reconstitutions of Austen and of England that I assemble here suggests that such common ground may in fact be found by considering what Mary A. Favret has identified as "the consequences of constructing a home for art" (1994, 61). It may be found by considering the attitudes to the domestic, private, and feminine that make Literature a place where one convalesces from history, and also, conversely, an object one protects from the taint of domestic consumption.

"Little England" and the "Little Bit of Ivory"

As they recoiled from the bellicose imperial ideal that had led them into the First World War, English people scaled down their idea of the nation (without actually giving up England's colonies). "There is . . . a patriotism that calls out for size," the Little Englander C. E. Montague conceded in an essay of 1925, but, he continued, the English loved their country with a love that "clings instinctively to things that are within the reach of sense, and small enough to be held in one grasp" (qtd. in Grainger 1986, 90). Englishness, it was agreed, found fullest expression in the little touches of comfort that made up life in the English home. Indeed, the effect of new forms of consumer credit, hire-purchase systems, and low-interest mortgages meant that it did not offend credibility as it formerly would to image an ideal England as something experienced behind closed doors. England was reenvisaged as a nation of single-family dwellings and walled gardens (Miles and Smith 1987, 14–18).[3] A new enclosure movement of sorts, this remapping of the nation was publicized by fictions like E. M. Delafield's *Diary of a Provincial Lady* (originally published in 1930) and Jan Struther's *Mrs. Miniver* (originally published in 1939). Those texts made an art form of documenting what Englishwomen (with their servants' help) did in houses. They displayed a mocking affection toward ordinariness, as in the Provincial Lady's case, or all-out reverence, as in Mrs. Miniver's. When Mrs. Miniver turns her house key in the lock and muses over the "minute tactual intimacies, whose resumption was the essence of coming home," or when she wonders about the source of the pleasure that is afforded by the tiny presents she's put into the children's Christmas stockings and decides it is "the sense of limitation within a strict form" that is also afforded by "the sonnet," it is hard to miss how hospitable the Little Englandism of the interwar period was, with its love of small things, to an ethos and aesthetics of private ownership (Struther 1940, 5, 46). As her increasing prestige in this period suggests, Austen was a beneficiary of that hospitality.

In the course of explaining that the image of John Bull will suffice no more, and that for typical Englishness one must resort instead to "the cottage homes of England," Stewart Dick shows how an early effort to imagine a scaled-down, closed-in nation could extend to questions about literary genre: "It is an age not of the drama, but of the novel . . . [W]hat before was presented visibly on the stage . . . is now hidden between the two boards of a book" (1909, 3). There is more than a conflation of subjectivity with private property at stake in this convergence between a new idea of the English person's homeland and an old idea of the novel, or in this convergence between the miniature toys that hold deep meaning for Mrs. Miniver and the painting on "a little bit of Ivory" that was Jane Austen's most famous image for what she did in her books. Austen's comparison between her nephew's "manly . . . Sketches full of Variety and Glow" and her own small-scale chronicles of daily doings was in the interwar period cited by almost all who wrote on Austen. In some ways, citation of Austen's reflections on her work accredited efforts to restrict "the" woman's novel to a particularly home-centered construct of women's experience;[4] it likewise helped to appropriate the language of home for the language of a single propertied class. While in these ways Austen's commentaries on her art supported articulations of discursive and social institutions that must make feminist critics uneasy, the other uses to which Little England put the Austen novel are harder to dismiss. In 1918, almost fifty years after the establishment of universal male suffrage in Britain, the Representation of the People Bill extended the franchise to married women over the age of thirty. A decade later Britain corrected the inequities perpetuated in this "matron's bill" and admitted a remaining 5.5 million women over the age of twenty-one into the company of British citizens. One response to these shifts in women's relation to the nation, as to History written under the sign of the nation-state, was to revalue the claims to "realism" made by and on behalf of domestic fictions. This meant reevaluating representations concocted in the crucible of the local: representations showcasing small talk and narratives that went "over the same ground again," like the story of the union between Emma and Knightley, which each resident of Highbury had "always foreseen" (Austen 1971a, 425), or like the story of Marianne Dashwood, whose "extraordinary fate" consisted in growing up (Austen 1967, 366).

Such reevaluations of everyday meaningfulness found support in *Northanger Abbey* especially, the novel in which Austen counterpoints her customary courtship plot with the story of a heroine's education out of Radcliffean "alarms of romance" and into the "anxieties of common life" (Austen 1971b, 161). Early in that narrative, when the heroine, Catherine Morland, is still in the grip of Gothic romance, she describes her distaste for "real, solemn history":

> "it tells me nothing that does not either vex or weary me. The quarrels of popes and kings, with wars or pestilences, in every page; the men all so good for nothing, and hardly any women at all—it is very tiresome: and yet I often think it odd that it should be so dull, for a great deal of it must be invention. The speeches

that are put into the heroes' mouths, their thoughts and designs—the chief of all this must be invention, and invention is what delights me in other books." (84)

Austen's novel could be redeployed in the interwar period to unsettle the gendered arrangements according to which people weighed the knowledge effects of different discourses and divided them into "manageable portions of fiction and fact, dream and reality" (Light 1991, 4). Catherine depreciates History (and Austen extols the truths of novelistic realism) in two ways: pointing up History's constitutive exclusion of women's lives and perspectives; hinting at History's debt to fiction's representations of real experiences and inner lives.

The English between the wars invested in Austen precisely because she seemed to snub History as much as History snubbed women. Their readings of the Austen novel stressed the words "as usual" ("the abracadabra necessary to summon happiness" [Kaye-Smith and Stern 1943, 192]); and Austen's emphasis on "common life" seemed to them the more inspiring, insofar as she, like them, lived in unusual, event-full times. Austen's was an epoch distinguished by almost unceasing war, as well as multiple political and economic revolutions: and yet, "there was no room for them and their big crudities on . . . 'the little bit . . . of ivory,'" as many a commentator emphasized (Bailey 1931, 13). Indeed, that the Regency became a byword for romance among English readers of the 1920s and '30s was the result in a roundabout way of the perception that the turn of the nineteenth century was a period more replete with public events, more "historical," than others. To give femininity the lead role in the representation of the national past was a more significant and iconoclastic gesture if that past was one in which, as the story usually went, the nation's survival and even the shape of the modern world were at stake. Georgette Heyer's Regencies performed this gesture: they irresponsibly refrained from acknowledging the epoch-making deeds of Bonaparte, Wellington, Prime Minister Pitt, and Admiral Nelson and established their period settings through allusions to the latest things in dress and decor (as Heyer titles like *Sprig Muslin* suggest). The many romances fictionalizing the life of Emma, Lady Hamilton, mistress to Nelson, operated to similar effect in the mass culture of interwar England, as they balanced between public-mindedness and the desacramentalizing and peaceable pleasures to be derived from substituting emotional crises—or wardrobe crises—for national crises and from showing the great to be made of common clay. Alexander Korda's 1941 film romance *Lady*

Hamilton, recasting Nelson's (Laurence Olivier's) campaigns as dry runs for the Battle of Britain, and assimilating both histories into a story of private life on the home front, routed its audience's access to history through the point of view of an aging Emma (Vivien Leigh). *The Man in Grey*, the Gainsborough Studio's 1943 blockbuster costume melodrama (directed by Leslie Arliss), privatized history even more thoroughly. The transition in the film from the wartime present—a prologue set in a London auction room that has contravened blackout regulations—to the past—a story of adultery among Regency beaux and belles—is effected by way of a close-up view of a Georgian trinket box that has yet to find a buyer. A fan, snuffbox, and needle case are enshrined in this box. These "bits and pieces . . . must have meant something to someone once," the khaki-clad hero avers: the "historical" narrative that follows illuminates their significance.

As Lillian Robinson notes in her essay on Austen and Heyer, through selectively reworking "a historical period when great public events were in the making," such historical fictions affirm what Catherine Morland says when she complains about history—"that the personal *matters*" (1978, 221). But the political import of this proposition is difficult to determine, because what the personal signifies is so nebulous. Contemplating the popularity of the numerous interwar romances and films revealing "the woman in the monarch," Sarah Waters argues that these texts indirectly acknowledged the new anxieties about women's entrance into the polis that followed enfranchisement. In playing out the histories of, for instance, Queen Christina, Elizabeth I, and Mary of Scotland as so many variations on a narrative invariably structured by the conflict between public duty and love, the historical romance invited its female reader or spectator to view her political agency and her personal fulfillment as incompatible goals. The fact that Queen Christina and Queen Mary fashions were hot sellers in the 1930s further demonstrates how the privatized desires instituted in and through the romance genre could easily be reinscribed as consuming passions of the most anodyne sort (Waters 1994, 51–54). As Waters's research suggests, to grant priority to the personal does not necessarily transform the gendered categories through which the historical is constructed. It may do no more than reverse the values assigned to either side of the gender divide while leaving the private-public opposition intact. England's new rhetoric of a domestic nationality may have granted, concurring with the Austen novel, that *real* life was at home with the women, but that concession seldom entailed reenvisioning the private sphere, in terms more consonant with masculinist inscriptions of history and citizenship, as a site of transience and activity in its own right.

That Austen's example of how to make the personal matter could in Little England support the most conservative agendas becomes apparent when we consider a remark the novelist Dame Ivy Compton-Burnett made during the Battle of Britain. (Dame Ivy's modernist domestic fictions—black comedies filled with the repartee of distressed gentlewomen who don't get out enough—were published between 1925 and 1971, making her an almost exact but more literary contemporary of Georgette Heyer.) Dame Ivy used the occasion of her relocation from bombed-out London to quiet Lyme Regis to reread *Sense and Sensibility* and to celebrate her own secure settlement in the "feminine" domain of private and personal meanings: "how much more important in the long run," she mused, "was the twisted ankle of a young girl than all the clamouring of leaders in far off countries" (qtd. in Light 1991, 46). This domestic novelist's blithe insularity might be coupled with the unapologetic individualism prompting Oxford lecturer Mary Lascelles to praise Austen for not representing "collective humanity": "it was well that she avoided even indirect representation of public disturbance, which gives abnormal importance to humanity in the gross" (1939, 132). The two remarks should alert us to just how treacherous a territory the domain of personal (and normal) lives can be. Scouted by Jane Austen in the Regency period, recognized as especially rich in resources after 1918, this is a territory in which feminist and conservative preoccupations can be hard to differentiate, in which statements about the significance of psychic as well as social structures too easily slide into the proposition that *only* the personal counts as the political.[5]

Like the nostalgia that made the Home Counties into the archetype of timeless England, Dame Ivy's appropriation made "Austen-Land" into (to borrow Raymond Williams's words from *The Country and the City*) "a rural backwater." Such readings of Austen's courtship plots and devices for rearranging the populations of her country houses suppress "the continual making and remaking of these houses and their families"; they create the conditions under which, Williams continues, "Jane Austen's world can . . . be taken for granted . . . as if it were a simple 'traditional' setting. And then if the social 'background' is in this sense 'settled,' we can move to an emphasis on a fiction of purely personal relationships" (1975, 141).[6] It is within just such interpretive parameters, though, that Austen could in Dame Ivy's lifetime become a figure of the home that England's soldiers and sailors were fighting for. Rudyard Kipling's war story "The Janeites," in which officers and men bond in the trenches through their love of Jane, makes Austen's emblematic, nationalized status evident. The story culminates with an account of how, after their trench is shelled and the narrator finds himself the " 'on'y Janeite left,' " that " 'Jane business' " saves his life. A well-timed reference to a character in *Emma* wins him the attention of a society lady and secures him a place on a hospital train (Kipling 1926, 185).

That Kipling's Janeites were not fighting, and would never have expected to fight, for a specific political claim or ideology but rather were fighting for our Jane and "our way of doing things" was itself reflective of a very English disdain for political theorizing (Nairn 1990, 94). The differential grid that established the specificity of Englishness did so by defining other peoples' nations as at once united and blighted by a doctrinaire adherence to abstract principles: and, as Lord Peter Wimsey, Dorothy Sayers's quintessential English gentleman, warns, " 'the first thing a principle does . . . is to kill somebody' " (1986a, 339). By contrast, Englishness was a matter of intuitions and images, tethered to the concrete by what was touted as the English person's characteristic diffidence in the face of big ideas (Nairn 1990, 304). Englishness was a concatenation of certain sounds or sights—"the tinkle of the hammer on the anvil in the country smith," Prime Minister Stanley Baldwin averred (Priestley 1931, vi); a view of the white cliffs of Dover; or a peep inside one of those "ramshackle" and "queer" cottages in which Constance Hill persistently installed Austen (1902, 135).

As a surrogate for more politicized notions of nationhood, literary discourse could function identically to landscape discourse: H. G. Wells finished up his own enumeration of domestic totems with a reference to "Jane Austen and chintz covers" (qtd. in Beauman 1983, 68). Indeed, it was by virtue of replacing dogmatic forms of ideological expression with this vague idiom, which minimized debate and privileged "the implicit and intuitive properties of . . . sensibility," that the study of classic English literature became a key mechanism of civic consensus for the twentieth-century state (Baldick 1983, 228). And by virtue of writing, as Austen scholars still emphasize, novels of manners while her Frenchified compatriots wrote novels of polemics, Austen had created classic English literature. "She had some unconscious instinct of the truth that individual men and women . . . are the true subject of the novel, and not theories or propaganda of any kind" (Bailey 1931, 105).

Good Housekeeping and the Future of Fiction

As they installed Austen's fiction inside the true home others' novels left at their peril, and as they imaged "Austen-Land" as the homeland the English waged war for, figures like John Bailey helped reorganize cultural hegemony. Nationalizing Austen was a means to borrow on her prestige and so underwrite the claims to unity that state-sponsored ideas of the nation enforced. By offering the Austen novel as an access route to the national past, these figures helped affirm a redesigned national present.

Rather than culture providing the medium through which "the nation" expresses itself, James Donald observes, culture produces that nation, "but always as if it were anterior to these processes of production." What was obtained when Austen's commentators defined English to and for the English and legislated the characteristic chronotopes of the national mentality was not simply a means of fixing "an identity" founded on a "uniaccentual order of perception and expression." Indeed, as Donald argues, what culture produces in producing the nation is not so much *identity* as "hierarchically organized values, dispositions, and differences" (1992, 50). What is at stake within the lived culture of the nation, what lies behind the concession that members of this imagined community are formally equal, is a set of unequal class and region-based dispositions toward the standard language and the national Literature that enshrines it, an organized dissensus according to which some are schooled to see their language use as vulgar and inarticulate, at the same time others experience literary language as their own (Donald 1989, 16). It is this second constituency that can read Austen and get the cozy feeling the novelists Sheila Kaye-Smith and Gladys Stern describe in *Talking of Jane Austen:* they can feel as if they were "walking in their own garden" (1943, 190). Though variously located and experienced, "home" is still a catchall concept with room for "disregarded needs and potentials" that have "no opportunity for realisation in the world as it is outside" (Wright 1985, 11). This is why the designation of the Austen novel as *every* English person's permanent residence is a problem. The cultural imperative that has required nondominant groups at once to identify with and dissociate themselves from this shared social referent occasions dislocations and deprivations that are all the more painful inasmuch as a national culture maintains aesthetic property to be open to all.

Involved in English education via the English Association, and in the English heritage industry via the National Trust for Places of Historic Interest, John Bailey might be said to have equated the Austen canon with the country houses he helped to protect. As viewed by the National Trust, disinclined to question the privileges of class, those privately owned yet "stately" homes were worthy of veneration and tax exemption because they were places where time had stood still. The country houses' survival, through reassuring evidence of historical continuity, could also (in conformity with the illogic particular to nostalgia) offset a notion of history as a process of decline, as a process in which the heritage was always in danger. And like the eighteenth-century manors that focused preservationist initiatives following the Georgian Group's establishment in 1937, the Austen novel could also function in a variety of narratives as a paradise lost and a means to discredit the present: narratives about, as we have seen, town dwellers' accelerating dereliction of the countryside, as well as narratives about cultural decline in an age of mass education and entertainment. Thus in Q. D. Leavis's *Fiction and the Reading Public,* an entropic literary history structured by a concept of a golden age of cultural homogeneity, Austen is portrayed as the last novelist who could "use quite simply . . . phrases like 'honour,' 'manly virtue' [and] . . . be sure of being understood" (1939, 125).

Images of the late-eighteenth-century countryside (dominated by stately homes, dotted with cottages) connoted a harmonious refuge from the modern world between 1918 and 1945—when that scene was reviewed in light of a conservative animus against the democratizations of interwar culture. At that same time, however, this Georgian countryside also represented "an historic precedent of orderly and progressive design" (Matless 1990, 203). That Home Counties landscape, which had replaced uninhabited (Lake District) beauty spots as *the* visual emblem of Englishness, was frequently reseen in the interwar period as the very image of "order and health appropriate to a rationally modernised society," and an image that might best be preserved via synoptic planning and the development of the national grid and arterial roads (Potts 1989,

167, 175).[7] As such an instance of double vision suggests, preservationism can "generaliz[e] bourgeois into national culture" (Wright 1985, 55) and can help consolidate the capitalist state's hegemony, because it is a system of retrospection that operates via a highly flexible (or contradictory) sense of time. Janeism operated that way too. For some highbrow readers in interwar England, Jane Austen could evoke the kind of emotional charge usually associated with a family heirloom or endangered species. At the same time, by contrast, other fractions of the dominant classes could invoke Austen as they expounded the tenets of literary modernism. The Austen novel could focus arguments against novelty, but whenever it was found that it had a "modern outlook" (Kaye-Smith and Stern 1943, 4), it also became useful to the hegemonic projects maintained through the idea of a progressive literary history, a literary history in which something that could still be considered "the English novel" kept rising.

It is Virginia Woolf who most explicitly links Austen's classical novel to an avant-garde "future of fiction." In *A Room of One's Own* (originally published in 1929), Woolf's narrator broaches the topic of the fate of the novel with the hypothesis that because "the book has to be adapted to the body," "women's books should be shorter, more concentrated than those of men" (1992b, 101). Since this conjecture follows a description of how Jane Austen looked at a tradition of masculine sentences, laughed, and "devised a perfectly natural, shapely sentence proper for her own use" (100), Woolf's text seems to cast Austen's fiction as the closest thing yet to the compact ideal that women's novels of the future will strive toward. Woolf emphasizes that quality of economy elsewhere in her readings of Austen. In 1918 she associated her with the eighteenth century's "shorter, denser, richer form of literature," and in 1925 she explained in *The Common Reader* that Austen's was not "a prolific genius"—"humbly and gaily she collected the twigs and straws out of which the nest was to be made and placed them neatly together" (Woolf 1986b, 324; 1937, 174).

For some, tidy economy like this epitomized a chic minimalism: it could be touted as a component of a specifically feminine and patrician modernity. Austen's comment about the "bit of ivory" and her observation that "three or four families in a country village" were the very thing for the aspiring novelist to work with were easily assimilable, for instance, to the promotion between the wars of a new, stripped-down style of interior decoration in which a *few* classic pieces of Regency furniture would replace the overupholstered and overnumerous accouterments of the Victorian home (Light 1991, 34–36). Figures like Margaret Jourdain, cofounder of the Georgian Group and the domestic partner of Ivy Compton-Burnett, encouraged the "present desire for simplicity and economy" as they wrote books on the decoration and furniture distinguishing the "smaller houses" of the Georgians (Jourdain 1923). Though patently licensed by a raid on the past, the new look that Jourdain and others concocted from Sheraton and Chippendale furniture, carpetless floors, and pastel-toned chintzes (instead of plush) was also the product of a modernization that accommodated Georgian tastes to a high-tech aesthetic of rational rectilinearity. In the meantime, the Austen novel was recruited into an analogous modernist campaign against the overdecorated gushiness of Victorian fiction. Woolf, who had her own family quarrel with the Victorians' "mounds of plush" (Light 1991, 34), had in *Orlando* described the onset of tumid prose Victorianism: "sentences swelled, adjectives multiplied, lyrics became epics, and little trifles that had been essays a column long were now encyclopaedias in ten or twenty volumes" (1992a, 229–30). Austen's streamlined Georgian fiction (her little bit of ivory) showed how a new English novel might recover from the Victorian age.

For some debating the future of fiction, the excess baggage that a new novel would have to shed included emotion—more precisely, emotion insufficiently subordinated to form. The running contrast in *A Room of One's Own* that pits Austen against Charlotte Brontë consistently assigns feeling, like excess, to the Victorian side of the divide: where Brontë typifies the woman writer who has passions to vent, Austen is dispassionate; where Brontë "write[s] of herself when she should be writing of her characters" and renders her books "deformed and twisted," Austen's impersonality links her to Shakespeare (Woolf 1992b, 90, 88). (As Bailey averred, Austen "was not in the habit of giving herself away' " [1931, 6].) When Woolf's *Room* compares the complete "match" between Austen's "gift" and her narrow "circumstances," on the one hand, with Brontë's "war with her lot," on the other (88, 90), the terms in which Austen is valued in fact suggest something like the criterion of "truth to materials" promulgated in modernist aesthetics. Austen is commended in conformity with the same criterion that elevated the orderly line and span of modern construction—of the *new* Georgian landscape of streamlined trains and electricity towers—over the unplanned chaos and "dreary horrors of Victorian sham-gothic" (Jenkins 1949, 1).

That "contentment" within a confined place which Woolf ascribes to Austen contributes, like Bailey's reference to Austen's self-restraint, to a familiar portrait of a prim and passionless authoress, but the characterization has served less blatantly conservative purposes as well. In praising Austen's detachment commentators also echoed the talk of "form," "harmony," "proportion," and "fitness for purpose" that throughout the 1920s and '30s dominated calls for a modern movement. By this means discussion of the Austen novel at times provided a site for efforts to reconcile a traditional Englishness with a specifically twentieth-century aesthetic—and so to formulate a concept of good taste that might help an elite English reading audience cope with the process of reimagining social forms, as well as art forms and machine forms, as something to be subjected to the functional rationality of the engineer. Mary Lascelles thus wrote of Austen's "delicate precision, resulting from control of the tools chosen" (1939, 115). Making the customary remarks on Austen's impersonality, Jenkins noted that even the adolescent Austen had "no time for vague, subjective outpourings," perhaps because at that time of her life she was tutored by her clergyman-father, someone "acutely sensitive to the construction of an English sentence" (1949, 35, 7).

To some degree Austen retained this exemplary status in the period's discussions of "good form" in that she was persistently associated with genre and the laws of genre. (She chose "her kingdom," Woolf wrote, and "kept to her compact; she never trespassed beyond her boundaries" [1937, 171–72].) Accordingly, her example underwrote the particular enterprise in redistributing cultural capital that was at stake in thinking of "the" novel as a genre, and in thinking of novels (in keeping with the axiomatics that posed functionalism against ornamentalism) as working best when they served the intrinsic laws of the form. Austen was the novelist who understood that the function of a novel was to be purely, quintessentially "novelistic." She appeared frequently in this guise in interwar culture, though not always cutting the same austere and undemonstrative figure she does in Jenkins's commentary. Indeed, if some found Austen's rigor to be good for a backsliding English novel, for others, the attraction of her good form resided, by contrast, in the knowingness she seemed to display in at once complying with convention and informing her readers that she did so. The detachment touted was in this case that of a novelist who, playing to and off a novel-reading constituency's habits, could playfully skirt the intimacies expected in a proposal scene and supplant her heroine's voice entirely: "She spoke then, on being so entreated.—What did she say?—Just what she ought, of course. A lady always does" (Austen 1971a, 391). In similar fashion, while Catherine Morland's happiness still lies in the balance, the narrator of *Northanger Abbey* nonchalantly dissolves the impediments to her marriage, acknowledging that it is high time to do so: "my readers . . . will see in the tell-tale compression of the pages before them, that we are all hastening together to perfect felicity" (1971b, 203).

In view of this coolly modern way of reducing the marriage plot's moments of affective intensity to empty gestures, it would not have been inappropriate to ally Jane Austen with the flapper or the bright young thing. In "Women and Fiction," Woolf contributed to a modernization of the idioms of Englishness and of gender that made jokiness about sentiment or a stiff upper lip into defining characteristics of the modern Englishwoman: she looked forward to a future when women's fiction would no longer be "the dumping ground for personal emotions." And at the same time, unwittingly, Woolf also gave ammunition to the numerous women writers of her period who, determined to write from a less feminine place in the culture, had taken up the purveying of whodunits to a mass market (Light 1991, 162). Through its skepticism about sentiment and its generic self-consciousness, the detective novel also aspired to represent—like the reconstituted Austen novel—a modern instance of good form. That claim to modernity and desire to shape the female future of fiction may be most apparent in the ways that crime writer Dorothy Sayers sorts out female character in *Have His Carcase* (first published in 1932). The trials of Sayers's flapper heroine include a discomfiting acquaintance with the betrothed of the carcass: some decades Harriet Vane's senior, the fiancée is wont to characterize herself as living "for [her] emotions." The acquaintance between the two begins, markedly enough, in the lounge of the Hotel Resplendent, where the female staff mount exhibition dances wearing the long skirts and ostrich fans of the 1870s, and where Harriet is set musing on the distance separating Victorian femininity from the independent womanhood of the day (1986b, 67, 41).

Myriad associations link English detective fiction to the Austen novel. With its interest in the daily timetables and topographical divisions that order lives in an enclosed locale, lives in a Home Counties village above all, the genre has, for a start, taken Austen's characteristic chronotope as its own. (It may be by this means that the whodunit is qualified to serve as a literature of convalescence right alongside the Austen novel.) Ruth Rendell's Inspector Wexford is in the habit of quoting *Sense and Sensibility* at his subordinates (see Rendell 1988), and the prime suspect in Peter Lovesey's *The Last Detective* (1991) is an Austen scholar, targeted because he has come to possess some hitherto undiscovered letters of Jane's. Reginald Hill, the author since 1970 of the series of mysteries chronicling the detections of Andrew Dalziel and Peter Pascoe of the West Yorkshire Constabulary, has under a different pseudonym published a sequel to *Emma:* his most recent Dalziel-Pascoe mystery, *Pictures of Perfection* (1994), borrows its title from a passage in Austen's letters in which she archly declared allegiance to realistic characterization—"Pictures of perfection as you know make me sick and wicked." And when, in the interwar period, this mode of writing was still new (and when the idea of "light" reading—the erstwhile "wicked" idea that a novel could be constructed of flimsy materials, be thrown away at the end of the day, and still rank as a good read—was new also), it would have been easier yet to see how the whodunit manifested the formalism, modern clarity of outline, and impersonality that contemporary reconstructions of Austen also privileged. As Alison Light explains, after the carnage of the First World War, the genre had little room for either graphic violence or moralizing melodrama, "relying [instead] upon a kind of inturned and internal ratiocination" (1991, 70). The puzzle plots of English detective fiction in fact draw attention to the contrivances of their construction. As we pursue those story lines our expectations are regulated (as they are, too, when we're engaged by a marriage plot) by our awareness of how many pages are left (of "the telltale compression of the pages"), and this in a way that makes reading a whodunit "a precursor, perhaps, of the antics of the *nouveau roman*" (Light 1991, 89). In 1880 the Victorian mothers of the Queens of Crime would have been appalled at the irreverence of the reader who can be amused by a "murder in the vicarage" (title in 1930 of Agatha Christie's first "Miss Marple" mystery) (Light 1991, 71). The Jane Austen with whom the first readers of Sayers, Christie, and Marjorie Allingham were acquainted would have been able to take such an innovation in stride, and might even have considered "murder in the vicarage" as a plausible sequel to *Pride and Prejudice*'s account of Charlotte and Mr. Collins.

In suggestive terms, the critic Herbert Read declared himself highly taken with Christie's "housewifely neatness in the slaughterhouse" (qtd. in Light 1991, 94). Other aficionados of the tale of detection declared its defining features to be "economy, tidiness, and completeness" (Wrong 1946, 24). Dorothy Sayers's prediction that the future would reveal how the genre's true affinities resided with "the novel of manners" rather than "the adventure story" suggests the investment in domesticating public taste that lay behind these customary terms of praise (Sayers 1946, 108). A parallel and equally familiar expression of conservatism—the recall to (neoclassical) order—was at stake when Columbia professor of English literature, Marjorie Nicolson, noted in 1929 that the rise in popularity of detective fiction must have the same source as "the recrudescence of interest on the part of thoughtful readers in that most mature age of writing, the eighteenth century" (Nicolson 1946, 115).

Nicolson's "The Professor and the Detective" suggests something else: that the whodunit in its English mode may be a form possible only in the wake of the institution of a national literature and of a literature-centered national curriculum. As its quantity of allusions to not only Austen but also Shakespeare, Scott, and Dickens suggests, it may be a form that depends, for its defining breeziness, on its saunters through the canon and on the appearance of overtly bookish unreality it acquires through this means (Lennard 1994, 30). It depends accordingly on the existence of a readership schooled in (and also taking pleasure in) the plot-recall and quotation-spotting skills requisite to the taking of exams. When, in *Gaudy Night,* Sayers's Harriet Vane returns to her Oxford college to investigate a series of crimes, she resumes the life of an English literature student and occupies her spare hours with research on Sheridan Le Fanu. This passage sees Harriet keeping late hours at her desk:

> "Wilkie Collins," wrote Harriet, "was always handicapped in his treatment of the supernatural by the . . . lawyer's fatal habit of explaining everything. His ghaisties and ghoulies"—no; worn-out humor—"His dream-phantasies and apparitions are too careful to tuck their shrouds neatly about them and leave no loose ends to trouble us. It is in Le Fanu that we find the natural maker of—natural master of—the master of the uncanny whose mastery comes by nature. If we compare—" Before the comparison could be instituted, the lamp went suddenly out. (1986a, 193)

The passage restages the moment in *Northanger Abbey* when that novel's levels of story and discourse collapse into one another. Then, Catherine

Morland, who has all the while been interpreting her experience through the framework of the Gothic novel (much as Harriet interprets *her* experience by thinking of what the detective in her own novels would do), seems to undergo a Gothic experience in good earnest.[8] Sayers here indicates that Austen's allusiveness—Austen's way of pointing to how she is not simply writing but writing within the generic coordinates proper to "the novel"—is her own model for how gracefully to work over an already well-worked genre.

Minority Culture, Mass Civilization, and the Descendants of Catherine Morland

As Sayers's breezy allusions to Austen suggest, the institution of a national literary curriculum brought into being reading audiences for whom canonized texts featured not just as objects of patriotic veneration but also as the raw materials for the pleasures purveyed in an equal degree by crosswords, acrostics, and charades. Yet if a salutary lesson about readers' inventiveness and about the limits of their interpellation is exemplified here, this does not mean that those new pleasures could not in turn reinforce old-fashioned forms of social division. To return to James Donald's formulation, culture, as it produces a nation, produces not so much a single consciousness as an organized dissensus. When it played games of self-reference and put the literary heritage on display, the new whodunit was providing, apart from new pleasures, new means by which readers might assert their degree of social standing and assert their distinction from others. The snobbery inspiring the Queens of Crime as they set up their country-house murders is, of course, notorious. Likewise, readers who "got" the whodunit's allusions to the classical novel simultaneously got confirmation that they were reading a "superior class" of best-seller—commercial fiction, to be sure, but of a kind that required more mental work from them than the run-of-the-mill pulp novel. The whodunit provided an arena in which one could (as Bourdieu puts it) distinguish oneself by making distinctions, a process that was pursued, at a time of mass literacy, with greater gusto than ever. Women writers who promoted detective fiction's well-made plots over what Woolf had called romance's formlessness, and promoted detective fiction's cerebral pleasures over romance's pathos, were registering the impact of the interwar period's sexual politics as they claimed cultural cachet in that way. They were also conforming to the value hierarchies that ordered the era's class politics. While the English working classes became more publicly sexualized (a consequence of the intersection between new public health policies and a new sexology), romance went downmarket. All the more inescapable now that fiction "had become infected with film technique," romance became *the* stuff of a debased, and also Americanized, popular culture (Jameson 1939, 18).

Stuart Hall has warned against viewing the popular as a homogeneous, static space, of and for the populace, rather than as a continually shifting and mediated relation between different social groupings. And, underscoring Hall's point, attempts to impose a map of taste on the cultural production of interwar England and to establish impermeable lines of demarcation between the classes and genders falter whenever we recall, for instance, that Agatha Christie used the alias Mary Westmacott to publish romance novels in the 1930s and that, simultaneously, Georgette Heyer published crime novels when she was not romancing the Regency (Light 1991, 162–63). The ways in which participants in the era's wars of position wielded Jane Austen's image are correspondingly complicated. On the one hand, the Leavises insisted that Austen's was a pattern novel: thus for F. R. Leavis in *The Great Tradition* (originally published in 1948) it is an axiom that the Austen novel inaugurates and epitomizes the English novel. And this pattern novel was of signal importance now, when, as Q. D. asserted, "for the first time in . . . our literature the living forms of the novel have been side-tracked in favour of the *faux-bon*" (Leavis 1939, 39). (For the Leavises, the latter category included detective fiction, notwithstanding mysteries' much-vaunted place on other professors' bedside tables.) To illustrate and firm up this distinction between authentic literature and cheap simulacra, Q. D. Leavis arrayed Jane Austen and Dorothy Sayers against one another when she reviewed *Gaudy Night*. Complaining particularly of Sayers's oversexed "indecency," she wrote:

> you sense behind it a sort of female smoking-room (see the girlish dedication to [Sayers's] *Busman's Honeymoon*) convinced that this is to be emancipated. (How right, you feel, Jane Austen was not to attempt male conversation unless ladies are present.) (1937, 336)

On the other hand, when (expatriate Englishman) Raymond Chandler invoked Austen to different effect, it was in the course of repositioning the boundary line between the high and the low so that instead of excluding detective fiction, it effected a division inside the genre. "The Simple Art of Murder," the essay in which Chandler complains in his turn about Sayers, begins with a reference to Austen's realist "chronicles of highly inhibited people" (Chandler 1946, 222). But as Chandler continues, a process of condensation occurs, so that the inhibition Austen portrays becomes a trait she and her gender embody. Chandler's thesis is that detective fiction has declined under the influence of "old ladies" who like murderers to observe etiquette and murders to be "nice." The remasculinization that Chandler, as a champion of Dashiel Hammett, prescribes for the genre will also return it to realism (235). Indeed, the habitual gendering of gentility that makes it easy for Chandler to conflate Austen with her characters also has a place in the history of Austen's reception, at the same time that it allows the many cultural-studies admirers of Chandler's quasi-Marxist essay to overlook how, thanks to a history of domestic violence, *ladies* especially do not need "to be reminded that murder is an act of infinite cruelty" (236). Hostility to Austen in this century, as a "gentry author," a symbol of a prissy high culture, often seems underpinned by the same little old lady bashing that Chandler undertakes, the same sense that a Regency old maid's combination of economic vulnerability with unassailable class credentials renders her fair game.[9]

While remembering Austen as classic allows Leavis to decry Sayers, Chandler elides the distinctions between the two "lady novelists" in order to cast Austen as the prototypical instance of a feminizing of fiction that he would undo by making detectives male and hard-boiled. That Chandler ends up at odds with Leavis in his way of deploying Austen's image—even though their common cause is an attack on Sayers, carried out by both in the name of realism—demonstrates how useful the gender hierarchy can be to the critic who needs to bolster the rather less stable hierarchy of the literary versus the popular. In the interwar era, when "the modern bestseller was popularly regarded as a feminine artefact, . . . a form of communication between distinctive feminine writing and reading publics" (Melman 1988, 45), it was only if the critic agreed to tolerate inconsistencies of the kind dividing Chandler and Leavis that Austen, perceived as a *lady* writer through and through, could be represented as an exemplar within debates on the future of the novel. These debates owed their urgency to the changes in the structure of the book market and the diversification of reading audiences that occurred following the First World War. What the editor of the *Daily Express*, reacting in 1927 to the new phenomenon of the best-seller, decried as "the mercenary demobilisation of the English novel" (Melman 1988, 44) was, in fact, the consequence not so much of the war as of a recently instituted system of compulsory education, the founding of a British Book-of-the-Month Club and of the Mills and Boon line of romances, and the new marketing strategy in which the release of a motion picture hiked the sales of the novel on which it was based (McAleer 1992). Yet the terms in which the *Daily Express* editorialized on the best-seller align it with those demonized figures created by the war, the "superfluous" women who were overnumerous (compared with a male population that had been reduced by warfare) and whose new earning power supported, as opponents to women's suffrage opined, desires ranging far outside the confines of marriage and home. F. R. Leavis's description, in *Mass Civilisation and Minority Culture* (1930), of cinemagoers' pleasure—"surrender, under conditions of hypnotic receptivity, to the cheapest of emotional appeals"—tapped fears about the overreceptiveness of a demonized and demobilized female sexuality (Leavis qtd. in Miles and Smith 1987, 93). The new forms of entertainment and the new consumers were condemned alike as cheap and easy (Light 1991, 161). Elizabeth Jenkins follows these Leavisite lines and compares "the girl of today who can see life only in terms of the cinema" to her counterpart in Austen's lifetime, when such a girl would have spoken "in the accents of Lydia Languish."[10] It is no surprise that the modern consumer, who might well belong to the working rather than the traditional "leisure" classes, is judged inferior: "Could there be drawn a more vivid, more compendious comparison?" (1949, 5).

Counterbalancing the difficulties that Austen's gender posed in a discursive context dominated by the trope of mass culture as woman—by a semantic circuit in which the inferiority of the feminine explained the inferiority of the popular and vice versa—readings of Austen's life and the Austen canon carried out by the academic culture of the interwar period develop a parable about the Austens as an embattled minority (in a tight place, but preserving their stiff upper lips and their family values). For critics like the Leavises, the Austen novel, which assembles through its narrative transformations a "small band of true friends" (Austen 1971b, 440), found its natural fulfillment in the heroic narrative that sees twentieth-century critics preserve "minority civilization" in an age of "mass culture."

In 1930s England, both the political left and the political right sought elitist remedies to what F. R. Leavis had identified as "the general dissolution of standards" effected by mass culture. For both, such remedies represented not so much a project to wrest "the benefits of culture away from some broader social base" as a strategy "to secure, on behalf of all, the guardianship of a disappearing culture among at least a few" (Miles and Smith 1987, 86). To conform to this presupposition that tradition was that which disappeared, assertions about the Austen novel's status as the heritage of *all* the English were consistently hedged with suggestions that Janeism was a minority position—with affirmations that she, "unlike Dickens," made "no mass appeal" (Kaye-Smith and Stern 1943, 5). And some found cause for congratulation, as well as melancholy, in the idea that, as Kipling's narrator put it, there was only one Janeite left. Woolf thus wrote half-nostalgically of how a taste for Austen novels had formerly been "a gift that ran in families and . . . a mark of rather peculiar culture" (1986c, 10).

In their joint work on the Cambridge journal *Scrutiny* especially, the Leavises did much to promote the (wishful) view that the Austen novel was the property of a minority. In her "A Critical Theory of Jane Austen's Writings" (first published in 1941), Q. D. portrayed Jane and her sister Cassandra, who had "too much penetration to be comfortable" and lacked "elbow-room" in their rural society, as the counterpart to the embattled Leavis household (1983, 144). The Leavises' belief in family and their defense of critical values in the face of the laxity of the industrial working class, the London intelligentsia, an amateurish, mystery-reading professoriate, and so forth, were, Q. D. Leavis seems to have believed, prefigured in the Austen correspondence. In the literary history that the Leavises delineated, the organic community that alone produced real Literature persisted longest in "the English countryside," where people ensconced in isolated villages, lacking the motorcars or bicycles that menace an integrated way of life, had once had little choice but to stay at home (1939, 209). Presumably resembling in this respect Leavisite criticism as well, Austen's novels, "A Critical Theory" averred, were critical of moral backsliding and yet did not lapse into "irritation." This was precisely because, inside *her* country cottage, Austen found her "own private society," where her language was spoken and her standards were endorsed (1983, 146, 144).

In her earlier attempt to recruit Austen to the defense of minority civilization, Q. D. laid out a contrast between Austen and Brontë reminiscent of that found in *A Room of One's Own*. In this case, what divided the Regency from the Victorian writer was the criterion that also divided Literature, in Q. D.'s view, from best-sellers. A change in the use of fiction occurred between Austen's era and Brontë's, *Fiction and the Reading Public* proposes, and the text demonstrates that change by juxtaposing Austen's "well-regulated mind" and her concern to "destroy any . . . illusions the reader may cherish" with Brontë's "shameful self-abandonment to undisciplined emotion" and her novels' fables of "wish fulfillment" (1939, 130, 138). The enduring centrality within Austen studies of juvenile burlesques like *Love and Freindship* [*sic*] and of *Northanger Abbey* may be ascribed to these efforts by interwar critics like Leavis who sought to wield the concept of "realism" in a way that would rescue the novel form from its popularity. Such critics argued that from her earliest work on, Austen was cognizant of her historical mission, which was to target those novels (sentimental fiction in the juvenilia; Gothic romance in *Northanger Abbey*) which give *the* novel a bad name. Noting the juvenilia's topicality, Elizabeth Jenkins remarks that "writers of [that kind of novel] exist in unequalled numbers at the present time" (1949, 28–29). At the start of *Jane Austen and Her Art* Mary Lascelles proposes that a "burlesque element"—the juxtaposition of a "caricature of the world of illusion" with "a faithful delineation of the actual world"—is the staple of Austen's work (1939, 55–56).

To describe the Austen novel as mediating and representing the novel's rise out of romance and into realism sanctifies and stabilizes that very opposition. In the interwar period, that description also commented implicitly on the future of fiction—its future as the property of an elite. Lascelles ends her book by insisting that first-rate fiction be distinguished from second-rate ("it is this twofold capacity of the novel that has kept all fiction so long in disrepute") and by worrying over whether the *good* novel can still secure a reader's sympathy for its characters without eliciting a gush of feeling that will "overflow into the channels which bad fiction has worn for it" (1939, 217 n. 4, 216).

Leaving Home/Escapism

Much as nationality is internationally defined, so that specifying Englishness is a matter of contrasting it with other identities, a value term like realism can most easily be defined relationally. In the interwar literary system, realism was defined by being privileged over romance and, also, because that literary system was organized by a reciprocal arrangement between genre differences and national differences, by being privileged over the foreign import. When between the wars romance went downmarket, it also, in keeping with that arrangement, left the country: for instance, the romance-reading "shopgirl," who was so often scapegoated for the depravities of mass culture, was frequently perceived to have sold her soul to Hollywood, and faulted for speaking "Cinema American."

As we have noted, to establish her distance from romance and so obtain high-culture credentials for the mystery form, Dorothy Sayers recycled Austen's debunking domestications of the Gothic. Sayers also had recourse to the reciprocal circuit of exchange linking national and generic differences, pointedly making the victim of the murder that Harriet and Lord Peter Wimsey investigate in *Have His Carcase* a Russian émigré and "hotel gigolo" whose death turns out not to involve, as at one stage it seems, a Bolshevik conspiracy but rather to be the result of his fatal, and un-English, addiction to pulp historical fiction. Indeed, the family tree that Harriet and Peter discover in his lodgings, "between the passionate leaves" of the novelette *The Girl who gave All*, suggests that the pretext for the plot that killed off Paul Alexis Goldschmidt was a family legend, much embroidered by Paul Alexis, and finally very like a Regency romance: "colourful, vivid stuff," in Lord Peter's words, "with costume effects and plenty of human interest," narrating how, in 1815, Paul Alexis's great-great-grandmother Charlotte secretly married Tsar Nicholas I of Russia, and how, in short, she and Nicholas lived romantic private lives altogether hidden from public histories of the post-Napoleonic political settlement (Sayers 1986b, 421). Aware of Paul Alexis's reading habits, the murderer lured him to his death by playing on the latter's naive trust that he could be proven the heir to the Romanovs.

Paul Alexis thus falls victim to Sayers's satire on popular historical fiction. Indeed, the family romance he concocts from the materials of that fiction is rendered all the more bathetic by virtue of its anachronism. His working-class girlfriend had pointed out to him early on that " 'they've done away with all these royalties now' " (Sayers 1986b, 414). An archive of audience response to the 1943 costume melodrama *The Man in Grey* preserves the comment of a male "technical researcher, aged 20," who was all in favor of the "escapist" pleasure (his term) that was supplied by the historical film's presentation of Regency high life: "we forget the present to dwell in the past when young ladies were taught just what to say to men who asked their hand in marriage, even though the latter were scoundrels" (viewer qtd. in Richards and Sheridan 1987, 231). The value of this imagined past seems to inhere in its satisfaction of conservative desires: in 1815, not only were there still "royalties," but women confined themselves to a set script in conducting relations with the opposite sex. Like Dorothy Sayers, cultural studies has some problems with the historical romance—with the Tory imagination of a genre that sets bygone aristocratic glamour against a lackluster present. Identifying modern egalitarianism with national decline, historical romance at once plays to its popular readership's discontents and aspirations and repowers an atavistic ethos of deference (Light 1989, 58–59). Lillian Robinson thus notes with scorn how high life in Georgette Heyer's novels is, snobbishly, much higher than anything to be encountered in Austen's (1978, 212).

Yet to assume that it is *simply* conservative or nostalgic can occlude the feminist interest of the historical romance's embrace of bygone aristocratic mores. Feminine mass entertainment's turn to the Regency, to what was pointedly the last era before the onset of Victorian values, enabled a cavalier stance toward marriage and monogamy. When James Mason's eponymous "man in grey" arrives at the ball that is meant to provide him with a wife and the means to continue the Rohan line, he sneers, "Plenty of fillies in the paddock tonight." However offensive, the versions of masculinity authorized by the Regency setting—cynical rakishness like the scoundrelly Lord Rohan's or, in a different way, dandiacal narcissism—could "free women to experience their own sexual pleasure without the inhibitions induced by tenderness and concern" (Aspinall 1983, 32–33). Similarly, the best-sellers that the Gainsborough Studios adapted for the screen found in Regency England a veritable catalogue of psychosexual options. Lady Eleanor Smith's Clarissa Rohan, wife of the Man in Grey, suspects herself of a "frigid abnormality that must set her apart . . . from women more fortunate than herself" (Smith 1942, 97). The episode of Norah Lofts's *Jassy* (1944; filmed in 1947) that is narrated from the point of view of the proprietress of a school for young ladies is titled "Complaint from Lesbia"; the subsequent chapter, "Neurosis in Arcady," takes up the point of view of a pupil at the school, whose story suggests one of the case histories of "nymphomania" that made up popular sexology at midcentury. The market success of these romances was a manifestation both of nostalgia *and* of a modernization of Victorian femininity as thoroughgoing as the one at stake in the middlebrow creation of the realist woman and her stiff upper lip. The feminine position within culture from which romance is written and read is not, in the 1940s at least, so fixed a position, not so much a matter of simple sentimentality, not so bounded by the polarities of heterosexuality, as highbrow critics, dons, or defensive mystery writers understand it as being.

Echoing statements made by Georgette Heyer herself, Jane Aiken Hodge, Heyer's biographer, expressed frustration at how, from the 1930s on, "a ravening fan public" incessantly demanding romance had put off a rather more select company of readers "who might have enjoyed [Heyer] as they do Jane Austen or even Ivy Compton-Burnett" (1984, 10–11). As this animus against the romance-reading woman suggests, Georgette Heyer was as proud as Dorothy Sayers of her knowledge of the intricate codes of the literary system and her competence in manipulating those codes. Heyer produced tamer stuff than contemporaries like Norah Lofts or Eleanor Smith, but she, too, could echo Austen's debunking of the alarms of romance, just as well as Sayers could. Parading her generic inheritance was Heyer's means of marking her literary savoir faire and of setting her own detached tone of formalist breeziness. Were we not accustomed to thinking of Austen as burlesquing romantic conventions, and unaccustomed to thinking of her as establishing them, we might notice the nod to *Northanger Abbey* that Heyer makes when she has the fugitive heroine of *The Corinthian* (first published in 1940) explain that she had chosen to escape from her guardian's townhouse via a second-story window, not because she was gothically locked into her room but because of an "anxiety of common life": she didn't want to set her pug dog barking (1966, 65).

In condemning Heyer's social upgrading of Austen's country-house set, Lillian Robinson impugns Heyer's Regencies as escapist fables of wish fulfillment—as romances of precisely that kind which a sardonic Dorothy Sayers uses to supply her detectives with a corpse. Still, we might wonder—since Harriet Vane marries a Lord, since Austen herself was not immune, at least not in *Northanger Abbey*, *Pride and Prejudice*, or *Mansfield Park*, to the charms of a rags-to-riches narrative—how much "realism" and "romance" have to do with stable categories of writing and whether these terms do not instead index the varying uses to which readers can put a single text. Everyone's art is somebody's escapism (Light 1990, 343).

As a term used to depreciate the writings readers use to distract themselves from an inadequate everyday existence, "escapism" is itself an invention of the 1930s. (The term's power to psychologize, and spirit away, a mass audience's material deprivations would first have been exploited during the Great Depression.) "Escapism" also implies mobility, which one might associate with the scope for female action that is revealed in the historical romances, especially when they are juxtaposed with contemporary realists' chronicles of feminine fortitude in the face of humdrum domesticity.[11] Escapism in this sense is also a term applicable to the experience of reading Regency romance. Practitioners of the genre, from Heyer on, have, in calling attention to the research that backs up their descriptions, endowed the romance with "an air of learning" (Light 1989, 60). The present-day community of romance fans interviewed by Janice Radway (1984) refer to the genre's informativeness to justify their reading, casting romance reading as an activity that leads to self-improvement and social mobility. (Likewise, although Heyer's heroines are usually well born, her plots also allow these provincial ingénues to achieve social éclat via makeovers that equip them to set the fashion in millinery or snuffboxes. Consumption supplements genealogy, in a way that might well have struck a chord with the reading audience of the interwar period, when, in an unprecedented manner, the acquisition of a New Look dress would for many have symbolized personal initiative and dignity, instead of serving only—as in numerous discussions of mass consumption—as the catalyst of envy and social one-upmanship [Steedman 1986].) And whatever snobbish nostalgia Heyer was acting on as she remade the turn of the nineteenth century into a time of social harmony and settlement, that nostalgia was counterbalanced by the ultramodern conditions of production under which she turned out her line of "Georgette Heyers." The tempo of serial recurrence that saw Heyer (re)producing one Regency romance after another also mobilized readers, enabling them to view the books as temporary accompaniments to commuting or vacation travel—light reading suited to traveling light. And Heyer's plots unfold in lodgings at Brighton or in the course of stagecoach journeys as often as they do in homes; her heroines learn to drive four-in-hands.

By contrast, Austen's home-loving attachment to a green nook was an article of faith with interwar commentators, who insisted that she loved country life, who told and retold the story of how Jane swooned when Reverend Austen announced his intention to move the family to Bath (see, e.g., Bradley 1929, 71–72). Without downplaying the ethical call inscribed in notions of home and neighborhood, and drawing on the experience of mobility that shaped him as a scholarship boy, and on his knowledge of how many other natives of Wales had been forced by agricultural depression and deindustrialization to leave home too, Raymond Williams continually contested the idealizing of settlement that such hegemonic constructions of English ordinariness inscribe. *The Country and the City* was his riposte to the proposition that the real England is the structure of feeling to be experienced from inside the rural retreat. Retreat for whom? Williams asked, as he identified the "self-regarding paternalism" that informs the (visitor's) demand for a timeless countryside and countryfolk, and the "insolent indifference to most people's needs" that informs such "idealization of settlement"—idealization of tradition and of those who stay put (1975, 107). In fact, the wars, economic restructuring, and mass migrations and expulsions (and educational reforms) marking Williams's youth made migrancy and mobility into ordinary experiences.

As the interwar editorials recommending emigration as a solution to the problem of the "superfluous woman" suggest, and as moral panics aroused after 1939 by the mobilized woman, the female war worker, and the war bride suggest in addition, these were also the experiences shaping the Englishwoman's life. Indeed, it may be argued that the feminized category of everyday life as such came to be characterized, subsequent to economic and technological modernization, less and less by the image of home and family and more by mobility. The time-space of "ordinary" women's homemaking, Meaghan Morris emphasizes, is expressed not so much in the upkeep of the heirlooms of an interior life but rather in the practices, like shopping or driving or orchestrating the itineraries of family recreation, through which women have produced modernity (1988).

Lillian Robinson unwittingly calls attention to that mobility and modernity in the course of her comparison of Jane Austen and Georgette Heyer. And, while she very nearly replays Elizabeth Jenkins's diatribe against the tourist whose consumerism despoils the English countryside, Robinson also unwittingly demonstrates the staying power of the paradigm that both understands literature as a private refuge and banishes the taint of female consumption from that home. After worrying that readers of Regencies will simply not notice the superiority of Austen's characters, incidents, and analysis and that the categorical difference, which underpins her essay, between Austen's literature and Heyer's trash is now a difference only for the few, Robinson concludes like this: "The problem is becoming acute. . . . I recently saw a vending machine called a Convenience Center in the lobby of a Holiday Inn. It dispenses such items as body lotion, hair spray, tampons, deodorant, and copies of *Pride and Prejudice*" (1978, 221n). As Elizabeth Jenkins's opening to her life of Austen shows, the classical novel can appear the way Williams says the Georgian "stately home" does: as an image of splendid isolation that "break[s] the scale," producing an effect of "social disproportion . . . meant to impress and overawe" (1975, 133). Alternately, the classical novel can appear, as it does for Robinson, in spite or because of her homesickness in the Holiday Inn, as the refuge where the novel reader returns to the first principles of literariness or Englishness. What both those perspectives occlude, by virtue of their familiarity to the professionally educated, are the other ways of being at home with Jane Austen—those I have tried to delineate by stressing the difference it made once English Literature was put to use in new venues, by new readerships, and read through lenses provided by new forms of commercial fiction like the romance or whodunit. Feminist literary history and cultural studies cannot do without the classical novel either. But if it is to provide us with a common ground, we need both to study the classical novel's effectivity as a classic and also, releasing it from that closed context, to return it to its multiple historicities and multiple textualities, to what John Frow calls the "realm of heterosignification." There we might encounter vantage points from which home, too, might be apprehended differently: not as private property to be defended from trespassers, not as the place of an idealized inheritance, "not as an enclosure, but [as] a way of going outside" (Morris 1992, 454).

Notes

For various kinds of assistance, I am indebted to Homer Brown, Nancy Glazener, Stacy Carson Hubbard, Tom Keirstead, Katie Trumpener, William B. Warner, and the undergraduates in my 1992 and 1994 classes on Austen, Janeites and anti-Janeites alike.

1. On the reinvention of rural England, see Potts 1989, Miles and Smith 1987, and Howkins 1986; on Quiller-Couch's part in this cult of the nation, see Brooker and Widdowson 1986.
2. In *Regency Buck* (originally published in 1935), Heyer stakes her claim to what her publicists called the tradition of Jane Austen, when she has her heroine take up *Sense and Sensibility* from a shelf of the circulating library, read a passage at random, and exclaim: "Surely the writer of that must possess a most lively mind? I am determined to take this book. It seems all to be written about ordinary people, and . . . I am quite tired of Sicilians and Italian Counts who behave in such a very odd way" (1991, 114).
3. Consumption levels increased in the Home Counties and Midlands in the 1920s and '30s, though not, after 1929 especially, in deindustrializing Northern England.
4. There were, of course, resistances to such efforts to domesticate women's fiction. In her historical novel *Troy Chimneys* (originally published in 1953), Margaret Kennedy at once acknowledges how Austen's example was used to underwrite that domestication and nonetheless manages, through her Regency-period setting and her allusions to the romance of second chances in Austen's *Persuasion,* to pay homage to that example. (Kennedy published a life of Austen in 1950.) Miles Lupton, the narrator of *Troy Chimneys,* cannot make the novel's heroine share his esteem for *Emma* and *Mansfield Park:* "she complained that they kept her continually in the parlour, where she was obliged, in any case, to spend her life. A most entertaining parlour, she allowed, but: 'That lady's greatest admirers will always be men, I believe. For, when they have had enough of the parlour, they may walk out, you know, and we cannot'" (Kennedy 1985, 200).
5. For important discussions of the overlap between conservatism and feminism see Light 1991.
6. As feminist critiques of Williams might suggest, the tone of this passage —Williams's slighting reference to "purely [merely?] personal relationships"— points up the limitations of his method of reading in its turn. Relations *within* the families, and inside the houses, of the Austen novel are not placed in history in the way that other relations are—those referenced when Williams discusses the enclosure movement in Hampshire or Austen's "preoccupation with estates, incomes, and social position" (1975, 141).
7. For an account of modernist-preservationist arguments, see Matless 1990 and the discussions of the interwar renovation of "Constable country" in Potts 1989.
8. Thus *Northanger Abbey:* "She seized, with an unsteady hand, the precious manuscript, for half a glance sufficed to ascertain written characters; and while she acknowledged with awful sensations, this striking exemplification of what Henry had foretold, resolved instantly to peruse every line before she attempted to rest.

The dimness of the light her candle emitted made her turn to it with alarm;

but there was no danger of its sudden extinction, it had yet some hours to burn; and that she might not have any greater difficulty in distinguishing the writing than what its ancient date might occasion, she hastily snuffed it. Alas! it was snuffed and extinguished in one" (Austen 1971b, 135).

Catherine's manuscript was, of course, merely a laundry list, so the terrors she undergoes with it alone in the dark merely underscore Austen's lesson that it is the anxieties of common life rather than the alarms of romance that concern the Englishwoman. Harriet's poltergeist, similarly, proves to be the college maid, and so, to use a term that the class-conscious Sayers would sanction, rather more "common" than Harriet had first believed.

9. I am indebted here to Adela Pinch's account (forthcoming) of how the specter of a Victorian old lady haunts contemporary thinking about culture and gender.

10. Lydia Languish, a girl notorious for her excessive reading of sentimental novels, is a character in Richard Sheridan's play of 1775, *The Rivals.*

11. I owe this point to Light 1989.

Katie Trumpener

6 The Abbotsford Guide to India

Romantic Fictions of Empire and the Narratives of Canadian Literature

The View from Abbotsford: Colonial, Postcolonial, Transcolonial

> Abbotsford is the centre of Canada & India is the centre of the world.
> Both India and Abbotsford missed the Industrial Revolution.
>
> . . . .
>
> Abbotsford & India were once agricultural societies.
> There are more Sikh temples in Abbotsford than in Madras.
> Abbotsford & India are targets of multi-national corporations.
>
> . . . .
>
> In Canadian fiction there are more scenes set in India than in Abbotsford.
>
> . . . .
>
> When Indians & Abbotsfordians dream of a common language they dream of their own language.
> —Frank Davey, "Abbotsford and India"

> "The seasons in this colony," said the Judge, "are not only accompanied by the ordinary mutations of weather observed in other countries, but present a constant and rapid succession of incidents and people. From the opening of the ports to the close of navigation, everything and everybody is in motion, or in *transitu*. The whole province [of Nova Scotia] is a sort of railroad station, where crowds are perpetually arriving and departing. It receives an emigrant population, and either hurries it onward, or furnishes another of its own in exchange. It is the land of 'comers and goers.' "
> —Thomas Chandler Haliburton, *The Old Judge; or, Life in a Colony*

In his 1986 volume of prose poems, *The Abbotsford Guide to India*, Canadian poet and theorist Frank Davey describes his travels through an India constantly measured back against his hometown of Abbotsford, British Columbia, a suburb of Vancouver best known for its large Sikh community. In Abbotsford Davey finds a double point of reference from which to evoke a bifurcated tradition of colonial views of the British empire. As a small, literally peripheral settlement, perched on the farthest edge of the North American continent, Abbotsford seems to afford a vantage point on India of laughable provinciality and presumption, a suburb reading a subcontinent—were it not, simultaneously, that its Sikh population represents a long-standing and live connection to South Asia. Manifesting what this essay will call a "transcolonial" consciousness, *The Abbotsford Guide to India* begins to fill in the historical preconditions for Canada's encounter with India, by evoking the parallel histories that link these two far-flung outposts of the British empire. In the course of retracing the lost routes of empire, Davey also begins to retrieve the lost, but crucial, history of an imperial mentalité. Formed during the eighteenth and early nineteenth centuries in the process of trans-continental traverse, this state of mind informs not only the shape of colonial life and literature throughout the nineteenth century but also, perhaps more surprisingly, the postcolonial thinking of the late twentieth century as well.

An empire lives from the existence of peripheries: its economy and trade depend on the underdevelopment of the peripheries in relation to the imperial center. Yet the large-scale social displacements that result from such economic asymmetries, as well as the need to anchor colonial authority with imperial armies and administrations, result in the permanent connection of the peripheries one to another, as well as to the center. If on one level, empires function by fixing a hierarchy of place, as by instituting legal and penal codes that keep colonized subjects in their places, on another level empires can function only by remaining in a kind of perpetual motion. What Nova Scotia satirist Thomas Chandler Haliburton described in 1849 as the characteristic "comings and goings" of the colonies—the circulation of explorers, missionaries, traders, administrators, immigrants, prisoners, soldiers, and poets back and forth between the empire's most "remote" places—brings along with it a corresponding circulation of ideas and ideologies, goods and customs, languages and literary tropes. The Sikh temples of Abbotsford are one concrete trace of such migrations. On account of its imperial history, Abbotsford is a place simultaneously of deep provinciality and of surprising internationalism, a place that is historically marginal but that also has symptomatic historical significance. Davey's guide can be read as a manifesto from Abbotsford about a signal by-product of the empire: the cultural cross-pollination of its most distant colonies, and the emergence of a trans-peripheral view that bypasses or opposes the empire's nominal "center."

Yet with the very name of Abbotsford Davey also evokes a different, more hegemonic kind of imperial memory. His British Columbia hometown recalls a literary memorial half a world away, the famous "stately home" in the Scottish Borders that novelist Walter Scott built with the proceeds of his world-famous series of historical novels. Published from 1814 to 1831, the twenty-five Waverley novels together form a chronicle of Scottish and British history. Describing a succession of national turning points (such as the 1707 Union between England and Scotland and the Jacobite Uprising of 1745), the novels at once mourn the growing erosion and Anglicization of indigenous cultural traditions and celebrate the course of historical progress.

Recapitulating his novels' antiquarian reconstruction and reinvention of Scottish tradition in the face of British incorporation, Scott's Abbotsford is designed as a monument to British Scottishness, displaying side by side the memorials of ancient Scottish life, the trophies of British military campaigns, and the mementos of Scottish emigrant settlements throughout the empire. During Scott's lifetime, friends and admirers involved in the colonization of Africa and Australia turned Abbotsford quite literally into a repository of empire, by sending him their first spoils: the skin of their first lion, a flock of emus, the first works of colonial literature, dedicated to the author of the Waverley novels. At the same time, throughout the nineteenth century, they and a host of novel-reading emigrants, settlers, and administrators continue to transplant the ideals of Abbotsford all over the empire. As Canadian Anglo-Indian satirist Sara Jeanette Duncan notes in 1903, the typical British official in Simla, the summer capital of British India, is still living in

> a ridiculous little white-washed house made of mud and tin, and calling itself Warwick Castle, Blenheim, Abbotsford! They haven't a very good hold, these Simla residences, and sometimes they slip fifty yards or so down the mountain side. (1984, 105)

In fact Scott's Abbotsford is not, like Warwick or Blenheim, a historically rooted national institution but rather a cobbled-together private home that Scott renamed, rebuilt, and almost lost through bankruptcy.

Scott actively fostered the cult of Abbotsford, guiding visitors through his house and grounds as if they were visiting a museum and shrine of Scottish history. And throughout the nineteenth century, from Scotland to Simla, Abbotsford continues to conjure a national and imperial ideal—even if, in India, the stately edifice has been miniaturized and transformed back into a bungalow, with only a precarious hold on the colony's unstable political terrain.

Throughout the British empire, the cult of Abbotsford accompanied, articulated, and mystified the new kind of transnational culture created by imperial emigration and circulation. The empire-wide influence of the Waverley novels lay in their ability to harmonize Scottish materials with British perspectives, as they enacted and explained the composition of Britain as an internal empire. The novels describe the historical formation of the Scottish nation, the simultaneous formation of the Britain that subsumes it, and a Scottish cultural nationalism that survives because it learns to separate the preservation of cultural distinctiveness from the memory of political autonomy (and can therefore be completely contained within the new transnational imperial framework). Scott's presentation of the ideological capaciousness of empire, and his ability to reconcile nationalist allegiances and imperialist mandates, made him popular at once with the British public, with imperial advocates and administrators, and with colonial readers throughout the empire searching for ways to describe their own sense of identity.

But the apparent ubiquity of Scott's influence should not obscure the coexistence either of alternative Romantic novelistic modes for describing nation and empire (particularly the "national tale," a genre developed by Anglo-Irish novelists in the decade before *Waverley* (1814), and propelled in its wake in more militantly nationalist and anti-imperialist directions) or of alternative currents within early-nineteenth-century colonial literature itself.[1] In British North America, in a literary culture heavily dominated by Scottish immigrants (many personal friends or associates of Scott himself), Scott's example is apparently all-powerful. Yet much of the early fiction of both Upper Canada and Nova Scotia, particularly the works of John Galt, Thomas McCulloch, and Thomas Chandler Haliburton, contains significant challenges to Scott's vision of national and imperial history. Crucially different from the Waverley novels in their mode of explicating empire, their fiction is grounded quite explicitly in a rejection of Scott's historiographic models, his optimism about Britain, and his investment in the project of empire itself. Where Scott's novels depicted the subsumption of nation into empire as a melancholy but inevitable and irrevocable process, some of Scott's colonial counterparts follow his Irish and Scottish contemporaries in developing new characterological models to describe the permanent fragmentation of the body politic in the wake of imperialist occupation and colonization. Scott describes a moment of cultural suffering and loss, which then gives way to a future full of unexpected compensations. His contemporaries, in contrast, insist that, on the psychic level if not on the political, the traumatic experience of colonization can never be completed, exhausted, or recovered from: instead, they describe a host of collective mental illnesses—neurotic obsessions and repetition compulsions, cultural schizophrenia, memory losses, permanent inabilities to "settle" or to form affective bonds—suffered in perpetuity by a host of collective and individual "national characters." Particularly in *Guy Mannering* (1815), the second Waverley novel, Scott aligns the formation of internal and overseas British colonies, the modernization of Scotland, and the conquest of India, presenting these developments as harbingers of political and economic progress. Building their own sustained critique of empire on a prior tradition of Jacobin analysis, many of Scott's contemporaries, in contrast, insist on viewing both the empire and Britain itself as economic systems grounded on slavery and economic oppression.

Quietistic and critical respectively, the two traditions give rise to very different literary-historical posterities. The Scott tradition feeds into the colonial formation of a new imperial nationalism, of new imperialist national literatures, national historiographies, and national literary historiographies that play up their nationalism at the expense of a critical analysis of their initial imperial context. The alternative fictional tradition is equally rooted in Scottish regional writing but explicitly critical of Scott, resolutely transnational in vantage point yet acerbic in its view of the workings of empire. Not easily assimilated to latter-day nationalist narratives of genealogy, this countertradition has never been revived and has never received the critical attention it deserves. In Canada, the rediscovery and canonization of colonial literature was motivated by the cultural nationalism of the 1960s and '70s; English Canadian literary historians described a literary tradition in terms that stressed its strong nationalist teleology and the vital influence of Scott and his Canadian imitators on the development of Canadian fiction. As if the novelistic tradition of a modern nation could only begin with a Waverley novel, they treated John Richardson's 1832 *Wacousta; or, The Prophecy: A Tale of the Canadas* (with its Highland subplots and its open derivation from Scott and James Fenimore Cooper) as the first "real" Canadian novel, despite earlier English-language novels set or written in Canada, and championed Philippe Aubert de Gaspé's 1862 *Les Anciens Canadiens,* derived formally and thematically from *Waverley,* as the first important French Canadian novel.[2] What Gaspé's historical novel best exemplifies, perhaps, is the appeal of the Waverley model for the literature and literary historiography of empire. Imitating Scott's antiquarian footnotes and ethnographic excurses, *Les Anciens Canadiens* assembles a veritable compendium of information about pre-Conquest French Canadian life. Through the national allegories of its plot (after Culloden, a Jacobite Highlander finds refuge in Québec, is forced in 1763 to participate as a British Army officer in its military conquest, and finally, in the new British colony, is reconciled with his adoptive French Canadian family), the novel simultaneously reenacts the political conflicts and eventual unity of the two Canadas and provides a foundational myth of the modern state. Like the Waverley novels, *Les Anciens Canadiens* at once chronicles the defeat of a national culture and, through its own acts of reconstruction, tries to save that culture from oblivion. At the same time (particularly for English Canadian readers and critics committed to a "unified," English-dominated Canada), Gaspé's sustained homage to Scott provides gratifying evidence of the final ascendancy of British narrative forms and Scottish novelistic traditions over French Canadian material.

"Canadian literature like Canadian history is largely Scottish," George Bowering put it sardonically in 1977. "To get into Canadian literature it helps to be . . . named Alex or Ian or Malcolm" (166). Yet the works of McCulloch, Haliburton, and Galt suggest a different kind of imperial imaginary than Scott's and together form a crucially counternationalist model of Canadian writing: the two Nova Scotia satirists emphasize the transmutative logic of empire, and John Galt uses the backwoods as a place from which to reassess the imperial project and through it, the Scottish and the British experience of modernity. If Scott provides the model for a national and imperialist Canadian literature, it is this countertradition, with its vision of an imperially constructed and empire-locked Canada, that forms the most important precedent for contemporary postcolonial Canadian writing.

Glen Tilt: From Internal to External Empire

> Peggy Bruce was the daughter of a respectable Irish farmer, and had made a runaway match with a handsome young Scotch sergeant. She had accompanied her husband through the various campaigns of the revolutionary war, and at the peace, his regiment being disbanded, they set up a small public house [in Upper Canada], which when I knew her as a widow, she still kept. The sign was a long board, decorated by a very formidable likeness of St. Andrew at the one end, and St. Patrick at the other, being the patron saints of the high contracting parties over whose domicile they presided and the whole surrounded by a splendid wreath of thistles and shamrocks.—William "Tiger" Dunlop, "Recollections of the American War," 1812–1814

Britain's conquest of a vast new overseas empire in North America, Asia, and Africa during the late eighteenth and early nineteenth centuries was anticipated by, then meshed with, the formation of Britain itself as a multinational inland empire. In his influential survey of English expansionism within Britain, Michael Hechter (1975) has argued that the modern British state came into being through the internal colonization of Wales, Ireland, and Scotland and built its own economic strength on the systematic underdevelopment of these domestic colonies. One British imperialism produces another. On the one hand, the administration of domestic colonies served as a trial run for the colonization of the British overseas empire. And on the other hand, the unfavorable economic situation in the domestic colonies meant that impoverished Scots and Irish continued to find disproportionate representation both in the British Army, which conquered and occupied various overseas colonies, and among the British colonists who settled these colonies throughout the nineteenth century.[3]

Their strong presence in the British colonies resulted in the export of intranational tensions into a new setting, particularly when—as with the tens of thousands of seventeenth-century Irish whom Cromwell "evicted" and sold into slavery in the West Indies, with the eighteenth-century Highlanders "cleared" to the Maritimes, with the tens of thousands of Irish felons and political prisoners transported to New South Wales, and with the hundreds of thousands of Irish starved out of Ireland over the course of the nineteenth century—their forced emigration from the British Isles had clear ethnic or political causes. At the same time, these emigrations also effected the transposition of nationalist plots and tropes into the colonies, where they often formed the basis of early colonial literature.

As reflected in these nascent colonial literatures, the model of cultural and literary nationalism developed in Ireland and Scotland reveals its potential both for radical anti-imperialist critique and for political accommodation. Many of the nineteenth-century emigrants from the internal to the external colonies of Britain retained a sense of considerable aggrievement. From Australia to Canada, Irish emigrants in particular insisted on the link between Britain's repressive domestic and imperial policies: in "Port McQuarrie Toweringabble Norfolk Island and Emu plains," Ned Kelly laments of the Australian penal settlements, "in those places of tyranny and condemnation many a blooming Irish man rather than subdue to the Saxon yoke was flogged to death and bravely died in servile chains" (qtd. in Hughes 1988, 443–44). In the transportation of Irish convicts and impoverished laborers to the outposts of the overseas empire, and in "genocidal" episodes like the 1847 Grosse-Isle cholera epidemic (in which thousands of Irish immigrants to Canada died in government quarantine), Fenian nationalists saw a deadly replication of Britain's uneven power relations (Mitchel [1845]).

Yet for other immigrants, particularly those from Scotland, transplantation ultimately brought new social mobility and political influence. Such colonists were often transformed, morally, politically, and economically, into colonizers. Generalizing from their own experience, subsuming their nationalist pride and their ambivalence toward "English" culture into generalized support of the empire, they embraced the compensatory cosmopolitanism it fostered and bestowed. In the case of the Scottish engineers, doctors, officers, and missionaries so ubiquitous in the Victorian literature of empire, they even worked actively to extend its spread.

In *His Natural Life,* the famous 1870 novel that describes the injustices and hypocrisies of nineteenth-century Australia, Marcus Clarke sarcastically describes an about-face that amounts almost to a somersault: "Glen Tilt—it was wonderful how Scotland was turned upside down in the antipodes!" (1970, 614). To still militant Irish and Scottish nationalists, the colonial conversion to the British and imperial cause appears as an unforgivable act of betrayal, the negation of a hard-won historical heritage. How, asks Nova Scotia politician and writer Joseph

Howe in 1839, "can an Englishman, an Irishman, or a Scotch man, be made to believe, by passing a month upon the sea, that the most striking periods of his history are but a cheat and a delusion?" (Howe 1964, 76). "How was it," Canadian novelist Graeme Gibson asks further in his 1982 novel *Perpetual Motion*, that

> common folk who'd fled tyranny in their homelands submitted here [in Canada], embracing it at that moment when like their American cousins they might have driven it yelping from the land? And how the swine who celebrated the hangings of Lount and Matthews, Scots whose grandfathers died at Culloden, whose families were harried from the glens, and Irish too, men and women who should have known better, how they were then rewarded, advancing in leaps and bounds until now, not thirty years later, they minced and postured everywhere, comfortable arse-lickers, bum-faced servants of the Crown. (113)

For a long line of prescient colonial and then postcolonial writers, this colonial "tilt," this collective amnesia whereby Scottish and Irish settlers misplace in transit their age-old anti-English, anti-British, and anti-imperialist hatreds, appears both as the central mystery of empire and as its cornerstone. It is also, for them, what gives the empire its structural instability—erected on a fundamentally wobbling and unsteady foundation, the edifice of empire threatens, in moments of storm, to topple over again. For what would happen if the settlers ever regained their collective memories and understood themselves to be replicating the injustices they themselves had once suffered? And what, conversely, are the psychic consequences of a continued repression of the structural parallels between themselves, with their traumatic experience of conquest, and the native peoples they displace through their settlement? In *The Diviners* (originally published 1976), one of English Canada's most influential postcolonial novels, Margaret Laurence traces the unacknowledged similarities between the Scottish settlers in Manitoba (forcibly cleared from the Highlands to the Red River colony) and the prior Métis inhabitants whom the Scots, in turn, displace, persecute, and marginalize. What keeps the Scots safe from a disturbing self-knowledge of their own complicity in empire is their proprietorial attitude toward historical suffering, and a nationalist nostalgia that is too specific in its objects of veneration and memorialization.

The ideology of the "tilt," at the same time, presents itself not as a mode of repression but rather as a spirit of conciliation, largesse, and plurality: old partisanships are sublated into new national and imperial identifications, so that a genuinely shared society emerges out of disparate immigrant nations. The colony thereby becomes *not* a site of imperialist struggle at all but rather a place in which Britain is successfully reconstituted, in miniaturized form. "The Thistle, Shamrock, Rose entwine" to form a single national culture—and the problem of Britain's internal unity is solved, at least on a symbolic level, thousands of miles from Britain itself, through and in the formation of new, transnational colonial cultures.[4] "In Canada," writes Susanna Moodie in 1853,

> where all religions are tolerated, it appears a useless aggravation of an old national grievance to perpetuate the memory of the battle of the Boyne. What have we to do with the hatreds and animosities of a more barbarous age? These things belong to the past: "Let the dead bury their dead," and let us form for ourselves a holier and truer present. The old quarrel between Irish Catholics and Protestants should have been sunk in the ocean when they left their native country to find a home, unpolluted by the tyrannies of bygone ages, in the wilds of Canada. (1989, 26)

Joseph Howe (1973), by contrast, argues in "Acadia" (originally published in 1874) for an ethnic politics based on nostalgia rather than cultural amnesia. Once all British emigrant groups grasp that, at least on the new terrain of Nova Scotia or British North America, their military interests and cultural assumptions are largely shared ones, each group remains free to cultivate particular memories of home: as Scots and Irish band together to defend British interests in the colonies, their collective memory of past aggrievements will fade into nostalgic melancholy. Yet nostalgia is inherently quietistic, as the earliest colonial literature of the Cape Colony makes clear. Dedicated to Walter Scott, Thomas Pringle's 1834 *African Sketches* (the first work of African literature written in English) is shaped by the struggle between Pringle's abolitionist obsession with the evils of slavery, as with the problematic effects of European imperialism on the lives and cultures of Africa's native peoples, and a conventional Scott-ish literary-political agenda whose reigning preoccupation is nostalgia. In the end, although Pringle does attempt a critical description of a "new" colonial landscape, the main effect of *African Sketches* is the transplantation of Scottish literary tropes and literary landscapes into Africa. Although ostensibly set in the African veldt, "The Exile's Lament," for instance, is set to the air of "The Banks of the Clyde" and rehearses its Scottish—and Scott-ish—details more pressingly than its African ones:

> By the lone Mankazàna's margin grey,
> A Scottish maiden sung
> And mournfully poured her melting lay
> In Teviot's Border tongue. (Pringle 1834, 66)

The emotional center of "Narrative of a Residence in South Africa," the prose work that fills half of the *African Sketches* volume, is its carefully staged scenes of national recognition and identification: a Scottish settler, in South Africa for twenty years, encounters a party of new Scottish immigrants and is overwhelmed by the almost forgotten sound of Scottish voices; the Highland regiments of the British Army, on hand to help a fleet of immigrant boats land off the coast, respond to Pringle's hailing in "broad Scots." "The name 'Auld Scotland' was a sufficient pass-word to their national sympathies," and the Highlanders bring the Lowlanders' boat to shore with particular caution and care. Far from home, the recognition of joint national identification transcends differences that once seemed decisive and divisive. Ethnic, regional, even linguistic differences—and with them the whole problem of imperialism itself—melt away under the dulcet tones of "broad Scots" and the naming of "Auld Scotland" (128).

In 1840, Captain Maconochie, the Scottish governor and first reformer of Norfolk Island (hitherto the most feared prison in the Australian penal archipelago) is moved by a similar spirit to purchase Scott's Waverley novels for the use of his Scottish inmates, a set of Maria Edgeworth for his Irish prisoners, and the works of Robert Burns, George Crabbe, and Mary Mitford for the edification of the entire prison population. The reading of these works was intended to encourage patriotism, to repair a damaged sense of national pride, and "to invest country and home with agreeable images and recollections . . . too much wanting in the individual experience of our lower and criminal classes" (Maconochie qtd. in Hughes 1988, 506). Full of faith in the power of literature to rehumanize even severely brutalized prisoners, Maconochie aims here at a more particular political rehabilitation. When Scottish and Irish prisoners are exposed to their respective "national" literatures, the nostalgic homesickness these works necessarily produce when read in exile will make "England's Exiles" into more loyal subjects of the

British Crown.[5] What Maconochie's program suggests is a reading of Edgeworth's national tales and Scott's historical novels as works that can be counted on to excite a constructive national pride among the convicts, without inciting national rebellion against their British jailers. Like Edgeworth before him, Scott pleads for a reconciliation between tradition and progress: conservative and progressive by turn, these authors' novels enact the process by which national histories are to be subsumed into a new imperial social contract, with familiar customs and communities easing the transition into a new order. And what the Waverley novels, in particular, give the inhabitants of all the British colonies is a model of how to negotiate a conflicted sense of identifications and identities.

Anne Monkland's 1828 novel *Life in India; or, The English at Calcutta* thus repeatedly invokes Scott's novelistic and poetic presence in the new colonial settlements of India, to several ideological ends. Scott symbolizes the ongoing cultural connection between imperial outposts and imperial centers:

> We can, in Calcutta, command many of the requisites of good society. . . . For those who chose literature there was Sir Walter Scott, Lord Byron's works, and the last Romances from Paris, in splendid morocco bindings. (1:135–38)

The Waverley novels at once entertain and educate colonial administrators: when Monkland's Anglo-Indians plan to act out parts of Scott's *Kenilworth,* they are thinking primarily of their own amusement—but the novel's elaboration of the chivalric code also provides a model for their own imperial duties. Scott's poetry, too, promises to have talismanic properties, evoking national feeling as a means of inoculation against the allures of the colony: on "the plains of Hindostan," two of Monkland's characters, a Scottish doctor and a Scottish major, thus express their gratitude "to our own bards [Byron, Campbell, and Scott] for the pictures of our native land they have given, though half the globe lies between" (3:24–25).

Such invocation and functionalization of national poetry, to serve the present purposes of homesick imperialists, of course runs the danger of falsifying what it invokes as a touchstone. Only twenty years before, indeed, it had been Scottish Anglo-Indians who financed the publication of the fraudulent Gaelic "originals" of James Macpherson's *Poems of Ossian,* for they were anxious to see those poems, which they had so often heard recited in their youth, printed in the language of their ancestors. (Macpherson 1807, lxxxviii)

Such "long-distance nationalism," as Benedict Anderson (1994) argues in his recent "Exodus," the nationalist sentiments felt by the immigrant or exile, often involves the distillation, stylization, or falsification of collective cultural memories to meet present needs. Monkland's homesick imperialists depend on Scottish Romantic poetry both to keep alive their memories of home and to forestall an emotional investment in the alien landscape that surrounds them—but to do so, they must neutralize the political differences between a "national poet" like Byron and one like Scott.

As the author of novels that explicitly celebrate the British conquest of India, Scott appears to Monkland as to other contemporary chroniclers of a new British imperial culture as the British writer most clearly engaged by the imperial project. Byron, in contrast, is famous as a champion of national freedom, one who risks his own life in another nation's war of independence. Yet in the eyes of the Scottish imperialists, longing for moors on the plains of India, both poets evoke national nostalgia together. So too Captain Maconochie will conjoin Edgeworth and Scott, Burns and Crabbe, as purveyors of national sentiment despite obvious differences in their forms of nationalism. For Monkland, for Maconochie, and for early colonial authors writing under the sign of Abbotsford, the empire appears unproblematically inclusive: as a supranational political system that permits the extension, continuation, and enhancement of national feeling itself, it seems able to subsume and absorb far more critical attitudes toward imperialism, apparently without any contradiction or difficulty.

Comings and Goings: Early Canadian Literature of Empire

> Canada, from its position on the map, its hardy climate, its grand natural scenery, its dramatic and stirring historical association should be the Scotland of America. . . . It should produce the great historical novelist; the Sir Walter Scott of the New World. Has the Sir Walter Scott of Canada appeared? And if so, is he unrecognized? If he has not yet come forward, what are the chances for his materialization? If Scott came to Canada,

> how long would it be before he starved to death? . . . Commercially, nothing pays a country better than lavishly to subsidize an author. A Sir Walter Scott would bring millions into Canada every year. Scotland could well have afforded to bestow on Sir Walter Scott a hundred million dollars for his incomparable Waverley Novels. His works have made Scotland the dearest district in the world in which a traveller can live, and have transformed it from a poverty-stricken land into a tourist-trodden country, rolling in wealth.—Robert Barr, "Literature in Canada"

Nova Scotia satirists Thomas McCulloch and Thomas Haliburton, and John Galt, a Scottish colonizer of Upper Canada, join the Scott-ish imperialists in seeing the empire as a political structure that conjoins a disparate and far-flung array of cultures. Yet the empire, in their view, with its enormous disparities of wealth, political power, and freedom, seems more likely to forge literal bonds of slavery, servitude, and dependence than to create a lofty new sense of cooperation, joint mission, and mutual understanding. To these writers, the empire represents economic exploitation, moral disconnection, and psychic dislocation. Each of the three, in fact, shows himself particularly obsessed with one of these imperial effects, according to his own occupational perspective on the empire. Minister, judge and parliamentarian, territorial administrator respectively, McCulloch, Haliburton, and Galt criticize the empire from different sectors of the colonial elite. Sent from Scotland to Nova Scotia by the colonial missionary service of the Presbyterian Church, Thomas McCulloch was instrumental in establishing higher education in the colony, becoming the first president of Dalhousie University. As a man of learning and of God, McCulloch bases his critique of empire on a condemnation of slavery and of commerce itself as sources of moral and civic contamination. His *Letters of Mephibosheth Stepsure* (published 1821–23 in the *Acadian Recorder*) chronicle the life of a small Nova Scotia town populated by Scots settlers. Yet the work involves more than the simple transposition of the modes and motifs of Scottish into a Scots Canadian setting. For even at the most local level, McCulloch argues, colonial life is implicated in the project and problem of empire. The letters begin, indeed, with a cautionary fable about the way commerce breeds commerce, colonies colonialism, and slavery slaves. Through the agency of one Calibogus, a West India merchant who trades in the goods of slavery and colonial oppression, Nova Scotia settler Solomon Gosling sets himself up as a storekeeper and thereby introduces credit, consumerism, and a new class division into his town. In the meantime, he bankrupts himself, becomes dissatisfied with the economic opportunities Canada offers, and resolves to emigrate with his family to a more promising British colony. As Gosling laments to his family:

"The truth is . . . the country does not deserve to be lived in. There is neither trade nor money in it, and produce gives nothing. It is fit only for Indians, and emigrants from Scotland, who were starving at home. It is time for me to go elsewhere, and carry my family to a place that presents better prospects. . . ."

The whole family agreed that, then, with the rest of his property, they would go to a country better worth the living in. . . . Miss Dinah preferred the Cape of Good Hope, but she was afraid of the Caffres, who sometimes carry off white women. . . . Upon the whole, they seemed to think the opinion of Miss Fanny most feasible; that it would be best to go to Botany Bay, where every genteel family like the Goslings, receives so many white niggers, sent out every year from Britain by Government for the supply of the colony. (McCulloch 1960, 12–16)

At the end of the letter, as the family rehearse possible colonial destinations, they are drawn to a situation in which their own status as white settlers will give them automatic privilege: in Botany Bay, with its unending supply of convict-slaves, their sense of mastery will be complete. McCulloch's fable functions as an indirect but powerful indictment of an imperial economy built on, implicated in, and connected by slavery. Rather than seeing political domination (as symbolized in Caliban's struggle with Prospero over the possession of the colonized island) as the crux of empire, McCulloch focuses on the economic complicity it creates, and on the alluring Calibogus, whose far-reaching trade routes double the routes of slavery itself.

Like McCulloch, Thomas Chandler Haliburton is haunted by the specter of slavery. His working life was spent in the colonial administrative caste (as a lawyer, justice, supreme court judge, a Member of the Nova Scotia Legislature, and of the British Parliament), and the political preoccupation of his fiction (perhaps under the influence of Galt's Scottish novels) is with the nature, distribution, exercise, and self-deceptions of political power. Haliburton's most famous work, *The Clockmaker* (originally serialized in 1836), targets the young United States, whose insistent rhetoric of individual liberty covers over its murderously capitalist economy, its mixture of Caribbean-style slave labor and equally brutalized industrial wage labor. The Irish whom famine forces to immigrate to the United States, Haliburton argues, find themselves caught in a second death trap, as they are paid true starvation wages, and literally worked to death.

"Upon my soul . . . [explains the narrator] the poor labourer does not last long in your country. . . . you'll see the graves of the Irish each side of the canal, for all the world like two rows of potatoes in a field that have forgot to come up."

"[The United States] is a land, sir, . . . [says Sam Slick] of hard work. We have two kinds of slaves, the niggers and the white slaves. All European labourers and blacks, who come out to us, do our hard bodily work, while we direct it to a profitable end; neither rich nor poor, high nor low, with us, eat the bread of idleness. . . . An idle fellow . . . who runs away to us, is clapt into harness afore he knows where he is, and is made to work; like a horse that refuses to draw, he is put into the teamboat; he finds some before him and others behind him; he must either draw, or be dragged to death." (1958, 17)

But Haliburton is also critical of the networks and circuits of power within the British empire itself, where a rhetoric of allegiance and merit is belied by a network of colonial favoritism. The empire harnesses indigenous talents but refuses to give them their due, and drains indigenous riches without giving enough back. "Calcutta keeps me, . . . [says Sam Slick] and Bot'ney Bay keeps me, and Canada keeps me, and Nova Scotia keeps me" (Haliburton 1844, 117).

Even more than *The Stepsure Letters,* Haliburton's fiction is preoccupied, epistemologically and formally, with the centrality of a traveling perspective for colonial consciousness. In *The Clockmaker,* the cultural differences between Canada and the United States are articulated by the pushy, peripatetic Yankee peddler, Sam Slick. *The Letter-Bag of the Great Western: or, Life in a Steamer,* which appeared in 1840, collects letters written during the Atlantic passage of a huge variety of travelers, from cabin passengers to steerage passengers, servants, slaves, and sailors. The book's formal structure suggests the radically heterogeneous character of colonial life, with nothing holding it together except the passengers' temporary destination; the boat itself includes settlers who refuse to stay settled and who restlessly migrate between settler colonies. In *The Old Judge; or, Life in a Colony* (originally published in 1849), Haliburton argues that colonial government is based on the interchangeability of postings and that colonies therefore breed an insidious habit of perpetual motion, which renders quite impossible the development of a colonial national character. Yet in his last major work, *The Season-Ticket* (1860), which describes a journey across Britain, Haliburton pleads for a better imperial transport and communication network to link the outposts of empire. More than Haliburton's other works, *The Season-Ticket* evokes the loss, in transit, of a coherent or distinctive sense of place:

> Everything has altered its dimensions, except the world we live in. The more we know of that, the smaller it seems. Time and distance have been abridged, remote countries have become accessible, and the antipodes are upon visiting terms. There is a reunion of the human race; and the family likeness, now that we begin to think alike, dress alike, and live alike, is very striking. The South Sea Islanders, and the inhabitants of China, import their fashions from Paris, and their fabrics from Manchester, while Rome and London supply missionaries to the "ends of the earth," to bring its inhabitants into "one fold." (1)

Yet the tone here is celebratory rather than critical. In *The Clockmaker*, thirty years earlier, Haliburton had seen the American development of railroad technology as the murderous advance of American capitalism; here, mechanized transport is indispensable to imperial commerce, cultural interchange, and a new transcolonial cosmopolitanism.

For John Galt, in contrast, the net effect of new technologies and economic modernization, both within Britain and throughout the empire, is to derail the political struggle for democratization. Galt's own parallel professional careers, as merchant and lawyer, colonizer and writer, at various nodal points of Britain's internal and overseas empire (Greenock, London, Upper Canada) inform his most famous novels. Taken together, Galt's 1821–32 series of historical case studies—a family chronicle (*The Entail*) that details the social history of eighteenth-century Scotland and the annalistic "autobiographies" of a Presbyterian minister (*Annals of the Parish*), a zealous Covenanter (*Ringhan Gilhaize*), a corrupt local politician and improver (*The Provost*), a laird impoverished by the advent of modernity (*The Last of the Lairds*), an optimistic businessman who emigrates to America (*Lawrie Todd*), a depressive merchant who emigrates to Canada (*Bogle Corbet*), a Tory MP (*The Member*), and a Chartist reformer (*The Radical*)—form a panoramic, materialist survey of modern Scottish society worthy of a Balzac or a Zola.

Several of these novels explore the influence of the British imperial economy on Scottish history. *The Entail* (first published in 1822) opens with the 1700 failure of Scotland's Central American colony at Darien: its sabotage by England caused a crash of the Scottish economy and the impoverishment of large sectors of Scottish society, and created the economic preconditions, Galt argues, for Scotland's forced 1707 Union with England and for its subsequent fiscal and political colonization. And *The Last of the Lairds* (from 1826) traces the opposite, yet related, social displacement caused when the influx of wealth generated from colonial revenues—personified by Mr. Rupees, the nouveau riche nabob who returns from Bengal to settle in Renfrewshire—establishes a mercantilist challenge to the traditional political authority of the Scottish aristocracy and threatens to introduce the political imperiousness of the empire back into Britain itself.

If these novels express suspicion about the influence of the British empire on Scottish culture and consciousness, Galt's own career becomes inextricably bound up with the imperial cause. In 1824, Galt was hired to help United Empire Loyalists gain recompense from the British government for the damages they sustained during the War of 1812. His proposal to the government that it raise the money by colonizing several large tracts of government land in Upper Canada resulted in his appointment as superintendant of the new Canada Company and his move to Canada in 1826 to supervise the settlement of the Ontario Townships.[6] Three years later, however, he had run afoul of the Family Compact (the powerful oligarchic clique governing Upper Canada), and his career as a colonist unraveled completely. Recalling him to Britain, the Canada Company fired Galt without paying his back salary and forced him into debtors' prison for several months, where he began the two contrasting novels that reflect upon his North American experiences.

The optimistic narrator of *Lawrie Todd; or, The Settlers in the Wood* (1830) recounts his emigration from Scotland to the United States, his initial struggle to establish himself, and his eventual successes as a settler and businessman in upstate New York. *Bogle Corbet; or, The Emigrants* (first published in 1831) tells a more complex and sober story. In the first two volumes, Bogle Corbet recounts failed industrial and mercantile careers in Britain and in the West Indies; in the third, a fictionalized account of Galt's own experiences, he emigrates to Upper Canada, oversees the construction of a Scottish settlement in the forest, and struggles to maintain political control over the new community. What he confronts are not only the republican influences of the nearby United States (with its twin allures of economic and political liberty) but, more important, the old Jacobin ideals of the settlers, Glaswegian artisans with a shared history of political struggle in the 1790s. Once a Jacobin himself, Bogle Corbet now extols the oligarchic, socially hierarchized, and socially controlled mode of Scots British settlement, in sharp contrast to what he depicts as the anarchic individualism of the nearby American settlements. In important ways, the final volume of *Bogle Corbet* hinges on the contrast between a colonial Upper Canada, proudly loyal to the empire, and a republican United States, proudly defined by its act of rebellion against the British colonial government.

The peculiar, nationally inflected history of *Bogle Corbet*'s modern reception has enshrined this contrast as the single point of the book. In 1977, during a period of intense anti-American sentiment and equally intense literary nationalism in Canada, *Bogle Corbet* received its first modern and first Canadian printing, as part of the canon-forming New Canadian Library issued by McClelland and Stewart, "the Canadian publishers." The "reprinting," however, involved a severe abridgment of the original, omitting the first two-thirds of the novel, so that only Bogle Corbet's final, Canadian sojourn remained. Taking the final volume more or less at face value (and at moments conflating Galt with his narrator) the novel's few subsequent commentators have tended to read it as an affirmative account of imperial growth that demonstrates how a settler colony reroots old-world virtues in a new colonial situation. Yet both the structure of the full novel and the overall thrust of Galt's oeuvre, with its extensive experiments with personification allegory (as individual representative characters come to stand for a whole class, a historical moment, or a historical force) and with accretive, annalistic modes of historiography, demand a more subtle reading. Like many of Galt's novels, *Bogle Corbet* uses the developmental history of its first-person narrator to explore the internal development and historical force of an ideological position, even while the shifts, breaks and prevarications within the narrator's speaking voice point up the ideology's internal inconsistencies, blind spots and hypocrisies.

Galt's full novel frames its extended comparative study of disparate colonial cultures within nuanced historical analyses of the relationship between capitalist and imperialist expansionism, the development of imperialism as an ideology in relationship to mercantilism and Jacobinism, and the emergence of the second British empire in relationship to both the Industrial and the French Revolutions. Like McCulloch and Haliburton, Galt insists on placing the settler colonies of British North America in relation both to other parts of the British empire (particularly the slave colonies of the West Indies) and to the mercantile functioning of the empire as a whole. For the first half of the story, Corbet sees the empire from the perspective of Glasgow. An early nodal point of imperial trade—and therefore one of Britain's earliest industrial centers and shock absorbers of modernity—Glasgow experienced boom periods punctuated by recurrent, devastating crashes, often precipitated by events in the colonies. The tobacco trade, the first base of the city's mercantile fortunes, collapsed in the 1780s in the wake of the American Revolutionary War, while the crash of the 1790s was brought on by the collapse of a major Glasgow West India house. In an unsuccessful attempt to corner the slave trade, Alexander Huston and Co. had shipped thousands of Africans in chains to the West Indies. When there proved no market for them and no further capital for their support, a large number of slaves starved to death, the West India house was bankrupted, and the Glasgow banks failed (Oakley 1990, 10). What Glasgow's economic life made visible was how the enormous financial gains of empire were matched not only by equal financial risks but also by the erosion of social stability and moral values.

As his unabridged narrative makes clear, Corbet is a product of empire on every level. Born into the Scots British plantation society of Jamaica, his earliest and deepest bonds are to his slave nurse Baba. Orphaned while still very young, and traumatically separated from Baba, he is sent back to Scotland to be educated. Under the guardianship of Mr. MacIndoe, a merchant who made his fortune in the East and West Indies, Corbet enters the cotton business. Yet MacIndoe's mercantilist and imperialist teachings cannot completely replace the sympathies formed at Baba's breast.

> When I heard the merchants talk of their West Indian articles, I used to speculate not in them, but on what, in time, would become of the islands when the Negroes got understanding; and when I heard the proud things in the coffee-room which the king's men talked in their newspaper politics, about heroes and glory, I could never help thinking that soldiering was only a trade, and that the man who was paid for carrying a musket was but little different from the pale weaver that earned his living driving a shuttle. . . . [R]eflections of that kind were neither favourable to the making of money, nor to the attainment of eminence in Glasgow. (Galt 1831, 1:73–74)

At work in a Glasgow cotton mill during the last decades of the eighteenth century, Corbet witnesses the rise of large-scale manufacturing, the emergence of a new industrial working class, and of a working-class Jacobin movement—a confluence of developments that leads him to reflect not only on the uncontrollability of historical change once set into motion but also on the apparent inevitability of revolutionary unrest in the West Indies. Yet by the beginning of the nineteenth century, Corbet's democrat friends have become Whigs. And despite his own youthful anticipation that the whole imperial system would soon be ended by colonial revolution, Corbet himself has become a West India merchant in London, fully involved in the business of empire.

When his business founders and he must travel to Jamaica himself, his native land leaves him disturbed, confused, and full of his old doubts. For although he finds the "degradation" of slavery not as harsh as expected (especially compared to British wage slavery), Jamaica's history of slavery has permanently undermined its stability as a colony: the white settlers' continual fear of black uprisings and retributions leads them to see the island as "only a scene of temporary possession . . . [with] everything prepared for departure" (2:305). With this the colonization project has already failed, emotionally and ideologically, even in advance of any actual revolution—and this failure marks human as well as political relations on the island. Although Corbet is happily reunited with his nurse Baba and an affectionate foster sister, he also has an unnerving encounter with a "deformed" old woman whose peculiar dialect proves to be a "Negro Scotch." In her youth, as a slave captive, she had been the mistress of a Scottish plantation overseer. Then, without warning, she and her "African lover" rose up against their master's authority, murdering him, burning down his house, and escaping to join the "Maroons" (as the British called the many groups of escaped slaves who waged continual guerilla warfare against plantation slaveholders and against British colonial authority). In Corbet's continuing ties to his black foster family, the system of slave-holding appears to have kept its paternalist promises and actually forged familial bonds between master and slave women. Yet the old Maroon woman's "wild mockery of language," with its taunting traces of Scots phrases and inflections, eerily evokes both the coercive circumstances under which such affective and cultural transferences take place and the rebellious violence that continues to lie beneath the colony's surface (1:299).

If in Jamaica the slave-holding system means that property relations underlie all personal relations, Corbet sees Scotland itself undergoing a comparable commercial transformation as it moves from a feudal to a capitalist society: even the lairds, who formerly defined themselves in relationship to their clan, now "stoop from their dignity to pick up commercial money," sending their youngest sons "into the armies as subalterns, or as cadets to India" (1:74). On his return from Jamaica, Corbet travels to the Hebrides and Highlands, where he meditates on the collapse of clan culture and traditional local economies, on the "disease of depression and lassitude" that has replaced them, and on the resulting mass emigration to the New World. In light of such experiences, Corbet's own eventual immigration to Canada, and his reconstruction there of a self-consciously traditional mode of Scottish settlement, seems both compensatory and ambivalent.

Corbet is still settled in Upper Canada at the end of the novel, and his final stance is that of a stalwart Tory and a firm believer in the immutable stability of British order. At the same time, however, Corbet sinks into recurring, almost suicidal depressions, so that the book ends on a note of profound pessimism.

> But though many days are here blank leaves in the book of life, let me not be misunderstood; I have no cause to regret my emigration; I have only been too late. . . . Emigration should be undertaken at that period when youths are commonly sent to trades and professions: the hardships are too heavy an apprenticeship for manhood, and to riper years penalty and privation. (Galt 1977, 198)

If Canada is meant to be the salvation of the imperial system, it certainly fails to save Corbet himself. For with its passage to Canada in the third volume, the novel offers not so much a new beginning as a restaging of all its political and economic issues within a fresh colonial context. The phenomenon of mass emigration from Britain itself arises from British industrialization, since "agricultural changes, and the introduction of new machinery, is [*sic*] constantly throwing off swarms of operatives who have no other resource" (1977, 11). For such workers North America represents the hope of renewed economic and political agency. But Corbet's own sympathies lie with middle-class emigrants, "individuals in impaired, or desperate circumstances, unable to preserve their caste in the social system of this country, wrecked and catching at emigration as the last plank" (1977, 11). Thus even while British industrialization depends on the capital produced by the colonies, the colonies themselves come, for an impoverished gentry, to seem a final refuge from economic transformation, as from the threat of a political and social leveling that would deprive them of their caste privileges.

Yet even emigration cannot guarantee protection from the indignities of modernity. When he founds his town in the forests of Canada, Corbet attempts to institutionalize a genteel ascendancy. The majority of "his" settlers, however, have emigrated in search of new political freedoms; refusing to assent to his plans, they continue to agitate for a different, radically egalitarian form of government. On the eve of the passage of the First Reform Bill, this backwoods conflict over the future form of political life and social organization reiterates the British class struggles fought throughout the 1790s between Jacobins and property holders. At stake in this new struggle is nothing less than the political and social temporality of the new colony. Will the colony understand itself as a new Eden, an attempt to form a new social contract and a new social order? Or, on the contrary, as a last refuge from modernization, will it insist, at all costs, on the transplantation and preservation of the British social order as it once was (or at least as it is now remembered)? Will the new immigrants from Paisley, the Highlands, Ireland, continue to stick to themselves in order to preserve their old clan structure? Or will they instead mix together to form a new whole? If this formulation invokes, once more, the old allegory of British national reconciliation in the new context of the empire, Galt's framing of the colonial situation of Canada insists more generally that the weight of history and of the imperial system itself makes a truly fresh beginning, a truly new union, a virtual impossibility.

Chronically depressed throughout his time in Canada, Corbet is at least subconsciously aware that his suffering has historical sources. But he also seems psychically committed to historical repetition compulsion. Born into the plantation system, bred into mercantilism, Corbet asserts his intellectual autonomy for the first and only time during his brief turn to Jacobinism before the British power structures reabsorb him. When he establishes his own settlement in the Canadian wilderness, the feudalist-capitalist model he chooses seems ultimately derived from the plantation system itself. Despite his fundamental doubts about the authoritarian forms of power that accompanied imperialist expansion in the Caribbean, and his wish to escape to a part of the empire that is not yet marked by them, when he arrives in the Canadian forests, he is compelled to construct the new colony in the image of the old.

Bogle Corbet represents one of Galt's most virtuoso uses of the annalistic form, as the changing texture of the narration invites both psychological and historical readings of the life story and suggests important links between them. Read as a psychological novel, *Bogle Corbet* narrates the story of a traumatic early separation from a beloved (although enslaved) love object, the native nurse; the reinvestment of affectional energies in a political movement that fails; two unhappy marriages; the replacement of human attachments by mercantile ones, and of a settled emotional life by an accelerating circulation between places; and finally, recurring bouts of disorienting despair. If these same elements are read historically and annalistically, the novel can be seen to progress from an emotional attachment to an idealized noble slave and a political commitment to European and colonial emancipation to mercantile ventures and commercial failures, recurring crises of imperialist conscience, and finally complete ideological and financial investment in the settler colony as a fresh start, chronicling the development and growing false consciousness of British imperial attitudes.

As the narrator of his autobiography, Corbet's continuous efforts to buttress his position amount to an ideological filter, through which we as readers are shown a particular vision of imperial and Canadian life. At regular intervals, however, Galt allows us to see the limits of the narrative perspective, and to guess at how much it systematically leaves out of consideration. What Galt attempts to work out in this novel is the way in which Corbet's personal repetition compulsions—and the British compulsion to repeat the fundamental injustices of colonization—are accompanied by a profound amnesia that both fuels a neurotic sense of disorientation and imparts a temporary, stabilizing illusion that the contradictions of ideology and experience can actually be reconciled. Any sense of being at home or at rest in the colony derives from this mirage, and is therefore precarious and short-lived.

Seized with a particularly virulent form of emigrant's amnesia, Corbet ends his autobiography without referring back to anything that happened before Canada, as if unable to remember anything but the present or anything about where he comes from. It is this same amnesia, of course, that at once enables and informs the McClelland and Stewart abridgment and the subsequent Canadian reception of the novel. A "transcolonial" writing of empire is preserved and studied so partially that only "national literatures" remain.

Calibogus and Caliban

> The island of his birth, on which [Indian Trinidadian businessman Alistair Ramgoolan] had grown up and where he had made his fortune, was transformed by a process of mind into a kind of temporary home. Its history ceased to be important, its present turned into a fluid holding pattern which would eventually give way. . . . [He] could hope for death here but his grandchildren, maybe even his children, would continue [in immigrating to Canada] the emigration which his grandfather had started in India, and during which the island had proved, in the end, to be nothing more than a stopover.—Neil Bissoondath, "Insecurity"

From the 1940s onward, famously, a postcolonial tradition has used Caliban's struggle with Prospero in Shakespeare's *Tempest* as a metaphoric starting point for a consideration of power relations within the European colonies, one that views the latter as an ongoing Manichean struggle between colonizer and colonized (Nixon 1987). The problem with this allegorization of empire is that it tends to be static, in that it sees the terms of imperial interaction as largely fixed and secured from an early moment of discovery, contact, conquest, or subjection.[7] Yet the more dynamic model of imperial interaction that derives from the developmental narratives of nationalism soon proves itself problematic as well. As Benedict Anderson (1983) and Partha Chatterjee (1986) have argued, it is the empire itself that creates a sense of national cohesion and nationalist resistance where there may have been none before, that catalyzes the classic process of nation formation as well as the national liberation struggles that sometimes result in autonomy from the empire. It is thus European rule that apparently shaped Arab and African nationalism out of regional or tribal identities, and the empires of the Moghuls and then the Raj that shaped the multiethnic South Asian subcontinent into a single "India." Even those colonies which are not formed historically from already existing nations become potential nations through the colonizing process itself.

The political analysis of colonial life has tended to situate it between two moments: its helpless or reluctant subordination, on the one hand, to the directives of a distant imperial center, which would transform the whole empire in its own image, and on the other, its resistance to imperial efforts at homogenization, the revival of indigenous leadership and social forms, the launching of campaigns for national autonomy. Literary historians have used similar categories to discuss (and canonize) colonial literary production. The early literature of the colony is characterized in terms of its imitative, reactive, subordinated relationship to the literature of the imperial center. Then, as time and distance increase the separation between "home countries" and colonies, and as the colonial educational system produces an indigenous intelligentsia and reading public, the growing influence of indigenous material and literary forms begins to shape a distinctive, increasingly autonomous colonial literature. At some point, each colony sees a second kind of literary beginning, with the emergence of a more clearly "national literature"; literary historians of the British empire often seem to place such developments in synchronicity with the domestic publication, in the late nineteenth century, of an extensive body of triumphant, racialist, or ambivalent literature of empire. With their typical emphasis on the Victorian period as the "real" imperial period, and their replication of both strictly imperial and strictly national principles in their attention to the subordination and reemergence of nations in empires, such investigations have left virtually unexamined a significant body of earlier British and colonial literature that describes the experience of empire in rather different terms. Rather than focus on the subordination and reemergence of nations in empires, this literature analyses the transcolonial consciousness and transperipheral circuits of influence that empire gives rise to.

The past thirty years have seen the emergence, throughout the former British empire, of a new wave of self-conscious literary reckonings with the legacies of imperialism. And the academic study of the English-language literature of empire has undergone a conceptual and political shift, moving away from "Commonwealth literature," the shared colonial reception of imperial traditions, to the history of resistant, indigenous literatures within each "colony," and to the contemporary "postcolonial" literature being produced both by expatriots and within the new nation-states of Africa, South Asia, and the Caribbean. The dual preoccupations of this new model are the indigenous and the creolized, and these in some ways are collapsed into one another, as the historical problem of national political autonomy becomes merged with the quest to identify the situated specificity of new colonial cultural forms. Under the sign of postmodernity, at the same time, the new field of "postcolonial" literary studies has also begun to address the diasporic, internationalized character of contemporary writing, often the work of deterritorialized intellectuals and often read not only by local readers but also by a worldwide audience of expatriates and other "serious" readers.

The danger of such emphasis is that the patently transcolonial and international character of much emergent literature will be read as a new development, an effect of this particular globalized moment, rather than as a constituent and thus constant feature of empire itself. The parallel danger, at the same time, is that in each individual "postcolony," literary interpretation will proceed much as usual, with parochially "historical" procedures (still territorialized searches for "indigenous voices" to claim for the national canon or countercanon) alternating only with cosmopolitan "theoretical" ones (deterritorialized intertextual readings that emphasize the sophistication, Europeanization, and mutual influence of postcolonial writers). But it is rather the pull of nation against empire over the *longue durée,* of the recurrent gap between the experienced specificity of culture or place and the rhythm of comparison in the traverse of "parallel" places, that gives colonial and then postcolonial literatures their texture. National(ist) narratives situate them too easily, after and as the outcome of disconnected struggle, not as the center of a still active force field. Arjun Appadurai (1990) has persuasively described the global flow of population, knowledge, tastes, and goods as a quintessential condition of late capitalism and postmodernity. Such flows tend to traverse the former British empire not only in straight lines back and forth between "periphery" and "center" but also through a large number of thoroughly transcolonial circuits, many as old as the fact of colonial settlement itself. In Canada, as in other parts of the former British empire, much of the most interesting English-language literature written over the last fifteen years is the work of immigrants, often from other British postcolonies; their pathbreaking discussions of Canada's structural racism as an explicitly imperial and colonial legacy is based on their own transcolonial experiences.[8]

"In Canadian fiction," as Frank Davey noted sardonically in 1986, "there are more scenes set in India than in Abbotsford," a comment simultaneously on Canadian exoticism and on the uneven distribution of literary attention to the "peripheries." Today, of course, the fact of a Canadian literature as interested in India and "Indians" (West, East, and Native) as in the imperial legacies of Abbotsford seems thoroughly unsurprising. But now, instead, it may be the historical and imperial roots of this transcolonial perspective that threaten to be lost, as "globalization" is misunderstood as a late-twentieth-century phenomenon without historical precedent. The danger of a "postcolonial" literary history is that, as its name implies, it will emphasize the temporal caesura between the empire and the postindependence life of the individual nation-state, as if the process of nation-subsumed-into-empire that Scott enshrines at Abbotsford could simply be reversed and run backward. What the critical, cosmopolitan novels of empire of Scott's contemporaries should help us see instead is an important prehistory of postcolonial perspectives. At the same time, in the way they add Calibogus to Caliban as symbols for imperial experience, these novels also open up alternative ways of describing the formation of colonial, transcolonial, and postcolonial consciousness.

Notes

Many thanks to the transcolonial friends (especially Deidre Lynch, Loren Kruger, and Shamoon Zamir) who have informed my thinking about empire, and to Richard Maxwell for his tireless feedback as this essay took shape. This work was begun during a Mellon Postdoctoral Fellowship at the University of Pittsburgh; it was materially assisted by a National Endowment for the Humanities Travel to Collections Grant and by access to a number of rare book libraries, especially the British Library; the Newberry Library, Chicago; the Thomas Fischer Rare Book Library, University of Toronto; and the Bruce Peel Special Collections, University of Alberta. My interest in the transcolonial logic of the British empire was sparked, long ago, when I was an undergraduate at the University of Alberta, by a fragment of Indian statuary, the head of a bodhisattva, on display in Cameron Library. The statue, its label announced, was a present to the university from a British Army major who had "traded it for rifles in the Khyber Pass."

1. See Ferris 1991; Trumpener 1993.

2. On Scott's influence in English (and French) Canada, see Gerson 1989, esp. chap. 5; Kroeller 1980; MacLulich 1988, esp. chap. 2. McGregor's *The Wacousta Syndrome* (1985) argues for the centrality of *Wacousta* for subsequent Canadian fiction; Davey's poem "Wacouster" (1985) parodically demythologizes it.

3. See Calder 1981; for the Scottish cultural and literary presence in the empire, see Bryant 1985; Bumstead 1982; Gifford 1988, esp. Alan MacGillivray, "Exile and Empire," 411–27, Paul H. Scott, "'The Last Purely Scotch Age,'" 13–21, and John Macinnes, "Gaelic Poetry in the Nineteenth Century," 377–95; Smailes 1981; Waterson 1976. For the Irish presence in the empire, see Hughes 1988; Power 1991.

4. The phrase forms the chorus of "The Maple Leaf Forever," a patriotic anthem written by the Scottish Canadian Alexander Muir in 1867 to celebrate Canadian confederation. Laurence's *Diviners* (1976, 69–70) contains a famous postcolonial gloss on the song, suggesting that it functions to reinforce the long-standing social marginalization of French, Eastern European—and especially Native—Canadians from "English" Canada.
5. The phrase comes from Colin Arrott Browning's *The Convict Ships and England's Exiles* (1847), in which Browning, a convict hull chaplain, describes his own program for the spiritual reformation, inner transformation, and resocialization of prisoners during the period of transport itself.
6. For Galt's work as a colonizer, see Timothy 1977; Waterson 1985, esp. Gilbert A. Stelter, "John Galt as Town Booster and Builder," 17–43.
7. For the hypostatization of the moment of contact into a general metaphor for colonial relations, see, for instance, Peter Hulme's otherwise learned and helpful *Colonial Encounters* (1986).
8. Daphne Marlatt, for instance, whose 1976 long poem "Steveston" was one of the first literary explorations of West Coast Canadian Japanese settlement as an ethnic history shaped for generations by official anti-Asian racism (culminating in the World War II expropriations and relocation camps), is white, born in Malaya, and a longtime resident of Australia before she emigrated to Canada; Marlatt's understanding of the situation of Asian Canadians is thus informed by her knowledge of the British colonies in Asia itself. Sam Selvon's work is similarly informed by several layers of diasporic experience in various corners of the old British empire: a member of the long-standing Indian community in Trinidad, he accompanied and chronicled the first wave of postwar West Indian emigration to Britain in the 1950s (*The Lonely Londoners*) before moving on to Canada.

James A. Fujii

7 Writing Out Asia

Modernity, Canon, and Natsume Sōseki's *Kokoro*

❧ I was invited to present a paper at a symposium, held at the National University of Singapore in April of 1991 and devoted exclusively to Natsume Sōseki's 1914 *Kokoro.* The venue (a land once occupied by Japan) prompted me to consider the meaning of such a conference, focused on perhaps *the* canonical work in modern Japanese literature, with invited scholars from Japan, Singapore, Canada, Australia, Taiwan, South Korea, and the United States. Mine was the only paper (out of twelve) that addressed these enunciative contingencies, and, not surprisingly, it was to be one of the few that were omitted from the subsequent special conference issue of the journal *Mugentai.*[1] In this revised version of that paper, I have juxtaposed Sōseki's travelogue *Man-Kan tokorodokoro* (Here and There in Manchuria and Korea) with *Kokoro* (the Heart/Mind) as a way to intervene in the current, ongoing reproduction of amnesia that underwrites our reception of this *shōsetsu* (prose narrative) today.

As is common when a literature with a substantial critical tradition is studied by critics of another, a finely honed scholastic topography mediates between Japanese literature and (Western) Japanologists. Texts chosen for reading and study, issues that are raised, and implicit agendas that are held by Western scholars of Japanese literature are all deeply influenced by native sedimentation, both academic and popular.[2] Such overdetermination is particularly marked in the case of Natsume Sōseki (1867–1916) who, perhaps with Mori Ōgai, towers over the landscape of modern Japanese literature. Today Sōseki's portrait graces the thousand-yen note, every Japanese youngster is made to read from his corpus, and the annual polls of school children continue to confirm his high standing among the "most admired" figures in Japanese history. His range is broad, as he has left us with essays on literary criticism, short stories, travelogues, satirical novels, and social criticism, but his lofty position in the pantheon of greats in Japanese literature owes chiefly to his later prose narratives (beginning with *Sanshirō,* from 1908), which focus on the alienated individual in early-twentieth-century urban Japan. And, among these works, *Kokoro* has earned a singular prominence, whether this privilege be assessed by enduring readership, critical attention (well over three hundred studies of varying length in Japan alone),[3] or security in the school curriculum.

While Sōseki is not widely read by the general public on this side of the Pacific, critical acclaim has mirrored the Japanese lead in celebrating his works as native expressions of the Western psychological novel. The reified conception of modernity and its individuated subject that underwrites such prose narratives has been reproduced yet again in a recent instance of canonizing in this country. Part of an ambitious series (projected for thirty volumes) called the Library of Japan, the volume entitled *Kokoro: A Novel and Selected Essays* includes a reprint of Edwin McClellan's translation of *Kokoro* (widely available in paperback) and Sōseki's essays "My Individualism" and "The Civilization of Modern-Day Japan."[4] Originally presented by Sōseki as lectures addressing the pernicious effects of "Western civilization" on Japan, as companion pieces to *Kokoro* these essays ostensibly address why it is that the protagonist in his longer works (such as *Kokoro*) must suffer so.[5] The imprecise answer to this question, inevitably, is to be found in the disjunction of East meeting West, with its most profound manifestation in the figure of the "modern individual." Sōseki and his texts have been repackaged yet again in the familiar Eurocentric oppositional terms that the writer himself exhorted his lecture audiences to question. Sōseki cannot be prized from the issue of modernity, but to avoid the worn formula exemplified by the Library of Japan, we must ask ourselves what the fixed conceptions of the "modern" and the "individual" have effectively valorized and suppressed for almost a century. What the naturalized connection of Sōseki to modernity conceals is the focus of the present essay.[6] We, as inheritors of and ongoing contributors to a particular discursive production of Sōseki, are the subject of this work.

While Sōseki's *Kokoro* is one of the most studied *shōsetsu* in modern Japanese literature, to my knowledge it has not been tied to the journalistic account of this author's travels on the Asian continent, *Man-Kan tokorodokoro.* The pairing is useful in illustrating what would become a relatively common experience for the modern Japanese writer—to experience firsthand the Japanese occupational presence in Asia, without letting it touch her/his literary production. The global exfoliation of nationalist sentiment today suggests more urgently than might have been the case even a scant five years ago the value of historicizing *Kokoro,* perhaps Sōseki's most enduringly popular work, in a way that has been avoided to date: to show how its privileged position at the heart of the Japanese literary canon owes much to the fact that it belonged to the discourse of modernism—particularly imperialism—that in modified form continues to order the world that we live in today. No more than we can step "outside" of Orientalism or other relations of domination, we cannot grasp Sōseki's text outside a nearly century-old practice of appropriation found in the discursive identity labeled "Japan." Our own position must be taken with the recognition that "it is no longer a question of judging the past in the name of a truth that only we can possess in the present" (Foucault 1977a, 164). The following discussion of *Kokoro* addresses the novel's canonicity, because that is what mediates our relation to this text written almost a century ago (deforming it to its present, familiar dimensions). More significantly, it brings the matter of responsibility for forgetting history to the present moment.

Ever since Japan was impelled to admit Western material, cultural, and intellectual practices at the beginning of the Meiji period (1868–1912), a stubborn pair of oppositions has shaped discourse on twentieth-century Japanese literature: in premodern literature it was China and Japan and in modern literature the West and Japan. The second division reflects the unquestioned assumption of Western humanist-realist conventions as the basis for reading modern Japanese texts. Thus, in spite of an apparent diversity of critical approaches to such works as *Kokoro,* most take as their theme the emergence of a modern, individuated, and hence deeply troubled subject in postfeudal Japan. With repetitions of the same theme, this critical discourse has coalesced into an interpretive template that displaces more politically informed perspectives. While Sōseki's later novels have been institutionalized as expressions of the dislocation wrought by the currents of late Meiji history (with Etō Jun's work [e.g., 1970] serving as a kind of imprimatur to this practice),[7] *Kokoro* continues to be read in ways that ignore the specific conditions of Japanese modernity and nationness that give rise to this text. What must be endeavored is to bring into focus the oft-neglected relationship between Japan and its Asian neighbors as a way of thinking about Japanese modernity and "modern Japanese literature" (which is always marked by the West).[8] While *Kokoro* continues to be read as one of the most sensitive portrayals of a modern Japanese intellectual failing in his attempts to negotiate the complications of Japan's modernization, the very notion of the modern is generally left unexamined, treated as if it were self-evident and fixed. My concern is with the aspects of Japan's experience of modernity that remain conspicuously absent from the secondary literature on *Kokoro:* the vital links between the discourse of nation building, Japan's colonialist behavior on the Asian continent, and the sense of lost history that deeply colors Japan's particular experience of the modern (and would lead to the fifteen-year Pacific war between Japan and its Asian neighbors).[9]

Partly to rectify the imbalance—critics continue to invoke Sōseki's links to the West, including his sojourn in London, while his trips to Asia receive scant attention—and for reasons given above, let us take a quick look at *Man-Kan tokorodokoro,* Sōseki's account of a trip he took to the Asian continent in 1909. This trip has always been described as a junket commissioned by the *Asahi* newspaper, but, in fact, Sōseki's trip had its source in the author's close friendship with Nakamura Zekō, who was president of Japan's South Manchurian Railway Company (SMR). An essay of 117 pages in the Iwanami *zenshū* ("complete" works) that is typically classified as a *kikōbun* (travelogue), *Man-Kan* remains generally ignored by readers and critics alike.[10] This is a piece meant to entertain more than to satisfy any curiosity the reader may have had about Japan's activities in Asia. Aside from occasional observations about hardworking *kūrii* (coolies) or an account of a pilgrimage to Port Arthur, where the critical battle in the Russo-Japanese War took place, the text is a breezy record of Sōseki's travels that is concerned far more with the author's many reunions with friends from his school days than with observations about foreign cultures. This personal focus, coupled with frequent mentions of the stomach ailments that plagued the writer throughout the trip, is probably what prompted one contemporary (Komiya Toyotaka) to quip that the travelogue would more aptly be titled "Sōseki Here and There" (*Sōseki tokorodokoro*). Joshua Fogel (1989) argues that "in literary terms, [Sōseki] consciously chose a highly objective style of reportage [for *Man-Kan*] in opposition to the naturalism so prevalent in Japan at the time. The roots of modern Japanese realism, it has been argued, can be found in this reportage style" (581).[11] It is noteworthy that this historian makes his observation to deflect what is clearly embarrassing to confront by giving the piece high marks for prefiguring later literary practices. I might also add parenthetically that, contrary to Fogel's characterization, at the level of stylistics *Man-Kan* is a chatty, impressionistic piece that resembles Sōseki's *Botchan* (The Little Master) in its tone, language, and use of humor.

There is little question that Sōseki probed the effects of modernity on Japanese society as no other writer of his time, but like the growing ranks of fellow intellectuals and writers during the first two decades of the twentieth century, he also displayed significant lapses in what might have been a more critical perspective on Japan's presence in continental Asia. The Russo-Japanese War, concluded just four years before Sōseki's trip to Manchuria, China, and Korea, had been a popular one, and to the Japanese living in Japan international tensions headlined in the press did not seem directly threatening to domestic order. Even so, it is hard to ignore Sōseki's condescension toward other Asians as he travels through their lands or the humorous tone of his work, which shows little sensitivity to conditions in which one nation is occupying another. In *Man-Kan,* Sōseki uses such pejoratives as "chan" (short for "chankoro") when referring to the Chinese, and he shows little self-consciousness in availing himself of the considerable facilities (hotels, tour guides) of the South Manchurian Railway, a government organ that played a key role in Japan's eventual colonization of Asia. Even the celebratory tone of schoolboy camaraderie between Sōseki and his close friend who presides over the SMR is excused by the historian Fogel, who says that Sōseki was simply "unable to transcend the prejudices of his time" (1989, 582). But this is to reify Sōseki the literary figure, ignoring his connections to his own particular moment and, more important, to the next eight decades, when the collective labor of canonization made him and his work a part of ongoing, contemporary history.

It is not simply a matter of resurrecting Sōseki's embarrassing lapses or of how difficult it is to step outside of an imperialist ethos that formed quickly in post-Restoration Japan. The concern of this paper is the more "inadvertent" but nonetheless troubling act of forgetting, the role of memory loss (both individual and collective) in cultural production—and its place in modernist and postmodernist society. If *Man-Kan* illustrates the forgetting that is done by those involved in the process of canon formation (all the critics "remember" Sōseki in London), *Ko-*

koro shows Sōseki's proclivity to gesture uneasily toward, without overtly criticizing, the larger forms of modernity, as he chooses instead to focus on problematizing bourgeois individualism.

Kokoro, Canon, and Modernity

To understand a work's canonicity is to address disparate strands of institutionalization, such as the conditions of a text's production, its reception over the years, and the extended process that is inherent in the term "canon." The focus of this paper prevents a proper examination of these areas, compelling me to address canonicity only rather narrowly as an inescapable condition that shapes our reading and interpretation of a text whether we openly acknowledge it or not. I touch upon the question both because the enormity of the investment made in *Kokoro* over the years cannot be ignored by any contemporary study of this text and, most important, because discussion of *Kokoro* as a canonical text reveals connections between narration and the modern nation-state that have been overlooked in previous studies. The link between textual expression and nation has been captured by Fredric Jameson's relation of national allegory to writing: "the telling of the individual story and the individual experience cannot but ultimately involve the whole laborious telling of the collectivity itself" (qtd. in Bhabha 1990a, 292). Aijaz Ahmad's criticism (1987) of Jameson's rigid alignment of "national allegory" to Third World countries notwithstanding, I have appropriated these words to suggest the hegemonic force that binds writing to canon within the framework of national borders. In the context of the twentieth century, the collectivity that canons narrate is the nation. *Kokoro,* like virtually every other text from the modern Japanese literary canon, refuses or is unable to address the imperialist dimensions of Japanese modernity.

The aspect of canonicity that concerns me here is not the production and maintenance of a literature as belles lettres but the social function or significance of canonization. Frank Kermode notes that "canons are essentially strategic constructs by which societies maintain their own interests, since the canon allows control over the texts a culture takes seriously and the methods of interpretation that establish the meaning of 'serious'" (1979, 78). This view of the literary canon resists the common practice of banishing it to the realm of aesthetics set apart from the vital contestation that marks any modern society. While canons are erected from texts of the past, they speak far more to the prevailing values that reign over the selection of the texts they include. Lost under the assumption of consensus is the contest that Charles Altieri puts this way: canons are "simply ideological banners for social groups: social groups propose them as forms of self-definition, and they engage other proponents to test limitations while exposing the contradictions and incapacities of competing groups" (1983, 39).[12] At the lowest level of differentiation, the canonization of Sōseki's work was carried out in competition with a literature that today might best be designated *shizenshugi-shishōsetsu* (naturalist) narrative, an approach to literature that flourished in various forms particularly from the turn of the century to well into the 1920s; at a higher level, *Kokoro* is defined by canons drawn in competition with other canons divided by national borders. *Kokoro* can be designated as a site on which issues of canon and nation meet in the particular shape we can discern as Japanese modernity. Put differently, as the canon that is today designated *kindai bungaku* (modern literature) began to take shape early in the twentieth century, it was closely associated with the forces of modernity that helped construct a modern Japanese society that could accommodate Western ideas, material, and practices. What was sought was the fusion of existing cultural and social identities to a modern European form of the nation-state. The notion of a literary canon is important for anyone reading *Kokoro* in the late twentieth century, because canonicity permits us to discern *Kokoro*'s exclusion of the Japanese state increasingly defining its own contours in international terms, or, more explicitly, as an imperialist power.

The very idea that a body of literature becomes a canon rests upon a unity constructed from a shared culture and a sense of a social whole inscribed within national boundaries. Thus, viewed paradigmatically in relation to other (national) canons, a particular literary canon will appear unified and even stable. But just as the constituent conditions of canonicity change over time, so does a category like the canon. In a passage reminiscent of Mikhail Bakhtin's description of heteroglossia, Richard Ohmann draws our attention to the mutability of categories (be it "the English Novel," or "American Literature") and the struggle that often attends their change:

> At any given moment categories embody complex social relations and a continuing historical process. That process deeply invests all terms with value: since not

everyone's values are the same, the negotiating of such concepts is, among other things, a struggle for dominance—whether between adults and the young, professors and their students, one class and another, or men and women. (1983, 199)

The notion of a literary canon, like many of the other terms we use to discuss Japanese literature in the West, is fraught with difficulty.[13] If canon is to designate a privileged mainstream literature in modern Japan, it must arise from such considerations as the literary coterie, the Monbushō (Department of Education) and its policies, reader reception, publishing firms and their relation to writers, the production of *zenshū* (collected works) so widespread in Japan, and even popular media attention to literature.[14] The text called *Kokoro* as we see it today has been "produced" by the combined effects of these forces; it should be readily apparent that what we assume to be a completed and stable product (this text) is hardly immutable and fixed and will continue to bear the effects of changing times. No one can deny that *Kokoro* has negotiated the various sectors mentioned above in such a way that *today* it continues to command a privileged place in modern Japanese literature.

The process of canonization unfolds over time across a variety of social sectors (publishing, the accumulation of scholarly ratification, etc.), making it hazardous at best to represent the process as resting on a set of stable criteria. *Kokoro* shares with other early-twentieth-century works an unstated imperative to ignore the aspect of Japanese modernity that shapes the nation's relations with other non-Western (i.e., Asian) lands. Stated differently, this work owes its place in the canon to the part it played in installing what would become the central figure in modern Japanese fiction—the isolated, bourgeois figure who will quickly come to outgrow the confines of "class" to stand for the whole of Japanese society. Such disregard of contention-ridden difference (class) is not fortuitous, and it does not simply reflect the appropriation of values implicit in Western literary practices (those of Romantic and realist literature, for instance). Modern Japanese narratives that come to occupy what we can only call, however metaphorically, the heart of the canon observe a kind of social contract to occlude such differences as those of class and political allegiance in Japanese society—that is, to shun the serious engagement of alterity, whether it be conceived in domestic or international (writ non-Western) terms. A text like *Kokoro* does not simply or neatly eliminate traces of social and political differentiation; but the contradictions and differences internal to the text must be suppressed so that it can be made to belong to, and to construct, a modern Japanese literary canon. To restate the matter in terms that exceed the structures of textuality, one might argue that *Kokoro* has been accorded a privileged place in the modern Japanese literary canon because the text confronts important issues that grow out of Japan's experience of the modern. But the text's ambivalence in addressing some of the more troubling contradictions of Japan's modernity—most pointedly the refiguration of the nation's relations to its Asian neighbors in colonialist terms—also tacitly underwrites the venerated status of this particular text. The repeatedly invoked hagiographic image of Sōseki spending mornings in his study writing what would become the canonical works of modern Japanese literature while devoting afternoons to penning Chinese-style poetry is telling. It seems to complicate the writer by showing him negotiating otherness from two directions, but it has in fact served to neatly contain Asia in an antiquated aesthetic realm with no relation to the twentieth century. Before we pursue the question of *Kokoro*'s complicity in this diminution of Asia, let us consider briefly the notion of the modern, a vast topic that defies adequate treatment within the space of this study.

The modern subsumes a collective diversity of events, developments, shifts in perception, and altered relations among things and people; the centrality of change makes modernity an extended moment whose nature and limits are difficult to specify. Its defining paradox—foregrounding the juxtaposition of present moment to the past—is captured in David Harvey's identification of Baudelaire as a key European modernist figure: modernity, said Baudelaire, "is the transient, the fleeting, the contingent; it is the one half of art, the other being the eternal and the immutable" (qtd. in Harvey 1990, 10). The subjective experience of such disjunction is captured by Marshall Berman, who endows the modern with a "paradoxical unity, a unity of disunity: it pours us all into a maelstrom of perpetual disintegration and renewal, of struggle and contradiction, of ambiguity and anguish. To be modern is to be part of a universe in which, as Marx said, 'all that is solid melts into air'" (1982, 15). In a spirit of passionately committed humanism, Berman sees modernity as universal, cutting "across all boundaries of geography and ethnicity, of class and nationality, of religion and ideology" (15).[15] While undoubtedly modernism as it has migrated from its European context maintains this universality, as many historians have pointed out, it is essential to see the specific inscription of a hegemonic West in the very notion of the modern in discussing Japan's modernity (see Sakai 1988).

Berman's attribution of contradiction to the modern may very well characterize all "modernities," but one of its central expressions in Japan can be located in the conjuncture of the sense of history made inconsequential and the desire to narrate an immediate history that would move beyond Japan's own borders. The demographic upheavals that accompanied rapid urbanization, the quickening rhythms of daily life, the insinuation of a new urban culture into the everyday life of virtually everyone—those conspicuous signs of modernity—are all familiar matters in the discussion of Japan's emergence as a modern nation-state. But what has continued to be relegated to later in the century (the 1930s)—Japan's encroachment onto the Asian continent—is one of the most striking features of Japan's modernity and already forms the fabric of the nation-state at the time of *Kokoro*'s appearance in 1914.

Used to apprehend early-twentieth-century Japan, the term "modern" almost always erases Japan's own reproduction of imperialist behavior and instead signifies the introduction of Western thought and material goods. While the forced subjugation of a foreign people is not a practice specific to modernity, the modern nation-state has typically engaged in such conduct. Japan begins actively to position itself as an agent of such behavior around the turn of the century, at a time when the Japanese are forced to conceptualize their own unity in the context of global imperialist contest. The coincidence of Japan's experience of modernity and the consolidation of "modern" nation-states is hardly accidental. Like its predecessor forms in Europe, Japanese modernity is closely linked to the establishment of a mass urban population. Rural life promotes a sense of community by differentiating its own small locale from other localities (villages, valleys, towns). A sense of connection will have to come from some other source in the city, which forces a vast number of strangers to share a large, variegated living space in which the conduct of daily life typically requires frequent movement. Sandwiched between the emergence of a vigorous popular culture in the Edo period (1600–1867) and the rise of a new mass culture in the 1920s and '30s, Sōseki's Tokyo is not so much a cluster of disconnected villages, a frequent characterization, as a population transformed into new social relations. Benedict Anderson suggests how an even larger space, the nation, achieves wholeness:

> I propose the following definition of the nation: it is an imagined political community—and imagined as both inherently limited and sovereign. . . . It is imagined because the members of even the smallest nation will never know most of their fellow-members, meet them, or even hear of them, yet in the minds of each lives the image of their communion. (1983, 15)

In his study of nationalism, Anderson goes on to show the importance of "print communities formed around newspapers and novels" in constructing such imagined community. It is worth noting that during the Meiji period, the print community facilitated the emergence of culture heroes that were discursively created and that such figures were often employed in ways that (sometimes intentionally, at other times unintentionally) served the cause of national consolidation. Thus the image of the Meiji Emperor was given different spins according to the needs of the moment, and the representation of General Nogi Maresuke (1849–1912) quickly shifted from that of an inept strategist responsible for heavy casualties among the Japanese army on the Asian continent to that of a war hero-cum-educator and guardian of such virtues as selflessness, military valor, and dedication to the nation.[16]

For our discussion, the salient characteristics of Japanese modernity are these: the rise of nationhood given shape by the growth of cities and such manifestations of urban culture as the "development of print-as-commodity[,] . . . key to the generation of wholly new ideas of simultaneity" (Anderson 1983, 41), and the exploitation of the means to create and circulate ideas or images (e.g., of General Nogi) within a short time period to a mass populace. Such are the conditions that gave shape to Sōseki's *Kokoro,* which appeared initially as a newspaper "novel" serialized in 110 installments from 20 April to 11 August 1914. While the tale itself is fictive, it is tied to its moment by the incorporation of the two figures mentioned above, Emperor Meiji and General Nogi; not simply important historical personages, these were figures whose much larger than life dimensions had been created by a commodified print culture. In a gesture of atonement for the heavy casualties suffered by his soldiers during the Russo-Japanese War of 1904–1905, Nogi committed ritual suicide upon the death of the Meiji Emperor in 1912. In accordance with the Tokugawa-era samurai code of following one's lord to the grave, Nogi's wife took her own life after overseeing her husband's suicide. Despite the ambivalence that Sōseki seems to have shared with his countrymen at the time regarding Nogi's anachronistic suicide, *Kokoro* ultimately appropriates an image of General Nogi associated with military valor, moral rectitude, and unflinching loyalty.[17] Sōseki was well aware that these images were at odds with the history of a soldier who had been suspended from the military on three different occasions, a man who had been dismissed from his post as governor of occupied Taiwan for administrative ineptitude, and a general whose outdated strategies and intransigence caused the senseless slaughter of nearly fifty-eight thousand of his own men at the battle of Port Arthur, a battle won only after Nogi was replaced by another commanding officer.[18] Despite these facts, the eventual Japanese "victory" over the Russians helped elevate Nogi to mythic proportions, and in 1907 he was appointed as director of the Peers School, "because the government maintained popular respect for Nogi's image as hero of Port Arthur while excluding the failed general from the inner circles of power" (Lifton, Kato, and Reith 1979, 54). In *Kokoro* such reversals, which link Nogi to the inaugural events of Japanese expansionism, are replaced by a "media"-created general whose final image has been imprinted on the public mind by his suicide. Characteristic of modern fiction, *Kokoro* treats the everyday life that is also the moment occupied by the text. More important, in the way that *Kokoro* fails to depict Nogi as a complicated historical figure at odds with his ideologically motivated image, we confront the text's complicit silence concerning Japanese adventurism on the continent.

The process of canonizing a modern Japanese literature directly overlaps with the period of Japanese confrontation with Western culture, a confrontation that provided both a model for the Japanese to emulate and an object to resist; but it soon became clear that successful resistance to Western material and cultural incursions, that is to say, the maintenance of national sovereignty, would require appropriation of the very things being resisted. *Kokoro* narrates the experience of modernity transplanted onto Japanese soil at once as something radically foreign that was forced upon Japan and as a new moment signaling the sudden irrelevance of Japan's own history, a history that might have helped the Japanese negotiate the present. Perhaps, like the modernity that was experienced on its native ground thousands of miles removed, Japan's modernity can only be perceived as confirming one of the irreducible facts of modern life—that it is radically contradictory. In any case, not unlike the upheavals of nineteenth-century Europe occasioning Nietzsche's declaration of the death of God, the events following the Imperial Restoration of 1868 spawned alternating, sometimes even simultaneous gestures toward repudiating the past, questioning it, and resurrecting it as the enduring repository of what is essentially Japanese.

Kokoro textualizes the irony of its protagonist's inability to speak within a modernity that ostensibly redefines time and space in such a way as to permit increased opportunity to meet and interact with others. And in the very transformation of a serialized one-part newspaper narrative into a book with three parts (and 110 chapters), *Kokoro* reproduces the attempt to narrativize something called a "modern" Japanese history. Within the next decade, such narrative activity would be depicting an imperialist mapping of Asia rivaling that of the Western powers.

Synopsis

Kokoro is narrated in the first person by a student who befriends an older man at a beach where they are both vacationing. The Student is drawn to Sensei by the mystery of the latter's unexplained loneliness, and the gradual revelation of Sensei's life provides a way for the Student to shed his innocence and confront the dangers that lie in following the stirrings of his own heart. The first part, titled "Sensei and I," tells the circumstances that lead to the friendship between Sensei and the narrating Student. It serves mainly to raise questions that remain unanswered until the revelations of Sensei's testamentary letter in part 3: Whose grave does Sensei dutifully visit alone every month? In spite of the love between Sensei and his wife, why is there no joy in his life? Despite his education, why does Sensei live with no job, almost completely cut off from society?

Part 2, "My Parents and I," recounts the Student's return to his home in the country to be with his dying father, a man whose unreflective security in his own conventionality contrasts sharply with the anguished intellectual figure of Sensei. As the Student's vigil lengthens into summer, the long testamentary letter arrives from Sensei. The impending death of his father prevents the Student from reading the letter from beginning to end, but in quickly skimming it, he is stung by the line that reads "by the time this letter reaches you, I shall probably have left this world—I shall in all likelihood be dead" (Natsume 1978, 122). In an act that leaves the door open for the Student to relive the same sense of guilt and despair that consumes Sensei, he immediately leaves his dying father and rushes back to Tokyo. Part 3, "Sensei and His Testament," consists entirely of the letter Sensei has written to the Student, one that presumably clarifies the mysteries of a man who lived each day tormented by his past. It reveals how, left in the care of his uncle after the death of his parents, the school-age Sensei is subsequently tricked out of his inheritance. With what money he has left, Sensei comes to study at the university and falls in love with the daughter of a widow in whose house he takes room and board. As his attraction to Ojōsan (young mistress) grows, Sensei worries about a classmate whom he identifies solely by the initial K. Concerned about this friend whose ascetic spirituality makes daily living a hazardous ordeal, Sensei persuades K to move in with him. Despite K's puritanical insistence on living a spiritual life, he too falls in love with the widow's daughter, Ojōsan. Upon hearing K confess his feelings for her, Sensei is seized with panic for having missed the opportunity to declare his own feelings (and presumably, to make prior, more legitimate claims on Ojōsan). Fueled by the jealousy he feels on those occasions when he perceives Ojōsan to be favoring K, Sensei plays on K's sincerity and ridicules him for straying from his path of the mind and spirit. Whether moved by his own heart, goaded by jealousy toward K, or influenced from some other direction (the text is ambiguous), Sensei quickly asks for Ojōsan's hand in marriage but is unable to tell K about doing so. When K discovers what has happened, he takes his own life. There is no accusation in his short suicide note, which simply ends with "why did I wait so long to die?" Sensei later marries Ojōsan, but he never confesses his part in the drama of K's death—out of fear, he writes in his last letter, that telling her would "taint her whole life with the memory of something that was ugly" (237). As a result, Ojōsan must suffer through living with a man who has renounced any intention to live, never certain how she herself might have been involved in his unexplained misery.

Death, Text, and the Problem of Lost History

Kokoro's use of a mythic General Nogi, together with the cameo appearance of a Westerner in the second chapter that has baffled critics over the years, alerts us to the text's refusal to admit any meaningful consideration of events outside of Japan's borders. Only because he is noticed by the

Student does the Westerner become visible in the text, but his abruptly truncated appearance serves only to signal the absence of the West from the work. What strikes the narrator-Student about this Caucasian male is his attire, which distinguishes him from other foreigners—he is wearing a genuine Japanese *yukata* [junsui no Nihon no yukata], a casual robe which he discards to reveal a "white body covered only by a loincloth that we Japanese wear" [kare wa ware ware no haku sarumata hitotsu no hoka nanimono mo hada ni tsukete inakatta] (Natsume 1983, 366; my translation). A succession of incongruities confronts the Student's gaze, from a white man in a crowd of Japanese to a foreigner unlike other foreigners (the Student notes the contrast between this *seiyōjin* [Westerner] and the others he had seen two days earlier at another beach who had worn Western-style swimming outfits that covered much more of their bodies). In this passage the Westerner enacts a series of subverted connections between outward appearance and expectations. The narrative focus on suggestive details that frame the Student's initial encounter with Sensei recalls the detective-mystery story frame employed in many of Sōseki's works and throughout this one. The association of this Westerner with Sensei is part of *Kokoro*'s attempt to maintain narrative interest by appearing to reveal more and more of Sensei. But just as other expectations are overturned, this detail, the curious Westerner, turns out to be a false lead that tells us nothing about Sensei.

If thematically this apparently dead-end appearance of the Westerner inadvertently reveals an aspect of its time that the text is not prepared to pursue, viewed formalistically the false clue serves to reveal the text's status as fiction. Despite the intrusion of actual historical figures like the Meiji Emperor and General Nogi, *Kokoro* aspires to a kind of mimesis for mimesis's sake. We can apply Simon During's characterization of Jane Austen's novel to Sōseki's work:

> With this lack of motivation comes a new principle of organization and delimitation—organic unity. . . . It operates a formal requirement of autonomous texts intent on providing a scene adjacent to the nation-state. The text's unity is the unity of culture—a set of overlapping, unprogrammable connections and analogies within the strictly delimited frame of the work itself. (During 1990, 147)

Described here is the realization of textual convention affirmed in the modern era, where narrative practice is "accorded" its own status by being relegated to the realm of cultural creation. If realism values the apparent likeness of literature to "the real world," it also rests on the presumption that the two are finally separate. It is the ambivalence of Sōseki's text, the way in which it gestures toward historical events and people while affirming mimeticist views of art as autonomous, that distinguishes *Kokoro.*

The relationship of Sensei to the Westerner, particularly as it remains a mystery, raises the suspicion that Sensei is not as isolated and asocial as the Student presents him to be. But insofar as the text rests on the promise of gradual disclosure, it must do what it can to thicken the mystery. For that sense of mystery is the textual strategy that *Kokoro* uses to realize its primary task: to interrogate the relationship between Sensei and the Student.[19] Earlier interpretations attribute inconclusiveness or irresolution to this text, largely because Sensei's death is not adequately explained by his testament. In my reading, the problem of indeterminacy is most vividly inscribed in this relationship between "teacher" and "student." Absence marks their relationship—absence of a firm ground for knowledge and knowing (which a teacher ought to impart to students), of a modern history, or of awareness that one's own country seeks nationness through colonial expansion. As the narrator, the Student presents the monologue of a dead father (Sensei) whose words must steadfastly focus on the private (the urban, nuclear family with little contact with the outside world), and whose only links to the social consist of orchestrated images of the emperor and his former general. The state, its modern history, and knowledge are disavowed or pointedly absent from Sensei's private account, and it is through the Student's relationship to him that we can recognize these "absences." It is from this perspective that the brief appearance of the Westerner in the beach scene makes more sense when viewed as signaling an absence.

Kokoro's opening lines inaugurate the process of confronting modernity by problematizing the student-Sensei relationship:

I always called him Sensei. I shall therefore refer to him simply as "Sensei," and not by his real name. It is not because I consider it more discreet, but it is because I find it more natural that I do so. Whenever the memory of him comes back to me now, I find that I think of him as "Sensei" still. And with pen in hand, I cannot bring myself to write of him in any other way. (Natsume 1978, 1)

Literally denoting priority by birth (born before), "sensei" is most commonly used by students to refer to their teachers or as a term of direct address that signals the respect one has toward a person who is knowledgeable and wise by virtue of his or her age and experience. *Kokoro*'s opening lines make sense only if the person referred to by this term does not properly fit the conditions of the appellation, thus requiring a disclaimer. The narrator is a college student, and while we are told that Sensei is a graduate of the university and has conducted research, he does not teach or work at all. Sensei's attitude toward scholarship and learning is expressed when he is asked why he is no longer interested in books: "Perhaps it is because I have decided that no matter how many books I may read, I shall never be a very much better man than I am now" (1978, 54).[20] The thematics of *Kokoro* indicate a favoring of matters of the heart over learning and knowledge, but *Kokoro* is a text whose narrative quest for deeper understanding ultimately signals the valuation of the latter. If the disjunction between content and form bespeaks the ambiguities of modernity, the split also signals Sōseki's singular ability to straddle what has been a rigid divide in Japanese letters between serious and popular fiction.

Sōseki represents the erasure of what in later years would become a widely accepted opposition between serious literature (*jun bungaku*) and popular narratives. It is not surprising that such a writer's work looks critically upon the separation of lived experience from knowledge and learning, an interrogation set in motion by focusing on the status of the "sensei." Among the unspoken requirements for inclusion in the canon of serious literature is a text's ability to contribute to the cultivation of a literate and intelligent reading population that is bound together by common discourses of knowledge (and its transmission). In *Kokoro,* "sensei" is constructed to overlap the domains of scholarly knowledge and wisdom gained through personal experience. But the very ground in which both of these are rooted—Japan's past—has been shaken by the incursion of the historical phenomenon called modernity. In large part, the value accruing to knowledge comes from its claims to represent time-tested practices of the distant past. History as the guarantor of knowledge has been undercut by the experience of modernity, leaving in *Kokoro* a "sensei" without the traditional roles given to a person with his title. *Kokoro*'s strategic response to this dilemma consists of the narrating Student's act of framing Sensei's death note with his own narrative act.

There is special meaning, then, in the way the questioning of knowledge and its transmission is linked to muteness and death as responses to the overwhelming contradictions of an era that Sōseki's text unsuccessfully attempts to comprehend. *Kokoro* invokes a narrative of patriarchy for this task of comprehension, letting family ideology be tested by the new age. Doris Sommer's discussion of Latin American novels can help defamiliarize *Kokoro*'s confrontation with modernity. After acknowledging Anderson's connection of nation building to print communities, Sommer argues that in order to explain why these novels are so "relentlessly attractive," we must not overlook in them the romance that "legitimates the nation-family through love." She continues:

> I suggest that this natural and familial grounding, along with its rhetoric of productive sexuality, provides a model for apparently non-violent national consolidation during periods of internecine conflict. To paraphrase another foundational text, after the creation of the new nations, the domestic romance is an exhortation to be fruitful and multiply. (1990, 76)

Kokoro contrasts sharply with this construction of "nation-family" and a "rhetoric of productive sexuality." Instead, it reduces Ojōsan, the sole female who might have played a larger part in the text, to a figure who cannot contribute to what is ostensibly the central objective of this work: to explain Sensei.[21] While Sōseki's text suggests the deterioration of the "traditional" Japanese family (by way, for example, of the Student's family living in the countryside), it cannot write out the narrative of patriarchy that the Meiji state institutionalized through the promotion of a "family" modeled on the samurai family. *Kokoro* displays the effects of a relentless state policy to govern its citizenry by reappropriating filial discourse, the law of the father, in post-Restoration Japan.

The narrator-Student interrupts his study to return to the countryside and his ailing father, who closely follows the daily newspaper accounts of the dying Meiji Emperor. The death of the monarch causes his father to fade rapidly, as if their fates were somehow linked. It is the father who first sees the news of General Nogi's death in the paper. A few days after the emperor's death, Nogi had taken his own life in part to atone for having lost a banner during battle, resurrecting a practice called *junshi* (following one's lord to the grave), which had been outlawed since the 1600s. Like the Student's father, Sensei himself will link his own impending death by suicide to these two public figures representing the tumultuous years of the Meiji period. Here are Sensei's thoughts on the emperor's death:

> I felt as though the spirit of the Meiji era had begun with the Emperor and had ended with him. I was overcome with the feeling that I and the others, who had been brought up in that era, were now left behind to live as anachronisms. . . . I had almost forgotten that there was such a word as junshi. . . . I did feel that the antiquated word had come to hold a new meaning for me. (Natsume 1978, 245)

While Sensei mourns the passing of an age, his suicide is not cast as the re-creation of a traditional, public act. Within the line of male figures linked by death—Emperor Meiji, General Nogi, the Student's father, and Sensei—are we to insert the narrator-Student, who appears to ensure himself a future fraught with guilt and torment by leaving his father on the brink of death?

Let us remember that the break between Sensei and the Student is anticipated by the questioning of the very notion of "sensei," a word that signals its own relationship (mentor-student). We must shift registers in the way we view Sensei's death in order to see how its signification escapes a "traditional" meaning of death and also shapes the text as a whole. My students have often been baffled by Sensei's inability to "simply communicate," whether with Ojōsan, his close friend K, or with the Student to whom he finally writes his long epistle. Differences in time, place, and sensibility clearly separate Sensei from today's inquisitive Western readers of *Kokoro,* but the question can guide us to matters that bear on the canonization of this work.

It is worth noting that the inability to express feeling recurs frequently. In part 2, the Student returns to his parents in the countryside, sitting in vigil with his older brother, who has rushed home from western Japan to be with their dying father; the two sit and wait, unable to admit that both of them await their father's death. When K confesses to being in love with Ojōsan, Sensei can say nothing in response to the revelation. Instead, he seeks out Ojōsan's mother and asks for her daughter's hand without mentioning anything to K. Several days after hearing of Sensei's action, K quietly kills himself. To the very end, Sensei shields his wife from the truth about K's suicide, revealing his tale of betrayal solely to the Student by way of his last testament.

The final instance of broken communication is, of course, the death of Sensei. *Kokoro* explores the relationship between speaking and death, making the latter the precondition for the former. Sensei's death is almost always attributed to such markers of Japanese modernity as the disintegration of the family unit, the ascendance of self-oriented conceptions of society, and the pernicious effects of an industrialized, increasingly materialistic nation. However, Sensei's death must also be seen together with the frustration of speechlessness, the loss of voice, and the erosion of the familiar ways in which a sense of subjectivity could be affirmed that must have assailed many of Sensei's generation. More functionally viewed, death engenders the production of Sensei's letter and, in turn, the Student's act of textualization. Put differently, it is the very possibility of textualizing life, of organizing it in accordance with the laws of writing and narrativizing that paradoxically gives rise to the impossibility of speech.

Sensei's life, which is governed by an inability to speak and communicate with others, is revealed in the form of a last will and testament—a document that reinforces new signifying relations governing narrativizing and death. For a man who remains trapped in his own silence to the end, only the immediate emptiness of death can engender the production of a long letter to break that silence. As if "he were listening to his own death," Sensei produces a written account tracing the events that lead him to live life as if he were dead—a life punctuated by his own suicide. Foucault's discussion of the function of language in the *Odyssey* can help us illuminate the status of language in *Kokoro.*

> The limit of death opens before language, or rather within language, an infinite space. Before the imminence of death, language rushes forth, but it also starts again, tells of itself, discovers the story of the story and the possibility that this interpretation might never end. Headed toward death, language turns back upon itself; it encounters something like a mirror, and to stop, this death which would stop it, it possesses but a single power: that of giving birth to its own image in a play of mirrors that has no limits. (Foucault 1977b, 54)

The Student to whom the testament is written inserts himself at the very point at which a stop might be put to endless interpretation. But he is not positioned as an authoritative interpreting agent, nor is he "next" in the chain of filial transmitters of knowledge. *Kokoro* speaks to the limits of such institutionalized intellectual labors. And, much like what Roland Barthes (1968) calls a writerly text, *Kokoro* invites the reader to assume the very position given to the Student, to narrativize and hence to interpret the story of Sensei.

In a sense, Sōseki himself "reinterpreted" the text when he took the serialized newspaper version, which was one continuous narrative subtitled "Sensei and His Testament," and reissued it in book form after dividing it into the three parts we know today.[22] The structural division sharpens the sense of contest that defines the relationship between Sensei and the Student. The first two parts provide background information on the Student, the circumstances of his encounter with Sensei, and his abbreviated visit to his dying father in the country. Parts 1 and 2 are also replete with hints about Sensei's past, his impending suicide—in short, about those matters that await revelation in part 3, "Sensei and His Testament." There, in his own voice, Sensei recounts the process leading to his own death, which provides the point from which the past (whether that of Sensei, that of the Student, or Japan's immediate history) must be narrated or created anew.

In *Kokoro,* death generates such narrative activity in a form that evinces its own status as writing. Note that the Student's narrative is a response not to the death of Sensei but to the narration of his dying (Sensei's epistolary testament). And it is not the veracity of Sensei's disclosures that matters, for overwhelmingly the text speaks to the nature of representation and its uses in modern civil society. Thus the revelation of Sensei's past occupies the thematic center of this text, but the real focus of interest shifts from Sensei to the Student who responds to him, first by befriending him and then by narrating his story. The text "owes" its existence to the Student's "narrative response" to Sensei's death, and the thematic weight of the text falls on the Student—what will be his fate?

Kokoro was written during the years when in spite of the existence of a wide range of writing, the prevailing practice consisted of literature claiming to record real life in an unmediated way. We must recognize that Sōseki's work, however, eschews the designation *shizenshugi* (naturalist) literature, contributing instead to a body of writing whose " 'truth' or 'falsity' is secondary to the task of representation itself." I have borrowed Simon During's words used to describe English literature of the "civil Imaginary," works that reenact everyday life, typically assuming the form of letters, memoirs, and other written forms. Such literature, During states, "reproduces representations of manners, taste, behavior, utterances for imitation by individual lives" (1990, 142).[23] Like his English counterparts, *Kokoro*'s narrator "is explicitly socially located in the writing, the text's occasion being made apparent" (During 1990, 143). Reinforcing the effect produced by the Westerner's brief presence in the text, the narrator-Student—whose function is limited to that of witness and writer—serves to highlight fabulation by gesturing to the very conditions that engender the narrative. The central contradiction in Sōseki's text, which is narrativized by a character whose participation in the production of text clearly differentiates him from the protagonists of *shizenshugi* literature, is expressed as a break between Sensei, for whom "truth" is primary, and the Student, whose concern is representation (here, storytelling).

By framing Sensei's confessional testament with the first-person account of the student, *Kokoro* leaves the generic domain of *shizenshugi* and becomes a text self-consciously about representation. (The anticipatory hints in the first two parts concerning developments that are more fully revealed in the testament section might well be read as awkward and at times uncertain duplications of a self-adequate text.) In what formalists would call a motivated text, both the prominence of private confession and the insertion of a perceiving writer to whom the confession is directed affirm the troubled status of the individual in Meiji society and the highly privatized way in which the text must write itself—namely, motivated by suicide. But, just as death is ambivalently associated with both the private (Sensei and his quiet suffering) and the public (the Meiji Emperor and General Nogi) spheres in *Kokoro,* the status of the individual subject remains in question.

When Ojōsan is left behind by an overprotective husband who leaves his wife with no explanation for his own death, the student's options are few. Passing references in the first two parts of *Kokoro* indicate that he has kept his promise to Sensei and has not conveyed to Ojōsan even the existence of the testament, let alone its contents. In effect, Sensei has left the Student with the imperative to remain mute, to continue down the path of betrayal, self-loathing, and despair. The Student's response to this imperative is an act of fabulation, the narrative-creation of a text that goes beyond the borders of Sensei's own testament.[24] Such transgression, it appears, is the only way in which the Student can avoid becoming yet another link in a chain of institutionalized patriarchy and death. At the same time, the Student's act comes marked as the kind of "creative destruction" that is central to the concept of modernity (see Harvey 1990, 18–19). Destruction may clear away tradition, reduce human relations to a depersonalized calculus of money and profit, and manifest itself in wars that subject people to colonial rule, but it is also tightly implicated in the dialectic of creation and destruction that defines modernity.

Kokoro is written in relation to other texts that constitute the field of literature, but that realm does not exist apart from larger contexts. Japanese naturalist literature—confessional writings that signaled their own veracity by way of the luridness of the author's revelations—peaked in 1908. Such prose, resurrected as the "I novel" of the 1920s and '30s, would largely determine the shape of the Japanese canon. Sōseki's *Kokoro* overtly challenges the naturalist I-novel trend by centering on death, for death can have no role in a narrative devoted to the unmediated depiction of the writer's own ongoing life. Death establishes *Kokoro* as derisively gesturing in the direction of *shizenshugi-shishōsetsu* literature and its practitioners, who continued to occupy key positions within the Japanese literary establishment. Death also plays a role in situating the novel in the world. *Kokoro* raises questions about the Japanese experience of modernity; its juxtaposition of silence, textuality, and death relate the text not only to the literary currents of its time but to the modern sense of nationness defined in global terms. In the coming decades, Japanese intellectuals would articulate more explicitly their concerns with a "world history" that excluded Japan.[25] Sōseki's work can forecast only by way of oblique gestures (the fleeting appearance of a Westerner) through a text marked by absence (the dead father-Sensei) the complicity of intellectual and military responses to this exclusion, which would lead to heightened expansionist activity on the Asian continent.[26] As surely as a helpless silence and death fuel and encourage narrative activity in *Kokoro,* confrontation with Japan's own mordant history would lead that country to emulate the imperialist activities of the Western powers and to narrate its own history of coercion onto the map. Here again, *Kokoro* contests Japanese *shizenshugi* literature, which displaced historical awareness with the "present," or contemporaneity, as a signifier of modernity. By linking Sensei's suicide with the Meiji Emperor's death, Sōseki's work attempts to create what is absent from *shizenshugi-shishōsetsu* literature and from the Meiji era itself—a history of modern Japan. In *Kokoro,* death urges us to look back at the events leading to that null point, and to seek meaning in individual lives from such a frame, thereby memorializing the first (Meiji) epoch of post-Restoration Japan.

As Sōseki's work almost heroically confronts the challenge to find meaning in a time when past history has lost its authority, it ends up engaging its moment with certain troubling blindnesses. Sharing space in the newspaper *Asahi Shimbun* with the later installments of *Kokoro* are articles and photographs of European mobilization for war. Photographs of impressive German and British officers and implements of war alternate with images of Japanese men of war in the July and August 1914 editions of the *Asahi*. Sōseki's text shared space not only with such visible records of military behavior abroad but with prominent ads for "Lion" toothpaste for boys and girls, "miruku-meido" (milk), and Dunlop tires.[27] By covering such international events and advertising these new products, the *Asahi* was unmistakably projecting itself as the purveyor of modernity. What Sōseki's prose fiction (including *Kokoro*) demonstrates is a blindness to the connection between Japan's experience of modernity, about which the author felt tremendous ambivalence, and Japan's extraterritorial activities. Thus what we might observe as one condition of the canonization of works such as *Kokoro* (appearing as it did on the pages of a mass-circulation daily urging readers to become consumers of new "modern" goods) is a narrowly constricted focus on minute nuances of private perceptions, thoughts, and feelings. At a time when Japan itself was searching for subjecthood, seeking to proclaim its place in world history, Sōseki's canonized works would pointedly ignore the grammar of nationness within which Japan sought recognition. Yet the text's engagement with the issues of modernity that arise in the narration of silence and death unwittingly reproduces the concurrent narratives of nation and of empire that construct "modern" Japanese history—the very conditions that governed the simultaneous creation of a new literary canon. Sōseki, of course, did not canonize *Kokoro*. As agents of an ongoing process of canonizing, it is our responsibility to question Sōseki's texts as the inaugural moment of literary high modernism in Japanese literature.

Notes

I am grateful to Norma Field, Edward Fowler, William Haver, Komori Yōichi, Masao Miyoshi, Leslie Pincus, Ellen Radovic, Naoki Sakai, Miriam Silverberg, Marilyn Young, and an anonymous reader, who, in varying ways, helped shape this paper.

1. *Mugentai* 89 (winter 1991), published by IBM Japan. I was never allowed to

read the actual comments made by a reader for *Monumenta Nipponica;* its editor conveyed to me only the "essence" of a negative review of the paper as polemical and too reliant on irrelevant theory from outside the field. I owe to this dismissal far more serious and useful comments from a subsequent reader for *positions,* where this article first appeared. Naoki Sakai's intervention led to the appearance of a shorter, Japanese-language version in *Bungaku* 3, no. 4 (fall 1992). An English-language version of that paper appears as chapter 5 of Fujii 1993, 126–50.

2. The critical literature on Sōseki and his works, even limited to *Kokoro,* is extensive, and he has always attracted attention beyond those working in the field of modern Japanese literature. If literary critics such as Komiya Toyotaka, Ochi Haruo, Ino Kenji, and Etō Jun represent the "mainstream," Karatani Kōjin might be seen as both heir to and critic of such Sōseki criticism. Among Karatani's many studies touching on Sōseki are his award-winning essays "Ishiki to shizen" (Consciousness and Nature) and "Uchigawa kara mita Sei" (Life Viewed from Within); see "Sōseki shiki ron I, II" in Karatani 1979 and "Sōseki no tayōsei—*Kokoro* o megutte" in Karatani 1989, 29–44. A more pointedly historicist meditation on Sōseki is found in Karatani 1980, esp. 7–22.

What might be called a new generation of theoretically sophisticated studies of Sōseki's work is represented by Komori 1991 and Ishihara Chiaki's work, including Ishihara 1990 and Ishihara 1991.

3. Compiled in Ishihara 1988, 157–68. Karatani claims that *Kokoro* remains somewhat devalued by virtue of its status as a confessional-epistolary (hence pre- or protonovelistic) novel. See Karatani 1989, 32–33.

4. Edward Fowler launches a carefully documented criticism of the personal politics that underwrite this project. See Fowler 1992. The unseemliness of the conservative canonizing enterprise married to commercial gain is even more tellingly and unwittingly revealed in Frank Gibney's subsequent reaction to Fowler's study. Gibney's letter and Fowler's impressive response are both in the winter 1993 issue of the *Journal of Japanese Studies.*

5. Natsume Sōseki, *Kokoro: A Novel and Selected Essays,* vol. 1 in the Library of Japan (New York: Madison Books, 1992).

6. As Mary Layoun observes, Sōseki's texts "raise a darkly despairing and contradictory objection, not to modernization and the foreign, not to nationalism . . . , but to the stultifying social and cultural effects of the specific direction that modernization, nationalism, foreign 'importation,' and capitalism took" (1990, 117).

7. Etō's subsequent anti-American books and essays might even be seen as a kind of recantation of his earlier work (his career and reputation were established on Sōseki criticism), which, perhaps unwittingly, at once belonged with and contributed to the discourse of modernization.

8. As Etienne Balibar observes, "every modern nation is a product of coloniza-

tion: it has always been to some degree colonized or colonizing, and sometimes both at the same time" (1991, 89).

9. This is *not* to argue that Sōseki's texts refuse to acknowledge Asia. *Shumi no iden* (The Heredity of Taste, 1905) celebrates the memory of a close friend made all the more glorious because of his self-sacrificial death for the imperial cause at Port Arthur. Manchuria appears in several works (including *Sanshirō* and *Higan sugi made* [Until After the Equinox]) in which characters seek escape from financial troubles in Japan; in *Meian* [Light and Darkness] another figure chooses to flee Japan for Korea to seek work. My concern in this essay is with the signification we might give to these references in the context of a process called canonization.

10. For a brief discussion of Sōseki's literature and *Man-Kan,* see Izu 1989. Izu attempts to temper Sōseki's prejudicial remarks by observing, for example, that while the author may have used pejoratives such as "chan," Sōseki deepened his identification as a fellow Asian during his trip to the Asian continent. Izu further notes that Sōseki commends the Chinese for battling the British and praises their unwillingness to embrace all things Western willy-nilly as the Japanese have tended to do.

11. In the afterword to the *zenshū* (collected works) volume that includes *Man-Kan,* Komiya Toyotaka echoes the widespread sentiment that Sōseki is a very obtrusive figure in this piece. See Sōseki 1975, 529.

12. It must be noted that Altieri's description describes a scenario that its author sets up to explicitly challenge. Positioning himself critically against what he calls a "critical historicism" and a "hermeneutics of suspicion," Altieri argues that "the past that canons preserve is best understood as a permanent theater helping us shape and judge personal and social values, that our self-interest in the present consists primarily in establishing ways of employing that theater to gain distance from our ideological commitments" (1983, 40).

13. The term "canon" defies easy translation into Japanese society, where relationships governing the reader, writer, publisher, and so on, not to mention the social dynamics of differential power, are different from our own. My reference to such matters as Japanese currency and school-age children's polls is meant to hint at the "noninstitutional" contours of Japanese canonicity. I employ the term here for its utility in conceiving a public, mediating space in which the private (whether author or reader) meets the public.

14. Brownstein (1987) discusses the canonization of classical Japanese texts in the Meiji era by focusing on the institutionalization of literary histories. For a thoughtful consideration of canonicity and *zenshū,* see Silverberg 1991.

15. For a thoughtful critique of Berman's book, see Perry Anderson (1988).

16. Carol Gluck addresses the changing figuration of the Meiji Emperor (1986, 221–26). Telling confirmation of the prominence of worldly events in late Meiji

society is found in the memoirs of Nakano Shigeharu. In her discussion of his *Nashi no hana* (Pear Flowers, 1957–58), Miriam Silverberg observes that the "expansion of empire, the execution of Kōtoku Shūsui, and the passing of the Emperor are embedded in the narrative, as Meiji history enters the village through the eyes of a child giving meaning to his immediate surroundings" (Silverberg 1991, 18). For an extended discussion of print culture and political consciousness in Meiji-Taishō Japan (1868–1925), see Silverberg 1991, 16–30.

17. Gluck surveys the ambivalent reaction to Nogi's *junshi* (1986, 219–56).

18. Lifton, Kato, and Reith note that during the Russo-Japanese War, "Nogi was denounced as an inept, 'no-policy' general who was senselessly murdering the nation's youth" (1979, 51).

19. While removed from the focus of the present study, the relationships between Sensei, his close friend K, the Westerner, and the Student suggest homoerotic affinities. This matter is pursued in Doi 1976.

20. Over the years, many critics have examined the relationship between the Student and K, some arguing that the latter signifies a pre-Meiji spirit, others that he is a symbol of a modern orientation to learning and knowledge. For a discussion of the relationship as governed by an "objectifying gaze," see Ishihara 1990.

21. Several critics rightfully point to a more significant function for Ojōsan. For example, Komori Yōichi suggests that the Student returns to Tokyo as he reads Sensei's testament in order to enter into a relationship with Ojōsan that is more than that of mentor's wife and student. This act of following one's heart, he argues, demonstrates a way to overcome the family-centered patriarchy continuing to order Meiji civil society. See Komori 1988, esp. 312–17.

22. While there are minor stylistic revisions, the original newspaper version and the Iwanami book edition remain virtually the same.

23. Simon During (1990) locates the origins of such literature in eighteenth-century England.

24. Ishihara Chiaki focuses on the dissension between the Student and Sensei in his provocative essay "*Kokoro* no Oedeipusu: Hanten suru katari" (Ishihara 1991).

25. Such culturalists of the 1920s and '30s as Watsuji, Kuki, and Nishida immediately come to mind.

26. While the Sino-Japanese War of 1895 is a convenient way to date the beginnings of Japanese adventurism on the Asian continent, we must remember that an increasing government presence in Korea can be discerned from the 1880s. See Myers and Peattie (1984). By all accounts it is the Russo-Japanese War of 1904–5 that clearly marks the early moments of "social acceptance" for colonialist behavior on the part of Japan.

27. See, for example, *Asahi Shimbun*, 11 Aug. 1914.

Susan Z. Andrade

8 The Joys of Daughterhood

Gender, Nationalism, and the Making of Literary Tradition(s)

> It is not to defend imperialist domination to recognize that it gave new nations to the world, the dimensions of which it reduced, and that . . . in spite of or because of the prejudices, the discrimination and the crimes which it occasioned, it contributed to a deeper knowledge of humanity as a moving whole, as a unity in the complex diversity of the characteristics of development.—Amilcar Cabral, *Return to the Source*

> Why is it that nationalism achieves the ideological effect of an inclusive and putatively macropolitical discourse, whereas the women's question—unable to achieve its autonomous macropolitical identity—remains ghettoized within its specific and regional space? . . . Faced with its own repression, the women's question seems forced either to seek its own separatist political autonomy or to envision other ways of constituting a relational-integrative politics without at the same time resorting to another kind of totalizing umbrella.—R. Radhakrishnan, "Nationalism, Gender, and the Narrative of Identity"

Novel writing from Francophone and Anglophone Africa exploded in the 1950s and early 1960s, coinciding with African agitation for independence, contributing to the birth of most of the continent's nation-states, and prefiguring Benedict Anderson's thesis (1983) that the origins of nationalism are bound up with those of the novel. Colonial triumphalism had represented Africa as a sign without a history, as an absence, or, occasionally, as the fertile ground of European subject consolidation. In response, the writers whom Anthony Appiah (1992) calls "the first wave" of modern African novelists wrote anticolonial realist narratives that articulated and celebrated a communal history. Appropriating the language and symbolic systems of the colonizers, writers such as Camara Laye, Ferdinand Oyono, Chinua Achebe, and Mongo Beti reinvented themselves and their communities in narrative, partly in response to colonial silencing, and partly because it seemed an ideal means by which to consolidate racial, religious, ethnic, and class differences into a single national identity.

According to Mary Layoun, this narrative of nationalism not only "privileges its own narrative perspective" but postulates a narrative past and "constructs a telos, presumably one deriving from the structure and content of the narrative—and the nation—itself" (1992, 411). The national allegories of this first wave, however, narrated only male stories, because, in the words of Jean Franco, male authors "psychoanalyzed the nation" in terms of masculine identity (1989, 131). The results of colonial violence, both physical and epistemological, were and have continued to be signified as masculine impotence. As Abdul JanMohamed (1985) and others have argued, the relations of power between colonizer and colonized took on a Manichean form: within the implied gender dynamics, the colonizer always occupied the masculine position, the colonized always the feminine.[1] Franco has suggested that "women became the territory over which the quest for (male) national identity passed, or, at best, . . . the space of loss of all that lies outside the male games of rivalry and revenge" (1989, 131).

From its inception, then, discourses of gender and sexuality have been imbricated in the African novel. Feminists, particularly those committed to African feminism, have been unable to ignore this logic and have begun to explore its implications in the work of male and female writers alike. My concern here is to trace a particular narration of the African literary tradition that corresponds to and underwrites the plotting of the anticolonial struggle. The two narratives in question efface female agency, featuring women primarily as forms of coinage or exchange between men. Intentionally or not, the historiographic tradition has suppressed the feminine in its writing or telling of history, much as literary history has failed to comprehend women's novels that did not explicitly inscribe themselves within the nationalist text. These (invented) traditions have been unable to account either for the female anticolonial uprisings that predated nationalism or for women's novels, because neither feminine discourse participated in the nationalist story as so named.

One means by which the erasure of women as subjects can be made visible is through an examination of Achebe's first novel, *Things Fall Apart,* published in 1958. Reading this most canonic of African novels and its reception through the critical lens of gender offers a view of male anxieties manifested in nationalism. Reading it along with current feminist analyses of an indigenous women's uprising, the Igbo Women's War of 1929, to which it has a complex and vexed relation, and also next to two later Igbo women's novels, illustrates nationalism's tendentious and gender-marked schemes for regulating the field of postcolonial African writing and for distributing cultural capital within it. Achebe's fellow Igbo writers Flora Nwapa and Buchi Emecheta must, according to hegemonic understandings of African literary production, either plot themselves into a nationalist literary history whose outlines are masculinist or be consigned to the heap of marginal writers.

Nwapa is the classic example. Patently lacking the power to change the nationalist story or to enter into a dialogue with it, Nwapa, the first Nigerian woman novelist, seemingly refuses engagement with national politics. Her *Efuru,* published in 1966, captures Nwapa's imaginary resolution of a contradiction in the male-dominated, nationalist ideology of the writers of her generation and employs a self-consciously feminine style and domestic subject matter to do so. It is only with the 1979 publication of *The Joys of Motherhood* by the more assertively feminist and openly nationalist Emecheta, and with the advent of both another literary generation and the outlines of a counterdiscourse in the African literary tradition, that Nwapa's imaginary resolution of the contradictions of male-dominated nationalist ideology is made visible. *The Joys of Motherhood* establishes an explicitly intertextual relationship with *Efuru,* one that acknowledges Nwapa's historical status and secures the earlier novel a place in literary history—while indirectly exposing the older novelist's ambivalent representation of female independence.

In this essay I examine the differing ways in which these novels, *Things Fall Apart, Efuru,* and *The Joys of Motherhood,* participate in the genealogy of an (Igbo) African literature, as well as in its putative "master" discourse, nationalism. The manner in which feminist anthropologists, historians, and now literary critics have reread the 1929 Igbo Women's War, rescuing it from semiobscurity and reinscribing it as an indigenous feminist challenge to colonialism, serves as a metaphor for my readings of these two women-authored novels. For if the act of writing is one of the most powerful means by which women can inscribe themselves into history, then the acts of African women writers inscribing themselves and (re)inscribing their precursors into literary history function as a powerful response to Hegel's infamous dictum on the exclusion of Africans from history. Moreover, when juxtaposed against the canonical *Things Fall Apart,* the popular rebellion of the Women's War invites an alternative reading of African literary historiography, by pointing to the convergence of gendered and nationalist politics, and by offering a lens through which to view both male anxieties about gender and female silences about nationalism.

Historians and anthropologists generally agree that the decentralized polities that constituted nineteenth- and twentieth-century Igboland in Nigeria afforded significant economic and social mobility to their people, particularly to their women. Two Igbo social institutions that helped protect women from patriarchal excesses were the *inyemedi* (wives of the clan) and the more influential *umuaada* (daughters of the clan) (Van Allen 1976; Amadiume 1987). Although most women could not own land, they could and were expected to make money in trade and, moreover, could exert economic and political pressure if they had prospered.

The 1929 Igbo Women's War, called in Igbo Ogu Umunwanyi, constitutes one such instance of pressure. Archivally recorded by the British as the "Aba Riots," this uprising may be read as the violent culmination of traditional manifestations of Igbo women's power.[2] In her essay on the Women's War, Judith Van Allen explains some of the mechanisms of precolonial Igbo women's power:

> To "sit on" or "make war on" a man involved gathering at his compound at a previously agreed-upon time, dancing, singing scurrilous songs detailing the women's grievances against him (and often insulting him along the way by calling his manhood into question), banging on his hut with the pestles used for pounding yams, and, in extreme cases, tearing up his hut (which usually meant pulling the roof off). This might be done to a man who particularly mistreated his wife, who violated the women's market rules, or who persistently let his cows eat the women's crops. (1976, 61)

This raucous and destructive behavior on the part of women was usually directed at men who were perceived to threaten their personal or economic security.

Contrary to what the name implies, the British system of Indirect Rule under which these women lived did not retain traditional forms of government. The British established a system of Native Courts and designated Africans to serve on them. Called Warrant Chiefs, these men rarely held traditional positions of respect, were ultimately beholden only to the British, and were, because of their linguistic abilities, powerful intermediaries between colonizer and colonized. British reliance on these intermediaries was compounded by the fact that the British rarely spoke the Igbo language. Under these conditions, the colonial juridical system soon became hopelessly corrupt.

With the onset of world economic depression in 1929, and the resulting fall in the price of palm oil, a crucial resource in the women's economy, the political scenery was complete. When the British indicated that they would extend direct taxation to the eastern provinces, the women took collective action. In November-December of 1929, tens of thousands of Igbo and Ibibio women from the Calabar and Owerri provinces "made war on" the Warrant Chiefs as well as on the British overlords. They originally mobilized around the issue of women's taxation, but their demands soon included abolition of the Native Courts (or the inclusion of women on them) and the return of all white men to their own country. Information and money for the uprising had been conveyed through an elaborate system of women's market networks.

These uprisings were conducted in a manner consonant with women's traditional exercise of power in the village setting. Van Allen describes the Women's War in the following manner:

> Traditional dress, rituals and "weapons" for "sitting on" were used: the women wreathed their heads with young ferns symbolizing war, and sticks, bound with ferns or young palms, were used to invoke the powers of the female ancestors. The women's behavior also followed traditional patterns: much noise, stamping, preposterous threats and a general raucous atmosphere, all part of the institution of "sitting on" a man. (1972, 175)

The war ended violently, however; approximately fifty women were killed and another fifty were wounded by the gunfire of police and soldiers. According to Van Allen, "the lives taken were those of women only—no men, Igbo or British, were even seriously injured" (174). Significantly, the women did not believe that they would be hurt, so culturally appropriate were their actions.

Of the archival (mis)representations of the Women's War as the "Aba Riots," a name that limits the scope of the action and depoliticizes its feminist impetus, Van Allen notes that the control of language means the control of history, saying that

> the British "won," and they have imposed their terminology on history. Only a very few scholars have recorded that the Igbo called this the "Women's War." And in most histories of Nigeria today one looks in vain for any mention that women were even involved. "Riots," the term used by the British, conveys a picture of uncontrolled irrational action. . . . "Aba Riots," in addition, neatly removes women from the picture. What we are left with is "some riots at Aba"—not by women, not involving complex organization, and not ranging over most of southeastern Nigeria. (1972, 60–61)

These uprisings can more usefully be read as one of the many blows dealt the colonial state by the natives than as a devastating political reverse. The women succeeded in toppling the corrupt system of the Warrant Chiefs, though none of their other demands were met. As a result of the women's efforts, the British attempted to emulate the precolonial Igbo model through a new system of administration.

Though other Africans had published novels before *Things Fall Apart*, it is generally accepted that, as C. L. Innes puts it, Achebe "may be deemed the father of the African novel in English" (1992, 19). Simon Gikandi suggests that Achebe was unique in his ability to recognize the function of the novel both as a depiction of reality and as a vehicle of limitless possibility for constructing and representing a new national identity:

> Achebe's seminal status in the history of African literature lies precisely in his ability to have realized that the novel provided new ways of reorganizing African cultures, especially in the crucial juncture of transition from colonialism to national independence, and his fundamental belief that narrative can indeed propose an alternative world beyond the realities imprisoned in colonial and postcolonial relations of power. (1991, 3)

Gikandi insightfully reads Achebe's contradictions as inherent to the anxieties of an early anticolonial nationalist. Nevertheless, like Achebe, he too accepts unchallenged the idea that nationalism consolidates itself through gendered formations. I would like first to read the gendered inflection of those relations and then to reexamine some of the relations of production—relations in which the Women's War plays a crucial role—that constitute the cultural history of *Things Fall Apart*.

Feminist readers of the novel have long noted that female characters are generally absent from—and when they do appear, silent in—this novel.[3] Okonkwo's mother, whose lineage affords the novel's hero seven years of protection, is unnamed, as are his senior wife and almost all of his daughters.[4] This is more than a simple inattention to women, for the absent presence of women is necessary to the construction of the novel's nationalist ideology. While women are not represented in any significant numbers, anticolonial nationalist subjectivity operates in a gendered social space defined by male bodies.

Igbo women's social organizations and their "war-making" are effaced in official anticolonial history, in order that masculine anticolonial rebellion might avoid occupying the role of female to the colonizing male. Achebe's novel is structured by erasures in a roughly analogous manner and attempts to avoid the representation of colonial relations in gendered terms by inscribing an excessively masculine Igbo man. Moreover, the category of the masculine, namely Okonkwo's hypermasculinity, is outlined not against the femininity of women but against that of other men, particularly against his own father and son, Unoka and Nwoye. Both Unoka and Nwoye prefer the "womanish" activities of storytelling and/or playing the flute. Neither is particularly interested in the warlike exploits that move Okonkwo. It is generally recognized that Okonkwo, the "tragic hero," is tragic precisely because his life is driven by the obsessive fear of becoming his feminine father. The irony of Okonkwo's anxious reaction to his paternal inheritance is that the violent masculinity of Okonkwo's life path leads to a death equally as shameful as that of the lazy and effeminate Unoka. Neither can be given a proper burial, and instead both father and son are cast into the Evil Forest. Moreover, Okonkwo's tendency toward violence and rigidity is juxtaposed against the more "gender-balanced" characteristics of his best friend, Obierika. Though a great warrior like Okonkwo, Obierika also resembles the inexorably feminized Nwoye in his pity for the sacrifice victim Ikemefuna and in his critique of some violent Igbo customs, particularly that of the infanticide of twins.

In the Manichean allegory of anticolonial struggle that I outlined earlier, the colonial/European side is characterized as masculine, while the weak and disorderly native/African side is necessarily feminine.

Achebe thus confronts a dilemma: how to narrate the brutality of imperialism without reifying the model that inscribes African men as submissive or "feminine." The result is his hypermasculine protagonist Okonkwo, a character who is violent and inflexible in his relations with others. In diametrical opposition, son Nwoye, who, as Biodun Jeyifo points out, has the most affinity for the "feminine" arts of storytelling, is also the one who "goes over to the colonizers and more or less embraces the colonialist ideology of the 'civilizing mission'" (1993, 855). Paradoxically, Achebe's preoccupation with the implicitly gendered pattern of colonial relations means that he can only imagine a negative masculinity; he has no room for a celebratory femininity.

Gender is represented exclusively through the relations of exchange between men, thus providing an African example of Eve Sedgwick's paradigm of homosocial relations (1985). With the exception of the priestess Chielo, all the women in *Things Fall Apart* function as objects of exchange in this homosocial yet rigorously heterosexual system. While women serve to maintain the institution of heterosexuality, gendered identity, spanning the excessively masculine to the excessively feminine, is embodied only by men.

While, as I have noted, the Igbo Women's War might have significance as a metaphor for a hidden Igbo women's literary tradition, I would like to suggest at this point that the uprising has a more direct—and problematic—significance for a masculine genealogy. Although the war ended violently, its scope and radical potential nevertheless posed a sweeping challenge to British authority and might well have been etched in the memory of the Igbo still living during the period when Achebe authored his first novel. Testifying to the link between colonial power and knowledge, Igbo historian S. N. Nwabara declares that "the revolt was therefore a major factor that led the government to encourage the study of Ibo indigenous society" (1978, 201).[5] In fact, anthropologist Sylvia Leith-Ross, who in the 1930s formed part of the British group sent down to study Igbo culture in the service of the colonial state, indicates that she was particularly interested in "how much the Riots were still remembered and what shape they took": "I believe that as palm-oil dominates the economic-social situation, so do the Aba riots still dominate the psychological situation" (1939, 174).

In a reading of the impact of Westernization on *Things Fall Apart*, Rhonda Cobham (1991) suggests that Achebe's investment in a type of

Victorian ideal of feminine decorum makes it possible for him to elide not only the Women's War but feminine Igbo institutional structures such as the *umuaada* that helped give rise to it. Because in his nonfiction prose Achebe has named Joseph Conrad and Joyce Cary as significant (negative) literary influences, much has been made of his response to the racism of European realism and modernism. Extending the work done by Cobham, I suggest that a literary influence on *Things Fall Apart* at least as telling as that of the English novelists can be found in the anthropological texts generated by Leith-Ross and others—which, themselves constitute a discursive action to the Igbo Women's War.[6] Nowhere is the response to colonial self-consolidation in *Things Fall Apart* more trenchant than in Achebe's description of the District Commissioner, whose projected book, *The Pacification of the Primitive Tribes of the Lower Niger,* reduces Okonkwo's tragic story to "a reasonable paragraph" (Achebe 1969, 191). The novel's closure, then, in this way overtly sets itself against the discourse of Leith-Ross and other anthropologists.

Things Fall Apart offers a history, a subjectivity, and a narrative voice that have been excluded from or misprized in imperial history. This male voice speaks, however, albeit unwittingly, over the silenced voices of the raucous Igbo women who came before. Within the reframed literary history I suggest here, the absence of a novelistic trace either of the Women's War or even of the women's organizations that facilitated it becomes glaring.[7]

Sociologist Ifi Amadiume, who comes from and did her field work in Nnobi, Achebe's home town, points out, for instance, how Achebe rewrites gendered behavior as he transposes it from history to literature, always obscuring the "feminine." One example involves his making a local water goddess—the same divinity that Efuru worships and that, in turn, gives her license to remain unmarried and childless—into a water god in *Things Fall Apart* (Amadiume 1987, 121). By investigating the local history that Achebe used as a source for the novel, Amadiume illustrates other elisions of the feminine. In the course of representing the Umuofian response to the imported religion that threatens to envelop them, the novel recounts the story of a fanatical Christian who kills a python, a sacred Igbo totem, then narrates the community's violent response to the incident. According to the village annals Amadiume consults, that particular historical event was very specifically gendered as feminine. It was the women who had been affronted by the killing of the python: their response was to "sit on" the man.[8] In *Things Fall Apart*, by contrast, the transgression is answered violently by the entire village (147–50).

Despite its paradigmatic status as the first Nigerian women's novel and as one of the first African women's novels, relatively little critical attention has been paid to *Efuru*.[9] Critics, most of them male, have dismissed Nwapa's writing as trivial, useful only for an understanding of domestic village life. Conversely, defenders of Nwapa, most of them female or feminist, argue that it is precisely *because* she offers a narrative of Igbo domesticity that she deserves her place in the African canon.[10] My interest here lies less in the authenticity of Nwapa's representation of village life than in the tensions that a woman-authored novel—in this case the first one—must confront when written in a colonial or neocolonial situation. Nwapa manipulates the language and narrative form of the colonizer while narrating the story of an "authentic" and independent female character against the backdrop of frequently pejorative representations of female characters by male authors.

Efuru tells the story of a woman notable for her noble birth, beauty, and poise as well as her remarkable skill in trading and making money. The novel's eponymous protagonist is also distinguished for her inability to bear children. (Though she does in fact give birth to a daughter who dies in infancy, Efuru is consistently characterized as barren.) Moreover, each of the men she marries lets her down at some crucial moment in her life, and it is the female village community that sustains her. Efuru's marriage to Adizua, with which the novel opens, is not initially sanctioned, so she helps her new husband earn the brideprice that will satisfy her father and tradition. While she becomes increasingly more successful at trading, then gives birth to their daughter, he spends increasingly less time at home, then disappears altogether. Shortly afterward, their daughter dies; Adizua does not return for the burial. Nor does he return later for the more important burial of Efuru's father. Later, Efuru takes up with and marries Gilbert. Though this marriage initially appears more promising and is accorded more space within the narrative, Gilbert also reveals himself to be an irresponsible husband by staying away from home, fathering a child without informing Efuru, even believing the unsubstantiated rumors of Efuru's adultery. For her part, Efuru devotes increasingly more time to the worship of the female/feminist water goddess Uhamiri, as she continues to prosper. Instead of celebrating her apotheosis, however, the novel ends ambivalently, juxtaposing her economic and social success to her failure at motherhood.

Efuru's entry into the male-dominated canon of African texts marks the beginning of an Igbo dialogue on gender, one in which Emecheta will later participate. The male-authored text that Nwapa appears most obviously to interrogate is Cyprian Ekwensi's extremely popular Onitsha market novel of a middle-aged prostitute, *Jagua Nana*, published in 1961. Lloyd Brown called Jagua "one of the most frequently discussed heroines of African fiction."[11] Ekwensi depicts a deracinated and narcissistic—if personable—woman, whose economic independence derives from her physical desirability and her constant search for sexual gratification. Despite her unorthodox success, Jagua yearns for a conventional married life. She attempts to bribe Freddie, her young lover, into marrying her by financing his college education abroad. Moreover, Jagua's economic independence is explicitly interwoven with her rejection of ethnic identity and her embrace of the vices of urban living: she and Freddie "always used pidgin English, because living in Lagos City they did not want too many embarrassing reminders of clan or custom" (Ekwensi 1961, 5).[12] Efuru and Jagua both become quite wealthy, but there the comparison ends. Efuru stays in the village, acquiring economic and social success through the traditional—and sanctioned—method of trading. She is untainted by employment or location and so is of commanding moral stature. And unlike Jagua, who uses her male partners for economic gain, Efuru is deserted by hers, though she accepts this abuse with dignity.[13]

In that it is a historical novel set in a rural rather than urban environment, and in that it is published after *Things Fall Apart*, *Efuru* does conform to the "Achebe school."[14] Unlike most of its male counterparts, however, it does not openly address what C. L. Innes and Bernth Lindfors consider a defining characteristic of that school, "the conflict between old and new values in Iboland" (1978, 5–6). The dialectic of tradition and modernity and its relation to both the new state and European colonialism is emblematic of nationalist discourse. But because nationalism is such a problematic terrain for women writers, neither it nor any of its avatars (the tradition-modernity opposition) are openly engaged in *Efuru*. The patriarchal narrative of nationalist literary history has ignored altogether the gendered logic according to which it operates. As Franco notes, much less was it able to acknowledge differently emplotted women's narratives:

> Without the power to change the story or to enter into dialogue, [early women writers] have resorted to subterfuge, digression, disguise, or deathly interruption. [These situations are prefeminist] insofar as feminism presupposes that women are already participants in the public sphere of debate. This makes it all the more important to trace the hidden connections and continuities, the apparently isolated challenges and disruptions of the social narrative which testify to a history of struggle and disruption, though not necessarily of defeat. (1989, xxiii)

Franco exposes the gendered logic that undergirds much nationalism and perceptively points out that though masculinism merely "invents" traditions, masculinist discourse nevertheless functions to circumscribe much of women's literary response. By rereading *Efuru* as Nwapa's initial and imaginary resolution of contradictions in the masculine nationalist ideology, we may put in perspective the ambivalent representation of her protagonist's subjectivity.

While Nwapa's primary object of implied critique is masculinist nationalism, her novel also indirectly implicates Eurocentric feminism. At the moment of *Efuru*'s publication, Europe and the United States were witnessing the birth of the second wave of European feminism: Simone de Beauvoir's *The Second Sex,* originally published in 1949, appeared in English translation in 1952, and Betty Friedan's *The Feminine Mystique* appeared in 1963. That Efuru's life appears to have no contact with Europe, certainly none with European-style feminism, means that the narrative's prototype of female power is Igbo—a notable statement in the face of a post–Second World War feminism which implied that the global liberation of women would begin in the West. Indeed, as the example of the Woman's War of 1929 suggests, Igbo culture contains sanctioned opportunities for women's gendered social expression, opportunities which permitted critiques of male power. Understanding this obviates locating Europe "as the primary referent in theory and praxis," to use Chandra Mohanty's phrase (1991b, 52), and it illustrates a recent historical example of just the localized feminist modes of analysis Mohanty advocates.

Nwapa's novel operates in a feminine register depicting a world of domestic activity where dialogue is privileged over action and where, in the words of Carole Boyce Davies, "men are shown to be intruders" (1986, 249). Cooking, fashion, proverbs, rumors, child-rearing, and marketing stratagems, the defining discourses of rural Igbo femininity, occupy narrative center stage. Elleke Boehmer celebrates Nwapa's expression of "a self-generating orality" and declares that this author uses "choric language" to enable and empower, to evoke "the vocality of women's everyday experience" (1991, 12, 16). Masculine tales of adventure and male social space itself are relegated to the peripheries of the novel. Men are portrayed as desirable and occasionally admirable but are often seen as completely incomprehensible, as in the examples of the three unreliable husbands, Adizua, Adizua's father, and Gilbert.

A folktale Efuru tells some of the village children on a moonlit night serves as a metaphor for the larger novel's investment in a women's community—and reveals that community's anger toward men. The tale's only male character is the villain. The (unnamed) protagonist is "so beautiful that she was tired of being beautiful"; Nkwo, the protagonist's youngest sister, is also very beautiful and "the kindest of them all" (Nwapa 1966, 106). When the protagonist is pursued for marriage by a maggot-eating blue spirit so strong that her mother cannot protect her, she turns for help to her sisters, whose names correspond to the names for the days of the Igbo week. Eke, Afo, and Orie refuse her request for help, but Nkwo takes in both her sister and her sister's new husband, helping the girl negotiate around a dinner of maggots. At night the two sisters trick the sleeping spirit, run out of the house, and burn it down with the spirit inside. At the tale's end, Efuru tells Gilbert (and the readers) that women spend Nkwo day buying and selling then collecting their debts (116).

Efuru recounts the tale directly before her upcoming marriage to her second husband and soon after she formally leaves the house of the first. Positioned liminally, the tale foreshadows the end of her marriage to Gilbert. It claims unambiguously that women's relationships with each other are the most secure and that, like the days set aside for them, these relationships are imbricated in an economy of exchange, particularly in the trading of commodities. It is in trade (and thus through relations with each other) as much as in marriage and childbirth that women obtain power in Igbo society.

While *Efuru*'s outer frame of narration offers a more subdued challenge to the institution of marriage, it nevertheless substantiates the embedded tale's claims about gender solidarity through its presentation of the friendship of Efuru and Ajanupu, and it binds the feminine exchange of gossip and advice with the (equally feminine) exchange of goods and money. Ajanupu, a character who frequently advises Efuru on domestic matters, early on in the novel offers to collect some of Efuru's debts, since the younger woman is not as practiced at this art. Ajanupu is intransigent with Efuru's debtor however, and, upon her return home, finds on her doorstep one of her own debtors, who, rather fittingly, is equally intransigent with her. This episode illustrates the novel's circulation of the overlapping discourses of domestic economy (and power) and market economy (and power).

It is only at the novel's end, however, that the power of a feminine community is made manifest—and then only in response to masculine perfidy. Efuru's unknown illness is rumored to be the result of her adultery, although no sexual partner is ever named. Gilbert believes the rumors, and Ajanupu vigorously comes to Efuru's defense, questioning his judgment, education, and even his family history for believing such a scandalous thing of his wife. Angered, he slaps her so hard that she falls down. Her response evokes the traditional power of Igbo women: "She got up quickly for she was a strong woman, got hold of a mortar pestle and broke it on Gilbert's head. Blood filled Gilbert's eyes" (Nwapa 1966, 217). The pestle, an important domestic tool, is also the instrument brandished by angry Igbo women when they "sit on" a man. In its position at the end of the novel's penultimate chapter, this incident underscores Efuru's move toward a women's community, which culminates in the eventual worship of Uhamiri.

Only with a great deal of ambivalence can the novel bring itself to represent an economically and socially powerful woman who is desirable to men, *at the same time* as it represents many of those men as lacking. Precisely because *Efuru* has no strong female-authored precursors (as Efuru, the character, herself had no strong female role models while growing up), Nwapa can only inscribe such a strong woman if she inscribes her tragically—and the logic of the text, which strongly validates femininity, appears to lead Efuru to the quintessential marker of femininity, (biological) motherhood. Unlike Achebe's Okonkwo, whose "tragic flaw" was psychological, Efuru's "tragic flaw"—her barrenness—is utterly biological. Given the flexible construction of sex and gender in Igbo societies, this gender mark is ironic indeed.

Nwapa's (feminist) critique is launched not upon the institution of motherhood as much as upon that of marriage (or of heterosexual relations in general); more accurately, it confronts all obstacles to female strength and self-sufficiency. What is most incomprehensible within the narrative is why Efuru's two ex-husbands should spurn such an extraordinary, desirable, and accommodating woman. This unanswered/unanswerable *psychological* question about marital relations gets displaced onto the *biological* problematic of childlessness. In fact, marriage as such is a narrative casualty, while child rearing is not. Not only do Efuru's two marriages end in failure, but so does that of her first husband Adizua's parents; in fact, few successful marriages are visible. Neither marital relations nor the presence of husbands keeps Ajanupu or other significant female characters from their trading, socializing, or child rearing. The novel's doubts about male-female relations are displaced onto their fundamental biological consequence, that of reproduction—with the result, ironically, that biology appears to determine destiny for the first Nigerian woman's novel. Because the text cannot bring itself to reject the normative discourse of marriage, it posits failed or absent versions of the married couple and endows its protagonist with the "tragic flaw" of barrenness, which removes her from marital circulation. Yet the novel also challenges marriage as women's only avenue to power by staging a confrontation between married life and participation in an independent female community (represented here by the different women of the village and culminating in Uhamiri worship), and it couples Efuru's failing within marriage (her infertility) with her exercise of another traditional, female-gendered virtue, that of making money.

Although *Efuru* moves toward a celebration of the protagonist's independence, economic success, and goodness, the novel displays a constant undercurrent of doubt, ending on a note of profound ambivalence about the ability of any woman without children to be completely happy. In the Bakhtinian sense, *Efuru*'s dialogism comprises the competing discourses of economic independence and maternal satisfaction, the latter of which, I have argued, is a result of displaced concern regarding male-female marital relations. Repeatedly, the text offers advice on what a woman should do in order to conceive, on how she should conduct herself during pregnancy, childbirth, and the upbringing of the child. In fact, Oladele Taiwo calls the narrative, "almost a manual of mothercare" (1984, 54).[15] But motherhood is the one condition that the otherwise perfect Efuru cannot satisfy.

The ambivalence over motherhood resonates most audibly in the novel's closing lines, which have been read by several critics (e.g., Condé 1972; Brown 1981; Holloway 1992) as key to an understanding of the text.

Although Uhamiri appears to have everything she needs, the narrative suggests that motherhood is necessary to completely fulfill her—and, by extension, her disciple Efuru:

> Efuru slept soundly that night. She dreamt of the woman of the lake [Uhamiri], her beauty, her long hair and her riches. She had lived for ages at the bottom of the lake. She was as old as the lake itself. She was happy, she was wealthy. She was beautiful. She gave women beauty and wealth but she had no child. She had never experienced the joy of motherhood. Why then did the women worship her? (Nwapa 1966, 221)

Though published only thirteen years after Nwapa's novel, *The Joys of Motherhood* (1979) emerges into an already existing women's literary community and does not exhibit the same hesitancy or ambivalence as its forebear.[16] While acknowledging her debt to *Efuru* through the similarity of the protagonist's stories, Emecheta revises and extends that novel and launches a biting critique of both indigenous patriarchy and colonialism. Henry Louis Gates (1984) might say that the later writer was engaged in an act of signifyin(g), of renaming and revisioning the earlier text, for it is from the paragraph above that Emecheta derives her title. Of greater importance is *The Joys of Motherhood*'s recognition of its precursor's ambivalence about the childless woman's possibilities for happiness. The later narrative revises its forebear by giving *its* protagonist, Nnu Ego, Efuru's primary unfulfilled wish—many times over, to the point of misery. By arranging the phenomenon of Nnu Ego's "barrenness/fecundity" to coincide with her change of husbands, Emecheta interrogates Efuru's "tragic flaw" by shifting responsibility for conception onto the man. This textual move is especially noteworthy in African literature, where the theme of motherhood is extremely important, and infertility routinely assumed to be the "fault" of the woman. Moreover, by the very act of writing this novel, Emecheta draws attention to the irony of *Efuru,* named after its "barren" protagonist, as the "mother" text of (Anglophone) African women's literature.[17] In so doing, she deftly appropriates the (male) domain of the production of texts by conflating it with the (female) production of children—and comments on the exclusion/absence of women from the tradition of African letters. She also rescues Nwapa from domestic oblivion and reintroduces her as a political actor.

The protagonists of *Efuru* and *The Joys of Motherhood* have generally similar personal and family histories. Both Efuru and Nnu Ego come from Igbo villages. Both are very attractive women, the cosseted only daughters of their fathers. The fathers, Nwashike Ogene and Nwokocha Agbadi respectively, are wealthy warrior-athletes, important men who are highly respected in the community. Each daughter is also her father's favorite, in part because she is the only child of his favorite woman. The determining narrative similarity appears to be that the mothers of both protagonists are dead at the time the narratives open, leaving their daughters with no strong female models on which to pattern their search for independence. Indeed, both daughters are particularly attached to their fathers. Perhaps because they are brought up by conservative fathers, Efuru and Nnu Ego begin as somewhat docile young women. They are invested in attaining the respect that deferral to authority offers.[18] Perhaps because of their privileged backgrounds, neither is particularly rebellious. Both marry twice; in each case, the husband terminates the first marriage. And for at least a short time, both women are stigmatized by an inability to bear children. Lastly, both are skilled market women who achieve (some measure of) economic independence through successful trading.

Emecheta's depiction of a female character who shares so much of Efuru's background must inevitably call attention to the difference between the two. Through the character of Nnu Ego, Emecheta interrogates Nwapa's idealistic portrayal of female struggle, and of Efuru as the perfect (Igbo) woman. Rachel Blau Du Plessis suggests that celebrating a female character because she is exceptional only reinforces the norm of prescribed behavior for other women, setting "in motion not only conventional notions of womanhood but also conventional romantic notions of the genius, the person apart, who, because unique and gifted, could be released from social ties and expectations" (1985, 84–85). Apparently adhering to this logic, Emecheta questions the ease of Efuru's success by presenting a much less exceptional female character. In contrast to the noble, talented, and indomitable Efuru, who overcomes her problems and eventually determines her own destiny, Nnu Ego is substantially weaker, more petty in her dealings with others. Also in contrast to Efuru, Nnu Ego leaves the village (and any protection it might offer) for Lagos. It is there that she experiences the brunt of indigenous patriarchy and the brutal effects of poverty under imperialism. Ultimately, she dies an ignoble death, alone.

Emecheta also responds to Nwapa's more subtle treatment of the effects of imperialism on the Igbo people by representing two less idealized feminine figures in *The Joys of Motherhood:* first Ona, a woman of the precolonial period, and then her colonial daughter, Nnu Ego. The historical specificity of the later text indicates that Efuru's contemporary is not Nnu Ego but her mother, Ona. Emecheta thus comments both chronologically and tropologically on her predecessor's protagonist, for while the events of Efuru's life parallel those of Nnu Ego's, it is with Ona that Efuru shares a certain precolonial, culturally sanctioned independence in village life.[19] *The Joys of Motherhood* affirms *Efuru*'s claim that precolonial Igbo women enjoyed more freedom than did their colonized descendants. Of the difference between the two generations, the later narrator says: "To regard a woman who is quiet and timid as desirable was something that came after his [Ona's lover Agbadi's] time, with Christianity and other changes" (Emecheta 1979, 10). However, acknowledging that Igbo women enjoyed far less freedom under colonialism, does not blind Emecheta to their subjection under indigenous patriarchy. Ona's struggles with her lover, Agbadi, occasionally result in her public humiliation. Moreover, being a "male daughter" accords her status and permits her to contribute sons to her father's diminishing line but prevents her from marrying.

Reading *The Joys of Motherhood* from the perspective of *Efuru* offers a different vantage point on the effects of European imperialism than does reading the text solely on its own terms. Though the later narrative vividly depicts the misery of colonialism, it represents it as an act perpetrated *on* Africans, declining to comment on African complicity with or resistance to the phenomenon. And while *The Joys of Motherhood* does not depict the precolonial period as paradisiacal, it barely examines colonial relations of power within the Igbo village hierarchy. *Efuru,* by contrast, offers a perceptive, albeit narratively marginal, account of the events that preceded colonialism and aided in its acceleration; in so doing, it manages a subtle critique of the protagonist's family history. Efuru's family is secure in the village hierarchy, as it has historically had both stature and wealth: "her family was not among the newly rich, the wealth had been in it for years" (Nwapa 1966, 19). Toward the end, however, the novel undermines that stature by revealing at her father's death the manner in which he obtained his riches:

> It was the death of a great man. No poor man could afford to fire seven rounds of a cannon in a day. . . .
>
> The cannons were owned by very distinguished families who themselves took

part actively in slave dealing. . . . Now the shooting of the cannon did not only announce the death of a great man, but also announced that the great man's ancestors had dealings with the white men, who dealt in slaves. (200–201)

Not only is Efuru's family prestige put into question, but the novel suggests that the construction of Igbo history—indeed of Igbo patriarchy—is determined by the interests of hegemony. Because of both Nwashike Ogene's stature and the chronological remove of their ancestors' histories, Nwosu and the fishermen do not connect the death of this great man with the cannon that celebrates his greatness. His role in the slave trade will probably slip through the cracks of historical discourse; only his wealth and stature will be remembered. Thus *Efuru* rejects the nostalgic approach to Ogwuta's past, pointing instead to traces of colonial violence evident in the structures of the current hierarchy. In the more active narrative style of *Things Fall Apart,* imperialism signifies a sudden cultural collision. Nwapa, by contrast, intimates the gradual ways in which European violence permeated and transformed Igbo culture. In dialogue with this male predecessor, then, *Efuru* illustrates the complicity of some Africans with the European colonialist enterprise, the commodification of Africans that developed from the slave trade, and the resulting colonial conquest of the continent.

Though the precolonial period is not idealized, *Efuru* is idealistic in its representation of a supportive women's community. Buchi Emecheta interrogates that idealism by representing both the great desire for—and continual frustration of—such a community. She also engages Nwapa's idyllic depiction of rural Igbo life by conjoining it to a depiction of urban life as it develops under the conditions of colonialism. For Nnu Ego, the lack of a female community partly results from the absence of other, older women. The cross-generational protection from male power that Ajanupu, Efuru's mother-in-law's sister, offers Nwapa's heroine is rewritten as the unsuccessful attempt of Nnu Ego's mother, Ona, to secure a greater degree of freedom for Nnu Ego than she herself had enjoyed. On her deathbed Ona asks Agbadi "to allow [their daughter] to have a life of her own, a husband if she wants one" (Emecheta 1979, 28). Agbadi agrees but soon begins arranging one marriage after another for their pliant daughter. Later on Nnu Ego moves to Lagos; there her friendship with Cordelia is cut short when the latter's husband finds work far away. Since Cordelia had helped Nnu Ego survive the loss of her first baby and had explained gender and racial power relations in Lagos, the loss of this friendship is especially painful. Nnu Ego's friendship with the Yoruba woman Iyawo, who saves Nnu Ego and her son from starvation, is always tenuous because of the economic inequality of their situations.

It is through the figure of Adaku, Nnu Ego's co-wife in Lagos, that *The Joys of Motherhood* explores most thoroughly the possibility of a neocolonial urban Igbo women's community; and it is also through her that the text illustrates such a community's failure. The tension between the co-wives is due partly to their competition for limited resources in the urban colonial context. The cramped single room in which the Owulum family lives in poverty contrasts with the clearly delineated women's living space that is part of the rural life described in *Efuru,* and with the greater control that *Efuru*'s rural women claim over their economic resources and sexual activity.[20] Through its depiction of the failed cooking strike mounted by the co-wives, *The Joys of Motherhood* challenges the patience with which Efuru waits for her husbands to behave responsibly. In an attempt to force Nnaife to give over all of his money to his hungry family instead of spending much of it on alcohol, Adaku instigates a cooking strike and convinces Nnu Ego to join her.[21] Within a village economy, men would have no recourse other than to capitulate or do their own cooking. In the city, however, Nnaife's male coworkers share their lunches with him. The women's strike is soon abandoned.

The quiet acceptance and waiting characteristic of Efuru are proven ineffective in the new urban context, and *The Joys of Motherhood* suggests that in new contexts different modes of women's resistance have to be adopted. Adaku's departure from the Owulum family and her brief period of prostitution may be read as just such a strategy of resistance. By becoming a prostitute, Adaku is able to accumulate enough capital to begin a more prosperous cloth-vending business and move out of the room, leaving little doubt that she is happier in her new living arrangement. Moreover, her new economic security represents a significant measure of success in the context of the Igbo valorization of women as good traders, and it contrasts sharply with Nnu Ego's continued poverty. Through Adaku, *The Joys of Motherhood* responds to and subverts the authority of Jagua, the "naughty" Igbo prostitute of Ekwensi's earlier novel. Through his titillating representation of Jagua as a violator of traditional taboos, Ekwensi upholds the patriarchal discourse his character is supposed to subvert. Emecheta's text, by contrast, does not linger over the details of Adaku's prostitution. It depicts only her decision to engage in the practice and the subsequent horror of the Ibuza community in Lagos.[22] By emptying prostitution of glamour, and by foregrounding it as a variant of commodity exchange, the feminist narrative thus refigures the topos of the prostitute. Most important, unlike Jagua (or Efuru or Nnu Ego), Adaku is not interested in (re)marriage, choosing to live outside the boundaries of patriarchal protection: " 'I want to be a dignified single woman. I shall work to educate my daughters, though I shall not do so without male companionship.' She laughed again. 'They do have their uses' " (Emecheta 1979, 170–71).

The Joys of Motherhood interrogates Efuru's easy success and her adherence to one version of indigenous tradition by separating passive acceptance of tradition from the active pursuit of power and locating them in rival characters. The former is represented by Nnu Ego (who bears the children Efuru desires), the latter by Adaku (who controls her destiny and matches Efuru's economic independence and her status as a successful trader). This strategy permits Emecheta to privilege the latter over the former, thus valorizing Efuru's independence without undercutting her success, as does Efuru's creator, Nwapa. In this light, the final passages of *The Joys of Motherhood* constitute a response to the infamous last paragraph of *Efuru*. If one of the most important moments of ideological negotiation in any work resides in the choice of a resolution, then Nwapa's resolution of her novel deserves special consideration. The ambivalence characteristic of the later part of *Efuru* becomes so acute, and the discourse of motherhood so elevated by the time one reads the concluding paragraph that the success of the divinity Uhamiri, and by extension that of Efuru, is subverted. In response, Emecheta blatantly criticizes her precursor's privileging of motherhood through *her* last lines. The poignant depiction of Nnu Ego's death represents the final undermining of *Efuru*'s maternal discourse. Devastated by her sons' silence, Nnu Ego begins wandering about Ibuza:

> After such wandering on one night, Nnu Ego lay down by the roadside, thinking that she had arrived home. She died quietly there, with no child to hold her hand and no friend to talk to her. She had never made many friends, so busy had she been building up her joys as a mother. . . .
>
> Stories afterwards, however, said that Nnu Ego was a wicked woman even in death because, however many people appealed to her to make women fertile, she never did. . . .
>
> Nnu Ego had it all, yet still did not answer prayers for children. (224)

By highlighting Nnu Ego's abnegation of self in favor of children, *The Joys of Motherhood* responds to its precursor's last line, "Why then did the women worship her?" Emecheta thereby signals a return to the discourse of economic independence that the childless Uhamiri represents in *Efuru*.

A closer look reveals, however, that Emecheta is most invested in critiquing women who passively accept oppressive institutional structures under the guise of adherence to "tradition." It is adherence to "tradition," for example, that informs Efuru's self-doubt about marriage and motherhood. Moreover, *The Joys of Motherhood* argues that while it might have been possible to be compliant during precolonial (and even colonial) times, imperialism and neocolonialism demand a vigorous (and different) response. Though passive in reacting to her husbands' indifferent treatment of her, Efuru is protected by the larger women's community. In *The Joys of Motherhood,* the lack of such a community, the result of the ravages of colonialism, modernization, and the constant uprooting the two factors together engender, is named as a cause of Nnu Ego's suffering. And what might appear to be "modern" in Adaku, her entrepreneurial spirit, independence, and stamina, are in fact traits intimately associated with the audacious market women who rose up in the Women's War.

If Emecheta divides Efuru's discourse between Nnu Ego and Adaku, she also favors the latter character.[23] By foregrounding the passivity and misery of Nnu Ego, the narrative suggests that Adaku's rebellion contributes to her greater happiness. Adaku's break with the conventions of Ibuza society also means her exclusion from it, however, and, ultimately, from the narrative itself. Although independent and well-to-do, she and her daughters nevertheless live apart from the community of Ibuza emigrants, which disapproves of her. Once she leaves the Owulum family, she virtually disappears from the narrative. The last times she reappears are special occasions for Nnu Ego's children, and on both occasions Adaku gives them expensive presents. Adaku's subsequent behavior suggests that had Nnu Ego been willing, a friendship free from the strain of close quarters and food shortages might have developed between the two women. Despite her curiosity about Adaku's new lifestyle, Nnu Ego is too proud and worried about her standing within the community to maintain a friendship with her former co-wife. As a result of the break, no news of Adaku's personal life or business dealings is offered. It is as if the text cannot contain so radical a choice as becoming a prostitute. Consigning such rebellious acts to the margins allows Emecheta to articulate their potential and also prevent them from dominating the rest of the narrative.

The topos of rebellion links *Efuru* and *The Joys of Motherhood.* Nwapa's creation of a heroine who is both an independent and an authentically Igbo feminist is an act of rebellion against an Igbo literary tradition dominated by male writers and female absences. Yet this assertive depiction of Efuru marginalizes the day-to-day struggles that such a character must confront. Moreover, Efuru's desire to be traditional (to uphold the institution of motherhood) threatens to subvert the text's manifest assertion of female independence. Thirteen years after the publication of *Efuru,* Emecheta interrogates Nwapa's elision of indigenous patriarchy and the colonial oppression of Igbo women, an oppression that her precursor's insistence on the valorization of tradition reinforces. Despite the critique of *Efuru* made by *The Joys of Motherhood,* the relation of the second text to the first does not entail a violent rewriting. Rather, it ultimately emphasizes the affinities that marginalized women writing in a shared tradition must acknowledge. In its rebellion against the "mother text," *The Joys of Motherhood* inscribes the conservatism of its precursor into the text through Nnu Ego and escorts its rebelliousness out of it through Adaku. The silencing of Adaku's radicalism need not be equated with its failure, however. Instead that radicalism can be read as eluding textual compromise. The near silent presence of Adaku, like that of the historical phenomenon of the Women's War, resists narrative closure, and thereby marks a rebellious potential that has not yet run its course.

Although gender should constitute a primary category of analysis, it is (still) too often conceived of as a marginal and private discourse within African letters. Both African historiography and African literary history have pretended to be gender-neutral, when, in fact, their genealogies reveal an implicit ideology of gender. As a result, the "feminine" has been elided, and until now nationalism has lacked the means by which to integrate either the 1929 Women's War or the first Nigerian woman's novel into its narrative. The "real" Women's War, which serves as a historical link between *Things Fall Apart* on the one hand and *Efuru* and *The Joys of Motherhood* on the other, also serves as a reminder to the male-dominated nationalist tradition of the rebellious potential of the feminine. The Women's War erupts, challenging conventional, patriarchal, and top-down historiographies. Similarly, the notion that there is no African women's literary history is undermined by the ways in which (Igbo) African women novelists have self-consciously inscribed themselves and their predecessors into a literary history; for before there is an official women's literary history, there is often an intertextual one.

Notes

My thanks to Uzoma Esonwanne, Nancy Glazener, Greg Diamond, and especially Deidre Lynch for their conversations and comments. An earlier version of this essay appeared in *Research in African Literatures* 20, no. 1 (1990): 91–110, and is reprinted here in altered form by permission of Indiana University Press.

1. JanMohamed outlines this model uncritically in his landmark book *Manichean Aesthetics* (1983) and in "The Economy of Manichean Allegory" (1985). Fanon, in *Black Skin, White Masks* (1967), his first engagement with anti-racist politics, explicitly links gender to political power and implicitly objects to the demasculinization of black and brown men that underpins white male masculinity. Even Said, in *Orientalism* (1978), objects to being the bottom (i.e., disempowered and feminized) half of the binary.
2. According to Isichei (1973) the 1929 uprising was not isolated; other documented women's rebellions took place in 1925 and in 1919. See Van Allen's two essays (1972, 1976) as well as the rather different interpretation of the Women's War given in Ifeka-Moller 1985. For British records of the events, see Leith-Ross (1939). And for a native feminist and more recent anticolonial reading of women's organizations and female access to power in Igbo societies, see Amadiume 1987.
3. One reading here is Davies 1986, which suggests that there are traces of a larger feminine narrative in the Chielo-Ezinma story. I would add that the contradiction that this narrative line in *Things Fall Apart* engenders (e.g., by developing a female subjectivity that does not depend on the male) must be relegated to the margins of the text in order for the novel to produce the illusion of coherence. For other feminist readings, see Cobham (1991) and Jeyifo (1993).
4. Okonkwo's third wife, Ojiugo, is named primarily so that a discrete identity may be attributed to the woman whom he beats during the sacred Week of Peace, thereby proving his violent masculinity. Okonkwo's second wife, Ekwefi, who leaves her first husband for him, has a distinct identity; she may be read as a cipher for a Western-style romance (Cobham 1991). And Okonkwo's favorite daughter, Ezinma, is so smart and spirited that he often wishes that she were a boy.

5. Nwabara offers some details: "Dr C. K. Meek was temporarily transferred from the anthropological department in the northern provinces to help with the study. Margaret Green and Sylvia Leith-Ross were also members of the study group, while Ida Ward concentrated on the Ibo language. These studies were published as books. In addition administrative officers were busy gathering information about the people (known as intelligence reports) which, by the end of 1934, had amounted to about two hundred" (1978, 201).
6. Achebe responds to Conrad in "An Image of Africa" and responds more directly to anthropological discourse in "Colonialist Criticism," his essay on a scathing (and racist) critique of *Things Fall Apart* by a British woman; here, Achebe indicates that he is well aware of the conflation of colonial anthropology and state hegemony, observing that the critic's literary style "recalls so faithfully the sedate prose of the district-officer-government-anthropologist of sixty or seventy years ago" (1975, 5). C. L. Innes's book (1992) examines Achebe's oeuvre as a rejoinder to Cary.
7. Having been taken to task for his gender politics in writing, Achebe has taken pains to depict women as active political agents and as protagonists in his most recent novel *Anthills of the Savannah* (1987), written after a gap of almost twenty years; this novel even includes references to the Women's War.
8. Amadiume recounts the story as follows: "When news reached the women, they demonstrated their anger by bypassing the local court, controlled by equally fanatical Christians, and marching half-naked to the provincial headquarters, Onitsha, to besiege the resident's office. He pleaded for calm and patience and asked the women to go home, saying that he would look into the case. The women considered this a feeble response, so they returned to Nnobi, went straight to the man's house and razed it to the ground. This was the indigenous Igbo female custom of dealing with offending men. . . . Two weeks after the incident, the man is said to have died" (1987, 122).
9. This statement is less true in 1996 than when the first version of this chapter was published (Andrade 1990). Since then, see the chapters on Nwapa in Wilentz 1992, Holloway 1992, and Stratton 1994. Nevertheless, in contrast to the attention given to the novelists Mariama Bâ, Bessie Head, Ama Ata Aidoo, or Emecheta, Nwapa is usually addressed only in broad comparative studies of African women's literature.
10. For critics see Ojo-Ade 1983 and Gordimer 1973; for defenders see Emenyonu 1970 and Taiwo 1984. Feminist readings include those by Davies 1986, Banyiwa-Horne 1986, Condé 1972, Brown 1981, and Nnaemeka 1989.
11. See Brown's introductory chapter to his classic text *Women Writers in Black Africa* (1981). Even Emmanuel Obiechina argues that "Jagua's personality shines through the vicissitudes and corruption of the city" (1975, 104).
12. That Brown reads Jagua's "redemption" at the end of the narrative as cor-

responding to her pregnancy and new interest in "rural living" only supports my point here (1981, 7).

13. In a comparative reading of *Efuru* and *Jagua Nana,* both of which address "the woman question," Uzoma Esonwanne in a letter to me addresses the dilemma of the "united front" stance adopted by cultural nationalists. "The problem was: how to articulate the specificity of women's oppression at precisely the moment when the dominant ideology eschewed internal critique? Those of us who grew up in Nigeria in the late '60s and '70s remember so well how this problem was resolved: Ekwensi's *Jagua* was the literary symptom of a pervasive attempt by men to displace this problem from the realm of the political economy dominated by men to that of an abstracted sexual probity of women themselves. Read against *Jagua,* then, *Efuru* emerges as a far more serious, but ultimately unsatisfactory, attempt through literary art to resolve this contradiction in the ideology of nationalism."

14. The "Achebe school" comprises Igbo writers Nwapa, Nkem Nkwankwo, John Munyone, E. C. C. Uzodinma, and Clemen Agunwa, all influenced by *Things Fall Apart.* See Innes and Lindfors 1978, 5–6.

15. Taiwo illustrates, citing from the novel: "For example, a pregnant woman should 'not go out alone at night. If she must go out, then somebody must go with her and she must carry a small knife. When she is sitting down, nobody must cross her leg.' . . . If at birth the child does not cry at once, you 'took hold of its two legs, lifted it in the air and shook it until it cried.' . . . The mother should put her legs together or else she will not be able to walk properly in the future. Breastfeeding should go on for a year or more" (1984, 54).

16. In addition to *Efuru,* Nwapa had published *Idu;* Bessie Head had published all three of her novels; and Emecheta herself had already published *The Slave Girl,* which contains specific references to the Women's War. 1979 is also the year in which Mariama Bâ published *Une si longue lettre,* for which she would win the first Noma award.

17. Florence Stratton (1994) correctly points out that Nwapa shares the honor of being the first black African woman novelist with Kenyan Grace Ogot; both published their first novels in 1966.

18. Efuru does run away with first husband, Adiuza, without first obtaining approval or going through the formality of brideprice. However, she, her husband, and mother-in-law work hard to earn the necessary money, and her father, Nwashike Ogeue, immediately sanctions the marriage.

19. While *Efuru* is not set in the precolonial period, it also refuses to date its narrative. What colonial presence it implies has not yet begun to wear at the fabric of Igbo social life.

20. Amadiume relates how separate gender space in the village could encourage autonomy for women and hinder marital rape: "Sex was not forced upon a

woman; she was constantly surrounded by children and other people. Men did not enter the women's quarters freely or casually. Avenues were open for 'politicking.' . . . Indigenous architecture and male/female polygyny made these choices possible" (1987, 114).

21. Amadiume points out that according to tradition women could refuse to give their husbands food if they "did not contribute meat or yam for the meal" (1987, 114). Van Allen explains the manner in which cooking strikes were traditionally utilized by women: "all the women refused to cook for their husbands until the request was carried out. For this boycott to be effective, *all* women had to cooperate so that men could not go and eat with their brothers" (1972, 1970).

22. So understated is the text's treatment of prostitution that some critics refuse to acknowledge it. Eustace Palmer (1983) denies that Adaku becomes a prostitute—without offering any textual evidence to the contrary. Palmer's attempt to read sympathetically feminist texts coupled with a certain morality make his approach similar to Emenyonu's.

23. Since Adaku has two children, Emecheta's text clearly does not argue against motherhood as such, merely against adhering to a notion of it as essential no matter what the context.

III
The Romance of Consumption

William B. Warner

9 Formulating Fiction

Romancing the General Reader in Early Modern Britain

❧ The global circulation and undisciplined plurality of novels so evident from other essays in this collection may have first become visible on the print market of the early eighteenth century in Britain. Such a speculation should *not* be assimilated to the dominant narrative of the novel's rise. There and then, according to a narrative given its definitive formulation in Ian Watt's *The Rise of the Novel* (1957), it is supposed that Defoe, Richardson, and Fielding authored the first genuinely modern novels. This narrative of origination constitutes the novel as an object of literary value so that it may be inserted into the pedagogy of the literary classroom and, in turn, confirm the self-evident form of several institutions: that of literary studies, the novel, and the university. In such a reciprocally supporting circuit, endemic to the conservative function of so many institutions, what gets lost? what's missing? In *Institution and Interpretation* (1987), Sam Weber argues that the appearance of a stable disciplinary institution like literary studies, with its proper objects, method, and boundaries, depends upon a prior, often obscured moment of active instituting, where the marking of limits and boundaries casts out cultural objects and inhibits some cultural practices while legitimizing others. How then do I answer my own question, what's missing from the hegemonic account of "the" novel's rise in Britain? This essay will argue that what is lost is the eighteenth-century vogue for the novels of amorous intrigue authored by Aphra Behn, Delarivier Manley, and Eliza Haywood, which begins in the 1680s and culminates in the institution of formula fiction in the early 1720s. This alternative "institution" of another kind of "novel" precedes, and in fact helps to motivate, the cultural elevation of the novel in Britain in the 1740s around the reception of Samuel Richardson and Henry Fielding. But the later, finally hegemonic institution of the novel erases the earlier novel and co-opts and detours the reading pleasures it had licensed.

The plausibility of Watt's "rise of the novel" thesis depends upon two hundred years of the cultural institution of the novel as moral, English, and realist. Through the lens of that progressive narrative of the novel's birth, and the literary histories that tell of the novel's progress, Behn, Manley, and Haywood were grouped together as a "notorious trio" of novelists unreadable because they were sexually immoral, too French, and either scandalously factual or abandoned to fantasy (Saintsbury 1913; Baker 1924). These oppositions between the first real novels and their abjected precursors are fortified and extended when literary histories code the true novel in English as "masculine," the novels of amorous intrigue as all too "feminine." It has been the project of a revisionist feminist literary history to challenge this masculinizing of the novel consolidated by Watt's *The Rise of the Novel* but also found to be working, in updated theoretical garb, in the more recent histories of the novel of Lennard Davis (1985), Michael McKeon (1987), and J. Paul Hunter (1990) (see Gardiner 1985; Ballaster 1992; Straub 1994). The occasional feminist response—to align the genre of the novel with the female gender—simply reverses a tendentious mapping of culture. This essay suggests reasons why the early novel, in fact, cannot be gendered.

In the essay that follows I will argue that the new formula fiction of Eliza Haywood achieves its distinctive popularity and scandal by appealing not to any particular type of reader but to what I will call the general reader. What do I mean by general reader? Haywood's reader is "general" in the negative sense of "not being limited in scope." Joined only by their engagement with the novel, a diverse plurality of readers can align their activities by reading a novel, so its reading can become "general" in the second sense of "widespread," "common," or "prevailing." It is clarifying to specify what the general reader is not. The general reader does not have a clearly delimited ideological position within the cultural field; nor is the general reader a subject with a defining difference of class, race, gender, sexual preferences; nor does the general reader have a specifiable identity, such that a novelist would know in advance how to move her or him. Instead, the sort of formula fiction that I will be investigating in this essay requires thinking of the reader as plural in interests and pleasures, a perversely polymorphous being capable of being "hooked" by many zones of readerly enjoyment. The general reader is not a vague or capacious universal; the term does not, as Joan Copjec argues about the general subject, "poorly or wrongly describe a subject whose structure is actually determinate but precisely indicates a subject that is in some sense objectively indeterminate" (Copjec 1994, 147). For the writer and bookseller working the early modern print market, this indeterminate but alluring "general reader" becomes the phantasmatic object the successful appeal to which assures monetary advantage. It has been so for publishers ever since. The popularity of Eliza Haywood's 1719 best-seller *Love in Excess,* and the notoriety of the many novels she published throughout the following decade, seems to depend upon her formulation of fiction with traits appealing to this "general reader."

To read the early novel through its appeal to the general reader will help overcome some of the difficulties that have arisen within recent feminist literary histories of these early novels. Since the 1970s, the feminist study of early writing by women has brought the novels of Behn, Manley, and Haywood back into print, critical discourse, and literary histories of the novel. But this project of feminist reappropriation has been guided by political values and conceptual terms that have obscured the actual significance of Behn, Manley, and Haywood in early modern culture. One strand of feminist criticism has considered these three novelists as early instances of "women's writing," writing, that is, by a female author who writes as a woman for other women so as to reflect upon, and sometimes contest, life within patriarchy. Even when the feminism of these early women writers is open to sustained questioning, as in the work of Jane Spencer (1986) and Judith Kegan Gardiner (1985), the goal is to isolate a more or less autonomous current of women's writing for inclusion in the canon of valued literary works (see Todd 1989; Schofield 1990). It is this pluralistic representational model (Guillory 1993) that leads critics to dub Behn the first real novelist in Britain (Duffy 1987; Gardiner 1985). A second strand of feminist criticism reads novels of amorous intrigue backward from the contemporary Harlequin romance so as to situate them as an early instance of women's popular culture. Developed out of the Marxist understanding of the various ways narrative can express the legitimate utopian longings of subordinate groups, and following modern cultural studies of women's romance by Tania Modleski (1984), Janice Radway (1984), and others, this mode of reading enables critics to put aside questions of literary genre or aesthetic value and focus on the fantasy life of early modern women (Bowers 1994). By assuming that these novels originate in the expressive efforts of an explicitly feminine subject, these strains of criticism seek to secure these texts for a modern imagining of early modern women's identity.

In the first sustained study of the novels of amorous intrigue, *Seductive Forms: Women's Amatory Fiction from 1684 to 1740*, Ros Ballaster offers critiques of both these alternative feminist ways of reading. Faulting that criticism which assumes "that women readers identify solely with the dominant female subject position . . . of the embattled heroine" (1992, 28), Ballaster finds another way to chart the compositional strategies of Behn, Manley, and Haywood. Lacking British models for their fiction, these authors looked to seventeenth-century France, where they found a broad band of "feminocentric" narratives that they could popularize (66). Because we don't know the precise ways in which these novels were read by their consumers, Ballaster undertakes an "analysis of the specific address that Behn, Manley, and Haywood make to female readers and the interpretative conflict between the genders that is the structuring feature of their amatory plots" (29). However, it is Ballaster, not Haywood, who destines this genre for women; it is she who puts the apostrophe *s* after the first word in her generic designation, "women's amatory fiction." The term "feminocentric" allows Ballaster to obscure the fact that the French romances, secret histories, scandalous chronicles, and novels that offered models for Behn, Manley, and Haywood were written and read by both men and women, and often centered upon the affect and adventure of the male characters who love and serve the relatively remote women they aspire to win. Are these texts centered on the women they monumentalize or the men who love them? It is difficult to know what Ballaster means by the "address" to "female readers." Like Behn and Manley, Haywood dedicates books to men; all three feature men as well as women as central characters; at the beginning of the second part of *Love in Excess*, the poet Richard Savage celebrates Haywood as a mistress of passions for both sexes. Only much later in Haywood's career, does this author's writing become more clearly directed at female rather than male readers. After 1740, Haywood may participate in a market segmentation for which there is no evidence earlier in the century.

When Ballaster turns to reading Behn, Manley, and Haywood, it becomes obvious why she wants to suppose these texts have a female address: the movement from Behn to Manley to Haywood is interpreted as a gradual gendering of "women's amatory fiction." In writing of Manley's autobiographical writing, Ballaster develops a heroic celebration of a resistant woman writer that she elsewhere complicates and historicizes: "*Rivella* and the story of Delia read side by side constitute a resistance to the madonna/whore opposition imposed on women by masculinist ideologies, subverting them by exposing their status as 'fictions' and insisting on the prerogative of the woman to write her own fictions of the female self" (1992, 151). Over the course of *Seductive Forms,* the more political writing of Behn and Manley evolves into an increasingly sustained engagement with the plight of the female heroine striving to desire in a system rigged against her. By seeking to gender the origin, content, and address of these novels—as from women, about women, to women—Ballaster aligns her study with the project that underlies virtually all post-Enlightenment feminist and Marxist interpretation of popular culture: how does the subject who would be free (here woman) resist or negotiate some compromise with the power of an oppressive system (here patriarchy) in order to win authority in view of (some possible future) liberation? In order to sustain the female address of these texts, Ballaster must underestimate what we will find repeatedly in the novels of amorous intrigue, that their inventive complications of the ordinary courtship plot, through the use of masquerade, incite a desire that is polymorphous and that exploits the pleasures of cross-gender identification. By blurring the identity of subject positions, these fictions can interpellate a general reader.

There is another, albeit more circuitous, way to articulate the novels of amorous intrigue with feminism. Although they cannot be assimilated to a consistent feminist politics, Behn, Manley, and Haywood's novels develop the motifs of gendered sexual power essential to a later, post-Enlightenment feminism. Like their precursors on the Continent, Behn, Manley, and Haywood articulate new comic situations with a cynical "modern" libertine ethos in a manner that intensifies the erotic tension, gender strife, and sexual explicitness of the conventional love story. The discourse of liberation propounded in their novels is also indebted to particular Restoration and eighteenth-century contexts—the realist political discourse developed out of Hobbes, Machiavelli, and Mandeville; the Tory individualism and libertinism epitomized by Restoration rakes like the First Earl of Rochester; and a baroque aesthetics of excess. Behn, Manley, and Haywood weave these elements into tightly plotted narratives that represent sexualized bodies and amoral egos scheming to secure their own pleasures at the expense of others. The formal traits of these novels—their brevity, their subordination of all narrative interest to intricate plotting, and the shell-like emptiness of their protagonists—support their ideological content—a licentious ethical nihilism and a sustained preoccupation with sex, explicitly rendered. The popularity of these novels seems to depend upon turning the empty ego of the central protagonist into a "reader's seat" from which anyone can follow a blatantly self-interested quest for victory on the field of amorous conquest. Even after they lose their explicit relation to politics, the novels of amorous intrigue retain the agonistic assumptions, the necessary duplicities, and the cruel realism of political discourse.

By eschewing the anachronism of depicting Behn, Manley, and Haywood as women writers contesting women's subordination as understood by contemporary feminism, we can suggest their crucial early role in the formation of an Enlightenment subjectivity. By transporting the continental novella to the British market, Behn, Manley, and Haywood played a decisive part in establishing the early novel as the first formula fiction on the market. As a type of private entertainment their texts incite desire and promote the liberation of the reader as the subject of pleasure. Later in the century, Richardson and Fielding set out to reform and replace the novels of amorous intrigue, and all these early novelists—from Behn to Fielding—become, as Habermas has argued, a crucial factor in the formation of the bourgeois public sphere, the Enlightenment critique of the self's self-imposed tutelage, the late-century revolutions, and modern feminism. This is, I will argue, the actual sense in which Behn, Manley, and Haywood contribute to the formation of modern feminism. Rather than anticipate the feminism that begins with Wollstonecraft, as do the French Querelles des femmes and Mary Astell's *Serious Call,* the novels of amorous intrigue do something more general and global: as early instances of formula fiction they teach readers, men as well as women, to articulate their desire and "put the self first," in the same way their characters do.

In order to tell my alternative story of the novel's early institution as formula fiction, in the following essay I will describe the important changes undergone by the novels of amorous intrigue between 1684 and 1740. In texts like Behn's *Love Letters* and Manley's *New Atalantis,* the novel of amorous intrigue develops a coded system of reference to "great men and women" so as to use fiction to inflict scandal upon political opponents (Ballaster 1992; Gallagher 1994). By separating these novels from the context of early political party writing, and shaping stories of thin fictional characters into complexly plotted action, Haywood develops "formula fiction" addressed to a market of general readers. As streamlined and autonomous vehicles of fictional entertainment, the novels of amorous intrigue elude the post-Enlightenment conception of a coherent political identity and predate the narrative of liberation and enslavement, subversion or co-optation, that provides the Urplot of Marxist and feminist accounts of popular culture. In order to read these novels as not written from or toward any definable collective or individual subject position, whether women, the bourgeoisie, the people, or the author, I will argue that the novels of amorous intrigue are an early instance of what I suggest we call "media culture," provisionally defined as the cultural practices associated with the consumption of print media. This culture of, by, and for a print market is more polyvalent and promiscuous in its address and effects than feminist and Marxist readings have allowed. Media culture does not exclude ideology of different sorts; instead, it offers an infrastructure for the diverse ideologies and class positionalities contending in culture in the early modern period. Its only consistent ideology is the ideology of pleasure itself. The novel of amorous intrigue—through the plotting of its pleasure-seeking protagonists—supports the pleasure-seeking reader sequestered in a more or less private act of reading.

Behind the scandal produced by Haywood's novels is a worry about a fundamental shift in the purpose of reading. If an earlier, reverential practice of reading was grounded in the claim that books represented (some kind of) truth, Haywood's novels seemed ready to deliver nothing more than pleasure (Woodmansee 1988). In formulating the first disposable books for the market, and winning extraordinary popularity, Haywood produced novels that won effects of cultural authority without any grounding legitimacy. So from the *Tatler* (1709–11) and *Spectator* (1711–14) to Pope's *Dunciad* (1728), and in the innumerable defenses of fiction formulated in the prefaces to novels written by Manley, Haywood, Aubin, and Defoe, novels become a focus of a public sphere debate about reading: how is culture to license—that is, sanction but also control—the powerful new reading pleasures these novels produce? As both novelists and their critics align and conflate the dangerous pleasures of reading novels with those associated with the sexualized body, the debate that swirls around the novel of amorous intrigue becomes embedded within the novels of Manley and Haywood. Reformers of the novel like Aubin, Defoe, and Hogarth, and then Richardson and Fielding, would challenge and overwrite the novels of Behn, Manley, and Haywood.

Political Intrigue, Novelistic Intrigue

What is a novel of amorous intrigue? Near the end of Behn's *Love Letters* (1684–87), Sylvia carries on an intrigue with a young nobleman named Don Alonzo. Not only does this affair offer an extension and simplification of earlier intrigues in the novel; within the context of the novel's account of Sylvia's movement from impassioned lover to jaded libertine, it suggests her gradual moral debasement. Sylvia's character becomes flattened and simplified as character is subordinated to the intrigue and the wit of artifice, coolly and cunningly performed. This episode offers a relatively self-contained example of the sort of narrative formula that Behn uses in her short novels (e.g., *The Fair Jilt, The Unlucky Chance,* etc.), a formula that Manley would modify and incorporate into the anthology of adventures making up the *New Atalantis* and that Haywood perfects in the numerous novels she publishes after the success of her best-seller and first novel *Love in Excess* (1719–20). By describing Sylvia's affair with Don Alonzo *as if* it were an autonomous novel and suggesting what makes it typical of many novels published by the notorious trio of Behn, Manley, and Haywood through the 1730s, I can develop a general description of the novel of amorous intrigue, and clarify the moral scandal of its popularity.

Here is a brief sketch of the Don Alonzo adventure. Sylvia, "going on a frolic to divert herself a day or two," disguises herself as a young man attended by a page and sets out on the road. At a small tavern she is struck by the appearance of a young Don Alonzo, who, according to the master of the hotel, is a man of quality but is now "incognito, being on an intrigue." At supper Don Alonzo and Sylvia, posing as Bellumere, drink wine and share stories of erotic conquest. Don Alonzo tells Bellumere/Sylvia of the wager he entered into at court with one Philander (Sylvia's first love) that he can seduce a countess about whose favors Philander had been bragging. Don Alonzo describes his successful intrigue—which involves deflowering the countess's maid and then receiving, on three successive nights, the favors of the lady herself. Sylvia is fired with passion, meditates exposing her true sex, but conceals herself for fear of his proven "inconstancy." She then asks, "Were you never in Love?" Don Alonzo denies having ever been subject to love but reports his passion at the sight of a woman he had seen passing on the street in Brussels, the "whore" of a man who had recently taken orders (Octavio, Sylvia's second love), who turns out, of course, to be Sylvia herself. Sylvia blushes. Forced to share a bed with Don Alonzo in the crowded inn, Sylvia delays going to bed, avoids discovery, and stays awake, looking at Don Alonzo asleep, while reading "a little Novel, she had brought." After exchanging rings as a token of friendship, each goes by a separate road to Brussels. The second part of the episode begins with Sylvia's diversion of the money Octavio had offered her for a respectable retirement from the world so that she may appear in lavish equipage and apparel on the "Toure." Don Alonzo and Philander fall in love with this anonymous beauty. Sylvia then assumes a masker's garb to follow Don Alonzo into the park. She contrives for him to see upon her ungloved hand the ring that Don Alonzo has given Bellumere (Behn 1993, 418). After an artful duel of wits, Sylvia refers the aroused and ardent Don Alonzo to Bellumere's apartment. Sylvia believes "her Conquest was certain: he having seen her three times, and all those times for a several person, and yet was still in love with her: And she doubted not when all three were joyn'd in one, he would be much more in love than yet he had been" (420). At her apartment, Sylvia greets Don Alonzo as Bellumere, leaving him ravished and confused to hear the same voice emanating from this man that he has just heard issuing from the fair incognito in the park. Sylvia/Bellumere offers to introduce her/his "sister" to Don Alonzo, retires to get the "sister"/the anonymous court beauty/the incognito, and returns in "a rich nightgown" as Sylvia (421). Now Alonzo renarrates the desire he felt on their night in the tavern as a homoerotic temptation he had resisted (422). After eight days and nights of erotic pleasure, Sylvia arranges a temporary return to her affair with Philander and pays off with sex Philander's retainer, Brilliard, a slavish admirer of Sylvia's who has been an invaluable assistant throughout the intrigue. The novel's last page offers a final postscript on the affair: Sylvia and Brilliard take such good advantage of Don Alonzo that "they ruined the fortune of that young Nobleman" (439).

In the Don Alonzo episode of *Love Letters* one can follow the emergence of the distinctive contrivance of the novels of amorous intrigue: narrative action comes under the sway of the intriguer's intrigue. The adventure begins with a disguised encounter that produces a strong and immediate erotic charge. Alonzo's arousing narrative (the story of his wager with Philander) embeds a "brag"—his absolute erotic mastery—and issues in a claim—not to have ever been in love. Finding her ambition piqued, the protagonist is called to a particular action: the seduction of Don Alonzo. Although contingencies of setting and situation (with the two forced to share the same tavern bed) are fraught with erotic potential and open doors to a promiscuous and polymorphous sexuality where anything might go, sexual resolution is blocked. The libertine's aim is not merely a physical possession but a psychic mastery won through the other's confused erotic surrender. This requires an organized imbroglio or entanglement of the action, achieved through an "intrigue," allowing the intriguer to prevail over the dupe and communicate that victory to a third party, the "ear of the social"—sometimes a general public, sometimes a select intimate—who can register, enjoy, and applaud the intriguer's skill. To develop such an action and circuit of communication, part 2 of the Don Alonzo episode shows the intriguing protagonist developing a scheme—pivoting upon a succession of cross-gendered masquerades—that takes control of the action. The intriguer develops probabilistic calculations of his or her opponent's behavior out of a Machiavellian anthropology that assumes "the uniformity of human nature, the power of the animal instinct and emotions, especially emotions of love and fear" (Wilhelm Dilthey, qtd. in Benjamin 1963, 95–96). The mastery of the schemer depends upon a general knowledge of human nature, psychology, and even physiology; the intrigue becomes a test of this mastery. Over the shoulder of the intriguer, the reader watches the social exchange illuminated and refracted through the harsh, artificial light of the scheme.

The intriguer's machinations, consolidated into a scheme, become the plot's engine; this mechanism requires a sadistic flattening of the social field and its agents that assures the cynical superiority of the intriguer. While embedded in intrigue, the protagonist cannot have the luxury of a "deep" identity; a shifting set of social masks allows him or her to manipulate the social, as if from the outside, as a fixed and limited set of codes, conventions, types. The intriguer is essentially alone and self-interested in his or her intriguing; alliances of purpose are provisional and open to disruption; the scheme is shaped to divide all others into solitary agents. By becoming an artist of disguise and manipulation, the intriguer turns plot into plotting, the theater of "history" or politics that plot often denotes into a spectacle of theatricality. Issues of point of view, epistemology, or narrative framing so important in other types of novels are here subordinated to a direct narration of the headlong rush of the action. The very simplicity of character and motive—characters come freighted with almost no history, each agent automatically seeks to expand his or her power vis-à-vis others—gives these novels a strong sense of ludic transparency. At the same time, the plotting of rivalrous egos produces an accelerating complication of the action that none can fully control. For the duration of the intrigue, the plot produces variety, interest, and absorption, offering a kind of performance by intriguer and author for the reader. The plot "hooks" the reader. Whether the scheme succeeds (as here) or misfires, results in sex (as here) or death (as in other novels), an unveiling of identities closes the action. The fiction often ends with a movement out of the magic circle of intrigue to the banality of the ordinary, here signified by Don Alonzo's financial ruin.

To adapt Karl von Clausewitz's famous adage, the novel of amorous intrigue suggests that not war but sex is politics pursued by other means. Behn composed the first novels of amorous intrigue in Britain by splicing together several distinct elements: the stingingly abusive satiric discourse of early English party politics; the secret histories of Lafayette and Bremond in France, with their disguised references to public figures; and the Spanish dramas and novellas of court intrigue, with their scheming protagonists. In this chiasmic binding of love and politics, the machinations of the schemer at first are articulated with the ground rules and ruses of political strife but end up transforming the love plot into a kind of political discourse. Critics have suggested how Behn's *Love Letters,* as well as her most famous novel *Oroonoko* (1688), lends itself to being read as a political allegory of the betrayal of a monarch by his people (Brown 1993, 56). But when Behn publishes several novels of amorous intrigue that have no overt political reference—*The Fair Jilt, Agnes de Castro, The History of the Nun: or, The Fair Vow-Breaker*—one finds an ethos of power, rivalry, and cunning consonant with the diplomatic and military maneuvering of the early modern state.

Formulating Fiction

Why did novels written in English move away from the political allegories Behn and Manley used to such effect? Every so often a runaway success changes the shape of media on the market. For example, the use of special effects, stunts, and quick-cut editing in *Star Wars* changed a broad band of Hollywood production after 1977 (Warner 1992b). With the extraordinary success of her three-part best-seller *Love in Excess* (1719–20), Eliza Haywood builds upon the market potential already evident in the novels of amorous intrigue written by Behn and expands the number and popularity of novels on the market through a set of compositional changes. First, by abandoning the political rationale and address of the earlier novelists, Haywood expands the appeal of her novels beyond the context of party politics and patronage.[1] The apolitical address of her novels means Haywood can drop or simplify those narrative elements which had linked earlier novels to political culture. Thus Haywood can dispense with the disguised secret history that allows Behn's *Love Letters* to reference and influence the direction of the Succession Crisis. At the same time, Haywood drops the Theophrastan "character" that Behn uses to deepen and complicate her presentation of Sylvia at the beginning of the third part of *Love Letters.* What results is character simplified into a function of social place and narrative position. Settings—like the lush nocturnal garden—are abstracted into generality. By eliminating any specific social-political reference, mimetic pretensions take on the vague and general form of claiming that "the foundation of this story is laid in truth." While love and lust figure prominently in the novels of Behn and Manley, Haywood gives a programmatic privilege to love over every other social, moral, and narrative value and subordinates traditional claims to improve the reader to the relatively new one of offering "diversion" and "entertainment." All these changes slim down the novel of amorous intrigue into a repeatable formula on a market oriented toward the private life of a reader. Haywood's repositioning of the novel of amorous intrigue is both cause and effect of her remarkable novel production during the 1720s and '30s, and it enables her to become the most prolific British novel writer of the century. It is the quantity and scope of Haywood's production in this period that help give the "bad name" to "novels" throughout the century.

In order to expand the range of readers ready to buy and read novels for entertainment, Haywood develops a new kind of formula fiction for the market. Her novels of amorous intrigue have the signal traits of formula fiction on the market recognizable from the eighteenth century to the present day, from the Gothic to detective fiction, from science fiction to contemporary romance. I will restrict my description of formula fiction, rather arbitrarily, to an interlocking set of general traits. Formula fiction often unfolds around didactic messages. The main characters in formula fiction are divided into heroes and villains, the good and the evil. In formula fiction, action, incident, and plotting take precedent over ideas or character: what's most crucial here is less the nature of the action than the way in which action is organized and paced according to a "rhetoric of expectation" that keeps the reader asking, "what will happen next? . . . I must know." By following preestablished formulas, this fiction requires no justification on grounds outside itself. Because the basic exchange formula fiction promotes is that of entertainment pleasure for money, readers of such fiction are not expected to be disconcerted by signs of incompleteness, fragmentariness, or last-minute revision. Finally, although formula fiction does not feature the self-reflection familiar from highbrow culture, we shall see that it may incorporate a certain defense of itself. Thus, because *Love in Excess* contends with the resistance it expects to produce in the culture of its reception, Haywood's novel develops a rather complex account of the pleasures of novel reading.

This brief description of formula fiction allows us to see how Haywood, by abstracting and simplifying the novels of amorous intrigue, opens those novels to a potentially endless repetition on the market. With this reformulation of fiction Haywood reaches beyond the implied audiences of earlier novels: the courtly coteries addressed by the *precieuse* with the French *grands romans* and the secret histories of Lafayette, the party political audience of Behn's secret histories and Manley's scandalous chronicles. Haywood's overt didacticism and schematic treatment of character clear the path for an intricate development of absorbing action. The novel becomes an entertainment machine. The very elements of the novels of amorous intrigue that drew the scorn of cultural critics—their thinness and shallowness, their opportunistic seriality and shameless repetition, their absence of compelling ethical justification—all fitted this new commodity to thrive in an urban print market of diverse buyers ready to pay cash for entertainment. Because it established Haywood's fame and set the type that she varied in her novels of the following decades, I will explore the logic of formula fiction through a reading of Haywood's first and most popular novel, *Love in Excess.* Only if we read *Love in Excess* with some detail and care will we apprehend what this commodity delivers to its reader, and most especially, how it both figures and hails a general modern reader. Then we can see how Haywood's novels anticipate the products of what Adorno and Horkheimer pejoratively dub "the culture industry," products I shall try to describe in less tendentious terms as media culture.

Through the way Haywood's *Love in Excess* opposes virtuous love to intriguing lust, "persecuted innocence" (Richetti 1992) to the rapacious ego, characters come to personify certain values readied for action. At the center of the action is Count D'Elmont, the gay and noble but somewhat enigmatically susceptible hero, who gradually changes from a superficial sexual opportunist to a passionate and high-souled lover. Around this figure are arranged a set of contrasting characters. D'Elmont's magical attractions become the test for the noble, virtuous, and innocent victims of love (Amena in part 1 and Melliora in parts 2 and 3) and the goal for the voracious rivals for D'Elmont's love—the restless, domineering, overpassionate Alouisa (in parts 1 and 2) and the extravagant Italian Ciamara (in part 3). Nothing appears more central to the novel of amorous intrigue than these improperly desiring women; both Alouisa and Ciamara are presented as powerful, obscenely desiring mothers descended from the resourceful schemers of Manley novels. Although D'Elmont is positioned to desire women, his early inexperience and his later depth of feeling mean that he contrasts with the heartless male libertine, the Baron D'Espernay, who cares not for love but for mere physical possession. The virtuous heroines, whose whole being becomes ensnared by love, are opposed to the trivial coquette Melantha, who puts only her vanity in play in the erotic games of the "Beau Monde."

What is the function for the reader of this didactic iconography of character? What does the simplification of character—in comparison, for example, to Behn's *Love Letters*—enable? In his extended discussion of *Love in Excess* in *Popular Fiction before Richardson,* John Richetti develops a key insight about the effectiveness of Haywood's novels as popular entertainment. Haywood's extravagant idealization of love alibis her heroine's imprudent actions and pathetic suffering (Richetti 1992, 201). To describe the action, Haywood deploys techniques of arousal and suspense that exert certain mechanical effects upon the reader, whom the novel thus constructs as a kind of automaton. The mechanical automatism at work in novels of amorous intrigue like *Love in Excess* may be suggested through the headlong propulsion of the action which is controlled by none but influenced perversely by all. The automatism of this novel derives from Alouisa's scheme to capture D'Elmont: her anonymous letter to D'Elmont declaring her love, and asking that he look for her at the ball the following night, incites D'Elmont's desire, which, because he arrives at the ball when he does, comes to rest upon the virtuous Amena, with whom he starts an intrigue. Here the disguise intended to assure Alouisa's control of the action (her anonymity) misdirects the love intrigue toward another. While the narrative follows D'Elmont's erratic and rather incompetent pursuit of Amena, Alouisa works to abort the affair: she warns Amena's father of the danger to her, has D'Elmont trailed, interrupts the lovers' tryst by having her servant cry, "fire," at Amena's house, poses as a rescuer of Amena's honor, and secretly convinces Amena's father to have his daughter put away in a monastery. The ambiguity and errancy of Alouisa's opening letter to D'Elmont enables all the business of *Love in Excess,* part 1. When Amena demands the return of a letter *she* has sent D'Elmont, and D'Elmont accidentally returns to her Alouisa's anonymous love letter to him, Amena recognizes her "friend's" handwriting and in a fit of reproach allows both Alouisa and D'Elmont to see the errant letter. At this moment of hidden desire exposed, Alouisa's letter finally arrives at its proper destination, as a signed love letter to D'Elmont, and the plot can achieve closure. The ending of part 1, with D'Elmont acquiescing in a marriage of interest to Alouisa, a woman he does not love, offers a complete victory for the scheming Alouisa.

This simple outline of part 1 of *Love in Excess* recalls the machinery we found working in the Don Alonzo episode of *Love Letters:* The plotter and the dupe are linked by the scheme and its necessary disguises. The use of the scheme sets a rigorous mechanics in motion, arranging characters in certain roles or positions of knowledge or ignorance. Disguises are used (here, Alouisa's initial letter) to control the perception of the dupe (D'Elmont) and the direction of the action. Whether plots are known in advance or disclosed only as they unfold, the reader's suspense derives from wanting to know if the scheme will succeed. Schemes against the unknowing produce plots with a complicated distribution of sympathy between the plotter and the dupe: the former is favored for his or her mastery and wit, the latter for his or her vulnerability and innocence. In *Love in Excess* no one character has the predominant authority and power that Manley often confers upon her intriguers, so feelings appear more spontaneous and the action less predestined. The comparative openness and ludic "play" of this plot encourage surprising turns of events. Plots sometimes misfire, appearing as sudden bad fortune for the plotter or good fortune for the dupe. Such reversals seem to be one of the main pleasures of the novels of amorous intrigue. Often the dupe may become knowledgeable and reverse the action through a counterplot. Part 2 of *Love in Excess* is based upon just such a set of reversals, as they issue in a new set of schemes.

By describing the way these reversals unfold, we can grasp the traits that make *Love in Excess* especially well adapted to the early modern print market. Central motifs of Haywood's fiction—misdirected communication, interruption just before the moment of sexual climax, accidental detours of the action—have the effect of deferring narrative climax, so as to require more novel writing. In this way, what links these novels to the market—seriality and repetition—gets woven into the workings of the plot. Part 2 of *Love in Excess* repeats the action of part 1, with characters now positioned differently, reversing its effects. On his deathbed Mr. Frankville asks D'Elmont to accept his daughter Melliora as a ward. In relaying his daughter to his friend, Frankville cannot complete a sentence, thereby producing a fatal ambiguity in Melliora's mind: "Therefore, my last command to thee shall be to oblige thee to endeavor to deserve the favours he is pleas'd to do us in accepting thee for—" (Haywood 1719–20, 2:4). Commanded by her father to receive the man he intends as her guardian but whom she misconstrues as a husband, Melliora is thrown together with D'Elmont, and the two are precipitated into love for one another. This turn of events fixes D'Elmont in the position of the lover, with a new innocence, sensitivity, and charm but also a new interest in scheming. But the jealousy of his wife Alouisa motivates *her* schemes to learn the secret of D'Elmont's love, a secret known to his friend—her admirer—the Baron D'Espernay. The action of part 2 follows the development, intensification, and near consummation of the love of the two good and innocent lovers, who are interrupted in their amorous pursuits first by Alouisa and then by the Baron's coquettish sister Melantha. Alouisa's determination to discover the object of D'Elmont's love, and the Baron's determination to win Alouisa's sexual favors, leads to the "deal struck"—he will show her ocular proof of D'Elmont's infidelity in return for sex—and to two ironically divergent schemes. The Baron enlists his sister Melantha's help in allowing D'Elmont access to Melliora at night, but when she puts herself in Melliora's place in order to have sex with him the first plot misfires. Alouisa enlists D'Elmont's brother Brillian to save her from the Baron's sexual attack after she has learned the secret of D'Elmont's love. When a fatal duel ensues, the Baron is killed by Brillian and Alouisa accidentally runs into D'Elmont's sword. The automatism of the action is the effect of schemes and machinations contending in a space that, from the position of agents, may appear aimlessly mechanical. But from the vantage point of readers this action is both absorbingly suspenseful and surprising, at the same time that it achieves a pleasing moral design: the villains are hoist on their own petard, while the good characters go to monasteries and on a tour of the Continent. By not resolving the love problem—the two virtuous lovers are still separated—part 2 of *Love in Excess* invites the sequel its market success turns out to warrant.

Figuring the General Reader

Although Haywood does not justify her fiction as productive of political or moral improvement, she does defend the reading and writing of novels. Over the course of three linked debates about reading, and one "big" sex scene in part 2 of *Love in Excess,* Haywood defends novel reading as an autonomous pleasure of the private reader engaged in erotic fantasy. In her defense of novel reading, Haywood figures the general reader of her novels as one free of particular ideological and moral investments, and open to the diverse play of fantasy. D'Elmont initiates the first discussion when Melliora, absorbed in reading in a garden, becomes an object of fascination. With D'Elmont watching her unawares and gradually approaching her to interrupt her reading, Melliora appears to be possessed of the charming self-completeness that Freud ascribes to narcissism and its attractions to others: "he looked into the garden (and) perceived Melliora lying on a green bank, in a melancholy but a charming posture, . . . her beauties appear'd if possible more to advantage than ever he had seen them, or at least he had more opportunity thus unseen by her, to gaze upon them . . . he stood for some moments fixed in silent admiration. . . . Melliora was so intent on a book she had in her hand, that she saw not the count 'till he was close enough to discern what was the subject of her entertainment" (Haywood 1719–20, 2:24). The circular relay of gazes in this scene defends reading by eroticizing it: the gaze of the reader of Haywood's novel is borne, through the "silent" and "fixed" gaze of the central character, to the body of the heroine, herself absorbed in reading. In an autoerotic movement Freud associates with the ego's turning around upon itself in narcissism, reading (Melliora's reading of a book, D'Elmont's reading of Melliora, and the reader's reading of the whole scene) enfolds and completes the reading subject. Finding that she is reading the philosophy of Fontenelle, D'Elmont frames an elegant conceit: if that gentleman had known her, he would have written of love and Melliora. When she refuses the compliment by "blushing extremely" and affirming the value of serious reading, D'Elmont adds that she is lucky to be born in an age that has these treatises from the previous age, "since (I am very confident) this, and a long space of future time will have no other theme, but that which at present you seem so much adverse to" (i.e., love) (2:25). With the words of her lead character, Haywood reflects upon the vogue for novels of love like her own, which pose a threat to the reading of serious authors like Fontenelle. This debate produces a silence and "disorder" in the heroine, which D'Elmont reads as the first sure sign of her love for him. He holds her in his arms but ventures no further.

The second debate about reading casts Melliora as the strict censor of "softening" and amorous reading. When the Baron D'Espernay's sister Melantha seeks "to divert the company with some verses on love," Melliora uses the occasion to condemn the "passion" as well, the narrator tells us, as "to conceal it in her self" and "check whatever hopes the Count had." But her austerely moral condemnation of the verses all others have enjoyed allows her to become the witty and intellectual woman whose condemnation of love merely incites desire for herself: "[Melliora] now discovered the force of her reason, the delicacy of her wit, and the penetration of her judgment, in a manner so sweetly surprizing to all that were strangers to her, that they presently found, that it was not want of noble, and truly agreeable thoughts or words to express them, that had so long deprived them of the pleasure of hearing her; she urged the arguments she brought against the giving way to love, and the danger of all softening amusements, with such a becoming fierceness, as made every body of the opinion that she was born only to create desire, not be susceptible of it her self" (Haywood 1719–20, 2:34). By discovering the fierce force of penetrating reason behind the modest reticence of the beautiful woman roused to speech, this scene does more than give Melliora a phallic power that fascinates. Melliora's chaste arguments against love and softening amusements also invoke the law that makes those amusements all the more delicious. "More than a little alarmed" to see her "appear so much in earnest," D'Elmont seeks a private interview to explore what's behind the austere expressions of this aroused superego. There he finds a novel reader in undress (2:34).

Behind Melliora's high-minded condemnation of "softening amusements" there is another kind of reading practice and another kind of desire. As a novel reader Melliora is represented as neither virginally apart nor as a formidable polemicist but as an erotic object, just come from her bath, "lying on a couch in a most charming dissabillee" with her hair flowing down her shoulders. Her gown is white and her body, as open as a book, "discovered a thousand beauties." But D'Elmont is not enchanted just by finding her in "undress." He is also interested in her mind and reading, and anxious to make discoveries; "casting his eyes on the book which lay there, [D'Elmont] found it to be Ovid's *Epistles*. How Madam (Cry'd he, not a little pleased with the discovery) dare you, who the other day so warmly inveigh'd against writings of this nature, trust yourself with so dangerous an amusement? How happens it that you are so suddenly come over to our party?" To deflect this criticism, Melliora deploys arguments that have the contradictory logic of the three reasons Freud describes as being offered to the reproach of having chipped a borrowed tea pot: each reason contradicts the other two, but all three pursue the logic of the alibi. First Melliora insists it is only chance that she reads Ovid: "Indeed my Lord (answer'd she, frowning more disordered) it was chance rather than choice, that directed this book to my hands, I am yet far from approving subjects of this kind, and believe I shall be ever so." Then she bolsters her excuse by exempting herself from the dangers this reading might pose for other readers: "Not that I can perceive any danger in it, as to my self, the retirement I have always lived in, and the little propensity I find to entertain a thought of that uneasie passion, has hitherto secured me from any prepossession, without which, Ovid's art is vain." Then D'Elmont refutes this argument in such a way as to use the topic of reading to take her from representations to the reality of love: "Now you contradict your former argument, which was, that these sort of books were, as it were, preparatives to love, and by their softning influence melted the soul, and made it fit for amorous impressions, and so far, you certainly were in the right, for when once the fancy is fixed on a real object, there will be no need of auxiliary forces, the dear idea will spread it self thro' every faculty of the soul, and in a moment inform us better, than all the writings of the most experienc'd poets, could do in an age" (1719–20, 2:35–36). D'Elmont's rejoinder pushes Melliora to her third defense of reading novels. To deflect the central reason for condemning novels—that they prepare the fancy to move from fiction to reality—Melliora invokes the powers of the critical reader like herself, who is more intent upon noting the "misfortunes that attended the passion of Sappho, than the tender though never so elegant expressions it produced. And if all readers of romances took this method, the votaries of Cupid would be fewer, and the dominion of reason more extensive" (2:36). Melliora's opposition between love and reason is taken up and contested by D'Elmont, and allows the two to have a disguised discussion of their own forbidden love, in which Melliora asserts the constraints of their situation and D'Elmont uses the device of "a friend's" love problem to describe his own. He finally makes an explicit avowal of love, while she feels more sympathy for him than she should.

Haywood's staging of these interlocked debates does not merely follow the familiar if perverse economy according to which warnings about the dangers of novel reading lead to an enactment of those dangers. By incorporating the critique of novel reading that has anathematized her own writing, Haywood exploits the erotic potential of what we might call the scandal of the reading body. The scenes we have examined unfold three positions in the debate around novel reading: first, Melliora adheres to the improving reading of authors from the previous generation, lamenting the encroachment of new forms of reading; then she delivers a moral rant upon the baleful effect of those "softening amusements"; finally, she is "discovered" to be a novel reader after all, offering inconsistent casuistical arguments to exempt herself from her general proscription of novel reading. By mapping D'Elmont's seduction of the virtuous Melliora onto her own seduction of the reader who would abstain from novels, Haywood allows her heroine to become a figure for the general reader she would seduce. This rehearsal of the reading debate around novels prepares for the fictional climax Haywood uses to implicate her reader in the general desire she ascribes to her characters.

For when D'Elmont, with the help of his "friend" the scheming Baron, inserts himself into a plot from one of the novels whose reading he promotes—and secretly enters Melliora's room when she is sleeping, and for a moment resists waking and seducing her—he finds that Melliora, though she champions philosophy, condemns the danger of "softening amusements" in company, and claims the critical powers to resist emulating the amorous behavior found in novels, has desires indistinguishable from those of readers who succumb to the allure of novels. While she dreams, Melliora is implicated in the delusion she has mocked in both novel readers and lovers: "in a lover's mind illusion seems realities" (1719–20, 2:37).

Haywood's narrator defines, in the terms of a general psychology of human desire, that which makes all men and women susceptible while dreaming: "Whatever dominion honour, and virtue may have over our waking thoughts, 'tis certain that they fly from the closed eyes; our passions then exert their forceful power, and that which is most predominant in the soul, agitates the fancy, and brings even things impossible to pass. Desire, with watchful diligence repelled, returns with greater violence in unguarded sleep, and overthrows the vain efforts of day" (2:47). Freud never said it better. In terms remarkably close to the psychoanalytic understanding of fantasy and of the role of dreams in evading the moral censor, desire here allows Melliora to effect through sleep what others do through novel reading: "Melliora in spite of her self, was often happy in idea, and possessed a blessing, which shame and guilt, deterred her from in reality." This prepares Melliora, at the moment when the desiring hero lingers by her bedside, to act out her desire. Building toward the first erotic climax of the novel, Haywood's narrator tells us that when Melliora dreamt,

imagination . . . was active, and brought the charming count much nearer than indeed he was, and he, stooping to the bed, and gently laying his face close to her's (Possibly designing no more than to steal a kiss from her unperceiv'd) that action, concurring at that instant, with her dream, made her throw her arm (still slumbering) about his neck, and in a soft and languishing voice, cry out, O! D'Elmont Cease, cease to charm, to such a height—Life cannot bear these raptures! (2:47–48)

The modest and proper Melliora's dream-induced words and gesture expose her desire to D'Elmont in all its literality. By offering a parenthetical speculation about D'Elmont's intentions—"(Possibly designing no more than to steal a kiss . . .)"—the narrator assumes an uncharacteristic tentativeness about her hero. After Melliora's rapturous gesture, the narrator alibis his failure to leave his unconscious lover's side: "Where was not the resolution he was forming some moments before? If he had now left her, some might have applauded an honour so uncommon; but more would have condemned his stupidity, for I believe there are very few men, how stoical soever they pretend to be, that in such a tempting circumstance would not have lost all thoughts, but those, which the present opportunity inspired. That he did, is most certain, for he tore open his waistcoat, and joined his panting chest to hers" (2:48). There follow the virtuous protestations Melliora makes upon waking, protestations countered by D'Elmont's resolve not to leave her at the moment when her desire has become so transparent to him. As in the climactic sex scenes in Behn's and Manley's novels, this scene's narrative sponsors an eroticized, roving gaze that ravishes its object, invokes a lawful-conduct discourse to restrain sex, and deploys a euphemistic language for body parts that condenses the drive and the law in a baroque excess of purple prose (2:49). The interruption of Melantha, which "saves" Melliora, merely teases the reader (2:50).

The plot device upon which this scene turns—the coincidence of Melliora's dream about her lover and his presence during that dream—constructs an alibi for both lovers, and for the reader. Because Melliora speaks her desire in a dream, she is spared the charge of immodesty; her grasping D'Elmont at the very moment he is about to depart excuses him for acting on his passion. But these two excuses for the characters also operate within the reading debate about novels as an alibi for the reader. In other words, the readers who gratify their fantasy desire through reading novels do what the privately dreaming Melliora and the adventitiously fortunate D'Elmont do: respond to a desire represented as fateful, necessary, and natural. As Haywood's characters are absolved of the charge of blatant sensuality, the reader is freed to consume the purple prose and eroticized situations of this fiction. Additionally, a scene of intense sexual arousal like this one—by dissolving particularized subjectivity into automatized bodies—helps to generalize subject positions by blurring identity. The two characters and the reader all are swept together into a single experience of polymorphous sexual arousal, in which the drive exceeds the subject position through which it operates.

The Novel of Amorous Intrigue as Media Culture

How are we to define the cultural location of the novels of amorous intrigue? This essay's reading of Haywood suggests the inadequacies of the two main discursive paradigms for understanding the vogue for the early novel in Britain. The feminist readings of Haywood I have critiqued develop out of a Marxist valorization of popular culture as that which speaks of, for, and to a collective identity, "the people." Within this broad cultural theory, these novels are positively valued as means by which women writers can challenge the hegemonic aesthetic system that suppresses writing and reading that articulate women's utopian longings. But my reading of Haywood also suggests the liabilities of the literary paradigm for interpreting the novels of amorous intrigue. Any effort to place these novels under the rubric of literature ends by finding them lacking and falling short, paradoxically, by coming too soon. Thus the literary histories of "the" novel, like those of Saintsbury and Baker, feature Behn and Haywood as false starts and miscarriages on the way to the "real" legitimate novels that follow them (Warner 1994). But even when the high literary agendas of literary histories have been displaced by a more analytical study of culture, a discrediting of the novel of amorous intrigue continues. Thus the important studies of Richetti, Hunter, and McKeon position Behn, Manley, and Haywood as markers on the way to, but always falling short of, the truly novelistic, because they lack any claim to literary realism. Such a positioning of Manley and Haywood is explicit in the title and text of Richetti's pioneering *Popular Fiction before Richardson* (originally published in 1969 and republished in 1992), but it also persists in J. Paul Hunter's treatment of all three novelists as writers "before novels" in his 1990 book of that title. Michael McKeon (1987) allows Behn, Manley, and Haywood to figure in the "origins" but not the actual writing of novels; instead their narrative matter contributes to the ideological matrix out of which, through the dialectical machinery of McKeon's plotting, novels by Cervantes, Swift, Bunyan, Defoe, Richardson, and Fielding may arise. This repeats an old trope: women's bodies give birth to male genius.

Novels of amorous intrigue are different from and other than popular or high culture, and they throw that opposition into question. The very set of oppositions produced by the Marxist and literary historical paradigms—high/low, culture/subculture, legitimate/marginal, official/popular, colonial/subaltern—cannot accurately describe the cultural struggle that has produced those oppositions as explanatory paradigms. They are, as Ernesto Laclau and Chantal Mouffe have suggested, a set of antagonistic equivalents by means of which one side or the other seeks to map and hegemonize all of culture from one specific vantage point—that of high literary culture or that of "the people" (1985). But if the novels of amorous intrigue are neither an early form of "popular culture" nor a legitimate aesthetic object like "the" novel, neither the source of poisonous infection nor a food source for the high-cultural vampire, what are they? I am seeking a third way to map this terrain. The unease produced by Behn, Manley, and Haywood seems to derive from the way their novels launch a new set of reading practices repeatedly described as automatic. Scholars like Roger Chartier and Robert Darnton writing about eighteenth-century France, Martha Woodmansee and others writing about the reading debate in eighteenth-century Germany, and Margaret Jacobs (1993) and Lynn Hunt (1993) speculating about the "invention of pornography" have all described the new reading practices associated with the increased commodification of the book in ways that resonate with the vogue for the novel of amorous intrigue in Britain. In both France and Germany the traditional authority of classical and religious learning is challenged by a torrent of books that, like the novels of amorous intrigue, seduce a reader into making a purchase and dispense with the traditional rationales for reading (education, moral improvement, etc.). My reading of Haywood's best-selling novel suggests that novels became powerful and disturbing precisely because they did not interpellate a particular reader—whether female or male, whether aristocratic, bourgeois, or working class, whether popular or high-cultural. Addressing no single category of reader, Haywood formulates her fiction to appeal to a general reader, that is, to the open set of readers who would purchase a book for entertainment. Her novels' address to a general reader, and the atavistic consumption practices those novels were said to produce depend in turn upon the plot-centered rhythms, and ludic repeatability, of the novel of amorous intrigue.

The specter of the novel reader as automaton anticipates many later representations of media-addicted consumers (of film, TV, rock music, etc.) and suggests that the novels of amorous intrigue can be seen as one starting point for the powerful exchange between what these days we call "the media" and "culture," in the anthropological sense of an ensemble of social practices developed around consuming media. Thus the spectacular popularity and spectacular scandal of the early novel of amorous intrigue may be one of the first instances of what I suggest we call "media culture." This term avoids the normative pull of high "literary culture," the nostalgic, romantic imprecision of "popular culture," and the tendentious opprobrium of "mass culture." The term "media culture" fuses together two elements. In the early modern period, the "medium" in question was "print." Print media had always been characterized by (1) continuity of form (each printed text is the same) and (2) portability. In this period, new developments bring (3) important changes in the character and distribution of print media over the quickly developing eighteenth-century information highway: now circulation is regulated by a uniform postal code and facilitated by the new turnpikes and commercial lending libraries; uniformity in text production and the efficiency of the new distribution network promotes (4) a commodification that subordinates the particular ideological content of novels to variations on proven formulas intended to stimulate new purchases; finally, (5) the ductility and mobility of print media increase the speed of cultural exchange.

The novels of amorous intrigue expand cultural and social practices of reception and production in several ways. Because larger geographical and population units can be touched by the same media, printed texts enhance communication at a distance. The profitability of the new media commodities accelerates imitation, and a contradictory double demand—to produce the effect of the latest hit yet appear enticingly new; to be, quite paradoxically, recurrently new. Seduction of the reader depends upon the appearance rather than the fact of novelty. The compositional strategies that issue from this marketing imperative are familiar from Hollywood film production: a recourse to adaptations, translations, sequels, prequels, and so forth. While the profit potential of print media frees the author from the patron, it makes him or her dependent on the bookseller as an agent of the market. The dissemination of new styles, fads, fashions, and modes of living is accelerated and can become the focal point of collective identification. The circulation of the image or name of the author allows the author to become a secondary commodity as a "celebrity." In the scramble to become visible amid its increasingly numerous counterparts, the book comes to encode its own self-advertisement. Finally, the popularity of novels produces a new specter within the discourses of cultural criticism: the reader as pleasure-seeking automaton, liable to an imitative acting out of the novelistic plots—through rash elopements, erotic intrigue . . . or the release of his or her passions by way of a debilitating masturbation.

It should be evident by now that the separation implied in my parallel lists of the features of print media and of print culture cannot be sustained. By taking two terms—"media" as a reference to the print medium and distribution network of the early novel and "culture" as a reference to the cultural forms and practices associated with the vogue for novels—and making them one, "media culture," I'm seeking to suggest the synergistic feedback loop that is set going around the currency of the novels of amorous intrigue. Thus the term "media culture" suggests both a repertoire of objects in circulation (novels on the market in the early modern period) and an interrelated set of cultural practices (of readers, authors, printers, etc.), as each supports and expands the other. The very difficulty of distinguishing cultural objects from cultural practices in the media culture of the early novel suggests that they are in fact two sides of a common phenomenon. Understood in this way, "media culture" can be neither simply the vilified "other" of "real," "legitimate" literary culture (the hegemonic high-cultural position from Pope to Saintsbury) nor a neutral set of objects and practices (the position of those who would affirm the equivalence of every commodified form of culture). Instead media culture opens a plural and ambiguous ground for morally contested pleasures. The ambiguity and plural potential of media culture in the early eighteenth century infects those who would purify its practices. Thus Alexander Pope's *Dunciad* constructs a poem with epic pretensions upon the waste products of print culture, and many a critic has noted his dependency upon the media culture he condemns. Richardson's programmatic effort to replace the novel of amorous intrigue with a "new species of writing" can succeed only by producing a new, morally enlightened and enlightening species of . . . media culture. From the eighteenth century on, formula fiction of varying sorts—from Gothic to detective fiction, from sentimental novels to science fiction—will haunt "the" legitimate novel as its double, challenging its claim to be the only fiction worth reading and deferring, interminably, the consolidation of "the" novel's institutional authority.

Note

1. Richetti 1992, 159–67; Ballaster 1992, 151–58; Richetti notes the shift by which even Haywood's explicit imitations of Manley's *New Atalantis* turn political satire into a general social criticism of the great; Ballaster notes that of all Haywood's novelistic production only *The Adventures of Eovaai* (1736) attempts a pointed attack upon the Whig ministry (of Walpole).

Dorothea von Mücke

10 "To Love a Murderer"—Fantasy, Sexuality, and the Political Novel

The Case of *Caleb Williams*

❧ The popularity of William Godwin's novel *Things as They Are; or, The Adventures of Caleb Williams* (first published in 1794) was short-lived. One might wonder why this relatively unknown and inconsequential book should be of interest to anybody besides scholars of eighteenth-century literature. And yet, one of the first consciously "political" novels, this text provides a very interesting test case for an analysis of the relationships between literature and politics, ideology and sexuality. *Caleb Williams* challenges the reductionist understanding of the political that depends on a straightforward mimesis of history: it does so by constantly confronting its reader with the pragmatic aspects of language, that is, the ways in which language shapes subjective fantasies or organizes social hierarchies. Of course, to the extent that the novel provides a detailed first-person account of Caleb's suffering at the margins of society as the character attempts to escape being persecuted by his former employer, it can be read as a portrait of contemporary social injustice, a truthful representation that documents the necessity for political change.[1] Along these lines *Caleb Williams* might be read as a mere illustration of the detrimental effects of feudal inequality, as those effects had already been laid out in Godwin's treatise *Political Justice* (in 1793). However—and this is why I have chosen to analyze Godwin's novel in detail—*Caleb Williams* also parts with these limiting representational claims by drawing attention to the medium of fiction, the institution of literature, and poetic conventions. More than a neutral medium allowing the objective representation of "things as they are," language in this novel fundamentally shapes and informs both the realities observed and the observing and speaking subjects. "Things as they are," injustice, inequality, and the perception of these realities are all affectively supported and shaped by fantasy and ideology—in a manner that culminates in the "willing submission to inequality."

Though the three books of *Caleb Williams* are mainly narrated by Caleb himself, we must by no means take this first-person narrator's account as a simple reflection or expression of his own view. Rather, Caleb Williams becomes the victim of his infatuation with the discourse of another, Squire Falkland, and of the latter's poetic ambitions. The novel distinguishes various high and low rhetorical registers and discursive genres, making it clear that while reading habits and literary tastes have a great impact on one's expectations and values, not all genres are equally accessible to every speaker. From the moment when Caleb becomes Falkland's secretary, the poor and orphaned country lad is fascinated and seduced by what he perceives as his employer's enigmatic chivalric charm. Falkland's personality is repeatedly characterized in what the latter's half brother Forester calls "the language of romance." When Caleb flees his employment, he does not give up his obsession with this dark romantic hero. By then Caleb believes he has the key to Falkland's personality: he has confirmed his initial suspicion that it was Falkland who murdered the unbearably tyrannical Squire Tyrrel. Book 1 of the novel consists primarily of an account of Falkland's youth and early manhood up to his trial for murder, when the finding of his innocence culminates in a drastic alteration of his personality. In books 2 and 3 Caleb's dreary existence is described, consistently in relation to Falkland on the one hand and to the writing and publishing of some kind of heroic narrative on the other. As it gradually becomes clear that Caleb's narrative is distorted by paranoid delusions, that Falkland might not be constantly trying to hunt down Caleb, and that this persecution is partly Caleb's fantasy and partly the doing of Falkland's half brother Forester, we are forced to ask how we should apprehend the novel's representational claims and political aim, how fantasy is related to "things as they are."

Should one describe *Caleb Williams* as a novel about the ideological function of literature? Could one view the book as a fictional case study of the disastrous effects of a chivalric code and the "fictions of romance"? What exactly does Godwin mean by "chivalry" and "romance," and what is their political significance? At this point it might be useful to introduce a citation from a later essay in which Godwin situates the origins of both inequality and love in the feudal culture of chivalry:

Chivalry was for the most part the invention of the eleventh century. Its principle was built upon a theory of the sexes, giving to each a relative importance, and assigning to both functions full of honour and grace. . . . The woman regarded her protector as something illustrious and admirable; and the man considered the smiles and approbation of beauty as the adequate reward of his toils and his dangers. These modes of thinking introduced a nameless grace into all the commerce of society. It was the poetry of life. Hence originated the delightful narratives and fictions of romance; and human existence was no longer the bare, naked train of vulgar incidents, which for so many ages of the world it had been accustomed to be. It was clothed in resplendent hues, and wore all the tints of the rainbow. Equality fled and was no more; and love, almighty, perdurable love, came to supply its place. (Godwin 1831, 296)

It should be noted that in contrast to Edmund Burke, his political opponent, Godwin firmly believes that all inequality among men, be it inequality of wealth, power, or status, derives from culture, not nature.[2] For Godwin human nature is in principle infinitely perfectible. The means to perfection are to be found in education, an increased awareness of one's true motives, and an enhanced insight into the common good. To the extent that it relates inequality to the specific cultural construction of courtly love, the citation above fits into this political perspective. But the passage also makes the critique of the ideology of romance a complicated matter. For once the culture of chivalry and "the delightful narratives and fictions of romance" have become the idealized version of a heterosexual relationship, the ideology that cements social inequality becomes part of the very fabric of identity formation.

This glance at Godwin's critique of the ideology of love and romance should indicate that for Godwin the fictions of romance are to be understood not merely as "misrepresentations" of reality but also in terms of their production of a reality. Literary language and fiction, according to Godwin, must also be analyzed with an eye to their pragmatic effects. In fact, not only literary fictions and poetic idealizations but every discursive genre, literary or not, can be described in terms of its performativity. In this sense it would be impossible to reduce *Caleb Williams* or any other text to the constative function of stating "things as they are." If the exact historical representation of "things as they are" is integral to a genre like the confession, for instance, that generic rule will greatly influence the subjectivity and actions of all those who will have to construct their past within the rules of this genre. Although this observation might sound like twentieth-century speech-act theory, it is one that can be found in *Political Justice*. In the chapter entitled "Sincerity" Godwin recommends the following discursive practice of "mental hygiene" in the interest of crime prevention:

> Did ever man impose this law upon himself, did he regard himself as not authorized to conceal any part of his character and conduct, this circumstance alone would prevent millions of actions from being perpetrated, in which we are now induced to engage by the prospect of secrecy and impunity. *We have only to suppose men obliged to consider, before they determined upon an equivocal action, whether they chose to be their own historians, the future narrators of the scene in which they were acting a part, and the most ordinary imagination will instantly suggest how essential a variation would be introduced into human affairs.* It has been justly observed, that the popish practice of confession is attended with some salutary effects. (1946, 327; emphasis added)

Note how Godwin's description of the genre of the confession makes it a model of surveillance that would combine features of such innovations as Jeremy Bentham's panopticon with what was to become the psychiatric case history.

Besides the pragmatic considerations that prevent us from reducing a genre to a pure instance of representation, there is another problem with the title's claim that *Caleb Williams* relates "things as they are." As I have already noted, Caleb's account turns out to be the writing of somebody whom we would call paranoid, that is, although Falkland is furious about Caleb's spying and does threaten him, he is neither always nor exclusively in search of his former secretary. Thus James Thompson, a critic who discusses this novel as a prime example of the "paranoid gothic," writes:

> The theme of being watched, that is, the thematization of paranoia, is common to the gothic novel, with its noumenal world constantly on the verge of interpenetration with non-human agency. But the eeriness found in a Walpole, Reeve, Radcliffe, Lewis, or Maturin novel is nothing like the anguish of isolation which Caleb experiences in his world as Prison. The passage just quoted is often cited to illustrate the power of *Caleb Williams,*[3] with its terrible, Benthamite combination of isolation and surveillance, the terror of exclusion and separation that George Lukács analyzes as the objectification of social relations under capital. If surveillance is central to this novel, then the passages exposing the brutal condition of the prisons, and the interpolated episodes from the *Newgate Calendar,* and the notes to John Howard's *State of the Prisons* are not mere social

protest dragged into an otherwise psychological novel out of the reformer's sense of duty: on the contrary, Caleb's vision of his society as a vast prison is Godwin's central insight.[4] (1989, 183)

In attempting to appreciate Godwin's critical insight into contemporary society, Thompson's account of the novel in terms of the "paranoid gothic" is caught in a strange contradiction, one that might have to do with the rather complex representational claims and status of this text. On the one hand, the novel's sinister description of a world of perfect surveillance and persecution is supposed to portray rather accurately the actual state of affairs in Godwin's England. On the other hand, Thompson calls the description "paranoid," a term implying that this view of reality is distorted by an unwarranted recourse to an epistemology of conspiracy or a hermeneutics of suspicion. Furthermore, even when we use the term "paranoid" in this colloquial sense, we mean not only that somebody's sinister view of reality is inaccurate but also that the paranoid person has an ambivalent emotional investment in the situation of surveillance and even in the persecutor. Caleb's excessive fear of Falkland is not the only thing that needs accounting for; so too do Caleb's fascination with Falkland, his spying on him, and his intense admiration of what he takes to be Falkland's chivalric ethos. In brief, to deal with the politics of *Caleb Williams,* we shall have to come to terms with the protagonist-narrator's obsession with his persecutor and his affective investment in being under surveillance. Ultimately, this project requires coming to terms with the special frisson, with the particular pleasures that are connected with Falkland in his capacity as a dark romantic hero.

In order to explain the connection between delusions of persecution and fascination with the persecutor, Alex Gold (1977) has recourse to the psychoanalytic model of paranoia and derives Caleb's paranoid delusion, his excessive fear of being persecuted by Falkland, from Caleb's love for Falkland. He reads Caleb's story as the result of a homosexual love story that in turn is borrowed from Falkland's biographical account in book 1 of Emily's unrequited love for him. Gold emphasizes the parallels between Godwin's political novel and Freud's analysis of Daniel Paul Schreber's autobiography. Concurring with Gold, Eve Kosofsky Sedgwick writes:

The limited group of fictions that represent the "classic" early Gothic contains a large subgroup—*Caleb Williams, Frankenstein, Confessions of a Justified Sinner,* probably *Melmoth*, possibly *The Italian*—whose plots might be mapped almost point for point onto the case of Dr. Schreber: most saliently, each is about one or more males who not only is persecuted by, but considers himself transparent to and often under the compulsion of, another male. If we follow Freud in hypothesizing that such a sense of persecution represents the fearful, phantasmatic rejection by recasting of an original homosexual (or even merely homosocial) desire, then it would make sense to think of this group of novels as embodying strongly homophobic mechanisms. (1985, 91)

Gold's analysis of *Caleb Williams*, certainly one of the most sophisticated and detailed analyses of this novel, and Sedgwick's use of this reading in her broader argument about the disciplinary deployments of homophobia lead me to a question that is provoked by these critics' ahistorical approach to sexuality. Like Freud, whose model of paranoia partially depends on a normative model of sexual maturation, one that ideally involves the overcoming of a homosexual stage, Sedgwick refers to an "original homosexual (or even merely homosocial) desire." Foucault in his *History of Sexuality* (1978) has shown, however, that this notion of "sexuality" as a fundamental character- or personality-forming trait was merely a nineteenth-century discursive construct, one that found its first full theoretical articulation in Carl Westphal's article "On the Contrary Sexual Sensation" (1871). Analyzing a male transvestite, Westphal argued that there is something like a fundamental sexual orientation, a type of desire that shapes an individual even in its latency, doing so quite independently of the "sodomitical" practices that until the late nineteenth century constituted a quite different version of male-male desire and practices. The psychiatric and clinical construction of homosexuality hence provides some important parameters for its later uses in psychoanalysis and identity politics.

Having voiced my objection to this anachronistic use of sexuality, I hasten to add that my own reading will by no means reject what psychoanalytic theory has to offer literary analyses. If we distance ourselves from its normative tendencies, we will find productive models of sexuality that presuppose the ambivalent and irrational nature of pleasure. Indeed, a model of human sexuality as polymorphous perversion may both support and subvert its normative counterpart.[5] In other words, I shall not with Gold try to map Freud's analysis of Schreber onto *Caleb Williams*, an operation that—as Gold has proven—works, if anything, too well;

rather, I shall attempt to show why this operation works at all, and how this particular novel as an example of the "paranoid gothic" participates in the history of sexuality.

How should we understand the Gothic novel's literary use of paranoid fantasy in relation to extraliterary accounts of fantasy and delusion? What was the status of "paranoia" in the discourse of psychiatry, which was at the end of the eighteenth century still very new? The first psychiatric case history of paranoia was not taken down until about fifteen years after the publication of *Caleb Williams.* It was published by John Haslam (1764–1844), the apothecary of Bedlam. In his *Illustrations of Madness* (1810) Haslam states that with his book he wants to initiate a new genre, one advancing the science of psychiatry. He regrets that England does not yet have a richly documented library of cases of mental illness, of the sort that can be found in Heinrich Spieß's *Biographien von Wahnsinnigen* (Leipzig, 1795). It is not clear whether Haslam is aware that Spieß is not a medical authority but the author of popular entertainment fictions, primarily robber novels. Spieß's accounts of madness are melodramatic; and their chief interest seems less medical or scientific than sensationalist. This glance toward the psychiatry of the 1790s allows us to note that, since the field was barely emerging when *Caleb Williams* was published, it must have been from literary fiction that the clinical case history took its cues rather than vice versa.

Though there might be no psychiatric prototypes for this novel's approach to fantasy and delusion, we can certainly think of literary works that explore the delusions of madness in terms of the impact of fiction. To the extent that both Falkland's and Caleb's madness is channeled by the reading of fiction, one might even think of comparing *Caleb Williams* with *Don Quixote,* the paradigm of the novel as antiromance. Yet the two novels are worlds apart in the ways in which each contrasts "reality" with the distorting fantasy world shaped by romance's heroic ideals. Whereas Cervantes builds the novelistic counterreality on the sensuality and sense certainty of Sancho Panza and ultimately relies on a commonsense model of "natural" bodily sensations and pleasures, for Godwin the nature of pleasure is more problematic: certainly pleasure can no longer ground a world of sanity and reason. In fact, I will show throughout my analysis of *Caleb Williams* that this novel's exploration of subjectivity insists on the ambiguity and complexity of pleasure. It is here, in its complex, "unnatural" approach to pleasure that *Caleb Williams* acquires its significance for the cultural work of the novel. In what follows I shall analyze in detail how the protagonist's paranoia is constituted through a relationship to literature and language. I aim to demonstrate that this novel's treatment of its hero's mental and emotional state participates in the construction of the kind of subjectivity that a century later would become theorized and analyzable by psychoanalysis.

My argument has two stages. First I shall trace the development of Caleb's paranoia, beginning with the moment in the narrative when he flees a gang of robbers. Once I have shown how Caleb's persecution anxiety is worked out vis-à-vis his poetic ambitions, and the allure of sublime postures, on the one hand and the humdrum publishing realities of sensationalist popular literature on the other, I shall focus on the kernel of his narcissistic fantasy, on the specific organization of pleasure that underlies it. In the second part of this article I shall isolate the scenes that condense *Caleb Williams*'s approach to the relationship between subjectivity, knowledge, the organization of pleasure, and writing. These scenes elaborate traumatic relationships between self and other, between pleasure and pain, in an attempt to answer the question of the origin of Caleb's passion, and to motivate the writing and the publication of Caleb's memoirs. Ultimately, I hope to show how this novel is involved with nothing less than the construction of human sexuality as the individual's secret, an encrypted but fundamental perversion.

I

The onset of Caleb's paranoia is marked by a shift from a position of perfect invisibility to one of visibility, and by a shift from a position in which language seems to be a tool to one in which language becomes opaque and conditions one's view of oneself and the world. As Caleb escapes from Falkland's household he has valid reasons to fear his former employer: that is why he joins a gang of robbers who hide in a secluded forest. This episode is described from the position of a quasi-neutral observer; Caleb studies and analyzes these people, speculating on their behavior, character, social interactions, and organization as a group as if he were on an anthropological field trip. Shortly after having left the robbers, Caleb sits in a corner of an inn, disguised as a beggar, and listens to the tall tales that are being told concerning him. Initially, he is frightened, but as soon as he apprehends his own "invisibility," he begins to enjoy himself:

> By degrees I began to be amused at the absurdity of their tales, and the variety of falsehoods I heard asserted around me. My soul seemed to expand; I felt a pride in the self-possession and lightness of heart with which I could listen to the scene; and I determined to prolong and heighten the enjoyment. Accordingly, when they were withdrawn, I addressed myself to our hostess, a buxom, bluff, good humoured widow, and asked what sort of a man this Kit Williams might be? She replied that, as she was informed, he was as handsome, likely a lad, as any in four counties round; and that she loved him for his cleverness, by which he outwitted all the keepers they could set over him and made his way through stone walls, as if they were so many cobwebs. (Godwin 1977, 237)

Note how at the start his enjoyment is derived mainly from being an invisible observer, from being in control and knowing that he has exclusive access to knowledge. This self-reflexive enjoyment is described, in its autoerotic physicality, as narcissistic pride.

Immediately after this scene, Caleb encounters Forester's people, who are pursuing him. Although his beggar's disguise and assumed Irish brogue forestall his capture, he cannot remain calm:

> I could almost have imagined that I was the sole subject of general attention, and that the whole world was in arms to exterminate me. *The very idea tingled through every fibre of my frame. But, terrible as it appeared to my imagination, it did but give new energy to my purpose;* and I determined that I would not voluntarily resign the field, that is literally speaking my neck to the cord of the executioner, notwithstanding the greatest superiority in my assailants. (238)

Here, as in the scene at the inn, both autoerotic and narcissistic components are present, since Caleb's fear of being discovered can also be read as a wish to be discovered. His allusions to being "the sole subject of general attention" and "having the whole world in arms" against him reveal the close proximity of megalomania and paranoia.

This fear/wish of having everybody persecute him, of being the subject of everybody's attention, this sudden turn from a position of invisibility to one of total exposure, leaving one at the center of the gaze and under permanent surveillance, is at last realized in a manner that confirms Caleb's paranoia. Shortly after Caleb has boarded a boat in order to flee to Ireland, two officers come aboard and order his fellow passengers onto the deck for examination. "I was inexpressibly disturbed at the occurrence of such a circumstance in so unseasonable a moment. I took it for granted that it was of me that they were in search" (239). In fact, they are in search not of him but of two Irish mail robbers. His vague resemblance to the description of one of the robbers results in his arrest. This confusion confronts Caleb with the fact that no matter which identity he chooses, that identity is not determined by him, not expressive of what he would like it to be, but always determined by others, and in this sense an alienation.

Such an alienation of being within language can, however, be described in more specific terms. It is not Caleb's inability to create his own private language of expression that is at issue; rather, the matter needs to be understood in terms of the prevailing distribution of speaking and subject positions and the classed access to discursive genres. For the novel makes it clear that the variety of rhetorical and literary conventions and genres that Caleb wants to associate himself with, on the one hand, and those he can actually have access to, on the other, are distinguished according to class. When Caleb begins to listen with narcissistic pleasure to the tall tales being told about him as "Kit Williams," "a devilish cunning fellow," "breaking prison no less than five times" (236), he identifies with a stock character, the daring criminal who makes it into oral legends and ballads, a character encountered in print primarily on handbills, in prison and execution reports like the *Newgate Calendar,* and in fictional penny legends. Letting himself be interpellated this way, Caleb seems to be aware merely of the heroic status attached to the outlaw's subject position; he seems far less aware of the fact that, as Foucault argued in the essay "Lives of Infamous Men," for an insignificant man of the lower classes, there is no way of entering history, of entering any public record or discourse, except by coming into conflict with power (1979). Caleb despises his disguises as an Irish beggar and as a poor Jew as much as he despises the company of the robbers. Clearly he would prefer to fancy himself somebody more glamorous. In fact, when he emphasizes how much his early youth was influenced by books, he makes a point of "ennobling" his character by dissociating himself from the genres of common, everyday life: "I read, I devoured compositions of this sort. They took possession of my soul; and the effects they produced, were frequently discernible in my external appearance and my health. My curiosity however was not entirely ignoble: village anecdotes and scandal had no charms for me" (4).

Caleb's paranoid fantasy takes its cues from what Godwin would call "romance," that is, from what in the introductory pages I have characterized, with Godwin, as the "life-embellishing," ideological function of the "language of poetry." The plot of Caleb's trials and persecutions, however, draws on the genres associated with the "vulgar incidents" of everyday life. Although Caleb would like to associate himself with high heroic rhetoric, he cannot escape the popular robber legend. Disguised as a poor Jew he supports himself as a hack writer for a newspaper: "By a fatality for which I did not exactly know how to account, my thoughts frequently led me to the histories of celebrated robbers; and I retailed from time to time incidents and anecdotes of Cartouche, Gusman d'Alfarache and other memorable worthies, whose career was terminated upon the gallows or the scaffold" (259). Ironically it is his excellence in imitating the robber genre that attracts the attention of the thieftaker Gines, who happens to be the printer's brother:

> After having listened for some time upon this occasion to the wonderful stories which Gines in his rugged way condescended to tell, the printer felt an ambition to entertain his brother in his turn. He began to retail some of my stories of Cartouche and Gusman d'Alfarache. The attraction of Gines was excited. His first emotion was wonder; his second was envy and aversion. Where did the printer get these stories? This question was answered. (264)

Note how the paradoxical formulation, "my stories of Cartouche and Gusman d'Alfarache," undermines both the notion of authorial originality and an expressive textual model. What matters both in terms of exciting Gines's mimetic desire and in terms of establishing Caleb's "identity" is not the actual story, which can just as easily be borrowed, or the particularities of its narration but merely the position from which it is circulated.

After Caleb manages to escape and change his identity once more, Gines, in order to find him, finally makes Caleb's megalomaniac/paranoid fantasy of universal persecution literally true. Gines imitates in his turn the genre of the robber legend and publishes a halfpenny legend about Caleb Williams, together with a previously published handbill promising a hundred guineas for the latter's apprehension: "It was no longer Bow Street, it was a million of men, in arms against me," Caleb laments (270). Gines's publication is used twice against Caleb. The first time it leads to his arrest and brief imprisonment; the second time Falkland employs Gines to distribute the legend wherever Caleb wants to settle and by this means repeatedly destroys Caleb's reputation. So far, the compulsive, repetitive nature of Caleb's megalomaniac and paranoid plot can be described in terms of a desire to cast his life as a heroic romance, a narrative of fighting wild beasts and resisting terrible enemies, whereas in actuality the script available to him is merely that of the trivial penny legend, of the runaway prisoner, robber, or traitor. Yet this distribution of speaking and subject positions according to social class does not suffice to explain all the dynamics of Caleb's involvement with Falkland or the way that interpersonal relationships and affective economies are worked out in the novel.

In fact, even before Caleb is set on his paranoid course, before his escape from prison, this novel makes it clear that much as individuals are determined by their participation in different types of speech genres, their most secret wishes, avowed desires, and hidden fantasies also depend on the discourse of others. Consider, for instance, this passage in which Falkland disagrees with Forester on how to deal with Caleb:

I care not for consequences, replied Mr. Falkland, I will obey the dictates of my own mind. I will never lend my assistance to the reforming of mankind by axes and gibbets; I am sure things will never be as they ought, till honour and not law be the dictator of mankind, till vice is taught to shrink before the resistless might of inborn dignity, and not before the cold formality of statutes. If my calumniator were worthy of my resentment I would chastise him with my own sword, and not that of the magistrate; but in the present case I smile at his malice, and resolve to spare him, as the generous lord of the forest spares the insect that would disturb his repose.

The language you now hold, said Mr. Forester, is that of romance, and not of reason. Yet I cannot but be struck with the contrast exhibited before me of the magnanimity of virtue and the obstinate, impenetrable injustice of guilt. While your mind overflows with goodness, nothing can touch the heart of this thrice bred villain. I shall never forgive myself for having once been entrapped by his detestable arts. (175)

In both cases the attitude toward Caleb is primarily a reaction to a narcissistic injury. Falkland's speech betrays in particular the narcissistic charge that attaches to the construction of the other as an opponent. From a sociological argument against the efficacy of laws in the improvement of men, he tips over into a hyperbolic discourse that recalls God's final boasting in the Book of Job. His opponent is unworthy to be touched by his own sword, and hence he smiles at him like the "lord of the forest" at the insect.

Whereas I have emphasized so far the degree to which Caleb is driven by a narcissistic desire to identify with heroic stereotypes, now I would like to point out that not just any heroic stereotype will do; instead Caleb will borrow almost literally Falkland's own "language of romance." A good example can be found in the hyperbolic language Caleb uses to describe Gines's hostility toward him after he has left the gang of robbers: "I had fastened upon myself a second enemy, of that singular and dreadful sort, that is determined never to dismiss its animosity, as long as life shall endure. While Falkland, was the hungry lion whose roarings astonished and appalled me, Gines was a noxious insect, scarcely less formidable and tremendous, that hovered about my goings, and perpetually menaced me with the poison of his sting" (261). As Caleb ventriloquizes Falkland's "language of romance," Falkland's heroic position remains uncontested; the lowly insect's place is no longer filled by Caleb, however, but is now filled rather by Gines. Caleb dramatizes the danger of his own position by making Gines "scarcely less formidable and tremendous" than Falkland. He thus not only creates a rather incoherent, unintentionally comical picture of the "sublime insect" but also marks Gines as a stand-in for Falkland.

Why is Caleb obsessed with Falkland? Caleb demonstrates not only a strong narcissistic investment in being persecuted by some horrendous foe but also a certain obsession with this enemy as a physical threat, with being "stung," overwhelmed, or mortally wounded by him. Shortly after he has left the gang of robbers, when he still sees himself as an "invisible" hero with superhuman powers, he encounters Forester's people: "It was fortunate for me that my disguise was so complete, that the eye of Mr. Falkland itself could scarcely have penetrated it" (237). If his disguise is to give him any feeling of power and invulnerability, it has to protect him, not against Forester's people, who are indeed searching for him, but against "Falkland's penetrating eye." This substitution points toward the kernel of his paranoid fantasy: he not only wants to be the center of Falkland's attention, but he also derives physical excitement and pleasure from Falkland's threat to the protective layers surrounding him.

At this point it is possible to describe Caleb's paranoid construction of reality with more precision. His fear of being/wish to be persecuted can be broken down into two aspects: (1) it is articulated in terms of the fear that "everybody is in search of me, watching me, and trying to hunt me down," a fear that can be translated into the megalomaniac wish "I am a superman, a hero, terribly important, on everybody's mind and everywhere sought after," a wish informed by the narcissistic desire to assume the heroic postures of the "language of romance"; and (2) it entails a fixation on Falkland: "I have the most terrible foe, he might suddenly overwhelm me because he can penetrate all the protective layers of disguise by which I have surrounded myself." It is not immediately clear how this fear might be translated into a wish. As opposed to the first aspect of Caleb's paranoia, which can be discussed in terms of ideology or as an interpellation through the discourse of romance, this second aspect is fundamental in representing the mechanism according to which the experience of inequality is anchored in an economy of pain and pleasure. Once pleasure and pain are no longer quasi-natural opposites, once pleasure becomes connected with a state of excitement that originates in the fantasy of the painfully violent disruption of those layers of clothing and skin that would protect the body and the self, we are confronted with a position that in psychoanalytic terminology would be called masochistic.

One scene that explores Caleb's fear of being overwhelmed by somebody like Falkland is exemplary in showing the interdependence of Caleb's *fantasy,* this peculiar economy of pleasurable excitement derived from physical threat, with Caleb's apprehension of *reality.* It is through scenes like this that the novel comes closest to the fantastic, because it is here that a model of a rationally apprehensible universe is most thoroughly undermined. This scene is also prominently placed within the development of the plot. As I have mentioned, Caleb's "plot of paranoia" begins with his departure from the gang of robbers. This scene brings about his flight. Caleb is alone in the robbers' hiding place: he is exhausted, dreams of rest, peace, and quiet, and falls asleep. During his sleep he is frightened by a nightmare from which he wakes only to discover that an ugly old woman, hostess and housekeeper for the robbers, is about to murder him with a "butcher's cleaver." That he should defend himself against an ax murderess and flee her does not seem strange but seems perfectly rational, in line with the interests of self-protection. However, a closer look at the sequence of scenes preceding Caleb's flight makes us doubt precisely this rational economy of pleasure and pain, in which pain seems naturally opposed to pleasure, and in which avoidance of pain, self-protection, and the maximization of pleasure seem to belong together. Whereas the rational model of pleasure would presuppose clear distinctions between a daydream, a nightmare, and waking reality, the following sequence explores the interdependence of these phenomena and, ultimately, exposes the fantastic kernel of waking reality itself.

The passage can be divided into three main phases:

1. Reverie
   a. "I sighed for that solitude and obscurity, that retreat from the vexations of the world and the voice even of common fame, which I had proposed to myself when I broke my prison."
   b. "I pulled out a pocket Horace, the legacy of my beloved Brightwell! I read with avidity the epistle in which he so beautifully describes to Fuscus the grammarian, the pleasures of rural tranquility and independence."
   c. "The sun was rising, . . . the scene soothing the mind. . . . a confused reverie invaded my faculties. . . . [I] fell asleep."
2. Dream
   d. Some person, the agent of Falkland, was approaching to assassinate Caleb.
   e. "I imagined that the design of the murderer was to come upon me by surprise, that I was aware of his design, and yet by some fascination had no thought of evading it. I heard the steps of the murderer as he cautiously approached. I seemed to listen to his constrained, yet audible breathings."
3. Awakening
   f. "The idea became too terrible, I started, opened my eyes, and beheld the execrable hag before mentioned standing over me with a butcher's cleaver."
   g. "Her vigour was truly Amazonian, and at no time had I ever occasion to contend with a more formidable opponent." (231)

Since Caleb's nightmare is introduced by a daydream, it does not take much familiarity with Freudian psychoanalysis to see that the nightmare is also a disguised wish fulfillment. The issue gets more complicated, however, if we ask what kind of wish the dream is supposed to fulfill. Is the dream meant to protect the self-sufficient contentment of the sleeper, that state of narcissistic bliss, solitude, independence, and withdrawal from the world that is invoked in quotation 1a? In this case the dream would provide protection against awakening, a means of integrating external reality and the noise of the approaching footsteps into the dream world and of securing a state of contented passivity. Yet this understanding of the dream's function for the dreamer's psychical economy seems incomplete. It cannot explain why we are dealing with a nightmare rather than a happy dream, nor does it explain why the dreamer wakes up after all. First we should note that the longing for peace and quiet is not immediately fulfilled through a sleepy reverie; rather, it is elaborated and modified through a scene of reading. What appears to be the most intimate and strictly subjective wish—the fantasy of self-sufficiency—is in fact mediated, informed by the discourse of the other in the guise of the pocket edition of Horace that Caleb had received from a dear friend. Is it possible that the "agent of Falkland," the murderer, takes the place of that longed-for other, especially since the dream seems not frightful but captivating instead? "I imagined that the design of the murderer was to come upon me by surprise, that I was aware of his design, and yet by some fascination had no thought of evading it." As if he were a voyeur spying on himself at a moment when he was about to be overpowered in a passive and helpless position, Caleb's first affect is fascination, not fright. Furthermore, the awakening is triggered not by Caleb's attempt to flee his persecutor but by "the idea [that] became too terrible"—that is, Caleb flees from the scene of the fulfillment of his own wish. Waking becomes a denial of his wish—or a slightly modified version of his nightmare. Reality then for Caleb is both an escape from his desire and a censored version of it. It wasn't Falkland who was approaching, but merely the horrible old hag. She is both terribly frightful, a castrating witch with a butcher's cleaver, and also just an ugly old woman who seems safely undesirable. Although he describes her from the start as an object of repulsion and contempt, she is also an object of fascination (comparable to the robbers and especially Gines) because of her fierce energy.

In this reverie-dream-awakening sequence, the transition from phase to phase must be understood in terms of the tension between a narcissistic desire for self-sufficiency and independence, on the one hand, and an intensified longing for a masochistic physical pleasure derived from the shattering of the ego's boundaries or penetration of the cutaneous layer, on the other. Whereas phase one (quotations 1a and 1c) would mean perfect stasis and self-enclosure, phase two (1b, 2, and 3) involves contact with a social dimension, through the discourse of the other. Since phase two seems to be fundamentally organized along the lines of a disruptive, if not transgressive, fantasy, it seems that it is exactly here, within the realm of intersubjectivity, that fantasy becomes a force in the construction of reality or "things as they are." This nexus between fantasy and the social dimension, between *Caleb Williams*'s bizarre economy of pleasure and communication, will be the focus of the following section.

2

In this section I shall analyze *Caleb Williams*'s irrational economy of pleasure in relation to practices of communication. I shall also show how this novel foregrounds its own production in terms of a staging of sexuality. By sexuality I do not mean, of course, anything naturally related to genital intercourse or human reproduction; I refer rather to what, according to Foucault (1978), was being discursively fabricated and managed during the nineteenth century: the secret, key to the individual, that needed to be incessantly confessed, therapeutically treated, normalized, and liberated. One precondition for the discursive production of sexuality was the break with instinct: human beings were in principle free to choose; even what was unfit for them could become an object of desire; only on these grounds could human reason and perfectibility develop.[6] Another precondition was the fascination with the secret of the individual. It is here that I would locate the contribution of the genres of the Romantic fantastic and of the novels of Gothic paranoia like *Caleb Williams*, Hogg's *The Confessions of a Justified Sinner*, or Shelley's *Frankenstein*.

Let me begin with an exemplary passage in which Caleb explains why as Falkland's employee he tolerated a position of servile submission:

> When I first entered into Mr. Falkland's service, my personal habits were checked by the novelty of my situation, and my affections were gained by the high accomplishments of my patron. To novelty and its influence, curiosity had succeeded. Curiosity, so long as it lasted, was a principle stronger in my bosom than even the love of independence. To that I would have sacrificed my liberty or my life; to gratify it, I would have submitted to the condition of a West Indian Negro, or to the tortures inflicted by North American Savages. (143)

This passage weaves together the elements we have noted in considering Caleb's relationship to an other: curiosity, admiration, voluntary submission, and a willingness to endure pain. Does "curiosity" then mean for Caleb what "love" means in Godwin's essay "Of Love and Friendship," that is, the end of equality, the willing submission to hierarchy, intimidation, and the other's ability to inflict physical harm? To a certain degree, yes. Yet, whereas in Godwin's essay love and inequality arise from an idealized heterosexual relationship, here the willing submission to inequality and the pleasure-pain ambivalence are the side effects of any truly functioning and hence interesting social contact. The opposite of this relationship of inequality is not brotherly love and understanding but utter indifference. Consider Falkland's indifferent and cold relationship with his half brother Forester, which Caleb glosses in this manner: "They had scarcely one point of contact in their characters; Mr. Forester was incapable of giving Mr. Falkland that degree either of pain or pleasure, which can raise the soul into a tumult and deprive it for a while of tranquility and self-command" (140). Whereas the age of sensibility would also have celebrated the "frisson" of a certain "je ne sais quoi" that could make a relationship interesting and intense, it would never have done so at the cost of the familial and familiar. For Rousseau, for instance, the presupposition of mutual sympathy and understanding is that one conceives of one's fellow being as somebody similar to oneself. In *Caleb Williams* a lack of contact and communication is blamed not on dissimilarity but on a lack of difference or even an absence of inequality: any functioning social contact or bond presupposes a certain amount of friction or irritation, the ability of one partner to jolt the other out of a state of calm and control. Note both Caleb's emphasis on the disruptive impact required for the establishment of social contact and the fact that pleasure and pain seem here to be exchangeable.

Although there is no question that Caleb's desire is primarily worked out as male-male desire, we still have to examine whether and how this matters. If Caleb is at all defined in terms of his desire, the object of desire is subordinated to its aim. The fact that the object of his desire is male is of little importance in comparison to the fantasmatic component of his desire, a component visible in the scenarios that define the type and the nature of the specific pleasure that Caleb seeks. To put it crudely, this novel is not yet about "sexual orientation" as an issue of "identity politics." Against Sedgwick's reading of *Caleb Williams* and Hogg's *Confessions* in terms of homophobia and "repressed homosexuality," I would argue that the object of desire has not yet become a problem. Instead, these novels are about the production of sexuality in the first instance: by joining a confessional, autobiographical genre to a notion of the sexual that is devoid of any "natural," "instinctual," or "rational" prototype, this novel provides a model for constructing an individual's identity in terms of his specific, highly problematic, organization of pleasure.

If indeed *Caleb Williams* participates in the creation of "sexuality" as the subject's defining mark, his or her innermost secret and determining feature, we shall have to describe in greater detail the axes along which such "sexuality" unfolds. In the beginning there was a transgression. It is not desire for a forbidden object of love that defines Caleb but the intrusive desire for a "forbidden" knowledge. Caleb is puzzled by Falkland's inexplicable moods. After he inadvertently surprises Falkland kneeling before a trunk and witnesses Falkland's excessive anger over this intrusion, he comes to believe that the trunk holds the key to Falkland's enigma:

> After two or three efforts, in which the energy of uncontrollable passion was added to my bodily strength, the fastening gave way, the trunk opened, and all that I sought was at once within my reach. (132)

> No spark of malignity had harboured in my soul. I had always reverenced the sublime mind of Mr. Falkland; I reverenced it still. My offence had merely been a mistaken thirst of knowledge. (133)

This confessional moment directs us toward a transgressive thirst for knowledge, fueled by a combination of intense physical and emotional excitement, as a crucial clue to Caleb's subjectivity.

Caleb's account of how he managed to confirm his suspicion that Falkland was Tyrrel's murderer represents an intensely climactic moment in the novel. First Caleb observes Falkland while the latter serves as judge in a murder trial. Then Caleb finds himself alone in a garden. It is in this overdetermined locale that he enjoys the knowledge he has gained from Falkland's visible uneasiness during the trial. The allusion to the biblical fall is obvious, yet the connection between the enjoyment of the forbidden fruit and the knowledge gained from the transgression deserves further commentary. The distribution of the two scenes onto different locales divides the issue of transgression, enjoyment, and knowledge into two stages, a primary one of immediacy and absorption and a secondary one of reflexivity. Surprisingly, however, full enjoyment is part of the second stage, during which Caleb is alone in the garden.

Caleb hopes to be able to study Falkland during the trial from the vantage point of an invisible, neutral spectator: "I will watch him without remission. I will trace all the mazes of his thought. Surely at such a time his secret anguish must betray itself. Surely, if it be not my own fault, I shall now be able to discover the state of his plea before the tribunal of unerring justice" (126). However, this Olympian gaze is very quickly replaced by a most intimate exchange of looks:

> The examination had not proceeded far before he chanced to turn his eye to the part of the room where I was. It happened in this, as in some preceding instances; we exchanged a silent look by which we told volumes to each other. Mr. Falkland's complexion turned from red to pale, and from pale to red. I perfectly understood his feelings, and would willingly have withdrawn myself. But it was impossible; my passions were too deeply engaged; I was rooted to the spot; though my own life, that of my master, or almost of a whole nation had been at stake, I had no power to change my position. (126)

Although the moment of mutual transparency of feeling and of a silent exchange of meaningful looks is rendered in the language of sensibility and love, this scene is taken to a very different conclusion. The fact that each knows what the other is thinking and feeling does not establish the equal and symmetrical relationship that we know from Enlightenment models of friendship and understanding—quite the contrary. Caleb is hurled from a position of superiority into one of paralysis, in which a passion stronger than he takes over and cancels any rational concerns that might fall under the rubric of self-preservation. Caleb's indiscreet, voyeuristic gaze is not the lone source of the all-powerful sensation that immobilizes him. That sensation is irresistibly intensified when Caleb is caught in mid-gaze by the one whom he is painfully invading. It is only because Falkland returns his look that Caleb's gaze acquires a sadistic component, while at the same time his own passivity bears a masochistic trait. Thus this scene rehearses the sexualization of the desire to know, to see, to observe, by investing this drive with a passion, energy, and intensity that have no regard for the calculus of happiness, or even for the preservation of the lives of those involved or for the survival of the nation at large. If one were to pinpoint what triggers this sexualization, one would have to conclude that it is the moment of interruption, of loss of control, of a momentary intrusion from the outside.

In the garden the traumatic emotions of the courtroom scene are transformed into a combination of visceral knowledge and intense physical pleasure:

> I no sooner conceived myself sufficiently removed from all observation, than my thoughts forced their way spontaneously to my tongue, and I exclaimed in a fit

of uncontrollable enthusiasm: "This is the murderer! The Hawkinses were innocent! I am sure of it! I will pledge my life for it! It is discovered! Guilty upon my soul!" While I thus proceeded with hasty steps along the most secret paths of the garden, and from time to time gave vent to the tumult of my thoughts in involuntary exclamations, *I felt as if my animal system had undergone a total revolution. My blood boiled within me. I was conscious to a kind of rapture for which I could not account. I was solemn, yet full of rapid emotion, burning with indignation and energy. In the very tempest and hurricane of the passions, I seemed to enjoy the most soul-ravishing calm. I cannot better express the then state of my mind, than by saying, I was never so perfectly alive as at that moment.* (130; emphasis added)

The conclusion Caleb draws from observing Falkland during the trial, his certainty about Falkland's guilt, is not reached through a rational process; rather it emerges from what seems an involuntary chant accompanied by an intense physical arousal composed of the contradictory sensations of satisfied calm and energetic passion. The knowledge he has gained through this transgressive act, moreover, entails something more than confirmation of his old suspicion that Falkland was guilty of Tyrrel's murder. What matters is not merely factual confirmation but the erotic and self-reflexive dimension of this knowledge: "I felt, what I had no previous conception of, that it was possible to love a murderer, and, as I then understood it, the worst of murderers" (130).

Whereas the climax of Caleb's curiosity is played out in these two scenes in the courtroom and the garden, the "origin" of Caleb's transgressive desire for knowledge lies elsewhere. From the start he is fascinated by Falkland's enigmatic character: "He appeared a total stranger to everything which usually bears the appelation of pleasure" (6). Caleb gains access to Falkland's enigma, his entirely different relationship to pleasure, through three consecutive encounters, each promising to hold the key to the preceding enigma. Yet, instead of resolving the riddle of Falkland's relationship to pleasure, this sequence of encounters radically reorganizes Caleb's own relationship to pleasure.

Let me quote at length from the narration of Caleb's accidental encounter with Falkland beside the mysterious trunk:

Who is there? The voice was Mr. Falkland's. The sound of it thrilled my very vitals. I endeavoured to answer, but my speech failed, and being incapable of any other reply, I instinctively advanced within the door into the room. Mr. Falkland was just risen from the floor upon which he had been sitting or kneeling. His face betrayed strong symptoms of confusion. With a violent effort however these symptoms vanished, and instantaneously gave place to a countenance sparkling with rage. Villain, cried he, what has brought you here? . . . Do you think you shall watch my privacies with impunity? I attempted to defend myself. Begone, devil! rejoined he. Quit the room, or I will trample you into atoms. (8)

What is emphasized is the suddenness of this first traumatic encounter. Caleb is caught off guard: he becomes an accidental witness to Falkland's guilty behavior, and Falkland threatens him as if he had been spying on his "privacies" deliberately.

The next encounter is no less enigmatic and sudden; however, the emotional tenor of the scene has changed.

His behaviour, which was always kind, was now doubly attentive and soothing. He seemed to have something of which he wished to disburthen his mind, but to want words in which to convey it. I looked at him with anxiety and affection. He made two unsuccessful efforts, shook his head, and then, putting five guineas into my hand, pressed it in a manner that I could feel proceeded from a mind pregnant with various emotions, though I could not interpret them. Having done this, he seemed immediately to recollect himself, and to take refuge in the usual distance and solemnity of his manner. (8)

This scene establishes Caleb's complicity with Falkland's guilty secret: he now retrospectively learns to associate Falkland's outburst of violence with an outpouring of attentiveness. To compare Falkland's behavior toward Caleb with the behavior of a child molester toward his victim does not seem that far-fetched. Alternately, one might think of a more generalized scenario of the infant's sexualization as seduction through the encounter with adult sexuality, the enigmatic, guilty adult unconscious.[7] Certainly the second enigmatic scene suggests to Caleb that Falkland wants something from him, that he is implicated in Falkland's desire. This encounter transforms Falkland's enigma, "what does he want?" into Caleb's question, "what does he want from me?"

The third and last element in the metonymic chain of enigmatic elements is the biographical narrative about Falkland recounted by Collins, Falkland's steward. (It constitutes almost the entirety of book 1.) Caleb is told this story after he confides to Collins the confusion he felt over Falkland's offer of the five guineas. Thus the question that motivates Falkland's biography becomes "What is Falkland's secret, which he has paid me to keep silent about?" Falkland's story is supposed to solve the riddle of his personality, explain his inability to enjoy normal sociability and its pleasures. At the same time it is to provide Caleb with information that requires his utmost discretion. Its effect on Caleb, however, is utterly different. Instead of answering his questions about Falkland, it provokes his determination to spy on him. And instead of ensuring his discretion, it leads to Caleb's retelling and publicizing of Falkland's biography. Note that for the most part it is Caleb who, for the sake of simplifying the speech situation—as he tells his reader—takes over Collins's role as narrator of Falkland's story. Caleb's ventriloquizing, of course, also supports our sense of his strong identification with that story.

Against the backdrop of the two traumatic encounters motivating it, namely, the trunk scene and the scene in which Falkland offers money to Caleb, Falkland's story is the narrative articulation of guilt and adult sexuality, a "case history" of individual pathology beyond a rationally accessible pleasure principle. At least this is the way it is viewed by Caleb, whose desire and sense of pleasure it fundamentally reorganizes. It is Falkland's story that makes Caleb articulate his suspicion/fantasy "what if Falkland were a murderer?" for the first time. And it is in the same context that his desire for knowledge and sense of pleasure are sexualized:

> the idea having once occurred to my mind it was fixed there forever. My thoughts fluctuated from conjecture to conjecture, but this was the centre about which they revolved. I determined to place myself as a watch upon my patron.
>
> The instant I had chosen this employment for myself, I found a strange sort of pleasure in it. To do what is forbidden always has its charms, because we have an indistinct apprehension of something arbitrary and tyrannical in the prohibition. To be a spy upon Mr. Falkland! That there was danger in the employment served to give an alluring pungency to the choice. I remembered the stern reprimand I had received, and his terrible looks; and the recollection gave a kind of tingling sensation, not altogether unallied to enjoyment. The farther I advanced, the more the sensation was irresistible. I seemed to myself perpetually upon the brink of being countermined, and perpetually roused to guard my designs. The more impenetrable Mr. Falkland was determined to be, the more uncontrollable was my curiosity. (107; 108)

Caleb is actually less concerned with gaining knowledge about Falkland than with enjoying the titillating intimacy that being his spy entails.

The source of excitement lies in the anticipated repetition of Falkland's anger. He states quite explicitly that to be Falkland's spy is a way to replay the traumatic scenario of surprising him at the trunk.

When Caleb seeks out Falkland's company, when he lures him by way of an assumed naïveté into conversations that have an unmistakable pertinence to Falkland's story, when he seduces him into forgetting himself and betraying his emotions, he is quite aware of the asymmetry of their situations:

> There was indeed an eminent difference between his share in the transaction and mine. I had some consolation in the midst of my restlessness. Curiosity is a principle that carries its pleasures as well as its pain along with it. The mind is urged by a perpetual stimulus; it seems as if it were continually approaching to the end of its race; and, as the insatiable desire for satisfaction is its principle of conduct, so it promises itself in that satisfaction an unknown gratification, which seems as if it were capable of fully compensating any injuries that may be suffered in the career. But to Mr. Falkland there was no consolation. What he endured in the intercourse between us appeared to be gratuitous evil. (122)

In this formulation we find probably the most elaborate articulation of the special kind of pleasure at stake in this novel. Neither the antithesis of pain nor a physical sensation that resembles the state of peace resulting from the satiation of some vital function, pleasure for Caleb is, on the contrary, a state of arousal and excitement informed by traumatic disruption, a shattering of the ego's sense of security and self-preservation. In fact, if there is any "organ" or erogenous zone involved, it is one related not to the body but rather to the mind which receives the stimuli. This purely mental and fantasmatic aspect of sexuality is also relevant to the "sexual relation" between Caleb and Falkland. Our analysis of the courtroom scene has revealed that to the extent that Caleb's pleasure involves an other and escapes its autoerotic confinement, it is informed by both sadistic and masochistic traits. The citation above confirms this: as Caleb enjoys the thrill of imagining himself threatened by Falkland's violent passions, and enjoys a masochistic fantasy of suffering the infliction of pain from a superior opponent, he also enjoys his own mental torture of Falkland.

The last passage I want to examine is from the end of the novel and traces Caleb's thoughts as he takes the decision to come out of hiding. Having moved from place to place, incapable of escaping Grimes's persecution of him, Caleb at last decides to break his loyal silence about Falkland's secret. He decides to make use of Falkland's confession and accuse him of Tyrrel's murder. The postponement of this decision provided the material for a large portion of the novelistic plot, notably, for Caleb's attempts to live a fantasy life of romance and to flirt with being persecuted by a sublime enemy. When I described Caleb's struggle to insert himself into some glamorous heroic genre, a struggle ultimately thwarted when the cheap robber legend and the broadsheet catch up with him, I referred to Foucault's "Lives of Infamous Men" (1979). In this essay Foucault argues that the only opportunity to enter history and acquire a momentarily heroic stature that is accessible to the common, insignificant man lies in a brush with power and a subsequent court hearing. It is finally exactly that speech situation—the courtroom confrontation—that Caleb resorts to. This courtroom scene not only puts an end to the paranoid romance but also, as we shall see below, provides Caleb with a rationale for becoming an author, at least for documenting his miserable life.

The actual courtroom scene—which culminates in Falkland's breakdown and acknowledgment of Caleb's version of events as well as in Caleb's overwhelming sense of guilt toward Falkland—is relegated to the postscript of the novel.[8] The last page of the novel before the postscript relays Caleb's reflections as he prepares himself for the coming confrontation. Breaking my quotation of this passage into numbered sections, I shall mark three different "truth scenarios," each of which is reminiscent of prior episodes of the novel:

1. No, *I will use no daggers! I will unfold a tale—*! I will show thee for what thou art, and *all the men that live shall confess my truth!—*Didst thou imagine that I was altogether passive, a mere worm, organized to feel sensations of pain, but no emotion of resentment? . . .

I will tell a tale—! The justice of the country shall hear me! The elements of nature in universal uproar shall not interrupt me! I will speak with a voice more fearful than thunder—Why should I be supposed to speak from any dishonourable motive? I am under no prosecution now! . . . Thou hast shown no mercy; and thou shalt receive none!—I must be calm! Bold as a lion, yet collected!

2. This is a moment pregnant with fate. I know—I think I know—that I will be triumphant, and crush my seemingly omnipotent foe. . . . His fame shall not be immortal, as he thinks. *These papers shall preserve the truth:* they shall one day be published, and then the world shall do justice on us both. . . . *How impotent are the precautions of man against the eternally existing laws of the intellectual world?* This Falkland has invented against me every species of foul accusation. . . . He

has kept his scenters of human prey for ever at my heels. He may hunt me out of the world,—In vain! *With this engine, this little pen I defeat all his machinations; I stab him in the very point he was most solicitous to defend!* . . .

3. *The pen lingers in my trembling fingers!*—Is there anything I have left unsaid?—*The contents of the fatal trunk from which all my misfortunes originated, I have never been able to ascertain.* I once thought it contained *some murderous instrument or relique* connected with the fate of the unhappy Tyrrel. I am now persuaded that *the secret it incloses is a faithful narrative of that and its concomitant transactions, written by Mr. Falkland,* and reserved in case of the worst, that, if by any unforeseen event his guilt should come to be fully disclosed, it might contribute to redeem the wreck of his reputation.

But the truth or falsehood of this conjecture is of little moment. If Falkland shall never be detected to the satisfaction of the world, such a narrative will probably never see the light. In that case this story of mine may amply, severely perhaps, supply its place. (314–16; emphasis added)

The first scenario is the anticipated confrontation in the courtroom: Caleb invests himself with the sublime rhetoric of God thundering at Job, depicting the courtroom scenario as a heroic combat or duel between himself and Falkland. Whereas the first truth scenario relies on speech, Caleb's oral account of Falkland's murder of Tyrrel, the second scenario assigns to Caleb's autobiographical memoirs the function of securing his reputation sub specie aeternitatis, should the courtroom confrontation fail. Here the scenario of the duel is replaced by one of murdering, in which Caleb's published account will "stab" Falkland's reputation. In this slide from a duel to a murder, Caleb imitates Falkland's relation with Tyrrel. He also imitates the court case Falkland judged, which concerned a peasant lad who, having been challenged, agreed to combat and then immediately killed his challenger. Indeed, the third and last truth scenario spells out the parasitic relationship between Caleb's and Falkland's stories: Caleb speculates that Falkland's account of Tyrrel's murder might very well be replaced by his own story. This substitution is considerable: whereas in the second scenario Caleb's writing is supposed to kill Falkland's reputation, in the third it is supposed to supplant a text written to rescue Falkland's reputation. Both expectations are actually met after the courtroom confrontation: Falkland dies of grief and shame, Caleb feels like his murderer and publishes his memoirs with the intent that Falkland's "story may be fully understood" (326).

By the end of the novel, to be sure, fame and reputation are no longer at issue; instead we find a hermeneutic concern for understanding an individual in his particularity. And it is here that we can situate the proximity of this novel's generic conventions to the psychiatric case history and the detective novel. Henceforth what defines an individual is not an exceptional life, a list of heroic achievements. Rather, it is some mysterious quality that exerts an intense fascination upon others. Caleb's hermeneutics is that of the detective who is determined to decipher an unreadable text, to find the heinous crime at the bottom of a riddle. It is not an open-ended search for knowledge but one driven by a desire to investigate and represent something horrible and unspeakable. I have shown how the traumatic encounter with the enigma is closely related to what we might call "sexuality." In the passage quoted above one crucial element of Caleb's obsession and involvement with Falkland reappears. The trunk with the secret becomes the link between the truth status of the narrative and sexuality. Earlier I described the trunk as a metonymy for mysterious adult sexuality and the guilty unconscious, which are first encountered in an accidental and traumatic way but subsequently become a seductive lure and pretext for the fantasmatic organization of pleasure. Earlier, Caleb tells us, he thought the trunk contained "some murderous instrument or relique"; now he believes "the secret it incloses is a faithful narrative" of Tyrrel's murder, which, he concludes, can just as well be replaced by his own narrative. Recalling the well-established eighteenth-century usage of "instrument" and "engine" for the male genitals, and insisting on the double entendre of "trunk," we can spell out the metonymic-metaphoric chain that has been set up through these truth scenarios and their recombinations: Caleb can finish his narrative, the novel has almost reached its conclusion, once Caleb's own adult sexuality can take the place of Falkland's. Note, however, that the kernel of the secret, be it the pen, the engine, the instrument, or the written document, that which is behind the enigmatic signifier, Falkland's and then Caleb's sexuality, is not a signified but merely another signifier: a piece of writing.

Falkland's narrative and Caleb's are, of course, intricately interrelated. Indeed, Caleb's narration of Falkland's story constitutes a third of *Caleb Williams.* How do we understand the strange claim that on the one hand, Falkland's secret, the key to his subjectivity, is contained in his story, the kernel of which is his sexuality, while on the other hand, that story can be replaced or supplanted by another, namely, Caleb's story and sexuality? One conclusion we can draw relates to the way this novel constructs sexuality in the first place. Remember that sexuality is not something that is a priori proper to a particular individual. The notion of the sexual as the individual's secret, one awaiting confession or extraction, is already part of Caleb's own sexual fantasy. Rather, sexuality is first of all the effect of a traumatic encounter with an enigmatic signifier (with the other's opaque behavior, story, etc.). It then becomes fantasy's mechanism for regulating the pleasurable repetition of the traumatic encounter. Thus sexuality can neither be defined exclusively as the imposition of a cultural, political, or ideological code on the behavior and affect of an individual subject nor be reduced to something pertaining to a "natural" organization of bodily pleasure. Before the fall there is no natural sexuality that has a definite aim and object. Sexuality is highly problematic in terms of the concepts of pleasure and satisfaction, and its object differs from the one found in the standard heterosexual "romance" pattern. Thus Godwin's novel situates the constitution of subjectivity not only in the realm of the confessional, in the urge and incitement to discourse, but also within the technologies of power and pleasure. At the same time, indeed through the same moves, *Caleb Williams* invokes the discourse of individuality and freedom, the fall from instinct into freedom, as perversion and illusion or delusion.

Notes

1. See the preface to Godwin 1977: "The question now afloat in the world respecting THINGS AS THEY ARE, is the most interesting that can be presented to the human mind. While one party pleads for reformation and change, the other extols in the warmest terms the existing constitution of society. It seemed as if something would be gained for the decision of this question, if that constitution were faithfully developed in its practical effects" (1). This preface, dated 12 May 1794, was withdrawn from the original edition, in compliance with the alarmed wishes of the booksellers.
2. For an interesting analysis of *Caleb Williams* in terms of Godwin's relationship to Burke, see Butler 1982. Butler sees in Falkland a fictional version of Burke.
3. "It was like what has been described of the eye of omniscience pursuing the guilty sinner, and darting a ray that awakens him to new sensibility, at the very moment that, otherwise exhausted nature would lull him into a temporary oblivion of the reproaches of his conscience. Sleep fled from my eyes. No walls could

hide me from the discernment of this hated foe. Everywhere his industry was unwearied to create for me new distress. . . . My sensations at certain periods amounted to insanity" (Godwin 1977, 305–6).

4. "For myself I looked round upon my walls, and forward upon the premature death I had too much reason to expect; I consulted my own heart that whispered nothing but innocence; and I said, This is society. This is the object, the distribution of justice, which is the end of human reason. For this sages have toiled, and the mid-night oil has been wasted. This!" (Godwin 1977, 182).

5. Important in this respect is the work of Jean Laplanche, who attempts to rethink psychoanalysis without Oedipus—probably the most normative model for the development of the psychical apparatus and its different components. See especially *Life and Death in Psychoanalysis* (1976) and *New Foundations for Psychoanalysis* (1989).

6. See Immaneul Kant's "Conjectural Beginning of Human History" ("Mutmaßlicher Anfang der Menschengeschichte") in Kant 1963.

7. On primal seduction and the primal scene, see Laplanche 1989, 89–151.

8. To be precise: this is the second, published version of the postscript. Initially Godwin had written an ending that suggests that Caleb becomes entirely mad after Falkland denies everything.

Jann Matlock

11 The Limits of Reformism

The Novel, Censorship, and the Politics of Adultery in Nineteenth-Century France

> People of France! Great and generous people! . . . They insult your name, what does it matter to you! They spit in the face of your repudiated history and you laugh! They take away your children to send them to die from the plague and the Saharan winds, so you have other children! They imprison your writers, they ruin your press, so you stop reading. They close your theaters, so you do without and go drinking. They confiscate your liberties along with your honor, so you say that you had too many liberties and that honor is only a word! —Auguste Luchet, preface to *Le Nom de famille*

❧ As his fourth novel went to press in December 1841, Auguste Luchet could hardly have predicted that he would soon become one of those writers to whom he alluded in his preface, condemned to imprisonment by the July Monarchy government.[1] In March 1842, nevertheless, in an unprecedented move on the part of the state, Luchet was tried for every offense available to the censors—for "exciting hatred and contempt against the government, troubling public peace by exciting contempt and hatred of citizens against various classes of people, offending public morality, and deriding the religious values held by the majority of the French people."[2] In a trial that lasted only one day, Luchet was found guilty and condemned to the radical penalty of two years in prison and a one-thousand-franc fine. His novel was ordered destroyed. Hounded into exile, the novelist would be made an example for others who attempted to use the genre of the novel as an instrument of political protest.

The trial of Luchet's *Nom de famille* is remarkable for the way it cut across a series of battles—over adultery, divorce, class, national identity, and especially, the state's power to regulate morality—at a key moment in the transformation of the novel in France. Although we have traditionally looked to the 1857 trial of *Madame Bovary* as the watershed moment in state intervention in the novel, many of the problematics thematized in ironic ways by Flaubert's Second Empire novel were in fact articulated by novels of the July Monarchy, and in particularly trenchant ways by *Le Nom de famille* and its trial. As this essay will argue, the battle over Luchet's work not only fixed the stakes for the participation of the novel in politics and social reform for decades to come but also set new boundaries for literary and press transgressions that long fueled disputes among critics, novelists, and the state.

The trial of *Le Nom de famille* was a radical new departure for the July Monarchy state. Though Louis-Philippe's regime had years before betrayed the promises of free speech guaranteed by its Charter—as the preface to Luchet's censored novel lamented—pursuing the press with increasing rapacity, preventing the performance of plays, and policing visual imagery before its distribution, prior to 1842 the novel had escaped political prosecution.[3] And although some twenty works with explicit sexual content were censored annually—many of them reprints of eighteenth-century works like those of Sade and Mirabeau[4]—only three novels seem to have been seized for political reasons by the July Monarchy state. Luchet's was the first, followed almost immediately by the confiscation of an autobiographical novel by a youthful first-time author. Another "literary trial" would occur in 1847, this time of a *roman-feuilleton* in a Fourierist newspaper, with serious reprisals for the government.[5] While these later episodes of censorship seemed to assault a kind of novel and, in the later case, the kind of newspaper that published it, Luchet's unusually severe punishment spotlighted him as the kind of writer the state would no longer tolerate. As the author of three previous novels, former editor of *Le Temps* in 1830, and coauthor of several widely discussed plays, Luchet had a public presence that ensured that the prosecution of his work would not escape notice.[6] Most surprising given his harsh sentence, Luchet's contemporaries in the press did not rise up in vigorous protest as they had in previous cases of censorship. *Le Nom de famille* had touched a nerve, and even those living the daily threat of the censors were hesitant to condone its tactics.

Because Luchet's novel, like those of many of his contemporaries, took as themes several of the most disputed issues of his era, the trial must be read in the context of an ever-spiraling fear that literary texts could elicit resistance, revolt, and social change. Like the trial of Flaubert's *Madame Bovary* in 1857, the trial of *Le Nom de famille* turned on perceptions of private life and the possibility of literature to promote change in the most intimate spheres of society.[7] Also like Flaubert's trial, that of Luchet exposed the stakes of the battles in which the novel had come to participate and the fragility of the institutions it was seen to threaten. This essay explores the politics of both this novel and its condemnation in the context of mid-nineteenth-century debates about the novel. It seeks to explain the investments of the state of 1842 in censoring this text and the terms through which the novel as an increasingly legitimized cultural institution had come to threaten state interests. I look first, therefore, at this novel's position amid debates about the genre in July Monarchy France. I then turn to the specific social battle to which this novel lent its reformist plots, over the possible reinstitution of divorce after the Revolution of 1830. The social novel of adultery—of which Luchet's work is an exemplary manifestation—waged its own literary war in a battle particularly destabilizing to the July Monarchy regime. And yet, as I show in the third section of this essay, nothing about the content of Luchet's novel marks it as extreme enough to have warranted either the censorship of the state or the silence of the author's contemporaries. One must, I argue, look beyond its content at the aesthetic and political battles in which this novel set new boundaries. This essay argues, ultimately, that the trial of Luchet's novel is the culmination of a battle waged by and against the literary itself. If Luchet ultimately lost that battle, his censorship trial demonstrates how high the stakes had become. Read today, both for its literary criminality and for its participation in a network of battles over the novel as a cultural institution, Luchet's text has a curious way of refiguring the debates in which it became the scapegoat, and of illuminating the forces at work in the new novel itself.

Monarchy Plots

Luchet's 1841 work turned on a central dilemma of the nineteenth-century European novel: what is a woman to do whose marriage does not satisfy her desires? Like dozens of July Monarchy novelists before him, including Honoré de Balzac, George Sand, and Eugène Sue, Luchet positioned his characters amid moral dilemmas that seemed inevitably to lead to transgression of the accepted moral values of his era. If, as Tony Tanner (1979) has suggested, the nineteenth-century novel's preoccupation with adultery articulates in thematic terms the genre's very transgressive mode,[8] nothing could be more exemplary in this domain than the plot line of Luchet's *Nom de famille.* The Marquise de Tancarville, happily married to a man of similar interests and standing, finds herself unable to have a child. Although divorce, still legal in the Empire of the novel's opening moments, might have freed her to gratify her maternal desires in a new alliance, the Marquise instead throws herself into the river. She is saved by the novel's hero, Georges Maurice, who is referred to as *le républicain* by the narrator of a work that stolidly opposes Maurice's values to those of the aristocrats whose life he comes to transform. Believing himself loved, Maurice spends an idyllic period with the Marquise during her husband's absence from Rouen, only to find himself dropped flat when she becomes pregnant. Disconsolate, the Republican, who has never told his lover that his own father condemned hers to the guillotine during the previous revolution, turns to warfare against the aristocracy that has betrayed him. Appearing at the child's christening to announce his paternity, he is turned out as a madman. Years later, by a turn of events as typical of the July Monarchy novel as of the theatrical melodrama on which it drew, Maurice finds himself convalescing in the very chateau in which the Marquise lies dying. Summoned to her bedside, he witnesses her confession to her husband that the man driven from their home a decade before had indeed spoken the truth: the child they have been raising is not only the fruit of adultery but the result of the Marquise's desperate manipulations of her husband's legal responsibilities of paternity. Forgiven in her dying moments by the benevolent Marquis, she confides her son Ernest to the care of both "fathers." Maurice is to raise the boy, posing as his tutor, while the Marquis continues to confer his name, rank, and fortune upon his wife's adulterous offspring.

Unlike the forlorn children of aristocrats in other novels of this era, of which Sue's Fleur-de-Marie is a stunning example, who demonstrate their high birth through noble actions despite their fall into the most debasing of circumstances, Ernest de Tancarville is rotten to the core. Unable to appreciate his tutor's loving upbringing and contemptuous of social conventions, he refuses to bow to any moral code, whether that of his biological father or that of the man whose name he bears. Although Maurice's imprisonment for republican activities prevents him from blocking Ernest's marriage to a woman he believes his son does not deserve, the father miraculously escapes prison to discover the misery of the young woman, herself the adulterous progeny of his best friend, republican journalist Lagrange. No sooner do we learn Marie's true parentage than Ernest has embroiled himself in a newspaper scandal that leads him to kill the aging Lagrange in a duel. Horrified by her husband's murder of her father, Marie resists her husband's socially endorsed marital rights and refuses to return to his household. Overwhelmed by the corruption of his adopted son, the Marquis finally disavows Ernest publicly, naming for the first time his son's true parentage. But before the Marquis has finished the speech that would forever limit Ernest's political aspirations, the son runs Maurice through with a sword, leaving the stunned Marquis languishing from shock. At the end of the novel that, in the words of Luchet's prosecutor, has involved a triple patricide ("Justice Criminelle" 1842, 1), the name of the family borne by Ernest remains intact. The last two paragraphs of *Le Nom de famille* leave doubt that this now murderous character is ever prosecuted. After the death of the Marquis we are told, "There was no will: Ernest was the Marquis de Tancarville and master of two hundred fifty thousand pounds of income" (Luchet [1841], 2:196).[9]

Innumerable works contain political allusions "keener than those we find in Luchet's book," argued defense attorney Jacques Favre in the trial of 10 March 1842 ("Justice Criminelle" 1842, 2). Reading from the works of Théophile Gautier and Jacques Peuchet, Favre sought to demonstrate that any number of other novels contained "obscenities or political ideas contrary to the established order," none of which had led to censorship despite their potential offensiveness ("Justice Criminelle" 1842, 2).[10] His client's work, he argued, had been unfairly scapegoated. What, indeed, differentiated Luchet's novel from dozens of others published in the previous decade that waged frontal assaults on the family, marriage, the aristocracy, and the government?

To listen to the critics of the July Monarchy novel, any number of works might have been targeted for the same offenses as *Le Nom de famille*. Seen as heirs to the revolutionary demands of 1830 and precursors of those of 1848, the novels of this period were targeted for every imaginable social ill by conservative critics bent on salvaging what they called religious, family, and moral values. For prize-winning essayist Jules Jolly, "insurrection" had been forced to retreat after 1830, but it had found a home in literature (1851, 10). Speaking to everyone and comprehensible by all, the novel gave free berth to dogmatism and combative theories, wrote critic Eugène Poitou in 1857: "everywhere we . . . see the same idea, . . . the same falsifying of truth, the same slander against society" (1857, 9, 82). Writing in 1841 in the very month of publication of Luchet's novel, G. de Molènes of the influential *Revue des deux mondes* condemned popular novelists like Sue and Frédéric Soulié, whom he saw as tailoring their works to the taste of an ever more avid public in what he called an "equally disastrous double effect" of the public on writers and of writers on the public (1841, 1018).

The explosion of the *roman-feuilleton* into the daily press in 1836 had, as de Molènes suggested, radically transformed the ways novels were read. Appearing several times weekly in newspapers of all political persuasions, novels like those of Sue, Soulié, Balzac, and Sand alternated their episodes with reviews of the Salon, theater, and other novels, often authored by those, like Luchet, who continued to publish in volume form alone. The July Monarchy interest in the novel, fostered by its increasing visibility, was further spurred along by its very vitality. Some fifty to a hundred new novels were published in volume form annually, made affordable to a bourgeois public by cheaper paper and printing methods.[11] Reading rooms, rising in numbers from the late Restoration throughout the 1840s, permitted men and women of all classes to rent newspapers and books for a minuscule fee. Literacy rates rose sharply, especially for women and the working classes.[12] More important—possibly due to these transformed conditions for reading—the novel had begun to delve into new subjects, becoming ever more concerned with the present, the social world, and the potentially marginal individuals in the midst of polite society. The new novel of the July Monarchy, in both its serialized and bound forms, had gained a much greater public and with it a new legitimacy, even as conservatives complained that it compromised all that society ought to hold dear.[13]

The novel's critics above all attacked its novelty, its insistence on treating the contemporary world and the socially relevant, its concern with much debated issues like divorce, adultery, bastardy, the plight of workers, and paternal, marital, and women's rights. Sue was condemned for inciting the working class to revolution. Soulié was assaulted for tempting women to duplicity and crime. Balzac was criticized for seducing women into adultery. Sand was imagined to be the source of marital trauma in bourgeois households.[14] Few contemporary novelists were immune to criticism, yet few seemed to suffer much in popularity for all the attacks. Even as conservative critics like Charles Nisard and Alfred Nettement waged war against this new literature,[15] novelists prolifically produced chapter after chapter of melodrama and social commentary. By the middle years of the July Monarchy, the novel had become, like the press itself, a major instrument of social criticism, hardly univocal in its goals but caught up in exchanges that questioned the institutions on which the French state had hitherto been seen to rely.

The censorship of Luchet's novel came on the heels of a series of major press scandals and amid an increasingly violent discussion of the role of the novel in challenging social institutions. More important, it came dead center into debates about marriage and the family that the novel of the previous decade had avidly promoted. Luchet's work was, as we shall see, part of a more generalized trend in the novel toward a specific kind of social criticism that particularly targeted the institutions of the family and marriage. One could say that Luchet was censored both for pushing the limits of the possibilities for the new novel and for engaging in that novel's most typical moves. In the following two sections, I would like to examine the context for the July Monarchy novel's social criticism and to consider how Luchet's contemporaries involved themselves in its demands for reform.

Divorce Plots

"Marriage is *the* central subject for the bourgeois novel," Tony Tanner has argued. Because, for Tanner, marriage is "the all-subsuming, all-organizing, all-containing contract for bourgeois society," the bourgeois novelist cannot avoid somehow engaging the subject of marriage (1979, 15). Adultery, Tanner has contended, represents the main topic for the bourgeois novel because it provides a new ("novel") plot for the lives it transforms (377). Threatening the contract of marriage, it enables the novel generically to rehearse potential breakdowns in the contract between reader and text, and to represent the risks of refusing or evading either structure (17). Tanner's account of the "narrational urges" of adultery in the novel is persuasive for the examples he reads at length (Rousseau's *Julie,* Goethe's *Wahlverwandschaften,* and *Madame Bovary*), but it interprets the transgressions of adultery as existing in an ahistorical time warp. Tanner believes divorce, which he calls "the main way in which society came to cope with adultery," was rejected as a solution by the novels he considers because "the novelist realized that divorce was a piece of surface temporizing, a forensic palliative to cloak and muffle the profoundly disjunctive reverberations and implications of adultery" (18). Since for most of the nineteenth century, divorce was not even a *possible solution* for disrupted marital contracts, one might need to rethink its position in relation to the novel of adultery. Since divorce was not legal either in the *ancien régime* or between 1816 and 1884, it is hardly surprising that neither Julie nor Emma Bovary imagined it as an alternative. For the novel of the July Monarchy, and for the novel of the 1830s in particular, divorce was not only a central demand of characters but also a specific political goal of many authors. And if adultery turns out to be the topic par excellence of these novels, the breakdown in contracts it implies targets a much greater breakdown in contracts, between the July Monarchy state and the bourgeois supporters who believed they would be rewarded with a relaxing of the laws enforcing indissoluble marriages. The July Monarchy novel staged adultery as part of a political gesture, and when it was thwarted, as in the case of Luchet's *Nom de famille,* this seems to have occurred because adultery and divorce alike were imagined as deeply destabilizing to an already unstable regime.

Opponents of divorce in the July Monarchy made repeated appeals to three stories, each with a novelistic quality of its own. The first involved the social anarchy and libertinism they evoked as resulting from the 1789 revolutionaries' loosening of marital ties. The second story told by the *anti-divorciaires* revolved around the dangers of adulterous desire encouraged by the possibility of marital dissolution. The third story—relayed and reinterpreted by Luchet's novel—centered on the potential havoc created in families by transformations in the contractual obligations of marriages.

Those who believed the family had been radically transformed by the revolutionary freedom to divorce found ample statistical evidence to make their case. One marriage out of four was dissolved in Paris between the revolutionary legalization of divorce in September 1792 and 1803, when the first Napoleonic restrictions on divorce took effect. Approximately twenty thousand marriages were terminated in the nine largest cities in France in this same period. One might have concluded from statistics that French citizens had been looking for ways to rid themselves of unwanted spouses as eagerly as they had sought voting rights and a republican government (Phillips 1988, 257–60). Perhaps most striking was the number of women petitioning for divorce: 74 percent of the petitions filed in Paris were those of women.[16] Though no statistics tell how many of these women, whose average age was thirty-six (Phillips, 1988, 274), married again and had children by a second marriage, such decisions were more than plausible. In the twenty-four years during which divorce was possible, women were able to assert a power over their private lives that had hitherto been imaginable only through widowhood or marital infidelity fraught with scandal. From the stories told by statistics and echoed in the hysteria surrounding July Monarchy attempts to relegalize divorce, women were both imagining changes in the institutions of the family and demanding that those changes respond to their desires.

What Margaret Cohen has called, in relation to the feminine social novel of the July Monarchy, "a second chance at sex" (1995, 106)[17] haunted divorce legislation throughout the nineteenth century. If legislators balked, after the Restoration's abolition of divorce in 1816, at liberalizing marital laws, they appear to have done so precisely to thwart the desires of women and men who sought something more than their marriages offered. It is hard to say whether this recurring concern in divorce debates was religious puritanism or simply blind allegiance to marriage in whatever form it took—arranged by parents, imposed by families, or initiated by lovesick teenagers. Whatever their motives, the opponents of divorce were as dead set against offering individuals a second chance at sex as they were against the potential results of such unions, progeny from a second marriage.[18] With a coldhearted fatalism, hard-liners urged the unhappy woman to turn her heart to God, as if she deserved neither love nor sex, and as if a childless marriage—especially agonizing in an era when motherhood was elevated as the supreme fulfillment of a woman's nature—was either her fault or her just punishment for wanting more.

"Must we obliterate marriage from our institutions and our morals?" asked Antoine Hennequin in one of the many antidivorce pamphlets published during the July Monarchy. "Must we give weapons to seduction and encouragement and rewards to adultery?" (1832, 1). For Hennequin, who saw divorce as a source of ruses and lies and as the validation of extramarital license, changed laws would assure the adulterer, "tomorrow you won't have to blush anymore" (8–9), and thus foster the most dangerous urges in spouses. Divorce would not, he pointed out fervently, "make the dagger fall from the hands of the patricidal wife or turn her away from her plots to serve poison to her husband" (71).[19] Hennequin's depiction of violent women, desperately plotting the end of their marriages, is part of an argument that equated desire with criminality:

> The possibility of divorce by mutual consent, considered a way to reconcile the security of the victim with the impunity of his executioner, seems to say to spouses fit to hear such advice: Go ahead! Strike! If the scheme fails, divorce by mutual consent will enable you to achieve the goal to which crime failed to bring you. It's no longer the scaffold, it's the hope of a new marriage that will come to present itself to the thoughts of the guilty spouse. Thus divorce by mutual consent abets crime and does not prevent it. (76)

Hennequin's pamphlet offered few recourses to women (or men) whose sufferings in loveless marriages had not driven them to adultery and crime. His novelistic rendering of the plots encouraged by divorce suggested that he imagined no middle ground between desperation and resignation. If unhappy marriages had already hatched transgressive plots, Hennequin wanted the partners to such plots to answer to their crimes. If not, then certainly the partners of indissoluble marriages could find some reasonable means to honor their contracts.

The specter of marital breakdown haunted July Monarchy France in part owing to a series of highly public episodes that shed light on the problematic ways in which marriages were arranged, families constructed, and, especially, women asked to bear the burden of contractual obligations in which they had given no consent. Flora Tristan's separation from her husband and subsequent adulterous liaisons drew attention when he attempted to murder her on a Paris street in 1838. Marie Cappelle-Lafarge's disastrous marriage, arranged by a marriage broker in 1839, was imagined to have ended in murder in part because she lacked the options to extract herself from a contract with a man who wed her for a dowry to save himself from bankruptcy. Feminist journalist Poutret de Mauchamps, editor of *La Gazette des femmes* and author of a petition for the reestablishment of divorce (1837), was tried for moral corruption along with her lover in 1838 and sentenced to prison. George Sand's liaisons with de Musset and Chopin were read as evidence of her contempt for the institution of marriage and correlated to the political ideology of her novels in ways that inevitably made her a partner to adultery and marital breakdown.[20] Public expectations that the bourgeois monarchy would gratify its supporters with a liberalization of divorce laws were dashed annually from 1831 to 1834 as legislation zipped almost unanimously through the Chambre des Députés only to be quashed in the Chambre des Pairs.[21] By 1835, when the September Laws narrowed press options for protest of the regime, complaints over the corruption rooted in the very heart of the bourgeois family remained a prickly though acceptable way to take jabs at the monarchy. Caricatures of Louis-Philippe as a pearhead could no longer make it past the censors, but the monarch's henchmen could find few excuses to block the publication of images, like Gavarni's *Fourberies des femmes,* that hinted at the cuckolding of the bourgeoisie who upheld his regime.[22]

The discourse of adultery, especially when accompanied by explicit demands for divorce rights, became a powerful way of indicting the July Monarchy government for its failure to respond to the desires of its original supporters. It also emerged as a subtle tool for demonstrating the corruption of the bourgeoisie depicted as blind to the intrigues of its own interiors. In its propagandistic forms, in pamphlets, petitions, and press editorials, that discourse spun tales of woe around the plight of unhappy spouses, especially neglected wives. In its novelistic versions, including Luchet's *Nom de famille* and dozens of July Monarchy social novels, unhappy spouses began to demand and procure solutions in ways that spurned traditional marriage plots, putting in place—as we shall see in the following section—a literary aesthetic of didacticism and utilitarianism as much debated as the institution of marriage itself. The possibility of social change tendered by the July Revolution had unleashed social demands that altered the very forms in which those demands might be asserted. Marital breakdown haunted Louis-Philippe's regime, and the possible plots it took—adultery, bastardy, and especially divorce—gave shape to tools for political protest hitherto unimaginable as wielding such power. The political goals appropriated by the novel thus emerged as a logical extension of social reformism, and the genre's growing didacticism seemed a logical answer to state attempts to muzzle voices demanding an overhaul of social institutions.

Reforming Adultery

"When you forged our chains, powerful legislators, you did not foresee all our opposition, and it's too bad for you," rails Luchet's Marquise de Tancarville on her deathbed.

> "Women's honor! Women's duty! Words that echo because they are empty. When Napoleon saw a pregnant woman go by, he greeted her, they say, and did not ask her how she got that way. A woman's honor, a woman's duty, is to be a mother. It's her glory. It's her life! . . . For us, marriage is an institution as despicable as it is fierce; if we are faithful, it brings us scorn; if we are guilty, it destroys us." (Luchet [1841], 1:98, 101; "Justice Criminelle" 1842, 2)

This passage, indicting not only marriage as an institution but women's responsibilities within marriage, emerged in the trial of Luchet's novel as the prosecutor's evidence of its "offense to public morals." The Marquise's rationale for her adultery, here confessed as her desire to become a mother, provides no potentially redeeming features for the state. Hers is no elevation of maternal instincts, no confession of repentant passion, but rather an indictment of the social institutions that she saw as leaving her no choice but lies, manipulation, and adultery. Strangely enough, though her speech begins with an appeal to the ignorance of state legislators, her "crime" transpired in an era during which divorce was logistically possible, though neither she nor her husband chose to exercise that right. Distraught over their failure to produce an heir, the Tancarvilles entertain every option, the novel tells us:

> How many times the thought of appealing to divorce came to seduce them and shine like a beacon amidst the wreck of their life! But divorce was a revolutionary resource, an incentive to debauchery, voted by men full of crime and blood, and it could not be permitted that a Tancarville or a Croixmare seek salvation in a law representing treason against God. (1:27)

Ernest, heir to the "name of the family," is born into the Tancarville household on Christmas day 1809. By the time the Marquise lies dying, divorce has been definitively outlawed by the Restoration government. Her deathbed protest, nevertheless, seems directed at the very government that has, since 1830, failed to loosen the "chains" she imagines emptying out the meaning of "women's honor." Small wonder, perhaps, that her remorseless adultery was presented during the trial as an assault on the morality promoted by that government.

According to the prosecutor, Nouguier, the goal of Luchet's novel was to "dump insults and contempt on what makes up the family, from birth to death." In its very title, Nouguier saw its overall view, that "the name given by the family is only a lie." Its epigraph, "*Is pater ist quem nuptiae demonstrant,*" borrowed from Roman law, which held that a child born into a marriage was that of the husband, was read by the prosecution as further evidence that Luchet wanted nothing better than to destroy the very foundations on which society rested ("Justice Criminelle" 1842, 1). Interestingly, this very maxim had turned up a decade earlier as part of Hennequin's argument against liberalizing marital dissolutions. For Hennequin, "the interest of morals and the dignity of marriage" made it essential that if proof existed that "the child born during a marriage cannot belong to the husband," then no man should have to honor the child as his own: "an adulterous wife must not be able to award to the fruit of her licentiousness the advantages of legitimacy; marriage would be debased if it was condemned by laws to protect with its shield children who manifestly do not belong to it" (1832, 65–66). It is precisely this "debasement" which Luchet's novel, both in its epigraph and its plot line, is read by the state prosecutor as embracing. Both the children of adultery in this novel have been raised ignorant of their true paternity, their origins veiled by the lies of wives and the complicity or blindness of husbands. Into the Tancarvilles' aristocratic household, into the Wilds' bourgeois home, children have innocently come bearing names of families to which they do not, according to social norms, rightfully belong.

The failure of these family names to properly mask adulterous liaisons is, however, precisely what gives a plot to this and many other contemporary novels. The didactic urges of Luchet's novel can be fulfilled only through a narrative that dislocates the socially acceptable from its complacent foundations and plummets its characters into the disorders of intrigues that conventions disallow. The new plots provided for lives by adultery in the July Monarchy novel promoted a challenge to social institutions and demanded marital reform but simultaneously destabilized novelistic institutions in ways that endangered both reformist goals and literary aesthetics.

"Marriage is perjury," argues protagonist Léonie in an 1837 novel depicting three extramarital relationships (Auger 1837, 2:28). Given lengthy speeches opposing both marriage and society's particularly heinous treatment of married women, artist Léonie refuses the marriage arranged by her family in order to pledge her heart to a young man she has met painting alongside her in the Louvre: "I will defy the opinions of the hypocrite and vicious throng. What does its view matter to me? I have made myself a man. I want to be free. I am an artist!" (Auger 1837, 1:246). Called exemplary of the social novels of this era (Evans 1936, 144), Hippolyte Auger's *La Femme du monde et la femme artiste* uses scandalous plot lines and vociferous polemics to demonstrate didactically the failure of social institutions to serve the interests of women caught in their contracts. Michel de Masson's *Vierge et martyre* (1836) depicts the trials of the child of an adulterous union between a woman whose life is ruled by her abusive pimping husband and the man of noble heart who had once sought to marry her. Begging him on her deathbed to protect their child from her husband, the adulterous woman hopes to extract the girl from the physical and emotional battery that has precipitated her own untimely death. In order to prevent Clémentine's marriage to a corrupt, aging baron, Montlieu winds up forced to marry the girl himself, effectively entering into an incestuous relationship with his own daughter. Tormented by her husband's sexual rejection, Clémentine grows increasingly drawn toward adultery with a young man Montlieu pushes in her direction. Unable to break her marriage vows, however, she commits suicide, leaving her husband/father suspected of her murder.

Similarly, a series of novels from the 1830s pointedly demand the reinstitution of divorce. Madame Monborne's *Une Victime* (1834) depicts the torments of a young orphan married against her will to a profligate who spends his time either gaming or in prison. Unable to divorce him, she attempts to support herself to no avail, ultimately losing her child and sinking into ever greater poverty and desperation. She is saved by the man she had once hoped to marry and lives happily with him until her criminal husband has her imprisoned and tried for adultery. She poisons herself in court, begging only that her "death inspire toward [her] sex the indulgence of laws" (Monborne 1834, 366). Jenny Bastide's *Elise and Marie* (1838) likewise demands the legalization of divorce by showing the unfortunate results of an arranged marriage between an aging marquis and a girl who had hoped to marry another. Driven to violent jealousy when Elise draws happiness from intriguing with the young viscount, her husband kills his rival in a duel—only to discover he has murdered his own son from a previous adulterous liaison.[23]

The social novel of adultery and divorce has a striking tendency to depict women's suffering in terms that doom even their most heroic efforts to discover alternatives. The attempt of Auger's Léonie to "say an eternal goodbye to what is 'done' and to social tyranny" fails to bring her the happiness she expected. When social opprobrium finally drives her to ask her beloved to marry her, he rebuffs her in a scene that seems to warn others who might try to live so freely. Every love affair in Auger's novel ultimately ends disastrously for the woman. Every woman is betrayed, either by her lover or by social conventions that entrap her in a loveless marriage. Each woman is forced to admit, as one character portentously insists, that "society has its laws and we must respect them" (Auger 1837, 1:256). The power of such a novel's polemic lies, however, in its poignant account of the constraints on women's lives that, in Léonie's words, offer them only a choice between "guilty joys or sorrow" (2:275).

At the forefront of the literary maneuvers that transformed the July Monarchy novel into a political statement were two overlapping generic trends that seemingly culminated in Luchet's novelistic moves and his subsequent embattlement with the press and state. The first, a trend as much in the press and theater as in the novel, was a clarion call for the usefulness of art. The second emerged in what Margaret Cohen has called the "feminine social novel" (1995, 2). The former, its novelistic versions best exemplified by Sue's *Mystères de Paris,* explicitly called for social change, through either the ideas elaborated in its narration or plot lines that made characters the mouthpieces for specific political visions. The latter, emphasizing that these works had as goals "to demonstrate, to move, and to improve" (Cohen 1995, 98), engaged in a didacticism that almost inevitably resulted in the destruction of the female protagonist herself.

The heroine's demise—or at least the demise of her desires—enunciated the fullest demonstration of the imagined truth that women's lives fail to meet their needs.[24] Regardless of the politics of these novels, characters and their desires were sacrificed to plot lines that infallibly demonstrated the private sufferings of women. When the plots of the feminine social novel were allied with the reformist projects of the social novel—as was the case with the work of Luchet, Masson, and Auger—women's tragic plights were staged to demonstrate the need for social change. Female characters were made to suffer as part of a plot for the greater good, and with increasing fervency, as a justification for legislative reform.

The July Monarchy social novel seemed to have a peculiarly forceful need for the stories of women's entrapment in social institutions beyond their control. Whether these stories are told from the women's points of view, whether the works are penned by women or by men, and whether the women represented ultimately find some salvation, the novels that questioned the family and marriage repeatedly depended on women's transgressions to illuminate the limitations of current laws and practices. Whether the novel depicted such transgressions as inevitable, as did *Une Victime,* or as manipulative and duplicitous, as did *Le Nom de famille,* its representation of what Cohen calls the "socio-moral truth" of women's failure to live either inside or outside their own society (1995, 95) evoked demands for social and moral reform in a world beyond the novel. Like the antidivorce pamphlets that, as we have seen, turn on the dangers of women whom marital contracts cannot restrain, the social novels of marital reform need women out of line in order to articulate political positions. Only by projecting into the most intimate spheres of women's lives can legislators, courts, and novels imagine the disorders to be found there destabilizing enough to warrant change. As novels and divorce pamphlets alike suggest, men may suspect that women are intriguing according to their own laws, but only women know the real terms for the plots they have been breeding.

Luchet's novel, borrowing from the reformist urges of the utopian social novel and from the intimate visions of the feminine social novel, had a curious way of confirming the worst fears of the *anti-divorciaires.* Not only do its female adulteresses go unpunished, but their children are never exposed for usurping the names and positions of families to which they do not belong. Luchet's novel's depiction of adultery without reprisal is not, however, a singular one for its era. A comparison with a feminine social novel with a similar plot line suggests, in fact, that something beyond the content of Luchet's novel may have been at stake in the censorship it encountered.

Like *Le Nom de famille,* the short novel published in 1837 under the pseudonym "la Baronne de T . . ." revolves around the desires of a woman to become a mother outside the constraints of marriage. Unlike the Marquise de Tancarville, however, this novel's female protagonist is not herself married prior to the intrigue she engineers with a man she has courted over a winter of balls. Always hidden behind a mask, refusing to reveal her identity or explain her rejection of his marriage offers, she finally gives way to her desires and has him transported to her house where, under the cover of darkness, she commits the adulterous act that lets her bear his child. Her letter explaining her refusal of marriage and her desire to have his child only further convinces Pèdre of his desire to marry her, but despite valiant searches, he cannot find her. Pèdre at last grows bitter toward this woman whom he believes wanted nothing from him but a baby. When he is reunited with her at her château after being wounded in battle, he refuses all contact, contemptuous of her manipulations, until his daughter wins him over. He finally agrees to marry Lady Marie Dudley, whose name has at last been revealed to him, but only in order to have a claim over the child to whom he will now give his name. He plans to depart as soon as they are wed, in a ceremony during which he assumes that his bride will again remain veiled, expecting to return only when their daughter comes of age. But Marie reveals her face in the church and rides back to the château with her husband and child. Softened at last by her beauty, but especially by their daughter's pleadings, Pèdre cannot bear to leave. Instead, he falls into his wife's arms, at last becoming the husband she might have wanted so long ago had the plights of her own mother and aunt not hardened her against marriage.

One might ask why *Mystère* escaped the censors when some four years later a novel with such a similar content did not. Unlike Luchet's Marquise, Marie Dudley passionately loves the man she seduces. But also unlike the Marquise, this woman manages to have her cake and eat it too. Never obliged to renounce her original understanding of the limitations of marriage, even when she reconciles with Pèdre, she winds up using the mechanisms of masquerade to achieve a dream marriage with a man who understands her needs for independence, love, and respect. And though the child is represented as the goal to which she aspired, maternity is finally made irrelevant to love when the newlyweds set off for Paris on a honeymoon at the novel's conclusion, leaving the child with Marie's confidante. The novel's indictment of traditional views of marriage not only remains intact but is therefore validated by the results of the woman's plots. Unlike Luchet's novel, where the adulterous child wreaks havoc on the life of every parent in sight, this work uses the adorable child to procure the best of unions and suggests the creation of a nuclear family that will resemble any other despite the child's original bastardy and the mother's illicit sexual intrigues.

Mystère is in some ways more revolutionary than Luchet's *Nom de famille,* for it offers the protection of appearances to a woman who follows her own desires, acts according to her own code of conduct, and rejects social norms. Luchet's female protagonist winds up not only dead but the mother of a monster. Yet by embracing, in its conclusion, the appearances of the socially acceptable nuclear family, *Mystère* contracts the guise of the most happily ending bourgeois novel: everyone is in place according to the institutions of marriage and the family; what matter how they got there? Luchet's novel, as the censors pointed out, did its best to demonstrate the breakdown of the institutions it represented—the family, marriage, fatherhood, and the state—even as it rejected the solutions of its characters to the problems they confronted. If, in the words of the prosecutor, this novel showed the "name of the family" to be nothing more than a lie ("Justice Criminelle" 1842, 1), it failed to provide palliative fictions to replace it. One was left, instead, with the name of the family intact, but emptied of its meaning. Small wonder, perhaps, that the censors sought to put in its place the name of the state as a warning to any who would so devalue the institutions invested by it.

Such a conclusion is a risky one, however, for it has an uncanny way of reproducing the conclusions of Luchet's trial. Any comparisons we might make between Luchet's censored novel and its uncensored counterparts inevitably restage the interpretative gestures of the censors, placing his work again on trial and reading it under surveillance. The danger of such comparisons is that one can argue, like the state prosecutor, that Luchet's novel elicited the censors' acts, but one cannot prove with any certainty that it was unjustly attacked. One can hypothesize how it offended the state, but one cannot be sure of the reasons its leftist contemporaries left it all but undefended.

Nevertheless, one might imagine ways in which this novel failed the reformist and Republican goals it claimed to serve. By transforming the adulterous son into an agent of vengeance against society, Luchet ultimately undermined whatever influence, either genetic or environmental, the saintly Republican Maurice might have had upon his son. Despite the goodness of the adulterous man, the transgression of marital boundaries proves disastrous for all parties. It is as if the blood of the Marquise, an agent of duplicity and betrayal, has poisoned whatever nobility the Republican might have brought to their progeny. The sins of mothers are here visited upon both Ernest and his wife Marie. The novel was therefore unlikely to win fans among female readers used to the plot devices of the feminine social novel. Despite its apparent justification of adultery and demands for the reinstitution of divorce, this novel portrays both women who seek sex outside their marriages as manipulative, neglectful of duty, and hardhearted. The only female character spared by

Luchet's novel, ultimately, is the gentle Marie, who emerges as a pawn in a broader social attack rather than as a novelistic personality in her own right. She exists, it would seem, more to provide Ernest with another father to destroy, and to allow the novelist another mother to indict, than to demonstrate any possibility of social reform. Like the children imagined by the antidivorce pamphleteers, children caught up in struggles over family names and inheritance thanks to their parents' dissolution of social contracts, Marie is a victim for whom no solutions can be found. And although, in her married state, chained to the abusive Ernest, she serves as evidence of the need for divorce in July Monarchy society, she remains only a tormented victim. Unable to divorce her husband—even after his murder of their fathers—she serves only as a painful reminder that the very kind of adultery that has poisoned all their lives has become an inevitability. She can become at best a lure for readers of Luchet's promise, in the last paragraph of his novel, that he will write her love story as an alternative to the broken contracts in which this novel has engaged. But even that imagined story will remain—as long as the social novel fails in its reformist goals of forcing the government to legalize divorce—only another account of adultery and transgression like the one that set this novel in motion.

One might imagine that there is another story to tell about the censorship of Luchet's *Nom de famille* that goes beyond its Republican and antistate rhetoric, the subversive nature of its characters' acts, the narrator's attitude toward its impenitent women and ineffectual men, and the novel's failure to offer alternatives to the social institutions it attacks. That story, of Luchet's participation in the remaking of the role of the novel, is inevitably related to the novel's transgressive content. But it is even more so a story of the attempt of literature to move beyond the spheres of fiction into the realm of public life. As we shall see in the following section, the tensions wracking the novel of adultery and divorce became particularly visible in the battles around Luchet's novel because this text transgressed imagined contracts of what the novel might do, and incited terror over what might be done with novels.

The Limitations of Form

The year prior to Luchet's trial was an explosive one, both for Louis-Philippe's government and for the press that opposed it. In August 1841, eight newspapers had been seized for publishing "false news." Late that fall, the Chambre des Pairs condemned the editor of the leftist *Journal du peuple* to five years imprisonment for complicity in an antigovernment plot, the assassination attempt of Quénisset against the Duc d'Aumale in September 1841. The lack of proof of Dupoty's guilt left the press reeling: that newspapers could now be condemned as complicitous in plots against the regime simply on the basis of their views suggested a level of repression yet more ferocious than any previously seen during the July Monarchy.[25] More press trials and more scandals would follow in swift succession. Forty-eight days into the new year, *Le Temps* would claim that since 1 January, press trials in Paris and the provinces had witnessed condemnations amounting to sixty-eight thousand francs and eight years, eight months of prison time.[26] In January 1842, the director of *Le Charivari* was sentenced to two years in prison and a one-thousand-franc fine. Its publisher was also fined in a trial that condemned presses for agreeing to print material that might later be viewed as offensive to the state. In the course of the winter and spring, *Le Siècle, Le National, La Gazette de France, La Mode,* and *Le Temps* would find themselves hauled before the courts of France and subjected to heavy fines and imprisonment, almost always for protests technically allowed by the July Monarchy Charter.[27] One thing had become certain: the July Monarchy government was no longer willing to take risks with the opposition, from either the press or other agents demanding reform.

The press scandals of the July Monarchy in general, and of 1841–42 in particular, set the stage for a showdown with the reformist novel in three ways. First, because voices of protest in the press were increasingly under siege, individuals who might otherwise have opted to speak out in newspapers seem to have chosen increasingly to use the hitherto safe space of the novel for social commentary. Second, because the leftist press was running scared, embattled by several years of confiscated papers, heavy fines, and prison sentences, the government could expect editors to act cautiously in leaping to the defense of those it targeted for excessive indiscretions. Third, because the government was increasingly eager to shut down voices of dissent, it had begun targeting not only newspapers but their publishers, some of whom were simultaneously involved in the publication of novels.

Read as the trial of a novel, Luchet's heavy condemnation makes little sense. Other novels were launching boisterous attacks on the state and its institutions. Other authors were telling similar stories, often with similarly revolutionary outcomes. Even if other novelists masked their critiques by placing them in the mouths of characters, any number of Luchet's contemporaries challenged the government, the family, and women's roles in ways that could have been construed as immoral or subversive.

Read in the context of struggles over the press, Luchet's censorship has an altogether different valence. The battle over divorce and marital rights had given a political dimension to the novel of ideas that brought the genre in new ways into the cultural sphere. Its authors' desires for legislative change caused the divorce novel to take up explicitly questions previously articulated by the Chambres des Députés and Pairs, the press, and pamphlet literature. The result was not just a call for the utility of art and for social reform but a pretense to veracity that allied the novel with press goals and made it subject to similar kinds of scrutiny.[28] "Ambitious well beyond its powers," wrote Louandre of the didactic novel in 1847, "instead of confining itself wisely to the study of the human heart, it has set itself up as a reformer, as a political preacher; it has tried to intervene in all public affairs and to govern the world" (1847, 682). In order to achieve this mission, deplored by Louandre but held up as exemplary by critics like Emile Souvestre, the novel became increasingly "carried toward the true": "For the true in everything has its importance: it clings by a link more or less free to the useful, which is nothing other than the true in practice, and to the virtuous, which is nothing other than the true in the order of morality" (Souvestre 1836, 123).

Such a notion of the importance of veracity to the reformist novel was embraced by Luchet with even more vehemence than by most of his contemporaries. His preface to *Frère et soeur* claimed, for example, that "all the facts" making up this text "are real; with one exception, all the characters appearing in it are living" (Luchet 1838, 1:1). *Le Nom de famille* voiced a similar refusal of fictionality:

> *Le Nom de famille* is no more a novel than *Frère et soeur*. The characters who come into play in the action of this second work are living and contemporary like those who populated the first. The imagination of the author had nothing to do with the production of scenes or with the catastrophe that follows. (Luchet [1841], 2:72)

For Luchet to claim the reality of his works inscribed the novelistic within a generic mode that was as journalistic as it was politically subversive. And as soon as the novel answered to Souvestre's mission of becoming "journalism with art and reflection as well" (Souvestre 1836, 123), it found itself caught in new binds. Drawing on traditional novelistic devices, authors may have hoped to use literary machinations to mollify critics and avoid the condemnation of political views that in the press would surely have met with censorship. By allying themselves with the embattled press to convey demands for social change, and insisting on the contemporary realism and truth of their representations, novels could not continue to pass for inconsequential fictions.

Luchet's appropriation of the goals of political propaganda, pamphlets, or newspaper editorials may have heightened the novel's chances of achieving political change, but it also bound him to new codes. Walking the fence between journalism and fiction, he was pinioned simultaneously by the formal strategies of the narrative modes the social novel had infused with new life and by anxieties over what truth in a novel might imply. His novel's cross-class adultery, condemnations of the aristocracy, complaints over women's imprisonment in loveless marriages, snipes at religious values, and, especially, its bleak picture of the corruptions of the family offered few palliatives for state readers on guard against challenges to authority. Its plays on real names and potentially real corruption within ostensibly real French institutions engaged it more fully in the debates of its era but, as we shall see, also threatened its very survival. We could say that Luchet was tried, not just for depicting the subversion of cultural institutions, but for subverting cultural expectations of the novel.

"We can consider Mr. Luchet's novel from three very different points of view, as an argument about society, as a political pamphlet, and as a mere narrative," wrote the literary critic "Old Nick" in the republican newspaper *Le National* in November 1841. For this critic, whose paper's political views aligned most closely with those of the author of *Le Nom de famille,* Luchet's novel had gone too far:

> The argument about society calls for the abolition of the family—the primary basis of Fourierist theories; the pamphlet, which takes up the most room and holds the most important position in this new work, is an energetic, sincere, and virulent attack against certain men and certain principles; the novel, often sacrificed, is made up of a few scenes in which the dramatic effect is once in a while procured rather violently.

What *Le National*'s critic called an "impartial reading" culminated in an assessment of "this slightly bizarre whole" that assaulted the novel for attempting to answer difficult social questions with a generic form "Old Nick" believed inappropriate for "serious dialectic" (1841, 1).

Luchet was not new to such accusations. His previous novel, *Frère et soeur,* had been called a "political pamphlet in two volumes" by *La Revue française* (Review of *Frère et soeur* 1838, 389). As in 1842, his earlier novel had been used by the anonymous critic to articulate a more generalized attack on the genre's involvement in social questions:

> In the moral anarchy that is the brilliant side of our era, all true and false principles, good or bad, have their literary representation. The novel especially, that work so facile in the way it is treated over the passage of time, is like a tribune, familiar and accessible to all, from which all doctrines are professed, and all social and humanitarian questions are debated. (392)

Despite the critic's certainty that the novel lacked either charm or interest, he nevertheless accorded *Frère et soeur* a lengthy review that sought to oppose both its social commentary and the form it used to attack "religion, science, politics, morality, social bonds and the family, and individual and professional relationships" (389). In *Frère et soeur* he saw "a plan for revolt or, if one wants to soften the term, a plan for general reform, beginning with the family and ending with politics and religion" (390). The novel, one might have inferred from criticism on both the right and the left, had no business engaging in social reform, let alone social revolt.

Critical hostility toward Luchet's writings was sufficiently pronounced that the state action against *Le Nom de famille* had been all but tacitly authorized in advance. Despite vehement protests in 1842 over the various episodes of press censorship, most Parisian newspapers responded to Luchet's penalty with a few restrained lines announcing the results of his trial. The lone exceptions, a newspaper on the right—*La France*—and one on the left—*Le National*—ended up using Luchet's conviction as a way of lambasting each other rather than opposing the state's newest means of encroaching on freedom of speech. If press trials had promoted the solidarity of newspapers with the most furiously opposed views,[29] Luchet's trial had the curious result of dividing not only the left of which he was a part but the opposition press in general.[30]

Despite their ambivalence about the novel condemned by the state, the editors of *Le National* expressed outrage at this further attack on authorial freedoms. But their editorial expressed yet another worry, one that, in light of their harsh critique of November 1841, seemed decidedly justified: that the state had viewed the left's rejection of Luchet's new novel as permission to censor it. "What will serious criticism become, when it believes itself nothing more than the predecessor of public prosecution?" asked *Le National*'s editors two days after Luchet's condemnation. "What will happen to the writer who would dare to judge a book he fears that his arguments may be but the precursors of a prosecutorial indictment?" The failure of *Le National* to ask what might happen to *writers* who express their opinions in *novels* seemed oddly masked by another rhetorical appeal: what would happen to criticism if writers feared being allied with the censorship of novels? Why so much concern about critics? Why so little concern with novelists? Or why, at least, so little concern about this novelist?

Possibly, we could hypothesize, because this novelist was himself so little concerned with the press and its critics. Hell-bent on presenting the truth of his society in the interest of reforming it, Luchet's novel had declared its mission all the more necessary because of the failures of the contemporary press. "What we call the periodical press represents two quite separate kinds of men, those who write and those who pay," declared the narrator of *Le Nom de famille* in a diatribe that implicated far more than the corrupt Ernest de Tancarville who used his father's name to become editor of a nameless Parisian daily. Although the narrator attributed the corruption of the press to "those cunning wretches to whom we owe the penal and social organization of the press," he nevertheless imagined state constraints as having created writers and editors who were "almost all [forced] to bow down before capital." What Luchet's narrator called "that degradation of thought by money" (Luchet [1841], 2:138) had, he claimed, contaminated other means of expression as well, such as the pamphlet and the bookstore. Sooner or later, he promised, if the king's men had their way, "the novelist, the historian, and the poet will also be obliged to mutilate themselves in order to live" (2:139). Though such a pronouncement may have seemed farfetched in late 1841, its presence in a novel that those very king's men ordered destroyed seems more than prophetic. The very real censorship of this novel performed an all too real indictment of the press that was willing to look the other way.

But Luchet's adhesion to veracity went even further in its needling of the press and in its transgressions subversion of traditional novelistic codes. Luchet's narrator's depiction of corruption at every level of the press had a provocative way of pointing a finger at newspapers on both the right and the left without actually naming names. The novel's insistence on its truth value left readers trying to identify not only the potentially adulterous progeny of aristocratic families to whom Luchet had given recognizable, existing names but the corrupt newsmen embroiled in scandals like those detailed in the last sections of the novel.[31] Not surprisingly, *Le National*'s November 1841 review focused heavily on its discomfort with the climate of suspicion with which Luchet surrounded his characters and their potential models: "The personal attack, when mixed with a work of the imagination, is as a general principle, the most perfidious and the most dangerous of all," fulminated *Le National*'s critic, safely avoiding references to anyone in particular he saw this novel as attacking. "The liberty of the novel must not be confused with that of the newspaper: they are two very separate things" ("Old Nick" 1841, 2). The newspaper, explained "Old Nick," laid out all the facts at its disposition, not seeking to cover anything over with ambiguities. The individuals attacked therefore had the right to respond in their own defense, or even to take the writer before the courts. Similar attacks in a novel play havoc, he argued, for no one could prove that this supposedly fictional work had anything more than a circumstantial relationship to reality.

Cloaking his attacks on the aristocracy and press with potential fictionality, Luchet had nevertheless appropriated a language of realism and contemporary truth to launch his critiques beyond the range of the novelistic. As soon as we believe the narrator who condemns the state and its supporters for their preparedness to act against the novel, we find ourselves struggling to read this work against the grain of the generic category to which it only seems to belong. If, in the words of the state prosecutor, this is a novel according to which "family names are only lies," it is equally a literary work that makes use of the name of the novel to diffuse truths its form might belie. Through its author's attempts to stretch the social reformism of the genre, the name of the novel is strained into a fiction.

Luchet's violation of the implicit contract of the novel's fictionality had a significant role to play in each of the accusations leveled against *Le Nom de famille* by the state prosecutor in 1842. As evidence of the novel's "excitement of hatred and contempt against the government," state censors cited passages from its account of the cholera epidemic and the riots of 1832, which read more like a piece of editorial journalism than a chapter in a literary work. As proof of the novel's attempt to disturb public peace by inciting hatred against a class of people, the prosecutor read indictments of the nobility, and particularly of the existing Croixmare family of Normandy: "old nobility, pure line of descendants, arrogant race." Although the state censors made no explicit reference to the offense the novel may have represented for the aristocratic families whose names it borrowed, the fact that such families had a history that stretched back to the Middle Ages nevertheless inscribed the novel's accusations within a register of truth that its defenders had difficulty disavowing. "I have never heard those families mentioned in our history," declared Favre during the trial, suggesting that Luchet's choice of names was purely serendipitous. Like any author, claimed Favre, Luchet had to use some name: "If we refuse him the right to borrow names of famous families, why would we authorize him to give plebeian names to the actors of his drama?"

Such pleas, though logical out of context, nevertheless failed to move a jury that had been reminded, not only by the critics of *Le National* but by Luchet himself, that "the characters who come into play in the action of this work are living and contemporary." Luchet could not have it both ways: either his characters were real people, named with real aristocratic names, positioned in a landscape of contemporary events, surrounded by corruptions the narrator wished to depict as terrifyingly real, and therefore adulterous, corrupt, and debased, or they were pure fictions and therefore unable to make good on his promises of truth. Luchet was either guilty of pushing his fiction too far into the realm of truth, or a literary prevaricator whose claims of truth had no substance. Either way, Luchet's revision of the novel's contract of fictionality had a powerful way of provoking questions about the role of art in society, about the boundaries between fiction and journalism, and about the limits of both form and reformism.

The Trials of the Social Novel

"They'll bring a lawsuit against you," author Aloïse de Carlowitz is warned by her neighbor, who has just read the novel she is about to publish. "A lawsuit! Against me!" she retorts, insisting that her characters—even the republicans—ask only for "the triumph of their opinions by means of debate" (Carlowitz 1835, 1:31). Not only has Carlowitz, in her *Le Pair de France ou le Divorce,* rejected violence as a means for social change, but she has studiously avoided providing her own political opinions in any explicit form anywhere in her novel. This woman's novel "of no importance" simply repeats, she argues, what one "hears every day in meetings of petit bourgeois families and in the brilliant salons of high society" (1:37). Her novel's veracity lies in an attentiveness to what people already believe and desire: "I hope that people will be grateful to me for having tried to call the attention of the public to an important social question"—her society's need for a law allowing divorce (1:34–35).

If adultery in the novel signals a breakdown in the contracts of society and of literature, the July Monarchy social novel's appeals for divorce legislation require an appropriation of verisimilitude that might necessitate new contracts. For the characters of these loveless marriages of convenience to acquire the rights to make new alliances, the novel must assume a form that inserts it into the most fervent debates of real-life society. "For a quarter of a century," wrote critic Eugène Poitou in 1857 of the literature of the July Monarchy and early Second Empire,

> there has been no shortage of attacks, whether open or roundabout, insidious or violent; there has been no shortage of abuse, of slander, and of insults, of which marriage has not been the butt. It seems that all *false systems* and all immoderate passions have united in order to deliver an attack on marriage. It has been the common enemy; it once served as the living symbol of moral law, and at the same time as the Ark of the Covenant that guarded the trust of private and public morals. (67–68; my emphasis)

The novel, "false system" par excellence, had moved during the July Monarchy into a realm of truth that found it, in Poitou's words, putting the family—and marriage—on trial (179). The new contract of truth it pledged could not preserve the appearances on which the novel had so long depended to shield it from accusations of sedition and subversion. Like the adulterous liaisons it depicted in order to call for marital reform and divorce legislation, the new social novel of veracity had radically disrupted the terms on which society depended for order. The trial of words it elicited had revealed fears running far deeper than novelists or social critics might have imagined. "What is then that thing which they bring back into fashion again, all the while remaining afraid to name it?" asked Luchet at his trial. "Is the word more terrible than the deed?" ("Justice Criminelle" 1842, 2). *Le Nom de famille* had installed a grammar of aesthetics and social reform that left the state struggling to put its own version of truth in the place of what it claimed were egregious falsities. Refusing to authorize the new relationships, new contracts, and new terms for society that novelists like Luchet demanded, the July Monarchy government saw itself with no choice but to try to stem the flow of these novels with a mission of truth. Luchet was found guilty as tried.

"Literature reproduces the system that makes it what it is," argues Mary Poovey. Literature does not resist ideology but reproduces it, exposing the "system of social and institutional relations" that nourishes it. "Because literary texts mobilize fantasies without legislating action, they provide the site at which shared anxieties and tensions can surface as well as be symbolically addressed" (1988, 123–24). When the literary text presumes to move into the realm of legislative authority, demanding change, appropriating power, it may well expose more than shared anxieties and tensions.

Luchet's novel pledged to demonstrate the failings of the social institutions of his era, to name the meaninglessness of the family ties authorized by the state, and to articulate the very real catastrophes it imagined emanating from relationships reduced to empty fictions. Inscribed into the melodramatic causality of the novel tradition, however, Luchet could not entirely achieve either his own political goals or those attributed to him by the censors. Despite its narrator's claims that he would seek reform for women trapped, like the Marquise and Marie, in marriages that do not satisfy their needs, this novel has a peculiar way of entrapping its female characters even more firmly in the interstices of fiction and truth on which it rhetorically depends.

The novel of adultery serves in powerful ways to indict the governments of nineteenth-century France for their blindness to the desires of citizens, but it can do little more with the plots of marital breakdown than replicate the social mores that place women's desires under surveillance. Invading the private lives of families and the private thoughts of women, the adultery novel puts women's behavior under surveillance to stage it as transgressive. Demonstrating the dangers to women who want more, the social novel would call for social change, as it were, over their dead bodies. Despite its reformist goals, it institutionalizes a circumspect gaze that puts the private lives of women and men on trial and justifies increased state intervention into the private sphere. The censorship of novels—long imagined as works read privately in the closed spaces of the home—could be seen as a pendant of that intervention. But Luchet's novel was not penalized because of the dangerous desires it was imagined to breed in youthful readers. It was censored instead for making a public spectacle of the private sphere, and for using that spectacle to indict the most public of institutions, the state, for its abuses of private rights. Though its author would be only barely remembered among those who challenged, with literature and words, the social institutions of nineteenth-century France, the severity of his penalty was adequate proof that his challenge had been read as not only one of words but somehow, also, one of deeds.

"May the warrant of the Assize Court put a brake on all those works of scandal that multiply in swarms around us!" demanded the Monarchist *La France* the week after Luchet's trial. Inviting the state to seek out other novelists and journalists who engaged in similar forms of blasphemy, the conservative newspaper reveled in the example made of this "republican work . . . of immorality and irreligiosity." Strangely uncritical of the politics of censorship to which other right-wing newspapers were regularly subject, *La France* applauded the widening of the net of repression around voices in opposition to its views. Literary criticism, it argued, was unable to meet society's need to silence authors like these. The state's intervention, it hoped, would be only the beginning of a repression that might end the "explosion of bad books that, beneath frivolous titles, deprave imaginations and trouble consciences."[32]

La France's wish was not gratified. With increasing furor, the French people and their press rose up to protest that, contrary to the words of Luchet's preface, they did not have "too many liberties." Though the July Monarchy state continued to pursue the press with venom throughout its remaining six years of power, the novel was only once more subject to censorship after March 1842.[33] And when the censors' next blow fell on a literary text, with the confiscation of *La Démocratie pacifique* for its roman-feuilleton, *La Part des femmes,* the press would rise up furiously to defend the small newspaper and its novelist. Only months later, the battles in which these novels engaged—over marital rights for women, improved conditions for the working class, and freedom of speech and press—would be played out on the barricades of February 1848. Though divorce would not be made legal, even amid the new dreams of the Second Republic, and freedoms of speech and press would flicker only briefly before the conservative crackdowns of the Second Empire, the reformist novel would be imagined for decades as having fueled the dreams of revolutionaries and as forming the political goals of a generation of republicans. That Luchet would return to Paris, in the wake of the Revolution, to help edit *La Réforme,* one of the most powerful leftist papers of 1848, was only further proof that the institutions of July Monarchy censorship had failed to meet their mark.

Read a century and a half later for its position in the battles of culture, the work of Auguste Luchet reminds us of the desires and anxieties trafficked through the novel form. *Le Nom de famille* may represent the failures of literature to achieve the reformist goals it touted so loudly. But at the same time, the censored text does not allow us to forget the powers the novel sought to appropriate, which for readers, writers, and the state of July Monarchy France, could not remain purely fictional.

Notes

I am grateful to Margaret Cohen and Frédéric Cousinié for stimulating discussions and research advice.

1. The monarchy of French Orleanist king Louis-Philippe came to power as a result of the Revolution of 1830, which brought an end to the restored Bourbon monarchy of Charles X. Promising greater liberties than either Napoleon Bonaparte's Empire or the Restoration, Louis-Philippe's "bourgeois monarchy," which gained its power through the support of bankers and landholders, found itself caught up in constant corruption scandals, including those involving the abridgment of liberties of speech and press, and ended in the fighting of the Revolution of 1848, which mobilized worker demands in explicit ways for the first time in the century.

2. A slightly abbreviated transcript of Luchet's trial of 10 March 1842 was published in the "Cour d'Assises de la Seine" section of *La Gazette des tribunaux,* 11 March 1842, 1–3. The accusations levied against his novel were detailed by the state prosecutor, Nouguier (see p. 1).

3. On the September Laws of 1835 and their repercussions for censorship, see Krakovitch 1985, 62–78; Collins 1959, 82–99; and Matlock 1994, chap. 6. Luchet had already felt the weight of those betrayals when *Ango,* the play he coauthored with Félix Pyat in 1835, was closed down by the ministry for ostensibly alluding to other scandals brewing in the government. On the censorship of *Ango,* see the authors' preface to the play (Luchet and Pyat 1835, vi); its censorship file in the Archives Nationales, F-21, 1134; Krakovitch 1985, 56; and Hallays-Dabot 1862, 307–8.

4. Virtually none of these works were discussed by critics or the press in the context of state limitations on liberties. For a substantive list of works censored in the July Monarchy, see Drujon 1879. According to James Smith Allen, 19.4 publications, including, I assume, books, journals, and illustrations, were censored annually during this period. Relatively few newly published books seem to have been censored (Allen 1991, 90). One example of a nonpornographic book censored for political reasons was Alphonse Esquiros's *Les Vierges folles* (1840), a socialist manifesto on prostitution and working-class women.

5. Both of the other novels that met with political prosecution, Marcellin de Bonnal's *Lamentations, ou la Renaissance sociale,* censored just after Luchet's in 1842, and Antony Méray's *La Part des femmes,* censored for two episodes of its *feuilleton* in 1847, were first novels by unknowns. Although the censorship of both works met with substantial press discussion, neither author was sufficiently well known to be a state target. I have discussed the censorship of *La Part des femmes* in Matlock 1994, chap. 7.

6. On Luchet's political and literary career, see Maitron 1965, 2:34–35; Hébert 1913; and Green 1990. His previous novels were *Henri le prétendant* (1832); with Michel de Masson, *Thaddéus le ressuscité* (1836); and *Frère et soeur* (1838). He also participated in the collections *Paris révolutionnaire* and *Le Livre de cent et un* and had published a work on Paris (*Paris, esquisses dédiées au peuple parisien* [1830]). He was considered sufficiently important to be asked to write prefaces for two other social novelists of his era, Elisa Billotey (*L'Agent de change* [1837]) and Ferdinand Vaucher (*Les Grisettes vengées* [1838]). He returned from exile to become editor of the leftist newspaper *La Réforme* and an active republican in 1848. Luchet's publisher, Hippolyte Souverain, was also placed on trial by the government, suggesting that the state was trying to use this trial to target other writers published by him: Balzac, Soulié, Sand, and Léon Gozlan. Defended furiously by Luchet, who claimed Souverain had never read the book he published, the house was acquitted of complicity in the 1842 trial.

7. On Flaubert's trial see La Capra 1982; Wing 1987; Leclerc 1991, 129–222; and Matlock 1995.

8. "The novel, in its origin, might almost be said to be a transgressive mode, inasmuch as it seemed to break, or mix, or adulterate the existing genre-expectations of the time" (Tanner 1979, 3).

9. In a final word, the narrator proposes that if he lives long enough he will "tell those who like the heroic story of Auguste and Marie" (Luchet [1841] 2:196). No such novel was ever published. All translations, unless otherwise noted, are my own.

10. Jacques Peuchet was the author of a number of works of scandalous "history," including the 1834 *Mémoires tirés des archives de la police.* Critic and novelist Théophile Gautier was best known for *Mademoiselle de Maupin* (1834).

11. Louandre claims there are an average of 210 new novels per year, with a high of 284 in 1833 and a low of 185 in 1841, excluding reprints of French novels from the previous two centuries and foreign novels (1847, 681). My estimates from an examination of the *Bibliographie de France* in these years are much lower. In 1841, for example, the rubric "Romans et contes" lists 234 works, of which fewer than sixty were novels printed for the first time in that year. See also Wood 1960.
12. On reading rooms and their transformation of the reading public of the Restoration and July Monarchy, see Parent-Lardeur 1982. On literacy rates and the transformation of the reading public, see Hébrard 1985; Allen 1991; and Furet and Ozouf 1982.
13. On the growing prestige of the novel in the July Monarchy, see Iknayan 1961, 50–84.
14. I analyze these attacks in Matlock 1994, chaps. 1 and 3 (Sue), chap. 5 (Balzac), chap. 8 (Soulié and Sand).
15. Nisard's attacks on the novel were published in the *Revue de Paris* (1833) and greeted by vigorous counterattacks by novelist and critic Jules Janin in the following year (1834). Nettement's attacks, especially on the *roman-feuilleton,* were published in the Monarchist, Catholic *La Gazette de France* and republished as *Études critiques sur le feuilleton roman* (1845).
16. Between two-thirds and three-quarters of the petitioners in other French towns were women, and 40 percent of those women in at least one town had been married before the age of twenty-one (Phillips 1988, 261, 271).
17. The best introduction to the nineteenth-century social novel remains Evans 1936.
18. In a divorce pamphlet appealing to the legislators of 1831, Jean Journel underlined the dangers of second unions in which children are produced. The "horrible disorder" of such arrangements, in which education, morality, and especially inheritance might be compromised led Journel to demand that the current legislation be soundly rejected (1831, 10).
19. Debates over divorce continued to turn on depictions of the homicidal wife up through the 1880s, though her crimes were often used as a plea for divorce, as in the case of Naquet's arguments ("Let the civil code liberate the wife. She will seek the protection of the law instead of taking vengeance with arsenic, sulphuric acid, or a revolver"), *Journal officiel,* Sénat, 1er trimestre 1884, 962 (26 May 1884), cited in Phillips 1988, 427. Emile Barrault, author of the novelistic plea for divorce, *Eugène,* published a further argument in 1847, entitled *La Pathologie du mariage,* claiming that had divorce been legal, the Duc de Choiseul-Praslin might not have needed to murder his wife in 1847. I have discussed the Choiseul-Praslin case in Matlock 1993.
20. On Flora Tristan, see Desanti 1972; Michaud 1984; and Strumingher 1988. On Cappelle-Lafarge, see Matlock 1994, chap. 8. On Poutret de Mauchamps,

see Moses 1984, 98–107, and the *Gazette des femmes,* 1 May 1837, 6. For indictments of Sand, see Poitou 1857, 74–82. Louis Maigron, writing in the early twentieth century, still eagerly attacked Sand for the destruction of a generation of marriages (1910).

21. On July Monarchy attempts to reinstitutionalize divorce, see Ronsin 1992, 27–110.

22. On the censorship of caricature during the July Monarchy, see Cuno 1985 and Goldstein 1989, 119–68. I have discussed Gavarni's equivocal position in the politics of censored caricature in a chapter of my book in progress, *Desires to Censor: Spectacles of the Body, Aesthetics, and Vision in Nineteenth-Century France,* a version of which will appear as Matlock 1996. I am grateful to my research assistant Sharon Haimov for sharing her observations on the *Fourberies des femmes* and divorce debates in the July Monarchy in her honors thesis (1993).

23. Unable to tolerate her fate, Elise commits suicide. Hortense Allart's *Settimia* (1836) calls for moral reform in both its preface and its plot line, which explicitly seek to demonstrate the need for divorce in order to liberate women's full potential. Likewise, Barrault's *Eugène* (1839) elaborates a series of intrigues in which an unhappily married woman increasingly turns her hopes to the passage of a law permitting divorce but is satisfied only upon the death of her husband. Despite the *Revue de Paris*'s ambivalence toward the social novel, Barrault's novel received a very positive review in that publication (B., A. 1839).

24. The feminine social novel, unlike classic narrative, does not present disorder that can be made into order or an enigma awaiting solution but rather, in Cohen's description, "an event instantiating the opening kernel of socio-moral truth" that will be borne out by the emphatic repetitions of its plot line (1995, 95–96).

25. See Ledré 1960, 179, and Collingham 1988, 294–95.

26. *Le Temps,* 18 February 1842, 3, col. 2.

27. By June, the centrist *Temps* had been forced to fold on a technicality of publication that may have been intended as much to warn other papers as to undo this upholder of Louis-Philippe's government. See *Le Temps,* 15–17 June 1842, as well as a particularly forceful critique of press censorship in *La Revue indépendante,* June 1842, 804–5.

28. In her study of the English novel between 1832 and 1867, Catherine Gallagher has argued that "narrative fiction, especially the novel, underwent basic changes whenever it became part of the discourse over industrialism" (1985, xi). The discourse of industrialism, Gallagher contends, "led novelists to examine the assumptions of their literary form." At the same time, "the formal structures and ruptures of these novels" revealed "paradoxes at the heart of the Condition of England Debate." Just as English industrial novelists transformed the "unsettled assumptions of the novel" into objects of scrutiny, the French social novelists of the same era found themselves making similar mimetic claims for

the novel and questioning its form in new ways—particularly when they turned to considerations of marriage and the family and the plight of women in society.

29. See especially the joint press declaration of 27 December 1841, printed in all of the papers that opposed the government's heavy censorship, among them *Le National, La Gazette de France, La Phalange, Le Siècle,* etc.

30. This result was further underscored by debates over Bonnal's censorship the following week. See Janin 1842 and Forest 1842.

31. The duel that ends in the death of Marie's newspaperman father undoubtedly resonated for July Monarchy readers with a veracity that recalled Emile de Girardin's killing, in a duel in 1836, of the leftist journalist Armand Carrel.

32. *La France,* 12 March 1842, 1, col. 3; 14 March 1842, 1, col. 1–2.

33. After Luchet's conviction, however, critics continued to call for increases in censorship of novels, as much of the fervor over Eugène Sue's 1842 *Mystères de Paris* attests: "As we wait for justice to be done," wrote Paulin Limayrac in the *Revue des deux mondes,* "this novel, which has caused much harm, is still dangerous" (1844, 96).

Nancy Glazener

12 Romances for "Big and Little Boys"

The U.S. Romantic Revival of the 1890s and James's *The Turn of the Screw*

"No literary movement could be more distinct than the romantic revival which has come about in the past few years," wrote an 1898 reviewer in the Chicago *Dial,* a periodical whose ambition was to rival the New York *Nation* in the excellence of its literary reviewing (Anderson 1898, 14; Nelson 1900, 351). Yet perhaps no literary movement has been so thoroughly effaced from U.S. literary history—effaced, that is, as a specifically literary movement affecting American readers in particular. It was easily recognized in its own time: *A Study of Prose Fictions* (1903), whose author Bliss Perry was formerly editor of the *Atlantic,* discusses a turn-of-the-century romantic revival at length, and a host of reviewers in major U.S. periodicals commented on the new version of romance that emerged in the 1880s and 1890s. Nevertheless, subsequent U.S. literary histories almost always identify naturalism and modernism as the only literary alternatives or successors to realist fiction that emerge at the end of the nineteenth century.

The main reason why the romantic revival disappeared from literary history is that the principal U.S. authors who participated in it are not part of the American canon, even though some of them—F. Marion Crawford and Lew Wallace, for example—were treated as "literary" rather than "popular" writers in their own time. Naturalism and modernism, by contrast, account for canonical U.S. writers such as Stephen Crane, Frank Norris, Gertrude Stein, and Henry James (in one phase). Occasionally, a late-century craze for historical romance is mentioned in literary histories, but as a separate popular phenomenon rather than as something bearing on the construction of the "literary."[1] Yet the *Dial* reviewer's reference to the revival as a "literary movement" needs to be taken seriously. In the most literary American periodicals of the era, the revived romance was posited as an important rival to the realist novel, even as a form whose appeal to literary-minded readers served as a reproach to realism. The main romancers whose works and public personae the romantic revival celebrated, however, were British. Crawford and Wallace, along with Amélie Rives and Edgar Saltus, were occasionally linked to the revival by reviewers, but overwhelmingly the romantic revival was associated with H. Rider Haggard, Rudyard Kipling, and Robert Louis Stevenson.

This effacement testifies in part to the artifice of organizing literary histories nationally, especially in the case of the United States, where British literature was and is widely read. It also highlights the limited usefulness of traditional schemes of literary periodization that were developed to account for sequences of canonical authors rather than to capture (say) the variable constructions of the "literary" and its relations with extraliterary forms, as Richard Brodhead has proposed (1993, 109–11). However, I would especially like to emphasize that the invisibility of the romantic revival is symptomatic of literary history's general inattention to reading practices. The romantic revival was not only a wave of American enthusiasm for certain British authors (a significant phenomenon in itself, given U.S. literary culture's usual anxious nationalism) but also a challenge to the reading practices that supported a system of literary value organized around the dominance of realism.

The relations between the revived romance and the realist novel form part of the genealogy of literary genres, a type of literary history that interrelates the production and reception of texts. For this purpose, a genre may be considered any "kind" of writing that is given a name and distinguished from other kinds by some readership.[2] Tony Bennett has usefully warned that trying to define genres stably "can only result in sets of institutionalized prescriptions for the regulation of contemporary reading practices," since a text can participate in a genre only according to readers' understanding of its generic identity, and these understandings are variable among readers and over time. Bennett's approach presumes that generic identities are not purely formal, not inherent properties of texts, but are rather produced by the ways in which texts with certain potentials for signification are read or activated. Therefore, a better task for cultural critics, in Bennett's view, is "to examine the composition and functioning of generic systems" (Bennett 1990, 112), an enterprise that necessarily involves attending to the public understandings of genre that shape readers' interpretations, on the one hand, and consequently writers' efforts to solicit their readership and make their work broadly legible, on the other. Even in eras during which readers are likely to imagine that their reading experiences are unique and personal, assigning genres (however casually) requires them to refer to clearly external and social categories, so that genres make important connections between individual and collective reading practices. For this reason, a genre can fruitfully be considered an institution, "a regulative principle or convention subservient to the needs of an organized community," so long as we remember that such regulative principles are always contested, likely to be the stakes in struggles for cultural dominance ("Institution," *The Compact Edition of the Oxford English Dictionary*, 1985, definition 6).

Since at least the late eighteenth century, newspapers and magazines have featured book reviews and other literary discussions that explicitly or implicitly disseminate generic distinctions. These prescriptions about genre provide paradigms for textuality that guide both readers and authors. The access we have to published discourses about genre allows us to organize a literary history of reception by tracing the public appropriations of particular generic categories: tracing public understandings of what it meant to write (for example) a realist novel and, equally important, to read *for realism*. The late-nineteenth-century paradigms this essay will examine were probably often resisted or applied idiosyncratically, and indeed they would have been hard to implement in any regular way. They were not really how-to guides that walked writers or readers through assembling the most fundamental elements of the text, the words on the page. Rather, they were ongoing conversations that modeled discourses—often abstract or metaphorical—for isolating textual features and classifying and evaluating texts. Like all discourses, they produced certain objects of knowledge and made others unspeakable, maybe even unthinkable, so that they helped to set parameters for reception.

It has become commonplace to assume that texts often engage their own conditions of production, figuring or meditating on the commodity status of books, the state of the literary marketplace, and other concerns central to their own making. Generic considerations are fundamentally involved in these conditions: they affect manuscripts' desirability for different kinds of publishers and the strategies used to market them. By analyzing the romantic revival as a discursive formation (though not a comprehensive literary "period," since the romantic revival affected only elite fiction) comprising the terms on which two competing genres, the realist novel and the late-century romance, were compared, this essay will demonstrate how intimately questions of genre were involved with a related set of issues affecting texts' conditions of production: the available concepts of authorship and readership and the boundaries of literariness that these concepts negotiated. To show how the romantic revival's construction of these issues can be located in a particular text, the essay will close with a case study. The critical rhetoric of the romantic revival produced a constellation of figures that turn up, rather surprisingly, in Henry James's *The Turn of the Screw,* attesting to the power of public critical discourses to direct and provoke even texts that proclaim their imaginative freedom.

The romantic revival can only be recognized as a distinct complex of critical discourses if it is situated as an intervention into the critical conversation that preceded it. As I mentioned, periodicals provide an important record of this conversation, as well as a crucial supplement to the small set of prefaces and essays by canonical authors that have usually been allowed to constitute the genealogies of the romance and the realist novel. Before contemporary literature or U.S. literature began to be taught extensively in colleges and universities, a group of American magazines had considerable power to influence what Americans with literary aspirations read and how they read it. I call these periodicals "the *Atlantic* group," because the *Atlantic Monthly* was their leading member for a long time, and because they had certain discourses in common, assumed similar kinds of cultural authority, entered into dialogues with each other, and published and reviewed fiction by many of the same authors. Along with the *Atlantic,* the group included the *Critic,* the *Forum,* the *Galaxy, Harper's Monthly, Lippincott's,* the *Nation,* the *North American Review, Putnam's, Scribner's Magazine,* and *Scribner's Monthly.*[3] Collectively, these magazines disseminated tastes. Between the 1850s, when these distinguished magazines of general culture began to proliferate, and the turn of the century, when U.S. literature began to be taught widely in the academy, they taught readers to value certain magazines, books, and publishing companies and to dismiss other cultural products and producers as low. They addressed an audience that was, or aspired to be, elite, even though in the United States elite culture must always be softpedaled.

Overwhelmingly, these magazines were concerned with the fate of the novel, and in particular with the distinctions among fictional genres: the romance, realism, sentimentalism, sensationalism, and so on.[4] And from the 1850s until the first stirrings of the romantic revival in the late 1880s, these periodicals mainly promoted realism. Even their contributors who quarreled with realism necessarily granted its status as a literary movement to be reckoned with.

During the late nineteenth century, many occupations sought professional status, which usually conferred greater financial stability as well as greater cultural authority on those who attained it, and authors were no exception. Perhaps the most important way in which the *Atlantic* cohort privileged realism over other kinds of fiction was by discursively aligning it with professionalism. Professionalism emerged as an answer to a crisis in authorship's status, since the mass-marketing of reading matter and the preponderance of writers whose livelihood depended on their succeeding in the marketplace meant that it was less and less plausible for writers to justify their cultural authority by appealing to the models of romantic seer or aristocratic amateur. The promoters of realism sought to keep capitalist culture at bay by claiming that realist authors, like physicians and other professionals, were not selling a product or a specific skill but offering instead a generalized expertise, usually figured as "vision" or "insight," which inhered in their person but approached the objectivity of scientific knowledge. Furthermore, their professional sense of civic responsibility was supposed to ensure that they would not abuse their power to advise and influence readers (Bledstein 1976, 107–8).

The realists' bid to monopolize professionalism meant that other kinds of fiction were scapegoated for the more threatening features of fiction's participation in consumer culture. Realism was specifically valued for promoting mature good citizenship and preparing readers for modern life in a democracy.[5] Its early promoters created a stark distinction between the (realist) novel and the romance, terms that had earlier in the century been almost interchangeable (Baym 1984, 430), and charged romances with being infantile, obsolete, and distorted by Old World social relations. But most important for realism's platform of professionalism, its advocates used the long-standing association between reading and ingestion to figure the difference between the products of realist-professionals and the products of inferior authors as a difference between wholesome food (realism) and addictive substances (sentimentalism, sensationalism, and—according to its detractors—the romance).

Elite readers were encouraged to cultivate a "taste" for realism, whose safety and decorum were underscored, whereas nonelite readers were pitied or faulted for indulging antisocial "appetites" for dime novels and other irresponsibly exciting kinds of fiction.

Closely related to prorealist rhetoric about the dangers of addiction to fiction was an ethic of productivity, the virtue so often used in the nineteenth century to sort the respectable and the aspiring from those disqualified from social success. Realist authors, as professionals, labored, though seemingly immaterially, and realist readers, consulting these authors, were also productive: they were supposed to use what they read to hone their moral sense, educate themselves about different sectors of society, and refine the tastes that authorized them to guide the tastes of their inferiors. Modes of reading that were compulsive, consumeristic, and therefore unproductive, insofar as they did not aim to improve readers or society according to the realists' criteria, were devalued, and during realism's ascendancy even romances issued by high-culture publishing houses risked being lumped with dime novels and other illegitimate kinds of fiction for offering only unproductive reading experiences. As the class-marked denigration of dime novels suggests, even though realist novels were sometimes called "democratic" for including nonelite characters, the social functions accorded to realist fiction by *Atlantic*-group magazines all presumed that it appealed to an elite readership who needed to know about "the people" but whose tastes were much better than the tastes of those same "people."

I have been sketching some of the discourses and figures that were deployed in polemics on behalf of realism in *Atlantic*-group magazines, but not all of the reviews and literary articles in these magazines fell in with these polemics. The romance, the only competing form that had historical claims to full literary status, continued to have its supporters, and intermittently critics threw up their hands about the contest, proposing some kind of compromise whereby romance and realism were both indispensable to legitimate fiction. (This move reveals the extent to which romance and realism constituted a dominant binary that successfully marginalized other forms such as sensation fiction [Hughes 1980, 48–49].) Realism was hegemonic, not because it was universally supported, but because its polemical promotion set the terms for debates about fictional legitimacy for several decades during the late nineteenth century. Promoters of romance could keep their place only by submitting to the discourses that had been put forth to legitimate realism: by claiming that romance writers could also be professionals, for instance, that romance's function of idealization was also necessary for mature good citizenship, or that romances, as Nathaniel Hawthorne's work had shown, could also be successfully adapted to the United States.

The Discourses and Figures of the Romantic Revival

During the 1880s, however, the romance began to be reformulated, and its promoters put forth their own protocols for determining the legitimate functions of fiction. For example, an anonymous reviewer of a novel by Jules Verne bristled at the dominance of realism, figured here as photography:

> M. Verne's position in literature may be a doubtful one, but there can be no question that the success of his romances—consisting as they do, not merely of improbabilities, but of the impossible, the untrue, the notoriously unreal—furnishes a strong indication of the strength of the imperishable appetite of the novel-reading public for something more exciting and idealistic than the dull photography of life which, according to the cant of the day, is all the future of fiction has in store for us. (Review of *Godfrey Morgan* 1883, 421)

The "Book-Talk" column of *Lippincott's* even more confidently proclaimed a change of literary tastes in 1889:

> We have all gone through our Howells and James fever, when a new book from the pen of either was a holiday occasion. . . . Booksellers report that Howells is rarely called for, and James as deliberately refused by a public which clamor with a loud voice for Haggard, for Stevenson, for Amélie Rives and Edgar Saltus. ("Book-Talk" 1889, 605)

As these statements suggest, the new version of romance was designed to delegitimate realism, not to appropriate realist standards of legitimacy. After several decades of the romance's being attacked by proponents of realism for being an aristocratic, immature, and addictive form whose authors were insufficiently professionalized, romancers recoded the charges so that they would backfire upon those who relied on them. Their recoding was organized around two interrelated figures taken to be exemplary readers, the boy and the worker, and the coordinated figure of the author as storyteller.

The ideology of professionalism upon which realism had drawn had been somewhat inhospitable to women, insofar as it centered on objectivity, distance, penetrating insight, and other masculine-coded qualities, but the theory of the new romance was more masculine yet. This phenomenon was, of course, part of that at least transatlantic surge of anxious masculinity that cast itself variously as a reaction against Victorianism, gentility, fin de siècle degeneration, the closing of the frontier, and other symptoms of overcivilization. Strenuous, manly exploits were supposed to be the best cure for these supposedly feminine malaises, and displays of militaristic prowess were their most characteristic form. The symbiosis between adventure fiction (which was being assimilated to the romance) and imperialism has long been recognized, and much productive work has been done analyzing the ways in which works of adventure fiction constructed imperialistic relations and inserted readers into them (Green 1979; Kaplan 1990). It is easy to see that fictions about pirates and forays into "primitive" places like Africa have imperialistic underpinnings, and I will be discussing some of the ways in which the theory of the new romance gave American readers new routes of identification with British as well as U.S. imperial activities. But more important for the kind of genre-oriented literary history I have proposed is that the theoretical apparatus of romance reading not only involved readers in imperialism, regardless of the subject matter of the romances they read, but also helped reconcile them to the consumeristic dimension of reading.

Henry James unwittingly helped to place boyhood at the center of generic controversy. At one point, James's "The Art of Fiction" (first published in 1884) contrasts Robert Louis Stevenson's *Treasure Island* with Edmond de Goncourt's *Chérie,* which James describes as "tracing the development of the moral consciousness of a child." Though preferring Stevenson's book to Goncourt's, he points out that he is in a better position to differ with Goncourt, having "been a child in fact" but having "been on a quest for a buried treasure only in supposition" (James 1984a, 61–62). James's essay denies that there is any important distinction between the realist novel and the romance, but Stevenson's response to James written the same year, "A Humble Remonstrance," zeroes in on James's remarks about childhood in the process of clearing a place for Stevenson's version of romance:

Here is, indeed, a wilful paradox; for if he [Henry James] has never been on a quest for buried treasure, it can be demonstrated that he has never been a child. There never was a child (unless Master James) but has hunted gold, and been a pirate, and a military commander, and a bandit of the mountains; but has fought, and suffered shipwreck and prison, and imbrued its little hands in gore, and gallantly retrieved the lost battle, and triumphantly protected innocence and beauty. (1950, 371)

Stevenson's essay, which was immediately reprinted in the United States, makes inroads on realist truisms about writing from experience and about the need to find new kinds of plots that work in democratic (that is, allegedly classless) settings. But because Stevenson clearly presumes that the child who provides imaginative access to these experiences is male, this passage sets up boyhood as a touchstone for imaginative adventuring. And even though Stevenson's most famous works have mainly been relegated to children's literature in our own time, his works and those of the other new romancers were reviewed at the time as adult reading: the reading of adults who had (re?)discovered their "inner boy," a prodigy of appetite and sensation, of imaginative responses and vivid wishes. H. Rider Haggard hinted as much when he dedicated *King Solomon's Mines* "to all the big and little boys who read it."[6]

Jacqueline Rose has suggested that the mediating fantasy figure of the child made it possible for turn-of-the-century adults to explore states that would otherwise be unduly threatening (1984, 9). In keeping with Rose's analysis, the figure of the boy reader made it possible for the romantic revivalists to redefine even the addictive aspects of reading, a target of great opprobrium under the realist dispensation, as desirable. "The significant fact is that the public taste has turned, and that that instinct which is as old as the children of Adam and Eve, the instinct for a story, has reasserted itself," proclaimed William R. Thayer in 1894 (478). Whereas an addiction was an artificial appetite, an "instinct for a story" was treated as an authentic appetite. The link between boyhood and primitivism enabled romancers to recast addictive reading as simple voraciousness: "The public is never more like a healthy child than in its thirst for the exceptional and the exotic," wrote Bliss Perry (1903, 276). And F. Marion Crawford, a U.S. author of historical romances, referred unapologetically to the world's having an " 'emotional habit' " needing to be satisfied by romance reading (1969, 102). These writers rhapsodically endorsed precisely the kind of exciting reading experience that was unlikely to shape people's ordinary lives. By the end of the century, reading had come into its own as a consumer pleasure.

This new emphasis on boyhood and its "instincts" marked the supplanting of the prorealist opposition between "high" and "low" culture by the romance-friendly preference for the "natural" over the "artificial." The realists' embrace of the "modern" over the "outmoded" was similarly countered by romancers' claim to represent the "lasting" rather than the "temporary," which meant that romances could be valued for embodying what was fundamental even if they did not fulfill realism's mandate to record contemporary life. Childhood, in turn, was identified with the primitive, an association compounded by the fact that some late Victorians interpreted the evolutionary principle that ontogeny recapitulates phylogeny to mean that children necessarily pass through the stages between primitivism and civilization (Forbush 1902, 9). Even though romances were often set in the medieval past or the colonial present, they were supposed to restore readers to a childlike state, which was imagined to be somehow an ancient and primitive state. By this means the (over)civilized could have their lost receptiveness and intensity restored to them: the romance supposedly had its "seeds . . . in the primitive passions and emotions," which had been weakened somewhat by "modern education," "the conventional uniformity of modern manners," and "the development of self-consciousness" ("Romance" 1881, 641).

Vicarious participation in the United States' widespread imperialist activity provided one outlet for these supposedly primitive or boylike impulses toward the end of the century. The link between the therapeutic effects of romance reading and imperialism was made explicit by many writers in periodicals, including this U.S. admirer of Rudyard Kipling:

> Civilization must contend with civilization that the more efficient, the more skillful, the more resourceful, may inherit the earth. And even those of us who believe this to be a moment when these deeply intrenched instincts should be restrained,—that the time has come when civilization will be the better advanced by such restraint, by coöperation rather than contest,—even they must grant, nevertheless, that the instincts to which he [Kipling] appeals, which have given our forefathers their preeminence, cannot be repressed without danger, must be guided rather than thwarted, must be made instrumental in the movement toward perfection, rather than crushed out and obliterated. (Marshall 1899, 376)

Not surprisingly, these promotions coincided with an upsurge in U.S. imperialist activity. Although the United States had been intervening in foreign affairs to protect its defensive and commercial interests for decades, and had fought a war against Mexico in the 1840s in order to gain much of what is now the American Southwest, the 1890s marked an increase in activity that was publicly recognized as imperialistic: the Spanish-American War and the acquisition of Hawaii, the Philippines, Cuba, Guam, and Puerto Rico as dependent colonies.

The economic and political interventions of the United States into cultures it deemed "primitive" were exploitative, but that by no means precluded Americans from making use even of fantasy versions of the peoples they were despoiling. In a breathtaking interplay of identifications, readers were invited by romance theorists to imagine themselves not only as boys needing imaginative outlets for their instincts of conquest but also as atavistic outcroppings of some kind of primitive community gathered around the clan's storyteller. For instance, a review article in the *Atlantic* about current novels by authors ranging from F. Marion Crawford to Henry James invoked the vague past when "the king, or the chief, or whoever had the ordering of his own entertainment, sent for the skald, the improvisator, the story-teller, or the jester, in the days when men were listeners, and not readers" ("A Few Story-Tellers" 1893, 693). Just as the realists' model of professionalism had played down authors' economic motives, the storyteller model insulated fiction from market forces in a similarly ideological manner. It implied that romancers' activity was not really conscious or calculated but rather proceeded from a racial memory, as if the transaction between writer and reader predated capitalism and eluded the market's structuring. The storytelling scenario recast the commercial transaction between author and reader as a personal interchange, and it similarly replaced the reality of privatized, individual reading with a fantasy of community—two ways to assuage late-century readers' discomforts about their conditions of reading.

The model of storyteller as tribal functionary, which was developed in relation to Haggard, Kipling, and Stevenson, helped the previously chauvinistic U.S. literary establishment forge a new cultural alliance with Great Britain through the myth of Anglo-Saxon origins. One of the rationales used to popularize imperialism was the notion of a providential design for Anglo-Saxon domination, a plan that included Americans not because of their recent dependent relationship with Great Britain but because of their shared ancient ties of blood and racial superiority. The romance model of bardic authorship underlined the ancient character of this relationship and provided a mediating fantasy for it. As

Richard Olney put it, justifying the United States' intervention in the Venezuelan Boundary Dispute on Great Britain's behalf, "There is a patriotism of race as well as of country—and the Anglo-American is as little likely to be indifferent to the one as to the other" (1898, 588). Converging with this construction of "Anglo-American" patriotism, romance theory allied U.S. literature with British literature, making it possible for American readers to find Kipling expressing their sentiments about America even though only a few years before the romance had been faulted for its roots in aristocratic, un-American cultures.[7] The new romance theory constructed, not William Dean Howells's progressive alliance of French, Russian, and Scandinavian writers who promoted democracy through realism—but a racial alliance among Anglo-Saxons (or Teutons) that predated national identities and imaginatively facilitated the subjugation or economic manipulation of other countries.

Romance theory shored up the imperialist project by inviting readers to revel in piracy (foreign trade made scary but exciting) and imperialistic adventures among subjugated nations craving American goods and ideals. And readers' identification with the healthy appetites of boys, conquerors, and "primitives" crucially allowed Americans to embrace consumerism without giving up their cherished identification as (mature, civilized) producers. The myth of "overproduction" was an important rationale for imperialism, since it blamed the economic crises of the late nineteenth century on the United States' inability to find adequate markets for what it produced (LaFeber 1963, 21). Since domestic consumption was also vital for turning "overproduction" from a weakness into a strength, one could argue that through the circuitous route of identifying with an imagined childhood appetite for fiction about foreign cultures presumed to be hungry for American products, Americans were able to internalize a consumerist appetite that served their economy (as its needs were understood or misunderstood at the time) without abandoning the productive virtues aligned with realism. Colin Campbell (1987) has stressed that an ethic of consumerism has always existed alongside the American ethic of production and deferred gratification, and he presents consumerism as a plausible development of the emotional intensity cultivated within pietistic Protestantism. However, the two ethics are kept from encountering and contradicting each other by being delegated to different sectors of society according to age, gender, occupation, and other demographic categories. In relation to his theory, one could view the opposing rhetorics of realism and romance as embodying this symbolic separation between the ethics of production and of consumption, which are systemically interdependent but have been psychologized in incompatible ways.

As a figure for the exemplary romance reader, however, the child was not only a transitional identification en route to Anglo-Saxon solidarity. In the late nineteenth century, children in the United States and in Great Britain were becoming a favorite index of society's ills and a favorite target of educators and social welfare reformers (associated in the United States with the beginnings of progressivism). Child prostitution and other forms of child abuse, including the "abuse" of raising children in poverty, were tackled by legislation, philanthropy, and government social programs. The concept of juvenile delinquency first emerged in this era, and juvenile courts were set up to handle crimes committed by minors.[8] Losing faith in the power of families to rear and socialize children properly, the schools began to address such extracurricular concerns as students' "health, vocation, and the quality of family and community life" (Cremin 1988, 229). The philosophers John Dewey and William James took up the task of helping teachers understand and influence students' most fundamental and intimate mental processes in order to advance their socialization.

Indeed, the general tendency of the new ideas about children and the institutions set up to deal with them in the late nineteenth century was to take into account all of the internal and external obstacles to proper socialization that existed in children's lives, in order to overcome them all the more effectively. No wonder, then, that the boy reader became at once an emblem of human potentiality whose resources were continually being discovered and appreciated anew and a metonymic reminder of the powerful apparatus of socialization designed to regiment and rationalize human life. Similarly, the fact that romance reading had been devalued by a realist-dominated cultural hierarchy allowed it to be constructed as natural and authentic, even though its revival was predicated on the complicated readjustment of readers' expectations I have been describing. Insofar as realism, as a form of social description, was aligned with social science, romance theory constructed its boy reader in oppositional but intimate relation to it.

Since the late nineteenth century was the era in which labor and capital most starkly emerged as opposed social forces, fueling bourgeois guilt though not bringing about a just reorganization of society, it is not surprising that the new polemic on behalf of romance allowed readers to identify themselves not only with male children and with both sides of the imperial project (conquerors and "primitives") but also with workers. Like the boy reader, the worker reader knew what he liked independently of what the experts thought (and this figure is also specified as male whenever gender comes up). Indeed, the worker reader became the occasion for romance theorists not only to accommodate consumerism but also to assert the inalienable rights of reader consumers. Building on the rhetorical stances of the labor movement and the Populist party, theorists of romance sometimes appeared to buck the literary establishment and grant "low" market preferences the status of a grassroots political movement taking on big government. G. R. Carpenter rejected the cultural authority of Brander Matthews, a professor at Columbia University, in these terms. Matthews had published a warning against historical novels in the *Forum* in 1897, calling them a "drug" for people who believe that "fiction is mere story-telling" and rejecting the claim that historical romances taught history (1897, 90). Six months later, the *Forum* published a rebuttal by Carpenter that challenged "Prof. Brander Matthews' " right to judge the tastes of others. Carpenter framed his rebuttal around the rights of working people to control their own leisure time:

> The attitude of all [experts, artists, literary histories] is, at bottom, dictatorial: they attempt to prescribe what we shall like,—which is as useless as to prescribe what we shall eat. Let these painters and dramatists and poets—so the simple-minded people has always said in its heart—offer us what they choose that is beautiful and interesting. So much is the privilege of the maker, the seller. But we are free to enjoy what we choose: that is the privilege of the consumer. . . . Art is your work; but it is our play. We have our work also, which is judged sternly by the laws of supply and demand: in our scant hours of leisure we must play as our nature bids us. It is, then, as one of the first rights of a citizen, that we hard-working people defend our hearty interest in the historical romance. (1898, 121)

On the one hand, Carpenter correctly identifies the manipulations and indoctrinations practiced in the name of high culture, which dissimulated its function of creating an economic demand for certain kinds of fiction over others. But on the other hand, he mystifies workers' right to determine their own pleasures under the guise of consumer choice, as if their preferences for certain kinds of marketed reading matter over others were natural appetites. Ironically, middle-class housewives, who were imagined not to work but who had been for most of the century envisioned as the primary consumers of novels, were not securely included in this manifesto of consumer rights.

Moreover, let us not forget that this rush to occupy the position of the worker was taking place within elite U.S. magazines. It is significant that G. R. Carpenter, serving here as a spokesman for workers, was actually a colleague of Brander Matthews's who held a chair of rhetoric at Columbia University, although the article mentioned only Matthews's status, not Carpenter's ("George Rice Carpenter" 1929, 511–12). The embrace of the worker reader, as Carpenter's remarks make clear, contributed to the positive recoding of reading as a leisure activity and a consumeristic activity, since it constructed unproductive leisure time as a necessary precondition for productivity at work. This logic provided another way in which the conflicting ethics of production and consumption could be accommodated to each other, in keeping with Colin Campbell's analysis. A passage from one of Agnes Repplier's essays exemplifies the slippage by means of which the work ethic was reconciled with a new valuation of leisure. "The god of labor does not abide exclusively in the rolling-mill, the law courts, or the cornfield," she wrote—squeezing a professional workplace between two less privileged settings. "He has a twin-sister whose name is leisure, and in her society he lingers now and then to the lasting gain of both" (1893, 63).

The revaluation of leisure that both Carpenter and Repplier are promulgating was part of an ideological formation that T. J. Jackson Lears has called "antimodernism." Antimodernism, a resistance to modern social and economic forms that surfaced around the turn of the century, often took the form of a fascination with medievalism (which Carpenter goes on to demonstrate when he especially promotes historical romances about the Middle Ages) and a desire to recover the control over one's work that medieval craftsworkers were believed to have had. Unfortunately, the subversive potential within the recognition that modern life excluded certain kinds of social relations—its potential to fuel reform movements—was all too often siphoned into the search for individual fulfillment through therapeutic activities, in this case, reading romances (Lears 1981, 93, 301). In keeping with Lears's analysis, Carpenter's use of the figure of the worker as a point of identification for readers is double-edged. It implicitly aligns itself with various kinds of workers' protests against systems that attempt to constrain them, but it elides the relations of production that give certain people who work—capitalists who might put in long hours at the office, for instance—structural advantages over other people who work—factory operatives, for instance. An 1892 *Atlantic* review functions the same way, claiming that fiction sets many persons "free from imprisoning circumstance, and makes them for a while masters of themselves because admitted to the freedom of another world" ("Recent American and English Fiction" 1892, 694). "Imprisoning circumstance" appears to be an existential inevitability, not the result of specific social and economic arrangements. In these formulations, reading has become a socially acceptable response to world-weariness, as if the civic functions it was previously accorded, its power to reform readers and thereby social institutions, were no longer imaginable. The romance theory of reader-consumer rights functioned only by denying the extent to which unsatisfactory working conditions and limitations on consumer choices resulted from socioeconomic relations that could have been different.

This sketch has only begun to analyze the rich set of figures and discourses that marked "the romantic revival," whose further historical connections are beyond the scope of this essay. My main purpose has been to show how works that were classified and read as romances were thereby brought in relation to certain cultural-political formations—most notably consumerism and imperialism. More precisely, the reviews and commentaries formulating the new romance constituted a tutelary apparatus producing this relationship. I do not mean to say that every book labeled a romance during this era simply or directly advanced these ideological projects. However, it seems fair to conclude that readers of romances during this era had to navigate these projects, not because they were "in the air," but because contemporary discourses that produced generic categories, and that offered readers accounts of why and how they ought to read romances, were riddled with them.

I especially do not wish to argue, as do proponents of the New Historicism, that texts and discourses which were roughly contemporaneous were therefore instantly and equidistantly related to each other, all being the products of a monolithic historical moment or of some unified "logic" or process underlying the moment in question.[9] Instead, I am suggesting that the genre "romance" as it was constructed in the American fin de siècle was an institution discursively implicated in the interrelated projects of consumerism and imperialism and that texts read as romances—especially those whose authors anticipated their being read as romances within this formation—had a necessary relationship to those projects, even if it was a relationship of negation or complication. This way of writing the literary history of genres posits specific intersections between literature and other areas of social life instead of viewing a genre as a technology that always operates according to the same ideological agenda.

Only one more discursive feature of the romantic revival deserves attention here. In keeping with the insistent masculinity of the boy reader, the worker reader, and the tribal storyteller, as well as of Haggard's, Kipling's, and (to a lesser extent) Stevenson's public personas, the new romance cast itself as a war on the feminine, a concept thereby compelled to signify the genteel, the mundane, the domestic, and the trivial. One of the most notorious outcroppings of this symbolic misogyny during the romantic revival was James Lane Allen's 1897 proposal that a "Masculine Principle" was currently restoring the equilibrium of culture previously marred, he claimed, by an excess of the "Feminine Principle." His description of these principles clearly bases their differences in conventions about masculine and feminine bodies, since the main characteristics of the Masculine Principle are "Virility as opposed to Refinement, Strength as opposed to Delicacy, Massiveness as opposed to Grace," and since its secondary features include "Largeness as opposed to Smallness, Obviousness as opposed to Rarity, Primary or Instinctive Action as opposed to Tact, which is always Secondary or Premeditated Action" (1897, 436). Allen claims masculinity for romance and leaves the feminine identification for realism, relying on realism's widespread association with detailed depiction and elite tastes.

However, proponents of realism had been equally zealous about constructing their preferred form and its practitioners as masculine within the matrix of professionalism. High culture was not remasculinized by the advent of romance. It was hypermasculinized, redundantly inseminated by the romance. In spite of Allen's claims, there wasn't really a heterosexual dialectic of culture at work at all; there was, rather, a kind of homosocial rivalry, to use Eve Sedgwick's terms. Realism was dismissed as effeminate, not genuinely relegated to women, although it is possible that this coding of realism made it easier for female regionalist realists to be recognized as legitimate practitioners toward the end of the century. The fact that unprofessionalism, within prorealist discourses, and overrefinement, within the discourses of the romantic revival, were both feminized exemplifies the way in which femininity—or effeminacy—can become a repository for the motley practices and values from which a dominant, and therefore masculine-identified, cultural bloc wants to distance itself.

In this way, the romantic revival linked the romance not only to consumerism and imperialism but also to a particular reconstruction of masculinity (routed through an identification with boyhood) entailing a special fear or condemnation of feminized cultural forces. A text that has often been read as embodying just this fearful condemnation of the feminine, Henry James's *The Turn of the Screw* (published in 1898), might seem to be otherwise remote from the discursive and figurative life of the romantic revival. This is precisely why its dialogue with the romantic revival is so productive to consider. *The Turn of the Screw*'s self-reflexivity has often been treated as a sign of James's mastery or, more complexly, of his exceptional capacity to dramatize the paradoxes of mastery. By reading *The Turn of the Screw* as a fiction powerfully shaped by the romantic revival, I hope to reposition this mystifyingly general "mastery" as an urgent response to the public critical discourses that produced the figures of readership and authorship James may have felt compelled to set in motion.

The Case of *The Turn of the Screw*

The audience depicted in the frame narrative to *The Turn of the Screw* has a hearty appetite for horror:

> "If the child gives the effect another turn of the screw, what do you say to *two* children—?"
>
> "We say, of course," somebody exclaimed, "that they give two turns! Also that we want to hear about them." (James 1980, 292)

The story that the audience clamors to hear turns out to be about a governess who comes to believe that her two charges, Miles and Flora, are in contact with the spirits of the previous governess, Miss Jessel, and her paramour, Peter Quint. The passage I have quoted from *The Turn of the Screw* can be seen to take up elements of the romantic revival quite explicitly: storytelling; fascination with children's receptivity, here extended to children's seeing ghosts; and unapologetic thrill seeking on the part of a fiction-consuming audience. Yet there is a certain irony in their implementation here. Douglas, the unlikely bard or skald who passes on the story, performs in an English country house to a small and elite audience (most of the women, significantly, having left by the time of the actual telling). He does not tell the story from memory but rather reads the governess's manuscript, so that only in his preparation for the story does he demonstrate performative oral inventiveness arising from his relationship with a particular group. Most ironically, in relation to the romancers' construction of childhood, the audience clearly plans to delight in the children's despoilment: they anticipate it with relish, and Douglas's emphasis on the children's innocent appearance within the story is foregrounded as a technique by means of which the audience will be made to experience an even more vivid surge of horror later on.

As early as 1865, Henry James had spoken out against the "degradation of sentiment by making children responsible for it," in a review of a novel that insisted upon the childlike innocence of the passion of two of its characters (James 1984c, 637). It seems likely that he was predisposed to be skeptical of romance theory's glorification of childhood three decades later. Douglas's preliminary remarks about the tale, emphasizing extraordinary events witnessed by children, signals the novella's ongoing preoccupation with key rhetorical figures of the "romantic revival"—which, by the way, is the exact phrase used by the governess to describe the architecture at Bly (James 1980, 310). How, after all, could James forget a recent contest in which he had been both a participant and a target?

For although James himself never unambiguously or permanently took up the cause of realism, William Dean Howells did, and he managed to drag James along with him. Howells wrote a profile of James for the *Century* magazine in 1882 that cast James as a realist revolutionary who eclipsed all writers of the previous dispensation. Predictably, Howells's claims met with ridicule and resentment on both sides of the Atlantic. The most incendiary passage from the essay is this one:

> The art of fiction has, in fact, become a finer art in our day than it was with Dickens and Thackeray. We could not suffer the confidential attitude of the latter now, nor the mannerism of the former, any more than we could endure the prolixity of Richardson or the coarseness of Fielding. These great men are of

the past—they and their methods and interest; even Trollope and Reade are not of the present. . . . This [new] school, which is so largely of the future as well as the present, finds its chief exemplar in Mr. James; it is he who is shaping and directing American fiction, at least. (Howells 1882, 28)

In the wake of this essay, James was everywhere paired with Howells and with Howells's pronouncements, and most of the romancers' volleys at realism's elitism and effeminacy aimed at these two writers. For example, a reviewer of James's *The Princess Casamassima* expressed longing for "the methods of those great masters whom Mr. Howells has told us are of the past" and accused James of aristocratic condescension: "he preserves throughout the calm, superior air of one who has outgrown emotions and enthusiasm; he looks upon his fellow-beings only as available literary material" (Review of *The Princess Casamassima* 1887, 359). A *Nation* reviewer who praised James nonetheless compared his work to that "of the cunning worker in ivory, or of the lapidary," neither of which was likely to capture the public imagination (Review of *Tales of Three Cities* 1884, 442). Taking a familiar proromance stance, a *Lippincott's* writer didactically propounded, as a corrective to James's and Howells's work, that "in health and vigor we are conscious of vivid feelings, lively passions. . . . [T]hese attributes claim their right to ministry, as well as the languid desire to know the material of a lady's dress or the precise way in which a man gets up in the morning" ("Our Monthly Gossip" 1887, 184). In short, James and Howells were precisely the writers neglecting the demands of healthy, manly, hardworking American readers.

It is curious, then, to see that James's New York preface, written eight to ten years after the work itself, aligns *The Turn of the Screw* with romance. James describes the work as "irresponsible," a "fairy-tale pure and simple," a "sinister romance" or "pure romance," and he protests, as he did in conversations and letters, that the work is anything but serious, the rhetoric of seriousness being essential to Howells's widely disseminated version of realist professionalism (James 1984b, 169, 171, 170, 175). And whereas Howells had once, (in)famously, declared that American literature should concentrate on "the more smiling aspects of life, which are the more American" (Howells 1983, 41), James's preface proclaims:

The thing had for me the immense merit of allowing the imagination absolute freedom of hand, of inviting it to act on a perfectly clear field, with no "outside" control involved, no pattern of the usual or the true or the terrible "pleasant" (save always of course the high pleasantry of one's very form) to consort with. (170)

Howells had claimed in his *Century* piece about James that in "one manner or other the stories were all told long ago," a claim often quoted mockingly by the proponents of romance (Howells 1882, 29); James counters Howells again when he recounts his fear, in the face of writing *The Turn of the Screw,* that the "good, the really effective and heart-shaking ghost-stories (roughly so to term them) appeared all to have been told" (1984b, 169). And James also harks back to a *Lippincott's* reviewer who claimed that James could not bring himself "to the vulgarity of a regular *dénouement*" (Review of *The Portrait of a Lady* 1882, 214) when, in the frame story, Douglas assures his audience that the story won't tell the secrets of the governess's heart " 'in any literal, vulgar way' " and one listener—not a sympathetic character—responds with open disappointment (James 1980, 294).

Yet despite his prefatory remarks about the tale's simplicity, James also points out its recursiveness, since he calls it "an anecdote amplified and highly emphasised and returning upon itself" (1984b, 172). It is very important for the purposes of genre history that this recursiveness be specified historically rather than be subsumed into textuality's necessary turn upon itself. Shoshana Felman has put *The Turn of the Screw* to wonderful use as an allegory of reading (1982), and her version of this allegory—in which readers seeking mastery are foiled and the text comments on the impossibility of the literal—functions beautifully as a heuristic fable for late-twentieth-century readers, teaching us, in effect, how to read *The Turn of the Screw* in a way that is satisfying and instructive. Her intention, however, is to analyze the text's continuities across historical moments rather than its engagement with any particular moment, as is demonstrated by the fact that she tracks reading effects that the text produces across generations of critics. In attending to the allusions made in James's preface to the polemics on behalf of realism and romance that structured the romantic revival, I am similarly emphasizing how much *The Turn of the Screw* comments on its own conditions of meaning. However, my interest is not only in the fact of the work's recursiveness, the Escher-like narrative design that Felman evokes, but also in the form that the recursiveness takes: its engagement with debates about reading that flourished at a particular historical moment, although they have left their traces in the present. Whereas Felman highlights scenes of reading that she glosses as ahistorical textual effects, I am highlighting the figures and discourses that mediated the readings James might have expected his novella to get and that shaped its public reception.

Interwoven with these allusions to the debate about romance is a discussion of James's relations with an imagined audience. Just after we hear about the text's recursiveness, we hear that "it is a piece of ingenuity pure and simple, of cold artistic calculation, an *amusette* to catch those not easily caught (the 'fun' of the capture of the merely witless being ever but small), the jaded, the disillusioned, the fastidious" (James 1984b, 172)—in other words, the overcivilized denizens of the late nineteenth century who longed for fictional rejuvenation. James goes on to specify two kinds of catching. One is that his fiction has exceeded the appreciation of a reader who "complained that I had n't sufficiently 'characterised' my young women engaged in her labyrinth" (1984b, 173), an objection that echoes more or less realist concerns with deep character and ethics. But James exults even more about having made readers construct for themselves the evils that menace the children, in a passage worth quoting at length:

> Only make the reader's general vision of evil intense enough, I said to myself—and that already is a charming job—and his own experience, his own imagination, his own sympathy (with the children) and horror (of their false friends) will supply him quite sufficiently with all the particulars. . . . There is not only from beginning to end of the matter not an inch of expatiation, but my values are positively *all blanks* save so far as an excited horror, a promoted pity, a created expertness—on which punctual effects of strong causes no writer can ever fail to plume himself—proceed to read into them more or less fantastic figures. (1984b, 176–77; emphasis added)

The reader here is given the opportunity to recognize how inextricable the idea of childhood innocence is from the idea of its corruption, since innocence is always innocence *of* certain kinds of knowledge and experience. The reader seeking a moral consciousness to emulate or internalize is not the only one taken in by this work. The romance reader expecting to reaffirm the originary innocence of childhood, which serves to guarantee the foundational innocence of the adult imagination, is led instead to produce materials more characteristic of the Freudian unconscious.

Of course, James's self-defense here is somewhat disingenuous. The danger of "vulgarity" to which he alludes in the preface is by no means so open to interpretation as to be a "blank." The word implies an infringement of very specific proprieties, a reference to sex or scatology, especially one that is semantically attributed to a subordinate class. The nobility of the children is overinscribed: they are "little grandees" or "princes of the blood, for whom everything, to be right, would have to be enclosed and protected," so that, the governess tells us, "the only form that, in my fancy, the afteryears could take for them was that of a romantic, a really royal extension of the garden and the park" (James 1980, 309).[10] Their tact, their refined manners (we hear that "whatever he [Miles] had been driven from school for, it was not for ugly feeding" [1980, 393]), and Miles's gentlemanliness testify to a quality about them in which aristocracy is conflated with innocence. Hence the importance of their corrupters, the ghosts, being servants; the danger of crossing class lines is demonstrated by the unhappy fate of Miss Jessel, who was "respectable" (296) until she mingled with the "base menial" (335) Peter Quint, the Master's valet.[11]

Significantly, the strongest proofs that the children have been corrupted are not sexual misbehaviors but lapses from the verbal propriety of their class: Miles has said things to boys he liked that were "too bad" to be written about (401), and Flora uses "appalling language" in speaking about her current governess to Mrs. Grose (388).[12] Since Miss Jessel's mingling with Peter Quint resulted in pregnancy, the expectation is created that the children's class-marked language also involves sexuality. And one question posed is whether their sexual fluency signifies real knowledge and real experience—knowledge and experience that they not only possess but recognize as illicit since, if they have it, they keep it from the governess. In this respect, the governess's fantasy that the children, especially Miles, have "no history" (314) is revealing, calling attention to another blind spot of the romance version of childhood. Only a few years before G. Stanley Hall's 1904 work *Adolescence* would explore the sexual capacities and feelings of children—an American advance that has been eclipsed in retrospect by Freud's 1905 essay "Infantile Sexuality" (Freud 1957)—the problem of whether the children at Bly have been corrupted by ghosts might well serve as a metaphor for the problem of whether children need anything but their own experiences to inform them about sexuality. Hall himself addressed this issue anxiously in discussing masturbation:

> There are well-authenticated cases where children of both sexes under two years of age have practiced it ["onanism"], and far more cases are on record for still later childhood years. In some cases it is taught by nurses, older children, or perverts, but there is abundant evidence that even with the very young, and still more with the older, the old view that it was not spontaneously learned, but due to example and moral infection, was wrong. (1914, 435)

It is only by erasing children's histories, especially the histories of their discovering and exploring their own bodies, that they can be posited as so very innocent, or ignorant, after all.

Readers ranging from Edmund Wilson to Martha Banta have pointed out some kind of eerie coordination between the governess and the ghosts, Wilson suggesting that the ghosts serve as projections of the governess's repressed sexuality (1960) and Banta suggesting that both the ghosts and the children, though real within the terms of the narrative, are playing out a dynamic within the governess's own desires (1972, 122). The governess's stance is not a personal idiosyncracy, though. Her relation to the children mirrors that of the *Atlantic*-cohort magazines, whose vying investments in realism and romance commit them both to discipline childhood and to revel in it. The governess has come to "watch, teach, 'form'" (James 1980, 300) the children and also "'to be carried away'" (301) by them. Her second motive is more easily satisfied than the first: "My attention to them all really went to seeing them amuse themselves immensely without me: this was a spectacle they seemed actively to prepare and that engaged me as an active admirer. I walked in a world of their invention" (326). She can be "plunged . . . into Flora's special society" (333); she acknowledges that "the surrender to their extraordinary childish grace" was "a thing I could actively cultivate" (338). They put on plays for her and tell her stories (339). No romance reader could have more successfully colonized the realm of childhood, as it was constructed at the end of the century, than this intrepid governess, who attributes the same motive to the ghosts. Her most positive statement about their designs on the children is that Miss Jessel wants Flora to share with her the torments of the damned (367), presumably to divert her and to filter her perceptions just as Miss Jessel's successor uses the children's play to distract her from her own sorrowful predicament. One might see in the governess an emblem of the uneasy resolution to a late-Victorian dilemma about childhood: she is trying to forget the disturbing specter of children's sexuality and self-consciousness by becoming absorbed in children's dutiful enactments of the sprightliness expected of them.

It would be overly simple to conclude that the novella is James's cold-blooded excursion into the kind of fiction that American elite reviewers were favoring, intended to catch readers who shared romancers' investment in childhood whether or not they ever realize that they had been caught. There seems to be a genuine desire in James's preface to invite reading practices associated with romance in order to gain some distance from realism: the narrative's use of some of the most conspicuous old and new marks of romance (such as ghosts and storytelling) underlines this invitation. *The Turn of the Screw* is not an antiromance, but neither is it "really" a romance. Indeed, from the point of view of the genre history I have been suggesting, it is impossible to locate any text squarely within a genre, although its genre attributions are part of its history, precisely because generic assignments are discursively so volatile. Nancy Armstrong has suggested that "the internal composition of a given text is nothing more or less than the history of its struggle with contrary forms of representation for the authority to control semiosis" (1987, 23). Taking her idea a step further, I am suggesting that texts struggle, not exactly with other forms, but with the representations of other forms, the discourses and figures on which the whole scheme of fiction's classification into forms depends. Accordingly, I have tried to present *The Turn of the Screw* as a fiction taking up key figures and discourses that had dominated public discussions of reading in the forum of the *Atlantic* cohort for more than a decade. And it is crucial to the kind of literary history I am proposing to recognize that not only works by "masters" are self-reflexive in this way, since this recursiveness is as much the product of the literary establishment's compulsive assigning and patrolling of generic identities as of individual authors' artful self-consciousness.

In closing, I would like to propose a way in which *The Turn of the Screw* pointedly interrogates one of the shibboleths of the romantic revival. One might imagine the novella to be organized around the competition between the governess and Peter Quint for Miles, since the governess's initial and final confrontations are with the ghost of Quint, and since the last one leaves Miles's heart "dispossessed" and stopped (James 1980, 403). A whole tradition of criticism that faults the governess for trying to cramp or feminize Miles reproduces the sexual politics of the discourses of the romantic revival, sometimes faulting the governess not only for repressing Miles's masculinity but even for unconsciously inventing the threatening masculinity of Quint.[13] However, the allegorical resonances of this struggle are subtler than this. For one thing, as I pointed out above, the governess plays out a bifurcation between the more or less realist desire to shape and discipline childhood and the more or less romantic desire to be submerged in it, neither of which can be reduced to a feminine or feminizing intent.

For another, presuming that only the governess's symbolic functions are thrown into question by the novella shortchanges the rich figures of Peter Quint and Miles. They are the only characters in *The Turn of the Screw* who have no counterparts in *Jane Eyre,* which Millicent Bell has described as the novella's "intertext" (1991, 224), and it is not too farfetched to assume that they were created as a result of James's experiences with the particular discourses that greeted his literary productions, discourses that still reverberate in his preface. Most significant, Miles and Quint are demonic versions of the figures idealized within the romantic revival. The innocent appetency of the boy reader and the consumeristic self-assertion of the oddly classless worker reader here spawn their sinister Others: the boy who knew too much and the man whose uncultured pursuit of leisure got out of hand. And of the two, Quint is the more revealing character, a means by which James embodies certain unacknowledged horrors that working-class males represented for elite readers, despite workers' having become fashionable as the icons of an in-group cultural rebellion.

In James's novella, Peter Quint is the origin of sexual contamination. He has contaminated Miss Jessel, and with her has contaminated the children; the struggle with him might even be contaminating the governess. It is precisely the nature of his contaminating influence that James's "blanks" prompt readers to surmise for themselves. Considered in this light, James's treatment of Quint, which makes a character from the social and narrative margins the absent center of the book, serves at least two purposes, both of which manifest a skeptical relationship to the romantic revival. On the one hand, the class degradation that James lavishes on Quint casts doubt on the idea that fiction would benefit by being renewed from its more "natural" margins, from cultural insiders' coming to identify with people who were less refined and more instinctual. Quint incarnates the elements of working-class masculinity, as it was culturally scripted, that were laundered out of the hypermasculine rhetoric of the romantic revival: vulgarity, since refinement had been feminized, so that the (imagined) uncouth workingman was therefore the most masculine; and sexual aggression, omitted in the idyllic all-male scenarios of adventure fiction. In short, Quint might be the slanderous antithesis of the worker reader: a more threatening, scarcely representable incarnation of James Lane Allen's "Masculine Principle" advancing on fiction, and a figure whose potential for cultural revitalization is dubious.

On the other hand, both the looming but silent presence of Quint and the absence of any explicit sexual references from the book, so that readers must be preoccupied with filling in these "blanks," point to the hypocrisy of a literary establishment that wanted to revitalize literature by drawing on society's earthy, unrefined margins but that still stringently limited public references to sexuality. Leon Edel's biography of Henry James shows that James had been frustrated by the extraordinary restrictiveness of U.S. high culture as recently as the winter of 1895–96, when an editor for the *Century* expurgated a mere reference to seduction in James's review of the works of Alexandre Dumas fils (1978, 156). If fiction was renewing itself by reclaiming certain transgressive pleasures of reading and certain materials that had been excluded from high culture during the preceding decades, what was being reclaimed was tame, indeed, in comparison with the sexual knowledge that was being produced at every turn but disallowed. Quint is also the specter of a set of social and sexual practices and meanings that was still effectively suppressed within high culture: suppressed by the mystifying enshrinement of the worker reader, which only papered over genuine class antagonisms and prejudices, and suppressed by the evacuation of open sexual discussion from high culture, which led elite readers to project sexual meanings and wishes they could not acknowledge as their own onto the working class.[14] No wonder James might pride himself on having readers furnish the content of the ghosts' depravities from their own thoroughly acculturated and class-bound consciousness.

Notes

This essay has benefited from the responses and suggestions of many of my colleagues at the University of Pittsburgh, who heard it delivered as a talk. Jayne

Lewis, Marianne Novy, Susan Harris Smith, and Katie Trumpener provided careful and instructive readings of the manuscript that were a great help. I am especially grateful to Deidre Lynch, who offered inspired advice and inspiriting enthusiasm at several crucial junctures, and to William Warner, whose shrewd editorial comments about the essay improved it considerably.

1. For example, Carl Van Doren's essay "The Later Novel: Howells" identifies the historical romance and naturalism as reactions against realism at the end of the century (Trent 1921, 3:89). Robert E. Spiller's *Literary History of the United States* bypasses the debate by casting realism and romance as fictional impulses that are likely to commingle in a given work; it omits any mention of a romantic revival (1963, 878). The *Columbia Literary History of the United States* likewise bypasses the debate. Amy Kaplan's excellent chapter entitled "Nation, Region, and Empire" in *The Columbia History of the American Novel* puts late-century historical romances in the context of imperialism but does not address the struggle over the romance form itself (Elliott et al. 1991:256–66). Peter Keating comes closest to engaging the public discourses about romance. He identifies "one strand of late Victorian fiction [that includes James, Hardy, Butler, and Corelli] in which children are portrayed as the victims of modern intellectual and moral restlessness" and another in which "adults were the enemy," although he does not relate this phenomenon to the debate over realism and romance (1989, 219). Keating also links these works to U.S. boy books such as those by Twain. Amy Kaplan's wonderful essay "Romancing the Empire: The Embodiment of American Masculinity in the Popular Historical Novel of the 1890s" (1990) comes closest to framing the phenomenon in terms of the gendered, imperialistic resonances of the romance, but Kaplan addresses works by American writers only, and the term "popular" in her title again reinforces the notion that this was a phenomenon running on a parallel track to properly "literary" history rather than a central feature of it.

Numerous works of British literary history make a place for the romantic revival, perhaps by another name, but the only example I know of an American literary history that does so since Bliss Perry's, which was Anglo-American in scope, is Martin S. Day's *A Handbook of American Literature* (1975, 146–47). And Day's handbook, which acknowledges the centrality of romantic fiction in late-century reading, does not seem to have influenced subsequent studies or histories of the period.

2. Given that the terms I am considering were used so variously—so that, for instance, sometimes the romance was distinguished from the novel, but at other times it was a subdivision of the novel—it would not be feasible for me to try to distinguish between more comprehensive and less comprehensive literary categories by giving them different names. Significantly, other writers emphasizing reception have also used "genre" in this way, most notably Bennett 1990 and Jauss 1982.

3. All of these magazines' publishing histories can be found in Frank Luther Mott's *A History of American Magazines* (1930–69), which has been indispensable for this project. Most of the magazines had somewhat long titles and even subtitles, so for convenience's sake I identify each by the briefest version of its name. All of my generalizations about the public discourses constructing genre are based on my research in the magazines named between 1850 and 1910.

4. In taking up the magazines in the *Atlantic* group as a source for certain dominant discourses about fiction reading, I do not mean to imply that this history on its own can represent reception (as it was dialectically related to literary production) during this era of U.S. history. It is crucial to combine this history with the histories of competing or resistant discourses about reading circulating in less elite publications, with histories of the foundational reading practices taught by primers and textbooks, and with other accounts of the relationship between reading and social life. For these histories, different methods will be appropriate, and questions of genre may not always be central. However, they were for the *Atlantic* group.

5. My limited space here prevents me from providing the kinds of textual evidence from the periodicals that would support and elaborate these claims about the prorealist discourses governing genre hierarchies, claims that I present more fully in my book-length project *Reading for Realism: The History of a U.S. Literary Institution, 1850–1910* (forthcoming from Duke University Press). However, they are based on the same kinds of texts—book reviews and literary and cultural articles in *Atlantic*-cohort periodicals—that I cite in characterizing the romantic revival in the next section of this essay. Realism's associations with maturity, modernity, and democracy run through countless reviews from this era, and William Dean Howells's critical writings include some especially notorious examples. An early article setting up a polarization between the romance and the implicitly realist novel provides an example of the extent to which realism was enlisted to serve middle-class citizens who live regular lives, however: "I have passed the period of romance. Only children wait for adventures. I do not look for sudden wealth or poverty. I do not expect to fall in love with a princess, a beggar, or an opera-dancer. I can earn my bread, and am not exposed to great misery in any turn of the wheel of fortune. Is life, then, for me no longer worth living? . . . The right novel, the true poem . . . will show the manhood, not the childhood, of the race. It will not need to elaborate a black background of misfortune to serve as a foil for doubtful happiness, but will exhibit an activity so splendid that it must shine in relief upon the dingy gray of ordinary circumstances, duties, and relations" ("Ideals in Modern Fiction" 1857, 96).

6. Despite this masculine reader identification, a surprising number of women critics (notably Agnes Repplier, a regular *Atlantic* contributor) supported the new romance. This fact becomes less surprising when one considers that their main alternative, realism, also depended on devaluing feminine-marked read-

ing ("addictions" to sentimental fiction, for example) and problematizing female authorship, as I indicate below.

7. Interestingly enough, Kipling sent his poem "The White Man's Burden," written in 1898 and subtitled "The United States and the Phillipine Islands," to Theodore Roosevelt, who had it published in the New York *Sun* on 5 February 1899. Kipling wanted Roosevelt to use the poem to help influence the debate about a treaty concerning whether the U.S. would take over the governance of the Philippines, which it had acquired from Spain (Hitchens 1990, 63–69).

8. On child saving and juvenile delinquency, see Platt 1982; on the British fight against child prostitution, see Weeks 1981, esp. 38 and 87; and on the Progressive movement in education and its prehistory, see the Hawes and Hines collection (1985).

9. The title of Walter Benn Michaels's *The Gold Standard and the Logic of Naturalism* (1987) exemplifies this assumption.

10. The text's emphasis on the children's aristocracy connects to Graham McMaster's (1988) reading of *The Turn of the Screw* as an example of the Indian orphan tale, a genre that thrived around the turn of the century and enacted a fantasy through which the profits of imperialism were laundered by descending to orphans, who were necessarily innocent of the colonial exploitation that had produced the profits. This argument suggests another way in which a text read as a romance might take up its implicit connection with imperialism.

11. Bruce Robbins's brilliant essay (1984) discusses how the novella's "blanks" point to the taboo subject of sexual relations across class lines in the story.

12. Edel also points out that Miles's "misdemeanor" is "in the realm of speech, not sex" (1978, 208).

13. Edmund Wilson kicked off this tradition with his famous essay "The Ambiguity of Henry James" (1960). But even Martha Banta, in an otherwise subtle reading, refers to the "Virgin governess who tried to impose her conscious, personal will upon those around her" (1972, 132). And Leon Edel, drawing on James's biography, claims, "The essential point the story makes is to show Miles's wish to be a boy among boys—and the fact that his expression of such a wish is deemed evil by the governess" (1978, 208).

The antidote to such readings that most closely approaches my own is Mark Seltzer's remark, in a brief discussion of *The Turn of the Screw,* that the governess, "in her roles of tutor, nurse, confessor, and analyst," occupies "in turn the power roles of the 'medico-tutelary complex'" (1984, 157), which Seltzer relates to the kind of textual preoccupation with achieving power through knowledge that Felman also raises.

14. My argument here is deeply indebted to Stallybrass and White's discussion (1986) of how the bourgeoisie projects elements of its own identity onto its social margins and can then transgressively reclaim them.

Lauren Berlant

13 Pax Americana

The Case of *Show Boat*

And if the things we dream about
don't happen to be so—
that's just an unimportant technicality.
—Oscar Hammerstein and Jerome Kern, "Make Believe"

The Unfinished Business of Sentimentality

This is an essay about the unfinished business of sentimentality. It asks why and how specific kinds of pain get turned into forms of modern entertainment; it asks what kind of theory or account of history the sublime object of sentimentality (of which the Urtext here is *Uncle Tom's Cabin*) offers its consuming and witnessing public; more broadly, it provides a case study in thinking through why sentimental texts must mask the aspiration they always embody to generate a public sphere of opinion and culture making. The disguise of "feeling" as a thing distinct from and superior to public-sphere norms of instrumental rationality requires the modern sentimental text's central moments of instruction and identification to appear only as sublime ephemera, fragile temporal material of feeling and memory that seems constantly to escape becoming knowledge that might inform, even revolutionize, the institutions and the common sense of official culture. These are the contradictions of modern American feminine sentimentality: a commitment to and revulsion caused by excesses of feeling in a world of politics, instrumental reason, and public-sphere mediation; the adoption of the commodity form to express the overwhelming predicament of subaltern identity in the face of the taxonomic and material violence of national capitalism.

By the phrase "unfinished business" I mean to designate the specific conjuncture of adaptation, commodification, and affect that distinguishes this modern and nationally inflected modality of expression. I also mean, here, to make specific historical arguments about how the semiotic substance of sentimentality has been used to produce a complicated account of modern American subaltern identity. I argue throughout that the culture—and the culture industry—of feminine sentimentality expresses, reproduces, and brings into critical representation some central contradictions and ambivalences of democratic culture in the United States.

We live in a modernity that appropriates in a kind of aversive blur the now mythified archaic authenticity of slave affliction: this is the argument of Edna Ferber's novel *Show Boat* (1926). The story of *Show Boat* follows the dissolution of the American color line into the linked crossover dynamics of the Harlem Renaissance, modernist youth culture, and middlebrow entertainments. Magnolia Hawks and her parents live on a showboat, the *Cotton Blossom,* that travels the Mississippi starting in the 1870s; Julie Dozier and Steve Baker, the romantic leading actors, are revealed to have committed miscegenation, with Julie passing as white. They are banished from the boat, with Julie resurfacing during the Columbian Exposition as the companion of Chicago's leading prostitute. Magnolia takes Julie's place as an actress; Gaylord Ravenal, the gambler who becomes the lead actor in the melodrama, falls in love with Magnolia, and as real-life lovers they dominate the theatrical scene of the river, their passion burning visibly through the plots their acting sells. They marry, and they go to the exotic and degraded Chicago of the Columbian Exposition, living the oscillating lives of gamblers on the economic periphery of the city. When they hit bottom, they return to the boat, and Magnolia gives birth to a child, Kim, named for the conjuncture Kentucky, Illinois, Missouri. They return to the city, go bankrupt again, and then Ravenal leaves Magnolia. To survive Magnolia joins the new entertainment form called vaudeville, marketing not the melodrama she performed on the showboat but the African American spirituals and popular songs Jo and Queenie, the ship's servants, had taught her as a child.[1] Magnolia makes these natal slave songs the rage in the North. The book begins and ends as a narrative about daughter Kim. She is a celebrity, a full-fledged star on Broadway, the third generation of Hawkses to capitalize on what she now delicately calls "southern" songs (Ferber 1926, 118); meanwhile, Magnolia returns to the showboat, and to immersion in the visibly unchanged and psychically unchanging interracial peasant South of her childhood.

Show Boat has been made into three films, six radio plays, the first American cast album, the first televised Broadway event, and more than thirty-five major revivals (Krueger 1977). As fiction-cum-star biography, the novel is a history of its own present tense masked as the saga of a celebrity family. In making this kind of mutual introjection of the personal and the historical drama, Ferber's *Show Boat* discloses some of the mechanisms by means of which American subaltern activity and in particular the public history of African Americans have been expropriated for the purpose of creating a "modern" American culture, one that might flaunt a rich past while feeling free from accountability to the past's ongoing activity in the present. The modern American moment is produced not through the official time line of national history, nor through a claim that family history is in any sense private, but through a genealogy of entertainments whose place in collective memory makes up a nation that takes on the shimmery, intimate, and distant quality of the commodity form. The effect of commodity "historicity" is generated, in *Show Boat,* by a national culture industry whose pleasure machines are the showboat on the Mississippi, the Columbian Exposition in Chicago, and the theater on Broadway. This culture industry is dedicated to substituting qualities of nationally coded experience and feeling for class reference and historical memory: as the novel stages the nation's recovery from the legacies of slavery, migration, urbanization, and industrialization, it develops an obsessive relation to futurity. The family form that mediates national culture and personal experience in the novel helps to do just that: hold a wedge open for the future and for reproduction in all its senses—biological, political, economic, aesthetic. In this way the novel tells the story of Americans' increasing dependence on tourism, entertainment forms, and leisure cultures for their own self-understanding and sense of possibility.

Show Boat's appraisal of modernist mass culture predicts the kinds of distortion the novel's meaning would undergo in its adaptation to drama: "It was Anodyne. It was Lethe. It was Escape. It was the Theatre" (Ferber 1926, 105). The novel's working contradiction arises from its attempt to narrate both critically and sympathetically the conditions of violence and optimism that have accompanied the adaptation of subaltern populations to national modernity. Trafficking heavily in racial, class, regional, and gender stereotypes derived from the bottom of the American class system, the novel aims to repopulate the image archive of modern American memory, intermixing scenes of elite life derived from the modern metropolitan public sphere with other American landscapes, other kinds of ordinary and extraordinary pleasure or suffering, other strange corporeal and cultural types. The archaism of the novel supports Ferber's use of the literary/printed stereotype to oppose the glamorous amnesiac spectacle with which she is also fascinated, a spectacle that represents the direction she sees America traveling.

In contrast, the plays (first performance 1927; book and lyrics by Oscar Hammerstein II; music by Jerome Kern) and the films (1929, dir. Harry A. Pollard; 1936, dir. James Whale; 1951, dir. George Sidney) that adapt the novel have made the text a classic vehicle for amnesiac narrative, an authentic piece of kitsch history. On behalf not of memory but of memorabilia. The narrative logic of *Show Boat*'s revisions cuts against the grain of the novel in two primary ways. First, the dramatic versions do not aspire to depict a national counterculture of sacred stereotypes: Ferber's peculiar collection and display of archaic Americana do not translate into the ways the theatrical songs and narrative of *Show Boat* display American personhood. Instead, the dramas actually give richer, more elaborate, and more nuanced subjectivities to the African American characters they foreground while casting into the dustbin of history the white peasantry and urban underclasses the novel gathers up.

Traces of the multiracial and class-fractured American historical past from the novel are replaced in the play by African American—but not always black—faces that sing with feeling, subjectivity, memory. African American history comes to stand for American history itself, at least insofar as history is a record of people and events that pass into pasts. But—and this is the second way the revisions erase the novel—having elaborated the African American stereotype more fully into theatrical personhood, the dramas nonetheless increasingly imagine a nation that pushes narratively toward the future, leaving its survivor cultures to a petrified obsolescence located in the space of the South and in the musical traces of popular song, the faint echoes of a classic sound track.

Thus while the dramas that adapt *Show Boat* differ from the novel, in which American histories provide the local color and rich past of the modern nation, the adaptations share the novel's contradictory impulses toward historical explanation and national culture making. The modernist desire for a past preserved in aspic can be detected in the place given feeling and passion in *Show Boat*'s historical sweep. All the versions of *Show Boat* show how one history of subalternity can become reconfigured into the materials for another: specifically, how the commodity code "romantic love"/"exotic sex" came to mark not only the erasure of slavery and Southern history from popular memory but also the creation of a sex class of exploited women across race and class divides.[2] Both Ferber and Hammerstein recount how women's domestic and sexual service to men, to entertainment culture, and to modern national identity became inextricably linked. At the same time, American "women's history" becomes white women's history, and white women's history becomes narrowed by being linked to a grander scheme of class amnesias: love plots and domestic fantasies come to saturate the narratives of experience with which women of a certain class identify.

The two subaltern codes of *Show Boat* thus diverge in their relation to modernity: the "race" code, central to knowledge but displaced from plot, represents a sign of the archaic origins of collective national consciousness; in contrast, the gender/sexuality code, which takes over the plot, represents both modernity and the transcendence of historical memory. Finally, *Show Boat* delivers a meaningfully incoherent account of whether white women represent a subaltern class in America. The very modes of shallow futurity Ferber questions in the novel become the means of production of modernity's celebration as a scene of entertainment.

To write about what I will call the "supertext" of *Show Boat*—the novel and its adaptations—is to stage a competition between the novel and other forms of leisure narrative over whose strategies for negotiating the relation between lived suffering and fantasy will produce the norms of American popular memory and lived culture. A specific scene of contradictory desire marks the narratives of modern capitalism: particular kinds of impossible fantasy are marketed as fantasies that truly superior, deserving, and lucky people will actually be able to live. Fantasy here operates not as a desire for a thing but as a desire for a life, as a sequencing of events that makes fabulous sense, a biography that, seen from the "outside," would appear to deserve a history.[3] The possibility that anyone's biography might tell of a lived fantasy is central to the ways the culture industry makes erotic, normal, and personal the risks and failures, the violences, deferrals, and impossible promises of democracy under capitalism. It does this first by referring the life-sustaining longing that people have to particular valued forms of intimacy—for example, the romantic couple, the conjugal family—and then by creating conventions of amnesia in which the costs of depending on these forms appear merely ordinary, necessary, or profitable.

In *Show Boat,* the very same vehicles that imagine the history of the present and the doggerel of the future—the culture industry and its plots of displacement and personalization—are also central apparatuses of violence and exploitation. This is much clearer in the novel, which is about the hard conditions of life that bring work into contact with play, than in the dramas, which focus on the plays of desire. Amnesias, like so many other lacks, often appear to us in spectacular forms, forms radiant with the wish they ill express, fetishes. Fredric Jameson calls these "fantasy bribes": bribes of culture that displace history and condense longing the way a dream does (1979, 144). My interest here is less in the bribe than in the scene of its exchange: the ways in which narratives about intimate life construct fantasy norms that make simply ordinary and personal violences and uncertainties that are also structural, political, and collective. In reading across the supertext that *Show Boat* has brought into being, I aim to apprehend the aesthetics, politics, and techniques that make Ferber's/Hammerstein and Kern's bourgeois project paradoxically both normative and critical. To begin this case study in the history of national sentimentality, I start with another, earlier context in which stereotype and subjectivity meet.

Uncle Tom's *Show Boat*

Show Boat has been called, by Ferber herself and by critics, a fantastic piece of Americana (Ferber 1939, 288). Its status as Americana has been said, in an anonymous review, to rival that of *Uncle Tom's Cabin* (Review of *Show Boat* 1936). *Uncle Tom's Cabin* follows *Show Boat* around the reviews and the criticism in ways that establish it as a vital and complex pretext for the later work. The fictional showboat itself features *Uncle Tom's Cabin* as one of its stock melodramas; Harry Pollard's 1927 direction of the Universal Studios version of *Uncle Tom's Cabin* was explicitly considered to be training for the first *Show Boat,* which Pollard directed in 1929; more recently, Richard Dyer's chapter on Paul Robeson in his book *Heavenly Bodies* cuts across fiction, stardom, and history in actually extracting a passage from the novel that describes Uncle Tom's body to illustrate Robeson's own atavistic modernist physique (1986, 85, 89). This is to say that in addition to the specific historiography of its plot, *Uncle Tom's Cabin* has an almost typological function in American culture. Its brief explication here will help to foreground the scene of adaptation and Americanization I am tracing in *Show Boat*.

There are specific ways in which *Show Boat* extends *Uncle Tom's Cabin*'s assimilation of the material of slavery into the hardwiring of national identity. Both novels perform the cultural work historical fiction of the present tense always does: they construct a register of national nostalgia that (a) revises what constitutes modernity in the public sphere and (b) conflates citizenship and consumer activity. To be sure, ending slavery was for Stowe the fundamental pressure behind writing about national life. However, *Uncle Tom's Cabin* mainly envisions this end by representing not slavery's violence but rather its banal operation in everyday life, in ordinary ethical subjectivity, and in losses of property and family, of mothers and children, as well as of the body's autonomy and privacy. Slavery is cast as a scandal of displacement: of democracy, inciting corporeal and capital distress; of topography, as Stowe transports the Southern slave system from its symbolic place on the geopolitical periphery to a space where, metonymically, the South stands for the nation itself; and, finally, of national aesthetics, as Stowe uses the otherworldliness of the feminized Gothic and Christian universes to signify the contingency and fragility of the nation as it stands before the realistic, novelistic, masculine mode that dominates the political public sphere. Stowe's deployment of Gothic, melodrama, and comedy as modes of nostalgic history are therefore indices of the nation's present political failure. A truly enlightened nation would produce novels without these temporalizing genres of displacement and excess.

Uncle Tom's Cabin intervened directly in a contemporary crisis of knowledge and national power and has therein come to stand for how a novel can work to change the course of history. Its status as a liberal democratic classic has everything to do with the way it cut across the distance between privacy and the public sphere. But its status as *Americana* derives from a slightly different domain, that of the nostalgic self-confirmation its stereotypes have provided as entertainment to postslavery America. George Aiken's stage melodrama of 1852 initiated hundreds of popular adaptations; at least six feature films have been made of *Uncle Tom's Cabin* (and more, if you count partial productions, as in *The King and I*), along with a few cartoons. All of these shuttle between comic and melodramatic racial representations and use the codes of black music and black death to signify some relation between personal and collective encounters with power.[4] For example, from the 1903 Edwin S. Porter/Edison adaptation on, slaves are constantly depicted while dancing. But their dance has an elastic meaning, signifying either slave humanity—dance as the only cultural production and site of pleasure the slaves own—or the greatest imaginable abjection to the master culture—as when slaves dance on the auction block, or little Harry dances his way into the slave trader Haley's heart in Pollard's 1927 production.

In addition, the black-white, slave-free, South-North formulas put into play by these "period" narratives paradoxically provide an achronic image of national taxonomy itself, onto which other forms of cultural domination became mapped. I take as an example the 1927 *Topsy and Eva,* which derives from but rings major changes on *Uncle Tom's Cabin. Topsy and Eva* opens in heaven, from which a stork carrying a baby in a diaper emerges. The stork drops Little Eva into a mansion; we see a beautiful angel write into the birth ledger, "Miss Eva St. Clare, Valentines Day 1842"; next, what the card calls "a stork of darker hue" emerges from the clouds, carrying a dark infant in a diaper. This stork tries to drop its bundle on a single woman's house, but she protests in defense of her reputation; the stork tries to drop the baby on a slave family, but they stone the stork, so that the baby is finally born in a trash can. In heaven the black angels are shooting craps; one of them gets up and writes "Topsy . . . ? 1842, April Fool's Day." This frame relocates the story of *Uncle Tom's Cabin* entirely within the realm of the personal: indeed, at the end of the film, Topsy's love for Eva revives her from her redemptive death, and the film closes with the two women cuddling in bed. The erotic prospects of this spectacle aside, *Topsy and Eva* banalizes contests over race, rank, and sexuality, making the scene of American history into a story of one baby everyone wanted and one baby no one wanted. That is to say, *Uncle Tom's Cabin,* and *Show Boat* after it, signifies both specific historical crises and the technologies of ambivalence—displacement, achronicity, or catachresis—made available by the power this tradition of the novel signifies, to recast and to change the world.

For Edna Ferber, writing in 1926 about a contemporary America whose modernity originates in the Civil War, the construction of Americana from slavery derives from different pressures to transform or to redistort national consciousness. Like Stowe, Ferber renarrates the nation by mobilizing the slave body, sexuality, American landscape, and fictive truths about subaltern peoples. But in contrast to *Uncle Tom's Cabin, Show Boat* aims directly at the field of nostalgic entertainment itself, locating in the banality of "Americana" the crisis of modernity. The true but imaginary America of *Show Boat* is generated by the Mississippi, with its "great untamed" life force (Ferber 1926, 9), its "ruthless, relentless, Gargantuan, terrible" capacity to endure violence and enjoy peace (240). The false but actually hegemonic nation is saturated by institutions of leisure and conventions of popular aesthetic identification that conflate the desire to survive, the aspiration to join a fantasy elite, and a wish to participate in democratic culture. This nation conflates citizenship with celebrity and its minor chord, consumption, in "a picture so kaleidoscopic, so extravagant, so ridiculous" that it virtually makes citizens into infants (240). "Americana" is the essentializing trivia of national culture. By making new signs appear as the ephemera of what already counts as "American" life, what *Show Boat* does is perform a radical act of tinkering with the national unconscious.

"You're Not the Type"

The cultural legacy of slavery Ferber describes has little to do with extracting a repressed subaltern history from the idealizing narratives of modern national culture; nor is Ferber interested in affirming the literatures or cultural practices of "peoples" across various margins of U.S. identity. Her critical consciousness constructs national culture by means of what remains, in the end, the stereotyping machinery of an American exotic otherness.[5] In this way the novel erratically succeeds and fails to gain a critical foothold on modernity. For its preferred mode of counterhistoricism relies on the very signs of racial violence, sexual suffering, and class exploitation that called out the sentimental machinery, as an apparatus of national self-healing and consolation, in the first place.

But in *Show Boat* and elsewhere, Ferber also stages a different kind of spectacle around American subalterns: here, African Americans, women, and workers are exploited by the mentalities, conventions, and institutions of modernity. Deploying modes of identification founded on the linked histories and social functions of stereotypes and commodities in America, Ferber depicts what we might call a *survival subculture* wrought from a bringing together of different collective experiences of social and political alienation, domination, and waste. How is it possible that the practice of stereotyping could further the project of narrative alliance building?

A digression into a later text by Ferber will highlight the kinds of affiliation among the bottom-dwellers of American culture she envisions in *Show Boat*. In a story called "You're Not the Type," which begins with the stuttering phrase "All her life—that is, all her professional life" (1947, 522), Edna Ferber tells the tale of a fading Broadway actress named Vivian Lande. Lande attributes her professional decline to the new conventions of youth and entertainment culture that dominated America in the 1930s. She rages at the way American youth has transformed the trauma of the depression into a style of acting, as though the ideal career of pain would be to produce new, commodified forms of marketable authenticity. In this scene, Lande has an attack of "resentment, jealousy, [and] fear." She has this attack in front of her maid, Essie, who responds:

> With the magic intuition of a race born to suffering the brown girl understood. She laughed. It was a superb imitation of mirth. "Land, everybody says they're going to be an actress. Look at me! I was going to be an actress, nothing would do, I was born to act. But I never did. That's how come I'm [a] maid. . . . It was the nearest to acting I could get." (528–29)

The narrator says that the "brown girl" who speaks was of a "race born to suffering." Essie says of herself: "I was born to act." When Edna Ferber details this double birthright, of suffering and of acting, she coordinates a variety of domains of activity, identity, and identification: the majestic ambitions of ordinary women, the theatrical labor of women in everyday life, the essential association of identity categories—race and femininity—with reactive affect—pain and laughter—and the modes of American entertainment culture that potentially turn these sites of experience into cultural capital.

But what is the relation, or the difference, between a maid and an actress, a brown girl and a star? Ferber here imagines for the brown girl a subjectivity—or, crucially, a "magic intuition"—which is collective and generic. She is barely distinguished by a proper name and a sketchy biography: because, in America, the semiotic field of the national stereotype *prenarrates* the story of any "brown girl's" particular life. There is no plot for the "brown girl," because a person "born" to a generic identity has neither the autonomy nor the prosaic specificity required for public narratives of personhood: and even in the scandalous event that a subaltern subject does speak the specific pain to which she is born, she deflects it with laughter, and therefore there is either no "story" of her own or else the story she tells is one of her identity's *other* birthrights—imitation, performance, acting. The horizon of identity designated by "brown girl" and "actress" stands for Ferber as the main available scene of desire and survival for female subaltern subjects in the national capitalist public sphere. But not all American subalterns have the same birthright: Ferber has it that "brown girls" are born both to *racial* suffering and to acting; it remains to be seen what compensation acting is for the white girls who, though born to act, are not, presumably, of a race whose painful confines they have collectively experienced.

"You're Not the Type" means to attribute both longing and critical consciousness to the subjects who are subjected to stereotypical personhood in the public sphere of American modernity. The contradictions of Ferber's liberalism in "You're Not the Type"—as the author attributes subjectivity to the stereotype who is nonetheless fated to subindividuality by being born to it—and its pressures on narrative are not as explicit in *Show Boat,* the novel, as they are everywhere in its dramatic adaptations. Yet even in the novel the resistance of the stereotype to narrative, to incorporation in a history of the present tense, marks the line between Magnolia's plot and Julie's plot: for example, the moment Julie is revealed as a black woman who passes, she is virtually expelled from the plot, and the narrative energy of romance, which Julie has been shown both to play on the river and to live in her romance with Steve, is transferred to Magnolia, in a tableau in which they embrace:

> And when they finally came together, the woman [Julie] dropped to her knees in the dust of the road and gathered the weeping child [Magnolia] to her and held her close, so that as you saw them sharply outlined against the sunset the black of the woman's dress and the white of the child's frock were as one. (Ferber 1926, 153)

The black woman's black dress and the white girl's white dress tell a "truth" about Julie and Magnolia that Ferber reinforces constantly: "In all the hurried harried country that still was intent on repairing the ravages of a Civil War, [the white people on the show boat] alone seemed to be leading an enchanted existence, suspended on another plane" (78).

I have proposed that *Show Boat*'s plays and films transform the novel's ambivalence—or perhaps it is merely sad resignation—about the attractions of modern life into a performance of fantasies of glamorous transcendence and that each revival revitalizes the view of *Show Boat* as a history of how slavery generated the wonders of love and the wonders of modernity. The memory of slave pain in the dramatic supertext provides, specifically, two kinds of cultural logic. The dominant and most elaborate one locates in the sexual and economic exploitation of slaves the melodramatic "problem" of American culture, which is "solved" in the narrative by a constellation of factors: the production of metropolitan life in the North, which appropriates and renames the material of what is alternately called Southern, coon, or nigger culture; the transformation of the divisions of race into productive forms of capital, spectacle, and sexuality; and the elevation of romantic love itself into the core bribe of modern entertainment culture.

The second textual logic of slave history and its national effects is much more muted in the novel and barely pulsates in the dramatic or cinematic spectacles. What we have called the "magic intuition" of the postslavery population is located in the characters who had been born into slavery—Jo, Queenie, and Julie Dozier, two servants and an actress. "Magic intuition" is everywhere present in the sound track as well, most famously in "Ol' Man River" but also crucially in the hauntingly beautiful song "Misery's Comin' Around." These songs causally link the experience of slavery and the organ of intuition; indeed, the songs are introduced lyrically and on the sound track to predict the plot right before it turns.

Yet African American modes of counterconsciousness become increasingly irrelevant and tacit in the adaptations. Take, for example, the complex scene of "Ol' Man River" sung by Paul Robeson in the 1936 film version. This scene comes early, establishing the distance between the naïveté of white people and African American wisdom, a wisdom derived from slavery, field labor, and life on the river's periphery. Narratively, "Ol' Man River" is not sung because Jo's capacity to master both voice and history and the trajectories of power in everyday life is valued or even apparent to his white bosses on the showboat. Magnolia has just sung "Only Make Believe" with her soon-to-be lover Gaylord Ravenal and asks Jo if he has seen the young man:

Noli: "Did you see the young man on the sheriff's buggy?"

Jo: "Yep I seen him. I seen lots like him along the river."

Noli: "Oh, but Jo, he was such a gentleman. Have you seen Miss Julie? I got to tell her. I got to ask her what she thinks."

Jo: "Ask Miss Julie what she thinks. Better ask the old river what he thinks. He knows all about them boys. He knows all about everything.

D'ere's an old man on the Mississippi,
that's the old man that I'd like to be.
What does he care if the world's got troubles?
What does he care if the land ain't free?
Ol' Man River . . ."

The context for "Ol' Man River," then, is the revelation of Jo's wisdom and Magnolia's simultaneous rejection of it as plot material. For if Magnolia were to listen to what she hears Jo say, both the love plot and the attendant historical narrative of *Show Boat* would be prevented from unfolding.

Thus when the song describes what it means to "say nothin'" and "know somethin'," it refers both to the suppressed and displaced history of American slaves and to the context of white misapprehension, the white will-to-not-know that supports the fantasy norms its romantic fictions express. Meanwhile, the medium of black magic intuition—which is only magic if history is merely a dream, a myth, or a feeling—about pain and suffering becomes essentially Cassandra-like in its profound irrelevance to anything that happens in the plot. As it turns the river into material for the shallow and ephemeral culture that saturates modern spectacle, "Ol' Man River" is also about the American subaltern experience of being made irrelevant to plot, to the present, and to the national future, by becoming "history," mere background.

The manifest content of "Ol' Man River" concerns not the African American knowledge that does not count but the intense physical labor that barely distinguishes free black life on the periphery of white wealth from life under slavery. The African American chorus sings about the material conditions of its modern life: "Don't look up an' don't look down, you don't dast make de white boss frown . . ."[6] As sung by Jo (Paul Robeson), "Ol' Man River" refuses to waste the energy of the wisdom Noli has rejected and instead enacts a change of address, one that replaces the text's white consumers and the actual dramatic audience with the film's ex-slave peasantry ("You an' me, we sweat an' strain, body all achin' an' racked wid pain"), thereby violating the characteristic classic Hollywood style with an expressionist mise-en-scène loaded with estranging angles and distortions of perspective. Its aesthetic referent is not *Uncle Tom's Cabin* but rather the film that had earned director James Whale his shot at directing this adaptation of *Show Boat*—the 1931 *Frankenstein*. Robeson is shot just as Frankenstein's monster is shot, and clearly the politics of monstrosity is meant to be read politically here, both to signify the estrangement of black reality from the white narrative spaces of the film and to address critically the forms of distortion and demonization that simultaneously produce the degraded life experiences and images of African Americans and make an icon of Robeson, singing his classic song.

Little in Ferber's novel would have predicted this intensity of paradox. If Ferber values the African American as Americana, the value of *specific* black people in the novel is to provide material for modern national culture, for the "American Theatre" (1926, 396) that Kim invents with the money she and her mother and her grandparents have earned in the minstrel business over four decades. Although "Queenie and Jo had been as much a part of [Magnolia's] existence as Elly and Schultzy" (269), Queenie's main legacy seems (appropriately for a story about the theater) to be about preparing ham:

> It was a fascinating process to behold, and one that took hours. Spices—bay, thyme, onion, clover, mustard, allspice, pepper—chopped and mixed and stirred together. A sharp-pointed knife plunged deep into the juicy ham. . . . Many years later Kim Ravenal, the actress, would serve at the famous little Sunday night suppers that she and her husband Kenneth Cameron were so fond of giving a dish that she called ham *à la* Queenie. (118)

Jo, meanwhile, teaches Magnolia "negro plantation songs, wistful with longing and pain; the folk songs of a wronged race, later to come into a blaze of popularity as spirituals" (120). The songs of "a footsore, ragged, driven race" that "always made her cry a little" are revised in the novel's memory to be material for the Harlem Renaissance (121–22). In short, Whale's staging of "Ol' Man River" gives it a kind of lyric power, which briefly interrupts the narrative mode of *Show Boat,* along with establishing an index with which we can measure the distances between any memory, any knowledge wrought from feeling, an American slave genealogy might offer and the technologies of modern (white) America's presentism. Ferber's take on the culture of black song predicts its subsequent textual status as sound track, not history.

By the 1951 adaptation, "Ol' Man River" denotes no monstrous difference—of race, class, body, or national fantasy: the song's status as "classic" overtakes entirely its plot and political function. It is no longer even putatively part of the story—until late in the film, when it is briefly sung as a bit of existential wondering by William Warfield, "Ol' Man River" is merely hummed by the disembodied chorus on the soundtrack, to remind the audience that there is "something" implicit the "river" knows that entertainment culture no longer needs to say. Here, as elsewhere in the score, the muffled music comes to signify a vaguely pervasive generic African American resistant subjectivity, which provides nebulous pedagogy for the white actors in the narrative. As for the audience, its pleasure in the dramatic spectacle of American history is now located in its mastery of *Show Boat* as a classic text: thus African American "magic intuition" and rememoration become themselves superseded or "unsung" in the dramatic adaptations.

You can see from this description that *Show Boat* follows a process of extracting "black style" from African American life and enfolding its traces into the pulsating present-tense culture of this book.[7] Because it is written as Kim's celebrity biography, and because Kim's talent is performing stylistic innovations on what the novel variously calls "nigger" (83), "negro" (122), "plantation" (155), "coon" (291), "American coon" (317), "real coon" (362), and "simple" (387) songs, imitation and renaming can be said to be the central aesthetic and ideological mechanism of the dominant and marginal American histories *Show Boat* tells. (Magnolia sings the songs to Kim, writes Ferber, "in unconscious imitation of the soft husky Negro voice of her teacher [Jo]" [1926, 291].) To be a name, of course, is to be a celebrity; to have one is to have a place in a cultural domain; to be restlessly, repeatedly renamed is simultaneously to be a register for someone's epistemic and ethical unease with both the word and the thing the word denotes, to be a structure that comes to mean serial obsolescence itself, and to designate as if from a source the collective amnesia that follows the trail of the "new" valorized by the narrative teleology.

The history of the word "nigger" in the adaptations of *Show Boat* reconfirms the instability of the text's scene of history—it is the sound track's first word: as Miles Krueger tells it, "First it was '*Niggers* all work on the Mississippi,' in the 1935 film it was '*Darkies* . . . ,' in the 1946 revival it was '*Colored folks* . . . ,' in *Till the Clouds Roll By* it was 'Here *we all* work on de Mississippi,' and by the 1966 revival it was—*Nobody* works on de Mississippi, because the Negro chorus was omitted altogether from the opening number" (1977, 211–12). Robeson, long identified with the role of Jo and the song "Ol' Man River," spent his life restlessly rewriting the lyrics to make them less abject, less complicit with the subordination of black history to the forms of American elite culture. For example, he frequently changed the lyric from "I'm tired of living / An skeered of dying" to "But I keeps laughing / Instead of crying / I must keep fighting / Until I'm dying": in so doing he asserts a performer's countermemory of the modes of racial and economic amnesia the dramatic texts of *Show Boat* disguise as Americana (Foner 1978, 481–82; Duberman 1988, 114, 604–5). Yet even Robeson embraced the power of celebrity, of personal commodification, to provide a spectacular model of what American citizenship might be.

The function of magic intuition in *Show Boat* is thus manifold, but clearly it serves the plot by providing wise discipline from the margins. It becomes, to be vulgar, the servant of the plot, glossing the emerging modern text of white melodrama—sex, love, and family trauma here merged with melodramas of celebrity and capital. In addition, the historical sweep of the play, and the construction of its black population as a chorus, sutures this instance of Americana with the form, though not the content, of national epic. Not uncritically, however: the peripheral consciousness of African Americans provides critical commentary on the spectacles of transcendence, imitation, consumption, and fetishism that dominate American mass culture. But even if the novel specifically seeks to ally its America with American racial and regional subcultures, the dramatic supertext of *Show Boat* builds its alliance, not with the wisdom or the ressentiment of chastised populations, but with technologies of fantasy.

What Love Has to Do with It

Show Boat eroticizes the history of the development of an apparatus of forgetting, in which modes of entertainment succeed each other, as dominant spaces do, along with the evolving lexicons of power that change slaves into "peasants" (101), peasants into consumers, consumers into career actors, or at least actors in the theater of everyday life, who play with the fantasy of being consumed, like a celebrity. The aesthetic code that supports this version of progress is the love story the novel tells, a story that integrates ex-slaves and gamblers into entertainment culture and that enables racial crossover, the repression of signs of labor, the development of new forms of capital, and the production of metropolitan nationalism as a force of nature, fate, libido, and "consent."

In the dramatic supertext, the vehicle for this crossover is the song "Can't Help Lovin' Dat Man." "Can't Help Lovin' Dat Man" directly follows the scene of "Ol' Man River" in the 1935 version, and repeats many of the themes Robeson intones as well, both musically and in the lyric. This repetition continues the pressure to displace slave history for love's sake. But the costs of the displacement are explicit in the film and the play's staging of this knowledge transfer, which has no analogue in the novel at all. Sung in the feminine space of the kitchen, this song is a female complaint, about the way love fates a woman to love one inadequate man and to suffer from that love (see Berlant 1988). The syllogism "Fish got to swim and / Birds got to fly / I got to love one man till I die" posits love as a force of nature, much like the river. This death drive of love is similar to the "river Jordan" that Jo would like to cross in "Ol' Man River," in an effort to escape his suffering in a beyond-life land of freedom (from pain and labor). But such repetition is also comic, substituting the situation or screwball comedy of heterosexual love for the tragedy of slavery and racism. Finally, the "magic intuition" of Jo emerges here as the commonsense philosophy of Julie, who has also learned from experience: "Love is such a funny thing, there's no sense to it."

In the original libretto and the 1936 film, Julie teaches "Can't Help Lovin' Dat Man" to Magnolia, in an act of loving sexual pedagogy. Yet when Queenie hears Julie sing it, she comments not on the epistemology of compulsory heterosexuality it sets forth but instead on the racial history embedded in the song: "ah didn't ever hear anybody but colored folks sing dat song. Sounds funny for Miss Julie to know it." Prior to Queenie's intervention, the song Julie sings appears to expose her intimacy with the ordinary tragic disappointments of love; but recast as an artifact of racial history, it comes to reveal her criminalized racial and sexual identity to the audience, initiating the juridical scandal that divides the plot into black diaspora and white romance.

As might be expected, in the 1951 version of *Show Boat* "Can't Help

Lovin' Dat Man" is extracted entirely from its racial context and is, likewise, transported from the basement kitchen to the public deck of the boat. Rather than affirm a long relationship between the older and the younger woman, this version simply signifies Julie's man troubles. Julie now teaches Magnolia the song as she sings it to her—on-screen, for the very first time. The women dance in this as in the other version; but as the dance they do here is simple and simply improvised around the song Magnolia newly hears, it is fair to say that this revision empties their bodies and the music of any relation to history—at least to the history of America, to the history of "Ol' Man River," and to race, for both Jo and Queenie are nowhere to be seen, their knowledge of the racial archive is irrelevant to what becomes an impromptu scene of female bonding over love's complexities. The history of *Show Boat*'s sound track thus powerfully reinforces the text's analysis of national amnesia: by displacing the "race" crisis onto a love story at every moment it can, and by refusing to specify whatever it is that Ol' Man River knows. Magnolia and Gay's love plot, intricately bound up *as realism* with the melodramatic love they perform as actors, thus coordinates a number of transformations: it retroprojects slavery as a nostalgic origin of the narrative of modern life; it establishes acting as a means of flight and of deliverance for women, who have no public access to power outside of careers on the stage, a stage that dominates the modern American public sphere; it establishes imitating what gets acted as a means of securing women's cultural and affective value; and it installs the love plot as an index of female subalternity in America, simultaneously expressing and deflecting desire as a fundamental condition of feminine identity. In this regard the revivals of *Show Boat* mark this text as a classic source of love's capacity to overcome nature and history, even as the show also provides a vehicle for female complaint.

The Consolations of Landscape

I have suggested that the supertext of *Show Boat* thrusts slavery and the South into the margins of the national diegesis. It does this, in part, by turning African American and Southern history into a property of the landscape we pass by, like tourists and space travelers, on our way to the national future. In contrast, fish that swim and birds that fly have a transitory relation to landscape: they move through time and space, and in this case, from the South to the North, the archaic to the emergent, from slavery and race codes to gender and entertainment, from coerced subordination to the simulacrum of free consent. One example of this resides in Magnolia's mixing up of "her" South with commodity aesthetics, thereby separating the region decisively from any aura of modernity. The dramatic supertext confirms the spatial cleavage between North and South with the song "It's Getting Hotter in the North." Kim performs this song on Broadway, in Southern drag and peasant blackface, while flecked with the metropolitan cool of the Harlem Renaissance. "Hotness" is the vehicle that both links and sunders the music from its lived context; the song tells the story of mass culture's foundation in African American culture and serves not merely as the virtuoso number in Kim's celebrity repertoire but also as the sum of her inheritance from her mother and America itself. The lyrics of "Ol' Man River" again prove instructive: as Miles Krueger has pointed out, the twelve-line refrain has only one true rhyme: "He don't plant 'taters, / He don't plant cotton, / An' dem dat plant 'em / Is soon forgotten, / But ol' man River, / He jes keeps rollin alon.' " "Cotton" and "forgotten" here clearly quote the historic instance of that rhyme, in Dan Emmet's Confederate anthem "Dixie's Land": "I wish I was in de land ob cotton, Old times there are not forgotten. Look away! Look away! Dixie land" (Krueger 1977, 54). *Show Boat*'s gloss on the Confederate/pseudo-black-vernacular/minstrel text evokes a breathtakingly complex set of revisions and elisions. It locates in turns of phrase the power to stimulate the transformation of slavery, and later of the Civil War, into the negative space of modernity in turn-of-the-century America. Look away—from what? Ferber has commented that the success of *Show Boat* was probably linked to Americans' desire to escape consciousness of the "blood and hate and horror" of the violent wars that marked the globe during the 1920s (1939, 301). The production of Americana in this light is indeed politics, war by other means.

The transformation of pain and labor into Americana is thus effected by the separation of racial or "historical" memory from love's forgettable, and therefore infinitely repeatable, performances. This dissipating function of the aesthetic commodity is telegraphed to the audience in other instances as well, by the staccato breaking apart of the consumption experience into memorial units like blackface numbers that evoke what Ferber calls "a glorious world of unreality" (1926, 104), in which the lines of power, desire, and identification are so morally and melodramatically clear they are overdrawn. The value of aesthetic experience here is also that it provides a forum for the exercise of agency: audiences of workers actually seek out the pleasure of unlearning or forgetting.

But if the novel of *Show Boat* exposes the relation between love plots, race, and the erasure of history as the cultural dominant of American modernity, it also promotes its own mode of cartography, one that resists the seeming inevitability of these deflections. Magnolia's consciousness is the locus of much of what we know about life on the Mississippi and its place in generating American culture. Lists of faces, of spaces that flow by the showboat and through her eyes generate a kind of counter-museum that holds the ephemera of American underclass life and experience, while also pioneering a mode of memory entirely adaptive to the capitalist public sphere. In particular, the specificity of local detail that overwhelms Magnolia's consciousness bridges the sensual experience of history and the commodity logic of serial consumption.

> As for geography, if Magnolia did not learn it, she lived it. She came to know her country by travelling up and down its waterways. She learned its people by meeting them, all sorts and conditions. She learned folkways; river lore; Negro songs; bird calls; pilot rules; profanity; the art of stage make-up; all the parts in the Cotton Blossom troupe's repertoire. (Ferber 1926, 83)

In this context, aesthetics are inseparable from everyday life: but their blending has many different implications for understanding the nationalist project of *Show Boat*. Magnolia's commodification of the songs she learned from her ex-slave servants links the exalted ambitions of the ordinary citizen to what Ferber calls the "weird spectacle of the commonplace" that underlies the aesthetics of the modern American culture industry (1926, 102). Magnolia creates patterns, mnemonics of social identity, through her short, object-dominated sentences: to live geography turns out to mean not experiencing the land but rather taking the peripheral traveling consciousness itself to be the source of a new modernity. "They were known to the townspeople as Show Folks, and the term carried with it the sting of opprobrium. . . . [But] [t]hey looked, Magnolia decided, as if they had just come from some interesting place and were going to another even more interesting" (1926, 53).

But having experienced both an acting and a laboring relation to body, landscape, and narrative, Magnolia imagines another way of inhabiting and transforming America. Repudiating history's disembodiment in the North and in mass culture at the end of the novel, she performs a *different* imaginary reconciliation of commodity logics, labor, desire, and national history. *Show Boat* investigates the cultural work of entertainment in part by representing entertainment *as* work, as an industry in which people labor. In one sense, this consciousness of the commodity's location in a system of production works against the text's representation of consumption, for popular and mass culture are cast as utopian spaces for audiences, places where labor, the thing that happens on land, away from the river and the metropole, is forgotten and where aesthetic consumption is seen as the *negation* of work, the only such activity—control over time, space, and the body—that the American peasantry has. Ferber's quarrel with the collusion of technological modernization and modernist art is that modernity requires an aesthetic that moves from place to place, name to name, according to the ideology of the new. In mass national culture, as it stands, there is no accumulation, no activity of public memory, but instead a shedding of prior knowledge on behalf of new promises and consolations. Thus the paradox of national memory in the culture industry: underclass populations consume melodrama and comedy to displace the absurdity, drama, and afflictions of their own lives; but these pleasures are momentary, in contrast to those of privileged metropolitan pleasure addicts, who consume as a means of generating and propping self-identity. Magnolia does not promote radical rememoration, however, or resistance to capital—nor indeed does she reimagine the American theater as a documentary form, a witnessing of the hard genealogical facts of national history. Instead, negotiating the contradictions of a critical bourgeois consciousness, she posits the value of fictive truths and strategic displacements to champion the cause of survival itself.

> But best of all [Magnolia] liked to watch the audience assembling. Unconsciously the child's mind beheld the moving living drama of a nation's peasantry. It was such an audience as could be got together in no other theatre in all the world. Farmers, labourers, Negroes; housewives, children, yokels, lovers; roustabouts, dock wallopers, backwoodsmen, rivermen, gamblers. . . . Seamed faces. Furrowed faces. Drab. Bitter. Sodden. Childlike. Weary. . . . They forgot the cot-

ton fields, the wheatfields, the cornfields. They forgot the coal mines, the potato patch, the stable, the barn, the shed. They forgot the labour under the pitiless blaze of the noonday sun; the bitter marrow-numbing chill of winter; the blistered skin; the frozen road; wind, snow, rain, flood. The women forgot for an hour their washtubs, their kitchen stoves, childbirth pains, drudgery, worry, disappointment. (1926, 101, 104–5)

The function of these lists of faces and lives in *Show Boat* is to provide the material for what Ferber, a sentimental nationalist, images as an American "survival subculture." This subculture is constructed not through collective struggle but in a mentality: in consciousness of collective pain, through a diasporic, aesthetically mediated identification with other survivors. In the face of the dissolution of American history by the mass culture that represents its modernity, survival seems to Ferber like an important victory over nature and nationality, a vital form of historicity, and material for a critical Americana. Thus in *Show Boat*, the "magic intuition" of "races born to pain" casts "acting" as a mechanism of survival, not mere celebrity; and it suggests that the audience's shared consumption of a memory of someone else's pain—the material of melodrama, sentimentality, and situation comedy—might take over the room political discourses typically inhabit to organize identity and identification in national life. And while this commodified mode of historicity is a form of accommodation to capitalist culture, to simply denigrate the utopian aspirations of affirmative culture would be, in her view, to impugn survival itself. For Ferber, the process of desubjectification becomes the price the reflective citizen pays for the protections of the stereotype or the performative role. In other words, the sentence "black faces dotted the boards of the Southern wharves as thickly as grace notes sprinkle a bar of lively music" amounts, here, to an episteme of survival politics (1926, 25). And *Show Boat* would argue that the capacity to survive in America, even protected by the shell of the stereotype, counters the same powerfully dislocating forces of modernity the dramatic texts virtually celebrate.

Show Boat demonstrates the cultural logics of what Antonio Gramsci calls "passive revolution," the means by which dominant parties persuade subordinated ones to perform acts of deference, perhaps through some notion of consensual democracy, thus affirming an incomplete hegemony as indeed a comprehensive one (1988, 246–74). *Show Boat* figures the transition from race plots to love plots as both a "natural" and a self-violating transition of American culture into modernity, with the love plot itself coming to serve as a subaltern sign for women, a sign of political, affective, and narrative displacement, and a utopian assertion of the tactics a survival subculture might use to endure the modern conditions of identity formation in which the stereotype, the commodity, and the history of collective pain collaborate in "democratic" mass culture. The novel resolves these contradictions of subalternity in a democratic space by separating out from "living" modern landscapes and narratives the archaic stereotypes whose resistance to representation according to the liberal biographical norms of modern personhood actually preserves them from annihilation in the amnesiac technologies and styles of the culture industry. The irony is that the compulsion to revive *Show Boat* as Americana has come to mean quite the opposite—a return to and celebration of the show as the source of crossover spectacles, the distillation of African American history into a vogue of black style, the celebration of women's erotic desire for publicity, and the supreme nostalgic fantasy of an America in which the pain of dominated classes was neither entertaining, nor entertainment.

Notes

1. In the Ferber novel, Jo is spelled without the "e"; in the plays and films, he is listed as "Joe." For consistency, I retain the Ferber spelling throughout.
2. I do not use the word "subalternity" casually here or seek to contribute to the emptying out of the specificity of that term for India and its historiography in the work of the subaltern studies group. Instead, I mean to deploy the anomalousness of this category to underline certain problems of analysis generated when hierarchies of self-representation and legitimacy in a mass democratic/capitalist culture are expressed outside the languages of caste, class, and rank that might otherwise index the failures of national-democratic *imaginaires* and practices. That is, my languages of identity are in competition with Ferber's "American" ones; and hers, in turn, stage a competition between the modernist logics of metropolitan identity and a whole host of corporeally specific and historically involved ones designating race, gender, region, and including an archaic category still in use in the U.S. 1920s and '30s, "peasant."
3. For discussions of fantasy in its relation to seriality, see Laplanche and Pontalis 1967, 314–19, and 1986; see also Kaplan 1986.

4. Here is the major archive from which I draw my conclusions about the film history of *Uncle Tom's Cabin:* 1903, Thomas A. Edison, Edwin S. Porter production, *Uncle Tom's Cabin, or Slavery Days;* 1914, *Uncle Tom's Cabin,* no studio given, dir. Robert Daly; 1927, United Artists, *Topsy and Eva,* dir. Del Lord; 1927, Universal, Carl Laemmle producer, *Uncle Tom's Cabin,* dir. Harry A. Pollard; 1927, E. A. Hammons, Paul Sullivan, "Felix the Cat in *Uncle Tom's Crabbin'*"; 1947, Tex Avery, *Uncle Tom's Cabana.* There is also a notable tradition of interpolated scenes from *Uncle Tom's Cabin* in films set in other periods: for example, the Shirley Temple vehicle *Dimples* (1936); Abbott and Costello's *Gay Nineties; Anna and the King of Siam* (1946); *The King and I* (1956).
5. Gerald Mast (1987) points out that this feature of naming and remaking was a standard habit of musical writing in the 1920s and after, especially with Jewish writers writing from within black traditions and minstrel, pseudoblack traditions of music. There is a story to be told, though not here, about the black-Jewish contexts for *Show Boat* that make this habit of music writing part of a larger arsenal of liberal/racist activities. See Mast 1987, 59.
6. The *Show Boat* industry is full of stories about the gratitude and amazement African Americans express that Hammerstein and Kern could have written such an "authentic" number. See, for example, Freedland 1978, 90–91; see also Mast 1987.
7. My thinking about the extraction of a racial style has been influenced by Mercer 1990 and Snead 1990.

Clifford Siskin

Epilogue

The Rise of Novelism

❧ By "novelism," I mean the now habitual subordination of writing to the novel. Witness Susan Sontag's efforts, as recounted in the *New York Times Magazine,* to describe the genre of her new book *The Volcano Lover:*

"In order to find the courage to write this book, it helped me to find a label that allowed me to go over the top," she explains. "The word 'romance' was like a smile. Also, the novel becomes such a self-conscious enterprise for people who read a lot. You want to do something that takes into account all the options you have in fiction. Yet you don't want to be writing *about* fiction, but making fiction. So I sprang myself from fictional self-consciousness by saying, "It's a novel—it's more than a novel—it's a romance!" She opens her arms and laughs un-self-consciously. "And I fell into the book like Alice in Wonderland. For three years, I worked 12 hours a day in a delirium of pleasure. This novel is really a turning point for me." (Garis 1992, 21)

Going over the top of the novel, it appears, is no easy task. Even as Sontag seeks to spring beyond that genre's self-consciousness, her own simile brings her back down to novelistic earth: she "fell . . . like Alice in Wonderland." And, her supposedly transcendent act of labeling—"it's a romance!"—is but a brief blip on the generic sonar as her final sentence about what the book "really is" relabels it a "novel."

One might argue that in this final usage Sontag simply means "book" or "piece of writing," but that's my point: we have so thoroughly conflated the novel with writing that even when we want to separate the two—as Sontag so passionately intends—we have trouble pulling them apart. Our habitual behaviors make them stick, from the common assumption that a would-be "writer" is an aspiring "novelist" to the professional celebration of the novel as the aesthetic (Great Tradition) or heteroglossic (Bakhtin) aspiration of writing itself. Stickiness, of course, can be quite pleasurable, as Sontag's three-year delirium suggests. With the novel securely in place, we can more easily, like her, use it to mark "turning point[s]" or simply enjoy what novels make and keep familiar: the flow from work to play as we reach for the bedside paperback; the pedagogical comfort of novels in multicultural syllabi. By ordering our experiences with and understanding of writing, novelism—as the discourse of and about novels—produces and reproduces private, public, and professional norms.

My focus here is on how that work first came to be performed; I am exploring not "the rise of the novel" but the advent of novelism. In fact, one of my primary tasks is to recover, from the histories of the novel that have metonymically displaced it, a history of writing. That recovery is a pressing problem for us now, since the particular configuration of writing, print, and silent reading with which we are familiar is presently undergoing change. "In the new cultural period we have . . . entered," argues Raymond Williams, "print and silent reading are again only one of several cultural forms, only one even of the forms of writing" (1983b, 7). The "again" turns us back to the eighteenth century, when the familiar form of writing first became, to use Williams's word, "naturalized."

By "us" I mean critics, novelists, and readers alike, for at the same time that the work of Armstrong (1987), Bender (1987), McKeon (1987), Warner (1992a), and others has helped critics to rethink the history of the novel, writers such as Sontag have taken the novel back into history. Not only was her turn to romance a turn to the eighteenth century, but *The Volcano Lover* was succeeded on the best-seller lists by a novel whose title explicitly points to the same historical moment. By calling her work *The Secret History,* Donna Tartt (1992) echoed one of the most popular phrases in late-seventeenth- and early-eighteenth-century fiction; in 1729, for example, Eliza Haywood sought in a preface to distinguish her work from "so many Things . . . which have been published under the Title of SECRET HISTORIES" (reprinted in Williams 1970, 85). The return to such "things" now—Deborah Ross introduces her recent study of the romance and novel as "A Secret History" (1991)—points to my specific concern in this essay. Their appearance as Williams's period of naturalization opened, and their reappearance at its apparent close, point to the ongoing correlation of novelism and the history of writing. To explore that correlation—what did the novel do to writing? what would writing be without it?—I will focus initially on the act that not only enables these returns to the eighteenth century but is, itself, a feature of that time—one to which we are now strangely returning: imitation.

Discussion of imitation in eighteenth-century studies has been fixed generically upon poetry, feeding upon Augustan poetic practice at the start of the century and Romantic mirror-and-lamp arguments at its end. Within novel criticism, however, when issues of imitation arise at all they appear in a different terminological guise, primarily, given the hegemonic power of Ian Watt's formal realism, as the problem of verisimilitude (Watt 1957). Rethinking imitation in regard to the novel, then, must be an act of recovery—of re-placing that issue of adherence to the real under a rubric that can link it to other concerns. To make those connections we must shift our attention outward from "the" novel as an object fated to "rise" to the discursive space I am calling novelism. With our teleological blinders removed, we can then opt not to subordinate the history of writing to tales of aesthetic improvement. Only when it is *in* that history can the novel be addressed in the manner called for by this collection: as an institution. To that end, I offer the following arguments:

First, *novelism is the discursive site on which the naturalization of writing is negotiated,* in large part through the rubric of imitation. I will show how attending to the fate of imitation allows for a new understanding of what "rose" in the eighteenth century. "Rise" narratives, that is, are themselves a part of my generic history of novelism—a history in which Neo-Classical tales of imitative decline from past masters give way to Romantic tales of developmental innovation.

Second, from the perspective of that shift to developmental histories, *Fielding and Richardson largely function as dead ends;* what William Warner calls their "programs" (1992a, 579) for the novel had, in important ways, to be written off before the novel as we know it rose up.

Third, what rose was "English," because *novelism helped to institute the form of nationalism peculiar to a newly united kingdom.* Rather than the standard scenario of a group aiming at political sovereignty, Great Britain was a sovereign state aiming to form a group. The success of that formation depended, in important ways, on the technology deployed to articulate it. Its foreign parts cohered into a newly domestic whole as that technology itself was—under the rubric of novelism—domesticated. It became comfortable with itself as a nation as it became comfortable with the technology—writing—in which that self was articulated.

Fourth, what we know as the English novel is tied to a particular way of knowing: *novelism is inextricably linked to modern disciplinarity, and that link is an important basis for the novel's ongoing institutional power.* This is why Sontag's discomfort with the novel—the need to "top" it—is occurring at the same moment that discomfort with disciplinary "limits" has led to widespread calls for interdisciplinarity. Novelism entails ways of behaving in writing that, like scientificity, become crucial to the making of modern knowledge—and thus the current rethinking of what we have made.

Having lived so comfortably and so long with writing, we must work to reconstruct the shock that accompanied its spread in Britain during the long eighteenth century. Writing proliferated then *as something new* through, in large part, writing about writing—that is, writers throughout the eighteenth century were so astonished by the sheer volume of writing they began to encounter that they wrote about it—and thereby astonished themselves. The engine here is not the oft-cited "growth of the reading public" or "rise in the literacy rate." Like Williams, I am using "writing" as shorthand for the entire "configuration of writing, print, and silent reading"; its proliferation is a matter not simply of when and how many learned a skill but of skills interacting in practice.

In fact, as J. Paul Hunter has pointed out, the most reliable studies suggest that, since the primary literacy "boom" occurred during the first three-quarters not of the eighteenth but of the seventeenth century, "it is not at all certain that a child in 1775 was more likely to learn to read than a child in 1675" (1990, 67). Thus while the proportion of literates may not have increased during the first eight decades of the eighteenth century, what did grow was the amount of writing—a rise in both kinds and quantity in print and in situations calling for that practice. That surge in print provoked Alexander Pope in *The Dunciad* and then alarmed Samuel Johnson, who, in writing up his age as the "Age of Authors," also linked writing's power to a sense of being overpowered: "the province of writing" was being invaded by "the busy part of mankind" (1963, 115). New forms of business—particularly the advent of modern professionalism—helped to fuel this increase in the practice of writing, whether the result was a novel, an account book, a contract, or an exam. More people had more occasions to write more.

A recurring topic of concern was the probable effect of this activity. Just as today we speculate and moralize about television's influence on attention spans, family values, and even scholarly productivity, so, back then, the new technology of writing gazed self-reflexively on its own unknown potential: a large part of *what* people wrote and *how* they wrote had to do with often discomforting expectations regarding the productive power of writing. Thus to classify the innumerable warnings against young women reading novels as simply a manifestation of Augustan conservatism is to miss the historical point—the particular attitude toward change was secondary to a primary issue: writing's capacity to produce that change.

When we keep in mind the historical sequence I've described above—the rise in writing occurring after the rise in the literacy rate—we realize that one fundamental form of change at issue was the transformation of reader into writer. To grasp its impact, a comparison of technologies is again useful. The current heightened concern with the behavioral consequences of electronic media is occurring—not surprisingly—at the moment at which more people are becoming more behaviorally invested in them. As they appear on stages, in the audiences, and on the telephones of talk shows, and as they star in, shoot, mail in, and show videos on network programs and local cable channels, formerly passive viewers become participants in, and partial producers of, what they consume.[1]

The middle decades of the eighteenth century saw parallel forms of investment in writing, particularly in the form that was proliferating most substantially at that time: periodicals. As I have discussed in detail elsewhere (Siskin 1994a), increasing numbers of readers became writers, the flow of contributions inducing the flow of capital, for this was the appropriation of surplus value in its purest form: almost all of this material was provided (and could be reprinted) for free. New periodicals could thus be launched and sustained with very little capital, making them a primary engine for the takeoff in overall publication levels in the latter part of the century. Writing, then, induced a fundamental change in readers—leading them to behave as writers—that, in turn, induced more writing. Writing's capacity to produce change, in other words, was, in this basic way, historically crucial to what I have been calling its proliferation—the production of more writing.

For those experiencing these specific historical changes—both the initial proliferation of writing and their own innovatively transformative roles within it—a central concern became who and what else would be changed and in what ways? Eighteenth-century readers/writers had to come to terms, that is, with what Michel de Certeau calls the "scriptural economy," his term for the workings of writing in the West in the "modern age." For de Certeau, writing—a "concrete activity" in which a "text" is "constructed" on a "blank page" that "delimits a place of production for the subject"—is necessarily transformative: as "the production of a system, a space of formalization," it "refers to the reality from which it has been distinguished *in order to change it*" (1984, 134–35). What I am trying to recover and index with terms such as "discomfort" is the eighteenth century's concern with writing as this relentlessly productive power—a power at issue in every act of writing, such as taking the exam that could change your occupation, and in every kind, such as the tracts of political economy that, in David McNally's words, constituted "an attempt to theorize the inner dynamics" of "changes [leading to capitalism] *in order to shape and direct them*" (McNally 1988, 1; my emphasis). Comfort levels, then, point not to deep psychological truths but to the specific ways in which Williams's "naturalization" rewrote that concern, turning writing itself into more of a cipherlike tool than a potentially threatening prescriptive technology.

Before that naturalization, however, the concern *with* writing was repeatedly articulated during the eighteenth century *in* writing, making writing as much an object of inquiry as a means. Writing about writing produced more writing in a self-reflexive proliferation. All writing became, in that sense, critical. To see criticism only as a separate kind is thus to miss the historical point: it was a condition and product of the act of writing itself, as long as that act was still experienced as new.[2] That is why, as Jürgen Habermas observes regarding the eighteenth century, "philosophy was no longer possible except as critical philosophy, literature and art no longer except in connection with literary and art criticism" (1989, 42).

The era's connections to the critical were both internal (e.g., digressions, tone) and external (e.g., prefaces, reviews), affecting every literary genre. An important manifestation in poetry was the spread of the lyric, which, as I have argued elsewhere (Siskin 1994b), was historically well suited to be a site for the experimental mixing of creative and critical features. The comparable location in prose at the turn into the eighteenth century was in fiction, where—in the discursive arena I have dubbed novelism—critical self-reflexivity permeated and accompanied the competing forms of romance, history, and novel. In Aphra Behn's *Oroonoko* (published in 1688), for example, writing is itself written up as the contractual tool of the white man, allowing the spoken word to function dishonorably as a weapon of deceit (Behn 1992, 131). The tale as a whole is itself a mix of various kinds of writing, from travel literature (115–17) to heroic myth (118–20). Framing these diverse parts is the overriding self-reflexive issue of whose pen—gender being the central issue—can "write" Oroonoko's "praise" most effectively (108, 140).

A more startling example of writing's self-reflexivity is Delarivier Manley's *The New Atalantis* (from 1709), a work that reads so strangely to us today precisely because where we expect characterological depth and agency, we find instead writing that relentlessly thematizes itself. In this supposedly amorous intrigue, the seducers are "airy romances, plays, dangerous novels, loose and insinuating poetry" (1991, 30). Charlot can act effectively only as an actress; the Duke is indifferent to her until an encounter "one evening at a representation" (32). He is aroused, but the work of arousing her remains the work of representation; in the actual seduction it is writing that works:

> She took the book [Ovid] and placed herself by the Duke; his eyes feasted themselves upon her face, thence wandered over her snowy bosom and saw the young swelling breasts just beginning to distinguish themselves and which were gently heaved at the impression Myrra's sufferings made upon her heart. (35)

Writing turns critically upon itself as a feature not only in these texts but also in one of the most prolific venues of novelism: the wide range of extratextual materials, from prefaces and introductions to footnotes and afterwords. In the preface to *The Secret History of Queen Zarah and the Zarazians* (published in 1705), Manley's writing about writing is again representative as she makes comparisons with France, defines history, and theorizes the probable (reprinted in Barnett 1968, 22–27). But, for us, that is only the first layer of self-reflexivity; we now know, thanks to John L. Sutton Jr., that Manley's preface is a translation of part of an essay published three years earlier, which is itself a paraphrase of a work that first appeared in 1683 (Sutton 1984). Considered within the critically inclusive rubric of novelism, this (unacknowledged) act can be seen as a variation of the same strategy that led Manley to acknowledge (falsely) *The New Atalantis* as a translation of a French translation of the Italian original (1991, 3). In both cases, she shares with writers of all forms at that time—Joseph Bartolomeo is right in calling the purloined preface "as prospective as it is retrospective" (1994, 23)—an overriding concern to contextualize and thus control writing's power.

Three areas of inquiry dominate discussions of that power:

> What can writing do?
> With what consequences?
> In whose hands?

How the questions were posed, the mode of pursuing them, and the kinds of answers varied from one sort of writing to the next. The shift within poetry to the lyric I noted earlier, led, through psychologizing strategies, to answers made familiar in works like William Wordsworth and Samuel Taylor Coleridge's *Lyrical Ballads:* writing's capacity to induce sympathetic "pleasure" could cure individuals and societies of their "savage torpor" when exercised by "a man speaking to men."

As poetry was lyricized, prose was novelized, with the competition among the forms of fiction adding a characteristic slant to the questioning of writing. Since, as Shaftesbury put it in 1711, the problem of "Human Fiction," was the problem of "Imitative Art" (1963), the queries cited above were posed within novelism as issues of imitation: "What can writing do?" became "Can the novel imitate real life?"; "With what consequences?" became, reversing the previous question, "Does real life imitate the novel?"; and "In whose hands?" became "Whom should novelists imitate?" The texts that directly address—or are configured by—these questions do resemble, as many recent critics have noted, conduct books; matters of imitation, particularly under the imperative of pleasurable instruction, prescribe behavior. But whether we read Manley's novels, peopled by "dangerous Books" (Manley 1991, 37), or her prefaces, addressed to "a *reader* who has any sense" (reprinted in Barnett 1968, 24; my emphasis), we realize that the behaviors at stake are all behaviors directed at, generated by, or mediated through writing. The results—the early products of novelism—are less conduct books than users' guides to that new technology.

Fielding and Richardson wrote the definitive guides for the eighteenth century. Actually, it was a matter of one comprehensive guide, since, as they responded to each other's efforts, they quickly constituted an inclusive binary. Samuel Miller could still use it in 1803, fifty years later, to summarize the fate of the novel during the previous century:

FIELDING is humorous and comic; RICHARDSON more grave and dignified. They both paint with a masterly hand; but FIELDING is perhaps more true to nature than his rival. The former succeeds better in describing *manners;* the latter in developing and displaying the *heart.* (1970, 2:159–60)

And so on. Like users' guides today, however, the shelf life even—or perhaps especially—of such an apparently comprehensive effort was determined both by its conceptual apparatus—the particular way it makes the technology make sense—and by changes in the technology.

The apparatus of writing at issue at that time was imitation. The "contingent decision" (Warner 1992a, 578) in favor of Fielding's and Richardson's work over that of Behn, Manley, and Haywood was so quick and definitive, not because these authors offered a thoroughly innovative *departure* from their predecessors, but because they so systematically foregrounded the *same* imitative concerns regarding writing. Although they introduced some innovative features, and some innovative functions for inherited features, their work was, in that important way, a culmination. Together, for example, they standardized writing's self-reflexive turns. Fielding, on the one hand, as Charles Jenner dutifully noted decades later (1770), made them regularly discrete parts of the novels themselves, declaring "introductory chapters"—of "observation and reflection"—"one of which he has prefixed to each book of his history of a Foundling, to be essentially necessary to this species of writing" (Jenner, qtd. in Barnett 1968, 124). Richardson, on the other hand, set standards for novelism's extratextual turns, critically contextualizing his novels by precirculating the manuscripts, gathering critiques, writing replies, and carefully assembling all of the materials in extended prefaces.

Both the embedded and the juxtaposed material used imitation arguments to tame the technology, and it is in that act of taming, domesticating, finding a home, making writing feel at home, that a home was made. The critical self-reflexivity in the discourse of and about novels turned relentlessly on the nation. Fielding's and Richardson's claims to be doing something "new" were not assertions of defamiliarizing difference as evidence of autonomous creativity; this newness was intended to make writing seem less strange, more acceptable, natural—in other words, in what became the critical shorthand of the day—English. Like Behn, Manley, and Haywood before them, Fielding and Richardson critically represented earlier and other forms of writing, particularly the French, as foreign, and they warned against the foreign—for example, the romance—as uncontrolled and, therefore, potentially uncontrollable—it might induce romantic behavior, behavior, that is, coded as not-English.

To suggest that British nationalism is, in a sense, a domesticating solution to the uncomfortable threat of writing is not to trivialize it. Doing so does not preclude the more conventional links to political issues of liberty, the conditions of war, or the state of the economy but, rather, offers up new angles from which to approach them. In regard to the economy, for example, James Raven has recently documented, with a particular focus on the place of novels in "the productive and distributive capacity of the book trades," how a "competitive literature industry" played a major role in "legitimiz[ing] specific modes of economic and social behaviour by upwardly mobile groups"; it "defined in practical terms," he argues, "acceptable and unacceptable methods of gaining, retaining, and deploying wealth during a period of often bewildering change and instability" (1992, 13). Wallace Flanders uses the novel to focus particularly on gender instability, seeing the critical transformations of that form in eighteenth-century England as crucial to working out the "severe contradiction between the dictates of egalitarian enlightenment thought on the status of the individual in society and the position of women" (1984, 180).

But the most important reason for putting British nationalism *in* the history of writing and *in* novelism is that it helps us understand the particular form that nationalism assumes in Britain. Doing so is no easy task; Gerald Newman reveals that a computer search in the mid-1980s came up with "only one document in the entire bibliography of nationalism which focuses squarely on the general problem of an English variety" (1987, xviii). He attributes that lack to "a manifestation in the academic world of the fond old idea that God is an Englishman. Other peoples—the French, the Germans, the Mexicans and Irish—have their nationalism, their amusing beliefs, and silly prejudices about themselves" but the English have, in a sense *are,* the truth (xix). The task, then, is twofold: to recognize that the English *did* have nationalism and then to specify *how.*

Otto Dann's description of "nationalism" is useful here. We apply "nationalism," he observes, "to any political movement by which a social group, regarding itself as a nation, aims at political sovereignty in its area of settlement and claims political participation and autonomy" (Dann 1988, 3). In eighteenth-century Britain, political sovereignty came first;

a group did not aim at political sovereignty, but a sovereign state aimed at forming a group. This process of group formation within a political frame was thus necessarily a process of self-critical accommodation. The Union with Scotland exemplifies this difference, for it was a political union of parliaments that left group cultural features of law, religion, and education initially untouched. They were then, however, as Robert Wuthnow has detailed (1989, 254–64), uncomfortably subject to ongoing revision to make the new form of sovereignty work. As the outpouring we call the Scottish Enlightenment makes particularly clear, the technology that lent itself—at that historical moment—to such self-critically productive work was writing. The discourse of nationalism, in turn, I am arguing, lent itself to the society's accommodation to that technology.

This mutual accommodation was completed[3] in the late eighteenth and early nineteenth centuries. As Gerald Newman points out, this period we call Romanticism was the moment of the "*mental unification, moral reformation, and social reorganization of the country*" (1987, 242). Although standard literary histories identify it as an age of poetry, it was also, from the perspective offered by the history of writing, a crucial moment for novelism. In fact, it saw the start of what I've termed the metonymic displacement of the former by the latter as two crucial events took place: (1) The *statistical* rise of the novel—growth until the 1780s had been slow and erratic. From an annual rate of only about four to twenty new titles through the first four decades, and remaining—despite Fielding's and Richardson's popularity—within a range of roughly twenty to forty for the next three, new novel production peaked briefly near sixty in 1770 before a steep decline to well below forty during the latter half of that decade. Within the next seven years, however, the output jumped—more than doubled—to close to ninety, and continued to increase sharply into the next century (see Siskin 1994a, 26). (2) The *generic* rise of the novel—the novel was a low form in the generic hierarchy until roughly the 1820s, when critics self-consciously noted a new attitude toward what was being described as the "new" novel (Siskin 1988, 127–38). This was not simply a matter of shifting opinions but, I shall suggest, a change in the narrative form of literary history.

To grasp what is at stake in these claims to being "new," particularly in regard to nationalism, we need to examine how Fielding's and Richardson's claims to "newness" became old. To make writing "new," in their sense, was, as we have seen, to domesticate it by containing it within the criteria of imitation; by bringing it into proximity with real life as something it could and should imitate, writing, they thought, could be held accountable for lives that imitated it. In Manley's borrowed words, the writer ought "to observe the probability of truth, which consists in saying nothing but what may morally be believed" (reprinted in Barnett 1968, 23).

That scenario of imitation, in which the novel negotiates the relationship between "truth" and "what may morally be believed," was what generated the normative binary of *Pamela/Shamela.* That was why statements about how good Fielding and Richardson were as novelists reposed throughout the century on assumptions about the novel's imitative relationship to moral goodness. Such statements were themselves features of the particular *kind* of historical narrative generated by the imitative imperative. Here, again, is Miller:

> The earliest productions of Great-Britain in this department of writing may be considered as her best. FIELDING and RICHARDSON have never been exceeded, and probably not equalled, by any novelists since their day. (1970, 2:159)

The shape of the argument is, of course, a familiar one: an Ancient-Modern story of imitative decline transposed into, and reduced to fit, the second half of the eighteenth century. Fielding's and Richardson's program to "elevate" the novel was, as Warner and others insist, "countersigned" by the public, but *not* as a "rise of the novel" as we now know it; the narrative had no upward curve but rather a sudden apotheosis and then a flattening failure to measure up. In fact, I should add, that flattening was preserved within the later developmental narrative of the Great Tradition as a temporary lack of genius. Its imitative function, however, was, once again, to domesticate writing; the narrative was invoked to demand more formal and moral discipline from those who were always already falling short.

The success of that tactic was, of course, its demise. As writing was made more familiar, it no longer had to be handled in imitative ways; in fact, imitative caution toward the end of the century seemed increasingly out of place. In 1778, for example, Clara Reeve introduced *The Old English Baron* in imitative terms as "the literary offspring of the *Castle of Otranto*"; however, the subsequent argument demonstrates how—as more writing produced more models—efforts to reconcile imitation of other novelists with imitation of the real produced almost disabling levels of distinction. Trying to define "the utmost *verge* of probability," Reeve says, of *Otranto:*

> we can conceive, and allow of, the appearance of a ghost; we can even dispense with an enchanted sword and helmet; but then they must keep within certain limits of credibility: A sword so large as to require a hundred men to lift it, a helmet that by its own weight forces a passage through a courtyard. (qtd. in Barnett 1968, 136)

Only by surrendering herself to this kind of argument—ghosts are okay but helmets over a certain size are not—can Reeve press forward with her plan to preserve and reform Walpole, fearing, even then, that "it might happen to me as to certain translators, and imitators of Shakespeare; the unities may be preserved, while the spirit is evaporated" (137).

Charles Jenner, a bit earlier in the decade (1770), turned to the same literary figure to articulate the difficulties of imitation, citing

> what Swift said of Rowe's Jane Shore: "I have seen," says he, "a play written in professed imitation of Shakespear, wherein the whole likeness consisted in one line, 'And so good morning to you, good Mr. Lieutenant.' " (qtd. in Barnett 1968, 126)

Unlike Swift earlier in the century, however, Jenner had another alternative to offer besides better imitations. Although his argument was itself part of an explicit imitation of Fielding—it is in an introductory chapter of "observation and reflection" in a novel entitled *The Placid Man*—it proposes a hierarchical distinction between those writers qualified for "original composition" and those, "in the next place," qualified "for imitation" (126). With the demotion of imitation came, as well, a reappraisal of the novel's moral imperative. Observing that "life is full of cares and anxieties" requiring "many expedients to make it pass on," Jenner argues that man "applies" various "schemes"

> for that purpose: one hunts, one shoots, one plays, one reads, one writes. Scarce anyone expects his mind to be made better by every one of them; happy if it is made no worse; and in this light what more pleasant, what more innocent than that amusement which is commonly called Castle-building? . . . For which species of amusement nothing affords so good materials as a novel. (127–28)

This increased emphasis on the novel's positive entertainment value was accompanied by a reformulation of its dangers. Writing in *The*

Lounger in 1785, Henry Mackenzie shares the imitative concern that real life can follow novels but claims not to be "disposed to carry the idea of the dangerous tendency of all novels quite so far as some rigid moralists have done." The issue for him is no longer the violation of absolute standards of behavior induced by wayward texts, for he brings additional terms into the equation: in judging novels, we need to "attend to the period of society which produces them. The code of morality must necessarily be enlarged in proportion to that state of manners to which cultivated eras give birth" (qtd. in Williams 1970, 329). With society and history in play, real life and morality are subject to change in which the novel naturally participates.

This naturalization is one of the most important effects of novelism. When writing becomes just like hunting and shooting, novels may still be dangerous, but we know how to handle them. As the technology is contextualized with respect to other concerns—society, history, the original mind of the author, the personal architecture of castle building—the old users' guide gathers dust on the shelf. Imitative imperatives—and fears—are qualified; epistolary novels wane after the 1780s, and, as Jenner indicates, imitators of Fielding's mixing strategies dwindle. What ensues is not so much a new chapter in the history of "the" novel but a new type of history, as the tales of imitative decline give way, early in the next century, to now familiar tales of ongoing improvement: the "rise" of the creatively autonomous aesthetic object called the *English* novel.

This sense of Englishness built upon, but was different from, the largely oppositional writing of the nation earlier in the eighteenth century. Whereas novelism's initial role in instituting nationalism in Great Britain turned on the generic identification of France with the older form of romance the novel claimed to supersede, this later stage depended on a different generic link—one that constructed national identity no longer as self versus other but as whole embracing parts. To be specific, the novel's quantitative rise at the end of the century occurred precisely when the audience of its close ally—the periodical—began, as Jon Klancher has shown (1987), to fracture. The politically and socioeconomically diverse audiences of this newly "complex" public appear, as I have argued elsewhere (Siskin 1994a), to have coalesced around the novel. In fact, the periodicals themselves, despite—actually, because of—their diversification, point to this increasing consolidation of the novel's cultural power.

At the moment of audience remapping, as Ioan Williams points out, not only were the established journals reviewing fiction more frequently, but new journals arose for which "novel-reviewing was an important activity" (1970, 22).

Novelism, embracing both the novels and the reviewing of them, was thus a primary arena for what Marilyn Butler calls the "war of ideas" (1975). What emerged was an Englishness that did not resolve but regulated difference, that in the 1790s accommodated both Godwin and Austen under the shared rubric of writing the regular: "things as they are," "bits" of the "ordinary." For the reviewers, these efforts were "singular" and "new," their detailings of "character and situation"[4] unlike those of their predecessors. And, when Walter Scott and Richard Whately wrote up Austen's newness, they did so in a new way: not as a return to the ancient heights of Fielding and Richardson but as an emerging "style," one that "has arisen" (Scott 1968, 63).

Novelism now featured, in other words, developmental narratives[5] within both the tales themselves (the eponymous Emma's "unit[ing]" the "best blessings of existence" in Jane Austen's novel) *and* the critical turns upon them (the novel's "rise"). The mix of development's imperative of progress with the stress upon the "common" that Scott praised in Austen—common not as low but as that which was ordinarily and locally shared by all—enabled the portrayal of Great Britain as a land that was itself united and rising. But as Scott's celebration of Austen's individual achievement, as well as Scott's own apotheosis as Author, shifted attention and concern from the writing to the writer, the technology itself was tamed. It came to be treated as a primarily reflective, rather than inherently productive, tool—a tool that in Austen's hand, for example, was increasingly understood to depict, not construct or change, the details of English life. Under the rubric of the newly triumphant novel, writing was domesticated at the same time as the society that depended on it. As Britain became comfortable with writing, it became comfortable with itself as a nation.

To emphasize the historical specificity and materiality of novelism,[6] I would like to conclude by identifying yet another institutional edge. Having connected novelism to the organization of the state, I want now to connect it to the organization of knowledge. Those formations are themselves, of course, connected; we still, for example, study novels primarily within the disciplinary bounds of "*English* Literature" and other nation-specific groupings. That is in fact the most obvious connection of novels to disciplinarity: they make up a significant part of the subject matter of particular disciplines.

Novelism, however, opens up historical and conceptual avenues of a different kind. By turning our attention from creative/critical distinctions to the hierarchical functions of competing categories of writing, we can begin to make sense of shifting categorizations of knowledge. The most recent shift left us with the modern disciplinary divisions between the sciences, the social sciences, and the humanities—divisions rationalized by seemingly natural discursive behaviors—behaviors that, since the eighteenth century, have been grounded in writing. Events in the history of writing, then, must in some way have been instrumental in the institutionalization of these divisions. And, given the central role I've ascribed to novelism in that history, we should be able to gauge its impact on disciplinarity.

The common ground linking novelism and disciplinarity is "fiction." On the one hand, the discourse of and about novels has been, in a sense, the workshop in which the various activities associated with fiction have been carried out, particularly those concerned with the problem of imitation. On the other hand, Michel de Certeau has pointed out fiction's generative role for modern disciplines, in terms of both the boundaries it sets (as that which "the historiographer constitutes as erroneous," fiction "delimits his proper territory") and, more important, the boundaries it opens: by "render[ing] possible," fiction generates possibilities "for producing or transforming reality" that distinguish disciplinary knowledge as that which is inherently progressive (1986, 201–2).

When certain disciplines *"fiction" in writing*—and thus enact the imperative of improvement as the transformative discovery of "truth"—we call it scientificity. But what do we call it when other disciplines *write fiction*—and thus enact the imperative as (remember Jenner) amusing self-development? "Novelism," I am suggesting, is a term that can help us come to terms with our disciplinary fates. By paralleling it to "scientificity," we can see that just as, within the sciences, the "fiction" has been subsumed within the "writing," so, within the humanities, has "writing" been subsumed within the "fiction." As historians of science and literary historians rewrite their respective pasts, recovering the fictive nature of science and the constitutive power of writing, these parallels will bear additional explanatory weight. Scientificity's valorization of "objectivity," for example, has its humanistic counterpart not in "subjectivity" (these terms constitute only a self-validating binary) but in novelism's heteroglossia: while objectivity posits all investigators always arriving at the same answer, and thus speaking with one voice, heteroglossia enacts truth as a multiplicity of voices.

The collection of essays that you now hold in your hand, as both the form for a new literary history and another example of novelism, has the potential to work in both ways. It can speak through the single title with one voice, even as it conveys different messages. I raise my own voice, then, in order to identify and participate in the institutional changes that are signaled not only by Susan Sontag's discomfort with the novel but by the appearance of this book.

Notes

1. I am not, of course, suggesting a heroic narrative in which the "people" are taking over the media. In fact, a key issue I am trying to address for writing and electronic media is the extent to which they "take over," such that even the modes of apparently active participation are behaviors scripted by the technologies they appear to affect.

2. Joseph Bartolomeo argues that "all too routinely, this critical commentary [on the novel] has been consigned to the footnote, the aside—or, occasionally, the chapter—and has been invoked largely for utilitarian purposes in literary histories, surveys of the genre, and critical biographies." He urges that we "mov[e] the discourse to the foreground" to "demonstrate the constitutive cultural role it played, its success in forging a place for the genre in literary and popular culture" (1994, 10). I share this desire to "foreground" the critical; for Bartolomeo, however, the concept of "genre" itself remains undisturbed, maintaining the novel's separate stature as a creative generic object whose "rise" his history of criticism helps to explain. I use the term "novelism" in an effort not just to foreground the critical but—in specific, historical ways—to confound it with the creative and thus denaturalize standard notions of genre and of literature. For the historicity of the creative/critical distinction, see Siskin 1988, 37–63.

3. The accommodation was also signaled by the redeployment of the critical elements in writing. They were not eliminated, of course, but increasingly partitioned off as a separate discourse: "criticism" came to serve the newly forming discipline of English Literature—a move that amounted, in national terms, to the institutionalization of a now comfortably loyal opposition.

4. The word "new" appears in a review of Austen by Scott (Scott 1968). The

other terms are from a review of *Caleb Williams* in the *Analytical Review* 21 (Feb. 1795), reprinted in Williams 1970, 396.

5. See my discussion of development in relation to the novel in Siskin 1988, 125–47.

6. I also hope this final argument helps to confirm the (nonpsychological) utility of the notion of "comfort" as a historical marker in the study of institutions.

Works Cited

Achebe, Chinua. 1969. *Things Fall Apart.* 1958. Reprint, Greenwich, Conn.: Fawcett.

———. 1975. *Morning Yet on Creation Day.* Rev. ed. Garden City, N.Y.: Anchor/Doubleday.

Advertisement for *Jazz.* 1992. *New York Times,* 29 Apr., national edition, B2.

Ahmad, Aijaz. 1987. "Jameson's Rhetoric of Otherness and the 'National Allegory.'" *Social Text* 17:3–25.

Allart, Hortense. 1836. *Settimia.* 2 vols. Paris: Arthus Bertrand.

Allen, James Lane. 1897. "Two Principles in Recent American Fiction." *Atlantic,* Oct., 433–41.

Allen, James Smith. 1991. *In the Public Eye: A History of Reading in Modern France.* Princeton: Princeton University Press.

Altieri, Charles. 1983. "An Idea and Ideal of a Literary Canon." *Critical Inquiry* 10:37–60.

Amadiume, Ifi. 1987. *Male Daughters, Female Husbands: Sex and Gender in an African Society.* London: Zed Books.

Anderson, Benedict. 1983. *Imagined Communities: Reflections on the Origin and Spread of Nationalism.* London: Verso.

———. 1991. *Imagined Communities: Reflections on the Origin and Spread of Nationalism.* Rev. ed. London: Verso.

———. 1994. "Exodus." *Critical Inquiry* 20:314–27.

Anderson, Margaret Steele. 1898. "A Modern Romancer." *Dial* 1:14–15.

Anderson, Perry. 1988. "Modernity and Revolution." In Nelson and Grossberg 1988. 317–33.

Andrade, Susan Z. 1990. "Rewriting History, Motherhood, and Rebellion: Naming an African Women's Literary Tradition." *Research in African Literatures* 20, no. 1:91–110.

Appadurai, Arjun. 1990. "Disjuncture and Difference in the Global Cultural Economy." *Public Culture* 2:1–24.

Appiah, Kwame Anthony. 1991. "Out of Africa: Topologies of Nativism." In *The Bounds of Race: Perspectives on Hegemony and Resistance,* ed. Dominick LaCapra. Ithaca: Cornell University Press. 134–63.

———. 1992. *In My Father's House: Africa in the Philosophy of Culture.* New York: Oxford University Press.

Arguedas, José María. 1978. *Deep Rivers.* Trans. Frances Horning Barraclough. Austin: University of Texas Press.

Armstrong, Nancy. 1987. *Desire and Domestic Fiction: A Political History of the Novel.* New York: Oxford University Press.

Armstrong, Nancy, and Leonard Tennenhouse. 1992. *The Imaginary Puritan: Literature, Intellectual Labor, and the Origins of Personal Life.* Berkeley: University of California Press.

Aspinall, Susan. 1983. "Sexuality in Costume Melodrama." In *Gainsborough Melodrama,* ed. Susan Aspinall and Robert Murphy. London: B.F.I. 29–39.

Auger, Hippolyte. 1837. *La Femme du monde et la femme artiste.* 2 vols. Paris: Ambroise Dupont.

Austen, Jane. 1967. *Sense and Sensibility.* 1811. Reprint ed. Tony Tanner. Harmondsworth: Penguin.

———. 1971a. *Emma.* 1816. Reprint ed. David Lodge. Oxford: World's Classics.

———. 1971b. *Northanger Abbey.* 1818. Reprint ed. John Davie. Oxford: World's Classics.

Axtell, James. 1985. *The Invasion Within: The Contest of Cultures in Colonial North America.* New York: Oxford University Press.

B., A. 1839. "Critique littéraire: *Eugène* par M. Emile Barrault." *Revue de Paris,* 3d ser., 1 (Jan.): 206–16.

Bailey, John. 1931. *Introductions to Jane Austen.* London: Oxford University Press.

Baker, Ernest. 1924. *The History of the English Novel.* New York: Barnes and Noble.

Bakerman, Jane. 1978. "The Seams Can't Show: An Interview with Toni Morrison." *Black American Literature Forum* 12:56–60.

Bakhtin, M. M. 1981. *The Dialogic Imagination.* Ed. Michael Holquist. Trans. Caryl Emerson and Michael Holquist. Austin: University of Texas Press.

Baldick, Chris. 1983. *The Social Mission of English Criticism, 1848–1932.* Oxford: Clarendon.

Balibar, Etienne. 1991. "The Nation Form: History and Ideology." In Etienne Balibar and Immanuel Wallerstein, *Race, Nation, Class: Ambiguous Identities.* London: Verso. 86–106.

Ballaster, Ros. 1992. *Seductive Forms: Women's Amatory Fiction from 1684 to 1740.* Oxford: Clarendon.

Banta, Martha. 1972. *Henry James and the Occult: The Great Extension.* Bloomington: Indiana University Press.

Banyiwa-Horne, Naana. 1986. "African Womanhood: The Contrasting Perspectives of Flora Nwapa's *Efuru* and Elechi Amadi's *The Concubine*." In Davies and Graves 1986. 119–29.
Barnett, George L., ed. 1968. *Eighteenth-Century Novelists on the Novel.* New York: Appleton Century-Crofts.
Barr, Robert. 1973. "Literature in Canada." 1899. Reprinted in *The Measure of the Rule.* Toronto: University of Toronto Press.
Barral, Carlos. 1978. *Los años sin excusa. Memorias II.* Barcelona: Barral Editores.
———. 1988. *Cuando las horas veloces. Memorias III.* Barcelona: Tusquets.
Barrault, Emile. 1839. *Eugène.* Paris: Delessert.
——— [Mme de Casamajor, pseud.]. 1847. *La Pathologie du mariage.* Paris: Comon.
Barthes, Roland. 1964. "History or Literature." In *On Racine.* Trans. Richard Howard. New York: Hill and Wang. 153–72.
———. 1968. *Writing Degree Zero.* Trans. Annette Lavers and Colin Smith. New York: Hill and Wang.
Bartolomeo, Joseph. 1994. *A New Species of Criticism: Eighteenth-Century Discourse on the Novel.* Newark: University of Delaware Press.
Barzun, Jacques. 1958. "The Scholar-Critic." In Leary 1958b. 3–8.
Bastide, Jenny (Madame Camille Bodin). 1838. *Elise et Marie.* 2 vols. Paris: Dumon.
Baym, Nina. 1981. "Melodramas of Beset Manhood: How Theories of American Fiction Exclude Women Authors." *American Quarterly* 33:123–39.
———. 1984. "Concepts of the Romance in Hawthorne's America." *Nineteenth-Century Fiction* 38:426–43.
Beatson, Peter. 1989. *The Healing Tongue.* Palmerston North, New Zealand: Massey University Press.
Beauman, Nicola. 1983. *A Very Great Profession: The Woman's Novel, 1914–1939.* London: Virago.
Behn, Aphra. 1992. *Oroonoko, The Rover, and Other Works.* Ed. Janet Todd. London: Penguin.
———. 1993. *Love Letters between a Nobleman and His Sister.* In *The Works of Aphra Behn.* Ed. Janet Todd. Vol. 2. Columbus: Ohio State University Press.
Bell, Millicent. 1991. *Meaning in Henry James.* Cambridge: Harvard University Press.
Bender, John. 1987. *Imagining the Penitentiary: Fiction and the Architecture of the Mind in Eighteenth-Century England.* Chicago: University of Chicago Press.
Benjamin, Walter. 1963. *The Origin of German Tragic Drama.* New York: Verso.
———. 1969. "Theses on the Philosophy of History." In *Illuminations.* Trans. Harry Zohn. New York: Schocken. 253–64.
Bennett, Tony. 1990. *Outside Literature.* London: Routledge.

Berlant, Lauren. 1988. "The Female Complaint." *Social Text* 19–20:237–59.
Berman, Marshall. 1982. *All That Is Solid Melts into Air: The Experience of Modernity.* New York: Simon and Schuster.
Bhabha, Homi K. 1984. "Of Mimicry and Man: The Ambivalence of Colonial Discourse." *October* 28:125–33.
———. 1990a. "DissemiNation: Time, Narrative, and the Margins of the Modern Nation." In Bhabha 1990b. 291–322.
———. 1991. "Race, Time and the Revision of Modernity." *Oxford Literary Review* 13:193–219.
———, ed. 1990b. *Nation and Narration.* New York: Routledge.
Billotey, Elisa. 1837. *L'Agent de change.* Preface by Auguste Luchet. Dieppe: Delevoye-Barrier.
Bissoondath, Neil. 1990. "Insecurity." In *Caribbean New Wave: Contemporary Short Stories,* ed. Stewart Brown. Oxford: Heinemann. 24–31.
Blackburn, Sara. 1973. Review of *Sula,* by Toni Morrison. *New York Times Book Review,* 30 Dec., 3.
Blades, John. 1993. "Nobel Panel Hails Morrison for Her 'Vision.'" *Chicago Tribune,* 8 Oct., sec. 1, pp. 1, 25.
Bledstein, Burton J. 1976. *The Culture of Professionalism: The Middle Class and the Development of Higher Education in America.* New York: Norton.
Boehmer, Elleke. 1991. "Stories of Women and Mothers: Gender and Nationalism in the Early Fiction of Flora Nwapa." In *Motherlands: Black Women's Writing from Africa, the Caribbean, and South Asia,* ed. Susheila Nasta. New Brunswick: Rutgers University Press. 3–23.
Bonnal, Marcellin de. 1841. *Lamentations de Marcellin de Bonnal, ou la Renaissance sociale.* Paris: published by author.
Bonus, Enrique. 1994. *Locating Filipino-American Identities: Ethnicity and the Politics of Space in Southern California.* Ph.D. diss., University of California, San Diego.
"Book-Talk." 1889. *Lippincott's,* Apr., 605–6.
Booth, Bradford A. 1958. "The Novel." In Leary 1958b. 259–88.
Bourdieu, Pierre. 1984. *Distinction: A Social Critique of the Judgement of Taste.* Trans. Richard Nice. Cambridge: Harvard University Press.
———. 1990. "The Intellectual Field: A World Apart." In *In Other Words.* Trans. Matthew Adamson. Stanford: Stanford University Press. 140–49.
———. 1991. "Rites of Institution." In *Language and Symbolic Power.* Ed. John B. Thompson. Trans. Gino Raymond and Matthew Adamson. Cambridge: Harvard University Press. 117–26.
Bowering, George. 1977. *A Short Sad Book.* Vancouver: Talonbooks.
Bowers, Toni O'Shaughnessy. 1994. "Sex, Lies, and Invisibility: Amatory Fiction from the Restoration to Mid-Century." In Richetti 1994. 50–72.

Bradley, A. C. 1929. "Jane Austen." 1911. Reprinted in *A Miscellany*. London: Macmillan. 32–72.
Brennan, Timothy. 1989. *Salman Rushdie and the Third World: Myths of the Nation*. New York: St. Martin's.
———. 1990. "The National Longing for Form." In Bhabha 1990b. 44–70.
Brodhead, Richard H. 1993. *Cultures of Letters: Scenes of Reading and Writing in Nineteenth-Century America*. Chicago: University of Chicago Press.
Brooker, Peter, and Peter Widdowson. 1986. "A Literature for England." In Colls and Dodd 1986. 116–63.
Brooks, Cleanth, and Robert Penn Warren. 1943. *Understanding Fiction*. New York: F. S. Crofts.
Brown, Laura. 1993. *Ends of Empire: Women and Ideology in Early Eighteenth-Century English Literature*. Ithaca: Cornell University Press.
Brown, Homer O. 1996. *Institutions of the English Novel*. Philadelphia: University of Pennsylvania Press.
Brown, Lloyd W. 1981. *Women Writers in Black Africa*. Westport, Conn.: Greenwood.
Brown, William Hill. 1970. *The Power of Sympathy*. 1789. Reprint ed. William S. Osborne. Albany: New College and University Press.
Browne, Nick. 1992. "Race: The Political Unconscious in American Film." *East-West Film Journal* 6, no. 1:5–16.
Browning, Colin Arrott. 1847. *The Convict Ships and England's Exiles*. London: Hamilton, Adams and Co.
Brownstein, Michael. 1987. "From *Kokugaku* to *Kokubungaku:* Canon Formation in the Meiji Period." *Harvard Journal of Asiatic Studies* 47, no. 2:435–60.
Bryant, G. J. 1985. "Scots in India in the Eighteenth Century." *Scottish Historical Review* 34, no. 1:22–41.
Bumstead, J. M. 1982. *The People's Clearances: Highland Emigration to British North America, 1770–1815*. Edinburgh: Edinburgh University Press.
Burgin, Victor, et al., eds. 1986. *Formations of Fantasy*. New York: Methuen.
Burnham, Michelle. 1993. "The Journey Between: Liminality and Dialogism in Mary White Rowlandson's Captivity Narrative." *Early American Literature* 28:60–75.
Burr, Esther Edwards. 1984. *The Journal of Esther Edwards Burr, 1754–1757*. Ed. Carol F. Karlsen and Laurie Crumpacker. New Haven: Yale University Press.
Butler, Marilyn. 1975. *Jane Austen and the War of Ideas*. Oxford: Clarendon.
———. 1982. "Godwin, Burke, and *Caleb Williams*." *Essays in Criticism* 32:15–28.
Cabral, Amilcar. 1973. *Return to the Source: Selected Speeches by Amilcar Cabral*. New York: Africa Information Service and Monthly Review Press.
Calder, Angus. 1981. *Revolutionary Empire: The Rise of the English-Speaking Empires from the Fifteenth Century to the 1780s*. New York: Dutton.

Campbell, Colin. 1987. *The Romantic Ethic and the Spirit of Modern Consumerism.* New York: Blackwell.
Carlowitz, Aloïse de. 1835. *Le Pair de France ou le Divorce.* 3 vols. Paris: Charles Lachapelle.
Carpenter, G. R. 1898. "The Neo-Romantic Novel." *Forum,* Mar., 120–28.
Caverly, Robert B. 1874. *Heroism of Hannah Duston, Together with the Indian Wars of New England.* Boston: B. B. Russell.
Certeau, Michel de. 1984. *The Practice of Everyday Life.* Trans. Steven Randall. Berkeley: University of California Press.
———. 1986. *Heterologies: Discourse on the Other.* Trans. Brian Massumi. Minneapolis: University of Minnesota Press.
Cha, Theresa Hak Kyung. 1982. *Dictée.* New York: Tanam.
Chakrabarty, Dipesh. 1992. "Postcoloniality and the Artifice of History: Who Speaks for 'Indian' Pasts?" *Representations* 37:1–26.
Chandler, Raymond. 1946. "The Simple Art of Murder." 1944. Reprinted in Haycraft 1946. 222–37.
Chandra, Bipan. 1980. "Colonialism, Stages of Colonialism, and the Colonial State." *Journal of Contemporary Asia* 10, no. 3:272–85.
Chase, Richard. 1957. *The American Novel and Its Tradition.* Garden City, N.Y.: Doubleday.
Chatterjee, Partha. 1986. *Nationalist Thought and the Colonial World: A Derivative Discourse.* Delhi: Oxford University Press.
Chevigny, Bell Gale. 1993. "Teaching Comparative Literature of the United States and Spanish America." *American Literature* 65:354–58.
Cheyfitz, Eric. 1991. *The Poetics of Imperialism: Translation and Colonization from "The Tempest" to "Tarzan."* New York: Oxford University Press.
Choi, Chungmoo. 1993. "The Discourse of Decolonization and Popular Memory: South Korea." *positions* 1, no. 1:77–102.
Chow, Rey. 1992. "Postmodern Automatons." In *Feminists Theorize the Political,* ed. Judith Butler and Joan Scott. New York: Routledge. 101–20.
Clarke, Marcus. 1970. *His Natural Life.* 1870. Reprint, Harmondsworth: Penguin.
Cliff, Michelle. 1984. *Abeng.* New York: Dutton.
Clifford, James L. 1958. "The Eighteenth Century." In Leary 1958b. 83–108.
Cobham, Rhonda. 1991. "Making Men and History: Achebe and the Politics of Revisionism in *Things Fall Apart.*" In *Approaches to Teaching Achebe's* Things Fall Apart, ed. Bernth Lindfors. New York: Modern Language Association.
Cohen, Margaret. 1995. "In Lieu of a Chapter on Some French Women Realist Novelists." In *Spectacles of Realism: Gender, Body, Genre,* ed. Margaret Cohen and Christopher Prendergast. Minneapolis: University of Minnesota Press. 90–119.

Collingham, H. A. C. 1988. *The July Monarchy: A Political History of France 1830–1848.* London: Longman.
Collins, Irene. 1959. *The Government and the Newspaper Press in France, 1814–1881.* Oxford: Oxford University Press.
Colls, Robert, and Philip Dodd, eds. 1986. *Englishness: Politics and Culture, 1880–1920.* London: Croom Helm.
Condé, Maryse. 1972. "Three Female Writers in Modern Africa: Flora Nwapa, Ama Ata Aidoo, Grace Ogot." *Présence Africaine* 82:136–39.
Copjec, Joan. 1994. *Read My Desire: Lacan against the Historicists.* Cambridge: MIT Press.
Crawford, F. Marion. 1969. *The Novel: What It Is.* 1893. Reprint, Freeport, N.Y.: Books for Libraries Press.
Crawford, Robert. 1992. *Devolving English Literature.* Oxford: Clarendon.
Cremin, Lawrence A. 1988. *American Education: The Metropolitan Experience, 1876–1980.* New York: Harper.
Cumings, Bruce. 1984. "The Legacy of Japanese Colonialism in Korea." In Myers and Peattie 1984. 478–96.
Cuno, James B. 1985. "Charles Philipon and La Maison Aubert: The Business, Politics, and Public of Caricature in Paris, 1820–1840." Ph.D. diss., Harvard University.
Dann, Otto. 1988. Introduction to *Nationalism in the Age of the French Revolution,* ed. Otto Dann and John Dinwiddy. London: Hambledon. 1–12.
Davey, Frank. 1985. "Wacouster." In *The Louis Riel Organ and Piano Company.* Winnipeg: Turnstone Press. 1–20.
———. 1986. "Abbotsford and India." In *The Abbotsford Guide to India.* Victoria: Press Porcépic. 3–5.
Davidson, Cathy. 1986. *Revolution and the Word: The Rise of the Novel in America.* New York: Oxford University Press.
Davies, Carole Boyce. 1986. "Motherhood in the Works of Male and Female Igbo Writers." In Davies and Graves 1986. 241–56.
Davies, Carole Boyce, and Anne Adams Graves, eds. 1986. *Ngambika.* Trenton: Africa World Press.
Davis, Lennard. 1985. *Factual Fictions.* New York: Columbia University Press.
Day, Martin S. 1975. *A Handbook of American Literature: A Comprehensive Study from Colonial Times to the Present Day.* New York: Crane, Russak.
Delafield, E. M. 1984. *The Diary of a Provincial Lady.* 1930. Reprint, London: Virago.
Derounian, Kathryn Zabelle. 1988. "The Publication, Promotion, and Distribution of Mary Rowlandson's Indian Captivity Narrative in the Seventeenth Century." *Early American Literature* 23:239–61.
Derrida, Jacques. 1989. "Psyche: Inventions of the Other." Trans. Catherine

Porter. In *Reading De Man Reading*, ed. Wlad Godzich and Lindsay Waters. Minneapolis: University of Minnesota Press. 25–65.

———. 1992. "'This Strange Institution Called Literature': An Interview with Jacques Derrida." In *Acts of Literature*, ed. Derek Attridge. New York: Routledge. 33–75.

Desanti, Dominique. 1972. *Flora Tristan: La Femme révoltée.* Paris: Hachette.

Dewey, John. 1964. *John Dewey on Education.* Ed. Reginald D. Archambault. Chicago: University of Chicago Press.

Dick, Stewart. 1909. *The Cottage Homes of England, Drawn by Helen Allingham and Described by Stewart Dick.* London: Edward Arnold.

DiPiero, Thomas. 1992. *Dangerous Truths and Criminal Passions: The Evolution of the French Novel, 1569–1791.* Stanford: Stanford University Press.

Doi, Takeo. 1976. *The Psychological World of Natsume Sōseki.* Cambridge: Harvard University Press.

Donald, James. 1989. "Beyond Our Ken: English, Englishness, and the National Curriculum." In *Dialogue and Difference: English into the Nineties*, ed. Peter Brooker and Peter Humm. London: Routledge. 13–30.

———. 1992. *Sentimental Education: Schooling, Popular Culture, and the Regulation of Liberty.* London: Verso.

Donoso, José. 1977. *The Boom in Spanish American Literature.* Trans. Gregory Kolovakos. New York: Columbia University Press.

Douglas, Mary. 1986. *How Institutions Think.* Syracuse, N.Y.: Syracuse University Press.

Dower, John. 1989. *War without Mercy: Race and Power in the Pacific War.* New York: Pantheon.

Dowling, David. 1989. "Historiography in Some Recent New Zealand Fiction." *Australian and New Zealand Studies in Canada* 2:37–62.

Doyle, Brian. 1989. *English and Englishness.* London: Routledge.

Drake, Samuel. 1990. "A Particular Account of the Captivity of Mrs. Jemima Howe." 1855. Reprinted in *The Indian Captivity Narrative: A Woman's View*, ed. Frances Roe Kestler. New York: Garland. 143–53.

Dreifus, Claudia. 1994. "Chloe Wofford Talks about Toni Morrison." *New York Times Magazine*, 11 Sept., 72–75.

Drujon, Fernand. 1879. *Catalogue des ouvrages, écrits, et dessins de toute nature poursuivis, supprimés, ou condamnés depuis le 21 octobre 1814 jusqu'au 31 juillet 1877.* Paris: Rouveyre.

Duberman, Martin Bauml. 1988. *Paul Robeson.* New York: Knopf.

Du Bois, W. E. B. 1971. "Criteria of Negro Art." 1926. Reprinted in *A W. E. B. Du Bois Reader.* Ed. Andrew G. Paschal. New York: Macmillan. 86–96.

Duffy, Maureen. 1987. Introduction to *Love Letters Between a Nobleman and His Sister*, by Aphra Behn. New York: Penguin. v–xvii.

Duncan, Sara Jeanette. 1984. *The Pool in the Desert.* 1903. Reprint, Harmondsworth: Penguin.

Dunlop, William. 1967. "Recollections of the American War 1812–1814." 1847. Reprinted in *Tiger Dunlop's Upper Canada.* Toronto: McClelland and Stewart.

Du Plessis, Rachel Blau. 1985. *Writing beyond the Ending: Narrative Strategies of Twentieth-Century Women Writers.* Bloomington: Indiana University Press.

During, Simon. 1985. "Postmodernism or Postcolonialism?" *Landfall* 39, no. 3:366–80.

———. 1990. "Literature—Nationalism's Other? The Case for Revision." In Bhabha 1990b. 138–53.

Dyer, Richard. 1986. *Heavenly Bodies: Film Stars and Society.* New York: St. Martin's.

Eagleton, Terry. 1978. *Criticism and Ideology: A Study in Marxist Literary Theory.* London: Verso.

Edel, Leon. 1978. *Henry James: The Treacherous Years, 1895–1901.* Vol. 4 of *The Life of Henry James.* New York: Avon.

Edel, Leon, and Mark Wilson, eds. 1984. *Literary Criticism: Essays on Literature, American Writers, English Writers, by Henry James.* New York: Literary Classics of the United States.

"Editor's Choice." 1970. *New York Times Book Review,* 6 Dec., 2.

Ekwensi, Cyprian. 1961. *Jagua Nana.* London: Heinemann.

Elliott, Emory, et al., eds. 1991. *The Columbia History of the American Novel.* New York: Columbia University Press.

Emecheta, Buchi. 1979. *The Joys of Motherhood.* London: George Braziller.

Emenyonu, Ernest. 1970. Review of *Efuru,* by Flora Nwapa. *Ba Shiru* 1, no. 1:58–61.

Etō Jun. 1970. *Sōseki to sono jidai.* 2 vols. Tokyo: Shinchō Sensho.

Evans, David-Owen. 1936. *Le Roman social sous la monarchie de juillet.* Paris: Presses Universitaires de France.

Fanon, Frantz. 1967. *Black Skin, White Masks.* Trans. Charles Lam Markmann. New York: Grove Press.

———. 1968. *The Wretched of the Earth.* Trans. Constance Farrington. New York: Grove Press.

Favret, Mary A. 1994. "A Home for Art: Painting, Poetry, and Domestic Interiors." In Favret and Watson 1994b. 59–82.

Favret, Mary A., and Nicola Watson. 1994a. Introduction to Favret and Watson 1994b. 1–19.

———, eds. 1994b. *At the Limits of Romanticism: Essays in Cultural, Feminist, and Materialist Criticism.* Bloomington: Indiana University Press.

Fee, Margaret. 1989. "Why C. K. Stead Didn't Like Keri Hulme's *the bone*

people: Who Can Write as Other?" *Australian and New Zealand Studies in Canada* 1:11–32.
Felman, Shoshana. 1982. "Turning the Screw of Interpretation." In *Literature and Psychoanalysis: The Question of Reading: Otherwise,* ed. Shoshana Felman. Baltimore: Johns Hopkins University Press. 94–207.
Ferber, Edna. 1926. *Show Boat.* Garden City, N.Y.: Doubleday.
———. 1939. *A Peculiar Treasure.* Garden City, N.Y.: Doubleday.
———. 1947. "You're Not the Type." In *One Basket.* Chicago: People's Book Club. 522–43.
Fergusson, Russell, et al., eds. 1990. *Out There: Marginalization and Contemporary Cultures.* Cambridge: MIT Press.
Ferris, Ina. 1991. *The Achievement of Literary Authority: Gender, History, and the Waverley Novels.* Ithaca: Cornell University Press.
"A Few Story-Tellers, Old and New." 1893. *Atlantic,* Nov., 693–99.
Fiedler, Leslie A. 1958. "American Literature." In Leary 1958b. 157–85.
———. 1960. *Love and Death in the American Novel.* New York: Criterion.
Fielding, Henry. 1987. *Joseph Andrews with Shamela and Related Writings.* Ed. Homer Goldberg. New York: Norton.
Fitz, Earl. 1991. *Rediscovering the New World: Inter-American Literature in a Comparative Context.* Iowa City: Iowa University Press.
Flanders, W. Austen. 1984. *Structures of Experience: History, Society, and Personal Life in the Eighteenth-Century British Novel.* Columbia: University of South Carolina Press.
Fliegelman, Jay. 1982. *Prodigals and Pilgrims: The American Revolution against Patriarchal Authority, 1750–1800.* Cambridge: Cambridge University Press.
Fogel, Joshua. 1989. "Japanese Literary Travel in Pre-War China." *Harvard Journal of Asiatic Studies* 49, no. 2:575–602.
Fogle, Richard Harter. 1958. "The Romantic Movement." In Leary 1958b. 109–38.
Foner, Philip S. 1978. *Paul Robeson Speaks: Writings, Speeches, Interviews, 1918–1974.* New York: Brunner/Mazel.
Forbush, William. 1902. *The Boy Problem.* Boston: Pilgrim Press.
Forest, P. 1842. "Un Feuilleton de M. Jules Janin." *La Phalange,* 20 Mar., 2–4.
Foucault, Michel. 1977a. *Language, Counter-memory, Practice: Selected Essays and Interviews.* Ed. Donald F. Bouchard. Ithaca: Cornell University Press.
———. 1977b. "Language to Infinity." In Foucault 1977a. 53–67.
———. 1977c. "Nietzsche, Genealogy, History." In Foucault 1977a. 139–64.
———. 1978. *The History of Sexuality.* Vol. 1, *An Introduction.* Trans. Robert Hurley. New York: Pantheon.
———. 1979. "Lives of Infamous Men." In *Michel Foucault: Power, Truth, Strategy.* Ed. Meaghan Morris and Paul Patton. Sydney: Feral Publications. 76–91.

———. 1986. "Of Other Spaces." Trans. Jay Miskowiec. *Diacritics* 16, no. 1:22–27.

Fowler, Edward. 1992. "Rendering Words, Traversing Cultures: On the Art and Politics of Translating Modern Japanese Fiction." *Journal of Japanese Studies* 18, no. 1:1–44.

Franco, Jean. 1988. "Beyond Ethnocentrism: Gender, Power, and the Third-World Intelligentsia." In Nelson and Grossberg 1988. 503–15.

———. 1989. *Plotting Women: Gender and Representation in Mexico.* New York: Columbia University Press.

Freedland, Michael. 1978. *Jerome Kern: A Biography.* New York: Stein and Day.

Freud, Sigmund. 1957. "Infantile Sexuality." In *Three Essays on the Theory of Sexuality.* 1905. Reprinted in *The Standard Edition of the Complete Psychological Works of Sigmund Freud.* Trans. and ed. James Strachey. London: The Hogarth Press and the Institute of Psycho-Analysis. 7:173–206.

Frost, John. 1976. *Heroic Women of the West.* 1854. Reprint, New York: Garland.

Frow, John. 1986. *Marxism and Literary History.* Cambridge: Harvard University Press.

Fujii, James A. 1993. *Complicit Fictions: The Subject in Modern Japanese Prose Narrative.* Berkeley: University of California Press.

Furet, François, and Jacques Ozouf. 1982. *Reading and Writing: Literacy in France from Calvin to Jules Ferry.* Cambridge: Cambridge University Press.

Gallagher, Catherine. 1985. *The Industrial Reformation of English Fiction: Social Discourse and Narrative Form, 1832–67.* Chicago: University of Chicago Press.

———. 1994. *Nobody's Story: The Vanishing Acts of Women Writers in the Marketplace.* Berkeley: University of California Press.

Galt, John. 1830. *Lawrie Todd; or, The Settlers in the Woods.* 3 vols. London: Henry Colburn.

———. 1831. *Bogle Corbet; or, The Emigrants.* 3 vols. London: Henry Colburn and Richard Bentley.

———. 1877. *The Radical: An Autobiography.* 1832. Reprint, London: James Fraser.

———. 1967. *Annals of the Parish.* 1821. Reprint, Oxford: Oxford University Press.

———. 1970. *The Entail, or, The Lairds of Grippy.* 1822. Reprint, London: Oxford University Press.

———. 1973. *The Provost.* 1822. Reprint, London: Oxford University Press.

———. 1975. *The Member.* 1831. Reprint, Edinburgh: Scottish Academic Press.

———. 1976. *The Last of the Lairds.* 1826. Reprint, Edinburgh: Scottish Academic Press.

———. 1977. *Bogle Corbet.* 1831. Reprint ed. Elizabeth Waterson. Toronto: McClelland and Stewart.

———. 1984. *Ringhan Gilhaize.* 1823. Reprint, Edinburgh: Scottish Academic Press.

García, Samuel. 1977. *Tres Mil Años de literatura en "Cien años de soldedad": Intertextualidad en la obra de García Márquez.* Medellín: Editorial Lealon.

García Márquez, Gabriel. 1971. (Orig. version, 1967.) *One Hundred Years of Solitude.* Trans. Gregory Rabassa. New York: Avon.

———. 1985. "Latin America's Impossible Reality." Trans. Elena Brunet. *Harper's,* Jan., 13–15.

———. 1988. "The Solitude of Latin America." Trans. Marina Castañeda. In *Lives on the Line,* ed. Doris Meyer. Berkeley: University of California Press. 230–34.

Gardiner, Judith Kegan. 1985. "The First English Novel: Aphra Behn's *Love Letters,* the Canon, and Women's Tastes." *Tulsa Studies in Women's Literature* 8:201–22.

Garis, Leslie. 1992. "Susan Sontag Finds Romance." *New York Times Magazine,* 2 Aug.

Gaspé, Philippe Aubert de. 1974. (Orig. version, 1862.) *Canadians of Old.* Trans. Sir Charles G. D. Roberts. Toronto: McClelland and Stewart.

Gasset, José Ortega Y. 1961. *Meditations on Quixote.* Trans. Evelyn Rugg and Diego Marin. New York: Norton.

Gates, Henry Louis, Jr. 1984. "The Blackness of Blackness: A Critique of the Sign and the Signifying Monkey." In *Black Literature and Literary Theory,* ed. Henry Louis Gates. New York: Methuen. 285–321.

———. 1988. *The Signifying Monkey: A Theory of Afro-American Literary Criticism.* New York: Oxford University Press.

"George Rice Carpenter." 1929. *Dictionary of American Biography.* Ed. Allen Johnson and Dumas Malone. Vol. 3. New York: Scribner's. 511–12.

Gerson, Carole. 1989. *A Purer Taste: The Writing and Reading of Fiction in English in Nineteenth-Century Canada.* Toronto: University of Toronto Press.

Gibson, Graeme. 1982. *Perpetual Motion.* Toronto: McClelland and Stewart.

Giddings, Paula. 1977. "The Triumphant Song of Toni Morrison." *Encore American and Worldwide News,* 12 Dec.

Gifford, Douglas, ed. 1988. *The History of Scottish Literature.* Vol. 3, *The Nineteenth Century.* Aberdeen: Aberdeen University Press.

Gikandi, Simon. 1991. *Reading Chinua Achebe: Language and Ideology in Fiction.* London: James Currey.

Gilbert, Sandra, and Susan Gubar. 1979. *The Madwoman in the Attic: The Woman Writer and the Nineteenth-Century Literary Imagination.* New Haven: Yale University Press.

Gluck, Carol. 1986. *Japan's Modern Myths.* Princeton: Princeton University Press.

Godwin, William. 1831. "Of Love and Friendship." In *Thoughts on Man, His Nature, Productions, and Discoveries.* London: Effingham Wilson. 273–98.

———. 1946. *Enquiry Concerning Political Justice and Its Influence on Morals and Happiness.* 1793. Facsimile of the third edition, corrected, edited, and with a critical introduction and notes by F. E. L. Priestly. Toronto: University of Toronto Press.

———. 1977. *Caleb Williams.* 1794. Reprint ed. David McCracken. New York: Norton.

Gold, Alex, Jr. 1977. "It's Only Love: The Politics of Passion in Godwin's *Caleb Williams.*" *Texas Studies in Literature and Language* 29, no. 2:135–60.

Goldman, Eric. 1960. *The Crucial Decade—And After: America, 1945–1960.* New York: Vintage.

Goldstein, Robert J. 1989. *The Censorship of Political Caricature in Nineteenth-Century France.* Kent, Ohio: Kent State University Press.

Gordimer, Nadine. 1973. *The Black Interpreters: Notes on African Writing.* Johannesburg: Ravan.

Gotanda, Neil. 1995. "Towards Repeal of Asian Exclusion: The Magnuson Act of 1943, the Act of July 2, 1946, the Presidential Proclamation of July 4, 1946, the Act of August 9, 1946, and the Act of August 1, 1950." In *Asian Americans in Congress. A Documentary History,* ed. Hyung Chan Kim. Westport, Conn.: Greenwood. 309–28.

Grace, Patricia. 1986. *Potiki.* Auckland: Penguin.

Graff, Gerald. 1987. *Professing Literature.* Chicago: University of Chicago Press.

Grainger, J. H. 1986. *Patriotisms: Britain, 1900–1939.* London: Routledge.

Gramsci, Antonio. 1988. *An Antonio Gramsci Reader.* Ed. David Forgacs. New York: Schocken.

Green, Martin Burgess. 1979. *Dreams of Adventure, Deeds of Empire.* New York: Basic Books.

Green, Nicholas. 1990. *The Spectacle of Nature: Landscape and Bourgeois Culture in Nineteenth-Century France.* Manchester: Manchester University Press.

Gross, Robert A. 1969. "The Black Novelists: 'Our Turn.'" *Newsweek,* 16 June, 94–98.

Grossberg, Lawrence, et al., eds. 1992. *Cultural Studies.* New York: Routledge.

Guerrero, Amado. 1979. "Specific Characteristics of Our People's War." In *Philippine Society and Revolution.* Manila: International Association of Filipino Patriots. 179–206.

Guha, Ranajit. 1988. "On Some Aspects of the Historiography of Colonial India." In Guha and Spivak 1988. 37–44.

Guha, Ranajit, and Gayatri Chakravorty Spivak, eds. 1988. *Selected Subaltern Studies.* Oxford: Oxford University Press.

Guillory, John. 1993. *Cultural Capital: The Problem of Literary Canon Formation.* Chicago: University of Chicago Press.

Gupta, Akhil, and James Fergusen. 1992. "Beyond 'Culture': Space, Identity, and the Politics of Difference." *Cultural Anthropology* 7, no. 1:6–22.

Habermas, Jürgen. 1989. *The Structural Transformation of the Public Sphere: An Inquiry into a Category of Bourgeois Society.* Trans. Thomas Burger. Cambridge: MIT Press.

Hagedorn, Jessica. 1990. *Dogeaters.* New York: Penguin.

Haggard, H. Rider. 1985. *King Solomon's Mines.* 1885. Reprint, New York: Tom Doherty Associates.

Haimov, Sharon. 1993. "The Personal Becomes Political: Divorce Debates in July Monarchy France, 1830–1848." Honors thesis, Harvard University.

Haliburton, Thomas Chandler. 1844. *The Attache; or, Sam Slick in England.* London: George Routledge and Sons.

———. 1860. *The Season-Ticket.* London: Richard Bentley.

———. 1958. *The Clockmaker.* 1836. Reprint, Toronto: McClelland and Stewart.

———. 1973. *The Letter Bag of the Great Western; or, Life in a Steamer.* 1840. Reprint, Toronto: University of Toronto Press.

———. 1978. *The Old Judge; or, Life in a Colony.* 1849. Reprint, Ottawa: Tecumseh Press.

Hall, G. Stanley. 1914. *Adolescence: Its Psychology and Its Relations to Physiology, Anthropology, Sociology, Sex, Crime, Religion, and Education.* Vol. 1. 1904. Reprint, New York: Appleton.

Hallays-Dabot, Victor. 1862. *Histoire de la censure théâtrale en France.* Paris: Dentu.

Hanson, Elizabeth. 1981. *God's Mercy Surmounting Man's Cruelty.* 1728. Reprinted in *Puritans among the Indians: Accounts of Captivity and Redemption, 1676–1724,* ed. Alden T. Vaughan and Edward W. Clark. Cambridge: Harvard University Press. 229–44.

Harss, Luis, and Barbara Dohmann. 1967. "Gabriel García Márquez, or The Lost Chord." In *Into the Mainstream.* New York: Harper. 310–41.

Harvey, David. 1990. *The Condition of Postmodernity.* Cambridge: Basil Blackwell.

Haslam, John. 1810. *Illustrations of Madness: Exhibiting a Singular Case of Insanity.* London: Hayden.

Hawes, Joseph M., and N. Ray Hines, eds. 1985. *American Childhood: A Research Guide and Historical Handbook.* Westport, Conn.: Greenwood.

Hawthorne, Nathaniel. 1941. "The Duston Family." 1836. Reprinted in *Hawthorne as Editor: Selections from His Writings in* The American Magazine of Useful and Entertaining Knowledge. Ed. Arlin Turner. Baton Rouge: Louisiana State University Press. 131–37.

Haycraft, Howard, ed. 1946. *The Art of the Mystery Story: A Collection of Critical Essays.* New York: Simon and Schuster.

Haywood, Eliza. 1719–20. *Love in Excess.* London: W. Chetwood.

Hébert, Félix. 1913. "Auguste Luchet (1805–1872)." *L'Abeille de Fontainebleau,* Jan.–Aug.

Hébrard, Jean. 1985. "Les Nouveaux lecteurs." In *Histoire de l'édition française,* vol. 3, ed. Henri-Jean Martin and Roger Chartier. Paris: Promodis. 470–509.

Hechter, Michael. 1975. *Internal Colonialism: The Celtic Fringe in British National Development, 1536–1966.* Berkeley: University of California Press.

Heidegger, Martin. 1977. "The Question Concerning Technology." 1954. Reprinted in *The Question Concerning Technology and Other Essays.* Trans. William Lovit. New York: Harper and Row. 3–35.

Henderson, Mae Gwendolyn. 1994. "Speaking in Tongues: Dialogics, Dialectics, and the Black Woman Writer's Literary Tradition." In *Colonial Discourse and Post-Colonial Theory: A Reader,* ed. Patrick Williams and Laura Chrisman. Hemel Hempstead: Harvester/Wheatsheaf. 257–67.

Hennequin, Antoine-Louis-Marie. 1832. *Du Divorce.* Paris: Gabriel Warée.

Heyer, Georgette. 1966. *The Corinthian.* 1940. Reprint, New York: Dutton.

———. 1991. *Regency Buck.* 1935. Reprint, London: Mandarin.

Hicks, Granville, ed. 1957. *The Living Novel: A Symposium.* New York: Macmillan.

Hill, Constance. 1902. *Jane Austen: Her Homes and Her Friends.* London: John Lane.

Hitchens, Christopher. 1990. *Blood, Class, and Nostalgia: Anglo-American Ironies.* New York: Farrar, Straus and Giroux.

Hodge, Jane Aiken. 1984. *The Private World of Georgette Heyer.* London: Pan.

Hogue, W. Lawrence. 1986. *Discourse and the Other: The Production of the Afro-American Text.* Durham: Duke University Press.

Holderness, Graham, ed. 1988. *The Shakespeare Myth.* Manchester: Manchester University Press.

Holloway, Karla F. C. 1992. *Moorings and Metaphors: Figures of Gender and Culture in Black Women's Literature.* New Brunswick: Rutgers University Press.

Howe, Joseph. 1964. *Joseph Howe: Voice of Nova Scotia.* Ed. J. Murray Beck. Toronto: McClelland and Stewart.

———. 1973. "Acadia." 1874. Reprinted in *Poems and Essays.* Toronto: University of Toronto Press. 5–40.

Howells, William Dean. 1882. "Henry James, Jr." *Century,* Nov., 25–29.

———. 1983. *Editor's Study.* Ed. James W. Simpson. Troy, N.Y.: Whitston.

Howkins, Alun. 1986. "The Discovery of Rural England." In Colls and Dodd 1986. 62–88.

Hubbard, George, and Robyn Craw. 1990. *Beyond Kia Ora: The Paraesthetics of Choice.* Auckland: Artspace.

———. 1992. *Cross-Pollination: Hyphenated Identities and Hybrid Realities.* Auckland: Artspace.

Hughes, Robert. 1988. *The Fatal Shore: The Epic of Australia's Founding.* New York: Vintage.

Hughes, Winifred. 1980. *The Maniac in the Cellar.* Princeton: Princeton University Press.

Hull, Gloria, Patricia Bell Scott, and Barbara Smith. 1988. *All the Women Are White, and All the Blacks Are Men, but Some of Us Are Brave: Black Women's Studies.* Old Westbury, N.Y.: Feminist Press.

Hulme, Keri. 1984. *the bone people.* Wellington: Spiral.

Hulme, Peter. 1986. *Colonial Encounters: Europe and the Native Caribbean, 1492–1797.* London: Methuen.

Hume, David. 1980. *A Treatise of Human Nature.* Ed. L. A. Selby-Bigge. Oxford: Clarendon.

Hunt, Lynn. 1993a. "Introduction: Obscenity and the Origins of Modernity, 1500–1800." In Hunt 1993b. 9–45.

Hunt, Lynn, ed. 1993b. *The Invention of Pornography: Obscenity and the Origins of Modernity, 1500–1800.* New York: Zone Books.

Hunter, J. Paul. 1990. *Before Novels: The Cultural Contexts of Eighteenth-Century English Fiction.* New York: Norton.

"Ideals in Modern Fiction." 1857. *Putnam's Monthly,* July, 90–96.

Ifeka-Moller, Caroline. 1985. "Female Militancy and Colonial Revolt: The Women's War of 1929, Eastern Nigeria." In *Perceiving Women,* ed. Shirley Ardener. London: Malaby. 127–57.

Ihimaera, Witi. 1985. "Interview with Witi Ihimaera." *Kunapipi* 7, no. 1:104–5.

———. 1986. *The Matriarch.* Auckland: Heinemann.

———. 1990. Discussion of *The Matriarch.* University of Auckland. 18 July.

———. 1994. Personal communication with Bridget Orr. 16 July.

Ihimaera, Witi, with Haare Williams, Irihapeti Ramsden, and D. S. Long, eds. 1993. *Te Ao Marama: Regaining Aotearoa: Maori Writers Speak Out.* Auckland: Reed.

Iknayan, Marguerite. 1961. *The Idea of the Novel in France: The Critical Reaction, 1815–1848.* Geneva: Droz.

Ileto, Reynaldo. 1988. "Outlines of a Nonlinear Emplotment of Philippine History." In *Reflections on Development in Southeast Asia,* ed. Lim Teck Ghee. ASEAN Economic Research Unit, Institute of Southeast Asian Studies. 130–59.

Innes, C. L. 1992. *Chinua Achebe.* Cambridge: Cambridge University Press.

Innes, C. L., and Bernth Lindfors, eds. 1978. *Critical Perspectives on Chinua Achebe.* Washington, D.C.: Three Continents Press.

Ishihara Chiaki, comp. 1988. *Kindai shōsetshū kenkyū hikkei.* Tokyo: Yūseidō.

———. 1990. "Manazashi to shite no tasha: *Kokoro* ron." *Nihon no bungaku,* Dec.

———. 1991. "*Kokoro* no Oedeipusu: Hanten suru katari." In Tamai and Fujii 1991.

Isichei, Elizabeth. 1973. *The Ibo People and the Europeans.* New York: St. Martin's.

———. 1976. *A History of the Igbo People*. New York: St. Martin's.
Ivask, Ivar. 1975. "Allegro Barbaro, or Gabriel García Márquez in Oklahoma." *Books Abroad* 47:419–40.
Izu Toshihiko. 1989. *Natsume Sōseki to tennō sei*. Tokyo: Yūseidō.
Jacob, Margaret C. 1993. "The Materialist World of Pornography." In Hunt 1993b. 157–202.
James, Henry. 1980. *The Turn of the Screw*. 1898. Reprinted in *The Turn of the Screw and Other Short Novels*. New York: New American Library. 291–403.
———. 1984a. "The Art of Fiction." 1884. Reprinted in Edel and Wilson 1984. 44–65.
———. 1984b. Preface to *The Aspern Papers*. 1908. Reprinted in *The Art of the Novel: Critical Prefaces by Henry James*. Boston: Northeastern University Press. 159–79.
———. 1984c. Review of *The Gayworthys*, by Adeline Dutton Whitney. 1865. Reprinted in Edel and Wilson 1984. 635–38.
James, Trevor. 1988. "Lost Our Birthright Forever? The Maori Writers' Reinvention of New Zealand." *Span* 24:107–21.
James, William. 1958. *Talks to Teachers on Psychology: And to Students on Some of Life's Ideals*. 1892. Reprint, New York: Norton.
Jameson, Fredric. 1979. "Reification and Utopia in Mass Culture." *Social Text* 1:130–48.
———. 1986. "Third World Literature in the Era of Multinational Capitalism." *Social Text* 15:65–88.
Jameson, Storm. 1939. *Civil Journey*. London: Cassell.
Janin, Jules. 1834. "Manifeste de la jeune littérature: Réponse à M. Nisard." *Revue de Paris*, Jan., 5–30.
———. 1842. "La Littérature et la Cour d'Assises." *Journal des débats*, 14 Mar., 1–3.
JanMohamed, Abdul R. 1983. *Manichean Aesthetics: The Politics of Literature in Colonial Africa*. Amherst: University of Massachusetts Press.
———. 1985. "The Economy of Manichean Allegory: The Function of Racial Difference in Colonialist Literature." *Critical Inquiry* 12, no. 1:59–87.
Jauss, Hans Robert. 1982. *Toward an Aesthetic of Reception*. Trans. Timothy Bahti. Minneapolis: University of Minnesota Press.
Jenkins, Elizabeth. 1949. *Jane Austen: A Biography*. 1938. Reprint, New York: Pellegrini and Cudahy.
Jeyifo, Biodun. 1993. "Okonkwo and His Mother: *Things Fall Apart* and Issues of Gender in the Constitution of African Postcolonial Discourse." *Callaloo* 16, no. 4:847–58.
Joaquin, Nick. 1988. *Culture and History: Occasional Notes on the Process of Philippine Becoming*. Manila: Solar Publishing.
Johnson, Samuel. 1963. *The Adventurer*. 1753. Reprinted in *The Yale Edition of the*

Works of Samuel Johnson. Ed. W. J. Bate, John M. Bullitt, and C. F. Powell. New Haven: Yale University Press.

Johnston, Arthur. 1964. *Enchanted Ground: The Study of Medieval Romance in the Eighteenth Century*. London: Athelone Press.

Jolly, Jules. 1851. *De l'influence de la littérature et du théâtre sur l'esprit public et les moeurs pendant les vingt dernières années*. Paris: Amyot.

Jones, Shane. 1994. "Waitangi and Maori Political Evolution." *New Zealand Herald*, 29 Aug., 5–6.

Jourdain, Margaret. 1923. *English Interiors in Smaller Houses: From the Restoration to the Regency*. London: Batsford.

Journel, Jean. 1831. *Considérations sur le divorce*. Lyon: Sauvignet; Paris: Dentu.

"Justice Criminelle: Cour d'Assises de la Seine, Audience du 10 mars, 'Affaire de Presse.—Roman intitulé *Le Nom de famille*.'" 1842. *Gazette des tribunaux*, 11 Mar., 1–3.

Kakutani, Michiko. 1987. Review of *Beloved*, by Toni Morrison. *New York Times*, 2 Sept., C24.

Kant, Immanuel. 1963. *Kant: On History*. Ed. Lewis White Beck. New York: Macmillan.

Kaplan, Amy. 1990. "Romancing the Empire: The Embodiment of American Masculinity in the Popular Historical Novel of the 1890s." *American Literary History* 2:659–90.

Kaplan, Cora. 1986. "*The Thorn Birds:* Fiction, Fantasy, Femininity." In Burgin et al. 1986. 142–66.

Karatani Kōjin. 1979. *Ifu suru ningen*. Tokyo: Tōjusha.

———. 1980. *Nihon kindai bungaku no kigen*. Tokyo: Kodansha.

———. 1989. *Kotoba to higeki*. Tokyo: Daisan Bunmei Sha.

Karetu, Timoti S. 1993. *Haka! The Dance of a Noble People*. Auckland: Reed.

Kawharu, Sir I. H., ed. 1989. *Waitangi: Maori and Pakeha Perspectives on the Treaty of Waitangi*. Auckland: Oxford University Press.

Kaye-Smith, Sheila, and G. B. Stern. 1943. *Talking of Jane Austen*. London: Cassell.

Keating, Peter. 1989. *The Haunted Study: A Social History of the English Novel, 1875–1914*. London: Sicher and Warburg.

Kennedy, Margaret. 1985. *Troy Chimneys*. 1953. Reprint. London: Virago.

Kermode, Frank. 1979. "Institutional Control of Interpretation." *Salmagundi* 43:72–86.

Kiely, Robert. 1970. Review of *One Hundred Years of Solitude*, by Gabriel García Márquez. *New York Times Book Review*, 8 Mar., 5.

Kim, Elaine, and Norma Alarcón, eds. 1994. *Writing Self/Writing Nation: Selected Essays on Theresa Hak Kyung Cha's DICTEE*. Berkeley: Third Woman Press.

King, Michael. 1993. "Ethnic Cleansing." *Metro* 139:133–35.

Kipling, Rudyard. 1926. "The Janeites." In *The Writings in Prose and Verse*. New York: Scribner's. 31:159–89.

Klancher, Jon. 1987. *The Making of English Reading Audiences, 1790–1832*. Madison: University of Wisconsin Press.

Komori Yōichi. 1988. "*Kokoro* o sesei suru haato." In *Buntai to shite no monogatari*. Tokyo: Chikuma Shobo. 293–317.

———. 1991. "*Kokoro* in okeru hanten suru 'shūki'—Kūhaku to imi no seisei." In Tamai and Fujii 1991. 304–15.

Krakovitch, Odile. 1985. *Hugo censuré*. Paris: Calmann-Lévy.

Kroeller, Eva-Maria. 1980. "Walter Scott in America, English Canada, and Québec: A Comparison." *Canadian Review of Comparative Literature* 7, no. 1:32–46.

Krueger, Miles. 1977. *Show Boat: The Story of a Classic American Musical*. New York: Da Capo.

Krupat, Arnold. 1992. *Ethnocriticism: Ethnography, History, Literature*. Berkeley: University of California Press.

Kwong, Peter. 1979. *Chinatown, N.Y.: Labor and Politics, 1930–1950*. New York: Monthly Review Press.

Lacan, Jacques. 1971. *The Four Fundamental Concepts of Psychoanalysis*. Ed. Jacques-Alain Miller. Trans. Alan Sheridan. New York: Norton.

La Capra, Dominick. 1982. *The Trial of Madame Bovary*. Ithaca: Cornell University Press.

———. 1985. *History and Criticism*. Ithaca: Cornell University Press.

Laclau, Ernesto, and Chantal Mouffe. 1985. *Hegemony and Socialist Strategy*. London: Verso.

LaFeber, Walter. 1963. *The New Empire: An Interpretation of American Expansion, 1860–1898*. Ithaca: Cornell University Press.

Lai, Him Mark, Genny Lim, and Judy Yung. 1980. *Island Poetry and History of Chinese Immigrants, 1910–1940*. San Francisco: Hoc Doi Chinese Cultural Foundation.

Lamb, Jonathan. 1986. "Problems of Originality; or, Beware Pakeha Bearing Guilts." *Landfall* 40, no. 3:352–58.

Laplanche, Jean. 1976. *Life and Death in Psychoanalysis*. Baltimore: Johns Hopkins University Press.

———. 1989. *New Foundations for Psychoanalysis*. Trans. David Macey. Oxford: Basil Blackwell.

Laplanche, Jean, and J.-B. Pontalis. 1967. *The Language of Psycho-Analysis*. Trans. Donald Nicholson-Smith. New York: Norton.

———. 1986. "Fantasy and the Origins of Sexuality." In Burgin et al. 1986. 5–34.

Lascelles, Mary. 1939. *Jane Austen and Her Art*. London: Oxford University Press.

Laurence, Margaret. 1976. *The Diviners*. 1974. Reprint, Toronto: McClelland and Stewart.

Lawrence, D. H. 1923. *Studies in Classic American Literature.* New York: Penguin.

Lawson, Alan. 1993. "Un/Settling Colonies: The Ambivalent Place of Discursive Resistance." In *Literature and Opposition,* ed. Chris Worth, Pauline Nestor, and Marko Parlysyn. Clayton, Australia: Clayton Centre for Comparative Literature and Cultural Studies. 67–82.

Layoun, Mary. 1990. *Travels of a Genre: The Modern Novel and Ideology.* Princeton: Princeton University Press.

———. 1992. "Telling Spaces: Palestinian Women and the Engendering of National Narratives." In Parker et al. 1992. 407–23.

Lears, T. J. Jackson. 1981. *No Place of Grace: Antimodernism and the Transformation of American Culture, 1880–1920.* New York: Pantheon.

Leary, Lewis. 1958a. "Literary Scholarship and the Teaching of English." In Leary 1958b. 9–21.

———, ed. 1958b. *Contemporary Literary Scholarship: A Critical Review.* New York: National Council of Teachers of English.

Leavis, F. R. 1954. *The Great Tradition.* 1948. Reprint, Garden City, N.Y.: Doubleday.

Leavis, Q. D. 1937. "The Case of Miss Dorothy Sayers." *Scrutiny* 6:334–40.

———. 1939. *Fiction and the Reading Public.* 1932. Reprint, London: Chatto and Windus.

———. 1983. "A Critical Theory of Jane Austen's Writings." 1941. Reprinted in *Collected Essays.* Ed. G. Singh. Cambridge: Cambridge University Press 1:61–146.

LeClair, Thomas. 1981. "'The Language Must Not Sweat': A Conversation with Toni Morrison." *New Republic,* 21 Mar., 25–29.

Leclerc, Yvan. 1991. *Crimes écrits: La Littérature en procès au XIXe siècle.* Paris: Plon.

Ledré, Charles. 1960. *La Presse à l'assaut de la monarchie (1815–48).* Paris: Armand Colin.

Lefebvre, Henri. 1991. *The Production of Space.* Trans. Donald Nicholson-Smith. Oxford: Basil Blackwell.

Leith-Ross, Sylvia. 1939. *African Women: A Study of the Ibo of Nigeria.* London: Faber and Faber.

Lennard, John. 1994. "The Redeemed Vicarage." *London Review of Books,* 12 May, 30–31.

Leonard, John. 1970. "Myth Is Alive in Latin America." Review of *One Hundred Years of Solitude,* by Gabriel García Márquez. *New York Times,* 3 Mar., 39.

Levin, Harry. 1963. *The Gates of Horn.* New York: Oxford University Press.

Lewis, R. W. B. 1958. "Contemporary American Literature." In Leary 1958b. 201–18.

Lifton, Robert J., Shuichi Kato, and Michael R. Reith. 1979. *Six Lives, Six Deaths: Portraits from Modern Japan.* New Haven: Yale University Press.

Light, Alison. 1989. "'Young Bess': Historical Novels and Growing Up." *Feminist Review* 33:56–71.

———. 1990. "'Returning to Manderley'—Romance Fiction, Female Sexuality, and Class." In *British Feminist Thought: A Reader,* ed. Terry Lovell. Oxford: Basil Blackwell. 325–44.

———. 1991. *Forever England: Femininity, Literature, and Conservatism between the Wars.* London: Routledge.

Limayrac, Paulin. 1844. "Simples essais d'histoire littéraire, IV: Le Roman philanthrope et moraliste. *Les Mystères de Paris.*" *Revue des deux mondes,* Jan., 75–97.

Lincoln, Charles H., ed. 1913. *Narratives of the Indian Wars, 1675–1699.* New York: Scribner's.

Lipking, Lawrence. 1992. "Inventing the Eighteenth Centuries: A Long View." In *The Profession of Eighteenth-Century Literature: Reflections on an Institution,* ed. Leo Damrosch. Madison: University of Wisconsin Press. 7–25.

Lloyd, David. 1987. *Nationalism and Minor Literature: James Clarence Mangan and the Emergence of Irish Cultural Nationalism.* Berkeley: University of California Press.

———. 1993. *Anomalous States: Irish Writing in the Postcolonial Moment.* Durham: Duke University Press.

Lofts, Norah. 1944. *Jassy.* London: Joseph Michael.

Long, Elizabeth. 1986. "Women, Reading, and Cultural Authority: Some Implications of the Audience Perspective in Cultural Studies." *American Quarterly* 38:591–612.

Loo, Chalsa M. 1991. *Chinatown: Most Time, Hard Time.* New York: Praeger.

Loomba, Ania. 1992. "Criticism and Pedagogy in the Indian Classroom." In Rajan 1992. 63–89.

Louandre, Charles. 1847. "Statistique littéraire: De la production intellectuelle en France depuis quinze ans: Littérature ancienne et étrangère, poésie, roman, théâtre." *Revue des deux mondes,* Nov., 671–703.

Lowe, Lisa. 1991a. *Critical Terrains: French and British Orientalisms.* Ithaca: Cornell University Press.

———. 1991b. "Heterogeneity, Hybridity, Multiplicity: Marking Asian American Differences." *Diaspora* 1, no. 1:24–44.

———. 1995. "Canon, Institutionalization, Identity: Contradictions for Asian American Studies." In *The Ethnic Canon: Histories, Institutions, and Interventions,* ed. David Palumbo-Liu. Minneapolis: University of Minnesota Press.

Luchet, Auguste. 1830. *Paris, esquisses dédiées au peuple parisien.* Paris: Barbezat.

———. 1832. *Henri le prétendant.* Paris: Canel.

———. 1838. *Frère et soeur.* 2 vols. Paris: Souverain.

———. [1841.] *Le Nom de famille.* 2 vols. N.p.: n.p., n.d.

———. 1842. *Le Nom de famille.* 2d (unmarked) ed. 2 vols. Paris: Souverain.

Luchet, Auguste, and Félix Pyat. 1835. *Ango.* Paris: Dupont.
Luchet, Auguste, and Michel de Masson. 1836. *Thaddéus le ressuscité.* 4th ed. Paris: Dupont.
Lyotard, Jean-François. 1984. *The Postmodern Condition: A Report on Knowledge.* Trans. Geoff Bennington and Brian Massumi. Minneapolis: University of Minnesota Press.
———. 1988. *The Differend: Phrases in Dispute.* Trans. Georges Van Den Abbeele. Minneapolis: University of Minnesota Press.
MacLulich, T. D. 1988. *Between Europe and America: The Canadian Tradition in Fiction.* Oakville: ECW Press.
Macpherson, James. 1807. *The Poems of Ossian.* London: W. Bulmer.
"Magic, Matter, and Money." 1982. *Time,* 1 Nov., 88.
Maigron, Louis. 1910. *Le Romantisme et les moeurs.* Paris: Champion.
Maitron, Jean. 1965. *Dictionnaire biographique du mouvement ouvrier français, 1789–1864.* Vol. 2. 1836. Reprint, Paris: Editions Ouvrières.
Manley, Delarivier. 1991. *The New Atalantis.* 1709. Reprint ed. Rosalind Ballaster. London: Penguin.
Marshall, Henry Rutgers. 1899. "Rudyard Kipling and Racial Instinct." *Century,* July, 375–77.
Marvin, Patricia H. 1970. Review of *The Bluest Eye,* by Toni Morrison. *Library Journal,* 1 Nov., 3806.
Mason, Theodore O., Jr. 1988. "The Novelist as Conservator: Stories and Comprehension in Toni Morrison's *Song of Solomon.*" *Contemporary Literature* 29:564–81.
Masson, Michel de. 1836. *Vierge et martyre.* Paris: Werdet.
Mast, Gerald. 1987. *Can't Help Singin': The American Musical on Stage and Screen.* Woodstock, N.Y.: Overlook Press.
Mather, Cotton. 1913. *Decennium Luctuosum.* 1699. Reprinted in Lincoln 1913. 169–300.
Matless, David. 1990. "Ages of English Design: Preservation, Modernism, and Tales of Their History, 1926–1939." *Journal of Design History* 3:203–12.
Matlock, Jann. 1993. "The Dead Duchess, the Dead Duke, and Bette Davis: The Scandalous Histories of the 1847 Choiseul-Praslin Affair." Paper presented at the Berkshires Conference on Women's History.
———. 1994. *Scenes of Seduction: Prostitution, Hysteria, and Reading Difference in Nineteenth-Century France.* New York: Columbia University Press.
———. 1995. "Censoring the Realist Gaze." In Cohen and Prendergast 1995. 28–65.
———. 1996. "Blagues Lithographiques et spectacles féminins: Les Rires de Gavarni et Baudelaire, et les regards de la modernité en France au dix-neuvième siècle." *Les Annales, E.S.C.* Forthcoming.
Matthews, Brander. 1897. "The Historical Novel." *Forum,* Sept., 79–91.

Matthiesen, F. O. 1941. *American Renaissance: Art and Expression in the Age of Emerson and Whitman*. London: Oxford University Press.

Mauchamps, Poutret de. 1837. "Pétition." *Gazette des femmes*, 1 May, 6.

McAleer, Joseph. 1992. *Popular Reading and Publishing in Britain, 1914–1950*. Oxford: Clarendon.

McCulloch, Thomas. 1960. *The Stepsure Letters*. 1821. Reprint, Toronto: McClelland and Stewart.

McGregor, Gaile. 1985. *The Wacousta Syndrome: Explorations in the Canadian Langscape*. Toronto: University of Toronto Press.

McKeon, Michael. 1987. *The Origins of the English Novel, 1600–1740*. Baltimore: Johns Hopkins University Press.

McMaster, Graham. 1988. "Henry James and India: A Historical Reading of *The Turn of the Screw*." *Clio* 18, no. 1:23–40.

McNally, David. 1988. *Political Economy and the Rise of Capitalism: A Reinterpretation*. Berkeley: University of California Press.

McRae, Jane. 1991. "Maori Literature: A Survey." In Sturm 1991. 1–24.

McWilliams, John. 1993. "The Rationale for 'The American Romance.'" In Pease 1993b. 71–82.

Mead, Hirini Moko. 1993. "Nga Timunga me nga Paringa o te Mana Maori." In Ihimaera et al. 1993. 199–209.

Mead, Robert G., Jr. 1970. Review of *One Hundred Years of Solitude*, by Gabriel García Márquez. *Saturday Review*, 7 Mar., 34–35.

Melman, Billie. 1988. *Women and the Popular Imagination in the Twenties: Flappers and Nymphs*. Basingstoke: Macmillan.

Méray, Antony. 1847. *La Part des femmes*. In *La Démocratie pacifique*, 27 May–1 July; 21 July–14 Aug.

Mercer, Kobena. 1990. "Black Hair/Style Politics." In Fergusson et al. 1990. 247–64.

Michaels, Walter Benn. 1987. *The Gold Standard and the Logic of Naturalism: American Literature at the Turn of the Century*. Berkeley: University of California Press.

Michaud, Stéphane, ed. 1984. *Un Fabuleux Destin: Flora Tristan*. Dijon: Presses Universitaires de Dijon.

Michener, Charles. 1982. "Latin American Laureate." *Newsweek*, 1 Nov., 81–82.

Miles, Peter, and Malcolm Smith. 1987. *Cinema, Literature and Society: Elite and Mass Culture in Interwar Britain*. London: Croom Helm.

Miller, D. A. 1990. "The Late Jane Austen." *Raritan* 10:55–79.

Miller, Samuel. 1970. *A Brief Retrospect of the Eighteenth Century Part First in Two Volumes Containing a Sketch of the Revolutions and Improvements in Science, Arts, and Literature during That Period*. 1803. Reprint, New York: Burt Franklin.

Miniata, Retimana. 1967. *Tukutuku and Kowhaiwhai.* Wellington: Department of Education.

Mita, Merata. 1984. "Indigenous Literature in a Colonial Society." *Republican* 52 (Nov.).

Mitchel, John. [1845.] *Jail Journal.* Dublin: M. H. McGill and Sons.

Modleski, Tania. 1984. *Loving with a Vengeance: Mass-Produced Fantasies for Women.* New York: Methuen.

Mohanty, Chandra Talpade. 1991a. "Cartographies of Struggle." In Mohanty, Russo, and Torres 1991. 1–47.

———. 1991b. "Under Western Eyes." In Mohanty, Russo, and Torres 1991. 51–80.

Mohanty, Chandra Talpade, Ann Russo, and Lordes Torres, eds. 1991. *Third World Women and the Politics of Feminism.* Bloomington: Indiana University Press.

Molènes, G. de. 1841. "Revue littéraire: Le Roman actuel." *Revue des deux mondes,* Dec., 1002–22.

Monborne, Madame B. 1834. *Une Victime: Esquisse littéraire.* Paris: Mouillefarine.

Monkland, Mrs. Anne Catherine. 1828. *Life in India; or, The English at Calcutta.* 3 vols. London: Henry Colburn.

Moodie, Susanna. 1989. *Life in the Clearings versus the Bush.* 1853. Reprint, Toronto: McClelland and Stewart.

Moretti, Franco. 1987. *The Way of the World: The* Bildungsroman *in European Culture.* London: Verso.

———. 1988. *Signs Taken for Wonders.* Rev. ed. Trans. Susan Fischer et al. London: Verso.

Morris, Meaghan. 1988. "At Henry Parkes Motel." *Cultural Studies* 2:1–47.

———. 1992. "'On the Beach.'" In Grossberg et al. 1992. 450–78.

Morrison, Toni. 1972. *The Bluest Eye.* 1970. Reprint, New York: Washington Square.

———. 1976. "A Slow Walk of Trees (as Grandmother Would Say), Hopeless (as Grandfather Would Say)." *New York Times Magazine,* 4 July, 104–5+.

———. 1978. *Song of Solomon.* 1977. Reprint, New York: Signet.

———. 1984. "Rootedness: The Ancestor as Foundation." In *Black Women Writers (1950–1980),* ed. Mari Evans. New York: Anchor. 339–45.

———. 1989. "Unspeakable Things Unspoken: The Afro-American Presence in American Literature." *Michigan Quarterly Review* 28:1–49.

Moses, Claire Goldberg. 1984. *French Feminism in the Nineteenth Century.* Albany: State University of New York Press.

Mott, Frank Luther. 1930–69. *A History of American Magazines.* 5 vols. Cambridge: Harvard University Press.

———. 1947. *Golden Multitudes: The Story of Best Sellers in the United States.* New York: Macmillan.

Mulhern, Francis. 1979. *The Moment of "Scrutiny."* London: NLB.

Myers, Ramon H., and Mark R. Peattie, eds. 1984. *The Japanese Colonial Empire, 1895–1945.* Princeton: Princeton University Press.

Nairn, Tom. 1990. *The Enchanted Glass: Britain and Its Monarchy.* London: Pan.

Nancy, Jean-Luc. 1991. "Myth Interrupted." Trans. Peter Connor. In *The Inoperative Community,* ed. Peter Connor. Minneapolis: University of Minnesota Press. 43–70.

Narrative of Mrs. Scott and Capt. Stewart's Captivity. 1978. 1786. Reprinted in *The Garland Library of Narratives of North American Indian Captivities,* ed. Wilcomb E. Washburn. Vol. 16. New York: Garland.

Natsume Sōseki. 1975. *Man-Kan tokorodokoro.* In *Sōseki zenshū.* Vol. 8. Tokyo: Iwanami Shoten.

———. 1978. *Kokoro.* Trans. Edwin McLellan. Tokyo: Charles E. Tuttle.

———. 1983. *Kokoro.* 1914. Reprinted in *Sōseki bungaleu zenshū.* Vol. 6. Tokyo: Shueisha.

Nee, Victor, and Brett de Bary Nee. 1972. *Longtime Californ': A Documentary Study of an American Chinatown.* New York: Pantheon.

Nelson, Cary, and Lawrence Grossberg, eds. 1988. *Marxism and the Interpretation of Culture.* Urbana: University of Illinois Press.

Nelson, Henry Loomis. 1900. "American Periodicals." *Dial* 1:349–52.

Nettement, Alfred. 1845. *Etudes critiques sur le feuilleton roman.* 2 vols. Paris: Perrodil.

———. 1854. *La Littérature française sous le gouvernement de juillet.* 2 vols. Paris: Lecoffre.

Newman, Gerald. 1987. *The Rise of English Nationalism: A Cultural History, 1740–1830.* New York: St. Martin's.

Ng, Fae Myenne. 1993. *Bone.* New York: Hyperion.

Nicolson, Marjorie. 1946. "The Professor and the Detective." 1929. Reprinted in Haycraft 1946. 110–27.

Niranjana, Tejaswini. 1992a. "'History, Really Beginning': The Compulsions of Post-colonial Pedagogy." In Rajan 1992. 246–59.

———. 1992b. *Siting Translation: History, Post-Structuralism, and the Colonial Context.* Berkeley: University of California Press.

Nisard, Charles. 1833. "D'un commencement de réaction contre la littérature facile à l'occasion de la Bibliothèque latine-française de M. Panckoucke." *Revue de Paris,* Dec., 211–28, 268–87.

Nixon, Rob. 1987. "Caribbean and African Appropriations of *The Tempest.*" *Critical Inquiry* 13:557–87.

Nnaemeka, Obioma. 1989. "Toward a Feminist Criticism of Nigerian Literature." *Feminist Issues* 9, no. 1:73–87.

Nwabara, S. N. 1978. *Iboland: A Century of Contact with Britain, 1860–1960.* Atlantic Highlands, N.J.: Humanities Press.

Nwapa, Flora. 1966. *Efuru.* London: Heinemann.

Oakley, C. A. 1990. *The Second City: The Story of Glasgow.* 4th ed. Glasgow: Blackie.

Obiechina, Emmanuel N. 1975. *Culture, Tradition, and Society in the West African Novel.* Cambridge: Cambridge University Press.

Ohmann, Richard. 1983. "The Shaping of a Canon: U.S. Fiction, 1960–1975." *Critical Inquiry* 10:199–223.

Ojinmah, Umelo R. 1993. *Witi Ihimaera: A Changing Vision.* Dunedin, New Zealand: University of Otago Press.

Ojo-Ade, Femi. 1983. "Female Writers, Male Critics." *African Literature Today* 13:158–79.

Okada, John. 1976. *No-no Boy.* 1957. Reprint, Seattle: University of Washington Press.

"Old Nick." 1841. "Critique: I. *Le Nom de famille,* par A. Luchet; II. *La Pension bourgeoise—La Marquise de Contades,* par A. de Lavergne." *Le National,* 19 Nov., 1–3.

Olney, Richard. 1898. "International Isolation of the United States." *Atlantic,* May, 577–88.

Omi, Michael, and Howard Winant. 1986. *Racial Formation in the United States: From the 1960s to the 1980s.* New York: Routledge.

Ong, Aihwa. 1991. "The Gender and Labor Politics of Postmodernity." *Annual Review of Anthropology* 20:270–309.

"Orchids and Bloodlines." 1970. Review of *One Hundred Years of Solitude,* by Gabriel García Márquez. *Time,* 16 Mar., 96.

"Our Monthly Gossip." 1887. *Lippincott's,* Jan., 184–86.

Palmer, Eustace. 1983. "The Feminine Point of View: Buchi Emecheta's *The Joys of Motherhood.*" *African Literature Today* 13:38–57.

Pandey, Gyanendra. 1988a. "Congress and the Nation, 1917–1947." In *Congress and Indian Nationalism: The Pre-Independence Phase,* ed. Richard Sisson and Stanley Wolpert. Berkeley: University of California Press. 121–33.

———. 1988b. "Peasant Revolt and Indian Nationalism." In Guha and Spivak 1988. 233–87.

Panther, Abraham. 1787. *A surprising Account of the Discovery of a Lady who was taken by the Indians in the year 1777, and after making her escape, she retired to a lonely Cave, where she lived nine years.* Norwich, Conn.: n.p.

Parent-Lardeur, Françoise. 1982. *Les Cabinets de lecture: La Lecture publique à Paris sous la Restauration.* Paris: Payot.

Parker, Andrew, et al., eds. 1992. *Nationalisms and Sexualities.* New York: Routledge.

Payne, Johnny. 1993. *Conquest of the New Word: Experimental Fiction and Translation in the Americas.* Austin: University of Texas Press.

Pease, Donald E. 1993a. "New Americanists: Revisionist Interventions into the Canon." In Pease 1993b. 1–37.

———, ed. 1993b. *Revisionary Interventions into the Americanist Canon.* Durham: Duke University Press.

Perry, Bliss. 1903. *A Study of Prose Fictions.* Boston: Houghton Mifflin.

Phillips, Roderick. 1988. *Putting Asunder: A History of Divorce in Western Society.* Cambridge: Cambridge University Press.

Pihama, Leonie. 1994. "Beyond Cannes: The Globalisation of the Maori Image." Unpublished paper delivered at Auckland University, 23 July.

Pinch, Adela. Forthcoming. "Rubber Bands and Old Ladies." In *In These Ruins: Essays on Cultural Theory,* ed. Nicholas Dirks. Ann Arbor: University of Michigan Press.

Platt, Anthony. 1982. "The Rise of the Child Saving Movement." In *The Sociology of Childhood: Essential Readings,* ed. Chris Jenks. London: Batsford. 151–67.

Plummer, Rachel. 1973. *Narrative of the Capture and Subsequent Sufferings of Mrs. Rachel Plummer, Written by Herself.* 1839. Reprinted in VanDerBeets 1973. 333–66.

Poananga, Atareta. 1986. "The Matriarch: Wahine Toa Takahia: Trample on Strong Women." Part 1. *Broadsheet* 145 (Dec.): 24–29.

———. 1987. "The Matriarch: Wahine Toa Takahia: Trample on Strong Women." Part 2. *Broadsheet* 146 (Jan.): 24–29.

Pocock, J. G. A. 1992. "Tangata Whenua and Enlightenment Anthropology." *New Zealand Journal of History* 26, no. 1:28–77.

Poirier, Richard. 1966. *A World Elsewhere: The Place of Style in American Literature.* New York: Oxford University Press.

Poitou, Eugène. 1857. *Du Roman et du théâtre contemporains et de leur influence sur les moeurs.* Paris: Auguste Durand.

Pomare, Sir Maui. 1989. *Legends of the Maori: Maori-Polynesian Historical Traditions, Folk-lore, and Stories of Old New Zealand.* 2 vols. Auckland: Southern Reprints.

Poovey, Mary. 1988. *Uneven Developments: The Ideological Work of Gender in Mid-Victorian England.* Chicago: University of Chicago Press.

Potts, Alex. 1989. "'Constable Country' between the Wars." In Samuel 1989b. 160–86.

Power, Thomas P., ed. 1991. *The Irish in Atlantic Canada, 1780–1900.* Fredericton, N.B.: New Ireland Press.

Prakash, Gyan. 1990. "Writing Post-Orientalist Histories of the Third World." *Society for Comparative Study of Society and History* 32:383–408.

Pratt, Mary Louise. 1992. *Imperial Eyes: Travel Writing and Transculturation.* New York: Routledge.

———. 1993. "Criticism in the Contact Zone: Decentering Community and Nation." In *Critical Theory, Cultural Politics, and Latin American Narrative,* ed. Steven M. Bell, Albert H. Le May, and Leonard Orr. Notre Dame, Ind.: University of Notre Dame Press. 83–102.

Prentice, Christine. 1991. "The Interplay of Place and Placelessness in the Subject of Post-Colonial Fiction." *Span* 31:63–80.

———. 1993. "Grounding Postcolonial Fictions: Cultural Constituencies, Cultural Credentials, and Uncanny Questions of Authority." *Span* 36:100–112.

Price, Reynolds. 1977. Review of *Song of Solomon,* by Toni Morrison. *New York Times Book Review,* 11 Sept., 1+.

Priestley, J. B. 1931. *English Humour.* Introd. Stanley Baldwin, M.P. 1929. Reprint, London: Longmans.

Pringle, Thomas. 1834. *African Sketches.* London: Edward Moxon.

Radhakrishnan, R. 1992. "Nationalism, Gender, and the Narrative of Identity." In Parker et al. 1992. 77–95.

Radway, Janice A. 1984. *Reading the Romance: Women, Patriarchy, and Popular Literature.* Chapel Hill: University of North Carolina Press.

———. 1989. "The Book-of-the-Month Club and the General Reader: The Uses of 'Serious' Fiction." In *Reading in America,* ed. Cathy N. Davidson. Baltimore: Johns Hopkins University Press. 259–84.

Rafael, Vicente. 1991. "Anticipating Nationhood: Collaboration and Rumor in the Japanese Occupation of Manila." *Diaspora* 1, no. 1:67–82.

Rajan, Rajeswari Sunder, ed. 1992. *The Lie of the Land: English Literary Studies in India.* Delhi: Oxford University Press.

Rama, Ängel. 1982. "El Boom en perspectiva." In *La Novela en América Latina.* Bogota, Columbia: Procultura. 235–93.

Ramsden, Irihapeti. 1993a. "Borders and Frontiers." In Ihimaera et al. 1993. 344–51.

———. 1993b. "Whakamaemae." In Ihimaera et al. 1993. 320–22.

Raven, James. 1992. *Judging New Wealth: Popular Publishing and Responses to Commerce in England, 1750–1800.* Oxford: Clarendon.

"Recent American and English Fiction." 1892. *Atlantic,* May, 694–707.

Reid, Alistair. 1976. "Basilisks' Eggs." *New Yorker,* 8 Nov., 175–208.

Reid, Roddey. 1993. *Families in Jeopardy: Regulating the Social Body in France, 1750–1910.* Stanford: Stanford University Press.

Renan, Ernest. 1990. "What Is a Nation?" Trans. Martin Thom. In Bhabha 1990b. 8–22.

Rendell, Ruth. 1988. *The Veiled One.* New York: Ballantine.

Repplier, Agnes. 1893. "Leisure." *Scribner's Magazine,* July, 63–67.

Review of *Frère et soeur,* by Auguste Luchet. *Revue française,* 7–8 Sept., 389–92.

Review of *Godfrey Morgan: A Californian Mystery,* by Jules Verne. 1883. *Nation,* 15 Nov., 421.
Review of *One Hundred Years of Solitude,* by Gabriel García Márquez. 1970. *Publishers Weekly,* 12 Jan., 58.
Review of *The Portrait of a Lady,* by Henry James. 1882. *Lippincott's,* Feb., 213–14.
Review of *The Princess Casamassima,* by Henry James. 1887. *Lippincott's,* Feb., 359.
Review of *Show Boat,* dir. by James Whale. 1936. *Picture Play,* Aug.
Review of *Tales of Three Cities,* by Henry James. 1884. *Nation,* 20 Nov., 442.
Reynolds, David S. 1989. *Beneath the American Renaissance: The Subversive Imagination in the Age of Emerson and Melville.* Cambridge: Harvard University Press.
Richards, Jeffrey, and Dorothy Sheridan, eds. 1987. *Mass-Observation at the Movies.* London: Routledge.
Richardson, John. 1987. *Wacousta; or, The Prophecy: A Tale of the Canadas.* 1832. Reprint, Ottawa: Carleton University Press.
Richardson, Samuel. 1971. *Pamela; or, Virtue Rewarded.* 1740. Reprint ed. T. C. Duncan Eaves and Ben D. Kimpel. Boston: Houghton Mifflin.
Richetti, John. 1992. *Popular Fiction before Richardson: Narrative Patterns.* 1969. Reprint, Oxford: Clarendon.
———, ed. 1994. *The Columbia History of the British Novel.* New York: Columbia University Press.
Richler, Mordecai. 1977. Review of *Song of Solomon,* by Toni Morrison. *Book-of-the-Month-Club News,* Sept., 1–4.
Rieder, John. 1994. "Wordsworth and Romanticism in the Academy." In Favret and Watson 1994b. 21–39.
Robbins, Bruce. 1984. "Shooting Off James's Blanks: Theory, Politics, and *The Turn of the Screw.*" *Henry James Review* 5, no. 3:192–99.
Robinson, Lillian S. 1978. "On Reading Trash." In *Sex, Class, and Culture.* Bloomington: Indiana University Press. 200–222.
Robinson, Michael. 1982–83. "Ideological Schism in the Korean Nationalist Movement, 1920–1930: Cultural Nationalism and the Radical Critique." *Journal of Korean Studies* 4:241–68.
"The Romance of Modern Life." 1881. *Atlantic,* Nov., 640–46.
Ronsin, Francis. 1992. *Les Divorciaires: Affrontements politiques et conceptions du mariage dans la France du XIXe siècle.* Paris: Aubier.
Rose, Jacqueline. 1984. *The Case of Peter Pan; or, The Impossibility of Children's Fiction.* London: Macmillan.
Ross, Deborah. 1991. *Romance, Realism, and Women's Contribution to the Novel.* Lexington: University Press of Kentucky.
Rowlandson, Mary. 1913. *Narrative of the Captivity of Mary Rowlandson.* 1682. Reprinted in Lincoln 1913. 107–67.
Said, Edward. 1975. *Beginnings: Intention and Method.* New York: Basic Books.

———. 1978. *Orientalism*. New York: Random House.

———. 1993. *Culture and Imperialism*. New York: Knopf.

Saintsbury, George. 1913. *The English Novel*. London: Dent.

Sakai, Naoki. 1988. "Modernity and Its Critique: The Problem of Universalism and Particularism." *South Atlantic Quarterly* 87:475–504.

Saldívar, José David. 1991. *The Dialectics of Our America: Genealogy, Cultural Critique, and Literary History*. Durham: Duke University Press.

Samuel, Raphael. 1989a. "Introduction: Exciting to Be English." In Samuel 1989b. xviii–lxvii.

———, ed. 1989b. *Patriotism: The Making and Unmaking of British Identity*. 3 vols. London: Routledge.

Samuels, Wilfred D., and Clenora Hudson-Weems. 1990. *Toni Morrison*. Boston: Twayne.

Sandoval, Chela. 1991. "U.S. Third World Women: The Theory and Method of Oppositional Consciousness in the Postmodern World." *Genders* 10:1–24.

Sangari, Kumkum. 1990. "The Politics of the Possible." In *The Nature and Context of Minority Discourse*, ed. Abdul JanMohamed and David Lloyd. Oxford: Oxford University Press. 216–45.

Sangari, Kumkum, and Sudesh Vaid. 1990. *Recasting Women: Essays in Indian Colonial History*. New Brunswick: Rutgers University Press.

San Juan, E. 1991. "Mapping the Boundaries: The Filipino Writer in the USA." *Journal of Ethnic Studies* 19, no. 1:117–31.

Santner, Eric L. 1990. *Stranded Objects: Mourning, Memory, and Film in Postwar Germany*. Ithaca: Cornell University Press.

Sayers, Dorothy Leigh. 1946. "The Omnibus of Crime." 1928. Reprinted in Haycraft 1946. 71–109.

———. 1986a. *Gaudy Night*. 1936. Reprint, New York: HarperCollins.

———. 1986b. *Have His Carcase*. 1932. Reprint, New York: HarperCollins.

Schofield, Mary Ann. 1990. *Masking and Unmasking the Female Mind: Disguising Romances in Feminine Fiction*. Newark: University of Delaware Press.

Scott, Sir Walter. 1906. *The Lives of the Novelists*. London: Dent.

———. 1968. Unsigned review of *Emma*, by Jane Austen. 1816. Reprinted in *Jane Austen: The Critical Heritage*. Ed. B. C. Southam. London: Routledge. 58–69.

———. 1972. "An Essay on Romance." 1824. Reprinted in *Essays on Chivalry, Romance, and the Drama*. Freeport, N.Y.: Books for Libraries Press. 127–216.

Sedgwick, Eve Kosofsky. 1985. *Between Men: English Literature and Male Homosocial Desire*. New York: Columbia University Press.

Selden, Rodman. 1969. "Literary Gold in South America." *Saturday Review*, 7 June, 25–26+.

Seltzer, Mark. 1984. *Henry James and the Art of Power*. Ithaca: Cornell University Press.

Shaftesbury, Third Earl of (Anthony Ashley Cooper). 1963. "Advice to an Au-

thor." In *Characteristics of Men, Manners, Opinions, Times, etc.*. Ed. John M. Robertson. Gloucester, Mass.: P. Smith. 103–234.
Sharpe, Jenny. 1993. *Allegories of Empire: The Figure of Woman in the Colonial Text.* Minneapolis: University of Minnesota Press.
Shorris, Earl. 1972. "Gabriel García Márquez: The Alchemy of History." *Harper's*, Feb., 98–102.
Silverberg, Miriam. 1991. *Changing Song: The Marxist Manifestoes of Nakano Shigeharu.* Princeton: Princeton University Press.
Siskin, Clifford. 1988. *The Historicity of Romantic Discourse.* New York: Oxford University Press.
———. 1994a. "Eighteenth-Century Periodicals and the Romantic Rise of the Novel." *Studies in the Novel* 26:26–42.
———. 1994b. "The Lyric Mix: Romanticism, Genre, and the Fate of Literature." *Wordsworth Circle* 25, no. 1:7–10.
Skube, Michael. 1993. "Nobel Cites Morrison's 'Epic Power.' Novelist Considered the Grande Dame of Black Literature." *Atlanta Journal and Constitution*, 8 Oct., D1, 9.
Smailes, Helen. 1981. *Scottish Empire: Scots in Pursuit of Hope and Glory.* Edinburgh: Scottish National Portrait Gallery.
Smith, Barbara Herrnstein. 1988. *Contingencies of Value: Alternative Perspectives for Critical Theory.* Cambridge: Harvard University Press.
Smith, Henry Nash. 1950. *Virgin Land: The American West as Symbol and Myth.* New York: Vintage.
Smith, Lady Eleanor. 1942. *The Man in Grey.* New York: Doubleday.
Smithyman, Kendrick. 1994. "Puzzling Over the Best Way to Tell It." *New Zealand Books* 4, no. 2 (Aug.): 6.
Snead, James. 1990. "Repetition as a Figure of Black Culture." In Fergusson et al. 1990. 213–30.
Soja, Edward. 1989. *Postmodern Geographies: The Reassertion of Space in Critical Social Theory.* London: Verso.
Sokolov, Raymond A. 1970. Review of *The Bluest Eye*, by Toni Morrison. *Newsweek*, 30 Nov., 95A–B.
Sommer, Doris. 1990. "Irresistible Romance: The Foundational Fictions of Latin America." In Bhabha 1990b. 71–88.
Souvestre, Emile. 1836. "Du Roman." *Revue de Paris*, Oct., 116–28.
Spencer, Jane. 1986. *The Rise of the Woman Novelist: From Aphra Behn to Jane Austen.* Oxford: Basil Blackwell.
Spengemann, William. 1989. *A Mirror for Americanists: Reflections on the Idea of American Literature.* Hanover, N.H.: University Press of New England.
Spiller, Robert E. et al., eds. 1963. *The Literary History of the United States.* London: Macmillan.
Spillers, Hortense. 1991. "Introduction: Who Cuts the Border? Some Readings

on 'America.'" In *Comparative American Identities: Race, Sex, and Nationality in the Modern Text,* ed. Hortense Spillers. New York: Routledge. 1–25.

Spivak, Gayatri Chakravorty. 1988a. "Can the Subaltern Speak?" In Nelson and Grossberg. 1988. 271–313.

———. 1988b. "Subaltern Studies: Deconstructing Historiography." In *In Other Worlds.* New York: Routledge. 197–221.

Stallybrass, Peter, and Allon White. 1986. *The Politics and Poetics of Transgression.* Ithaca: Cornell University Press.

Stead, C. K. 1985. "Wedde's Inclusions." *Landfall* 39, no. 3:289–302.

Steedman, Carolyn. 1986. *Landscape for a Good Woman: A Story of Two Lives.* London: Virago.

Steele, Ian K. 1986. *The English Atlantic, 1675–1740: An Exploration of Communication and Community.* New York: Oxford University Press.

Steiner, Wendy. 1992. Review of *Playing in the Dark,* by Toni Morrison. *New York Times Book Review,* 5 Apr., 1+.

Stevenson, Robert Louis. 1950. "A Humble Remonstrance." 1884. Reprinted in *The Essays of Robert Louis Stevenson.* New York: Coward. 365–75.

Stratton, Florence. 1994. *Contemporary African Literature and the Politics of Gender.* New York: Routledge.

Straub, Kristina. 1994. "Frances Burney and the Rise of the Woman Novelist." In Richetti 1994. 199–219.

Strumingher, Laura. 1988. *The Odyssey of Flora Tristan.* New York: Peter Lang.

Struther, Jan. 1940. *Mrs. Miniver.* 1939. Reprint, New York: Harcourt, Brace.

Sturm, Terry, ed. 1991. *The Oxford History of New Zealand Literature.* Auckland: Oxford University Press.

Sutton, John L., Jr. 1984. "The Source of Mrs. Manley's Preface to *Queen Zarah.*" *Modern Philology* 82:167–72.

T . . . , Baronne de [pseud.]. 1837. *Mystère.* Paris: Desforgues.

Taiwo, Oladele. 1984. *Female Novelists in Modern Africa.* New York: St. Martin's.

Takaki, Ronald. 1989. *Strangers from a Different Shore: A History of Asian Americans.* Boston: Little, Brown.

Tamai Takayuki and Fujii Hidetada, eds. 1991. *Sōseki sakuhin-ron shūsei: Kokoro.* Tokyo: Ofūsha.

Tanner, Tony. 1979. *Adultery in the Novel: Contract and Transgression.* Baltimore: Johns Hopkins University Press.

Tartt, Donna. 1992. *The Secret History.* New York: Random House.

Tate, Claudia. 1983. "Toni Morrison." In *Black Women Writers at Work.* New York: Continuum. 117–31.

Thayer, William R. 1894. "The New Story-Tellers and the Doom of Realism." *Forum,* Dec., 470–80.

Thompson, E. P. 1968. *The Making of the English Working Class.* London: Penguin.

Thompson, James. 1989. "Surveillance in William Godwin's *Caleb Williams.*" In *Gothic Fictions, Prohibition/Transgression,* ed. Kenneth W. Graham. New York: AMS Press. 173–98.
Thomson, James C., Peter W. Stanley, and John Curtis Perry. 1981. *Sentimental Imperialists: The American Experience in East Asia.* New York: Harper.
Timothy, H. B. 1977. *The Galts: A Canadian Odyssey.* Toronto: McClelland and Stewart.
Todd, Janet. 1989. *The Sign of Angellica: Women, Writing and Fiction, 1660–1800.* London: Virago.
Toulouse, Teresa A. 1992. "'My Own Credit': Strategies of (E)Valuation in Mary Rowlandson's Captivity Narrative." *American Literature* 64:655–76.
Trumpener, Katie. 1993. "National Character, Nationalist Plot: National Tale and Historical Novel in the Age of Waverley." *ELH* 60:685–731.
Ulrich, Laurel Thatcher. 1982. *Good Wives.* New York: Knopf.
Van Allen, Judith. 1972. "'Sitting on a Man': Colonialism and the Lost Political Institutions of Igbo Women." *Canadian Journal of African Studies* 4:165–81.
———. 1976. "'Aba Riots' or Igbo 'Women's War'? Ideology, Stratification, and the Invisibility of Women." In *Women in Africa,* ed. Nancy J. Hafkin and Edna G. Bay. Stanford: Stanford University Press. 59–85.
VanDerBeets, Richard, ed. 1973. *Held Captive by Indians: Selected Narratives, 1642–1836.* Knoxville: University of Tennessee Press.
Van Doren, Carl. 1920. "The Later Novel." In *The Cambridge History of American Literature,* ed. William Peterfield Trent et al. New York: Putnam's. 3:66–95.
Van O'Connor, William. 1958. "Modern Literary Criticism." In Leary 1958b. 221–33.
Vaucher, Ferdinand. 1838. *Les Grisettes vengées.* Preface by Auguste Luchet. Paris: Souverain.
Vico, Giambattista. 1970. (Orig. version, 1725.) *The New Science of Giambattista Vico.* Trans. Thomas Goddard Bergin and Max Harold Fisch. Ithaca: Cornell University Press.
Viswanathan, Gauri. 1989. *Masks of Conquest: Literary Study and British Rule in India.* New York: Columbia University Press.
Walker, Ranginui. 1994. "Te Karanga: Getting Real." *Metro* 158:134–35.
Warner, William. 1992a. "The Elevation of the Novel in England: Hegemony and Literary History." *ELH* 59:577–96.
———. 1992b. "Spectacular Action: Rambo, Reaganism, and the Cultural Articulations of the Hero." In Grossberg et al. 1992. 672–88.
———. 1994. "Licensing Pleasure: Literary History and the Novel in Early Modern Britain." In Richetti 1994. 1–22.
Washington, Leslie. 1987. "Toni Morrison Now." *Essence,* Oct., 137.
Washington, Mary Helen. 1990. "'The Darkened Eye Restored': Notes toward

a Literary History of Black Women." In *Reading Black, Reading Feminist,* ed. Henry Louis Gates Jr. New York: Meridian. 30–43.

Waters, Sarah. 1994. "'A Girton Girl on a Throne': Queen Christina and Versions of Lesbianism, 1906–1933." *Feminist Review* 46:41–60.

Waterson, Elizabeth. 1976. "The Lowland Tradition in Canadian Literature." In *The Scottish Tradition in Canada,* ed. W. Stanford Reid. Toronto: McClelland and Stewart. 203–31.

———, ed. 1985. *John Galt: Reappraisals.* Guelph, Ont.: University of Guelph Press.

Watt, Ian. 1957. *The Rise of the Novel.* Berkeley: University of California Press.

Weber, Samuel. 1987. *Institution and Interpretation.* Minneapolis: University of Minnesota Press.

Weeks, Jeffrey. 1981. *Sex, Politics, and Society: The Regulation of Sexuality since 1800.* New York: Longman.

Wellek, René, and Austin Warren. 1956. *Theory of Literature.* New York: Harcourt, Brace, and World.

Westphal, Carl. 1871. "Uber die conträre Sexualempfindung." *Zeitschrift für Neurologie.*

White, Hayden. 1973. *Metahistory: The Historical Imagination in Nineteenth-Century Europe.* Baltimore: Johns Hopkins University Press.

Wilentz, Gay. 1992. *Binding Cultures: Black Women Writers in Africa and the Diaspora.* Bloomington: Indiana University Press.

Williams, Ioan, ed. 1970. *Novel and Romance, 1700–1800: A Documentary Record.* London: Routledge.

Williams, Mark. 1990. *Leaving the Highway: Six Contemporary New Zealand Novelists.* Auckland: Auckland University Press.

Williams, Raymond. 1975. *The Country and the City.* London: Paladin.

———. 1983a. *Keywords.* 1976. Rev. ed. New York: Oxford University Press.

———. 1983b. *Writing in Society.* London: Verso.

Wilson, Edmund. 1960. "The Ambiguity of Henry James." 1948. Reprinted in *A Case Book on Henry James's* The Turn of the Screw, ed. Gerald Willen. New York: Crowell. 115–53.

Wing, Nathaniel. 1987. *The Limits of Narrative.* Cambridge: Cambridge University Press.

Wolff, Geoffrey. 1970. "Fable Made Flesh." Review of *One Hundred Years of Solitude,* by Gabriel García Márquez. *Newsweek,* 2 Mar., 88–89.

Wood, John S. 1960. *Sondages.* Toronto: University of Toronto Press.

Woodhull, Winifred. 1993. *Transfigurations of the Maghreb: Feminism, Decolonization, and Literatures.* Minneapolis: University of Minnesota Press.

Woodmansee, Martha. 1988. "Toward a Genealogy of the Aesthetic: The German Reading Debate of the 1790s." *Cultural Critique* 11:203–21.

Woolf, Virginia. 1937. *The Common Reader.* 1925. New ed. London: Hogarth.
———. 1986a. *The Essays.* 4 vols. Ed. Andrew McNeillie. London: Hogarth.
———. 1986b. "Mr Howells on Form." 1918. Reprinted in Woolf 1986a. 2:324–26.
———. 1986c. Review of *Jane Austen: Her Life and Letters,* by William Austen-Leigh. 1913. Reprinted in Woolf 1986a. 2:10–16.
———. 1992a. *Orlando.* 1928. Reprint ed. Rachel Bowlby. Oxford: World's Classics.
———. 1992b. *A Room of One's Own.* 1929. Reprint ed. Morag Shiach. Oxford: World's Classics.
Wright, Patrick. 1985. *On Living in an Old Country: The National Past in Contemporary Britain.* London: Verso.
Wrong, E. M. 1946. "Crime and Detection." 1926. Reprinted in Haycraft 1946. 18–32.
Wuthnow, Robert. 1989. *Communities of Discourse: Ideology and Social Structure in the Reformation, the Enlightenment, and European Socialism.* Cambridge: Harvard University Press.
Young, David. 1986. "An End to the Silence." *New Zealand Listener,* 7 June, 24–25.
Yúdice, George. 1991. "*Testimonio* and Postmodernism." *Latin American Perspectives* 18, no. 3:15–31.
Žižek, Slavoj. 1989. *The Sublime Object of Ideology.* London: Verso.

Index

Contributors

Susan Z. Andrade teaches at the University of Pittsburgh. Her interests are African and Caribbean literature and culture in English and French, feminist theory, and European travel narrative. Her essay here forms part of a book on the discourses of nationalism and sexual politics in Africa.

Lauren Berlant, who teaches at the University of Chicago, is the author of *The Anatomy of National Fantasy: Hawthorne, Utopia, and Everyday Life* and the forthcoming *The Queen of America Goes to Washington City.* Her essay on *Show Boat* is part of an ongoing study titled "The Female Complaint."

Homer Brown is the author of the forthcoming *Institutions of the English Novel* and a book on James Joyce's early fiction. He teaches literature and theory at the University of California, Irvine, and is working on British and American Romanticism.

Michelle Burnham teaches in the English department at Auburn University. Her essay forms part of the book that she is currently completing, titled *Captivity and Sentiment.*

James A. Fujii teaches modern Japanese literature at the University of California, Irvine. He is the author of *Complicit Fictions: The Subject in Modern Japanese Prose Narrative.*

Nancy Glazener teaches U.S. literature and women's studies at the University of Pittsburgh. She is the author of the forthcoming *Reading for Realism: The History of a U.S. Literary Institution, 1850–1910.*

Dane Johnson is working on a book entitled *Which Difference Makes a Difference: William Faulkner, Gabriel García Márquez, Toni Morrison, and the Creation of Literary Value.* He teaches in the Department of World and Comparative Literature at San Francisco State University.

Lisa Lowe teaches comparative literature at the University of California, San Diego. She is the author of *Critical Terrains: French and British Orientalisms* and *Immigrant Acts: On Asian American Cultural Politics.*

Deidre Lynch teaches British literature and feminist cultural studies at the State University of New York at Buffalo. She is completing a book on the British novel, the eighteenth-century consumer revolution, and "the economy of character."

Jann Matlock teaches in the Department of Romance Languages and Literatures at Harvard University. She is the author of *Scenes of Seduction: Prostitution, Hysteria, and Reading Difference in Nineteenth-Century France* and the coeditor of *Media Spectacles.* She is the recipient of a Guggenheim fellowship for 1996–97 for the book she is completing on vision, aesthetics, and censorship in nineteenth-century France.

Dorothea von Mücke teaches in the German department at Columbia University. She is the author of *Virtue and the Veil of Illusion: Generic Innovation and the Pedagogical Project in Eighteenth-Century Literature* and coeditor (with Veronica Kelly) of *Body and Text in the Eighteenth Century.* She is currently working on the Romantic fantastic.

Bridget Orr has taught in the English department at the University of Auckland in Aotearoa/New Zealand; she is currently at the University of Iowa. She recently completed *Civilizing the Stage: Colonization and English Drama from 1660 to 1700.*

Clifford Siskin teaches English and comparative literature at the State University of New York at Stony Brook. He published *The Historicity of Romantic Discourse* in 1988. His work on "novelism" is part of a project on changes in the divisions of knowledge and labor during Britain's long eighteenth century that will appear as *The Work of Writing: Disciplinarity, Professionalism, and the Engendering of Literature in Britain, 1700–1830.*

Katie Trumpener teaches comparative literature, German, English, and film at the University of Chicago. She is the author of the forthcoming *Bardic Nationalism: The Romantic Novel and the British Empire.*

William B. Warner teaches in the Departments of English and Comparative Literature at the State University of New York at Buffalo. His contribution to this volume forms part of a forthcoming book entitled *Licensing Entertainment: The Elevation of Novel-Reading in Britain, 1684–1750.*

Library of Congress Cataloging-in-Publication Data
Cultural institutions of the novel / Deidre Lynch and
William B. Warner, editors.
p. cm.
Includes bibliographical references and index.
ISBN 0-8223-1854-7. — ISBN 0-8223-1843-1 (pbk.)
1. Fiction—History and criticism. I. Lynch, Deidre.
II. Warner, William Beatty.
PN3353.C85 1996
809.3—dc20 96-19761
CIP